October 22–27, 2011
Portland, Oregon, USA

I0027533

**Association for
Computing Machinery**

Advancing Computing as a Science & Profession

SPLASH

SPLASH'11

Proceedings of the ACM International Conference Companion on
**Object Oriented Programming Systems Languages
and Applications**

Sponsored by:
ACM SIGPLAN

Supported by:
**IBM Research, CISCO, BlackDuck, Cloud9IDE,
& Amazon WebServices**

**Association for
Computing Machinery**

Advancing Computing as a Science & Profession

The Association for Computing Machinery
2 Penn Plaza, Suite 701
New York, New York 10121-0701

Notice to Past Authors of ACM-Published Articles
ACM intends to create a complete electronic archive of all articles and/or other material previously published by ACM. If you have written a work that has been previously published by ACM in any journal or conference proceedings prior to 1978, or any SIG Newsletter at any time, and you do NOT want this work to appear in the ACM Digital Library, please inform permissions@acm.org, stating the title of the work, the author(s), and where and when published.

ISBN: 978-1-4503-0942-4

Additional copies may be ordered prepaid from:

ACM Order Department
PO Box 11405
New York, NY 10286-1405

Phone: 1-800-342-6626 (USA and Canada)
         +1-212-626-0500 (all other countries)
Fax: +1-212-944-1318
E-mail: acmhelp@acm.org

Printed in the USA

Introducing the ACM International Conference on Systems, Programming, Languages, and Applications: Software for Humanity (SPLASH)

Welcome to SPLASH! SPLASH is the new umbrella for OOPSLA, Onward!, and the Dynamic Languages Symposium. This year, SPLASH also hosts the Scheme Workshop. As usual, a couple of other conferences chose to co-locate with SPLASH; this year, we have the conference on Generative Programming and Component Engineering (GPCE) and the Pattern Languages of Programming conference (PLoP).

SPLASH has emerged from OOPSLA with the underlying drive to expand from it and to include more contributions than those that were typically accepted at OOPSLA. This transition didn't have a master plan; we tried several models for SPLASH and its relation to OOPSLA and Onward!. One of them was the "federated conference" model, like the ACM FCRC, where several existing conferences co-locate in the same place at about the same time. But that didn't feel quite right—there has always been a strong connection between OOPSLA, Onward!, and DLS. Separating them while co-locating them might make them compete with each other, which would be exactly the opposite of what we intended SPLASH to be.

We realized that conferences have many possible views: there are at least internal and external views. The internal view is what the ACM uses for accounting and administration purposes; for this internal view, separation is a good thing, because it keeps every single event financially independent and accountable. This is what the federated conferences model does. The external view is what the attendees see; from the attendees' point of view, separation of all these events in the form of separate registration fees is bad, because people prefer to flow freely from session to session without having to make upfront plans about what to attend. We realized that we needed an accounting model that served the attendees better than the federated conferences model does. So let me explain SPLASH with a picture:

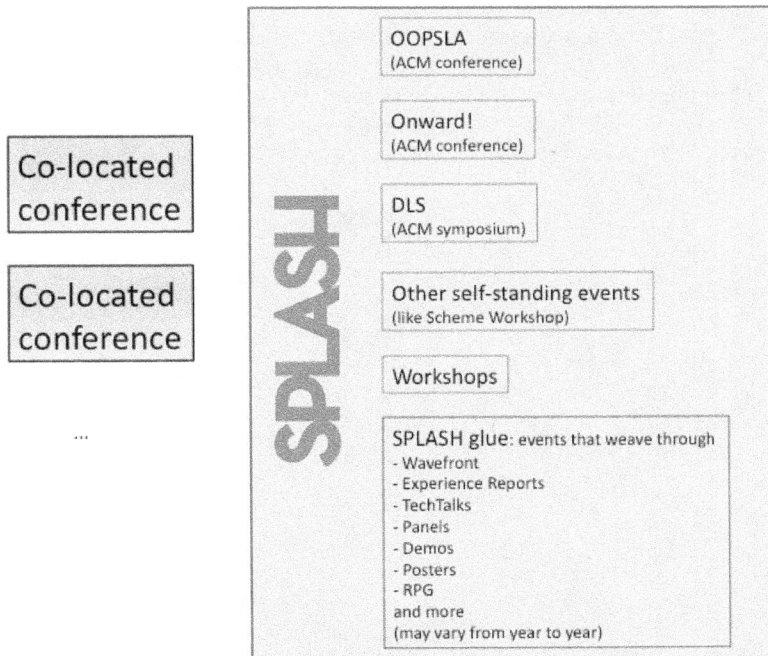

In the picture, the SPLASH box and the co-located conference boxes denote accounting borders. What this means is that SPLASH accommodates several conferences and symposia (OOPSLA, Onward!, DLS, etc.) within one single accounting box; participants see a simple registration fee that doesn't separate the different events, and whose price is proportional to the number of days that a participant decides to attend. As a consequence, during the SPLASH days, participants can freely roam to whatever sessions they want without having to register for individual events, which is exactly what all of us want to do!

There is one final detail concerning this arrangement: even though we are grouping conferences under the SPLASH administrative and accounting umbrella, we don't want to disturb the intellectual autonomy and branding of those conferences. We want the SPLASH conferences to continue to make their own decisions regarding topics, scope, and criteria for content selection, as well as produce their own separate proceedings. This is crucial for the success of the SPLASH model and the success of each of its conferences.

In short: SPLASH gives full autonomy to the different conferences in it, while minimizing their administrative overhead and serving participants the full spectrum of options about which parts to attend under one single registration fee. On top of this, it also supports the more traditional co-location model with other conferences that, for one reason or another, wish to remain financially independent. We hope that in the future more conferences join *the SPLASH* in whatever way they see fit.

Design conferences as you may, SPLASH is the premier conference for researchers, practitioners, educators, and students who are passionate about all aspects of software construction and delivery, and who seek to find deep insights about software that go beyond the shiny surfaces of the latest trends. There is no question that software is having a tremendous impact in Society. The SPLASH community should be proud of the fact that many of the technologies and methodologies that underlie modern software have emerged here at OOPSLA. I decided to choose a theme this year that captures the change in the order of magnitude of computing that happened over the past few years: *The Internet as the world-wide Virtual Machine*. We're operating at the global scale now. These days software systems are rarely designed in isolation; they connect to pieces written by 3rd parties, they communicate with other pieces over the Internet, they use big data produced elsewhere, they touch millions of interacting users through an ever larger variety of physical devices...in other words, the "machine" is now a global computing network. What does this entail for software development itself?

In this publication, you will find the collection of proceedings of the several sponsored conferences, as well as many papers and summaries of sessions that have a more informal arrangement within SPLASH. I believe we have assembled an impressive technical program, and I hope you enjoy it!

Organizing SPLASH was lot of work. The talent and enthusiasm of all the volunteers made it all possible. I am thankful, first of all, to the Organizing Committee — without them the conference would not have happened. I am grateful to the Program Chairs of the SPLASH conferences, symposia, workshops, and tracks who enlisted a large number of reviewers, and I am grateful to each and every one of those reviewers. Reviewing other people's papers is a time-consuming, largely thankless, task that ensures the intellectual health of any community. I am also grateful to the SPLASH Steering Committee for their guidance, to our corporate supporters for their trust, and to SIGPLAN and the ACM for sponsoring SPLASH.

Crista Videira Lopes
SPLASH 2011 General Chair
University of California, Irvine

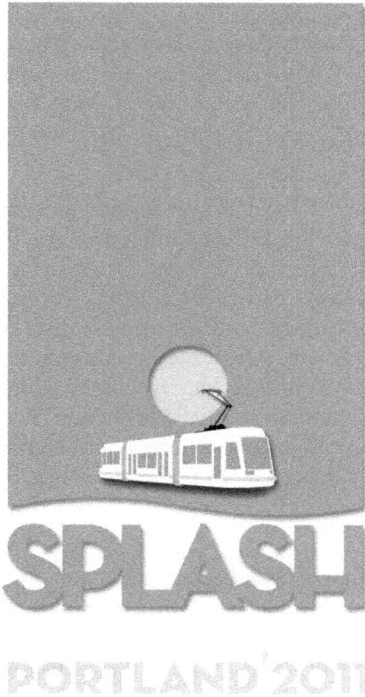

OOPSLA Program Chair's Welcome

On behalf of the OOPSLA program committee, it is my pleasure to welcome you to OOPSLA 2011! The conference is being held in Portland, Oregon on October 25-27, 2011. We have selected a diverse and interesting program of research papers for the 26th annual ACM SIGPLAN OOPSLA Conference. As in the past few years, the scope of the conference is quite broad, providing a venue for researchers from a wide variety of backgrounds to interact. The call for papers specified the scope as follows:

> Papers may address any aspect of software development, including requirements, modeling, prototyping, design, implementation, generation, analysis, verification, testing, evaluation, project cancellation, maintenance, reuse, regeneration, replacement, and retirement of software systems. Papers on tools (such as new programming languages, dynamic or static program analyses, compilers, and garbage collectors) or techniques (such as new programming methodologies, type systems, design processes, code organization approaches, and management techniques) designed to reduce the time, effort, and/or cost of software systems are particularly welcome.

The accepted papers cover almost all of these topics and contain many interesting and exciting results.

The OOPSLA program committee evaluated papers using one primary criterion: would it better for the research community to accept the paper than not, and have it presented at this year's OOPSLA. This criterion encompassed considerations such as:

- **Significance**: How well the paper addresses an important or useful problem.
- **Novelty**: How the paper extends the frontiers of knowledge and improves on previous work.
- **Correctness**: Whether the paper makes clear claims and how carefully it evaluates and supports those claims with proofs, an implementation, examples, or experiments.
- **Clarity**: How clearly the paper is written and organized.

Authors were not required to anonymize their submissions. At least three program committee members and one external program committee member reviewed each submitted paper. Additional reviews were solicited from the broader community as necessary to ensure that each paper was reviewed by an expert in the topic of the paper or to resolve differences of opinion amongst the original reviewers.

There has been concern in the OOPSLA community that the traditional review process inappropriately rejects innovative papers that "break the mold." To address this concern, each member of last year's program committee was allowed to unilaterally accept one paper. After extensive discussions with attendees at last year's OOPSLA and with this year's program and extended review committees, I decided not to allow unilateral accepts. The people I consulted were sympathetic to the goal of the unilateral accept mechanism, but there was concern that the mechanism was subject to abuse and did not necessarily accomplish its goals. This year we tried a different mechanism to accomplish the same goal. In particular, we added a new metric to the evaluation process, the *innovation score*, with the following meaning:

> **Q**: Quirky, breaks the dominate paradigm, provocative, possibly the start of Something New.
> **F**: I'm sitting on the fence.
> **B**: Another brick in the wall: solid, thorough, worthy, useful

The committee took the innovation score into account when discussing papers. The reader may judge from the accepted papers the extent to which this mechanism was successful.

Reviewers were asked to provide detailed feedback about each paper they reviewed, both about how they evaluated the paper and about how the authors might improve the paper. To ensure that the program committee had as much accurate information as possible during the program committee meeting, reviews were made available for an author response period from May 25-26, 2011. More than 99% of the originally assigned reviews were available at the time of the author response period. Additional reviews that came in after the author response period were also made available to the authors for comment as long as they were received more than a few days before the program committee meeting. Time did not permit showing later reviews to the authors. During discussions, the program committee took into consideration whether the authors had had a chance to see a particular review.

The in-person program committee meeting was held June 9-10, 2011 at IBM Almaden. The dates and location were chosen to leverage the fact that many PC members planned to attend the FCRC conference. All 35 members of the program committee attended the entirety of the PC meeting in person. We used the two-week period between author response and the program committee meeting to discuss papers with widely varying reviews and to solicit additional reviewers for papers where there was a lack of confidence, expertise, or agreement. Program committee members were not allowed to review papers with which they had a conflict, and they were required to leave the room while papers with which they had a conflict were discussed. Doug Lea led the discussion on papers for which I had a conflict. During the program committee meeting, we discussed all papers that had at least one A or two B reviews. We discussed all papers with no conflicts first and then the remaining papers. Within these two groups, we discussed the papers in an order not sorted by their initial scores.

In all, 165 papers were submitted, 94 were discussed at the meeting, and 61 were accepted. This 37.0% acceptance rate is significantly higher than the historical average. It does not reflect a decision to lower the acceptance standard for the conference, either by the steering committee or by the program committee. So how did the committee come to accept so many papers? I do not know all the factors, but one was that the program committee meeting took place in the context of a growing sense that SIGPLAN conferences should accept more papers because the submission quality for these conferences is generally so high:

- At POPL 2010, there was a business meeting attended by most conference participants.
  The sense of the participants was that POPL should accept roughly 50 papers.
- POPL 2011 and PLDI 2011 accepted 49 and 55 papers, respectively.
- OOPSLA 2010 accepted 45 papers.

All three of these conferences were double tracked. Feedback surveys indicated that most people were happy with the higher number of acceptances and tolerant of the double-tracking necessary to accommodate the increase.

Because of this context and knowing OOPSLA 2011 had the meeting space to double-track the technical program, I instructed the program committee that we could accept all papers for which we felt that it was better for the community to accept the paper than not. This instruction is consistent with instructions given by program committee chairs for OOPSLA, PLDI and POPL in previous years and did not constitute a change in standard, but rather a sense that we should not reject papers that met the quality threshold simply because they did not fit in the space constraints of the meeting location.

For each paper we accepted, there was at least one reviewer (and frequently more) who was excited about having the paper in the conference, and no one who thought it was a terrible mistake to accept the paper. We did not accept any paper because it was better than some previously accepted paper, so there was no "race to the bottom." All decisions were made by consensus without recourse to voting. At the end of the PC meeting, we discussed whether there were any accepted papers that should be reconsidered, particularly in light of the high acceptance rate. No one brought up any paper. Everyone was happy with the set of accepted papers and comfortable with the acceptance rate.

Program committee members were allowed to submit papers, but reviewing for PC papers was handled entirely by the external review committee, following the same procedures that PLDI has used for the past two years. Specifically, each PC paper was reviewed by at least four members of the external review committee, and the acceptance/rejection decision was made during on-line discussions amongst the paper reviewers prior to the in-person program committee meeting. Program committee members were notified of the decision after the program committee meeting. There were twelve program committee papers submitted, of which six were accepted.

At the request of this year's OOPSLA program committee, the SPLASH steering committee (which serves as the steering committee for OOPSLA) inaugurated a Distinguished Paper Award, to be given to at least one and up to 5% of the accepted papers. The procedure for selecting these papers worked as follows: (1) the program and extended review committees nominated accepted papers for consideration, (2) people on these committees who co-authored nominated papers were recused from the remainder of the process, (3) the remaining committee members read the final versions of the nominated papers and selected the winners using a combination of on-line discussion and voting. Program committee papers were eligible for the award. The committee selected 3 winners this year: *Reactive Imperative Programming with Dataflow Constraints* by Camil Demetrescu, Irene Finocchi, and Andrea Ribichini; *SugarJ: Library-based Syntactic Language Extensibility* by Sebastian Erdweg, Tillmann Rendel, Christian Kästner, and Klaus Ostermann; and *Two for the Price of One: A Model for Parallel and Incremental Computation* by Sebastian Burckhardt, Daan Leijen, Caitlin Sadowski, Jaeheon Yi, and Thomas Ball. Congratulations to these authors on their exemplary work!

OOPSLA also awards a Best Student Paper Award to a single paper with a student as a primary author. This year's award was selected using the same procedure as was used for the new, distinguished paper awards. The program committee felt strongly that the same paper should not receive both awards, and so the papers that were named Distinguished Papers were not eligible for the Best Student Paper award. The winner of this year's Best Student Paper Award is *Hybrid Partial Evaluation* by Amin Shali and William R. Cook. Congratulations to these authors, and in particular to Amin Shali.

It is a great honor and privilege to serve as program chair for OOPSLA 2011. The job involves coordinating the work of a great many people, all of whom deserve my thanks. In particular, I would like to thank the members of the broader OOPSLA community who agreed to write additional reviews for papers as necessary, occasionally on very short notice! I would like to thank the members of the program and extended review committees for their careful consideration of the submitted papers and for their detailed reviews. I would like to thank the members of the program committee for their efforts in attending the program committee meeting in person at their own expense. I would like to thank Crista Lopes, the SPLASH General Chair, for her support in providing technical and policy guidance. Finally, I would like to thank the authors of all the submitted papers for the interesting and exciting work that they offered for our consideration.

Please enjoy the conference!

Kathleen Fisher
SPLASH 2011 Program Chair
Tufts University
kfisher@eecs.tufts.edu

The views, opinions, and/or findings contained in this article are those of the author and should not be interpreted as representing the official views or policies, either expressed or implied, of the Defense Advanced Research Projects Agency or the Department of Defense. Distribution Statement "A" (Approved for Public Release, Distribution Unlimited)

Onward! 2011 General Chair's Welcome

It is my pleasure to welcome you to the 10th Onward!. This year marks its first year as a *bona fide* SIGPLAN symposium; its proper name is **ACM Symposium on New Ideas in Programming and Reflections on Software**. Its familiar name, though, remains **Onward!**—with the exclamation point.

"New ideas in programming" means that we are interested in ideas that can move us forward or radically sideways. A good Onward! paper has two characteristics: readers will wish they had thought of it, and they will believe "it might just work." We don't expect detailed proof the idea will work, but we don't accept pure claims. Onward! papers are well written, well argued, and compelling. They are generally bigger than technical papers, more radical, more visionary, wider ranging, more thought provoking, more frustrating even. Here is what they are **not**: ordinary OOPSLA papers with lousy validation.

"Reflections on software" means that sometimes the way forward begins by looking back and thinking hard, finding new (and better) ways to view what has gone before, in order to provide a new vector. We call such papers "essays." Essays are reflective, often personal, and cover a lot of ground in unexpected ways. Essays are hard to write. Very hard to write. Over the years we have had a good number submitted, but only a scarce few accepted. Here is what they are **not**: ordinary OOPSLA papers with lousy validation.

We welcome submissions about every and any aspect of programming, software, and software engineering. When what you want to say doesn't fit into the research papers or essays bucket, you can submit a film.

This year we accepted seven out of 23 research papers and five films for presentation and publications. While authors of research papers are proficient at writing technical papers, the essay form has proven to be more difficult, and this year, though we had 13 submissions, none were taken. We decided, then, that this year's essays track take the form of a writers' workshop in which a couple of good essayists will coach budding writers in the essay form.

Our keynote speaker is Markus Püschel who is well known for his work on **Spiral**, an automatic performance programming framework for a small, but important class of functions called linear transforms. In his talk he will draw attention to the performance / productivity problem for mathematical applications and make the case for a more interdisciplinary attack.

I wish to thank my organizing committee:

Eelco Visser, Research Papers Chair
David West, Essays Chair
Bernd Bruegge, Films Chair
Pascal Costanza, Workshops Chair
Tobia Pape, Web Chair
Constanze Langer, Designer
Richard P. Gabriel, Steering Committee Chair[†]

I am looking forward to an interesting and inspiring symposium.

Onward!

Robert Hirschfeld
Hasso-Plattner-Institut Potsdam
Onward! General Chair

---

† Ever vigilant but (mildly) annoying.

Onward! Program Chair's Welcome

It is my pleasure to welcome you to Onward! 2011, the ACM Symposium on New Ideas in Programming and Reflections on Software. At Onward! we are interested in papers that describe work with potential to change significantly the field. But Onward! is not a venue for just any old thing; an Onward! paper must say something substantially original, and must be sufficiently important and interesting to deserve the attention of the programming and software communities. An Onward! paper must present some supporting evidence, not pure conjecture. Evidence may be in the form of a compelling argument or analysis, a sketch of validity, or an initial implementation. The scope of an Onward! paper can be broad: It can be a single idea, a new approach, or a new paradigm. It can talk about programming languages, programming methodologies, process, software engineering, collaboration, and anything to do with programming and creating software. But above all, an Onward! paper must be well thought out, well-written, and compelling in its argument.

This year Onward! welcomed, in particular, papers reflecting on the future of software language design. Collectively the software language community is exploring the space of language designs. It often takes many years for a design (a point in this space) to be implemented, applied, and evaluated. Language design is very much an art. Can we speed up the process by more systematic methods? What properties do good language designs have? What are good language design patterns? How can we evaluate language design at an early stage, i.e., before an implementation exists? Can we (and should we) incorporate method from human-computer interaction in the evaluation of language designs? Can we use user-centered design methods to inform language design? Can programming language designers learn from the design methodologies of other disciplines such as architecture and industrial design? Are there principled ways to guide and evaluate software language designs other than empirical experiment and mathematical proof? What assumptions do we hold so dearly about programming languages that it would be heresy to question them?

The Programme Committee consisted of Jean Bézivin, Dave Clarke, Jonathan Edwards, Tim Finin, Robert Hirschfeld, Ralf Laemmel, Oscar Nierstrasz, Klaus Ostermann, Alex Payne, Lori Pollock, Jeremy Siek, Guy Steele, Tom Van Cutsem, Eelco Visser (chair), Markus Voelter, and Tao Xie. Additional reviews were provided by external reviewers Richard Gabriel, Jeehyun Hwang, Andoni Lombide Carreton, Jens Nicolay, Rahul Pandita, Fabrizio Perin, Jorge Ressia, Christophe Scholliers, Niko Schwarz, Yoonki Song, Andrei Varanovich, Toon Verwaest, Erwann Wernli, and Xusheng Xiao.

This year we received 23 submissions, of which 7 were accepted for publication in the proceedings and presentation at the conference. Together the Programme Committee and external reviewers wrote 74 reviews with at least three reviews per paper. The result is an exciting program including contributions to programming with touch devices, scripting of virtual worlds, interaction design for software languages, and the application of natural language concepts in programming languages.

Organizing *Onward!* required hard work from many individuals. I am very thankful for all the work performed by the Program Committee and the external reviewers, the organizing committee headed by General Chair Robert Hirschfeld, and last but not least, the authors of all submitted papers. I am grateful also to the Onward! Steering Committee for their guidance and support and to SIGPLAN and ACM for sponsoring the conference. Finally, I would like to thank all of the people who took part in *Onward! 2010*. Thank you!

Eelco Visser
Onward! 2011 Program Chair
Delft University of Technology, Delft, The Netherlands

Onward! Essays Welcome

It is my pleasure to welcome you to *Onward! Essays* - a forum for interesting, challenging, and provocative ideas and insights. An essay is a narrative, often personal, of a new idea, how it came into being and any implications arising from the idea. It is well argued, but does not require the kind of detail expected of a technical paper.

While SPLASH and Onward! authors are adept at writing technical papers, the essay form has proven to be more elusive. This year the Essays Track will take the form of a writer's workshop followed by presentation and publication. This means more work, with tight deadlines, for the authors and the Essays Committee.

Onward! Essays has a tradition of introducing ideas that become important themes in future conferences. Join us for the opportunity to be among the "first to know," or to stimulate your own thinking and ideas, or simply to begin an engaging discussion.

I want to thank the members of the Essays Committee for their diligent and thoughtful work. This year's format meant even more work than was expected when they accepted the assignment and they deserve special recognition for their efforts.

David West
SPLASH 2010 Onward! Essays Chair
New Mexico Highlands University

Table of Contents

SPLASH'11 Panels

SPLASH'11 Posters & Student Research Competitions

SPLASH'11 Wavefront Session

SPLASH'11 Workshop Summaries

SPLASH'11 Tech Talks

Author Index

SPLASH 2011 Conference Organization

General Chair:	Cristina Videira Lopes *(University of California, Irvine, USA)*
OOPSLA Program Chair:	Kathleen Fisher *(Tufts University, USA)*
Onward! General Chair:	Robert Hirschfeld *(Hasso-Plattner-Insitut Potsdam, Germany)*
Onward! Program Chair:	Eelco Visser *(Delft University of Technology, Netherlands)*
Onward! Essays Chair:	David West *(New Mexico Highlands University, USA)*
Wavefront Chair:	Allen Wirfs-Brock *(Mozilla Foundation, USA)*
Experience Reports:	Tim O'Connor *(K12, Inc. USA)*
Tech Talks:	Aino Cory *(University of Aarhus, Denmark)*
Panels:	Daniel Weinreb *(Google, USA)*
Onward! Films:	Bernd Bruegge *(Technische Universität München, Germany)*
Demonstrations:	Igor Peshansky *(Google, USA)*
Posters:	Eli Televich & Sushil Bajracharya *(Virginia Tech & Black Duck Software, USA)*
ACM Student Research Competition:	Eli Televich & Sushil Bajracharya *(Virginia Tech & Black Duck Software, USA)*
Doctoral Symposium:	Jonathan Aldrich *(Carnegie Mellon University)*
Educators' and Trainers' Symposium:	Ed Gehringer & Eugene Wallingford *(North Carolina State University & University of Northern Iowa, USA & USA)*
Hackathon:	Jeff Barr *(Amazon, USA)*
Dynamic Languages Symposium Program Chair:	Theo D'Hondt *(Vrije Universiteit Brussel, Belgium)*
Workshops:	Ademar Aguiar & Ulrik Pagh Schultz *(Universidade do Porto & University of Southern Denmark, Portugal & Denmark)*
Onward! Workshops:	Pascal Costanza *(ExaScience Lab, Intel Belgium, Belgium)*
Student Volunteers:	Joel Ossher & Rochelle Elva *(University of California, Irvine & University of Central Florida, USA & USA)*

Sponsor & Supporters

SPLASH Sponsor

SPLASH'11 Silver Supporters

SPLASH'11 Bronze Supporters

Friend Supporter – Videotaping Service

Support for the SPLASH'11 Hackathon kindly provided by

SPLASH 2011 Demonstrations Chair's Message

Welcome to the SPLASH 2011 Demonstrations track. We all know that it's better to see something once than to hear about it a hundred times. Live demonstrations show the impact of software innovation in a dynamic and highly interactive setting. This track is an excellent opportunity for companies and universities to share their latest work with an experienced and technically savvy audience – you.

We have received many interesting and diverse demonstration submissions from both industry and academia, and have compiled an exciting demonstration program consisting of tools, applications, and languages in various stages of development – from prototypes and proofs of concept to mature tools and systems. Each of them contains interesting and relevant technology and should appeal to the SPLASH community.

These demonstrations are not product sales pitches, but rather an opportunity for the authors to highlight, explain, and present interesting technical aspects of running applications. The sessions are intended to be two-way interactions with the audience, which has the opportunity to share ideas, interact with the authors in a small scale venue, and learn techniques used in developing innovative and high quality software. Presenters are encouraged to actively solicit feedback from the audience, which should lead to very interesting and entertaining demonstration sessions.

I would like to thank this year's demonstration presenters for their hard work in bringing live demonstrations to SPLASH 2011. I am also grateful to this year's demonstrations subcommittee for their efforts to shape the 2011 demonstrations program.

Demonstrations Committee Members:

Nicholas Chen *(University of Illinois at Urbana-Champaign)*

Erik Meijer *(Microsoft)*

Yannis Smaragdakis (*University of Massachusetts, Amherst*).

Igor Peshansky
SPLASH 2011 Demonstrations Chair
Google
demos@splashcon.org

Automatically Fixing Security Vulnerabilities in Java Code

Aharon Abadi

IBM Research – Haifa

aharona@il.ibm.com

Ran Ettinger

IBM Research – Haifa

rane@il.ibm.com

Yishai A. Feldman

IBM Research – Haifa

yishai@il.ibm.com

Mati Shomrat

Tel Aviv University

matis@cs.tau.ac.il

Abstract

Most kinds of security vulnerabilities in web applications can be fixed by adding appropriate sanitization methods. Finding the correct place for the sanitizers can be difficult due to complicated data and control flow. Fixing SQL injection vulnerabilities may require more complex transformations, such as replacing uses of `Statement` by `PreparedStatement`, which could include some code motion.

We have developed algorithms to place sanitizers correctly, as well as to transform `Statement` to `PreparedStatement`. These have been implemented as "quick fixes" in an Eclipse plugin that works together with a commercial tool that discovers security vulnerabilities in web applications.

Categories and Subject Descriptors D.2.7 [*Software Engineering*]: Distribution, Maintenance, and Enhancement—Restructuring, reverse engineering, and reengineering

General Terms Algorithms

Keywords Quick fix, security

1. Introduction

Security vulnerabilities in web applications can be very costly, and various tools exist for discovering such vulnerabilities. These use black-box testing methods, static analysis, or both. However, these tools offer little help remediating the vulnerabilities they discover.

In most cases, remediation consists of the insertion of calls to sanitization methods. These ensure that malicious user input cannot harm the application, typically by quoting characters that form part of the syntax (such as SQL or HTML) in which the input is embedded. For SQL Injection vulnerabilities, however, the preferred solution in many cases is to switch from the `Statement` API to `PreparedStatement`, which performs sanitization on all its inputs.

When scanning even medium-size applications, dozens of vulnerabilities may be discovered. Remediation can be non-trivial, because of subtle relationships between different parts of the implementation, as demonstrated below. Since going over many vulnerability reports and fixing them one by one is tedious work, developers are likely to make more mistakes than usual in the process. In order to alleviate this problem, we have developed algorithms for automatic remediation of security vulnerabilities, and implemented them in an Eclipse plugin that receives security-related information from a commercial security scanner. In the sequel we describe two types of difficulties in the remediation of security vulnerabilities, and sketch the way our algorithms deal with each.

2. Placing Sanitizers

The example of Figure 1(a) shows server-side code that contains a cross-site scripting vulnerability, in which an attacker can cause arbitrary HTML fragments to be embedded in the page presented to the user. In this example, the server writes the `sms` input it reads on line 1 into the generated page (line 5), including any scripts it may contain. This vulnerability can be eliminated by encoding any HTML syntax in the input so that it appears as text in the generated page.

Where should the sanitizer be placed? The input must not be sanitized immediately on reading (line 1), since the value of `sms` needs to be sent (line 2) using a protocol that does not treat HTML syntax in a special way, and HTML-related sanitization will appear verbatim in the output. Furthermore, it will incorrectly affect the length of the SMS message. The last value of `sms` on line 5 cannot be sani-

```
1 String sms = request.getParameter("sms");
2 if (send(sms) == ERR_TOO_LONG)
3   sms = "<span class=\"red\">Too long!" +
4       "</span><br/>" + sms;
5 response.getWriter().write
6       ("<b>SMS:</b><br/>" + sms);
```
(a)
```
1 String sms = request.getParameter("sms");
2 if (send(sms) == ERR_TOO_LONG)
3   sms = "<span class=\"red\">Too long!" +
4       "</span><br/>" +
5       URLEncoder.encode(sms, "UTF-8");
6 else sms = URLEncoder.encode(sms, "UTF-8");
7 response.getWriter().write
8       ("<b>SMS:</b><br/>" + sms);
```
(b)

Figure 1. A method with a cross-site scripting vulnerability.

tized, since it contains legitimate HTML syntax that should be written as-is. Therefore, the value of sms must be sanitized on line 4, just before it is prefixed with the warning. However, that is not enough. There is a path (the one in which the message is not too long), in which sms would still not be sanitized when written out. The value of sms on this path must also be sanitized; for example, by adding an else clause, as in Figure 1(b). (Alternatively, the value of URLEncoder.encode(sms, "UTF-8") can be extracted from the conditional and placed in a temporary variable prior to it; our algorithm supports this option, although our current implementation chooses the one shown in the figure.)

For each string in the program, the sanitizer-placement algorithm needs to know whether it is fully tainted, partially tainted, or untainted. A fully-tainted value is one that comes directly from user input, and must be properly sanitized before it reaches any *sink*, which is a security-sensitive operation, such as HTML output or a database query. A partially-tainted value consists of some fully-tainted string to which other, trusted, values have been added. An untainted value is one containing no user input at all. This information is supplied by the scanner that discovers the vulnerabilities. The algorithm then searches for all fully-tainted values that are on some path to a sink, and will place a sanitizer of the appropriate type exactly once on each such value. It also ensures that no sanitization happens on paths that do not lead to a sink.

Many security vulnerabilities can be fixed by an appropriate insertion of sanitizers, as in the cross-site scripting example shown here. These can all be fixed using our sanitizer-placement algorithm.

3. Replacing the Statement API

SQL injection vulnerabilities are similar to the example shown above, in that there is flow from a user input to an SQL query. While sanitizers can be used to fix SQL injection vulnerabilities, the preferred solution is to use the PreparedStatement API, which automatically encodes all inputs for SQL. To use a PreparedStatement object in Java, it needs to be initialized with a parameterized query. This has the usual SQL syntax, except that it may have question marks instead of some values; for example: SELECT * FROM users WHERE id = ?. Then, the values of the parameters can be set using call such as statement.setString(1, userid), which also sanitizes its argument. Finally, the statement is sent for execution in the database using a call such as statement.execute(). This differs from the more common but insecure Statement API, which is created without any specific initialization. An SQL query is created using the usual string operations, and sent to the database using the call statement.execute(sql).

In order to replace the Statement API by PreparedStatement, several changes are necessary: (1) replace the tainted inputs in the code that creates the SQL query by question marks; (2) move this code to precede the creation of the Statement object if necessary; (3) replace the creation of the Statement object by a PreparedStatement object; (4) add calls to set the parameters; and (5) remove the parameter of the execute() call.

In the second step, the code may need to be reordered, because the string query given to a Statement can be computed after the Statement object has been created; in contrast, the query must be computed before the creation of the PreparedStatement object, since it is required as a parameter to the constructor. Code-motion transformations are difficult because they need to preserve existing control flow and data flow in the presence of side effects, conditionals, and loops. Other factors that complicate this transformation, such as possible uses of the tainted values in non-security-sensitive situations, are similar to the sanitization case.

We have previously described an algorithm to fix SQL injection vulnerabilities by migrating from the Statement to the PreparedStatement API [1]. This algorithm performs any required code motion transformations, and adds new code necessary to preserve the control flow and data flow of the original program. For an example, as well as more details about the algorithm, see Abadi, Feldman, and Shomrat [1]. This algorithm has also been implemented in our plugin.

Acknowledgments

We are grateful to Dmitri Pikus and Adi Sharabani for their help with the implementation and the paper.

References

[1] A. Abadi, Y. A. Feldman, and M. Shomrat. Code-motion for API migration: Fixing SQL injection vulnerabilities in Java. In *Proc. Fourth Workshop on Refactoring Tools*, May 2011.

DrHJ – The Cure to Your Multicore Programming Woes

Vincent Cavé†   Jarred Payne   Raghavan Raman   Mathias Ricken   Corky Cartwright   Vivek Sarkar†

Department of Computer Science, Rice University

{vcave, vsarkar, jrp1, raghav, mgricken, cork}@rice.edu,   †Demo presenters

Categories and Subject Descriptors   D.1.3 [*Concurrent Programming*]

General Terms   Human Factors, Languages

Keywords   IDE, Language, Parallel Proramming, Data-Race Detection, Habanero-Java

Abstract

DrHJ extends DrJava with support for the pedagogic Habanero-Java language derived from X10, and used to teach parallel programming at the sophomore level. The demonstration will show how a rich and powerful set of parallel programming capabilities can be easily introduced to anyone familiar with the basics of sequential programming in Java.

1.   Habanero-Java Language

The Habanero-Java (HJ) language [2] was developed at Rice University during 2007-2010 as a pedagogic extension to the original Java-based definition of the X10 language [3][1]. In addition to its use as a research language in the Rice Habanero Multicore Software research project [6], HJ is used in a new sophomore-level course on "Fundamentals of Parallel Programming" (COMP 322 [4]) which has become a required course for all Computer Science majors at Rice. The code generated by the HJ compiler consists of Java classfiles that can be executed on any standard JVM.

The HJ extensions to Java are primarily focused on task parallelism. Similar extensions to C and Scala are being pursued in the Habanero C and Habanero Scala projects at Rice. A brief summary of the most commonly-used HJ constructs is included below. A number of recent papers have demonstrated that HJ programs can achieve comparable or superior performance to programs written using standard Java Concurrency features.

1) async: Async is a construct for creating a new asynchronous task. The statement async ⟨*stmt*⟩ causes the parent task to create a new child task to execute ⟨*stmt*⟩ (logically) in parallel with the parent task.

HJ also includes support for *async* tasks with return values in the form of *futures*. The statement, "final future<T> f = async<T> Expr;" creates a new child task to evaluate Expr that is ready to execute immediately. In this case, f contains a "future handle" to the newly created task and the operation f.get() (also known as a *force* operation) can be performed to obtain the result of the future task. If the future task has not completed as yet, the task performing the f.get() operation blocks until the result of Expr becomes available. *Data-driven futures* [10] extend futures by adding an *await* clause that specifies a set of future values that need to be available before the *async* task can be scheduled.

2) finish: The statement finish ⟨*stmt*⟩ causes the parent task to execute ⟨*stmt*⟩ and then wait until all sub-tasks created within ⟨*stmt*⟩ have terminated (including transitively spawned tasks). Operationally, each statement executed in an HJ task has a unique *Immediately Enclosing Finish* (IEF) statement instance [9].

3) isolated: The *isolated* construct enables execution of a statement in isolation (mutual exclusion) relative to all other instances of isolated statements. The statement isolated ⟨*Stmt*⟩ executes ⟨*Stmt*⟩ in isolation with respect to other *isolated* statements. Certain patterns of isolated statements can be replaced by semantically equivalent calls to java.util.concurrent (j.u.c.) libraries for atomic variables and concurrent collections. A new scalable implementation for HJ's isolated construct is described in [7].

4) phasers: The *phaser* construct [9] integrates collective and point-to-point synchronization by giving each task the option of registering with a phaser in *signal-only/wait-only* mode for producer/consumer synchronization or *signal-wait* mode for barrier synchronization[2]. These properties, along with the generality of *dynamic parallelism*, *phase-ordering* and *deadlock-freedom* safety properties, distinguish phasers from synchronization constructs in past work including barriers and X10's clocks [3]. In general, a task may be registered on multiple phasers, and a phaser may have multiple tasks registered on it.

5) forall: The statement forall (point p : R) S supports parallel iteration over all the points in region R by launching each iteration as a separate *async*, and including an implicit *finish* to wait for all of the spawned asyncs to terminate. A *point* is an element of an n-dimensional Cartesian space ($n \geq 1$) with integer-valued coordinates. A *region* is a set of points, and can be used to specify an array allocation or an iteration range as in the case of *async*.

Each dynamic instance of a forall statement includes an implicit phaser object (let us call it ph) that is set up so that all iterations in the forall are registered on ph in *signal-wait* mode. Since the scope of ph is limited to the implicit finish in the forall, the parent task will drop its registration on ph after all the forall iterations are created.

6) places: The *place* construct in HJ provides a way for the programmer to specify affinity among async tasks. A place is an abstraction for a set of worker threads. When an HJ program is launched with the command, "hj -places p:w", a total of $p \times w$ worker threads are created with p places and w workers per place.

---

[1] See http://x10-lang.org for the latest version of X10.

[2] The latest release of j.u.c in Java 7 includes Phaser synchronizer objects, which are derived in part from the phaser construct in HJ.

The number of places remains fixed during program execution. However, the management of individual worker threads within a place is not visible to an HJ program, giving the runtime system the freedom to create additional worker threads in a place, if needed, after starting with w workers per place. The main benefit of use $p > 1$ places is that an optional `at` clause can be specified on an async statement or expression of the form, "`async at(place-expr)` ...", where *place-expr* is a place-valued expression. This clause dictates that the child async task can only be executed by a worker thread at the specified place. Data locality can be controlled by assigning two tasks with the same data affinity to execute in the same place.

2. DrHJ

DrHJ extends DrJava with support for the HJ language. DrHJ builds on past experiences at Rice with developing the DrJava IDE [1] and the HJ language. DrJava is a free, open-source lightweight IDE for Java. It is designed primarily for students, providing an intuitive interface and the ability to interactively evaluate Java code in an *Interactions Pane*. It also includes powerful features for more advanced users, enabling (for example) the DrJava team to develop DrJava completely within DrJava. Since the inception of the DrJava project in 2002, it has been downloaded over 1.25 million times and is being used by many universities world-wide. DrJava has also been used as a teaching tool in books published by Pearson Education and Wiley Higher Education.

Figure 1 shows the general architecture of DrHJ, which can be divided into two main parts, the graphical user interface (GUI) and a collection of compiler plug-ins. It is composed of three elements: a Navigation Pane that shows documents currently opened; a Definitions Pane that contains the source code being edited; and a set of bottom panes that includes the Interactions Pane and panes for compiler messages and program output. The Definitions Pane allows users to edit HJ source code and provides syntax highlighting for HJ keywords. Compilation and execution of HJ programs can be done directly in the IDE.

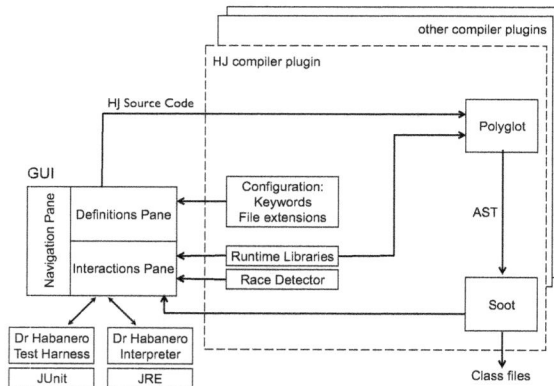

Figure 1. Architecture of the DrHJ IDE

3. Description of Demonstration

This demonstration shows how a rich and powerful set of parallel programming capabilities can be easily introduced to anyone familiar with the basics of sequential programming in Java using the HJ language and the DrHJ IDE. The demo will start with a publicly available download of a single jar file for DrHJ that requires no installation, assuming that a Java Runtime Environment (JRE) is available. We will step through a selected number of laboratory assignments from the COMP 322 class at Rice. For each example, we

will show how a sequential Java program can be easily converted to a parallel program. The HJ compiler is integrated with the DrHJ IDE using a standard plug-in interface. Compiler error messages are transferred back to the IDE and displayed in one of the bottom panes. If compilation is successful, the user can invoke the program by pressing the Run toolbar button, or by using the `run` keyword in the Interactions Pane, followed by the name of the program's main class, and an optional list of arguments for the program (for example: `run Fib 10`).

DrHJ also includes a tool to detect data races in HJ programs, based on the ESP-bags algorithm developed for HJ [8]. The ESP-bags algorithm is a generalization of the SP-bags algorithm developed for Cilk's spawn and sync constructs [5]. Like SP-bags, ESP-bags works by following a depth-first execution of a sequentialized version of the parallel program. The extensions in ESP-bags were necessary because the set of computation graphs generated by async-finish constructs in HJ is more general than the graphs generated by spawn-sync constructs in Cilk. The DrHJ data race detector currently supports HJ programs that contain only `finish`, `async` and `isolated` constructs, since those programs can be easily sequentialized. An important property of the DrHJ data race detector is that it uses the depth-first execution to report all *potential* races that may be encountered for a given input.

While this demonstration will show how multicore programming can be performed simply using the HJ language and the DrHJ IDE, a number of technical challenges had to be overcome in building this system. First, the compiler and the runtime system are all implemented in Java to ensure portability. In fact, HJ's parallel runtime system leverages a number of low-level capabilities in the `java.util.concurrent` library. Second, we have to distinguish between the main JVM that executes the DrHJ IDE, and the the "Interpreter JVM" that executes HJ applications. DrHJ's main JVM communicates with the Interpreter JVM using Java's Remote Method Invocation (RMI) API. Any output produced by the Interpreter JVM is forwarded back to DrHJ to be displayed in the Interactions Pane. Third, DrHJ includes a state-of-the-art data race detector that tracks locations in Java objects and arrays. Finally, all the parallel primitives have highly efficient and scalable implementations on multicore processors.

References

[1] Eric Allen, Robert Cartwright, and Brian Stoler. Drjava: a lightweight pedagogic environment for java. In *SIGCSE '02*, 2002. ACM.

[2] Vincent Cavé, Jisheng Zhao, Jun Shirako, and Vivek Sarkar. Habanero-Java: the New Adventures of Old X10. In *PPPJ'11*, 2011.

[3] P. Charles et al. X10: an object-oriented approach to non-uniform cluster computing. In *OOPSLA'05 Onward! track*, pages 519–538, New York, NY, USA, 2005.

[4] COMP 322: Fundamentals of Parallel Programming. https://wiki.rice.edu/confluence/display/PARPROG/COMP322.

[5] Mingdong Feng and Charles E. Leiserson. Efficient detection of determinacy races in cilk programs. In *SPAA '97*, pages 1–11. ACM, 1997.

[6] Habanero Multicore Software Research Project web page. http://habanero.rice.edu.

[7] Roberto Lublinerman, Jisheng Zhao, Zoran Budimlic, Swarat Chaudhuri, and Vivek Sarkar. Delegated isolation. In *Proceedings of OOPSLA '11*, October 2011.

[8] Raghavan Raman, Jisheng Zhao, Vivek Sarkar, Martin Vechev, and Eran Yahav. Efficient data race detection for async-finish parallelism. In *RV'10*. Springer, Nov 2010.

[9] J. Shirako et al. Phasers: a unified deadlock-free construct for collective and point-to-point synchronization. In *ICS '08*, 2008. ACM.

[10] Sagnak Tasirlar and Vivek Sarkar. Data-driven tasks and their implementation. In *Proceedings of ICPP'11*, September 2011.

Sensor Composer: Composing Intelligent Virtual Sensors for Collaborative Sensing

Hoi Chan

IBM T.J. Watson Research Center
109 Skyline Dr.
Hawthorne, N.Y. 10532
hychan@us.ibm.com

Abstract

Sensor networks have been gaining popularity with the proliferation of internet and wireless networks. Millions of sensors (physical, Webs and social Webs) are available in sensor networks via the internet around the globe collecting enormous amount of data. Generally, sensors provide information about various aspects of the physical world. They can provide information about weather, traffic conditions, efficiency of data center operation, enable autonomic management of smart buildings, and are being used in numerous mobile applications. Due to the diversity and the number of available sensors, it is practically impossible for the general users to manually define the set of sensors that best meets their application needs. The ability to select automatically and intelligently the best set of sensors to form a high level reusable virtual sensor will create a new class of applications and expand the horizon of numerous current applications. To meet these challenges, we developed the Sensor Composer, a foundation tool in which we treat each sensor as a sharable and reusable entity and assemble these sensors to form higher level abstract sensor based on the user requirements.

Categories and Subject Descriptors **H.3.4 H3.5 [Information Systems]: Systems and Software – distributed systems, information network. Online Information Services – data sharing, Web-based services.**

General Terms: Measurement, Design, Economics, Experimentation.

Keywords: demo, GUI, sensors, collaborative, composer, virtual, browser, Web, collaboration.

1. Introduction

Sensor networks have been gaining popularity with the proliferation of internet and wireless networks [1, 2]. Millions of sensors (physical, Webs and social Webs) are available in sensor networks via the internet around the globe collecting enormous amount of data, ranging from GPS enabled sensors to small localized surveillance systems [3]. Until recently, most of these sensors have been used in sophisticated military and industrial applications. Recently, with the widespread use of mobile computing devices and advanced Web browser technologies, these sensors to a large extent have begun to infiltrate people's everyday lives. In general, sensors provide information about various aspects of the physical world. They can provide information about weather, traffic conditions, datacenter operation efficiency, enable autonomic management of smart buildings, and are being used in numerous mobile applications. Due to the diversity and the number of available sensors, it is practically impossible for the general users to manually locate and define the set of sensors that best meets their application needs. The ability to select automatically and intelligently the best set of sensors to form a high level reusable virtual sensor will create a new class of applications and expand the horizon of numerous current applications. To meet these challenges, we developed the Sensor Composer, a foundation tool in which we treat each physical and virtual sensor as a sharable and reusable entity and assemble these sensors to form higher level abstract sensor based on the user requirements.

We use advanced XML and rule technologies to represent and describe sensors and utilize the REST architecture [4] for interactions and communication among various sensors and applications. The Sensor Composer's main user interface is Web browser based [5] and powered by an Apache Server [6]. We illustrate Sensor Composer in two practical scenarios (by constructing and operating a virtual sensor defined as "Comfort Sensor") via interactive GUIs, showcasing the unique features of physical and virtual sensor description, automatic composition and collaboration.

2. Scenarios

2.1 Scenario 1

The first scenario shows architecture and organization of the Sensor Composer, the representation of physical and virtual sensors via rules and other facets and in action the automatic composition of physical and virtual sensors to form a higher level virtual sensor based on its defined goal.

We also show via the interactive GUI the discovery of specific type of sensors, the construction of virtual sensors from various physical and virtual sensors and their description.

Figure 1 shows the home page of the browser based Sensor Composer. From the home page [5], all functions such as sensor locations, sensor composition and sensor management can be accessed with typical browser controls. Figure 2 shows the sensor discovery and location page [5] while Figure 3 shows sensor composition and management page [7].

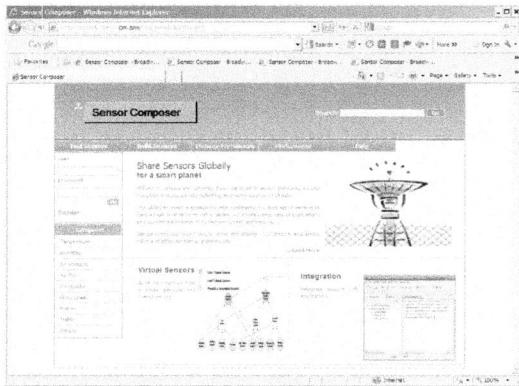

Figure 1 Sensor Composer home

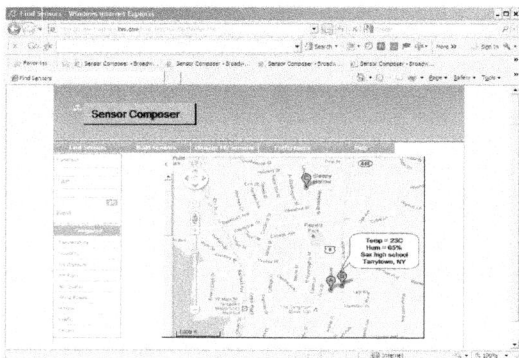

Figure 2 Sensor Composer: locate sensors

2.2 Scenario 2

Second scenario shows the integration of the virtual sensors integrated with a commercial application ITM (IBM Tivoli Monitoring) [8, 9]. ITM is a commercially available product for data monitoring and management and data from virtual sensors will be displayed in real time on ITM's monitoring console.

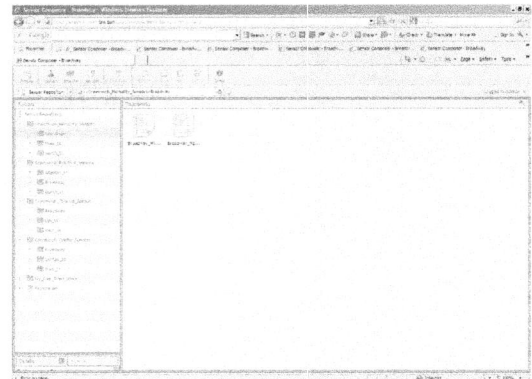

Figure 3 Sensor Composer: compose sensors

Acknowledgments

The author wishes to express his gratitude to Dr. Jeff Kephart who was abundantly helpful and offered invaluable assistance, support and guidance.

References

[1] Yick, J., Mukherjee, B., Ghosal, D.: Wireless sensor network survey. Computer Networks 52(12)(2008) 2292.

[2] Ware, R.H,, etl.al,. "SuomiNet: A real–time national GPS nework for atomspheric research and education," Bull Ameri.Meteror. Soc., 81, 677-694.

[3] M. Feng, S. Wen, K. Tsai, Y. Liu and H. Lai, "Wireless Sensor Network and Fusion Technology for Ubiquitous Smart Living Space Applications," in 2nd International Symposium on Univesal Communication, 2008, pp 295.

[4] http://en.wikipedia.org/wiki/ Representational_State_Transfer.

[5] http://www.freewebsitetemplates.com

[6] http://www.apache.org.

[7] http://www.ajaxplorer.info.

[8] http://www.ibm.com/software/tivoli/products/monitor/

[9] IBM, ITM are trademarks of IBM Coporation

A HIP and SLEEK Verification System

Wei-Ngan Chin, Cristina David, Cristian Gherghina

Department of Computer Science, National University of Singapore

Abstract

The HIP/SLEEK systems are aimed at automatic verification of functional correctness of heap manipulating programs. HIP is a separation logic based automated verification system for a simple imperative language, able to modularly verify the specifications of heap-manipulating programs. The specification language allows user defined inductive predicates used to model complex data structures. Specifications can contain both heap constraints and various pure constraints like arithmetic constraints, bag constraints. Based on given annotations for each method/loop, HIP will construct a set of separation logic proof obligations in the form of formula implications which are sent to the SLEEK separation logic prover. SLEEK is a fully automatic prover for separation logic with frame inferring capability.

Categories and Subject Descriptors D.2.4 [*SOFTWARE ENGINEERING*]: Software/Program Verification

General Terms Verification

1. Description

HIP is a separation logic based automated verification system for a simple imperative language, able to modularly verify heap-manipulating programs.

The system can handle programs with complex data structures. HIP accepts abstract descriptions for such structures in the form of inductive predicates. Predicates are represented as separation logic formulae that describe the shape of data structures together with their derived properties, such as length, height and bag of values.

Given annotations for each method/loop with one or more pre/post conditions[2], the HIP verifier constructs a set of obligations in the form of implication checks between pairs of formulae which are then sent to the SLEEK prover to be discharged. The specification language allows rich specifications[5] that contain both heap constraints expressed as separation logic formulae and several different logic fragments like Presburger arithmetic, bags, lists for the pure constraints[1]. By making use of set/bag solvers, the user can also encode reachability conditions as a set/bag of values that can be collected from some given data structure. Such conditions are then automatically discharged by HIP.

HIP relies on the SLEEK prover in order to discharge the verification conditions. SLEEK[7] is a fully automatic prover for separation logic with frame inferring capability. It takes as input two heap states represented by separation formulae, and checks if one formula (the antecedent) entails the other (the consequent). The antecedent may cover more heap states than the consequent, so a residual heap state which represents the frame condition can be returned by the prover. This residual heap state will include the pure state of the antecedent. SLEEK also supports instantiation of logical variables that appear during the entailment as existential variables in the consequent. As part of the implication check, SLEEK discharges the heap obligations, the obligations pertaining to the shape of data structures and translates the remaining pure obligations to pure constraints that can be discharged by theorem provers. The list of possible pure provers includes Omega (a Presburger prover), MONA (based on monadic second-order logic), CVC Lite, Z3, and Isabelle (a general purpose theorem prover that supports some automatic tactics).

2. Examples

In the current demo, we are going to present a suite of examples handling mutable data structures. Each example will contain the heap predicates describing the data structures used by the example, together with a few methods performing operations on the data structures. Each method is decorated with pre/post conditions. The task of the HIP verifier is to check each method implementation against the given specification. If the specification is not met then it reports the obligation that could not be discharged and the source of it. Furthermore in the process of verifying a method, pointer safety guarantees like null dereferencing are naturally enforced. Similarly, bounds checks, can be encoded and verified as well.

SPLASH'11 Companion,   October 22–27, 2011, Portland, Oregon, USA.
ACM 978-1-4503-0940-0/11/10.

Some of the examples presented in the demonstration are enumerated below:

- Examples involving an acyclic linked list (that terminates with a `null` reference). The heap predicate describing the list can be described by:

$$\text{root} :: \text{ll}\langle n \rangle \equiv (\text{root}=\text{null} \wedge n=0) \vee (\exists i, m, q \cdot \text{root}::\text{node}\langle i, q \rangle * q::\text{ll}\langle m \rangle \wedge n=m+1) \text{ inv } n \geq 0$$

The parameter `n` captures a *derived* value that denotes the length of the acyclic list starting from `root` pointer. The above definition asserts that an `ll` list can be empty (the base case `root=null`) or consists of a head data node (specified by `root::node`$\langle i, q \rangle$) and a separate tail data structure which is also an `ll` list (`q::ll`$\langle m \rangle$). The $*$ connector ensures that the head node and the tail reside in disjoint heaps. We also specify a default invariant $n \geq 0$ that holds for all `ll` lists. (This invariant can be verified by checking that each disjunctive branch of the predicate definition always implies its stated invariant. In the case of `ll` predicate, the disjunctive branch with $n = 0$ implies the given invariant $n \geq 0$. Similarly, the $n = m + 1$ branch together with $m \geq 0$ from the invariant of `q::ll`$\langle m \rangle$ also implies the given invariant $n \geq 0$.) Our predicate uses existential quantifiers for local values and pointers, such as `i, m, q`.

With the `ll` predicate we can, for example, specify the expected behaviour of a list append operation as follows:

```
void append(node x, node y)
  requires x :: ll⟨n₁⟩* y :: ll⟨n₂⟩ ∧ n₁>0
  ensures x :: ll⟨n₁ + n₂⟩;
```

This specification guarantees that if two lists of sizes n_1 and n_2 are appended then the result will be a list of size $n_1 + n_2$. Depending on the properties of interest and the precision required, the user provided specifications can be easily refined further. The specification language allows the user to supply varied granularities for the precision of the specification, by default coarser specifications can be used and more refined ones can be added only when required. For example, the previous specification does not require that the resulting list contains all the initial elements however if such a constraint is needed it can easily be added.

- Examples regarding sorted linked list operations.
- Examples involving AVL tree structures.
- We also investigate the benefits of immutability guarantees for allowing more flexible handling of aliasing, as well as more precise and concise specifications. Our approach supports finer levels of control that can localize and mark parts of a data structure as being immutable through the use of selective annotations on predicate and data declarations. Additionally, we support either partial or total immutability on each predicate. By using such annotations to encode immutability guarantees, we expect to obtain better specifications that can more accurately describe the intentions, as well as prohibitions, of the method. Ultimately, our goal is improving the precision of the verification process, as well as making the specifications more readable, more precise and as an enforceable program documentation.

- Conventional specifications typically have a flat structure that is based primarily on the underlying logic. Such specifications lack structures that could have provided better guidance to the verification process. In this demo we will also investigate three new structures to our specification framework for separation logic to achieve a *more precise* and *better guided* verification for pointer-based programs. The newly introduced structures empower users with more control over the verification process in the following ways: (i) case analysis can be invoked to take advantage of disjointedness conditions in the logic. (ii) early, as opposed to late, instantiation can minimize on the use of existential quantification. (iii) formulae that are staged provide better reuse of the verification process.

- Examples of entailments of separation heap constraints using SLEEK.

3. About the speaker

Cristina David is a PhD student at National University of Singapore, working under the supervision of Wei-Ngan Chin. During her studies, she participated in developing the HIP and SLEEK systems, and co-authored a few of the papers based on these systems [3, 4, 6].

References

[1] Wei-Ngan Chin, Cristina David, Huu Hai Nguyen, and Shengchao Qin. Automated verification of shape, size and bag properties. In *ICECCS*, pages 307–320, 2007.

[2] Wei-Ngan Chin, Cristina David, Huu Hai Nguyen, and Shengchao Qin. Multiple pre/post specifications for heap-manipulating methods. In *HASE*, pages 357–364, 2007.

[3] Wei-Ngan Chin, Cristina David, Huu Hai Nguyen, and Shengchao Qin. Enhancing modular oo verification with separation logic. In *POPL*, pages 87–99, 2008.

[4] Cristina David, Cristian Gherghina, and Wei-Ngan Chin. Translation and optimization for a core calculus with exceptions. In *PEPM*, pages 41–50, 2009.

[5] Cristian Gherghina, Cristina David, Shengchao Qin, and Wei-Ngan Chin. Structured specifications for better verification of heap-manipulating programs. In *FM*, 2011.

[6] H. H. Nguyen, C. David, S.C. Qin, and W.N. Chin. Automated Verification of Shape And Size Properties via Separation Logic. In *VMCAI*, Nice, France, January 2007.

[7] Huu Hai Nguyen and Wei-Ngan Chin. Enhancing program verification with lemmas. In *CAV*, pages 355–369, 2008.

Distributed Ray Tracing in X10

Dave Cunningham

IBM TJ Watson
dcunnin@watson.ibm.com

Abstract

We will demonstrate the maturity of the X10 programming language by implementing such a real-time ray tracer using a pile of low spec GPGPU laptops and a Gigabit Ethernet switch. Ray tracing is a rendering technique that can better simulate complex lighting situations such as reflections and refractions. It is typically too computationally expensive for real-time rendering on a single CPU and is non-trivial to implement in a distributed fashion.

Categories and Subject Descriptors   D [*3*]: 3

General Terms   Languages, Performance, Human Factors

Keywords   CUDA, GPU, X10, Heterogeneous, Distributed, Multicore, Parallel, High-level, Java.

1. Description

The difficulties of distributed / multi-core / GPGPU programming are well-known. We show how the X10[3] programming language can make them more tractable with its Asynchronous Partitioned Global Address Space (APGAS) [5] programming model and high-level Java-like aesthetic. To give weight to the argument that X10 is ready for real programs, we demonstrate a real-time distributed ray tracer, a complex piece of software that has strict performance requirements, written in pure X10.

The ray tracing is done in a distributed fashion using several cores on several laptops. To demonstrate the use of X10 for GPGPU programming, the ray tracer uses the GPUs of the laptops for fluid dynamics computations.

The audience will see the real-time scene rendered by the laptops. There will then be a short code review showing how the APGAS model is used to implement the ray tracer and take advantage of the various hardware available. Brave audience members can elect to take control and explore the scene.

The actual ray tracing algorithms are not novel. The novelty is the use of the X10 language for ease of writing such an application for commodity hardware. A ray tracer was chosen to exemplify X10 language constructs and the APGAS programming model because it is challenging to write, and engaging for audience members to see in action. Likewise, the fluid simulation exists only to demonstrate how a GPU-accelerated application can be written in X10.

SPLASH'11 Companion,   October 22–27, 2011, Portland, Oregon. USA.
ACM 978-1-4503-0940-0/11/10.

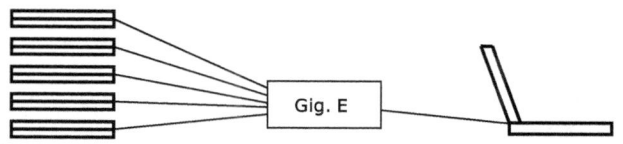

Figure 1. Laptop cluster

2. System

The ray tracer is written entirely in X10 and compiled using the X10 compiler's 'native' (C++) backend. About a half dozen dual core laptops form a portable x86 Linux cluster to run this demo. The networking infrastructure is Gigabit Ethernet.

One of the laptops is used for the display and for the keyboard/mouse input required to navigate the scene. A small amount of GL[1] pixel buffer code is used to blit the ray-traced output into video memory. We use GLUT for the keyboard / mouse processing.

3. APGAS model

The APGAS model divides the heap into a fixed number of places. Each place occupies its own address space, an operating system process. However, there are references between places and static checking to ensure objects are only accessed by code running at the right place. In X10, code switches place using a construct `at (p) S` where p is an expression that yields a place object and S is the statement to be synchronously executed remotely. S can use variables from the enclosing scope, in which case they are copied automatically by the runtime.

We can now express distribution but not parallelism. Parallelism is handled via the constructs `async S` and `finish S`, which together define a fork/join concurrency model. For synchronisation, there is an `atomic S` construct for mutual exclusion and a `when (c) S` construct that atomically waits for a boolean condition to be true. These basic constructs express the core language, but there are also libraries that provide more high level features and support optimised communication patterns such as remote array copies and barriers.

In the ray tracer, each laptop is a place, and the special laptop that is displaying the output is place 0.

4. Parallelisation

The top-level structure of the code is a frame loop that loops until program termination, each iteration consisting of the following steps: Mouse and keyboard events are interpreted by place zero, causing a new camera position to be computed, and distributed to the other places. Each place maintains a local copy of the scene to reduce communication costs. The rendering work is divided by carving the frame buffer into a grid of equally-sized rectangles, one for each place. These are then further subdivided to exploit multi-core. All these small rectangles are thus rendered in parallel, and

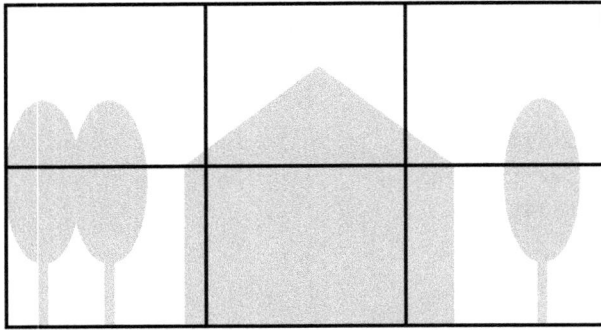

Figure 2. Partitioning of screen

when complete, each thread copies its colour data (using the remote array copy API) into the GL pixel buffer at place 0. After a global synchronisation barrier (another library), it is guaranteed that all frame data has been supplied, so place 0 signals to GL that the pixel buffer is populated and refreshes the screen.

5. Raytracing

The raytracing algorithm supports a simple set of primitives, currently spheres and triangles. To render a scene efficiently there is an octree datastructure [7] for efficient spatial queries. We have implemented simple textures and shading models to bring the scene to life. Water is rendered by intersecting rays with a heightmap. Ray tracers are able to easily implement reflection and refraction and we take advantage of this as well, using an object-oriented material framework.

X10's structs are used to implement a 3D vector library, and quaternion library, that store objects on the stack to reduce garbage collection overheads.

6. Water Simulation

The water is animated by simulating the wave motion using the GPU to compute the new values in the height field. The work is again divided among the places by carving up the water into equally-sized rectangles. It is possible to interact with the water to create simple splashes and observe the effects in the rendered output.

The GPGPU programming is achieved using additional places to represent the GPU memory spaces, and async/finish to represent the GPU programming model with its unique concurrency hierarchy. The implementation compiles X10 code to CUDA code and integrates the X10 runtime to the CUDA runtime to transparently launch kernels on the GPU and deal with memory DMAs.

7. Conclusion

We have written a real-time, distributed, and concurrent ray tracer with GPGPU water simulation in the X10 programming language. We believe that, especially for a program that uses such a wide range of concurrency idioms, X10's language constructs and AP-GAS programming model allow a simpler exposition of the core behaviour (i.e. tracing rays, materials, and lighting models) than would be possible using a fusion of low-level models, such as MPI[6], CUDA[4], and OpenMP[2]. The performance of the ray tracer demonstrates that the implementation of X10 is mature enough to be seriously considered by users outside the X10 team.

8. Bio

Dave Cunningham is a member of the X10 core team at IBM TJ Watson. He has worked on many areas of X10's language design, compiler implementation, and runtime implementation. Previously he completed a PhD at Imperial College London with Sophia Drossopoulou and Susan Eisenbach in the field of lock checking and lock inference for atomic sections.

References

[1] Open graphics library. http://www.opengl.org/, .

[2] The OpenMP API specification for parallel programming. http://www.openmp.org/, .

[3] The X10 Programming Language. http://www.x10-lang.org.

[4] NVIDIA Inc. Nvidia CUDA programming guide, version 3.0, 2010.

[5] V. Saraswat, G. Almasi, G. Bikshandi, C. Cascaval, D. Cunningham, D. Grove, S. Kodali, I. Peshansky, and O. Tardieu. The asynchronous partitioned global address space model. In *Proceedings of The First Workshop on Advances in Message Passing*, PLDI'10.

[6] M. Snir, S. Otto, S. Huss-Lederman, D. Walker, and J. Dongarra. *MPI - The Complete Reference, second edition*. The MIT Press, 2000.

[7] Wikipeida. Octree. http://en.wikipedia.org/wiki/Octree.

Parallel Programming by Hints

Chen Ding

Department of Computer Science
University of Rochester

Abstract

A sequential program is difficult to parallelize often due to the complexity in its implementation and the uncertainty in its behavior. *Behavior-oriented parallelization* (BOP) provides annotations for a user to mark possibly parallel tasks and a safe implementation to execute the annotated tasks in parallel if they produce the correct result — the same result as the sequential execution. The demonstration includes a description of the interface and two examples.

Categories and Subject Descriptors D.1.3 [*Concurrent Programming*]: Parallel programming

General Terms Languages

Keywords safe parallel programming

1. Introduction

BOP hints express likely rather than definite parallelism [1, 2]. They annotate possibly parallel regions (*PPR*) in a sequential C program. The hints divide a program into *PPR* tasks. *BOP* implementation uses first data copy-on-write to isolate each *PPR* task from its peers and then in-order commit to ensure sequential semantics. It may roll back and re-execute if necessary. The *BOP* execution always produces the same result as the sequential execution without hints.

2. BOP Interface

First, *BOP* provides hints of parallelism and dependence. Three are shown below. The use of these hints in a program affects its parallelism but does not change its output.

- bop_ppr{ code } marks a block of code and suggests task parallelism—the *PPR* block may be parallel with the code after the *PPR* block.

- bop_ordered{ code } marks a block of code and suggests an ordered execution when run by multiple *PPR* tasks— the ordered block should be run one task at a time and in the order of the original (sequential) program.

- bop_abort_spec is a speculation barrier. *BOP* terminates speculation before a barrier (so the code at the barrier is never speculated). A barrier is inserted before system calls and other unrecoverable operations.

Second, *BOP* provides two annotations to mark *PPR* accesses to shared data: one for read access and one for write access. The annotations are needed by the *BOP* run-time system to detect parallel conflicts. They affect program correctness and the cost of *PPR* monitoring.

- bop_promise(*addr, size*) is called by a *PPR* task to mark a block of memory that has been or will be modified by the *PPR* task. Only promised changes will be copied out when the task finishes.

- bop_use(*addr, size*) is called to mark a block of memory that needs the most recent value in sequential semantics—the same one as if the program is executed sequentially.

When annotating an access to a single datum, e.g. x, we abbreviate and mark just the name, which means $\&x, sizeof(x)$.

3. Demonstration

In the first example below, we use two *PPR*s to suggest that the two statements may be parallel. Then we annotate two data accesses. The first is a promise, which marks the write to $g[x]$. The second is a use, which marks the read of $g[y]$. The parallelism depends on whether the two array cells are the same, which is checked by the *BOP* run time. As mentioned before, the use annotation is an assertion that $g[y]$ must read the same value as in sequential execution (for the parallel execution to be correct).

Listing 1: two *PPR* tasks

```
# try setting g[x] and using g[y] in parallel
read x, y
bop_ppr {
    bop_promise( g[x] )
    g[x] = foo( )
}
bop_ppr {
    bop_use( g[y] )
    bar( g[y] )
}
```

SPLASH'11 Companion, October 22–27, 2011, Portland, Oregon, USA.
ACM 978-1-4503-0940-0/11/10.

The second example is a parallelized version of *strcmp*, part of the standard C library. In practice, it is useful only when two very long strings are compared. For this demo, the code is non-trivial yet short, so it makes a good illustration.

The example code divides the input strings into chunks. Each task compares a chunk. *Parallelization is both input and behavior dependent*: we do not know beforehand the length of the string or the location of the first difference. Using *BOP*, we suggest each chunk comparison as possibly parallel. Then we annotate the two accesses to the loop termination variable *done*: a use when it is tested at the start of each iteration and a promise when it is set in the last iteration. When a task executes the promise, *BOP* discards those and only those tasks working on subsequent chunks (because their use was wrong). The "promising" task continues and eventually exits the loop.

Listing 2: parallel *strcmp*

```
procedure strcmp( str1 , str2 ):
  done , ret = false , 0
  step = 2000000   # 2MB per chunk / task
  while ( !done ) {
    bop_use( done )
    ptr1 , ptr2 = str1 , str2

    bop_ppr {

      do {
        c1 = *ptr1++
        c2 = *ptr2++
      } while ( c1==c2 && ptr1<base1+step )

      if ( c1=='\0' || c1!=c2 ) {
        ret = c1 − c2
        done = true
        bop_promise( ret )
        bop_promise( done )
      }
    }
    str1 += step
    str2 += step
  }
  return ret
```

Through copy-on-write and sequential commit, *BOP* let each task maintains a local version of shared data. Errors in incorrect tasks do not affect other tasks. In this example, it does not affect correctness if a speculative task reads unmapped memory and triggers a segmentation fault.

The two examples have shown the hint and the annotation interface and the safety guarantee. The *BOP* system currently runs on x86 multi-core machines with 64-bit Linux or Mac OS X operating system.

Originally *BOP* has only the parallelism hint and uses a process for each *PPR* task [1]. It supports coarse-grained parallelism with hundreds of milliseconds per task. A recent version supports both parallelism and dependence hints and reuses a process for multiple *PPR* tasks [2]. Process reuse makes *BOP* profitable for finer grained parallelism with sub-millisecond length tasks.

4. Benefits

Hints based parallelization addresses the problems of uncertain parallelism due to either implementation or program input. It enables safe parallelization of programs that use legacy code and programs that have frequent but uncertain parallelism. Its sequential semantics means that there is no need for parallel debugging. Separately annotated modules can be composed without losing correctness as long as the composition of their sequential version is correct. The parallelized code can be run with other sequential code or automatically parallelized code. A program may be fully annotated so it no longer needs speculation. A *BOP* program can run on a cluster of machines without shared memory (not included in this demonstration). *BOP* supports incremental programming. Conflicts are detected and removed gradually based on feedback and testing. Finally, it supports safe specialization—a user can parallelize a program just for specific usage scenarios.

About the Speaker

Chen Ding (cding@cs.rochester.edu) is a Professor of Computer Science at University of Rochester. His research seeks to model and manage large-scale program behavior especially dynamic parallelism and locality. He received young investigator awards from NSF and DOE, co-founded the ACM SIGPLAN Workshop on Memory System Performance and Correctness (MSPC), and was a visiting researcher at Microsoft Research and a visiting associate professor at MIT.

Acknowledgment

Process reuse in *BOP* is developed by Chuanle Ke and Lei Liu at Institute of Computing Technology, part of the Chinese Academy of Sciences. The idea was inspired by Long Chen. Zachary Fletcher at Rochester provided the string comparison test. The author also wishes to thank the two reviewers for their comments and suggestions. This research is supported by NSF (Contract No. CCF-0963759, CNS-0720796), and IBM CAS Faculty Fellowships.

References

[1] C. Ding, X. Shen, K. Kelsey, C. Tice, R. Huang, and C. Zhang. Software behavior oriented parallelization. In *PLDI*, pages 223–234, 2007.

[2] C. Ke, L. Liu, C. Zhang, T. Bai, and C. Ding. Safe parallel programming using dynamic dependence hints. In *OOPSLA*, 2011.

The Language of Languages Research Project: Unifying Concepts Expressed Across Different Notations

James R. Douglass

The Boeing Company
jamie.douglass@boeing.com

Nicholas Chen   Ralph E. Johnson

University of Illinois at Urbana-Champaign
{nchen, rjohnson}@illinois.edu

Abstract

Maintaining the consistency of multiple notations used in large projects is daunting. Language of Languages(LoLs) is our experimental language workbench that fulfills a frequently overlooked but important role: *unify* the different notations so developers can better understand and evolve a project. Due to the impossibility of anticipating all the notations that may be used in a project, LoLs adopts a language agnostic view and supports different notations from freeform text to graphical forms and shapes. Our demo begins by illustrating the fundamental ideas of LoLs through building a calculator that supports multiple notations; the demo concludes with more advanced projects that exemplify the extent of our multi-notation support.

Categories and Subject Descriptors   D.2.2 [*Software Engineering*]: Design Tools and Techniques;   D.3.3 [*Programming Languages*]: Language Constructs and Features

General Terms   Design, Languages

Keywords   Language Workbench, Modeling, Smalltalk

1 Introduction

Different programming languages, libraries and frameworks provide **different** notations for representing components. For instance, state machines, a common component used in many engineering disciplines, can be expressed using VHDL code (text) or state diagrams (graphics). Large projects seldom, if ever, commit to just a single notation. Instead, multiple notations are used, with developers choosing the most expressive one for the task at hand.

Using multiple notations creates several challenges: (i) **communication** – how would my colleagues understand the notations that I have chosen? (ii) **correctness** – how would we verify that notations are consistent with one another? LoLs [1] has an ambitious goal: distill the core concepts from each component and attempt to unify these underlying concepts across different notations.

This unification maintains consistency and facilitates *virtual integration* of components as the project evolves. Virtual integration, done early and continuously, enables prompt detection of problems and reduces the cost of fixing them. Virtual integration is a key component of the System Architecture Virtual Integration (SAVI) project [3], and we see LoLs as one feasible approach for supporting it.

2 Language of Languages Approach

Consider the simple expression "3 + 4". There are different notations to represent this expression: in Western Numerals, Roman Numerals, or even using graphics. Regardless of the notation, the underlying *concept* remains the same: we are adding two numbers together. How can we represent this concept across different notations?

The fundamental building block of LoLs is the `Language Element`. Everything has a corresponding `Language Element`. In Figure 1, the symbols "3", "+" and "4" have corresponding `Language Elements`. These `Language Elements` form a `Language Element Tree`. Each `Language Element` has a corresponding `Concept`. In our example, we have two `Concepts`: Addition and Number. Each `Concept`, in turn, has several `Language Definitions` that it can select from. In our example, we have three `Language Definitions`: Western, Roman and Graphical. The Western Definition is being used in our example (indicated by the check mark).

The fundamental idea of LoLs is thinking in terms of reusable `Concepts` that apply across different notations. Each notation is supported by a particular `Language Definition`. `Language Defintions` do not stand alone; they can reference other `Concepts`. For instance, it is necessary for the `Addition Concept` to reference and use the `Number Concept`. Each `Language Definition` supports **three** operations: checking, parsing and projecting.

Checking The checking operation validates if a `Language Definition` is applicable for the current context.

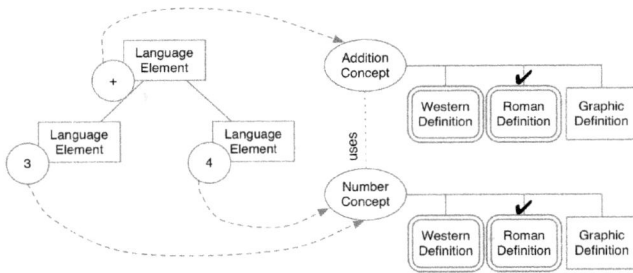

Figure 1. Fundamental building blocks in LoLs for the "3+4" example.

Parsing The parsing operation recognizes the notation that is being used and builds a `Language Element Tree` from each construct of interest.

Projecting The projecting operation interprets or transforms `Language Elements`. This operation can take a Language Element Tree and reduce it to a single value e.g. the tree in Figure 1 is reduced to the value 7. Or, it can transform a Language Element Tree from one notation (Western Numerals) to a different notation (Graphical).

Our approach allows us to easily "plug-n-play" different concepts. New `Concepts` and `Language Definitions` can easily be written by the developer or extended from existing ones. Judicious use of `Concepts` and `Language Definitions` in LoLs affords the developer a lot of freedom in expressing the underlying domain knowledge. It is an open research question to catalog the common concepts that apply to various projects.

3 Agenda for Demo

We begin by showing how to build a basic calculator in LoLs. We start with a calculator that only understands Western Numerals and show how to add support for graphical notations in a modular fashion. Starting with a simple example provides the audience with both a high-level overview of LoLs and also a deeper understanding of how our tool is implemented. Figure 2 shows the preliminary user interface for our tool. After familiarizing the audience with the basic ideas, we will demonstrate how to support projects that require the use of multiple notations. These projects illustrate the extent of our support for multiple notations.

The SPLASH community has always been at the forefront of new ideas and would be a befitting audience for LoLs. LoLs is a novel idea that presents not only a new way of thinking about programming but also a minimalistic yet flexible approach that is easily extensible. Our current bootstrap implementation in Squeak Smalltalk [2] makes good use of metacircularity (LoLs is defined in terms of itself) and well-known design patterns for its core. We leverage the Morphic graphic system in Squeak to support graphical notations. LoLs has a small core that is easy to understand and extend for different purposes.

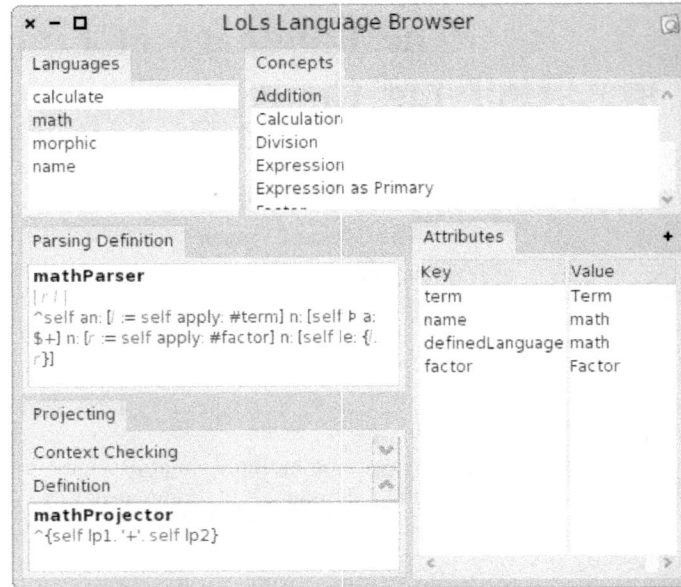

Figure 2. Language Workbench in bootstrap version of LoLs.

The LoLs bootstrap and examples presented will be available for download from `www.LanguageOfLanguages.org` after our demo. LoLs is an open source project under the MIT license and we encourage participation and contributions from the community.

4 Presenters

Jamie Douglass and Nicholas Chen are the main developers of LoLs. Jamie Douglass is an Architect and Associate Technical Fellow within the Office of IT Chief Engineer at the Boeing Company. His research interests include language based integration, modeling and software development. Nicholas Chen is a PhD candidate in the Software Architecture Group at the University of Illinois. His research interest lies in mining patterns of software evolution and creating flexible software engineering tools to support them.

Acknowledgments

The authors thank Jeff Overbey, Kathleen Chalas and Eric Reed for feedback on earlier drafts of this manuscript.

References

[1] J. R. Douglass. Language of Languages for Flexible Development. In *FlexiTools@SPLASH2010*, 2010.

[2] D. Ingalls, T. Kaehler, J. Maloney, S. Wallace, and A. Kay. Back to the future: the story of Squeak, a practical Smalltalk written in itself. *SIGPLAN Not.*, 32:318–326, October 1997. ISSN 0362-1340.

[3] D. Redman, D. Ward, J. Chilenski, and G. Pollari. Virtual Integration for Improved System Design. In *The First Analytic Virtual Integratio of Cyber-Physical Systems Workshop*, 2010.

Library-based Model-driven Software Development with SugarJ

Sebastian Erdweg*   Lennart C. L. Kats[†]   Tillmann Rendel*
Christian Kästner*   Klaus Ostermann*   Eelco Visser[†]

* University of Marburg
[†] Delft University of Technology

Abstract

SugarJ is a Java-based programming language that provides extensible surface syntax, static analyses, and IDE support. SugarJ extensions are organized as libraries; conventional import statements suffice to activate and compose language extensions. We demonstrate how programmers can use SugarJ to modularly extend Java's syntax, semantic analyses and IDE support.

Categories and Subject Descriptors   D.3.2 [*Language Classifications*]: Extensible languages;   D.2.13 [*Reusable Software*]

General Terms   Languages

Keywords   language extensibility, library, DSL embedding, language workbench

1. Introduction

With embedded domain-specific languages (DSLs) and language-oriented programming, two core requirements arise: Languages have to be extensible and language extensions need to compose easily. Programmers require language extensibility to break up the ties to a single (typically general-purpose) programming language and to benefit from all aspects of embedded DSLs (for instance, domain-specific syntax or IDE support). Furthermore, since software projects touch upon multiple domains, it is essential to support composing DSLs for the common case of conflict-free language composition. For example, it should be possible to extend Java with SQL, XML or regular expressions with regard to their concrete syntax, IDE support (e.g., code completion), static analyses (e.g., XML Schema validation), and so forth. It should be simple for programmers to use any combination of such language extensions within a single source file.

To address these goals, we propose to organize and implement language extensions as libraries in the object language itself. In contrast to conventional libraries, *language libraries* do not export functionality and data structures but rather stipulate an augmentation of the object language. Due to our library-based design, a programmer can easily activate and compose language extensions by simply importing the corresponding language libraries; no external configuration or reasoning is necessary to understand a given source file. Furthermore, programmers can readily implement a language extension themselves by writing a language library; no additional tools but the object language compiler are required. Lastly, language libraries inherit the self-applicability property from conventional libraries, that is, language extensions can be used for developing language extensions: domain syntax, IDE support and static analyses for the definition of syntactic extensions, IDE extensions, static analyses, and so forth.

We have developed an extension of Java—called *SugarJ*—which demonstrates the feasibility of our library-based approach for extending a language [2]. SugarJ supports the definition of syntactic sugar within libraries, where each syntactic sugar extends the grammar of the object language and specifies a transformation—called desugaring—from the extended syntax into the base syntax. Programmers can activate and compose (domain-specific) syntax extensions through simple import statements that bring the corresponding libraries into scope. Technically, we support library-based syntax extensions through an incremental parsing process that parses a file one top-level entry at a time and adapts its own grammar as it goes along. The finally resulting abstract syntax tree is desugared using all desugarings in scope.

For example, consider the illustration of a SugarJ source file in Figure 1. We extended the base language with syntax for XML through an import of the xml.Sugar library and compose the grammar of XML with SugarJ's base grammar, so that SugarJ parses XML documents as part of the surrounding Java syntax. Furthermore, the xml.Sugar library declares a desugaring of XML to Java, which SugarJ applies after parsing. Programmers can easily compose the XML embedding with other syntactic extensions such as SQL or regular expressions by adding more import statements.

As the screenshot furthermore highlights, we generalize our library-based extensibility mechanism towards IDEs [1]. Accordingly, we promote to organize and implement IDE extensions within libraries of the object language, so that simple import statements suffice to activate and compose editor services of several DSLs. In the example above, we import the xml.Editor library and the Book schema to bring syntax coloring and code completion for XML into scope. Such editor services compose with editor services for Java because each one only affects those fragments of the syntax tree that correspond to Java *or* XML, respectively. We have implemented a prototypical extensible IDE—called *Sugarclipse*—based on the Spoofax language workbench [3] and its support for the declarative configuration and dynamic reloading of editors. Sugarclipse provides editor services on a file-by-file basis, according to the libraries in scope.

In summary, SugarJ is a lightweight and scalable alternative to model-driven language workbenches: it is lightweight because it is

SPLASH'11 Companion,   October 22–27, 2011, Portland, Oregon, USA.
ACM 978-1-4503-0940-0/11/10.

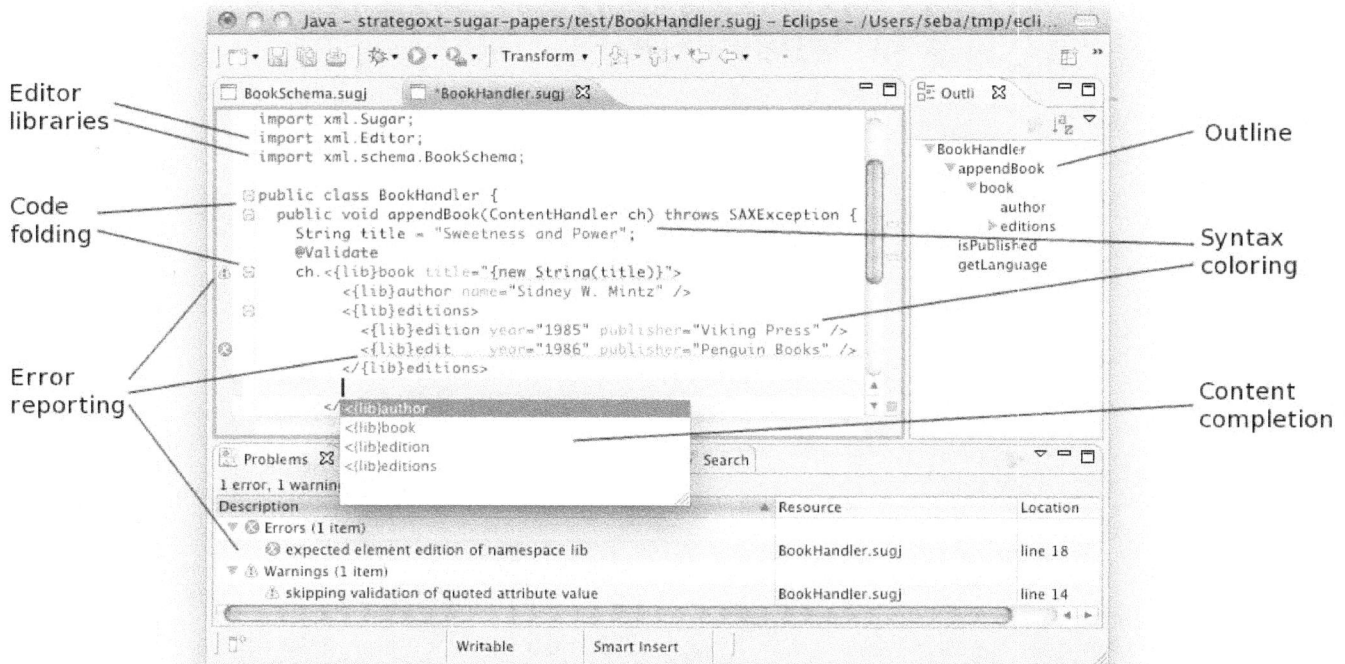

Figure 1. SugarJ extended with support for XML processing: The library xml.Sugar provides an integration of XML syntax, xml.Editor provides XML IDE support (e.g., code coloring, folding and outlining), and xml.schema.BookSchema integrates XML validation and auto-completion rules derived from an XML schema.

purely textual and aligns with the host language's module system; it is scalable because DSLs and their code generators can easily be combined and composed.

SugarJ is an open source project; its compiler, Eclipse plugin and case studies are publicly available at http://sugarj.org.

2. Demonstration description

In our SugarJ demonstration, we will illustrate how to grow a language's syntax, static checks and tool support using our library-based extensibility approach. In particular, we will demonstrate how to perform the following tasks with SugarJ:

- Extend Java with syntactic language extensions and DSL embeddings.
- Specify domain-specific static analyses on top of a DSL embedding.
- Provide domain-specific IDE support such as code completion.
- Compose language extensions to support multiple DSLs in single files.
- Incrementally build language extensions on top of each other.

In addition, we will elaborate on the technical challenges we encountered while realizing SugarJ. In particular, we will discuss our incremental parsing technique, which takes import statements into account when parsing the remainder of a file, and explain how this parsing technique co-operates with source location tracking as needed for error marking and syntax highlighting.

3. About the presenters

Sebastian Erdweg is a Ph.D. student in the programming language and software engineering research group at University of Marburg and leads the SugarJ project. He received an honours master's degree in computer science from Aarhus University. Klaus Ostermann is full professor at the University of Marburg and leads the programming language and software engineering research group.

Acknowledgments

This work is supported in part by the European Research Council, grant No. 203099, and NWO/EW Open Competition project 612.063.512, *TFA: Transformations for Abstractions*.

References

[1] S. Erdweg, L. C. L. Kats, T. Rendel, C. Kästner, K. Ostermann, and E. Visser. Growing a language environment with editor libraries. In *Proceedings of Conference on Generative Programming and Component Engineering (GPCE)*. ACM, 2011.

[2] S. Erdweg, T. Rendel, C. Kästner, and K. Ostermann. SugarJ: Library-based syntactic language extensibility. In *Proceedings of Conference on Object-Oriented Programming, Systems, Languages, and Applications (OOPSLA)*. ACM, 2011.

[3] L. C. L. Kats and E. Visser. The Spoofax language workbench: Rules for declarative specification of languages and IDEs. In *Proceedings of Conference on Object-Oriented Programming, Systems, Languages, and Applications (OOPSLA)*, pages 444–463. ACM, 2010.

BeneFactor: A Flexible Refactoring Tool for Eclipse

Xi Ge   Emerson Murphy-Hill

Department of Computer Science, NC State University, Raleigh, NC, USA 27695
xge@ncsu.edu, emerson@csc.ncsu.edu

Abstract

Although broadly available in major software development environments, refactoring tools are still underused. One of the reasons for this underuse is that existing refactoring tools assume that a developer recognizes that she is going to refactor before she even begins. In this paper, we present a flexible refactoring tool called BeneFactor that can be invoked after refactoring begins to safely complete a refactoring change.

Categories and Subject Descriptors   D.2.3 [*Software Engineering*]: Coding Tools and Techniques–Object-oriented programming; D.2.7 [*Software Engineering*]: Distribution, Maintenance, and Enhancement–Restructuring, reverse engineering, and reengineering

General Terms   Languages

Keywords   refactoring

1. Introduction

Refactoring is both an effective and commonplace way of improving non-functional requirements. Empirical studies of refactoring have found that it can improve maintainability [2] and reusability [3]. Not only does existing work suggest that refactoring is useful, but it also suggests that refactoring is a frequent practice [4]. Cherubini and colleagues' survey indicates that developers rate the importance of refactoring is equal to or greater than that of understanding code and producing documentation [1].

However, refactoring by hand is labor-intensive and error-prone. In order to help developers perform efficient and correct refactoring, various refactoring tools have been developed. These tools promise to help developers refactor faster and with a smaller probability of introducing defects. These tools have been integrated into most popular development environments, making them available in a variety of programming languages to a large population of developers. In spite of the wide availability, our previous study shows that refactoring tools are underused; according to two case studies, about 90% of refactorings are performed by hand [4]. As a result, this underuse of refactoring tools unnecessarily slows down software development and increases the potential for introducing new software defects.

One of the reasons for this underuse is that existing refactoring tools assume that a developer realizes that she is going to refactor before she begins. Our previous study indicates that this assumption may be false because a developer may have already started a refactoring manually by the time she realizes that she is refactoring. One software developer outlined this situation in our interview [4] as, "my hands start doing copy-paste... without my active control. After a few seconds, I realize that this would have been easier to do with a refactoring [tool]. But since I already started..., I just finish it and continue." In these situations, existing refactoring tools fail.

To address this issue, we present a novel refactoring tool named BeneFactor that can be invoked after manual refactoring begins. BeneFactor detects manual refactoring behavior, prompts developers to use automatic refactoring, and finishes the incomplete refactoring automatically. Currently, BeneFactor supports the rename refactoring and the extract method refactoring. Let us compare conventional refactoring tools against BeneFactor using an example.

Suppose Grace is a developer who works on the Mylyn project [5]. To improve understandability, she wants to change the name of the local variable *event* to *intEvent* in the code snippet showed in Figure 1. She starts doing this task manually from the last reference of *event* backwards through her code. After changing seven references to *intEvent*, she realizes that she is refactoring, but in order to use a conventional refactoring tool, she needs to either back out and undo her changes, or finish the refactoring manually.

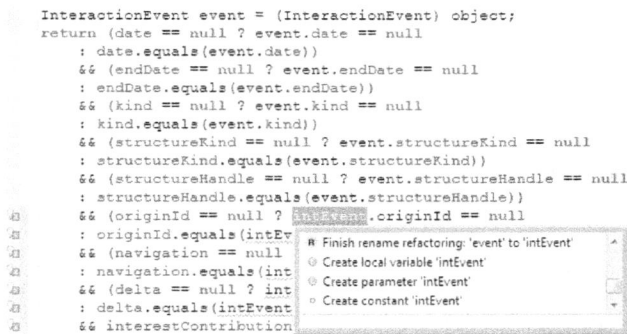

Figure 1. BeneFactor in use.

On the other hand, with BeneFactor, after Grace changes references of *event* to *intEvent*, BeneFactor detects that she is renaming a local variable. Therefore, it places a quick fix refactoring option on the problem markers at the lines where Grace did name changes, as illustrated in Figure 1, suggesting that she allow BeneFactor to finish this rename refactoring automatically. When Grace realizes that she is performing a rename refactoring, she then clicks the quick fix refactoring option. Finally, BeneFactor automatically renames all references of *event* to *intEvent*.

2. Approach

BeneFactor has two components: refactoring detection and code modification. The refactoring detection component runs silently in background of Eclipse, while monitoring code changes and a developer's editing actions. If a potential refactoring behavior is detected, the refactoring detection component adds a quick fix to automatically finish the refactoring that she has started. The code modification component takes the responsibility of finishing the refactoring automatically and safely.

2.1 Refactoring Detection

Most existing refactoring tools force a developer to recognize that she is going to refactor even before she begins. In order to shift this cognitive burden from the developer to our refactoring tool, we created a refactoring detection component for BeneFactor. In contrast to existing refactoring detection tools (for example, RefacLib [7] and RefFinder [6]), our refactoring detection component detects refactoring live rather than in the version control system. Once the refactoring detection component detects that a refactoring has begun, it can assist the developer in completing the refactoring automatically. We use two strategies to detect that a developer is refactoring: code-change based detection and action based detection.

Code-change based refactoring detection: The code-change strategy detects that a developer is refactoring by analyzing code base changes. We capture the changes as changes to the abstract syntax tree (AST), such as node addition, deletion, update and move. For example, by monitoring AST changes, BeneFactor is able to detect various kinds of refactorings, such as renaming a local variable. Renaming a local variable is detected whenever the developer updates an AST node whose type is local variable. The more references to a local variable that are changed, the more confidence BeneFactor has that the developer is performing a rename refactoring.

Action based refactoring detection: The action based strategy detects that a developer is refactoring by analyzing her editing actions upon the code base. Our refactoring detection component monitors a developer's editing actions, such as copy, paste, cut, and select. Once a sequence of editing actions matches a typical manual refactoring workflow, the developer is likely refactoring. For example, if a developer cuts a contiguous set of program statements, BeneFactor infers that she is probably starting an extract method refactoring.

2.2 Code modification

Once a developer's manual refactoring has been detected, BeneFactor allows her to automatically finish the refactoring that she has started. This user intervention allows the developer to safely perform the refactoring with the help of a refactoring tool, but without having to undo her changes. After the developer activates the quick fix, BeneFactor invokes the code modification component to finish the refactoring automatically. The code modification component consists of three steps, which are code recovery, information collection, and change creation. This component makes significant use of existing APIs from the Eclipse Language Tool Kit (LTK).

The **code recovery** step must modifies the code so that the existing LTK refactoring APIs can be applied. Because the existing LTK refactoring API can only refactor an un-modified code base, BeneFactor must transform the partially-refactored code base to its earlier state before manual refactoring began. For example, when a developer allows Benefactor to automatically finish an ongoing extract method refactoring, it is likely that the code statements to be extracted have already been cut out of the code base. BeneFactor must undo the cut command before using the existing API.

The **information collection** step collects configuration information when performing automatic refactoring. BeneFactor collects information by traversing ASTs of code base. Examples of such information include original and new name in rename refactoring and the range of code statements to be extracted in extract method refactoring.

The **change creation** step makes the actual code base change. In this step, BeneFactor first performs a set of precondition checks. These checks ensure that automatic refactoring can be successfully finished. After passing all the checks, BeneFactor calculates the actual code change of the refactoring and uses the code change to modify the code base.

3. Future Work

We plan to alter current condition checking mechanism of BeneFactor. Rather than checking all the preconditions before a change is made, we plan to adopt a more flexible precondition checking mechanism for BeneFactor. It will check the preconditions live, as changes are being made (either automatically or manually), so that the developer is kept aware of, but not forced to resolve, potentially behavior-modifying changes.

We also plan to add refactoring warnings to BeneFactor. According to our observations, developers sometimes prefer to make a change and let the compiler warn them about what pieces of code must be changed [4]. This is a convenient strategy, yet the compiler's warnings are not sufficient to tell the developer all the places that she must modify to complete the refactoring. In order to complement these insufficient compiler warnings, we plan to add refactoring warnings that augments the development environment by informing the developer of all the code that must be modified.

4. Demonstration Script

The presenter will demonstrate BeneFactor by refactoring an open source project using rename local variable and extract method. Each type of refactoring will include several demonstration cases in order to show how BeneFactor can help developers when manual refactoring workflow varies. For each case, the presenter will demonstrate how BeneFactor detects manual refactoring begins, how BeneFactor prompts developers to invoke automatic refactoring, and how the code base will look like after invoking the automatic refactoring.

Acknowledgments

Work partially supported by an NCSU FRPD grant. Thanks to Moin Ayazifar, Quinton DuBose, and Suprit Patankar for their participation in this project.

References

[1] M. Cherubini, G. Venolia, R . DeLine, and A. J. Ko. Let's go to the whiteboard: how and why software developers use drawings. In Proc. CHI, pages 557-566, 2007.

[2] R. Kolb, D. Muthig, T. Patzke, and K. Yamauchi. A case study in refactoring a legacy component for reuse in a productline. In Proc. ICSM, pages 369-378, 2005.

[3] R . Moser, A. Sillitti, P. Abrahamsson, and G. Succi. Does refactoring improve reusability? In Proc. ICSR, pages 287-297, 2006.

[4] E. Murphy-Hill, C. Parnin, and A. P. Black. How we refactor, and how we know it. IEEE TSE, 2011.

[5] Eclipse Mylyn Open Source Project, 2011.
http://www.eclipse.org/mylyn/.

[6] K. Prete, N. Rachatasumrit, N. Sudan, and M .Kim. Template-based reconstruction of complex refactorings. In Proc. ICSM, pages 1-10, 2010.

[7] K. Taneja, D. Dig, and T. Xie. Automated detection of API refactorings in libraries . In Proc. ASE, pages 377-380, 2007.

An 'Explicit Type Enforcement' Program Transformation Tool for Preventing Integer Vulnerabilities

Munawar Hafiz

Department of Computer Science and Software Engineering
Auburn University
Email: munawar@auburn.edu

Abstract

A security-oriented program transformation is similar to a refactoring, but it is not intended to preserve behavior. Instead, it improves the security of systems, which means it preserves the expected behavior, but changes a system's response to security attacks. This demo is about a tool for *Explicit Type Enforcement* transformation, which adds proper typecast to integer variables. The tool is built using Eclipse CDT and applies on C programs. Preliminary results show that it is very effective in fixing integer-related vulnerabilities. Power tools such as these can improve developer productivity and produce vulnerability-free software.

Categories and Subject Descriptors D.1.2 [*Automatic Programming*]: Program transformation; D.2.9 [*Software Management*]: Software maintenance

General Terms Security

Keywords Program Transformation, Integer Overflow.

1. Integer Overflow Vulnerability

When arithmetic operations mix the type of operands, the result may be unexpected. For example, a signedness bug occurs when an unsigned variable is interpreted as signed, or vice versa [2]. This type of behavior can happen because a computer makes no distinction between the way signed and unsigned variables are stored. Hence, the end result is not the one originally intended. If an unsigned integer is compared to a signed integer in a program, an attacker can carefully inject inputs to bypass the comparison. Similarly, if signed values are used in an arithmetic operation, an attacker may cause an overflow and store a value with a wrong sign. When this is used in an unsigned context, an error will occur.

Consider this very simple program snippet.

```
1    ...
2    char buf[80];
3    int s;
4    s = atoi(argv[1]);
5    if (s >= 80)
6        return -1;
7    memcpy(buf, argv[2], s);
8    ...
```

This very simple and apparently innocuous C program has a serious integer overflow vulnerability. The variable *s* is a signed integer, but it is compared with an unsigned integer in line 5. An attacker can bypass that check by providing a negative input, e.g., −1. Then in line 7, the signed negative value of *s* will be converted to a large unsigned value. Hence an attacker can load a large malicious payload in the buffer in line 7. A carefully crafted payload can cause a buffer overflow attack, and can allow the attacker to take control of the system.

Such integer related vulnerabilities have become very prominent in recent years.

2. Motivation for a tool

Most of the existing works on integer overflow vulnerability concentrate on detecting the vulnerability. Many sophisticated program analysis tools [3] [1] [4] are available for automatically detecting these vulnerabilities in the source code. There are compiler based detection tools, such as gcc with -ftrapv option, which forces gcc compiler to insert additional calls (e.g., _addvsi3) before signed addition operations to catch overflow errors. Also there are integer overflow detection tools that apply on binaries [7, 8].

While determining whether a particular vulnerability exists in source code is very important, we believe that researchers stop one step short of solving the problem, because they still require a programmer to manually add security checks in the program to prevent the attack.

Our research on program transformations explores how existing security solutions could be automatically introduced to an application to retrofit 'security on demand' [5]. We have been describing the mechanism of program transformations so that tools could be built for software developers [6],

SPLASH'11 Companion, October 22–27, 2011, Portland, Oregon, USA.
ACM 978-1-4503-0940-0/11/10.

similar to refactoring tools. This demo describes a tool for preventing integer related vulnerabilities.

3. *Explicit Type Enforcement* **Program Transformation Tool**

An *Explicit Type Enforcement* program transformation explicitly casts the type of operands so that they are properly handled in an operation.

In order to apply the program transformation, a developer has to specify a target input variable.

The program transformation tool checks whether the input variable has been used in an unsafe context. It explicitly casts the type of variables in an arithmetic operation.

A developer can apply an *Explicit Type Enforcement* transformation on the variable s in the listing in section 1. It explicitly forces typecasting in all the places the variable s is used.

```
1   ...
2   char buf[80];
3   int s;
4   s = (signed) atoi(argv[1]);
5   if (((unsigned) s) >= 80)
6       return -1;
7   memcpy(buf, argv[2], (unsigned) s);
8   ...
```

In line 5, the comparison mixes a signed integer with an unsigned integer. By explicitly promoting the type in the comparison operation, the program transformation ensures that an attacker cannot bypass the operation by passing a signed value.

4. Content of the Demo

During the demo, the presenter will introduce the tool and the research behind it. Then he will run the tool on open source C programs of varying size. He will run test cases on the unmodified and modified programs and demonstrate the similarity of their 'good path behavior'.

Some of the sample programs will have known integer overflow vulnerabilities. In that case, the presenter will run exploit codes on unmodified programs, apply program transformation on variables, and run exploit codes on modified programs. The exploit code will be ineffective on the the modified program.

A video demo of the tool is available at the author's webpage: https://netfiles.uiuc.edu/mhafiz/www/research/sopt/AddIntCast.avi.

5. Under the Hood

The program transformation is written in Java using Eclipse CDT framework. CDT has a program analysis package called CODAN that provides limited control flow analysis. The tool uses this to search for all instances of a chosen integer variable. The scope is always within a procedure. When all the instances of an integer variable is found, the tool analyzes the context of each instance to identify whether the

integers have been used properly. The tool keeps a ranking of all possible integer variables. The ranking is used to determine whether the integer usage has been proper. Whenever, integers of different rankings are used, the proper ranking is introduced as a type cast.

6. Conclusion

Security-oriented program transformations are real because they combine human ingenuity with the thoroughness of computers. The analysis and transformation performed by the tool is done in many places of a program. It is tedious and error-prone for a developer to manually check so many instances. Instead, developers remain at the policy level and the tool implements the structural change.

References

[1] K. Ashcraft and D. Engler. Using programmer-written compiler extensions to catch security holes. In *SP '02: Proceedings of the 2002 IEEE Symposium on Security and Privacy*, page 143, Washington, DC, USA, 2002. IEEE Computer Society.

[2] blexim. Basic integer overflows. *Phrack*, 60, 2002.

[3] E. N. Ceesay, J. Zhou, M. Gertz, K. N. Levitt, and M. Bishop. Using type qualifiers to analyze untrusted integers and detecting security flaws in C programs. In R. Büschkes and P. Laskov, editors, *DIMVA*, volume 4064 of *Lecture Notes in Computer Science*, pages 1–16. Springer, 2006.

[4] X. C. L. David Molnar and D. A. Wagner. Dynamic test generation to find integer bugs in x86 binary Linux programs. In *Proceedings of the 18th USENIX Security Symposium*. USENIX, Aug. 2009.

[5] M. Hafiz. *Security On Demand*. PhD thesis, University of Illinois Urbana-Champaign, 2010.

[6] M. Hafiz, P. Adamczyk, and R. Johnson. Systematically eradicating data injection attacks using security-oriented program transformations. In *Proceedings of the International Symposium on Engineering Secure Software and Systems (ESSoS-09)*, Feb 2009.

[7] T. Wang, T. Wei, Z. Lin, and W. Zou. Intscope: Automatically detecting integer overflow vulnerability in x86 binary using symbolic execution. In *NDSS*, 2009.

[8] R. Wojtczuk. UQBTng: A tool capable of automatically finding integer overflows in Win32 binaries. In *22nd Chaos Communication Congress*, 2005.

Presenter Biography. Munawar Hafiz is an Assistant Professor at Auburn University, AL. His research is on leveraging program analysis and program transformation techniques to improve application security. He has prototyped several program transformation tools applicable to C and Java [6], including this tool for preventing integer overflow attacks. Munawar has presented his research in various forms at previous SPLASHes, e.g., as part of a tutorial, as a poster, and as a finalist project in ACM student research competition.

Mobl: The New Language of the Mobile Web

Zef Hemel

Delft University of Technology, Could 9 IDE Inc.
z.hemel@tudelft.nl

Eelco Visser

Delft University of Technology
visser@acm.org

Abstract

Mobl is a new language designed to declaratively construct mobile web applications. Mobl integrates languages for user interface design, styling, data modeling, querying and application logic into a single, unified language that is flexible, expressive, enables early detection of errors, and has good IDE support.

Categories and Subject Descriptors D.2.4 [*Software Engineering*]: Software/Program Verification; D.2.11 [*Software Engineering*]: Software Architectures; D.3.3 [*Programming Languages*]: Language Constructs and Features

General Terms Design, Languages, Verification

1. Description

With the rapid growth in sales of modern smart phones and tablets, such as iPhone, iPad, Android, WP7 and Black-Berries, the web becomes available on an increasing number of powerful mobile devices equipped with modern web browsers. Recent advances in HTML and CSS enable the creation of web applications that offer a comparable experience to native applications by supporting application and data caching, detection of touch gestures and access to geographical position information (GPS). The portability and deployment advantages of web applications make the use of web technologies for building mobile applications very attractive.

While HTML5 *enables* the development of mobile applications, development exposes a number of problems, specifically: developers are required to use many loosely coupled languages (including HTML, CSS, Javascript and SQL) with limited tool support and application code is often verbose and imperative.

We will demonstrate *mobl* [1], a new, high-level, declarative language for programming mobile web applications, which addresses these problems. Mobl integrates languages

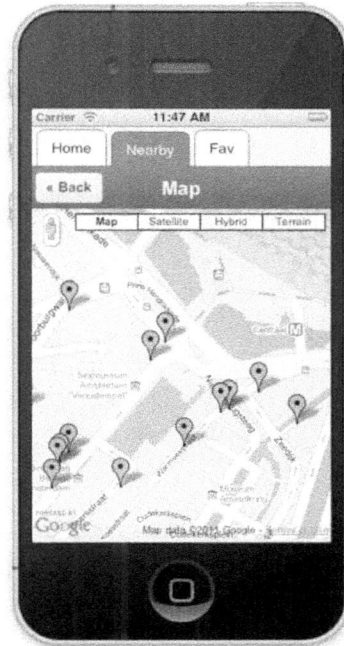

Figure 1. Example application built with mobl

for user interface design, styling, data modeling, query and application logic into a single, unified language. The language is *declarative* since it ensures automatic updates of the user interface through reactive programming and automatic persistence of data in the client-side database.

The mobl compiler compiles mobl code into a pure client-side web application, implemented using a combination of HTML, CSS and JavaScript. The resulting application can be deployed to any web server and is server-technology agnostic. Already, mobl is starting to be used in industry. An enthusiastic community is contributing to the development of mobl at `http://www.mobl-lang.org`.

2. About the presenters

Zef is the lead developer of mobl. He will soon finish his PhD in computer science from Delft University of Technology. His area of his research was the design and implementation of domain-specific language design. He currently works

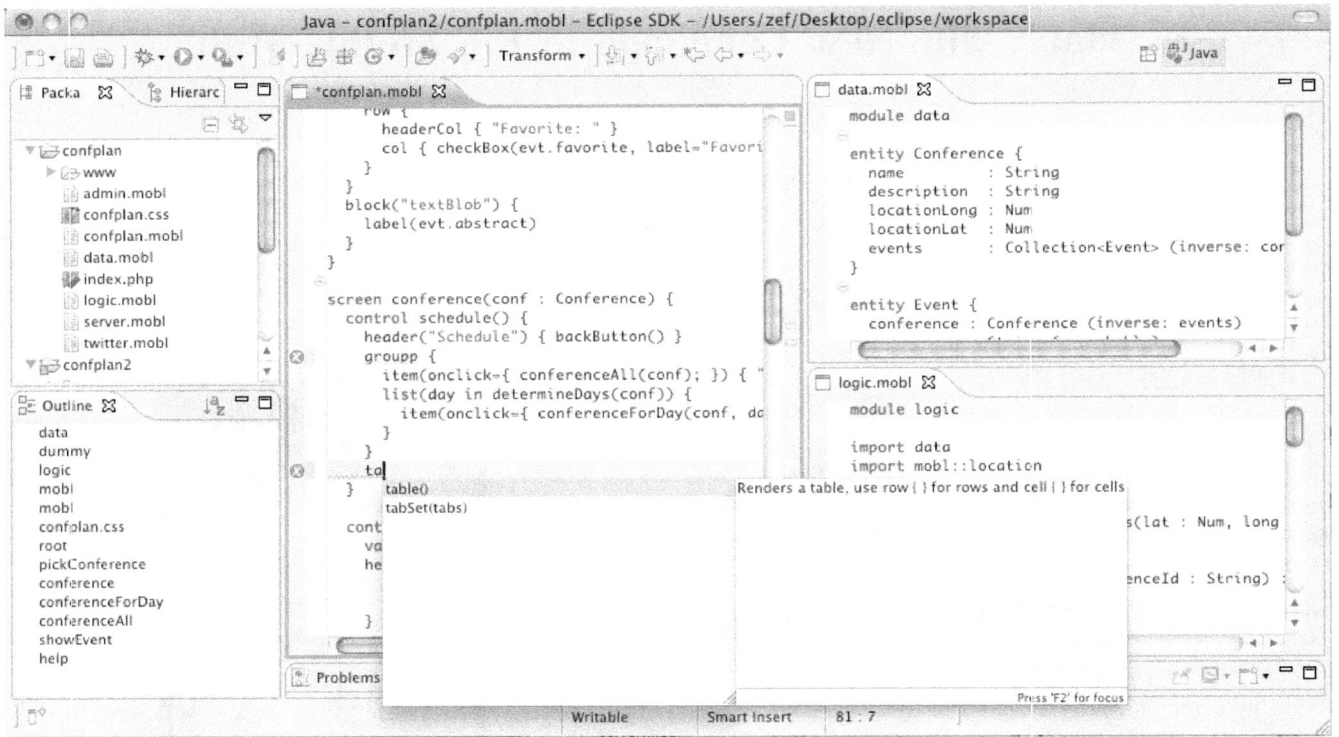

Figure 2. The mobl IDE is implemented as an Eclipse-plugin and features syntax highlighting, inline error highlighting, an outline view, reference resolving and code completion.

as senior developer on IDE language support for Cloud 9 IDE, Inc.

Eelco Visser is associate professor at Delft University of Technology, where he conducts research in the areas of language engineering, DSLs and software deployment. He is the project lead of the TraCE, TFA, MoDSE and PDS projects and published over 70 papers in peer-reviewed venues.

3. Acknowledgments

This research was supported by NWO/JACQUARD project 638.001.610, *MoDSE: Model-Driven Software Evolution.* We would like to thank Google for providing Android phones for testing and development.

References

[1] Z. Hemel and E. Visser. Declaratively programming the mobile web with mobl. In *Proceedings of the 26th Annual ACM SIGPLAN Conference on Object-Oriented Programming, Systems, Languages, and Applications, OOPSLA 2011*, Portland, Oregon, USA, 2011. ACM.

Testing Domain-Specific Languages

Lennart C. L. Kats

Delft University of Technology

l.c.l.kats@tudelft.nl

Rob Vermaas

LogicBlox

rob.vermaas@logicblox.com

Eelco Visser

Delft University of Technology

visser@acm.org

Abstract

The Spoofax testing language provides a new approach to testing domain-specific languages as they are developed. It allows test cases to be written using fragments of the language under test, providing full IDE support for writing test cases and supporting tests for language syntax, semantics, and editor services.

Categories and Subject Descriptors   D.2.5 [*Software Engineering*]: Testing and Debugging—Testing Tools;   D.2.3 [*Software Engineering*]: Coding Tools and Techniques;   D.2.6 [*Software Engineering*]: Interactive Environments

General Terms   Languages, Reliability

Keywords   Testing, Test-Driven Development, Language Engineering, Grammarware, Language Workbench, Domain-Specific Language, Language Embedding, Compilers, Parsers

1. Domain-specific Language Engineering

Domain-specific languages (DSLs) provide high expressive power focused on a particular problem domain. They provide linguistic abstractions and specialized syntax specifically designed for a domain, allowing developers to avoid boilerplate code and low-level implementation details.

The development of new DSLs comprises many tasks, ranging from syntax definition to code generation to the construction of an integrated development environment (IDE). The Spoofax language workbench [2] combines meta-languages for syntax definition, transformations, analyses, and editor services to form comprehensive *language definitions* that can be used to generate full interpreters, compilers, and IDE plugins.

2. Test-driven Language Development

In this demonstration we introduce the Spoofax testing language, a language-parametric testing language [1]. The testing language can be instantiated for a specific language under test, thereby integrating its syntax, semantics, and editor services into the testing language. This allows language engineers to write test cases in the language under test with full IDE support (Figure 1 (a, b)). The testing language also provides primitives for specifying assertions on tested fragments (Figure 1 (c)).

In this demonstration we show how tests can be used as the basis for an incremental, test-driven approach to language engineering. Test cases can be used to sketch and validate new syntax designs,

(a) Content completion for the language under test.

(b) Online evaluation of tests and error markers.

(c) Passing test case specifying negative test condition.

Figure 1. IDE support for test specifications.

through positive and negative test cases of small snippets written in the language under test. As a language definition evolves, tests can also be written for the semantics and editor services of the language under test. Test cases can check whether static semantic constraints hold (Figure 1 (c)), and can check the result of transformations and code generation. For editor services, tests can check whether hyperlinks resolve to the correct declaration, and whether services such as content completion and refactorings deliver the expected result.

Spoofax is an open source project and is publicly available at http://spoofax.org/.

3. About the presenters

Lennart Kats is a PhD student at Delft University of Technology, where he works on techniques and tool support for developing domain-specific languages. He is the lead developer of the Spoofax project. Rob Vermaas is a researcher and developer at Delft University and LogicBlox, and is a contributor to the Spoofax project. Eelco Visser is associate professor at Delft University,where he conducts research in the areas of language engineering, DSLs, and software deployment. He is the project lead of the TraCE, TFA, MoDSE, and PDS projects and published over 70 papers in peer-reviewed venues.

Acknowledgements This research was supported by NWO project 612.063.512, *TFA: Transformations for Abstractions* and the NIRICT LaQuSo Build Farm project.

References

[1] L. C. L. Kats, R. Vermaas, and E. Visser. Integrated language definition testing: Enabling test-driven language development. In K. Fisher, editor, *Proceedings of the 26th Annual ACM SIGPLAN Conference on Object-Oriented Programming, Systems, Languages, and Applications (OOPSLA 2011)*, Portland, Oregon, USA, 2011. ACM.

[2] L. C. L. Kats and E. Visser. The Spoofax language workbench: rules for declarative specification of languages and IDEs. In W. R. Cook, S. Clarke, and M. C. Rinard, editors, *Object-Oriented Programming, Systems, Languages, and Applications, OOPSLA 2010*, pages 444–463. ACM, 2010.

KonohaScript: Static Scripting for Practical Use

Kimio Kuramitsu

JST/CREST/DEOS Project
Yokohama National University, JAPAN
kimio@ynu.ac.jp

Abstract

This demonstration presents the language design of Konoha-Script, a statically typed object-oriented scripting language. KonohaScript provides the very similar scripting experiences compared to dynamic languages. In addition, it also preserves useful programming supports by static typing, such as automated verification of careless mistakes, improved readability of source code, better opportunity of optimized code generation. This demonstration will show how KonohaScript improved scripting experiences with static typing, using our open source implementation fully written in C.

Categories and Subject Descriptors D.3.2 [*Language Classifications*]: Object-oriented scripting languages

General Terms Design

Keywords scripting, language design, dynamic languages

1. Introduction

More recently, lots of applications have been developed with dynamic scripting languages, such as JavaScript, Python, PHP, and Ruby. Modern application developers enjoy flexibility and agility in their development style, while they suffer from lacks of several good features that static languages have provided. Several attempts to adding static typing or static type inference to existing dynamic languages are underway, but they are still far from practical programming.

KonohaScript is a newly designed scripting language to bridge the gaps between static typing and dynamic scripting. But our approach is opposite. We started from the static language basis, and made an attempt to adding dynamic features in order to augment scripting experience. Thus, KonohaScript works more practically than the extension of existing dynamic languages.

Dynamic and agile features modeled in KonohaScript are:

- Absence of type declaration
- Dynamic typing (by explicit dynamic type)
- Duck typing (by structural typing)
- Dynamic code loading (by eval)
- Runtime modification of existing classes
- Partial execution of incomplete program

KonohaScript, on the other hand, preserves useful programming supports by static typing, such as automated verification of careless mistakes, improved readability of source code, better opportunity of optimized code generation. This demonstration shows how KonohaScript improves scripting experiences with static typing, using our open source implementation fully written in C.

2. Language Design

The design of KonohaScript is based on a statically-typed class-based object-oriented language. All programs must be typed at compilation time, and compiled to type-specialized instructions. On the top of this static language basis, we have added flexible and agile features that dynamic scripting languages provided. We focus only on some of the interesting features of KonohaScript as a brief introduction.

2.1 Two Coding Styles

KonohaScript allows both *typed* and *untyped* styles of coding.

The following static `succ()` function shows a typed style of coding written in KonohaScript. For typed coding, we adopted Java's Grammar; approximately 90% Java's source code can be run on KonohaScript without any major modification.

```
int succ(int n) {
  return n + 1;
}
```

For untyped coding style, we adopt many grammatical features from JavaScript, such as `function` constructor and the absence of type declaration.

SPLASH'11 Companion, October 22–27, 2011, Portland, Oregon, USA.
ACM 978-1-4503-0940-0/11/10.

```
function dsucc(n) {
    return n+1;
}
```

KonohaScript generates the same compiled bytecode when `dsucc(1)` is called. At the same time, the latter definition allows to accept `fact(1.0)` as if the version of `float succ(float n)` is defined. The parameter of `succ(n)` is decided at the first calling time and then complied at that time. We call lazy compilation, which improves dynamic typing features and then allows static code generation only with simple type inference.

2.2 Static Type-Cheker for Incompletness

The strength of static type checker is to offer software verification, which is simple enough to avoid careless mistakes of programmers. However, the compilation policy of "all-or-nothing" code generation leads to the decreased agility of software development, because programmers want to try running code that they are programming even if incomplete. Ironically, the lack of type checker in dynamic languages allows the rapid cycle of coding and running.

KonohaScript models this "lack of type checker" feature by rewriting detected type errors with runtime exceptions. If a running program doesn't hit the errors, it goes normally. In the following example, the first if-then clause is replaced with throwing a runtime error, because a type error is detected within it. Without calling `serial(0)`, the function `serial(n)` works as usual.

```
int serial (int n) {
    if(n == 0) {
        InputStream in = new ("serial.txt");
        n = in.readLine(); // a type error
        in.close();
    }
    return n + 1;
}
```

In addition, as with other static compliers, KonohaScript (with −c option) allows static type checking without any program execution. This helps avoid unexpected runtime type errors before running scripts.

```
$ konoha -c script.k
- (script.k:8) (info) suppose v has type int
- (script.k:9) (error) v has type String, not
  int
- (script.k:12) (error) undefined method:
  Script.ssucc
```

2.3 Optimized Code Generation

As many know, static typing helps us make an interpreter faster and enables more optimized generation of native code. From the beginning, KonohaScript is designed to run its script in a byte-complied form on KonohaVM with having type-specialized instructions. In addition, we started to inte-

Table 1. Ambient Occlusion Rendering Benchmark: Performance of C++, Konoha LLVM, Lua5.1, Python3.1, Ruby1.9 in relation to Konoha VM

GCC4.4	0.15
Konoha LLVM	0.4
KonohaVM	1
Python 3.1	6.6
Lua 5.1	9.6
Ruby 1.9	30

grate the LLVM framework for JIT compilation. Preliminary performance studies show promising results. (See Table 1)

3. DEMO

KonohaScript is now designing and developing as a part of JST/DEOS project, or Japanese government-leading research program on dependable embedded operating system. We discuss several practical scenarios where static scripting would help application developers a lot. At the same time, many of middle-size experimental applications (including information appliance and intelligent robots) have been developed for now. From our development history, we will select some of small good code in order to better share static scripting experiences and script evolution.

- Language design hilighting static scripting with code examples
- Improved scripting experience with static typing
- performance comparison of scripting languages

KonohaScript is an open-source software written in portable C and available on major operating systems, such as Linux, MacOS X and Windows. The readers and the audience will try all the demonstration and its sample code by downloading the following site:

http://www.konohascript.org

Acknowledgments

The work was founded by Japanese Ministry of Economy, Trade and Industry: IPA "unexplored domain of software challenge" program, Japanese Ministry of Internal Affairs and Communications: SCOPE-R for younger researcher fund, a Japan Science and Technology Agency: CREST "Dependable Embedded Operating System for Practical Use" (led by Mario Tokoro).

References

[1] Kuramitsu, K.: Konoha: implementing a static scripting language with dynamic behaviors, *Workshop on Self-Sustaining Systems*, S3 '10, ACM, pp. 21–29 (2010).

Cedalion 101: "I Want My DSL Now" *

[Extended Abstract]

David H. Lorenz   Boaz Rosenan

Open University of Israel
1 University Rd., P.O.Box 808, Raanana 43107 Israel
lorenz@openu.ac.il   brosenan@cslab.openu.ac.il

Abstract

Cedalion is a research LOP language designed for hosting internal DSLs but with the look-and-feel of external DSLs. Cedalion demonstrates a novel approach that combines extensible logic programming with projectional editing. We shall demonstrate the ease of realizing a small, yet nontrivial, highly expressive DSL in Cedalion.

Categories and Subject Descriptors   D.2.6 [*Software Engineering*]: Programming Environments—Programmer workbench;   D.3.2 [*Programming Languages*]: Language Classifications—Specialized application languages.

General Terms   Design, Languages.

Keywords   Language-oriented programming (LOP), Language workbenches, Domain-specific languages (DSLs).

Short Biographies of Presenters

- *David H. Lorenz* is an associate professor in the Department of Mathematics and Computer Science at the Open University of Israel. His research interests include aspect-oriented software engineering and language-oriented programming, particularly involving multiple domain-specific languages. Lorenz has a PhD in Computer Science from the Technion–Israel Institute of Technology. He's a member of the ACM and the IEEE. Contact him at lorenz@openu.ac.il.

- *Boaz Rosenan* is a graduate student in the Department of Mathematics and Computer Science at the Open University of Israel and a lead software engineer in GE Health-

care, Israel. His research thesis, conducted under the supervision of Professor Lorenz, introduces Cedalion as a new language-oriented programming language. Rosenan has a B.Sc. in Computer Science from the Technion–Israel Institute of Technology. He's a member of the ACM. Contact him at brosenan@cslab.openu.ac.il.

Description

- *What problems are addressed?* Domain-specific languages (DSLs) are considered to be hard to implement and use. One approach aimed at making DSLs easier to implement is to embed them internally in a host language. Another approach aimed at improving their expressiveness is to build them externally and provide projectional editing. However, the two approaches are considered to be cumbersome and incompatible. In this demonstration, we will show how these approaches can be made to work together in a new way.

- *What will the audience be seeing?* The audience will witness the development of a complete, small, yet non-trivial, internal DSL in Cedalion [5], from inception to production, in a projectional editing setting.

- *What is unique about the design or implementation?* Cedalion [5] is a language-oriented programming (LOP) language made to be a host for internal DSLs. Unlike other languages that make good hosts for internal DSLs, Cedalion uses projectional editing to provide syntactic freedom. Cedalion's projectional editing is flexible enough to allow constructs that have not been defined to be used in DSL code. We will use this feature to gradually define a DSL, starting with an example, gradually building a language around it, and finally giving it meaning.

- *What underlying technologies are used?* Cedalion [5] is a logic programming language. It is based on and implemented in Prolog. Its projectional editor is implemented in Java as an Eclipse plug-in. It features type inference that allows the projectional editor to guide DSL users in writing well-formed code.

* This research was supported in part by the *Israel Science Foundation (ISF)* under grant No. 926/08.

- *What are the interesting technical details and challenges?* The concept of using DSLs as the main means of software development dates back to the 1960's, with internal DSLs over Lisp, implemented using macros. These DSLs were relatively easy to implement, but suffered from being bound to Lisp's syntax, consisting of S-expressions. The fact that Lisp allows the customization of the reader allows more flexible syntax, but comes at the expanse of DSL interoperability. Supporting both DSL interoperability and syntactic flexibility in internal DSLs is a challenge we address.

Language workbenches such as the Meta Programming System (MPS) [2], Spoofax [3] and the Intentional Domain Workbench (IDW) [11] are considered the state of the art in this field. They reduce the cost of implementing DSLs by providing DSLs for defining and implementing DSLs. They support DSL interoperability, both syntactic and semantic, by using a common representation for all DSLs, a feature that somewhat resembles internal DSLs although working on external DSLs.

On the syntactic level, they use different methods to avoid the problem of syntactic composition of languages. MPS and IDW use projectional editing, while Spoofax uses Generalized Scannerless LR parsing. Each method has its own way of coping with ambiguities that may occur when composing two DSLs together. The projectional DSLs disambiguate the code as it is being entered. DSL constructs are simply selected from menus or lists, and the user is responsible to choose the right one, e.g., based on its fully qualified name (as in MPS). Spoofax, however, can use a potentially ambiguous grammar and parse code successfully, as long as the parsing of this code is unambiguous. Ambiguous code emits a parsing error.

Cedalion takes the projectional editing approach, similar to MPS and IDW. However, Cedalion is not considered a language workbench, but rather a programming language. DSL constructs are implemented internally in Cedalion, not by transforming them into a lower-level language, as done in language workbenches. This makes the implementation of DSLs easier.

- *What makes it relevant to the SPLASH community?* Cedalion is the topic of a research paper [5] and a poster [7] to be presented at OOPSLA/SPLASH 2011. More technical detail on its potential and relevance can be found elsewhere [4, 6, 8–10].

Download

The Cedalion Eclipse plug-in is implemented as an open source project and publicly available [1]. Before the demo, participants are encouraged to visit the website and read through the Cedalion "Hello, World" tutorial [8].

References

[1] Cedalion. The Cedalion project homepage. Software Engineering Research Lab, The Open University of Israel, 2010. http://cedalion.sourceforge.net.

[2] S. Dmitriev. Language oriented programming: The next programming paradigm. *JetBrains onBoard*, 1(2), Nov. 2004.

[3] L. C. Kats and E. Visser. The Spoofax language workbench: Rules for declarative specification of languages and IDEs. In *Proceedings of the ACM International Conference on Systems, Programming Languages, and Applications: Software for Humanity (SPLASH'10)*, pages 444–463, Reno/Tahoe, Nevada, USA, Oct. 2010. ACM.

[4] D. H. Lorenz and B. Rosenan. Cedalion: A language oriented programming language. In *IBM Programming Languages and Development Environments Seminar (PLDE'10)*, Haifa, Israel, Apr. 2010. IBM Research.

[5] D. H. Lorenz and B. Rosenan. Cedalion: A language for language oriented programming. In *Proceedings of the ACM International Conference on Systems, Programming Languages, and Applications: Software for Humanity (SPLASH'11)*, Portland, Oregon, USA, Oct. 2011. ACM.

[6] D. H. Lorenz and B. Rosenan. Code reuse with language oriented programming. In *Proceedings of the 12th International Conference on Software Reuse (ICSR12)*, number 6727 in Lecture Notes in Computer Science, pages 165–180, Pohang, Korea, June 13-17 2011. Springer Verlag.

[7] D. H. Lorenz and B. Rosenan. A case study of language oriented programming with Cedalion (poster). In *Companion to the ACM International Conference on Systems, Programming Languages, and Applications: Software for Humanity (SPLASH'11)*, Portland, Oregon, USA, Oct. 2011. ACM. to appear.

[8] B. Rosenan. Cedalion hello, world tutorial. Software Engineering Research Lab, The Open University of Israel, 2010. http://sourceforge.net/apps/mediawiki/cedalion/index.php?title=Hello_World_Tutorial.

[9] B. Rosenan. Designing language-oriented programming languages. In *Companion to the ACM International Conference on Systems, Programming Languages, and Applications: Software for Humanity (SPLASH'10)*, pages 207–208, Reno/Tahoe, Nevada, USA, Oct. 2010. ACM. Student Research Competition, 2nd prize.

[10] B. Rosenan. Cedalion submission to the language workbench competition of 2011. In M. Völter, E. Visser, S. Kelly, A. Hulshout, J. Warmer, P. J. Molina, B. Merkle, and K. Thoms, editors, *Language Workbench Competition*. 2011. http://www.languageworkbenches.net/lwc11-cedalion.pdf.

[11] C. Simonyi, M. Christerson, and S. Clifford. Intentional software. *ACM SIGPLAN Notices*, 41(10):451–464, 2006.

Modularizing Crosscutting Concerns with Ptolemy

Hridesh Rajan[1]   Sean Mooney[1]   Gary T. Leavens[2]   Robert Dyer[1]   Rex D. Fernando[1]
Mohammad Ali Darvish Darab[1]   Bryan Welter[1]

[1]Department of Computer Science
Iowa State University
{hridesh,smooney,rdyer,fernanre,ali2,bawalter}@iastate.edu

[2]Department of EE and Computer Science
University of Central Florida
leavens@eecs.ucf.edu

Abstract

In this demonstration we show our language Ptolemy, which allows for separation of crosscutting concerns while maintaining modular reasoning. We demonstrate the benefits of Ptolemy over existing aspect-oriented languages and implicit invocation designs. Ptolemy's quantified, typed events provide a flexible quantification mechanism that acts as a declarative interface between object-oriented code and crosscutting code. Events are announced explicitly and declaratively.

Event types allow for compile-time errors and avoid the fragile pointcut problem of aspect-oriented languages. The interface provided by event types also allows for modular reasoning, without considering all aspects in the system. The declarative event announcement allows avoiding writing tedious and error-prone boiler-plate code that implicit invocation designs require.

We demonstrate several realistic examples that showcase the features of the Ptolemy language and show use of Ptolemy's compiler. The demonstrated compiler is built on top of the OpenJDK Java compiler (javac), providing full backwards compatibility with existing Java sources as well as ease of integration into the existing tool chains. We show how to integrate the compiler into both existing Ant and Eclipse builds.

Categories and Subject Descriptors   D.3.3 [*Programming Languages*]: Language Constructs and Features—Modules and Packages

General Terms   Design, Languages

Keywords   modular reasoning, aspect-oriented programming languages, implicit invocation, translucid contracts, aspect-oriented interfaces, Ptolemy

SPLASH'11 Companion,   October 22–27, 2011, Portland, Oregon, USA.
ACM 978-1-4503-0940-0/11/10.

1. Background

Maintenance and evolution of software systems is of extreme importance in software engineering. In order to evolve and maintain systems easily, a clear traceability of concerns from requirements to code must exist. Certain concerns lack such traceability due to their scattering across several modules and tangling with other concerns. Such concerns are called *cross-cutting concerns* in aspect-oriented (AO) terminology [4]. Being able to modularize such concerns is an important problem investigated by AO techniques as well as implicit invocation (II) techniques [6].

The key idea behind both AO and II techniques is to decouple components and allow for their composition at runtime using *events*. For example, in the observer design pattern, which is an adaptation of II techniques [6], the participants (*subjects* and *observers*) are decoupled in both the design and code and then composed at runtime. The subjects dynamically announce events which observers dynamically register event *handlers* (methods) that are invoked implicitly after the events are announced. This ensures that subjects are independent of any observers and allows for separate maintenance and evolution.

In AO languages such as AspectJ [5], the events are predefined by the language. Certain standard events, such as method calls, in the program's execution are provided. In AO languages, these events are announced implicitly and handlers are declaratively registered to sets of these events. This process is called quantification [3].

II techniques have two distinct advantages over AO techniques. First, all events are explicitly announced, which aids reasoning about modules announcing events as all points where such announcement may occur are explicitly marked. Second, event announcement is generally more flexible as any arbitrary point may announce an event.

AO techniques have advantages over II techniques as well. First, compared to II techniques the implicit event announcement in AO helps automate and decouple event announcers and handlers. Second, since modules announcing events do not explicitly name handlers, the handler code remains syntactically independent of all announcement code.

2. Ptolemy

The Ptolemy language [7] takes advantages from both implicit-invocation (II) and aspect-oriented (AO) techniques. It has three main design goals:

- Enable modularization of crosscutting concerns while maintaining the encapsulation of object-oriented code,

- enable a well defined interface between the crosscutting and object-oriented concerns and

- enable separate type-checking, compilation and modular reasoning of crosscutting and object-oriented code.

Achieving these goals using AO languages in the style of AspectJ is difficult. First, knowing for certain if advice may apply at a point in the code is difficult, as such potential locations occur frequently. At every such possible point, programmers must reason and account for the effects of all applicable advice. Second, in order to reason about control flow, programmers would have to reason about all potential control effects of advice at that location, including how different advice might interact with each other.

3. Benefits of Ptolemy

The event types provided by Ptolemy's design provides a declarative interface between the object-oriented and crosscutting code. Event types define the type for all announced events as well as the context information available during event announcement. Announcing events is declarative and explicit. The language design provides several software engineering benefits.

- Explicit event announcement aids in modular reasoning.

- The declarative event announcement syntax saves programmers from writing tedious and error prone boilerplate code. It also allows the compiler to statically check and optimize the event announcement code.

- Event types are statically checked during compilation, which avoids the fragile pointcut problem associated with AO techniques.

- Event types allow for specifying a contract between subjects and observers. Such translucid contracts [1, 2] expose some details of the observers, which allows programmers to understand an upper-bound on the behavior of subjects and observers by only inspecting the event type.

- Quantification over subjects does not require enumerating the subjects, which decouples the observers from subjects.

Ptolemy allows observers to declaratively express interest in certain events in the system. The bindings allow observers to refer to subjects without becoming name dependent on the subjects. This name independence allows for separate and independent maintenance and evolution of the subjects and observers.

4. Demonstration Overview

This demonstration showcases the features and benefits of the Ptolemy language through several realistic examples. The current infrastructure for developing Ptolemy programs is also demonstrated, including syntax highlighting in Vim/Emacs and use of Ptolemy's compiler. The compiler is built on top of the standard OpenJDK Java compiler (javac) and is fully backwards compatible with pure Java programs. Use of the compiler with both Ant and Eclipse is demonstrated.

5. Presenter Biographies

Hridesh Rajan is one of the two original authors and creators of the Ptolemy language. He has extensive experience in separations of concerns techniques and co-developed the aspect-oriented language Eos. He has given previous demonstrations on the Ptolemy language at AOSD'10, FSE'10 and ECOOP'11. He also taught a half day tutorial on the Ptolemy language at AOSD'11.

Robert Dyer helped develop the original research compiler for Ptolemy. He also was the lead researcher on an empirical evaluation of the Ptolemy language which involved developing Ptolemy versions of two medium sized, open source programs (MobileMedia and Health Watcher).

Acknowledgments

This work is supported in part by the US National Science Foundation (NSF) under grant CCF-10-17334 to Hridesh Rajan and grant CCF-10-17262 to Gary T. Leavens.

References

[1] M. Bagherzadeh, H. Rajan, and G. T. Leavens. Translucid contracts for aspect-oriented interfaces. In *FOAL '10*.

[2] M. Bagherzadeh, H. Rajan, G. T. Leavens, and S. Mooney. Translucid contracts: Expressive specification and modular verification for aspect-oriented interfaces. In *AOSD '11: 10th International Conference on Aspect-Oriented Software Development*, March 2011.

[3] R. E. Filman and D. P. Friedman. Aspect-oriented programming is quantification and obliviousness. In *OOPSLA 2000*.

[4] G. Kiczales *et al.* Aspect-oriented programming. In *ECOOP '97*.

[5] G. Kiczales *et al.* An overview of AspectJ. In *ECOOP '01*.

[6] D. Garlan and D. Notkin. Formalizing design spaces: Implicit invocation mechanisms. In *VDM '91*.

[7] H. Rajan and G. T. Leavens. Ptolemy: A language with quantified, typed events. In *ECOOP*, July 2008.

Guidance Trees

A New Programming Paradigm for Non-Programmers

Michael Rowley

CTO, Active Endpoints
Waltham, MA USA
michael.rowley@activevos.com

Abstract

Guidance trees are a new development paradigm that can best be described as a mix between decision trees and workflows that you work with like mind maps. This demonstration will show how a non-technical user can use a guidance tree to develop a sales guide that executes within SalesForce.com.

Categories and Subject Descriptors D.3.2 [**Programming Languages**]: Language Classifications – Specialized application languages.

General Terms Design, Human Factors, Languages.

Keywords decision trees, graphical programming, workflow

1. Demonstration Overview

Michael will talk about the design considerations that went into the development of a new graphical-oriented programming language that is based on a new construct called *guidance trees*. The users of the system would not think of what they are doing as programming, but because they are creating a formal description of what the computer should do, it is essentially programming. We were able to keep the language simple by leveraging the fact that we were designing for the creation of screenflows, which are a sequence of screens that may be intermixed with calls to *automated steps* that do any non-screen related work. In the example that will be demonstrated, guidance trees are used for guiding a user of Salesforce.com through part of a sales process.

Michael will also talk about the evolution of the language design. He will describe aspects of the system where the drive toward simplicity resulted in an overly simplistic approach to data handling. He will then describe how a new version of the language overcame the limitations of the first version by incorporating some simple object-oriented concepts into the system.

During the demonstration, Michael will show guidance trees running inside of the SalesForce.com application (where they are called "sales guides"). He will then show the development of a sales guide from scratch, deployed and then run in the context of a SaleForce object. The guidance tree design environment is web-based and dynamically presents the subset of the tree that is most relevant to expanding parts of the tree as the user navigates.

Michael will then open the hood and talk about the kinds of things that can and _can't_ be done in the design environment in order to provide the level of simplicity that is needed for the target user. He will describe the HTML-5 based implementation for the design environment and the techniques used to integrate it into SaleForce.com (without running on Force.com). He will also show how the guidance trees created execute on a BPEL-based BPMS and the advantages of this approach even though the guidance tree itself has few similarities to BPEL.

2. Bio

Michael Rowley is the CTO of Active Endpoints and is an expert in SOA and BPM technology. He was a contributor on the BPMN 2.0 specification and is an editor of the BPEL4People and WS-HumanTask specifications that are being finalized within OASIS. He is a key contributor and an editor on OASIS specifications for Service Component Architecture (SCA) and is also co-author of the book Understanding SCA (Service Component Architecture), which was published in July of 2009.

At Active Endpoints, Michael is the lead designer of Guidance Tree technology and the Cloud Extend product that is based on it. Before joining Active Endpoints, he worked at BEA Systems, where he was an architect on three products before moving to the office of the CTO, where he worked on innovative technology and standards. Michael received his Ph.D. in Computer Science from UCLA in 1994.

See more about guidance trees at http://CloudExtend.com.

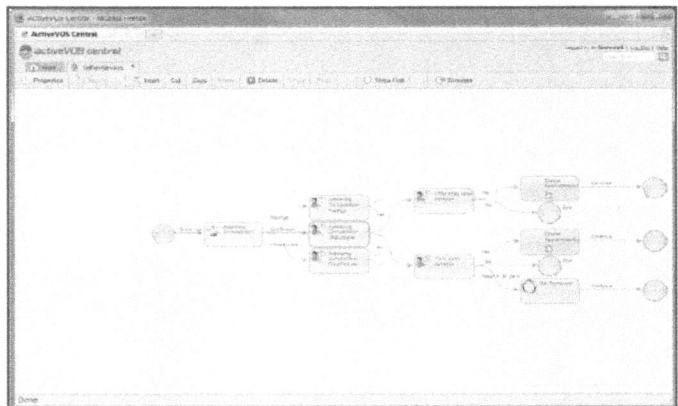

JP2 – Collecting Dynamic Bytecode Metrics in JVMs

Aibek Sarimbekov
Walter Binder

University of Lugano, Switzerland
firstname.lastname@usi.ch

Andreas Sewe   Mira Mezini

Technische Universität Darmstadt,
Germany
lastname@st.informatik.tu-
darmstadt.de

Alex Villazón *

Universidad Privada Boliviana
(UPB), Cochabamba, Bolivia
avillazon@upb.edu

Abstract

The collection of dynamic metrics is an important part of performance analysis and workload characterization. We demonstrate JP2, a new tool for collecting dynamic bytecode metrics for standard Java Virtual Machines (JVMs). The application of JP2 is a three-step process: First, an online step instruments the application for profiling. Next, the resulting profile is dumped in an appropriate format for later analysis. Finally, the desired metrics are computed in an offline step. JP2's profiles capture both the inter-procedural and the intra-procedural control flow in a callsite-aware calling-context tree, where each node stores, amongst others, the execution count for each basic block of code. JP2 uses portable bytecode instrumentation techniques, is Open Source, and has been tested with several production JVMs.

Categories and Subject Descriptors   D.2.8 [*Metrics*]: Performance measures

General Terms   Experimentation, Measurement

Keywords   Dynamic metrics, Java

1. Introduction

We demonstrate JP2, an open-source tool[1] for portable execution profiling in standard Java Virtual Machines (JVMs). Thanks to plugins that dump the collected profile in an appropriate format, it is easy to set up an evaluation workflow and compute a wide range of dynamic metrics. Recently, JP2 has successfully been used to characterize Scala workloads and to compare their execution behavior with the DaCapo benchmarks [5]; the results of this study are presented in a complementary research paper at OOPSLA 2011 [12].

In terms of implementation, JP2 is a significant improvement over the previous JP profiler [4]. In particular, it improves the completeness and accuracy of profiles in the presence of native methods [11]. Moreover, JP2 adds awareness of both individual callsites [11] and intra-procedural control flow; it thus collects much richer profiles than its predecessor. The collected profiles are complete in the sense that invocations of native methods as well as callbacks from native code into bytecode are all present in the profile. They are also accurate in the sense that for all methods, whether represented by bytecode or by native code, their invocations are counted. Additionally, for methods represented by bytecode, accurate basic-block execution counts are part of the profile.

JP2 arranges the profiles for individual methods in a so-called calling-context tree (CCT) [2], which represents the overall program execution. While rich in information, the resulting profile is therefore conceptually quite simple; the CCT contains only two kinds of objects: nodes representing the calling-contexts and arrays with basic-block execution counts for each context.

2. Step 1: Instrumentation

JP2 applies instrumentation to any method with a bytecode representation, including methods in the standard Java class library. To this end, JP2 uses polymorphic bytecode instrumentation (PBI) [10] to avoid infinite recursions which otherwise may occur when the instrumentation itself invokes methods in the instrumented class library. PBI achieves this using code duplication within method bodies; depending on the control flow, the correct version of the code (either instrumented or original) is executed. A thread-local flag indicates whether execution is at the level of the base program under analysis or at the level of the inserted profiling code. Using PBI requires no structural modifications of classfiles.

For profiling native methods, JP2 relies on native method prefixing, a feature of the JVMTI[2] introduced in Java 6, and statically inserts a bytecode wrapper for each native

---

* The work presented here was conducted while A. Villazón was visiting University of Lugano, Switzerland.

[1] See `http://jp-profiler.origo.ethz.ch/`.

[2] See `http://download.oracle.com/javase/6/docs/technotes/guides/jvmti/`.

method [11]. This is the only use of static instrumentation; otherwise all classes get instrumented dynamically, with classes already loaded during JVM bootstrapping being redefined after the bootstrap. If native methods are not of interest, this static instrumentation step becomes optional; all that is required is a Java-6-compatible JVM.

3. Step 2: Profiling and Profile Dumping

Although JP2 collects platform-independent dynamic metrics like method invocations or basic-block execution counts, it can also be used to collect platform-dependent metrics such as elapsed CPU or wallclock time. Momentarily, however, the focus is on dynamic metrics that are independent of both the specific JVM and underlying hardware architecture.

JP2 uses a plugin mechanism for dumping the collected profiles and ships with four different plugins: One pair of plugins uses a text-based output format. Another pair of plugins uses XML-based formats to output either the entire CCT or a dynamic call graph. This flexible plugin mechanism enables the user of JP2 to compute dynamic metrics offline, thus giving an opportunity first to collect the necessary data, then define the metrics of interest, and finally compute them (all from the same profile).

4. Step 3: Metrics Computation

During the live demonstration, JP2 will be applied to several Java and Scala applications, producing detailed profiles. These profiles will be dumped in an XML representation suitable for easy analysis with off-the-shelf tools. We will show several small XQuery scripts [6] that compute various dynamic bytecode metrics of interest, such as method and basic block hotness, callsite polymorphism, and others. The tool demonstration will present all necessary steps for setting up, running, and customizing JP2. Hence, the participants will be able to immediately start using JP2 for their own workload characterization tasks.

5. Related Tools

Dufour et al. [7] presented *J, a tool for collecting dynamic metrics, which relies on the obsolete JVMPI profiling interface.[3] It introduces high overhead and is thus not applicable to large-scale, real-world workloads. Other related tools use sampling techniques that compromise completeness and accuracy of the collected profiles [3, 13]. Finally, many profilers rely on modifications of a particular JVM, such as the Jikes RVM [1] or the Sable VM [8], and are therefore available only for a limited set of environments, such as the profiling framework for multicores devised by Ha et al. [9]. In contrast, JP2 is a tool for collecting complete and accurate dynamic metrics in any standard JVM; moreover, its use incurs only an acceptable overhead [11].

---

[3] See `http://download.oracle.com/javase/1.4.2/docs/guide/jvmpi/`.

References

[1] B. Alpern, D. Attanasio, A. Cocchi, D. Lieber, S. Smith, T. Ngo, and J. J. Barton. Implementing Jalapeño in Java. In *Proceedings of the Conference on Object-Oriented Programming, Systems, Languages, and Applications*, 1999.

[2] G. Ammons, T. Ball, and J. R. Larus. Exploiting hardware performance counters with flow and context sensitive profiling. In *Proceedings of the Conference on Programming Language Design and Implementation*, 1997.

[3] M. Arnold and B. G. Ryder. A framework for reducing the cost of instrumented code. In *Proceedings of the Conference on Programming Language Design and Implementation*, 2001.

[4] W. Binder, J. Hulaas, P. Moret, and A. Villazón. Platform-independent profiling in a virtual execution environment. *Software: Practice and Experience*, 39(1):47–79, 2009.

[5] S. M. Blackburn, R. Garner, C. Hoffman, A. M. Khan, K. S. McKinley, R. Bentzur, A. Diwan, D. Feinberg, D. Frampton, S. Z. Guyer, M. Hirzel, A. Hosking, M. Jump, H. Lee, J. E. B. Moss, A. Phansalkar, D. Stefanović, T. VanDrunen, D. von Dincklage, and B. Wiedermann. The DaCapo benchmarks: Java benchmarking development and analysis. In *Proceedings of the Conference on Object-Oriented Programing, Systems, Languages, and Applications*, pages 169–190, 2006.

[6] S. Boag, D. Chamberlin, M. F. Fernández, D. Florescu, J. Robie, and J. Siméon, editors. *XQuery 1.0: An XML Query Language*. World Wide Web Consortium, 2nd edition, 2010.

[7] B. Dufour, L. Hendren, and C. Verbrugge. *J: a tool for dynamic analysis of Java programs. In *Companion of the Conference on Object-Oriented Programming, Systems, Languages, and Applications*, 2003.

[8] E. M. Gagnon and L. J. Hendren. SableVM: A research framework for the efficient execution of Java bytecode. In *In Proceedings of the Java Virtual Machine Research and Technology Symposium*, 2000.

[9] J. Ha, M. Arnold, S. M. Blackburn, and K. S. McKinley. A concurrent dynamic analysis framework for multicore hardware. In *Proceedings of the Conference on Object-Oriented Programming, Systems, Languages, and Applications*, 2009.

[10] P. Moret, W. Binder, and E. Tanter. Polymorphic bytecode instrumentation. In *Proceedings of the International Conference on Aspect-Oriented Software Development*, 2011.

[11] A. Sarimbekov, P. Moret, W. Binder, A. Sewe, and M. Mezini. Complete and platform-independent calling context profiling for the Java virtual machine. In *Proceedings of the Workshop on Bytecode Semantics, Verification, Analysis and Transformation*, 2011.

[12] A. Sewe, M. Mezini, A. Sarimbekov, and W. Binder. Dacapo con Scala: Design and analysis of a Scala benchmark suite for the Java virtual machine. In *Proceedings of the Conference on Object-Oriented Programming, Systems, Languages, and Applications*, 2011.

[13] J. Whaley. A portable sampling-based profiler for Java Virtual Machines. In *Proceedings of the ACM 2000 Conference on Java Grande*, 2000.

Changing State in the Plaid Language

Joshua Sunshine[†]   Sven Stork[†*]   Karl Naden[†]   Jonathan Aldrich[†]

[†]Carnegie Mellon University   [*]University of Coimbra

{sunshine, svens, kbn, jonathan.aldrich}@cs.cmu.edu

Abstract

Plaid is a language in which objects are defined not by fixed classes, but by changing abstract states. We will overview the Plaid programming language through a series of examples drawing from domains like I/O code and web applications. Attendees will write Plaid code and experience its benefits.

Categories and Subject Descriptors   D.3.2 [*Programming Languages*]: Object-Oriented Languages

General Terms   Languages

Keywords   Plaid, typestate, state change

1. Description

Plaid is an emerging programming language with native support for *typestate*, which captures the changing states an object can be in. Each typestate defines its own interface (methods signatures), representation (fields), and behavior (method signatures); calling a method on the object may result in a transition from one typestate to another. Typestate is thus a powerful facility for modeling many different kinds of stateful abstractions.

In this presentation, we will provide an overview of the Plaid programming language through a series of examples drawing from domains like I/O code, user interfaces, web applications, and robotics. These examples will show how Plaid more closely models state-based design than traditional languages. Plaid code is smaller, easier to understand, less error-prone, and more reusable. We will demonstrate the open-source Plaid compiler, which is available at http://plaid-lang.googlecode.com/, and provide opportunities for attendees to try out the language themselves, either by downloading the compiler or by using the web-based Plaid terminal at http://plaid.isri.cmu.edu:8080/plaidWeb/.

Attendees should come away with an understanding of the core new ideas in the Plaid language. They should also

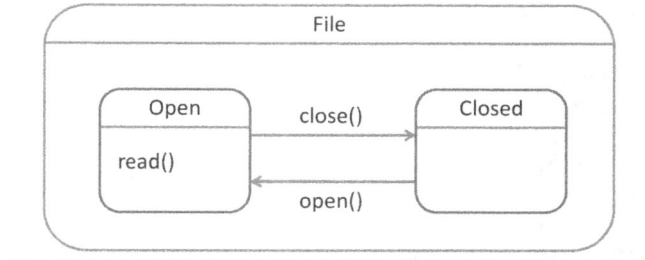

Figure 1. State space of File.

```
state File {
    val filename;
}
state OpenFile case of File = {
    val filePtr;
    method read() { ... }
    method close() { this <- ClosedFile; }
}
state ClosedFile case of File {
    method open() { this <- OpenFile; }
}
```

Figure 2. File states in Plaid

have an idea of how different problems can be effectively modeled with Plaid's constructs, and (for the adventurous) a taste of writing programs in Plaid. We hope some attendees will experiment with Plaid after the presentation, and perhaps find it useful. We also hope that Plaid's new ideas will in turn spur further innovation in other emerging programming languages.

2. File Example

To get a feel for the way that stateful abstractions are represented in Plaid, consider files, the canonical stateful protocol example [1]. We show the state space of files in Figure 1. Some files are open and some are closed. We close an open file by calling the close method and open a closed file by calling the open method. One cannot open an open file, so the open file state does not include the close method. Similarly, one cannot read a closed file so the closed file state does not include the read method.

```
method readFromClosedFile(f) {
    f.open();
    val x = f.read();
    f.close();
    x; //return
}
```

Figure 3. File client in Plaid

The state space of files can be encoded cleanly in Plaid as shown in Listing 2. The `state` keyword is used to define a state. The `File` state contains the fields and methods that are common between open and closed files. In this case, only the filename is shared. Fields are declared with the `val` keyword.

`OpenFile` and `ClosedFile` define the methods and fields that are specific to open and closed states. Both are substates of `File`. Specialization is declared with the `case of` keyword. In addition, `case of` implies orthogonality: files can either be open or closed, not both. Methods are defined with the `method` keyword. Open files have a `read` method, a file pointer field which is presumably used by the `read` method to read the file, and a `close` method. Closed files have the `open` method.

The `open` and `close` method bodies contain the most novel bit of syntax. An object referred to by a variable `x` can be changed to state `S` by writing `x <- S`. In the `open` method we transition the receiver, referred to as in Java by the keyword `this`, to the open state by writing `this <- OpenFile`.

An example file client is shown in Listing 3. The `readFromClosedFile` method takes a file as an argument, opens it, reads from it, closes it, and returns the value read from the file. All of the method calls are valid if a closed file is passed to the method. If an open file is passed instead the `open` method call will fail. The library writers do not need to write any special error handling code to handle this condition like they would in Java. This has the concrete benefit that Plaid code for the equivalent design is smaller. Furthermore, the errors can be more specific and relate the problem to the abstract state of the object.

3. Other Examples

Files provide a simple example of abstract states, but there are many more. Streams may be open or closed, iterators may have elements available or not, collections may be empty or not, and even lowly exceptions can have their cause set, or not[1]. State spaces may be complex: In `ResultSet` from the Java JDBC library, we found 33 unique states dealing with different combinations of openness, direction, random access, insertions, etc. [3]. States are also common: a recent study of protocols in Java suggests that almost three times as many types define protocols as define type parameters [2].

They also cause significant pain: for instance, in a study of problems developers experienced when using the ASP.NET framework, three out of four of the issues identified involved temporal constraints such as the state of the framework in various callback functions [4].

4. Biographies

Joshua, Sven, Karl and Jonathan are four of the principal designers, specifiers, and implementers of the Plaid programming language. Joshua is a software engineering PhD student at Carnegie Mellon University; his research focuses on the usability of programming languages. Sven is a software engineering PhD student at both Carnegie Mellon University and University of Coimbra; his research focuses on programming language support for concurrency by default. Karl is a computer science PhD student at Carnegie Mellon University; his research focuses on the design and development of the Plaid programming language. Jonathan Aldrich is an Assistant Professor in the Institute for Software Research at Carnegie Mellon University; his research focuses on providing novel ways to express and enforce structural and behavioral aspects of software design within source code.

Acknowledgments

We thank Nels Beckman and Robert Bocchino for their work on the semantics of Plaid; Manuel Mohr, Mark Hahnenberg, Aparup Banerjee, Matthew Rodriguez, and Fuyao Zhao for their work on the Plaid compiler; and the PLAID group for their helpful feedback and suggestions. This research was supported by DARPA grant #HR00110710019. Sven Stork is supported by the Portuguese Research Agency FCT, through a scholarship (SFRH/BD/33522/2008). Joshua Sunshine is supported by the Department of Defense (DoD) through the National Defense Science and Engineering Graduate Fellowship (NDSEG) Program.

References

[1] J. Aldrich, J. Sunshine, D. Saini, and Z. Sparks. Typestate-oriented programming. In *Proc. Onward*, 2009.

[2] N. E. Beckman, D. Kim, and J. Aldrich. An empirical study of object protocols in the wild. In *Proc. European Conference on Object-Oriented Programming 2011*.

[3] K. Bierhoff and J. Aldrich. Lightweight object specification with typestates. In *Proc. Foundations of Software Engineering*, 2005.

[4] C. Jaspan. Proper plugin protocols: Cost-effective verification of frameworks. Technical Report CMU-ISR-11-101, Institute for Software Research, Carnegie Mellon University, April 2011. Thesis Proposal, originally accepted April 2010.

---

[1] E.g. in Java, the cause of an exception can only be set once.

Keshmesh: A Tool for Detecting and Fixing Java Concurrency Bug Patterns

Mohsen Vakilian   Stas Negara   Samira Tasharofi   Ralph E. Johnson

University of Illinois, Urbana, IL, USA

{mvakili2, snegara2, tasharo1, rjohnson}@illinois.edu

Abstract

Developing concurrent software is error prone. Others have cataloged common bug patterns in concurrent Java programs. But, there are no tools for detecting complex concurrency bug patterns accurately, and concurrent programs are full of similar bugs. We have been developing a tool called *Keshmesh* for detecting complex concurrency bug patterns in Java programs statically. Keshmesh is the first tool that accurately detects a few of the top concurrency bug patterns of the SEI CERT catalog [3] and suggests automated fixers for some of them. Keshmesh is fast enough to be used interactively, produces few false alarms and helps Java programmers to quickly find and fix common concurrency bug patterns in their programs.

Categories and Subject Descriptors   D.2.4 [*Software Engineering*]: Software/Program Verification;   D.1.3 [*Programming Techniques*]: Concurrent Programming

General Terms   Algorithm, Design, Verification

Keywords   bug, pattern, detector, fixer, concurrency, parallelism, static analysis, program analysis

1. Introduction

Multi-cores have encouraged more programmers to write concurrent software. But, writing concurrent software is difficult and similar bugs keep showing up in concurrent programs. Cataloging common bug patterns in concurrent programs is an active research domain, and the SEI CERT catalog [3] is a recent and comprehensive catalog of concurrency bug patterns in Java. The existence of a bug pattern does not necessarily imply a bug. In other words, some bug patterns are considered as bad practices that might lead to future bugs as the software evolves. Nonetheless, it is valuable to detect such problems as early as possible.

Keshmesh is the first tool that automatically detects complex concurrency bug patterns and suggests ways of fixing them. Complex concurrency bug patterns usually cross the boundaries of methods and involve indirect accesses to shared data via references. The SEI CERT catalog has rated the *severity*, *likelihood* and *remediation cost* of each bug pattern. We have prioritized the bug patterns based on these three attributes and selected five of the top ten bug patterns. Keshmesh provides automated detectors

for the generalized forms of five bug patterns and fixers for two of them. Keshmesh improves the state of the art in static analysis for detecting concurrency bug patterns by looking for instances of the bug patterns interprocedurally and employing context sensitive points-to analysis. Keshmesh is an Eclipse plug-in that uses WALA [2] as its underlying static analysis engine and FindBugs [1] as its user interface. Keshmesh is open source and available at `http://keshmesh.cs.illinois.edu`.

2. Detecting and Fixing Bug Patterns

Keshmesh extends the Eclipse plug-in of FindBugs [1] by a few concurrency bug pattern detectors and fixers. By extending FindBugs, Keshmesh inherits all the nice features of FindBugs such as filtering and integration into build systems and becomes easily usable by the users of FindBugs. Even though Keshmesh extends FindBugs to report bug patterns and suggest fixes to the user, it does not use the analysis engine of FindBugs. Instead, Keshmesh uses WALA [2], which is a much more powerful engine for analyzing Java byte code.

WALA enables Keshmesh to detect complex bug patterns with high accuracy. WALA requires the user to designate some methods as entry points. Typically, the `main` methods and test methods serve as entry points. Keshmesh expects the user to specify the entry points by using the custom method annotation `@EntryPoint`. Knowing the entry points, WALA builds the call graph and computes the points-to sets starting from the entry points. Then, every Keshmesh detector inspects the results of WALA, i.e. the IR, call graph and points-to sets to find the bug patterns. Keshmesh reports the bug patterns to the user as FindBugs bug reports, and if an automated fix is available, the user can apply the automated fix using the quick fix mechanism of Eclipse. In the following, we briefly describe the bug patterns and their detectors and fixers in Keshmesh.

2.1 LCK01-J. Do not synchronize on objects that may be reused

Objects such as interned strings and primitive literals may be reused. Therefore, such reusable objects cannot be safely used as locks. Keshmesh examines the allocation sites to detect reusable objects, and reports any `synchronized` block whose lock expression may point to a reusable object as an instance of LCK01-J. For example, Keshmesh reports a `synchronized` block whose lock object is the variable `intLock`, where `Integer intLock = 0`, because this object is autoboxed and allocated inside `Integer.valueOf()`.

2.2 LCK02-J. Do not synchronize on the class object returned by `getClass()`

The bug pattern LCK02-J recommends not to use the return value of `Object.getClass()` as a lock.

Keshmesh detects an object returned by `Object.getClass()` by inspecting the allocation site of the object. If the type of the allocation is `Class` and the object is allocated inside `Object.getClass()`, Keshmesh recognizes the object as one returned by `Object.getClass()`. Keshmesh reports any `synchornized` block whose lock expression may point to an object returned by `Object.getClass()` as a instance of LCK02-J. Moreover, Keshmesh suggests automated fixes to the user to replace the lock expression by the class literal of the objects that it may point to, if there is only one possible class literal.

2.3 LCK03-J. Do not synchronize on the intrinsic locks of high-level concurrency objects

Instances of classes that implement `Condition` or `Lock` are high-level concurrency objects. And, using such concurrency objects as the lock objects of `synchronized` blocks is a bad practice.

Keshmesh reports `synchronized` blocks whose lock expressions may point to a high-level concurrency object as instances of LCK03-J. In addition, if the high-level concurrency object is a `Lock`, Keshmesh provides the user with an automated fixer that replaces the `synchronized` block on the high-level object by a block that invokes `Lock.lock()` and `Lock.unlock()` at the beginning and end, respectively.

2.4 LCK06-J. Do not use an instance lock to protect shared `static` data

Instance locks cannot protect shared `static` data because multiple instances of the class may make the locks different. Therefore, LCK06-J warns about the use of instance locks to protect shared `static` data.

Let S be the set of objects that the `static` fields may point to. A `synchronized` block is *safe* if the points-to set of its lock object is a nonempty subset of S. Similarly, a `synchronized` method is *safe* if it is either `static` or the points-to set of its lock object, `this`, is a nonempty subset of S. A byte code instruction is *unsafe* if it is not inside any safe `synchronized` blocks and modifies a non-`final` `static` field or an object that some `static` field may point to.

Keshmesh computes the unsafe instructions of each method and performs an interprocedural data flow analysis to propagate these instructions up the call graph. Finally, it reports the `static` fields affected by the unsafe instructions to the user.

2.5 VNA00-J. Ensure visibility when accessing shared primitive variables

An unprotected access to a non-`volatile` shared primitive variable is an instance of VNA00-J. We have generalized VNA00-J by not restricting the shared data to primitive variables. Keshmesh considers any class that extends `Thread`, implements `Runnable`, or contains `synchronized` methods or blocks as a thread-safe class. And, it treats all objects reachable from the fields of nonlocal instances of thread-safe classes as shared data. Keshmesh looks for unsafe accesses to the shared data and marks every line of code that directly or indirectly, i.e. through method invocations, makes an unsafe access as an instance of VNA00-J. Keshmesh propagates unsafe accesses across the boundaries of methods by solving a data flow problem. This formulation of the data flow problem propagates unsafe accesses from the callee to the caller if the call site is not protected by a `synchronized` block and at least one argument of the method invocation may be shared data.

3. Related Work

FindBugs [1] detects a variety of bug patterns, including several concurrency bug patterns. However, the capability of FindBugs for detecting bug patterns is limited by its intraprocedural analysis engine.

Luo et al. [4] developed a tool to statically find concurrency bug patterns in Java. Their tool finds most of the bug patterns intraprocedurally by AST pattern matching, and it uses WALA's points-to analysis only for one bug pattern.

Naik et al. [5] proposed a static analysis to find a specific kind of bug pattern, i.e. data races, in Java programs. Their tool looks for actual bugs rather than bug patterns that might lead to bugs in future.

4. Future Work

A challenge in developing an effective static analysis tool for finding bug patterns is to make the right balance between accuracy on one hand and performance and scalability on the other hand. We plan to evaluate Keshmesh on real-world software, adjust the identification criteria of its bug patterns and tune the context sensitivity of WALA [2] to improve the accuracy, performance and scalability of Keshmesh.

5. Description of the Demonstration

The SPLASH community has been actively participating in shaping the future of multi-core software engineering. Keshmesh is relevant to the SPLASH community since it is a step towards correct concurrent software.

In our demonstration session, we plan to present the bug patterns supported by Keshmesh. We will do a live demo of Keshmesh on some examples. Specifically, we will run Keshmesh on several example programs containing instances of some of the bug patterns supported by Keshmesh. Then, we will show how the results are presented to the user, including the fix information, where it is available. We will show the audience how to use Keshmesh to find instances of the bug patterns and fix them. Then, we will explain the underlying algorithms of Keshmesh for detecting the bug patterns. We will compare Keshmesh with an existing tool for detection of concurrency bug patterns such as FindBugs [1]. Also, we will describe the techniques that we have employed to achieve the right number of false alarms and tune WALA [2] for getting good precision and performance.

6. Presenters

Mohsen Vakilian and Samira Tasharofi are PhD students at the University of Illinois. Mohsen is interested in improving the programming environments for parallel programming. In addition to developing better tools for finding and fixing concurrency bug patterns, he has been working on tools for migrating sequential programs to parallel languages. Samira is interested in concurrency bug patterns and testing concurrent programs. She has been working on partial order reduction and tools for testing message-passing programs.

References

[1] FindBugs. URL http://findbugs.sf.net/.

[2] T.J. Watson Libraries for Analysis (WALA). URL http://wala.sf.net/.

[3] F. Long, D. Mohindra, R. C. Seacord, and D. Svoboda. Java Concurrency Guidelines. Technical report, 2010. URL http://www.sei.cmu.edu/reports/10tr015.pdf.

[4] Z. D. Luo, L. Hillis, R. Das, and Y. Qi. Effective Static Analysis to Find Concurrency Bugs in Java. In *10th IEEE Working Conference on Source Code Analysis and Manipulation*, 2010.

[5] M. Naik, A. Aiken, and J. Whaley. Effective Static Race Detection for Java. In *Proceedings of the conference on programming language design and implementation*, 2006.

Extending the Graal Compiler to Optimize Libraries

Thomas Wuerthinger

Oracle Labs
thomas.wuerthinger@oracle.com

Abstract

The Graal compiler is an optimizing just-in-time compiler written in Java that works with both the Maxine VM and the HotSpot VM. It allows Java libraries to extend its functionality for example by providing new intermediate representation nodes and new optimization phases. We demonstrate how to write such plug-ins for the Graal compiler.

Categories and Subject Descriptors D.3.4 [*Programming Languages*]: Processors - Code Generation; Compilers; Optimization; Runtime Environments

General Terms Algorithms, Performance, Languages

Keywords Compilers, optimization, plug-ins, JIT, Java, virtual machines

1. Introduction

The Graal just-in-time compiler [4] works with two different virtual machines and is designed for extensibility in order to support customization. Graal was originally derived from the HotSpot client compiler [2] and uses a linear scan register allocator [3]. The intermediate representation (IR) of the compiler is a program dependence graph [1] in static single assignment (SSA) form. The IR can be explored using the IdealGraphVisualizer [8]. Figure 1 shows the Graal IR of an example method as presented by the visualization tool.

Graal is built with a clean compiler-runtime separation [6] and is currently integrated in two virtual machines: The Maxine Research VM [5] and the HotSpot VM. Additionally, the compiler provides a Java API that enables fine-grained control of compiler phases and also allows the introduction of new phases or IR nodes. This allows for efficient implementation of new languages and the introduction of special optimizations for library calls. The demonstration focuses on this distinguishing feature of the Graal compiler.

SPLASH'11 Companion, October 22–27, 2011, Portland, Oregon, USA.
ACM 978-1-4503-0940-0/11/10.

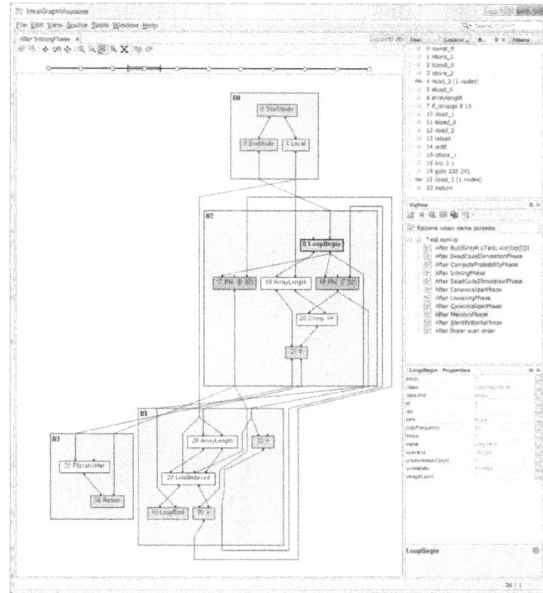

Figure 1. Graal IR for a method with a simple loop shown in the IdealGraphVisualizer.

2. Demonstration Outline

The presentation includes two examples of how to customize the Graal compiler:

- **New IR node:** We show how to introduce a new IR node for adding two integer values and efficiently guarding against overflow by directly lowering to machine code that checks the X86 overflow flags.

- **New optimization phase:** We show how to add a new optimization phase to the compiler that is capable of combining subsequent calls to a vector library if they match a specific pattern.

During the presentation, we write the Java source code that is necessary to achieve the compiler customizations. The result is demonstrated by executing the program using the new customized compiler. Additionally, the IdealGraphVisualizer is used to explain the transformations on the compiler intermediate representation.

3. Presenter Bio

The presenter received a PhD degree in Computer Science from the Johannes Kepler University Linz [7]. He joined Oracle Labs in April 2011 and started working on the Graal compiler. His research interests include graph visualization, compilers, and virtual machines.

Acknowledgments

The demonstration was prepared with the help of Lukas Stadler and Gilles Duboscq who also made signif cant contributions to the Graal compiler. Additionally, the presenter would like to thank the members of the Maxine team and the HotSpot team for their continuous support and contributing many helpful ideas and discussions that lead to the current design of the compiler.

References

[1] J. Ferrante, K. J. Ottenstein, and J. D. Warren. The program dependence graph and its use in optimization. *ACM Transactions on Programming Languages and Systems*, 9:319–349, July 1987. ISSN 0164-0925.

[2] T. Kotzmann, C. Wimmer, H. Mössenböck, T. Rodriguez, K. Russell, and D. Cox. Design of the Java Hotspot client compiler for Java 6. *ACM Transactions on Architecture and Code Optimization*, 5:7:1–7:32, May 2008. ISSN 1544-3566.

[3] H. Mössenböck and M. Pfeiffer. Linear scan register allocation in the context of SSA form and register constraints. In *Proceedings of the International Conference on Compiler Construction*, pages 229–246. Springer-Verlag, 2002.

[4] *The Maxine Project: Graal*. Oracle Labs, 2011. http://wikis.sun.com/display/MaxineVM/Graal.

[5] *The Maxine VM*. Oracle Labs, 2011. http://labs.oracle.com/projects/maxine.

[6] B. L. Titzer, T. Würthinger, D. Simon, and M. Cintra. Improving compiler-runtime separation with XIR. In *Proceedings of the ACM/USENIX International Conference on Virtual Execution Environments*, pages 39–50. ACM Press, 2010.

[7] T. Würthinger. *Dynamic Code Evolution for Java*. PhD thesis, Johannes Kepler University Linz, 2011.

[8] T. Würthinger, C. Wimmer, and H. Mössenböck. Visualization of program dependence graphs. In *Proceedings of the International Conference on Compiler Construction*, pages 193–196. Springer-Verlag, 2008.

Software Objects Fairy Tales

Merging design and runtime objects into the cloud with MyDraft

Michel Zam

KarmicSoft, Paris Dauphine University

m.zam@karmicsoft.com

Gilles Dodinet

KarmicSoft

g.dodinet@karmicsoft.com

Geneviève Jomier

Paris Dauphine University

Genevieve.Jomier@dauphine.fr

Abstract

This is the story of software objects living in a space-time continuum, where design and runtime activities are causally connected. Tracing their adventures gives new insights and draws the big picture of the Darwinian fable we all live in.

Categories and Subject Descriptors D.2.2 [Software Engineering]: Design Tools and Techniques.

General Terms: Design, Experimentation.

Keywords: meta-design, traceability, causality, time machine, rapid development, cloud computing

1. Speaker

Michel Zam, PhD, is co-founder and CSO of KarmicSoft, Associate Professor at Paris Dauphine University, and member of IEEE Computer Society. He holds innovation awards and patents on evolution and traceability of both data and software. He and his team build reflexive tools, flexible applications and traceable solutions. He faced design challenges, meta bugs, and knows the real story of aggressive software evolution from inside.

2. Description

The addressed problems involve data and application co-evolution. The audience will travel in space and time through the evolutionary process of an emerging and experimental self-made system, meant to let power users build data-driven web applications without technical skills. Runtime and design activities are merged and the system never stops. At each bus stop, new bold requirements are integrated in the application and the environment itself. Changes are impacted through the whole running system, down to its atoms. Both the application and the environment are continually enhanced. Their common log uncovers the DNA of a sustainable software environment. Instant jump back in time shows initial versions of data and earlier development stages of the application and the environment. Trace pattern mining stimulates insight, new ideas and better ways to rebuild the system. Changing the past is tempting, but this could alter the timeline and change the course of the history, including the mindset of the audience.

The demo is relevant to the pain and hope of splash community members that face upgrading software as a day-to-day challenge. The unique thing about the design is that data and programs co-exist in a causally connected system and their interactions are traced on the fly and used to impact changes.

Used techniques include meta-object protocols and reflecting metamodeling, object-relational mapping and server-side scripting. The technological stack covers RDBMS, JPA, JavaEE, and RIA. Interesting technical details: optimized bootstrap, balanced static and dynamic resources, full traceability features and matching web performance constraints.

3. Background

The classical way to build data-driven web applications is based on the standard edit-compile-build-deploy-run lifecycle. On the left-hand, design items are expressed through object-oriented and/or tag-based statements, using an IDE and stored in text files at design time. On the right hand, at runtime, persistent items are read by the server, transformed into web resources (html, css, jpg, json, etc.) and displayed through the user's web browser. Design time and runtime items live in isolated worlds and are incarnated in different formats. They remain loosely coupled, only through a fragile virtual chain of human conscience and will. Therefore, their co-evolution raises huge issues with consequences on cost, quality and time-to-market. In the long run, evolution cost becomes prohibitive and the application dies.

4. Motivation

Our motivation is to simplify the standard lifecycle and reduce the co-evolution issues by merging design time and runtime environments. Design and runtime items are managed through uniform object-oriented representations, i.e. causally connected objects that live together in the same perpetually running system [1].

As this approach was already experimented at different extents by RAD tools, WYSIWYG editors or reflective meta object tools, we started some time ago by setting several bold constraints:

- Target data-driven rich web applications, based on established standards, and be useful to as many end users as possible

- Allow building and evolving applications without technical skills, to address a broader community of power users

- Provide a dedicated evolution support, from the physical storage up to the users' screen, in order to simplify collaboration and change impacts.

Several man-years later, the result is a SaaS environment, called MyDraft [4] that let power users build and evolve data-driven web applications in minutes, with little or no code, only using the web browser.

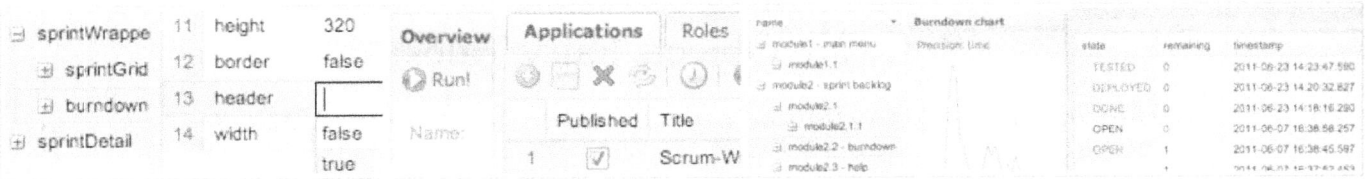

Figure 1. Merging design time and runtime activities into a unified high-level cloud-based environment where data, applications and the environment itself co-evolve peacefully in the same communitarian hive raise new questions about the evolution of object oriented concepts, agile methods and human ideas living together in the big virtual washing machine called internet.

The demonstration will first show a boring application built and run this way, and will emphasize the evolution support for both final data and design objects, including full traceability and time travel, as shown in Figure 1. Power users can perform online several design activities, such as:

- Display, search and create persistent business objects, then execute operations on them, using high-level RIA components.
- Define classes, attributes, associations and operations as regular business objects, and visualize them in UML class diagrams
- Design and preview complex GUI likewise, by choosing predefined fragment types like grids, forms, tabs, maps or charts
- Define roles, customize permissions for the GUI fragments, invite users to use the application and join the community
- Code client-side actions and server-side controllers, if needed
- Define new fragment types, declare libraries and web services
- Define user stories, add them into sprint backlogs and display burndown charts
- Inspect the history of any object and navigate instantly through time to any previous state of the system.

Evolution support includes refactoring features such as renaming any item in the system, changing the attribute's type or moving it to another class, changing multiplicity, adding or removing inheritance. Changes are propagated instantly through the whole currently running system, located in the cloud.

5. Emerging questions

The new paradigm shifts from code-based driven development to an integrated and self-described MDE environment. We discover that everything is stored as *atomic* data in a RDBMS, assembled on the fly as typed *molecule* and finally becomes executable scripted *object*. As the demonstration focuses on building such a system and learning form the experience, the sharp-eyed audience might ask:

- What about the storage strategy that supports both data and schema versioning? Is it meta-model dependent? How does this affect performance and storage space?
- If this is a meta reflective system, then does the evolution support apply to the environment itself? If so, can we go back to early development stages of the application and the environment? Can we redo the whole story, zoom in to important moments and learn from the past? Does the trace log reveal straight lines or interesting patterns?
- Are there any dinosaur object-oriented fossils? Which design concepts survived to the natural selection of the numerous iterations? By the way, did *multiple inheritance* finally make it?

- Can we change the past? What about temporal loops? Can we change the laws of software physics? Can we clone the universe?
- If everything can be changed without stopping the system, where is the remaining static part that supports the world?
- If you could rebuild the system, what would you change? If this is so efficient, what about testing new concepts and invent the future of object-orientation and agility?

In order to answer some of these questions, we will navigate through time and workspaces, experiment changes and observe the effects on data, application, on the whole environment and our own perceptions of the multiple reality.

6. Conclusion

Beyond the environment itself and the space-time travel features, will this free ride to the cloud development help solve the big issues? As a practitioner, can I let go my file-based IDE and my versioning system just like I already did with gmail and wikis? As a manager, will I survive the next generational jump and assemble applications in the cloud? As a researcher, can I spread my findings at warp speed? Social gardening in the cloud seems quite fun, remains available from any connected desktop or mobile device and does not hurt at all. The cloud itself – the biggest object we ever met – seems to grow faster from inside, blooming new applications, concepts and metaphors, ultimate proof that it's alive.

Acknowledgments

We would like to express our gratitude to professor Raymond Bisdorff from University of Luxembourg who encouraged us to boldly go where no man had gone before [2], for being the first power user of MyDraft and the first test pilot of the time-machine. We're very proud for rescuing him from the command-line era of the planet of the apes [3]. We would also like to apologize to our families. We have to confess that the impolite guys who type on their keyboards all day long and say mm-hmm when it comes to dinner are just our clones. We love you and we'll be back in your timeline, just after SPLASH 3011.

References

[1] Dodinet G, Zam M, Jomier G. *Coevolutive Meta-execution Support - Towards a Design and Execution Continuum*. ICSOFT 2010, Athens.

[2] Zam M, Bisdorff R. *Modern MCDA software: requirements and opportunities, EWG-MCDA Newsletter, fall 2011.*

[3] Zam M. & al. *Software Objects Nightmares: actually, we were all wrong back in 2011. Let's undo-redo it*, OOPSPLASH 2015 Paris, Texas, Earth v3.1, level 4.

[4] MyDraft, a reflective SaaS platform for building data-driven rich web applications: http://www.karmicsoft.com

SPLASH 2011 Doctoral Symposium Chair's Welcome

The SPLASH Doctoral Symposium provides students with guidance for completing their dissertation research and beginning their research careers. Doctoral students who attend the symposium are in one of two phases:

- *Apprentices*, who are just beginning their research, are not ready to actually make a research proposal, but are interested in learning about structuring research and getting some research ideas; and,

- *Proposers*, who have progressed far enough in their research to have a structured proposal, but will not be defending their dissertation in the next 12 months.

At the workshop, all students give a two-minute overview of their research describing the most critical issues (the "elevator talk"). Proposers also give a 20-minute description of their research, including its purpose, goals, and technical approach. The doctoral symposium committee then provides each student with constructive feedback on his or her research.

This year, I reviewed the 8 proposer and 2 apprentice submissions to the doctoral symposium in advance of selecting the doctoral symposium committee. As the topics discussed in the doctoral symposium are often quite diverse, this allowed me to ensure that the committee covered all areas in which students were working. After reading each submission, I decided to accept all 10 submissions.

I hope you enjoy their papers in this volume. In my view, they showcase the broad range of topics in the area of SPLASH, and the energy and creativity that students bring to the conference!

I would also like to think—on behalf of myself and the students as well—the distinguished committee who has agreed to serve as mentors to the students in this year's doctoral symposium. They are (besides myself):

- Michael Bond, from The Ohio State University,

- Ralph Johnson, from the University of Illinois at Urbana-Champaign, and

- Joseph Yoder, from The Refactory.

I appreciate their time and effort spent attending the doctoral symposium, as well as their careful thought and advice to the students. It is my hope that, through their mentoring, the students at the doctoral symposium will mature in their research, making an impact in the field and becoming the next generation of leaders in the SPLASH community.

Jonathan Aldrich
SPLASH 2011 Doctoral Symposium Chair
Carnegie Mellon University

Object Recognition in the Enterprise

Structural and Behavioral Capabilities of Patient-Centered Medical Homes

Nima A. Behkami
Portland State University
nima@pdx.edu

Abstract

The healthcare industry in United States is the largest delivery system in the world. However, this system is facing significant pressures to transform itself to operate more efficiently. It is generally accepted that the use of health information technology can assist in solving the problem by reducing cost and increasing quality of patient care. However characteristics of adopters and quality of implementations are not well understood and are an ongoing challenge.

Using an interdisciplinary study of healthcare and technology, the objective of this research is to measure the prevalence of health information technology capabilities and their impact on delivery of care. More specifically, this research will study health information technology adoption in context of Patient-Centered Medical Home implementations. By using as its basis the American Association of Family Physician recommendations for becoming a Patient-Centered Medical Home (one of the most widely disseminated models), the proposed research will survey health care providers for prevalence of structural and behavioral capabilities used to implement a Patient-Centered Medical Home.

The general objectives of the feasibility study includes demonstrating the larger research objectives and demonstrating that the right mix of theories and methodologies have been considered . The small field study was conducted at Oregon Health & Science University (OHSU) with the Care Management Plus (CMP) Team. CMP is a proven HIT application for older adults and chronically ill patients with multiple conditions and the innovation includes software, clinic processes and training. Use of qualitative research based case study, with application of diffusion theory and dynamic capabilities using the Unified Modeling Language (UML) notation are demonstrated in this field study. In the following sections data collection, analysis, results, conclusions and limitations of research along with propositions for future research are discussed.

Categories and Subject Descriptors H.1.1 Systems and Information Theory: Information theory, General systems theory.

General Terms Management, Measurement, Documentation, Design, Theory.

Keywords Health IT, Information Technology, Medical Home, Organizational Theory, PCMH, object-oriented systems

1. Fesaiblity Study Objectives

Objective.1: Identify some dynamic capabilities needed for successful implementation of HIT (Care Management Plus @OHSU).
Objective.2: Demonstrate that Dynamic Capabilities theory can be used and how to meaningfully extend Diffusion of Innovation Theory.
Objective.3: Use Software & System engineering methods including 4+1 View for perspectives and Unified Modeling Language to demonstrate documentation and analysis.
Objective.4: Build and run a small simulation of the DOI theory extension using System Dynamics. The simulation will be used to demonstrate the validity of the new diffusion framework.

2. Significance

The healthcare delivery system in the United States is facing a crisis and it is widely accepted that the use of Health Information Technology (HIT) can help by reducing cost and increasing quality of patient care. However, to date HIT adoption has been slow. For example, currently only about 20% of physician practices and 25% of hospitals use an Electronic Health Record (EHR) (Fonkych & Taylor 2005). Previous reviews have shown that broad use of Health IT may improve health care quality, prevent medical errors, reduce health care costs, increase administrative efficiencies, decrease paperwork and expand access to affordable care (Chaudhry et al. 2006). Additionally, interoperable HIT may improve individual patient care, and it may also provide other public health benefits including early detection of infectious disease outbreaks around the country, improved tracking of chronic disease management and evaluation of health care based on value, enabled by the collection of de-identified price and quality information that can be compared. However, these benefits are not consistently seen, and have mostly been achieved in so-called 'benchmark' institutions (Chaudhry et al. 2006; Sidorov 2006) rather than the broad mass of HIT adopters. All other paragraphs are indented.

To show any significant improvements in the population's health, the meaningful use of HIT needs to be far and wide. By examining the organizational science that enables diffusion of Patient-Centered Medical Home (PCMH) innovations, our contribution is expected to lead to an enhanced understanding of the possible means to accelerate HIT adoption. This research will measure the prevalence of recommended HIT capabilities for PCMH to determine how adoption varies among practices types.

Since its introduction in 1967 by the American Academy of Pediatrics (AAP), Medical Home concept has evolved and more recently the American College of Physicians (ACP) defined a Patient-Centered Medical Home as "a team-based model of care led by a personal physician who provides continuous and coordinated care throughout a patient's lifetime to maximize health outcomes. The PCMH practice is responsible for providing for all of a patient's health care needs or appropriately arranging care with other qualified professionals. This includes the provision of preventive services, treatment of acute and chronic illness, and assistance with end-of-life issues. It is a model of practice in which a team of health professionals, coordinated by a personal physician, works collaboratively to provide high levels of care, access and communication, care coordination and integration, and care quality and safety (American College of Physicians n.d.). "

This type of research requires an interdisciplinary approach that integrates the fields of Social Sciences, Engineering, and Medical Informatics. By addressing a problem at the intersection of technology management and healthcare, the main objective of this research is to help facilitate policy planning and decision making for the use of Health IT for improving patient health outcomes.

3. Innovation

While the concept of Patient-Centered Medical Home and the benefits of its associated Care Coordination functions have been accepted, evaluation of Medical Home adopters and the quality of their implementations are not well understood and are an ongoing challenge. A seminal study introduced the concept of PCMH structural capabilities and surveyed primary care physicians for their prevalence (Friedberg et al. 2009). One of the major findings of this study was that large primary care practices are more likely than small ones to adopt several recommended (Structural) capabilities. This study is a promising step towards better evaluating Medical Home implementation and understanding prevalence of its capabilities; however, the study examined everything as a structural capability without examining or distinguishing the so called behavioral capabilities of these providers. Structural capabilities are the static components of the practice, such as simply having an EHR in place (regardless of usage pattern). The Behavioral capabilities are the components of the practice that are dynamic rather than static, for example, the behavior or action to use EHR reminders and alerts.

Hence this is a gap; it is critical to look at the combination of structural and behavioral capabilities to understand the entire HIT adoption process. Therefore this research proposes to survey the field for structural and behavioral capabilities used in implementations of PCMH. The research proposed in this application is innovative, in our opinion, because it is an entirely different approach using capabilities. The proposal is the first research of its kind to combine the Resource Based Theory from the Strategic Management body of knowledge with Diffusion of Innovation Theory and apply it to Health Services. Diffusion is defined as the process where an innovation is communicated through specific channels over time among members of a social system (Rogers & Rogers 2003). Dynamic Capability theory defines the ability of firms to develop new competences that leads to superior firm performance (Teece et al. 1997).

4. Research Approach

With our focus on the Patient-Centered Medical Home (PCMH), the objective of this study is to facilitate understanding of potential interventions to accelerate Health IT adoption. A questionnaire will be sent out to a sample from set of over 8,000 clinicians nationwide to survey for prevalence of static and dynamic PCMH capabilities (Aim 1). Second, test whether recent policies for reimbursing for HIT use have been influential on Providers payer mix (Aim 2). Third, examine clinicians' satisfaction with PCMH implementation and how it pertains to number of recommended HIT capabilities implemented (Aim 3). Lastly, assess the impact of financial and organization barriers on implementation of HIT capabilities for PCMH (Aim4).

5. Preliminary Research

The Care Management Plus (CMP) model for primary care, developed by researchers at Oregon Health & Science University through funding from the John A. Hartford Foundation, uses specially trained care managers and tracking software to help clinics better care for patients with complex chronic illness. The model helps the clinical team prioritize health care needs and prevent complications through structured protocols, and it provides tools to assist patients and caregivers to self-manage chronic diseases. Specialized information technology includes the care manager tracking database patient summary sheet and messaging systems to help clinician's access care plans, receive reminders about best practices, and facilitate communication between the health care team.

CMP couples an ambulatory care team with health information technology (HIT). For seniors with complex needs, CMP demonstrated a 20% reduction in mortality, a 24% reduction in hospitalizations and a 15-25% reduction in complications from diabetes (DA Dorr et al. 2006; DA Dorr et al. 2005). CMP facilitates use of HIT to establish and track care plans and specific patient goals, to teach and encourage self-management, to measure and improve quality, and to manage the complex and interleaving tasks as patients and teams prioritize needs. Experience from the dissemination of CMP in more than 75 clinics across the country has led to a deep understanding of the barriers and benefits of such HIT. Barriers include the need to integrate systems, difficulty communicating with the entire team, and representation of workflow.

The feasibility study conducted at OHSU around Care Coordination and Medical Home adoption was valuable to verify the research and it lead to learning that have resulted in modifications to the proposed research design. As described below it includes 1) changing the research instrument from interviews to a survey 2) validating that using the concept of Capability would indeed be useful within the research framework and 3) focusing the research on a particular set of Medical Home functionally.

A major learning from the preliminary study was that a quantitatively based research instrument was more appropriate rather than the originally proposed qualitative instrument. The nature of the questions that are being asked require taking an inventorying of a large set of Medical Home adopters that is not feasible with a qualitative study. Prior to conducting the preliminary research there were some doubts whether or not using the concept of Capabilities was applicable to Health IT adoption. Analysis of scenarios encountered and documented in the preliminary work highlights that indeed using the Capability construct is appropriate for providing better understanding of Health IT adoption process. While this validated the research design, it also highlighted the need to divide the Capabilities into static and dynamic constructs. Structural Capabilities will be used to describe elements in the research subject organizations that were structural in nature and did not change overtime. Behavioral Capabilities will be used to describe elements that were behavioral and changed overtime.

In terms scope of research the preliminary work discovered a need to limit the focus on a practical set of functions rather than the general concept of the Patient-Centered Medical Home.

References

American College of Physicians, American College of Physicians - Internal Medicine - Doctors for Adults. Available at: http://www.acponline.org/ [Accessed November 1, 2010].

Chaudhry, B. et al., 2006. Systematic Review: Impact of Health Information Technology on Quality, Efficiency, and Costs of Medical Care. Annals of Internal Medicine, 144(10), pp.742-752.

Dorr, D. et al., 2006. Implementing a multidisease chronic care model in primary care using people and technology. Dis Manag, 9(1), pp.1-15.

Dorr, D. et al., 2005. Impact of generalist care managers on patients with diabetes. Health Serv Res, 40(5 Pt 1), pp.1400-21.

Fonkych, K. & Taylor, R., 2005. The state and pattern of health information technology adoption, Rand Corporation.

Friedberg, M. et al., 2009. Readiness for the Patient-Centered Medical Home: Structural Capabilities of Massachusetts Primary Care Practices. Journal of General Internal Medicine, 24(2), pp.162-169.

Rogers, E. & Rogers, E., 2003. Diffusion of Innovations, 5th Edition, Free Press. Available at: [Accessed October 7, 2009].

Sidorov, J., 2006. It Ain't Necessarily So: The Electronic Health Record And The Unlikely Prospect Of Reducing Health Care Costs. Health Aff, 25(4), pp.1079-1085.

Teece, D.J., Pisano, G. & Shuen, A., 1997. Dynamic capabilities and strategic management. Strategic management journal, 18(7), pp.509–533.

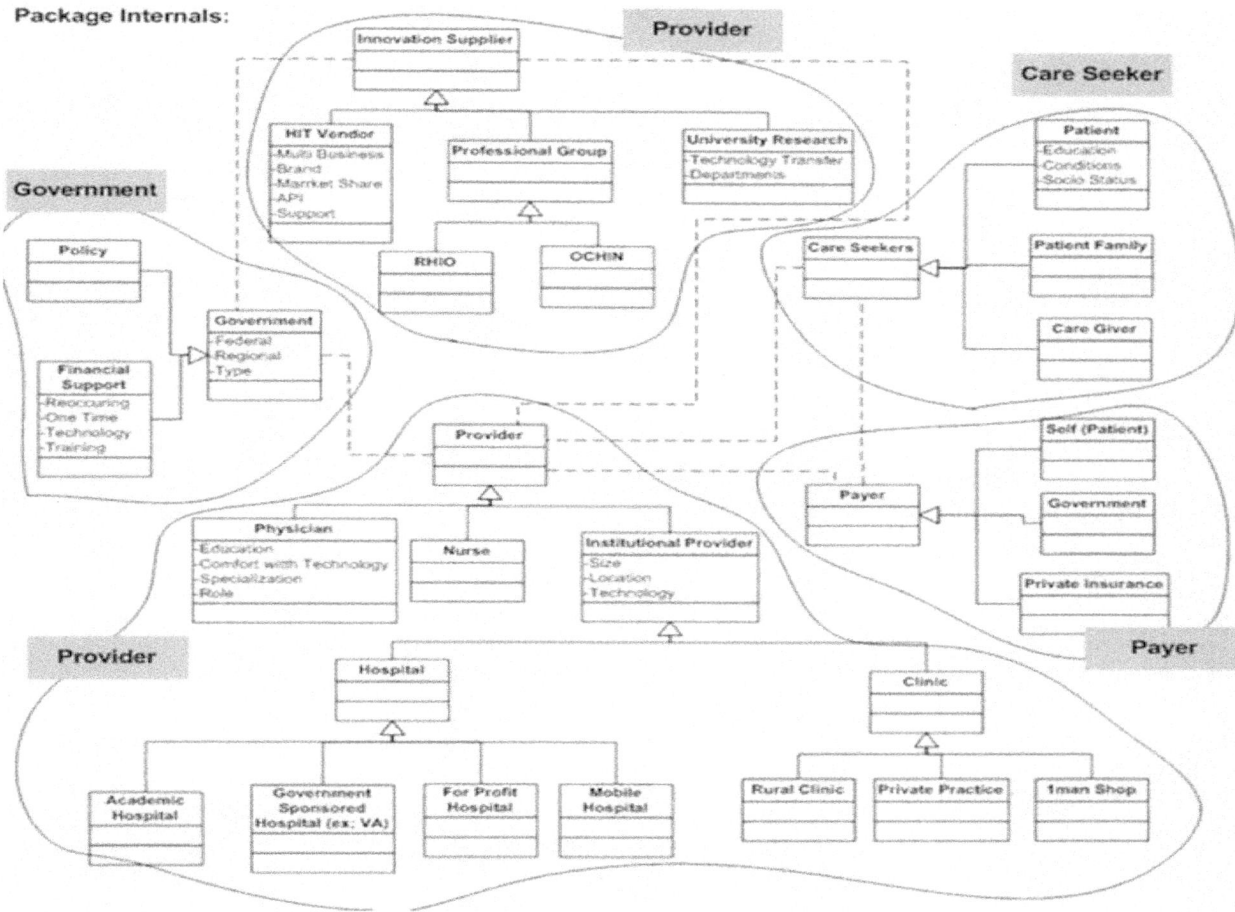

Figure 1 Field study packages

A Demonstration-Based Approach for Designing Domain-Specific Modeling Languages

Hyun Cho

University of Alabama
Department of Computer Science
Box 870290, Tuscaloosa, AL, USA
hcho7@ua.edu

Abstract

Domain-Specific Modeling Languages (DSMLs) have been recognized as a viable solution for reducing the gap between domain abstractions and computational expression within specific domains. In several domains and contexts, DSMLs have been applied successfully to various areas (e.g., finance, combat simulation, and image manipulation) and have shown improvements to productivity and quality. However, development of a new DSML is not an easy task for either computer scientists or end-users because designing and implementing a DSML requires profound knowledge of the domain and deep experience in modeling language development. To address the challenges of DSML development, this doctoral symposium abstract outlines a new approach for building DSMLs that represents a demonstration-based technique for specifying the details of a new modeling language. The approach provides an environment for describing and generating the abstract and concrete syntax of a DSML. Initial work on describing the semantics of a new DSML is also a focus of the work. The research represents an investigation into a technique that allows end-users to sketch (or demonstrate) a domain model with free-form shapes. The goal of the proposed research is to develop the underlying science and tool support to enable end-users to assist in designing a DSML for their domain, while minimizing the typical mundane tasks of DSML development involving many accidental complexities.

Categories and Subject Descriptors D.3.3 [**Programming Languages**]: Language Constructs and Features – abstract data types, Frameworks.

General Terms Design, Languages.

Keywords Domain-Specific Modeling Language; By-Demonstration; Flexible Modeling Tools.

1. Description of Purpose

Domain-Specific Modeling Languages (DSMLs) are languages that support encapsulation and abstraction of a particular domain. Normally, DSMLs provide notations tailored to the domain, and the customized notations offer substantial benefits, such as rich expressiveness and shortened learning curves for non computer scientists who need to express some computational task in a specific domain [9].

As an example, consider embedded report designers who do not have language development expertise, but

would benefit from a domain-specific language to capture the diagrams that they currently draw informally. The formats of reports slightly vary according to the characteristics of embedded devices and customer requirements, but much of the reports are common. The job responsibility of these designers is to customize report formats for each embedded device and link each data field with predefined APIs. However, it may be challenging for them to implement quality report formatting because report formats may be hard-coded with a specific programming language. Therefore, the report designers may desire a DSML that can customize a report format through a WYSIWYG editor.

The barriers that prohibit non-programming language experts from developing a DSML are that development of a DSML requires both domain and language development expertise. But learning language development techniques in a short time is difficult and hiring experts that have both domain and language development expertise may be challenging. Thus, in general, at least two experts (domain expert and language development expert) collaborate when creating a new DSML. In addition, DSMLs are often engineered with an iterative and incremental process, but the complexity of the process makes the DSML development tedious, error-prone and time-consuming. The purpose of the research described in this doctoral symposium abstract is to provide a framework that assists domain experts, who have domain knowledge but do not have language development expertise, in building their own DSMLs.

2. Goals of the Research

A DSML is developed by iterating over complex language creation tasks (shown in Figure 1) until the language meets the needed requirements and/or reaches desired quality.

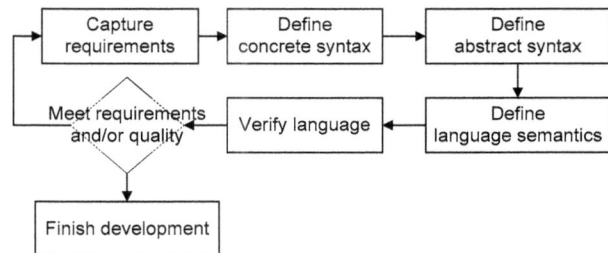

Figure 1. DSML Development Process

DSML development begins by identifying the requirements of a problem domain. After requirements are captured, domain experts and language development experts collaborate to design the concrete syntax, which represents a problem domain. Based on the concrete syntax definition, language development experts define the abstract syntax. In addition, the semantics of a DSML is attached to the abstract syntax (often represented as a metamodel). Finally, domain experts and language development experts collaborate to verify the correctness of the DSML. As described, DSML development requires language development expertise as well as domain knowledge so that domain experts who do not have language development expertise may face several challenges [3] if they try to develop their own DSMLs. From the DSML development process as shown in Figure 1, defining a DSML grammar (both concrete and abstract syntax) and its semantics are challenging tasks even for computer scientists, and automated and systematic approaches are crucial toward resolving the challenges of DSML development. Thus, the framework aims to simplify and automate DSML development by (1) capturing concrete syntax as end-users perform modeling tasks in their domain (or demonstrate their domain through modeling), (2) inferring abstract syntax from concrete syntax and model instances, and (3) associating semantics to abstract syntax.

3. Technical Approach

The overall process for developing a new DSML based on demonstration approach is shown in Figure 2.

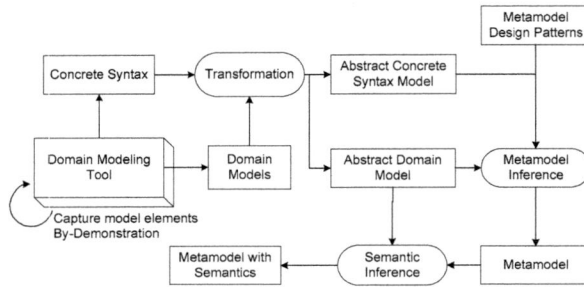

Figure 2. Framework of By-Demonstration Approach

The framework provides a modeling canvas that allows domain experts to draw their domain notations with free-form or sketch-level shapes. The framework infers a candidate concrete syntax by recording the actions of domain experts on the modeling canvas as they interact with the tool to describe example systems in their domain. After the concrete syntax is identified, the concrete syntax and domain models are transformed into an abstract model before the abstract syntax is inferred. The inference process induces abstract syntax in the form of a metamodel by comparing abstract models of the concrete syntax and the domain models with patterns representing common metamodel idioms. Metamodel design patterns represent a set of training data that are passed on to an abstract syntax inference engine. The framework completes its process by inducing and associating relevant static semantics to the inferred metamodel.

3.1 Technical Challenges and Possible Solutions

In this section, we identify four major technical challenges that this research may encounter. We describe the challenges and our candidate solutions below.

- *Support for free-form or sketch-level shapes*: Due to the likely preference of domain experts to work in more unconstrained environments (i.e., whiteboard and paper-based sketches) and advances in pen-based input devices, the need to support free-form or sketch-level shapes is a new challenge for language inference research. Chen et al. [2] developed a software design tool named SUMLOW to capture and formalize sketch-level UML constructs. Ossher et al. [10] introduced the concept of flexible modeling tools, which use predefined free-form shapes for modeling pre-requirements. They built a prototype to combine the advantages of office automation tools and traditional modeling tools. In our approach, we support a combination of these two approaches. At first, the framework will provide a shape authoring tool. End-users draw shapes that represent their domain and store them as pre-defined shapes. After that, we will add free-form recognition functionality to the framework, which is similar to Chen's work. With this functionality, end-users can use any free-forms without defining them prior to use.

- *Concrete syntax definition*: Concrete syntax represents the visual representation of a DSML. It should be designed to avoid ambiguity and assist with readability by domain experts. Concrete syntax typically consists of a set of domain notations and their relations. To define concrete syntax automatically, the framework captures the domain expert's operations when they demonstrate a new concept using the notation of a specific domain on the modeling canvas. Concrete syntax is finally defined after a domain expert reviews the candidate concrete syntax and annotates with appropriate names. The core technology for capturing and inferring concrete syntax for a DSML is based on a by-demonstration technique, which is similar to earlier work on Program By Example (PbE) or Query By Example (QBE) [5][12]. Technically, a by-demonstration approach can be implemented by hooking events into a recording tool (e.g., a plug-in for Visio or Eclipse). A challenge of the recording process is maintaining an optimized sequence of actions (i.e., pruning unnecessary actions) while preserving the demonstrators intent. For example, a domain expert may draw a rectangle as a symbol for some domain-specific process and tweak the size and appearance. The intermediate interactions in the editor are of little concern to the inference process.

- *Abstract syntax inference*: Inferring abstract syntax is a special case of inductive learning and represents a core research area for this doctoral research. The goal of this step is to generate abstract syntax (i.e., metamodel for a DSML) by applying machine learning algorithms to concrete syntax and domain models, which are created in a previous by-demonstration step of the process. To induce abstract syntax, many approaches have been proposed, such as genetic programming [6], Bayesian learning [1], hill climbing [4], and graph-based approaches [8]. In our research, we plan to adopt a graph-based approach to leverage the benefits of graphs (e.g., analysis of structural and dynamic properties, design for verification, and model transformation). Thus, before proceeding to abstract syntax inference, the domain models and concrete syntax will be rewritten as a (typed) graph grammar. Generally, to induce accurate abstract syntax, an inference engine requires a large set of training data (or model instances in our case). Presumably, it is not possible to provide a large set of model instances because a demonstration-based approach will ask domain experts to construct domain models manually, which can be a mundane and error-prone task. Thus, it is challenging to predict all possible cases of input for the inference process. To resolve this issue, we plan to investigate the notion of metamodel design patterns, which describe a set of patterns that are commonly used in metamodel design. Accordingly, the abstract syntax will be induced by searching and composing a set of maximum-likelihood patterns. The metamodel design patterns approach will help to infer accurate abstract syntax in the presence of insufficient training data.

- *Semantics inference*: Designing and implementing semantic inference are other core areas of the research. This will be the most challenging area of the research because specifying semantics in a formal way is difficult even for language development experts. For specifying modeling language semantics, several methods have been proposed, such as OCL [7] and Attribute Grammars [11]. The research goals of semantic inference of modeling languages will focus on (1) devising efficient and accurate algorithms for semantics inference, and (2) finding an appropriate method to associate the inferred semantics with the inferred abstract syntax, with representation of both abstract syntax and semantics in a (typed) graph.

4. Current status and Future Work

A prototype has been developed to understand the feasibility of the approach. The prototype was developed with Microsoft Visio because Visio provides various predefined shapes that support the creation and definition of user-specific shapes. The prototype was implemented with an understanding that a Visio template has a correspondence to the metamodel of a DSML. The prototype implementation focused on (1) the identification of concrete syntax, (2) creation of a Visio template, and (3) the identification of rules between shapes as a part of an initial static semantics.

Although we believe that the prototype demonstrates the feasibility of a "by-demonstration" approach to DSML creation, we will also develop our framework for other development platforms (e.g., Eclipse). The new framework will be developed according to the following schedule.

- Phase 1: The initial phase will focus on a preprocessor for the framework. During Phase 1, we will develop a by-demonstration technique on the new development platform and devise efficient algorithms for capturing concrete syntax and graph transformation.

- Phase 2. An abstract syntax inference engine will be implemented and compared to verify our approach in terms of accuracy and performance.

- Phase 3. Finally, semantic inference will be designed and implemented. At this phase, we will try to design efficient algorithm for inducing semantics as well as their association with abstract syntax.

Acknowledgments

This work is supported by NSF CAREER award CCF-1052616.

References

[1] Chen, S. F. 1995. Bayesian grammar induction for language modeling. *In Proceedings of the 33rd annual meeting on Association for Computational Linguistics (ACL '95)*, Stroudsburg, PA, USA, 228-235.

[2] Chen, Q., Grundy, J., & Hosking, J. 2008. SUMLOW: early design-stage sketching of UML diagrams on an E-whiteboard. *Software Practice and Experience*, vol. 38, no. 9, Jul. 2008, 961-994.

[3] Cho, H., Sun, Y., Gray, J., & White, J. 2011. Key Challenges for Modeling Language Creation By Demonstration, *ICSE 2011 Workshop on Flexible Modeling Tools*, Honolulu HI, May 2011.

[4] Cook, C. M., Rosenfeld, A., & Aronson, A. R. 1976. Grammatical inference by Hill Climbing. *Information Science*. vol. 10, no. 2, 59-80.

[5] Cypher, A., Halbert, D. C., Kurlander, D., Lieberman, H., Maulsby, D., Myers, B. A., & Turransky, A. (Eds.). 1993. *Watch what I do: Programming by Demonstration*. MIT Press, Cambridge, MA, USA.

[6] Dupont, P. 1994. Regular Grammatical Inference from Positive and Negative Samples by Genetic Search: The GIG method. *Proceedings of the 2nd International Colloquium on Grammatical Inference and Applications*, ICGI'94, LNAI, vol. 862, 236-245.

[7] Evans, A. S. and Kend, S. 1999. Core Meta-modeling semantics of UML: The pUML approach. *In Proceedings of the Second International Conference on the Unified Modeling Language*, B. Rumpe and R. B. France, Eds., Lecture Notes in Computer Science, vol. 1723.

[8] Jonyer, I., Holder, L. B., Cook, D. J. 2004. MDL-based context-free graph grammar induction and applications. *International Journal on Artificial Intelligence Tools (IJAIT)*, vol. 13, no. 1, 65-79.

[9] Kelly, S. & Tolvanen. 2008. *Domain-Specific Modeling: Enabling Full Code Generation*. Wiley-IEEE Computer Society Press.

[10] Ossher, H., Bellamy, R., Simmonds, I., Amid, D., Anaby-Tavor, A., Callery, M., Desmond, M., de Vries, J., Fisher, A., & Krasikov, S. 2010. Flexible modeling tools for pre-requirements analysis: conceptual architecture and research challenges. *Object-Oriented Programming Systems Languages and Applications (OOPSLA)*, Reno/Tahoe, NV, Oct. 2010, 848-864.

[11] Paakki, J. 1995. Attribute grammar paradigms-a high-level methodology in language implementation. *ACM Computing Surveys*, vol. 27, no. 2 (June 1995), 196-255.

[12] Zloof, M. M. 1975. Query-by-example: the invocation and definition of tables and forms. *In Proceedings of the 1st International Conference on Very Large Data Bases (VLDB '75)*. ACM, New York, NY, USA.

CUDACL+:
A Framework for GPU Programs

Ferosh Jacob

Department of Computer Science
University of Alabama
fjacob@crimson.ua.edu

Abstract

Graphical Processing Units (GPUs) provide an excellent execution platform for several classes of computation intensive problems. Even though there are vendor-specific Application Programming Interfaces (APIs) for GPU programming, they all share a high-level of similarity. In this extended abstract, we introduce a transformation framework through which sequential programs from legacy systems can be executed in any of the two common GPU programming APIs: OpenCL and CUDA. Our study shows that blocks of independent sequential code can be converted automatically to an equivalent representation in OpenCL and CUDA. In some cases, the transformation requires additional information from the programmer regarding the specific computation and the GPU configuration. Our approach provides the design decisions for a Domain-Specific Language (DSL) to specify the additional information.

Categories and Subject Descriptors   D.1.3 [**Concurrent Programming**]: Parallel Programming

General Terms   Performance, Design

Keywords   CUDACL, OpenCL; CUDA.

1.   Introduction

Parallel programming can be defined as the creation of code for a special class of problems that can be divided into smaller problems, such that each sub-problem can be solved concurrently. Generally, parallel programs in legacy systems are sequential programs with a few select sections of code that execute in parallel. The size of most parallel blocks varies between 2-57% of the total size of the program [10]. Hence, programmers prefer tools and frameworks that can work on these parallel sections without manually rewriting the entire program.

Graphical Processing Units (GPUs) provide an excellent platform for executing parallel programs, because of their highly parallelized structure. As revealed by a survey on general-purpose computation on graphics hardware, General-Purpose GPU (GPGPU) algorithms continue to be developed for a wide range of problems [13]. NVIDIA's Computation Unified Device Architecture (CUDA[1]), Microsoft's Direct Compute[2], and Khronos Group's Open Computing Language (OpenCL[3]) are some of the frameworks for GPGPU programming. CUDA is primarily supported for GPUs from NVIDIA, whereas OpenCL supports GPU programming for different vendors (including NVIDIA). Microsoft's Direct Compute allows GPU programming in Windows. Given the various languages and libraries for GPU programming, an abstract API would assist in creating programs that are transparent to the underlying specific concerns of each GPGPU programming environment.

In [9], we classified device functions executed on a GPU into class A, B, and C. In Class A functions, there is no communication between the threads (i.e., "Embarrassingly parallel" lines of code). Thread communication inside a Class A program represents a Class B instance. If there is communication between two such device functions within a host code, we call this a Class C function (the variables modified by a function are consumed by another device function).

Static code analysis can provide the input variables, output variables, size of each variable, and number of iterations required to complete the computation for a given block of code in a parallel program. In Class A functions, with this information the block of code can put much of the execution on a GPU. However, this is not always the case. There can be scenarios where programmers want to fine-tune the execution by specifying the grid size, block size,

---

[1] http://www.nvidia.com/object/cuda_home_new.html

[2] http://archive.msdn.microsoft.com/directcomputehol

[3] http://www.khronos.org/opencl/

mapping the threads with the size of computation, and restricting the memory transfer operations to and from the CPU. Ideally, a programmer who is informed about a specific computational problem for a specific GPU architecture should be able to convert the sequential code to GPU code (CUDA or OpenCL) without manually rewriting it, while also maintaining performance goals.

In this paper, we describe a dissertation plan focused on a framework called CUDACL+. The aim of CUDACL+ is to provide an environment through which programmers can execute sequential code on a GPU device with the help of a DSL, where a user specifies additional information for GPU execution. Section 2 gives an overview of our goals and the objectives of our proposed DSL. The tools used in our implementation are explained in Section 3. Section 4 describes initial experimental evaluation of our approach. Related works are overviewed in Section 6 and a conclusion is offered in Section 7 that enumerates future directions of this doctoral work.

2. Goals and Objectives

The proposed DSL is designed to achieve three goals, as summarized in this section.

2.1.1 Control memory transfers

An obvious observation is that for fast running programs, programmers must avoid unnecessary memory transfers. As an example, in the Integer Sorting (IS) program from the NAS Parallel benchmarks[4] the program has two hot spots: 1) Generating random numbers, and 2) Sorting the numbers. If both operations are executed on a GPU, there is no need for transfer in between the two steps. Hence, it is preferred to restrict these memory copy operations.

2.1.2 Thread to problem size mapping

Threads are launched in CUDA and OpenCL in a block (2d) of grids (3d). A programmer must manually configure and execute a program to discover the optimum configuration. There should be a configurable mechanism to fine-tune the block and grid size. In many cases, a programmer must map the size of a problem to the threads on a GPU. CUDA allows only 65,535 threads in one dimension, so in order to execute a program like BlackScholes [1] (which has 512K independent units of work), one thread has to process more than one unit of work.

2.1.3 Defining memory locations:

Accessing constant and shared memory on a GPU is faster than accessing the global memory. Hence, for optimum performance, programmers should be able to map units of

work to threads, define variables in different memory locations and access them in their device functions.

3. Proposed Methodology

In this section, we describe the tools that are needed to realize the proposed work. As mentioned earlier, because GPU memory is different from CPU memory, tool support is needed to find and copy the variables included in the selected code section. This is achieved by parsing the main program and creating a symbol table of all the variables in the main program. The selected section is further parsed to find out the read and write variables used in the selected section. The size and type of the variables are queried from the symbol table and passed to the tool. In our earlier implementation, Eclipse CDT[5] was used for parsing and refactoring C code. In our current implementation, we use ANTLR[6] for parsing and code generation to avoid dependencies with Eclipse (i.e., our tool can be invoked from a command line). The same tool can be used for design, development and code generation of the proposed DSL.

4. Experimental Evaluation Plan

A GPU may not be the best platform for many programs, even for parallel programs. This is mainly due to the communication between threads in a program and computations involved in the problem. Programs with less intercommunication and high computation are expected to perform better on a GPU. Our goal is to find programs that can benefit from porting to a GPU. Our approach is to find parallel (OpenMP[7] or MPI[8]) and serial versions of a program and compare the execution time of each. If the parallel version executing with n threads (OpenMP) or processes (MPI) finish in $T_p(n)$ time, and the serial version finishes in T_s time, speed up is defined as $T_s/T_p(n)$. The programs that can give speed up close to n are good candidates for execution on a GPU. For proper evaluation, we make sure the execution environment (hardware) can support n number of threads concurrently.

To evaluate our approach, we need to compare the generated code with handwritten code. In the case of Class A programs, the generated code is very similar to a handwritten program (i.e., the execution time difference between each would be same as the difference of the same program executing two times). In the other two classes, there can be a difference in execution time based on the implementation of device functions and configuration of the GPU. To evaluate this, we have to test the level of expressiveness and usefulness of the proposed DSL. Rewriting existing

---

[4] http://www.nas.nasa.gov/Resources/Software/npb.html

[5] http://eclipse.org/cdt

[6] http://antlr.og

[7] http://openmp.org

[8] http://www.mcs.anl.gov/research/projects/mpi/

CUDA programs can show the usefulness of the tool (a first-level metric could be lines of code). We plan to conduct a user study to compare the development time for the different versions.

5. Related Work

There have been several parallel programming refactoring efforts that offer support within Eclipse [3], [4], [8], [9]. We believe that programmers working on legacy scientific code often prefer command-line tools outside of the Eclipse editor. The work described in [3] applies to only CUDA and is restricted to NVIDIA GPU cards. Other related works include [6], [11], which convert OpenMP or OpenMP-like directives to CUDA code. However, the goal of our work is to convert sequential programs to GPU programs with minimum effort from the programmer. Many of the sequential to parallel converters [7] use data dependency and refactoring approaches that are similar to our current implementation. Many efforts [2], [5], [6], [11], [14] were based on the abstraction of GPU programs. Most of the work has concentrated on a particular device or language; for example, [2], [6], [11] and [14] all target CUDA. CGiS [5] provides support for multiple devices. Some of the features include parallel control structures and special vector operators.

6. Conclusion and Future Work

We have implemented the refactoring required for transforming Class A programs on a GPU in our earlier work. In this paper, we investigate some of the design concerns while converting Class B and Class C programs to a parallel version that can be executed on a GPU. We propose that this can be achieved by using a DSL to provide additional information required for the conversion.

As a next stage, we plan to select several GPU programs and design a DSL for these programs, such that the DSL has all of the required information to optimize performance and provide enough abstraction to hide the accidental complexities from the user. We will extend and implement new constructs in the DSL to transform and optimize additional types of programs using case studies from open source projects.

Acknowledgements

We thank the Alabama Super Computing (ASC) for allowing us to run our programs on their cluster.

References

[1] F. Black and M. Scholes, "The pricing of options and corporate liabilities," Journal of Political Economy, vol. 81, pp. 637-54, 1973.

[2] J. Breitbart, "CuPP: A framework for easy CUDA integration," Proceedings of the 24th IEEE International Parallel and Distributed Processing Symposium, Rome, Italy, May 2009, pp. 1-8.

[3] K. Damevski and M. Muralimanohar, "A refactoring tool to extract GPU kernels," Proceedings of the Workshop on Refactoring Tools, Honolulu, HI, May 2011, pp. 29-32.

[4] D. Dig, M. Tarce, C. Radoi, M. Minea, and R. Johnson. "Relooper: Refactoring for loop parallelism in Java," Proceedings of Object-Oriented Programming Systems, Languages, and Applications, Orlando, FL, October 2009, pp. 793-794.

[5] N. Fritz, P. Lucas, and P. Slusallek, "CGiS: A new language for data-parallel GPU programming," Proceedings of the International Workshop on Vision, Modeling, and Visualization, Stanford, CA, November 2004, pp. 241-248.

[6] T. D. Han and T. S. Abdelrahman, "hiCUDA: High-Level GPGPU Programming," IEEE Transactions on Parallel and Distributed Systems, vol. 22, no. 1, pp. 78-90, Jan. 2011.

[7] J. Hull, Options, futures and other derivatives. Upper Saddle River, NJ : Prentice Hall, 2009.

[8] F. Jacob, R. Arora, P. Bangalore, M. Mernik, and J. Gray, "Raising the level of abstraction of GPU-programming," Proceedings of the International Conference on Parallel and Distributed Processing Techniques and Applications, Las Vegas, NV, July 2010, pp. 339-345.

[9] F. Jacob, D. Whittaker, S. Thapaliya, P. Bangalore, M. Mernik and J. Gray, "CUDACL: A tool for CUDA and OpenCL Programmers," Proceedings of the International Conference on High Performance Computing, Goa, India, December 2010, 11 pages.

[10] F. Jacob, J. Gray, P. Bangalore, and M. Mernik, "Refining high performance FORTRAN code from programming model dependencies," Proceedings of the International Conference on High Performance Computing (Student Research Symposium), Goa, India, December 2010, 5 pages.

[11] S. Lee, S. Min, J, Seung, and R. Eigenmann, "OpenMP to GPGPU: A compiler framework for automatic translation and optimization," SIGPLAN Notices, 44, February 2009, pp. 101-110.

[12] M. Mernik, J. Heering, and A. M. Sloane, "When and how to develop domain-specific languages," ACM Computing Surveys, pp. 316-344, 2005.

[13] J. D. Owens, D. Luebke, N. Govindaraju, M. Harris, J. Krger, A. E.Lefohn, and T. J. Purcell, "A survey of general-purpose computation on graphics hardware," Computer Graphics Forum, pp. 80-113, 2007.

[14] S. Ueng, M. Lathara, S. Baghsorkhi, and W. Hwu, "CUDA-Lite: reducing GPU programming complexity," Proceedings of the International Workshop on Languages and Compilers for Parallel Computing, Edmonton, Canada, July 2008, pp. 1-15.

Generic Ownership

The Case of Java Collections

Ahmed Aziz Khalifa

Victoria University of Wellington

ahmkhal@ecs.vuw.ac.nz

Abstract

In recent years, several prototypes have been proposed to extend Java with ownership types. To varying degrees, these proposals omit many features of Java such as static declarations, enum types, arrays, exceptions, inner classes, constructors, interfaces, equals, clone, and wildcards. In this project, we will try to address these features. In order to evaluate the adequacy of generic ownership encapsulation, the general purpose implementations of the Java Collections Framework will be refactored; then, measurements of performance time overheads will be conducted using tools for Java benchmarking.

Categories and Subject Descriptors D.3.3 [*Programming Languages*]: Language Constructs and Features—Polymorphism

General Terms Languages, Experimentation, Performance

Keywords Encapsulation, Generic Ownership, Java Collections

1. Introduction

In mainstream object-oriented languages, such as Java and C#, references are the only possible approach to sharing objects. Programs can bundle data with the methods that control the functioning of that data, but the data will still not be hidden properly. In other words, the principle of information hiding can be violated when two or more objects refer to a single object which can be changed by any of the referrers, resulting in malfunction in parts of a system. Language's *access modes* restrict access to the names of the local state, but do not restrict access to the objects to which the names refer. An object's `private` internal representation can still be accessed and modified by its `public` methods that can directly return references to that `private` representation.

Noble et al. [2] describes the problem in the context of aggregation. An aggregate object's state is likely to change via an alias to any of the component objects that make up the aggregate's representation, while the aggregate itself is unaware of any aliasing. Any reference to an aggregate is subject to mishandling, and can mutate the state of the object's implementation, either by modifying a field or via method calls. So, it is essential for an aggregate to be capable of sharing its element objects, while its internal representation is kept hidden.

In the light of the Flexible Alias Protection model [2], the pioneer model for ownership types was introduced by Clarke et al. [1]. Any object should be owned by only one owner object, and can only be referenced from within that owner object. The set of objects owned by the same owner is named a *context*. A reference from within one context to a particular object in another context must pass through the owner of that particular object; this is known as the *owners-as-dominators* approach to encapsulation. Paradigms that adopt a fully nesting scheme of the owners-as-dominators approach are recognized as having *deep ownership types*. The notion of *object contexts* accommodates the capability to layout the heap into nested constructs (inside-outside relationships). Any representation object is virtualized as being inside its owner (enclosing object), and is disallowed from being exported outside.

As a combined mechanism to facilitate deep ownership types in conjunction with parametric polymorphism, Potanin et.al. [3] introduced *Generic Ownership* along with an extended version of Java, named *Ownership Generic Java* (OGJ). This combination provides the ability to constrain aliasing and detect errors statically, while neither demands an added syntactic extension nor imposes overheads at runtime. This is because OGJ treats ownership as a supplementary generic type. That is, Java Generics is extended by the ability to hold, and interpret, ownership information; which means that a valid OGJ program is, of course, a valid Java program. In OGJ, any class declaration should be type-parameterized by its ownership status (i.e., context locality). The *root context* is the set of objects owned by `World`. For example, to declare a class within the root context, it needs to be parameterized by a type variable (usually known as *owner parameter*) that is bounded by `World`. A possible declaration would read as:

SPLASH'11 Companion, October 22–27, 2011, Portland, Oregon, USA.
ACM 978-1-4503-0940-0/11/10.

```
class Foo<Owner extends World> {...}
```
OGJ uses the last type parameter to annotate a class's owner. For example, instantiating a container class, such as `List`, can read as: `List<String, Owner> lst =`
```
            new ArrayList<String, Owner>();
```

2. Goals

2.1 Ownership for all of Java

This project aims to address the issues that have not been addressed in OGJ. OGJ provides ownership support for classes and subtyping, inner classes, field access and assignment, methods, casts, and statics. This project is an attempt to deal with issues such as enum types, exceptions, constructors, interfaces, equals, clone, and wildcards.

One of the fundamental issues that any attempt to extend Java with ownership types encounters is arrays. Generic types are not covariant; on the contrary, Java arrays are covariant. Against the immediate apprehension by one's object-oriented sense that a `List<Manager>` is a `List<Employee>`, this is a serious logical error based on the assumption that `Manager` is a subtype of `Employee`. It is logically unacceptable to treat a list of managers as a list of employees, because otherwise users could add employees who are not managers to the list. Since there should be no dependency between two objects generated from a single generic class, so that `List<Manager>` guarantees that the members of the list are all managers, Java does not associate generics with a built-in conversion from `List<Manager>` to `List<Employee>`. However, Java arrays have such a conversion from `Manager[]` to `Employee[]`. The fundamental problem in applying Generic Ownership, as a static type-checking mechanism, to Java arrays is the covariance of arrays that cannot be dealt with until it is run-time. If `Manager` is a subtype of `Employee`, then `Manager[]` is a subtype of `Employee[]`. That is, handling arrays as covariant leaves the compiler totally uninformed about what is going on. This is an obvious reason why there is no generic array creation in Java; since generic type operators should be invariant.

Since there is no generic array creation in Java, array types are eliminated in our new compiler, and a wrapper called `OwnedArray` is implemented in order to be able to refactor the collection classes that are backed by arrays (e.g., `ArrayList`, `HashMap`), and to provide owners for the array elements as well as the `OwnedArray` objects themselves. Since array types became eliminated, the `main()` method is therefore adapted to capture the command line arguments in a `List` rather than in an array.

The resulting compiler is not intentionally implemented to make things easier for programmers since the purpose is to experiment how such a kind of restrictive compiler will work; what refactoring necessities will be needed for non-ownership programs to be ownership compliant; and what performance impact will be imposed on the refactored pro-

grams. Since Java Generics is a language level mechanism, there should not be any fundamental barriers as long as the challenges we are facing are on the language level. The arrays issue, mentioned above, is fundamental and we tried to address it with solutions at hand.

2.2 Generic Ownership Compliant Collections

The second goal of this project is to apply generic ownership to the Collections Framework to study the issues of converting non-ownership code to a generic ownership compliant code, and to estimate the performance time overheads.

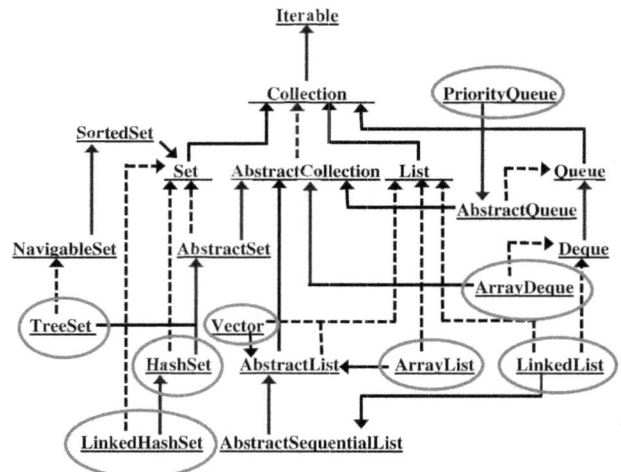

Figure 1. General-Purpose Iterable Collections

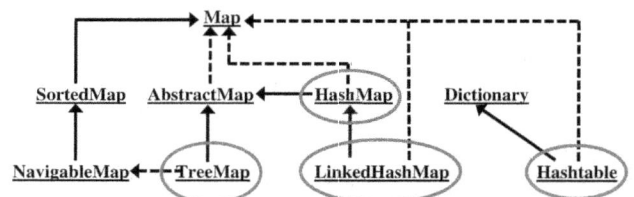

Figure 2. General-Purpose Maps

The concerns regarding the problem of representation exposure can be best described in the context of aggregation [2]. The phenomenon of representation exposure is plainly the side-effect of adapting reference semantics as a mainstay for flexible object sharing. *Rep exposure* is the inability of an aggregate object, or any such large component, to prevent references to objects that make up its internal implementation or *representation* from leaking outside its boundary. That is, rep exposure occurs as long as an object is by itself lacks the capacity to constrain aliasing sufficiently in order to enforce encapsulation. Breaking encapsulation boundaries can happen whenever an incoming alias manages to bypass the object's interface operations, and create an internal reference, while still being manipulated by arbitrary external objects. For example, the collections' `LinkedList` is considered one of the vulnerable containers, in terms of encapsulation. This is because the elements of the list, as can be plainly envisioned, are a number of objects placed into the heap with each of them having its own data plus pointers to the next and previous element objects; then, a `ListIterator`, as an outsider object, can bypass the `List` object's interface operations, and directly accesses the list's elements by pointing at any object in the chain. That is, a `LinkedList` is consistently available from any arbitrary entry point, since any element object is considered an entry point. This will still be the case with `LinkedList` as a generic ownership compliant implementation, since the incoming reference from `ListIterator` to the internal representation of `LinkedList` will be owned by the current instance of `LinkedList`, and hence cannot be manipulated by arbitrary external objects.

```
public class LinkedList<E>
    extends AbstractSequentialList<E>
    implements List<E>, ... {
    private transient Entry<E> header =
            new Entry<E>(null, null, null);
    ...
    private class ListItr
        implements ListIterator<E> {
        private Entry<E> lastReturned = header;
        ...
    }
}
```

Figure 3. `LinkedList`'s Inner Class `ListItr`

Generic ownership will be applied to the hierarchies of Figure 1 & 2. The classes to be experimented are the ones that are known as General-Purpose Implementations (in blue circles), namely `HashSet`, `TreeSet`, `LinkedHashSet`, `ArrayList`, `ArrayDeque`, `LinkedList`, `PriorityQueue`, `HashMap`, `TreeMap`, and `LinkedHashMap`. The legacy implementations (in red circles) `Vector` and `Hashtable` will also be experimented. Typically, the refactoring starts off by identifying the representation part of each collection class and making it owned by `This` (i.e., to be private and hidden). Owner `This` will not allow any access to that representation part unless through variable `this`. The other non-representation objects will be owned by the defining collection class, which means that these objects can only be shared with objects owned by the same owner as the current instance of the defining collection class. The only exception is when a representation object is being assigned to any of the other objects. In this case, such objects will need to be made owned by `This`, and thus they will need to be only accessed via variable `this`, which is not usually the intended receiver. Moreover, it is not possible to assign objects owned by `This` to inner classes' objects which are also owned by `This`. This is mainly the issue with iterators because all iterators are defined as inner classes inside their respective collection classes. Consider the example of Figure 3, `header` is a representation object of `LinkedList`, which means that `header` should be owned by `This`. `ListItr` is an inner class of `LinkedList`, and `header` is being assigned to `lastReturned` inside `ListItr`. If we are to make `lastReturned` owned by `This`, this does not mean that `header` and `lastReturned` are having the same owner. `lastReturned` belongs only to the inner class, not to the enclosing class. This is one of similar issues that will require careful refactoring when applying ownership to collections.

2.3 Generic Immutability

The third issue to be addressed in this project is Immutability [4]. An object is said to be immutable if its state cannot be modified after it is created. By default all objects are mutable in Java; fields can be annotated to be immutable using an attribute such as `final`. In Java, all primitive data types have their corresponding wrapper classes (e.g., `Integer`, `Long`, `Float`) in the Java standard library, and they are all declared `final`. Such classes are declared to be entirely immutable; the data contained within an object can never be modified by any of the class's methods. Such an object can be made immutable if all fields are of primitive types and are declared `final`. An immutable `String` contains an array of characters; `final` fields protect this internal array from being replaced by another `char` array; however, `final` fields do not protect the array elements from being replaced. Aliases to the internal `char` array can cause the string to be converted; this is mainly because Java's type system is not adopting any measures against exposing an array's representation. The goal is to try to add reference and object immutability on top of our generic ownership mechanism, and re-experiment the collections after being adapted to Generic Immutability.

References

[1] D. G. Clarke, J. M. Potter, and J. Noble. Ownership Types for Flexible Alias Protection. *ACM SIGPLAN Notices*, 33(10):48–64, Oct. 1998. ISSN 0362-1340.

[2] J. Noble, J. Vitek, and J. Potter. Flexible Alias Protection. In E. Jul, editor, *ECOOP '98—Object-Oriented Programming*, volume 1445 of *Lecture Notes in Computer Science*, pages 158–185. Springer, 1998. ISBN 3-540-64737-6.

[3] A. Potanin, J. Noble, D. Clarke, and R. Biddle. Generic Ownership for Generic Java. In *Proceedings of the 21st annual ACM SIGPLAN conference on Object-Oriented Programming Systems, Languages, and Applications*, OOPSLA '06, pages 311–324, New York, NY, USA, 2006. ACM. ISBN 1-59593-348-4.

[4] Y. Zibin, A. Potanin, M. Ali, S. Artzi, A. Kie, un, and M. D. Ernst. Object and Reference Immutability using Java Generics. In *Proceedings of the the 6th joint meeting of the European Software Engineering Conference and the ACM SIGSOFT symposium on The Foundations of Software Engineering*, ESEC-FSE '07, pages 75–84, New York, NY, USA, 2007. ACM. ISBN 978-1-59593-811-4.

Cloning in Ownership

Paley Li

Victoria University of Wellington

lipale@ecs.vuw.ac.nz

Nicholas Cameron

Victoria University of Wellington

Nicholas.Cameron@ecs.vuw.ac.nz

James Noble

Victoria University of Wellington

kjx@ecs.vuw.ac.nz

Abstract

Cloning is an essential feature in many object-oriented programs. Unfortunately, existing techniques generally copy too little or too much. We present an object cloning technique that uses the object structure enforced by ownership types to produce the clones.

Categories and Subject Descriptors   D.3.3 [*Software*]: Programming Languages—Language Constructs and Features

General Terms   Languages

Keywords   Ownership types, object cloning

1. Introduction

Object-oriented programs regularly need to copy objects (often called cloning). Since the time of Simula and Smalltalk, object-oriented languages have attempted to perfect cloning. Features in more recent languages such as the copy constructor in C++, the default cloning method in Java, and the use of value types in C#, are all implementations of cloning. Most cloning techniques are either shallow cloning or deep cloning. We purpose sheep cloning, a cloning technique that utilise ownership types to achieve the beneifts of shallow cloning and deep cloning. Below we will present sheep cloning, examples to illustrate the shortfalls of shallow cloning and deep cloning, and the benefits of sheep cloning.

2. Description of purpose

The purpose of this research is to develope a cloning technique that is guided by ownership types. Ownership types provide the necessary information for when the cloning technique comes to decide how deep to copy, and so producing a clone that takes into consideration the semantics of the object provided by the ownership types, while remaining more efficient than copying the entire object. For example, consider a window in a GUI that contains a scroll bar and a reference to a database:

```
class Window{
  Scroll scrollbar;
  Database database;
  ...
}
```

Shallow cloning copies only the values in the object, the clone aliases the references held by the object. In Fig. 1 we present a shal-

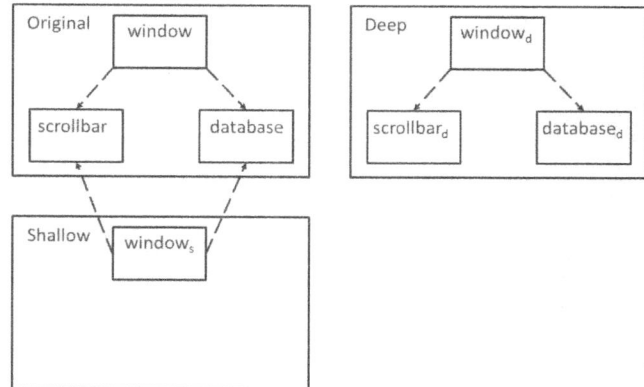

Figure 1. Deep and shallow cloning the car object.

low clone of our GUI example. When we perform shallow cloning on the `window` object, the new `window_s` object is created. The scroll bar of the `window_s` object will be an alias to the `scrollbar` of the original `window` object. Similarly, the database of the `window_s` object is the same database as the `window` object. The internal representation objects of `window_s` and `window` are the same, so any changes in either object will have an effect the other object. Hence when we move the scroll bar of the `window` object, the scroll bar of the `window_s` object will move as well.

Deep cloning eliminates any relationship between the original object and the cloned object, by creating the clone as an independent object to the original object. Deep cloning creates a duplicate of the original object, by copying the intended object and all reachable objects.

In Fig. 1 we perform an example of deep cloning on the `window` object. The `window` object is copied to produce the `window_d` object. Then the `scrollbar` is copied, producing the `scrollbar_d` object. Next the `database` object of `window` is copied, producing the `database_d` object.

If, however, we take a moment and step back from blindly copying every object, we might have realised that we probably should have not copied the database. It seems obvious that the scroll bar, the panels and the canvas are parts of the window, and that these parts should be copied when the window is cloned. The database for the items to be displayed on the window should not have been copied when the window is cloned.

So where do we draw the line on what should and shouldn't be copied? For shallow cloning and deep cloning, how deep we copy and which objects to copy are determined by the references and the depth of these references of the intended object. However, Fig. 1 shows that shallow cloning is not deep enough, where the two windows share the same scroll bar, and that deep cloning is too deep, where `window_s` contain a copy of the original `database`.

SPLASH'11 Companion,   October 22–27, 2011, Portland, Oregon, USA.

ACM 978-1-4503-0940-0/11/10.

2.1 Cloning with Ownership

Ownership types [2], ownership domains [1], and universe types [7, 8] each enforce an hierarchical topological structure on the objects in the heap. This descriptive property compartmentalises the heap, allowing for more modular reasoning and analysis of the heap. This will aid us in the development of our cloning technique that is not too deep or too shallow, but just right.

```
class Window<owner>{
  Scroll<this> scrollbar; //owned by the current window
  Database<o> database; //not owned by the current window
  ...
}
```

Above we have incorporated ownership types to the window class of our example. The window object now owns its scrollbar object, but not the database object, instead it contains a reference to the database object to retrieve the data.

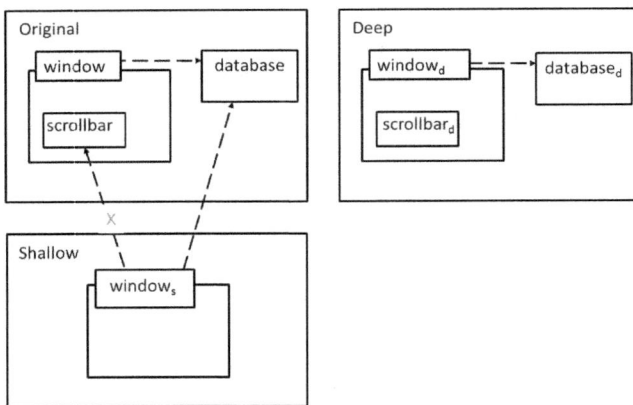

Figure 2. Deep and shallow cloning the car object in an ownership system.

In Fig. 2 we present a diagram that demonstrates shallow cloning and deep cloning on the window object with ownership types. Under the owners-as-dominators policy [2], shallow cloning the window object will result in an ownership error. After the $window_s$ object is created, the technique will attempt to create a reference to the scrollbar of the window object from the $window_s$ object. However, this is an illegal operation, the new $window_s$ object can not reference objects that are part of the representation of another object. Deep cloning on the ownership typed window object is the same as the deep cloning in Fig. 1, an exact replica of the window object is produced. The window object will be copied to create the $window_d$ object. The scrollbar is copied to create $scrollbar_d$. Finally the database is copied, creating a new $database_d$. However, like in Fig. 1, we have created an unwanted and undesired copy of the database.

Ownership types allow us to develop a cloning technique where the semantic, structure and internal representation of the object are respected when the object is cloned. The internal representation of an object is essentially everything that is part of the object, or in ownership types it's everything the object owns.

Sheep cloning is an ownership type directed cloning technique first introduced by Clarke et al [2]. Sheep cloning states that every object in the representation of the intended object is copied, and every reference in the representation of the intended object that point to objects outside the representation is aliased. In Fig. 3 we present a sheep clone of our window example in ownership types. The Window class states that the window object owns the

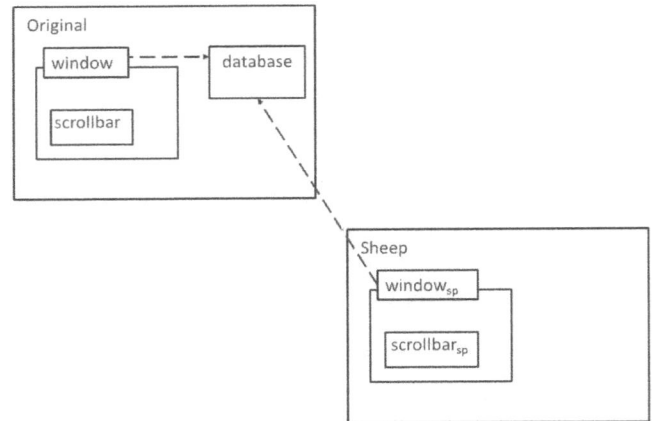

Figure 3. Deep, shallow and sheep cloning the car object in an ownership system.

scrollbar object, and not the database object. Sheep cloning will copy the window object, by creating the $window_{sp}$ object. Then it will create a duplicate $scrollbar_{sp}$ for the $window_{sp}$ object. Lastly it will create a reference from the $window_{sp}$ object to the original database, to allow $window_{sp}$ to display the same data as window.

The depth to which sheep cloning copies depends on the topological structure of the heap. Shallow and deep cloning are purely guided by references, where sheep cloning is guided by references and ownership information. When an object is sheep cloned, instead of copying the structure of the object, sheep cloning copies the representation of the object provided by ownership types.

2.2 Limitations

The biggest limitaion of sheep cloning is that sheep cloning can only be performed on objects with ownership types. This means to use sheep cloning on any non-ownership typed programs, the program will need to be annotated with ownership types, incurring at the very least a syntactic overhead. In addition, not all programs can have ownership types, because not all programs fit into an ownership structure [6]. Oof all programs that present an ownership-like structure, only a small amount of those structures are suitable for ownership based features like sheep cloning.

3. Goals

We have two main goals for this research. The first goal is to construct a formal type system that features sheep cloning, prove it is sound, and prove sheep cloning preserves correctness. The type system will be based on Featherweight Java with ownership types. Sheep cloning will be incorporated as a language feature of the type system. The second goal of this research is to determine how sheep cloning compares with shallow cloning and deep cloning. To achieve this, we purpose to conduct a series of empirical studies to on shallow cloning, deep cloning, and sheep cloning.

4. Technical Approach

We have constructed the operational semantics for sheep cloning. The next step is to build the type system, and to incorporate sheep cloning into the type system. Once we have completed the formal system, we will prove that it is sound, and prove correctness for sheep cloning. We have only so far outlined the correctness proof for sheep cloning. The outline of proof is to use subheaps and heap manipulation to show sheep cloning holds under three lemmas. The first lemma is that sheep cloning preserves ownership. The second lemma shows that the subheap of the original object and the subheap of the cloned object are disjoint. The final lemma shows that the heap from the concatenation of all the subheaps is well-formed. Another approach to prove correctness for sheep cloning is to utilise an observer. The observer will create observations of the original object and the cloned objects. The two observations must be equivalent for sheep cloning to be correct.

The most convincing way to compare sheep cloning against shallow and deep cloning is to perform a series of empirical studies. Wach technique will be judge on the behavior, time, and space taken to perform a task. Conducting an empirical study on sheep cloning will be difficult, as discussed in the previous section, programs are required to be ownership typed. Any studies with sheep cloning will require a corpus that is already ownership typed or can have ownership types inferred upon it.

5. Related Work

The idea of an ownership guided cloning technique was first introduced in "Object ownership for dynamic alias protection" by James Noble, David Clarke and John Potter [9], Noble called this cloning technique "sheep cloning". When you sheep clone an object, you copy all objects owned (transitively) by that object, while all objects outside the representation of that object are shallow cloned. Sheep clone provides the benefits of a deep clone with the possibility of performing shallow where appropriate, reducing the cost of the clone which would otherwise be a deep clone. Noble et al. detailed possible limitations of sheep clone. The cloning will be performed on a graph, rather than tree, and the existence of cycles within the object graph might hinder the feasibility of sheep clone.

One of the earliest papers to address issues surrounding cloning is "Copying, Sharing, and Aliasing" by Peter Grogono and Patrice Chalin [3]. Grogono et al. explain how there is confusion within programming languages between the semantics and implementations of copying. The paper goes on to describe that it is more important to know if the object you are copying is immutable or mutable than it is if you are copying a value or a reference. The paper then goes on to talk about the importance of containing and sharing objects, which later became known as representation objects and argument objects. Finally the paper concludes with ways to implement these principles, suggesting copying should be guided more by effect systems. Peter Grogono and Markku Sakkinen present a technique to automatic generate copying and cloning functions, this work is detailed in their paper "Copying and Comparing: Problems and Solutions" [4]. In the paper Grogono discuss some of the issues surrounding copying and comparing objects. Grogono then presents detailed examples of various cloning operations and types equality. Next Grogono explores the copying and comparing features of several programming languages. Finally Grogono presents how languages can partially automatic generate copying and cloning functions.

The issue of cycles within object graphs, was addressed in the paper "A type system for Reachability and Acyclicity" by Yi Lu and John Potter [5]. Lu et al. present a type system, called Acyclic Region Type System(ARTS), that allows programmers to restrict cycles within the heap, through the use of constraints on the reachability of references and pointers. The paper uses region-based types to achieve acyclic reachability for regions. Lu et al. describe regions as disjoint sets of objects, with the property that regions are acyclic reachable, while reference cycles are allowed within each region. A novel contribution of this paper is that whenever a new region is created, the existing regions will perform a refinement of the acyclic reachability ordering to incorporate the new region. That is because the ordering of the definition of each region ensures the regions are acyclic, similar to how the inheritance relationship is acyclic.

6. Conclusion

We have presented motivations for sheep cloning, through the use of our GUI example. We have also informally discussed our formal type system, by stating how we will construct, prove soundness, and prove correctness for he system. Finally we have presented our plan to conduct empirical studies on each of the cloning techniques, to investigate the viability of sheep cloning.

References

[1] Jonathan Aldrich and Craig Chambers. Ownership Domains: Separating Aliasing Policy from Mechanism. In *European Conference on Object Oriented Programming (ECOOP)*, 2004.

[2] David G. Clarke, John M. Potter, and James Noble. Ownership Types for Flexible Alias Protection. In *Object-Oriented Programming, Systems, Languages, and Applications (OOPSLA)*, 1998.

[3] Peter Grogono and Patrice Chalin. Copying, sharing, and aliasing. In *In Proceedings of the Colloquium on Object Orientation in Databases and Software Engineering (COODBSE)*, 1994.

[4] Peter Grogono and Markku Sakkinen. Copying and comparing: Problems and solutions. In *European Conference on Object Oriented Programming (ECOOP)*, 2000.

[5] Yi Lu and John Potter. Protecting representation with effect encapsulation. In *Principles of Programming Languages (POPL)*, 2006.

[6] Nick Mitchell. The Runtime Structure of Object Ownership. In *European Conference on Object Oriented Programming (ECOOP)*, 2006.

[7] P. Müller and A. Poetzsch-Heffter. Universes: A Type System for Controlling Representation Exposure. In *Programming Languages and Fundamentals of Programming*, 1999.

[8] Peter Müller and Arnd Poetzsch-Heffter. Universes: A Type System for Alias and Dependency Control. Technical Report 279, Fernuniversität Hagen, 2001.

[9] James Noble, David Clarke, and John Potter. Object ownership for dynamic alias protection. In *Technology of Object-Oriented Languages (TOOLS)*, pages 176–, 1999.

Composing Locks by Decomposing Deadlocks

Hari K. Pyla

Virginia Tech

harip@vt.edu

Categories and Subject Descriptors D.1.3 [*Programming Techniques*]: Concurrent Programming—Parallel programming; D.3.4 [*Programming Languages*]: Processors—Runtime environments; D.3.3 [*Programming Languages*]: Language Constructs and Features—Concurrent programming structures

General Terms Algorithms, Design, Languages, Measurement, Performance and Reliability

Keywords Concurrent Programming, Runtime Systems, Program analysis, Deadlock Detection and Recovery, Speculative Parallelism and Coarse-grain Speculation

1. Introduction

The evolution of processor architectures from multi-core to many-core requires programmers to use concurrency to achieve performance. Unfortunately, shared memory parallel programs are difficult to implement correctly, and so is detecting concurrency bugs (e.g., data races, deadlocks, order violations, atomicity violations). In practice, the most common concurrency bugs are a) data races that arise due to unguarded or improperly guarded memory updates and b) deadlocks that arise due to circular dependencies among locks. While data races can be ameliorated by appropriate synchronization (a challenging problem in itself), deadlocks require fairly complex deadlock avoidance techniques, which may fail when the order of lock acquisitions is not known a priori. Furthermore, due to the potential for deadlocks, programmers cannot arbitrarily compose lock based codes without knowing the internal locking structure. Hence, *composability* is limited by deadlocks. *The goal of this research is to achieve composability of lock based codes.*

We present Sammati [1] (*agreement* in Sanskrit), a software system that is capable of *transparently* and *deterministically* detecting and recovering from deadlocks in multi-threaded applications, without requiring any modifications to application source code or recompiling/relinking phases. Sammati is implemented as a pre-loadable library that overloads the standard POSIX threads (pthreads) interface and supports applications written using weakly typed languages such as C and C++. It guarantees the acquisition of mutual exclusion locks a deadlock free operation. Sammati supports arbitrary application level threading models, including those that use locks for concurrency control where serial lock elision does not result in a program with the same semantics.

Sammati associates the memory accesses with locks and privatizes memory updates within a critical section. The updates within a critical section are made visible outside the critical section on the release of the parent lock(s), viz. the containment property. On the acquisition of every lock, Sammati checks for deadlocks. If a deadlock is detected, the deadlock elimination algorithm breaks the cycle by selecting a victim, rolls it back to the acquisition of the offending lock, and discards its memory updates. Since our containment mechanism ensures that memory updates from a critical section are not visible outside the critical section until a successful release, we simply restart the critical section to recover from the deadlock.

Although the core idea behind Sammati is quite simple, there are several challenges in the details of this work. First, we need to provide a transparent mechanism for detecting memory updates within a critical section and privatizing the updates. Second, in the context of nested locks we need to define a set of visibility rules that preserve existing lock semantics, while still permitting containment based deadlock elimination and recovery. Finally, we need a deadlock detection and recovery mechanism that is capable of deterministically eliminating deadlocks without either (a) deadlocking itself or (b) requiring an outside agent. Additionally, Sammati can detect and report *write-write* races that occur between (a) guarded and concurrent unguarded updates to a shared value and (b) improperly guarded updates, where a single data value is guarded by two or more different locks. In this research we propose and implement techniques that address the above design objectives.

We evaluated its performance of Sammati using SPLASH, Phoenix and synthetic benchmark suites on a 16 core shared memory machine (NUMA) running Linux with 64GB of

RAM. We measured the number of locks acquired and lock-acquisition-rate (total locks acquired/total runtime) for all applications used in this study. While Sammati's runtime is impacted by lock acquisition rate, it shows speedup comparable to the native pthreads case even for applications that have large ($\approx 89,500$ locks/sec) lock acquisition rates. This is in contrast to transactional memory systems, which have significant impact on speedup, largely due to privatization at the instruction level and the need to guard every read from read/write conflicts. Additionally, the space overhead of our approach is O(W), where W is the write set (in pages) within a lock context. Finally, we also evaluated Sammati by running programs that were deadlock prone. We find that the native pthreads programs deadlock while Sammati deterministically detects and avoids the deadlocks, transparently recovers from them and successfully executes the program to completion. Our results indicate that for most applications the speedup of Sammati is comparable to that of native Pthreads with modest memory overhead.

Contributions and Impact

There are several aspects of this work that will significantly impact the usability of lock based programming for concurrency on multi-core architectures.

- **Handling Deadlocks:** Existing systems rely on program analysis, modifications to source code and/or operating system and, prediction techniques to identify the occurrence of deadlocks. In contrast, Sammati deterministically detects and recovers from deadlocks at runtime without requiring access or modifications to source code in applications with arbitrary threading models. Our proposed approach readily enables its use with existing applications. Additionally, Sammati's language transparency, enables its use with a wide variety of programming languages including unmanaged languages such as a C, C++ and Fortran.

- **Programmer Productivity:** Due to the non-deterministic nature of thread execution, it may not be feasible in practice to verify and test all possible interleavings of threads and their lock acquisitions in order to determine if a program is deadlock free. Programmers can write code to the best of their ability and rely on the runtime system (Sammati) to handle deadlock detection and recovery.

- **Mutual Exclusion Locks:** Most programmers are already familiar with lock-based programming as opposed to using transactional memory systems and addressing issues in lock based programming can benefit the large base of lock-based software artifacts in use today. Previously, lock based codes were not composable due to the potential of deadlocks –one of the primary motivations for transactional memory. Since Sammati provides a robust mechanism to address this problem, we believe that

this work will enable a new generation of composable lock-based codes.

2. Current and Future Directions

Several novel techniques proposed in the research opens way to solve important challenges faced in concurrent programming.

2.1 Program Analysis and Shadowing Memory

We are currently working on improving the performance of Sammati through compile time analysis and instrumentation. Sammati's overhead primarily stems from the protection and privatization of the virtual address space. We believe that we can reduce this runtime overhead by employing program analysis to accurately determine the write-set (i.e., data modified) within a lock even in the presence of nested and conditional lock acquisition and release sequences. There are several challenges in the details of this work. First we need a mechanism to identify locks and their scope in the program. Second, we need to accurately determine the write-set (i.e., data modified) within a lock. In situations where program analysis cannot determine control flow, the Sammati runtime can act as the fail-safe to provide deterministic deadlock detection and recovery. Third, we need to isolate the memory updates within locks to facilitate recovery on deadlock. We need a lightweight memory shadowing mechanism to accomplish isolation. Additionally, the ordering and integrity of the load and store instructions must be preserved in order to maintain program correctness. We plan on leveraging the LLVM compiler infrastructure to implement some of our proposed techniques. We will be evaluating our approach using SPLASH, Phoenix and PARSEC benchmarks.

Given the scope of this research, we expect the following key research deliverables from this work. First, a runtime infrastructure for transparent deadlock detection and recovery for POSIX threaded codes with any threading model, which enables composability of arbitrary lock-based codes. Second, reachability and flow analysis methods to minimize the performance impact of deadlock detection and recovery mechanisms in the common case of deadlock free operation. Third, novel methods to transparently eliminate priority inversion problems in threaded codes operating in realtime infrastructures. Fourth, mechanisms to support non-idempotent operations such as memory management and IO within critical sections that may be affected by deadlock recovery. Fifth, methods to guide deadlock victim selection based on a variety of performance and correctness metrics and techniques to ensure safe progress when threads abort while holding locks. To our knowledge, several of the proposed research deliverables present the only known solutions to the corresponding research problem and will complement existing research in the area of compilers and runtime systems.

2.2 Concurrency Bugs and Managed Languages

We are currently extending our work to detect other forms of concurrency bugs (e.g. data races) and provide concurrency bug detection and composability of lock based codes in managed languages such as Java.

2.3 Support for Speculative Execution

The impending multi/many core processor revolution requires that programmers leverage explicit concurrency to improve performance. Unfortunately, a large body of applications/algorithms are inherently hard to parallelize due to execution order constraints imposed by data and control dependencies or being sensitive to their input data and not scale perfectly, leaving several cores idle in the impending multi/many-core processor revolution. *The goal of this research is to enable such applications leverage multi/many-cores efficiently to improve their performance.* Our objective in this work is extend the lock/unlock semantics of Sammati to begin/commit/abort semantics and to provide programmers with a tool for exploiting parallelism in such applications.

Technical Approach

This work equips programmers with a powerful tool for exploiting parallelism by means of *coarse-grain speculation*. Our programming model can express computation at any granularity, so that any application unit can be executed speculatively without burdening the programmer from the subtleties of concurrency programming such as using the low level threading primitives to create speculative control flows, manage rollbacks, and recover in the event of mis-speculations.

We present a simple speculative programming framework, Anumita (*guess* in Sanskrit) [2], in which coarse-grain speculative code blocks execute concurrently, but the results from only a single speculation modify the program state. Anumita is implemented as a shared library that exposes APIs for common type-unsafe languages including C, C++ and Fortran. Its runtime system transparently (a) creates, instantiates, and destroys speculative control flows, (b) performs name-space isolation, (c) tracks data accesses for each speculation, (d) commits the memory updates of successful speculations, and (e) recovers from memory side-effects of any mis-predictions.

Anumita associates each speculation flow's (e.g., an instance of a code block or a function) memory accesses in a speculation composition (loosely, a collection of possible code blocks that execute concurrently) and localizes them, isolating speculation flows through privatization of address space. Ultimately, a single speculation flow within a composition is allowed to modify the program state. We present well-defined semantics that ensures program correctness for propagating the memory updates. Anumita supports a wide range of applications by providing expressive evaluation criteria for speculative execution that go beyond *time to solution* to include arbitrary *quality of solution* criteria.

Using Anumita requires minimal modifications (8-10 lines on average) to application source code. Additionally, the speculation-aware runtime manages memory and collects garbage from failed speculations. In the context of high-performance computing, with the prevalent OpenMP threading model, Anumita naturally extends speculation to an OpenMP context through a pragma. To our knowledge, Anumita is the first system to provide support for exploiting coarse-grain speculative parallelism in OpenMP based applications.

Our preliminary results [2] using real applications such as graph coloring problem, partial differential equation (PDE) solvers and combinatorial problems including sorting indicate that Anumita is capable of significantly improving the performance of hard-to-parallelize and input sensitive applications by leveraging speculative parallelism. For instance, in the PDE solver the speedup ranged from 0.84 to 36.19, for the graph coloring problem it ranged from 0.95 to 7.33, and for the sort benchmark it ranged from 0.84 to 62.95. Using Anumita it is possible to obtain the best solution among multiple heuristics. We found that in some cases where heuristics failed to arrive at a solution, the use of speculation guaranteed not only a solution but also the one that is nearly as fast as the fastest alternative. Anumita's preliminary results indicate that it is possible to exploit coarse-grain speculative parallelism without sacrificing performance, portability and usability.

3. Summary

In this dissertation we provide novel techniques to solve several challenges faced in concurrent programming. The contributions of the research will extend well beyond our core technical contributions. By providing usable and efficient deadlock detection and recovery for threaded codes, we will provide a critical tool to programmers designing and implementing (and debugging!) complex applications for emerging many-core platforms. In addition, our solutions to several hard problems in concurrent programming will each serve to broaden the set of codes, and even application domains that will benefit from the rise of manycore platforms. More broadly yet, this dissertation will impact the future of concurrent programming and assist in improving the productivity of application developers. We believe that our research efforts will help adapt and sustain the increasing core counts of multi/many-core systems.

References

[1] H. Pyla and S. Varadarajan. Avoiding Deadlock Avoidance. In PACT '10, pages 75–86, New York, NY, USA, 2010.

[2] H. Pyla, C. Ribbens, and S. Varadarajan. Programmable Coarse-Grain Speculative Execution. In OOPSLA '11, New York, NY, USA, 2011.

Towards Client-Aware Interface Specifications

Henrique Rebêlo

Federal University of Pernambuco, Recife, PE, Brazil

hemr@cin.ufpe.br

Abstract

Runtime assertion checking (RAC) is a well-established technique for runtime verification of object-oriented (OO) programs. Contemporary RACs use specifications from the receiver's dynamic type when checking method calls. This implies that in presence of subtyping and dynamic dispatch features of object-oriented programming, these specifications differ from the ones used by static verification tools, which rely on the specifications associated with the static type of the receiver. Besides the heterogeneity problem, this also hinders the benefits of modular reasoning achieved by the notion of supertype abstraction. In this context, we propose a more precise runtime assertion checking for OO programs that better matches the semantics used in static verification tools. While we describe our approach, we discuss how it can be used to avoid the heterogenous semantics problem and among others.

Categories and Subject Descriptors   D.2.4 [*Software/Program Verification*]: Programming by contract, Assertion checkers; F.3.1 [*Specifying and Verifying and Reasoning about Programs*]: Assertions, Pre and postconditions, Specification techniques

General Terms   Design, Languages, Verification

Keywords   Modular Reasoning, Runtime Verification, Client-Aware Interface Specifications

1. Introduction

Object-oriented programming (OOP) has been presented for many virtues, of which we can emphasize subtyping and dynamic dispatch. Both are useful and problematic in relation to the procedural approach that OOP replaces. They are useful because one can abstract away details in the specifications of subtypes using the supertype ones. This allows variations in data structures and algorithms to be handled uniformly with subtype polymorphism. They are problematic for reasoning about object-oriented (OO) programs, because dynamic dispatch selects different methods depending on the exact runtime type of an object. For example, a dynamically dispatched method call such as o.m() requires a case analysis to deal with all possible dynamic types of o's value. Hence, we need to re-specify or re-verify the method m whenever new subtypes are added to the program. However, such an approach is not modular, because it requires re-specifying or re-verifying existing code when the program is extended.

SPLASH'11 Companion,   October 22–27, 2011, Portland, Oregon, USA.
ACM 978-1-4503-0940-0/11/10.

In this context, Leavens and Weihl [7] proposed a strategy for modular reasoning, which they call "*supertype abstraction*". Such a strategy is modular in that it does not depend on receiver's dynamic type. For instance, What specification should one use to reason about a call, such as o.m(), given that the static type of o is T?. Based on the supertype abstraction technique, one should use the specification associated with the static type of o (T in this case) to reason about the correctness of a method call. As supertype abstraction does no depend on the o's dynamic type, the method m does not need to be re-specified or re-verified when the existing subtypes of T are changed or when new subtypes are added to a program.

The benefits of the supertype abstraction idea are related to the Liskov's invited talk at OOPSLA 1987 [9]. Liskov stated an easily-remembered test for subtyping, also called Liskov Substitutability Principle (LSP), (p. 25): "if for each object o1 of type S there is an object o2 of type T such that for all programs P defined in terms of T, the behavior of P is unchanged when o1 is substituted for o2 then S is a subtype of T".

Problems. Although supertype abstraction is a helpful technique to reason about object-oriented programs, current runtime assertion checkers use specifications from the receiver's dynamic type when checking client method calls. As a consequence, to reason about the method call o.m(), one need to perform a case analysis with all possible dynamic types of receiver o. This approach hinders modular reasoning and raises other problems. To illustrate, consider the code in Figure 1 from the canonical figure editor example [6, 10]. We use JML [8] as our formal interface specification language for concreteness, but the problems and solution we present can also be exploited to other interface specification languages (e.g. Spec# [2]). In JML, annotation comments start with an at-sign (@) and specification cases for methods start with a visibility modifier and **normal_behavior**, both appear before the method's header. Preconditions are introduced by keyword **requires** and postconditions by **ensures**.

Figure 1 gives protected specifications for classes Point and ScreenPoint. In the class Point, the method setX's precondition states that the argument x must be greater than or equal to zero. The postcondition ensures that the coordinate Point.x (the field x of Point class) is equal to the value of the argument x. The Point's subclass ScreenPoint overrides the inherited setX method and provides an additional JML specification case that describes how the method behaves for arguments that do not satisfy the precondition of the inherited protected specification case (in JML the keyword **also** means that the specification of Point.setX is inherited to ScreenPoint.setX). Hence, when the argument x is less than zero (precondition) the inherited coordinate Point.x must be zero (postcondition).

Heterogeneous Semantics Problem. The first problem with runtime verification of specified OO programs is that the specifications used to check the correctness of a method call is based on its dynamic type, thus hindering modular reasoning (supertype ab-

```
1  package p;                         12  package p;                                23  package p; // protected client
2  class Fig {}                       13  class ScreenPoint extends Point{          24  class clientClass1 {
3  class Point extends Fig {          14  /*@ also                                  25    void clientMeth1 (Point p) {
4    protected int x, y;              15    @ protected normal_behavior             26      p.setX(-1);
5    /*@ protected normal_behavior    16    @ requires x < 0;                       27    }
6      @ requires x >= 0;             17    @ ensures this.x == 0; @*/              28  }
7      @ ensures this.x == x; @*/     18  public void setX (int x) {                29  package q; // public client
8    public void setX (int x) {       19    if (x >=0) this.x = x;                  30  class clientClass2 {
9      this.x = x;                    20    else x = 0;                             31    void clientMeth2 (Point p) {
10   }                                21  }                                         32      p.setX(-1);
11 }                                  22  }                                         33    }
                                                                                    34  }
```

Figure 1. Behavioral contracts for the figure editor [6, 10] using JML [8].

```
1  package p;                         8   package p;                                16  package p; // protected client
2  class Point extends Fig {          9   // Behavioral Interface Specification     17  class clientClass1 {
3    protected int x, y;              10  class Point extends Fig {                 18    void clientMeth1 (Point p) {
4    public void setX (int x) {       11  /*@ protected normal_behavior             19      //@ assert -1 >= 0;
5      this.x = x;                    12    @ requires x >= 0;                      20      p.setX(-1);
6    }                                13    @ ensures this.x == x; @*/              21      //@ assume this.x == -1;
7  }                                  14  public void setX (int x);                 22    }
                                      15  }                                         23  }
```

Figure 2. Formulation of Client-Aware Interface Specifications.

straction) and resulting in a heterogenous semantics in contrast to some verification tools, which are static type reasoning-based [4]. For example, consider the call to method setX on line 26 (Figure 1). The technique of supertype abstraction [7] uses the specification of the static type of the receiver to reason about such a call. Hence, since p's static type is Point, supertype abstraction tell us to reason about the call p.setX(−1) using the specification given on lines 5−7. As a result such a call violates the precondition (line 6) when passing −1 as argument to method setX.

However, by using the classical JML runtime assertion checker (RAC) [4], we got no precondition violation when the receiver p represents the dynamic type ScreePoint. This happens because the effective precondition used is the specifications given on lines 5−7 is joined with the specification on lines 14−17 (this give us the effective precondition $(x >= 0) \parallel (x < 0)$). In other words, this problem happens because the instrumentation technique is done locally at the method declaration site. For instance, the JML RAC compiler (jmlc) uses an approach called *wrapper approach* [4]. This approach translates pre- and postcondition specifications into separate *assertion checking methods* which wraps the original method implementation with such assertion checking methods. Thus, all client calls now go to the wrapper method. In addition, the wrapper approach is responsible for calling corresponding assertion checking methods of supertypes if any. Because of that, the method call p.setX(−1) includes the specifications of type ScreePoint when the receiver p matches it (thus, going against supertype abstraction).

On the other hand, if we use the static checker ESC/Java2 [4] on the same method (call on line 26 in Figure 1), we can now detect the expected precondition violation based on the specifications of class Point (lines 5−7). Therefore, this causes another fundamental problem for program verification; the existing tools [4] use a heterogeneous semantics for program verification. For instance, the static checker is based on static type reasoning, whereas the runtime assertion checker is based on dynamic type reasoning.

Visibility Rules Checking Problem. Leavens and Müller [6] present rules for information hiding in specifications for Java-like languages. Their rules restrict proof obligations on method calls to only satisfy visible specifications. Consider the method call p.setX(−1) on line 32 (Figure 1). According to the supertype abstraction technique, the Point's specification must be used to rea-

son about the correctness of such a call. The Point's specification has a protected specification case for the method setX. Thus, only privileged clients (i.e. subclasses or code in the same package) are required to obey such specifications. Since the method call on line 32 is originated from a public client (the call is located in a different package), the effective precondition on such a call defaults to **true** [6, Rule 2].

However, the instrumented code generated by current RACs ignore visibility modifiers in specifications (our second problem). Hence, by using the jmlc [4] on the same method call (line 32) results in no contract violation, but the effective precondition (assuming that the dynamic type of the receiver p is ScreenPoint) that is checked is the disjunction of the precondition on line 6 with the one in line 16 $((x >= 0) \parallel (x < 0))$, instead of the default one explained. Due to the server side instrumentation approach adopted by RACs, all specifications (with different visibility levels) are checked without respecting the information hiding rules [6]. It is important to note that none of existing tools [4] check visibility rules properly in interface specification languages. According to Leavens and Müller [6], the practical enforcement of such visibility rules is future work.

Library Checking Problem. Nowadays we have a large-scale reuse of components. This is due to the standardization of large libraries and frameworks in popular programming languages such as C++, Java, and C#. Such a standardization and heavy use of libraries keep module specification important and useful. However source code of libraries is not available for proprietary libraries [5]. This issue poses our third problem with runtime verification of OO programs. Since the contemporary RACs (e.g. jmlc [4]) need the source code in order to generate the runtime checks, we can neither specify nor verify programs during runtime when source code is not available.

2. Client-Aware Interface Specifications

To solve the three afore-mentioned problems, we propose the notion of *client-aware interface specifications*, or CAIS. We call our approach client-aware because all clients must be aware of the formal specifications contained in a special interface. We say special

72

interface in the sense that specifications do not necessarily be written in the source code.

Formulation of Client-Aware Interface Specifications. Figure 2 illustrate the formulation of client-aware interface specifications. For simplicity, we just consider the type Point (lines 1−7), its specifications (lines 8−15), and a client (lines 16−23). In a program logic, CAIS are embodied by the proof rule for method calls, which allows us to derive $\{P\}\ p.m()\ \{Q\}$ only from a specification $(pre_m^T,\ post_m^T)$ associated with the static type T for the receiver p. Usually, an automated verifier uses weakest precondition semantics and achieves modularity by replacing a call $p.m()$ by the sequence of "**assert** $pre_m^T[\vec{a}/\vec{f}]$; **assume** $post_m^T[\vec{a}/\vec{f}]$" [1]. We use the notation $[\vec{a}/\vec{f}]$ to denote the substitution of the formal parameters by the actual ones. Since we are concerned with runtime verification, all the **assume** statements are checked like the **assert** ones. The instrumentation in the call site can be observed on lines 19−21 (Figure 2). Therefore we use a call site instrumentation approach in contrast to existing works [4, 11]. Another important concept of our CAIS is about abstraction. According to Liskov, we should specify the behavior, but keep it separated from implementation details [9]. This is an important concept when considering libraries specification and runtime verification.

Usefulness of Our Approach. Since our instrumentation mechanism is based on the static type of the receiver of a particular method call, we can again exploit all the benefits achieved with supertype abstraction (i.e. modular reasoning) during runtime verification. Moreover, since we adopt a static type reasoning for checking method calls, we can get similar results when using other tools like a static checker (**tackling our first problem**). As our approach is a call site driven, once our clients are known, we can instrument them according their interface specifications respecting the visibility rules (**tackling our second problem**). Finally, with client-aware interface specifications (as observed in Figure 2), one can detail specify and check during runtime the behavior of class libraries even if their source code are not available. The runtime verification is possible since our CAIS uses a client side instrumentation. Hence, we neither need the source code nor modify proprietary bytecode APIs (**tackling our third problem**).

Tool. We built these ideas on the Aspect-JML RAC compiler (ajmlc) [11] which is available online at `http://www.cin.ufpe.br/~hemr/JMLAOP/ajmlc.htm` (its current release is 3.0).

Evaluation. We intend to conduct experiments with real systems and compare the traditional runtime assertion checkers with our new approach proposed here and embedded in ajmlc [11]. So, we are looking for bugs that the contemporary runtime assertion checkers do not catch. Additionally, we want to analyze how precise is the error reporting including the visibility specifications. This is intended to blame different kinds of clients (e.g. subclasses). We also intend to evaluate the impact of our approach in relation to the classical ones in terms of source code and bytecode instrumentation sizes. Eventually, we are also interested to analyze the runtime performance of each approach.

Limitation. Since our approach is based on clients, the more new clients we have, more instrumentation code will be generated. On the other hand, in the classical approach the instrumentation is achieved only once at the declaration side which the methods being called are physically declared.

Future Work. We hope to increase expressiveness of the client-aware interface specifications to enable specifications of more complex design rules which are already found in JML [8]. We need to adapt our approach to use model program specifications [12]. Thus, this allows us to go beyond the traditional black box approach [3]. We also intend to investigate how to improve the separation of the design by contract concern in a separated interface. Preliminaries results can be found in [10].

Summary. Our hypothesis is that by using the client-aware interface specifications developers can achieve a more precise runtime verification of constrained OO programs. Our Benefits include: (i) modular reasoning by the use of supertype abstraction without drawbacks caused by runtime verification; (ii) the choice to switch from a static checker to a runtime assertion checker without surprises while getting error reporting; (iii) applying runtime verification including visibility levels achieved by information hiding principles, and (iv) precise specification and runtime verification of class libraries even if the source code is not available.

Acknowledgments

I would like to thank Professors Ricardo Lima and Gary T. Leavens (my supervisors) for the fruitful discussions we had about the ideas of my PhD thesis proposal.

References

[1] M. Barnett and K. R. M. Leino. Weakest-precondition of unstructured programs. *SIGSOFT Softw. Eng. Notes*, 31:82–87, September 2005. ISSN 0163-5948. doi: http://doi.acm.org/10.1145/1108768.1108813.

[2] M. Barnett, K. R. M. Leino, and W. Schulte. The Spec# programming system: an overview. In G. Barthe, L. Burdy, M. Huisman, J.-L. Lanet, and T. Muntean, editors, *Post Conference Proceedings of CASSIS: Construction and Analysis of Safe, Secure and Interoperable Smart devices, Marseille*, volume 3362 of *LNCS*. Springer-Verlag, 2005.

[3] M. Buchi and W. Weck. The greybox approach: When blackbox specifications hide too much. Technical report, 1999.

[4] L. Burdy et al. An overview of JML tools and applications. *Int. Journal on Soft. Tools for Tech. Transfer (STTT)*, 7(3):212–232, June 2005. URL http://dx.doi.org/10.1007/s10009-004-0167-4.

[5] G. T. Leavens. The future of library specification. In *Proceedings of the FSE/SDP workshop on Future of software engineering research*, FoSER '10, pages 211–216, New York, NY, USA, 2010. ACM. ISBN 978-1-4503-0427-6. doi: http://doi.acm.org/10.1145/1882362.1882407.

[6] G. T. Leavens and P. Müller. Information hiding and visibility in interface specifications. In *International Conference on Software Engineering (ICSE)*, pages 385–395. IEEE, May 2007. URL http://dx.doi.org/10.1109/ICSE.2007.44.

[7] G. T. Leavens and W. E. Weihl. Specification and verification of object-oriented programs using supertype abstraction. *Acta Informatica*, 32(8):705–778, Nov. 1995. doi: http://dx.doi.org/10.1007/BF01178658.

[8] G. T. Leavens et al. Preliminary design of JML: A behavioral interface specification language for Java. *ACM SIGSOFT Software Engineering Notes*, 31(3):1–38, Mar. 2006.

[9] B. Liskov. Keynote address - data abstraction and hierarchy. In *Addendum to the proceedings on Object-oriented programming systems, languages and applications (Addendum)*, OOPSLA '87, pages 17–34, New York, NY, USA, 1987. ACM. ISBN 0-89791-266-7. doi: http://doi.acm.org/10.1145/62138.62141.

[10] H. Rebêlo, R. Lima, and G. T. Leavens. Modular contracts with procedures, annotations, pointcuts and advice. In *SBLP '11: Proceedings of the 2011 Brazilian Symposium on Programming Languages*. Brazilian Computer Society, 2011. to appear.

[11] H. Rebêlo et al. Implementing java modeling language contracts with aspectj. In *Proceedings of the 2008 ACM symposium on Applied computing*, SAC '08, pages 228–233, New York, NY, USA, 2008. ACM. ISBN 978-1-59593-753-7. doi: http://doi.acm.org/10.1145/1363686.1363745.

[12] S. M. Shaner, G. T. Leavens, and D. A. Naumann. Modular verification of higher-order methods with mandatory calls specified by model programs. In *Proceedings of the 22nd OOPSLA*, OOPSLA '07, pages 351–368, New York, NY, USA, 2007. ACM. ISBN 978-1-59593-786-5. doi: http://doi.acm.org/10.1145/1297027.1297053.

Alternate Annotation Checkers Using Fractional Permissions

Chao Sun

University of Wisconsin Milwaukee
csun@uwm.edu

Abstract

Although existing annotation checker based on fractional permissions is powerful, it causes great space and runtime overhead. To address this issue, we propose to use a multi-layered approach for checking annotations. In addition to the heavyweight permission checker, we use two lightweight checkers: a conservative checker for those obviously correct cases, and a liberal checker for those obviously wrong cases. The type system for the conservative checker is more high-level, albeit less precise. To prove its soundness, we piggy-pack its proof to that of fractional permission, which is already proven sound. We also plan to implement both checkers on Fluid, an analysis framework for Java programs, and use various benchmarks to compare the performance of both approach.

Categories and Subject Descriptors D.1.5 [*Software*]: PROGRAMMING TECHNIQUES—Object-oriented programming

General Terms languages

Keywords permissions,twelf,fluid

1. Purpose

One common safety issue in imperative programming languages is *aliasing*, which happens when a data location in memory is accessed through different symbolic names in program. With the presence of aliasing, it is difficult to reason about program behavior, because write on a memory cell through one variable may affect the read by some another variable. The write action could happen at a totally unrelated point in the program, which makes program's behavior extremely hard to reason about.

Aliasing can have serious affect on *information hiding* and *encapsulation*, which are essential elements in object-oriented programming. For instance, a private member of an object may have aliases outside the scope that refers to it, thus violating the purpose. Modern softwares are often required to offer *implementation transparency*, which means the ability to change internal implementation without affecting the rest of the system.

To resolve this issue, many researchers have suggested using annotations. Unlike program types, which are "hardcoded" in the language, and concern more about low-level semantics, annotations are more about the high-level program behaviors. They usually will not change the run-time behavior, and therefore can serve two purposes: implementors can attach their *design intent* to the program, for better understanding, and maintainers can use them to extract more semantic information about the program, for better analysis of its behavior. In general, annotations enable a component supplier to offer *contract* in which certain *demands* are described, and clients are supposed to follow these requirements, to guarantee result of execution meets the expectation.

Another reason of using annotation is its flexibility. Rather than design a new language and add all the desired features, people can deploy annotations as an *optional type system*. Existing languages can be improved in this way without their essential elements altered, as well as the compiler and run-time system.

Several annotations have been brought into literature to address the aliasing problem. Among them, most widely discussed are uniqueness and ownership types.

The notion of uniqueness comes from linear types [18], and [15] is one of the earliest work which brought linearity into object-oriented languages. To prevent aliasing on unique variable, *destructive read* is used. That is, once a unique variable is read, it is immediately set to null. In this way, information is transferred via *moving*, instead of *copying*, therefore guarantees every unique pointer is the only copy to the object it refer to. Although destructive read preserves the uniqueness, it also causes many inconveniences in practical usage - not only that the null pointer has unpleasant side-effects, but language semantics also needs to be changed to accommodate the uniqueness.

Alias burying [3] resolves the above issue by delaying the nullification as long as no alias is *read*. When one alias is read, all other aliases are set to undefined, and cannot be used anymore. The advantage is that a separate static program analysis can be used to replace the need of modifying the compiler. Since aliasing is a global effect, to enable intra-procedure analysis, a borrowed annotation is introduced in this approach to grant temporary access to a unique variable.

Another branch is ownership types [8]. This approach, instead of *forbidding* alias, attempts to *confine* [2] aliases in a certain scope. Alias confinement is especially important when coping with large-scale software system, since it allows one to reason about one module at a time, independent of the others. In the ownership approach every object is inside the scope of another one (called the owner object), and all the objects on heap form a tree structure. In fact, the idea of restricting the scope of alias is similar to adoption [9], in which the adopter of a linear value can be seen as its owner. This idea is further made explicit in an object-oriented language setting [4], where ownership is established by *nesting* a linear value into a special data group [14].

One important consequence of the above is, for an object, it guarantees every access path from *root* to it has its owner as one of the node [7]. Therefore, the approach is also called "owners-as-dominators".

In contrast, another approach is "owners-as-modifiers". The difference is the latter allows an object be referenced by any other object, as long as the latter doesn't *modify* it.

SPLASH'11 Companion, October 22–27, 2011, Portland, Oregon, USA.
ACM 978-1-4503-0940-0/11/10.

Ownership Domain [1] is a further attempt on finding a balance between safety and expressiveness. Unlike previous ownership techniques, which impose a fixed structure on objects, Ownership Domain separates aliasing policy from ownership mechanism. In specific, a class can declare multiple *domains* to represent different encapsulation levels, and *links* can be established between domains to grant one access to the other.

Unlike previous works, which tend to introduce new annotations, give them with meanings, and propose a set of rules for checking them, fractional permission [5] provides a foundation for various annotations to ground. Based on separation logic, it provides a logic to reason about the semantic meaning of most annotations. Under this infrastructure, various annotations, such as `unique`, `nonnull`, data group, ownership and effects, can be expressed.

However, while fractional permission provides a powerful tool for checking annotations, the downside is its complexity. Currently, the implementation [17] has both high runtime and space overhead, and it may take a considerable amount of time to analyze a reasonable large program. This hinders its use in practice. Therefore, it is sensible for us to ask: can we implement a lightweight version of the fractional permission, which can check *most* of the annotated programs, while being much more efficient?

2. Goals

The goal of our research is not to invent some new annotations and provide meanings to them, but to make the existing annotation checking more *efficient*.

Currently, the implementation of fractional permission is on Fluid [12], which is an framework for program analysis. Due to the heavyweight nature of permission analysis, the implementation is rather complicated. For instance, to model base permission, the implementation needs lattices for both location and fraction, and has two separate maps for them. To model Java evaluation at a low-level, the transfer function needs to simulate stack operations, and therefore a stack lattice in which elements are of some other base lattices is used. One side-effect for this is that all the primitive types in Java, such as `int`, need to have a lattice representation too. Besides, along the control flow, the analysis also needs to collect various facts, like the equality (inequality) between object locations, as well as nesting situations.

Because of the large amount of information that needs to be tracked, and the operations on them (especially the join operation upon control flow merge), the analysis has high runtime and space overhead. This makes it impractical to use on reasonable large-size program.

To make annotation checking run faster, instead of applying the heavyweight checker on the input program directly, a better strategy is to use a more "conservative" checker first. The conservative checker should run much faster, albeit less precise. Instead of encoding fractional permission directly, it uses much higher-level types. The fractional permission type system, instead, serves as a foundation for the new type system to be built on. This approach gives us two benefits: first, we can have better understanding of semantics of annotations, using fractional permission, and therefore derive better type system to check them; second, we can build the soundness proof of the type system directly on that of fractional permission.

Besides the conservative checker, we also intend to use a "liberal" checker, which identifies those *obviously wrong* cases. Inside an annotated program, some methods may contain errors that are easy to detect. After failing the conservative checker, these methods are passed to permission checker, which makes the overhead even worse. Instead, by applying the liberal checker on these methods, we can reject these methods very quickly, without utilizing the

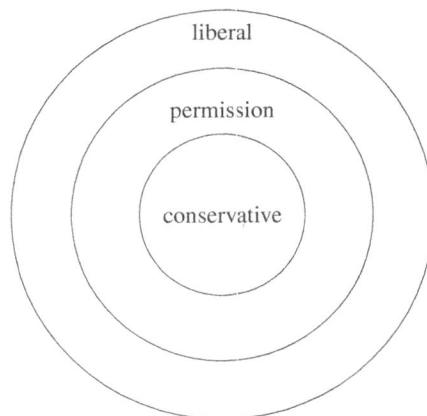

Figure 1. Multi-layered annotation checkers

```
class Node {
  @InRegion("Instance")
  @Unique Node next;
}

class List {
  @Unique Node head;

  @RegionEffect("writes_head")
  void prepend(@Unique Node n) {
    n.next = head;
    head = n;
  }
}
```

Figure 2. Sample annotated code in Fluid

heavyweight checker. Some obviously wrong cases include storing a `borrowed`-annotated method parameter into a `unique` field, or not returning the effects passed in to the method.

A type system can not be trusted without soundness property. For the conservative checker, we intend to use machine-checked proof, based on fractional permission system [6]. The proof is written using Twelf [16], which is a implementation of LF logical framework [13] that is especially useful for proving properties of programming languages and logics. Specifically, for the conservative type system, we piggy-pack its proof on the permission system. That is, for each term in the language, we show that if it can be checked under the conservative system, then it can also be checked under the permission system, and since the latter is already proved sound, this shows the former is sound too. With this approach, we avoid the need to prove progress and preservation, and the semantics of the language is also separated from the type system.

3. Technical Approach

Our approach will be in two directions. First, we will formalize the type system and use machine-checked proof for its correctness. Second, based on the type system we will implement a prototype annotation checker, and compare the performance with the single type system approach.

The related annotations that are currently supported in Fluid include `unique`, `shared`, `borrowed`, and effects. Although we do not support ownership parameters currently in either formalization and implementation, we believe it should be a straightforward extension to the above.

Formalization Compared to the permission type system, the conservative type system is designed to be mostly flow-insensitive. Although this will make several kinds of type errors difficult or impossible to detect, it guarantees the overhead of the checker to be low. However, for effect analysis, we need to track the source of local variables and record effects on them. This requires Binding Context Analysis (BCA) [11], which is flow-sensitive. However, BCA is independent of the main type checking process, and is much faster than the permission analysis. We also intend to use various optimizations to speed up this process.

A major part of our research is the machine-checked proof for the soundness of type system. Not only will this give us strong confidence on the correctness of the system, but also it will force us to address all the possible cases which one may not notice in a natural language proof.

As a pilot study, the author has first proved a simple non-null type system [10] based on fractional permissions. The system itself is a very simple extension of a standard type system, with the following additions:

- in a class, every field is either annotated as `nonnull` or `maybenull`. Also, every field is implicitly `shared`.

- the effects for methods is implicitly `writes shared`, which, combined with the first, grant them privilege to write every field.

- the constructor is especially restricted; the body of it must be a sequence of assignments to the fields, followed by returning `this`.

The type system is built on a Java-like kernel language for reasoning about concurrent imperative language, which, alone with its semantics, is already defined in Twelf. Both the existing proof for permission type system and the conservative type system are based on the assumption of single-threaded programs, although a proof for multi-thread programs is ongoing.

The proof is done by (roughly) first transforming all the relevant environments (class map, method map, etc) to the corresponding structures under the permission system. Then, we prove that for every program in the kernel language, if it's well-typed under consistent environments, then after converting these environments, the same program can also be checked under the system of fractional permission.

The machine-checked proof for the non-null system consists of 15 files and 769 KBytes. Although it seems large, over 500K of the code is automatically generated, and contains many unused theorems. The definition of types also occupies a reasonable part of the code.

Implementation Our implementation of the type system is based on the Fluid project, which is an analysis framework implemented as plugin for Eclipse IDE. In the previous work, the fractional permission type system has been implemented [17] by William Retert on it as control-flow analysis, and some case studies have also been done both on some simple code fragments and JEdit, a reasonably large sample of annotated Java code.

Because our goal is to improve the speed of annotation checking based on the current permission analysis, we need to collect various statistics to see the result using different measures. Currently, the main issue is lacking of sample annotated code. Although JEdit has a reasonably large size, the annotations on it are mainly used for thread and lock analyses (only six fields are annotated as `unique`). In future, we need more sample code for benchmarking. The result of this not only can provide us a general idea of how much improvement can be achieved with the multi-layered approach, but also can give us feedbacks for the cases that the lightweight checkers should handle.

References

[1] Jonathan Aldrich and Craig Chambers. Ownership domains: Separating aliasing policy from mechanism. In Martin Odersky, editor, *ECOOP'04 — Object-Oriented Programming, 18th European Conference*, volume 3086 of *Lecture Notes in Computer Science*, pages 1–25, Berlin, Heidelberg, New York, 2004. Springer.

[2] Boris Bokowski and Jan Vitek. Confined types. In *OOPSLA'99 Conference Proceedings—Object-Oriented Programming Systems, Languages and Applications*, volume 34, pages 82–96, New York, October 1999. ACM Press.

[3] John Boyland. Alias burying: Unique variables without destructive reads. *Software Practice and Experience*, 31(6):533–553, May 2001.

[4] John Boyland and William Retert. Connecting effects and uniqueness with adoption. In *Conference Record of POPL 2005: the 32nd ACM SIGACT-SIGPLAN Symposium on Principles of Programming Languages*, pages 283–295, New York, 2005. ACM Press.

[5] John Boyland, William Retert, and Yang Zhao. Comprehending annotations on object-oriented programs using fractional permissions. In Matthew Parkinson, editor, *International Workshop on Aliasing, Confinement and Ownership in object-oriented programming (IWACO)*, New York, 2009. ACM Press. To appear.

[6] John Tang Boyland. Semantics of fractional permissions with nesting. *ACM Trans. Program. Lang. Syst.*, 32:22:1–22:33, August 2010.

[7] David Clarke. *Object Ownership and Containment*. PhD thesis, University of New South Wales, Sydney, Australia, 2001.

[8] David G. Clarke, John M. Potter, and James Noble. Ownership types for flexible alias protection. In *OOPSLA'98 Conference Proceedings—Object-Oriented Programming Systems, Languages and Applications*, volume 33, pages 48–64, New York, October 1998. ACM Press.

[9] Manuel Fähndrich and Robert DeLine. Adoption and focus: Practical linear types for imperative programming. In *Proceedings of the ACM SIGPLAN '02 Conference on Programming Language Design and Implementation*, volume 37, pages 13–24, New York, May 2002. ACM Press.

[10] Manuel Fähndrich and K. Rustan M. Leino. Declaring and checking non-null types in an object-oriented language. In *OOPSLA'03 Conference Proceedings—Object-Oriented Programming Systems, Languages and Applications*, volume 38, pages 302–312, New York, November 2003. ACM Press.

[11] Aaron Greenhouse. *A Programmer-Oriented Approach to Safe Concurrency*. PhD thesis, School of Computer Science, Carnegie Mellon University, Pittsburgh, Pennsylvania, USA, 2003.

[12] Aaron Greenhouse, T. J. Halloran, and William L. Scherlis. Using Eclipse to demonstrate positive static assurance of Java program concurrency design intent. In *Proceedings of the 2003 OOPSLA workshop on eclipse technology eXchange*, pages 99–103, October 2003.

[13] Robert Harper, Furio Honsell, and Gordon Plotkin. A framework for defining logics. *Journal of the ACM*, 40(1):143–184, 1993.

[14] K. Rustan M. Leino, Arnd Poetzsch-Heffter, and Yunhong Zhou. Using data groups to specify and check side effects. In *Proceedings of the ACM SIGPLAN '02 Conference on Programming Language Design and Implementation*, volume 37, pages 246–257, New York, May 2002. ACM Press.

[15] Naftaly Minsky. Towards alias-free pointers. In Pierre Cointe, editor, *ECOOP'96 — Object-Oriented Programming, 10th European Conference*, volume 1098 of *Lecture Notes in Computer Science*, pages 189–209, Berlin, Heidelberg, New York, July 1996. Springer.

[16] Frank Pfenning and Carsten Schürmann. Twelf user's guide, version 1.4. Available at http://www.cs.cm.edu/~twelf, 2002.

[17] William S. Retert. *Implementing Permission Analysis*. PhD thesis, University of Wisconsin–Milwaukee, Department of EE & CS, 2009.

[18] Philip Wadler. Linear types can change the world! In M. Broy and C. B. Jones, editors, *Programming Concepts and Methods*. Elsevier, North-Holland, 1990.

SPLASH 2011 Educators' & Trainers' Symposium Welcome

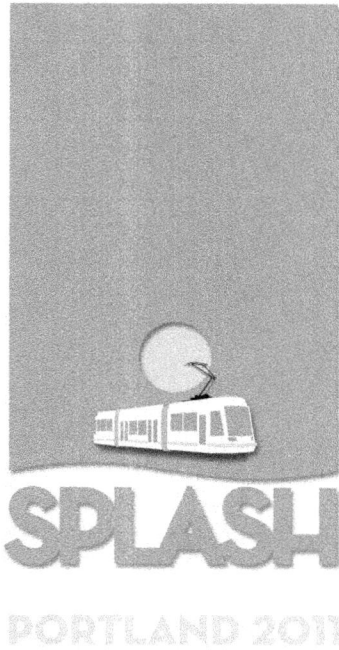

This year marks the 20th OOPSLA/SPLASH Educators' and Trainers' Symposium. The past two decades have witnessed several stages of evolution of o-o in education. At first, efforts were directed at getting objects into the curriculum. During the second stage, in the latter half of the nineties, o-o moved from being an advanced subject to one that dominated introductory courses. Since then, the discipline has become more research oriented, with studies on how best to teach o-o. In the early years of the last decade, pair programming and "objects first" were hot topics. While pair programming has become routine, the past few years have seen a retreat from the concept of "objects first." In the past five or six years, a recurring theme has been the need to effectively manage large projects undertaken by students. At the same time, the importance of parallelism has become increasingly obvious. That realization led to the change in conference name last year, from one devoted to o-o in particular, to one more generally devoted to advances in programming technology and teaching programming.

This year's symposium concentrates on programming teams and parallel programming. Kim Bruce talks on introducing parallelism and concurrency early in the curriculum. Rich LeBlanc gives a Curriculum 2013 steering committee report, along with an audience-participation exercise.

From the perspective of teams, Deer Run Software will present their CATME/Team Maker application, a popular engineering-education tool for creating teams and assessing the effectiveness of team members. One of the contributed papers, from the Technical University of Eindhoven, our other contributed paper, from Thomas Van Drunen of Wheaton College, explores teaching functional programming in a discrete-math course. Several contributed posters will explore other issues in teaching and learning programming.

Today's programming textbooks include more than just text. Add-ons like lecture slides, videos, and automated testing are becoming increasingly necessary for successful marketing. A panel of textbook authors will discuss ancillary resources for textbooks.

This symposium would not take place without the help of a dozen members of the program committee, notably Eugene Wallingford, who was to chair it, but had to step down for medical reasons. I would like to offer them my sincere gratitude.

Ed Gehringer
SPLASH 2011 Educators' and Trainers' Symposium Chair
North Carolina State University

The Case for Teaching Functional Programming in Discrete Math

Thomas VanDrunen

Wheaton College, Wheaton, IL
Thomas.VanDrunen@wheaton.edu

Abstract

Functional programming is losing its place in undergraduate computer science curricula, in part because of the attention given to many new ideas in the field. Nevertheless, undergraduates benefit from an early experience in a second programming paradigm, especially functional programming. The solution, advocated here, is to weave functional programming into the discrete mathematics course. Not only does this give a convenient, early occasion to teach functional programming, but it also allows the functional programming topics and discrete mathematics topics to illuminate each other. Furthermore, it provides a service course to students in mathematics and other majors.

Categories and Subject Descriptors   K.3.2 [*Computers and Education*]: Computer and Information Science Education—Computer and Information Science Education; G.2 [*Discrete mathematics*]: General

General Terms   Languages

Keywords   Discrete mathematics, functional programming

1. Introduction

There is a wide variety of pedagogical and curricular approaches to introducing the field of computer science. This can be seen by perusing the available textbooks for CS 1 or similar courses. Even though the core topics for undergraduate programs in computer science have been standardized in such reports as the IEEE and ACM Computing Curricula reports [13, 14], there remain considerable differences across programs regarding what first programming language or paradigm works best, the relative emphases for theory, systems, and software development, the ordering and pairing of topics throughout the curriculum, and which new trends

or advanced topics to integrate into the curriculum and how quickly.

In recent curricular trends, the topic of functional programming is being squeezed out of many undergraduate programs. In this paper we advocate retaining it as a core and early topic in the curriculum, specifically that the ideal place for it is in a freshman- or sophomore-level course in discrete mathematics. In Section 2 we make a brief defense for keeping (or reintroducing) functional programming in the undergraduate curriculum and observe the curricular pressures that make this difficult. Section 3 lays out the case for putting functional programming and discrete mathematics in the same course, showing that not only do the mathematical and programming content streams complement each other for computer science majors, but that they also together provide a useful service course for math majors and others. Precedents for this approach are briefly surveyed in Section 4. Section 5 addresses pragmatic aspects of implementing a course in discrete mathematics and functional programming, suggesting a course outline and reporting on the author's own experience. In Section 6 we conclude by reviewing the advantage of placing such a course in the curriculum.

2. Functional programming in the curriculum

2.1 The need for functional programming

Functional programming is vital to a well-rounded understanding of the field of computer science. Not only is the functional programming model of computation foundational to some approaches to the theory of computation, but important applications have been produced in it. Even if students end up programming primarily in an imperative or object-oriented setting, seeing another paradigm increases their understanding of the paradigm they use most. Moreover, many idioms and design patterns for object-oriented programming are essentially ways to import features or programming idioms from functional programming [7, 9, 12].

The SIGPLAN Workshop on Undergraduate Programming Language Curricula, meeting ahead of the 2008 revisions to Computing Curricula 2001, recommended a prominent place for functional programming:

> Shifting to functional programming is not merely about a change in syntax; rather, it forces students to approach problems in a novel way. This change increases their mental agility and prepares them for a life of practice in a world where languages continually grow, morph, and sometimes shift their perspective [2].

2.2 The squeeze on functional programming

The prevalence of functional programming surged in the 1980s with the publication of the original edition of *Structure and Interpretation of Computer Programs* [1], and many schools began using a dialect of Lisp as the first or primary programming language in their curriculum. Felleisen et al describe this popularity as short-lived because of the difficulty of then-available introductory material on functional programming and because of how greatly functional languages differ from dominant programming languages [6]. (They also propose a solution: Begin the curriculum with a functional language but follow it quickly with an object-oriented language. This way the students learn early how to think in both paradigms.)

With functional programming taken out of the introductory sequence, a typical student would be introduced to it in a sophomore- or junior-level programming languages course. This is where the IEEE and ACM Computing Curricula report (2001) places the topic (PL7) [14]. By that time, students have acquired the imperative or object-oriented paradigm (or a combination of them) as their native way of thinking about computation, and functional programming is viewed as a alternative curiosity.

Even that presence of functional programming in typical computer science programs is in jeopardy. Mark Bailey observes that as the field of computer science grows, new topics crowd for attention in a curriculum, and a core programming languages course is likely to absorb a lot of the pressure. "The emergence of offerings, at the undergraduate level, of courses in bioinformatics, wireless networking, security, game programming, robotics, and mobile computing...compete for a limited number of course slots in an undergraduate computer science major. ...Liberal arts colleges, in particular, have greater curricular pressures" because of limited time alloted to major courses [3].

For functional programming in particular, we note that Computing Curricula 2001 does not place PL7 as a core topic—in fact, one of the main goals of the Workshop on Undergraduate Programming Language Curricula for the 2008 update to the Computing Curricula report was "to make the functional programming unit (FP), PL7 in the curriculum, required rather than elective" [2]. Although the 2008 update does require exposure to more than one programming

paradigm, the CC 2008 Review Taskforce decided not to require functional programming in particular [13].

2.3 Other curricular needs to address

Some schools prefer to have an early course on the foundations of computer science that gives computer science majors the mathematical background to reason about computational models and their limitations and to appreciate the contributions of the theory of computation to computer science and to science in general. For example, the computer science program at Purdue University requires CS 18200, a freshman course that begins with discrete math topics and goes on to cover analysis of algorithms, proofs, automata, and computability. A course like this may also be of interest to students outside the computer science program.

Many computer science departments must provide programming or other computing courses to serve the needs of other programs at the school—most notably mathematics, engineering, and natural science. There is great advantage to giving the introductory courses for computer science majors double duty so that they also fill this need for service courses. Not only can they be used for recruiting (so that a few mathematics or engineering students can be "converted" to computer science), but for small departments it is a matter of efficient use of faculty load. Thus for many schools it makes sense for introductory computer science courses to be designed for other populations in addition to computer science majors.

3. Where should functional programming go?

In light of the need for functional programming in the computer science curriculum and its precarious position in either the introductory programming course or in a mid-level programming languages course, the question arises: Where should functional programming go in the computer science curriculum? We propose an answer: Put it in the discrete mathematics course. Call it, "Discrete Mathematics and Functional Programming," DMFP. Students can take it some time in their first three semesters *in parallel with* a traditional introduction to programming sequence.

Functional programming and discrete math are closely tied. It is immediately apparent that the two areas of study are related. To begin, functions and recursion are fundamental to both [11]. Moreover, proof by induction is an important topic of a discrete math course, which is also closely tied to recursion.

Functional programming illuminates discrete mathematics. The inclusion of functional programming in a discrete math course has a pedagogical benefit to the teaching of the discrete math topics. As Cong-Cong Xing has pointed out, the treatment of functions in discrete math differs enough from students' experience with functions in pre-calculus to cause a good deal of confusion. In particular, students have trouble differentiating between the name of a function and the function itself, and, along the same lines, trouble understanding functions as discrete objects or the idea of a higher-order function. A functional programming language gives a context in which to illustrate all these things [17].

Moreover, functional programming languages are good contexts for modelling other ideas in discrete mathematics. Types and lists each model sets, though in different ways. Lists also model sequences. Tuples model the elements of a Cartesian product. Relations can be modeled in many ways: lists of tuples, predicates, and matrices, to name three. Functions, of course, represent functions. Quantification can be illustrated algorithmically in functions that process lists.

DMFP puts functional programming early. It has become standard for students to take a course in discrete mathematics or discrete structures in their first or second year. The CC01 gives "Discrete Structures" 43 core hours, more than any other area. Putting functional programming here is a compromise between a functional-first approach and delaying functional programming until a later point; it incorporates the advantages of functional-first but still allows the introductory programming sequence to be taught in an object-oriented or imperative paradigm.

Specifically, by putting functional programming here, students will have experience in functional programming ideally in their first year, in their second year at the latest. This way they can digest it before a sophomore- or junior-level software development course and thereby appreciate the influence of functional programming on design patterns. Likewise, the students' experience in a second paradigm allows a later course in programming languages to be more advanced.

DMFP allows a thorough investigation of functional programming. If functional programming is not taught until a mid-level programming languages course, then that course likely spends only one unit on functional programming in a series of units on different programming paradigms. Students are unlikely to acquire a thorough understanding of, much less competency in, functional programming with merely a passing exposure. Functional programming would not get a full course's worth of attention in a DMFP course either, since it would be only part of the content stream. However, with functional programming topics being spread throughout the semester—and, more importantly, with students continually practicing functional programming—the students will gain and retain a more thorough skill base in the paradigm.

DMFP motivates discrete mathematics for computer science majors. Despite computer science and mathematics being kindred fields, computer science major populations include many math-averse students. Many are frustrated at the math requirements of the program and are slow to understand the relevance. The situation is more likely to be aggravated than remedied when the discrete math course is taught by the mathematics department. The functional programming component in a DMFP course provides a set of enjoyable topics and assignments to keep the computer science majors engaged. More importantly, the links between the mathematical topics and the pragmatics of programming are made explicit.

DMFP motivates programming for math majors. Computing is a vital topic for contemporary math majors. Many will need some level of competency in programming at some point in their studies, whether in professional practice as actuaries, to introduce algorithmic topics as high school math teachers, or in research as graduate students. Accordingly, math major programs typically include at least one semester of programming. Unfortunately, many math majors find programming to be foreign and become frustrated when they do not see any immediate relevance for their mathematical studies. Their frustration is especially understandable if they are dropped into a Java programming course that was not designed for their needs.

What better context to introduce programming to math majors than a math course? Just as the programming topics illuminate and motivate the math topics for computer science majors, the math topics do the same to programming topics for math majors.

The course easily can be designed to hit a sweet spot for both majors. There is a synergistic effect in bringing both student populations together. The slogan used in advertising the course taught by the author is *Computer science majors should learn to write proofs and math majors should learn to write programs **together***. Computer science majors who have had a previous or concurrent programming course will be at an advantage for learning functional programming, whereas math majors usually are better prepared for the course's proof-writing content. The two populations can partner and help each other.

DMFP provides a framework for talking about computer science foundations. Many computer science programs have an early course on the foundations of computer science that can give an overview of the field, especially of the theoretical aspects. Topics can include models of computation, automata, asymptotic growth of functions, correctness proofs, P vs NP, and the limits of computation. It is hardly possible to deal with these topics rigorously in an introductory course—in fact, for many programs these ideas appear in an elective if anywhere. However, touching on these ideas informally at the front of the curriculum allows the students to connect them with the practical material they see throughout the course of study.

A course in discrete mathematics provides the right framework for discussing these ideas, since they rely on sets, relations, functions, and graphs, not to mention logic and quantification. Moreover, even a smattering of functional programming provides simple illustrations of the computational issues and provides exercises accessible even to beginning students.

4. Precedents for this approach

Although the case for teaching functional programming and discrete mathematics together is here presented as a proposal—and it is not common practice—it is not altogether without precedent either. Roger Wainwright [15], Peter Henderson [8], Christelle Scharff and Andrew Wildenberg [11], and Cong-Cong Xing [17] have reported experiences in teaching Standard ML or Miranda in a discrete math course at five institutions for two decades. Moreover, the *Model Curriculum for a Liberal Arts Degree in Computer Science* by the Liberal Arts Computer Science (LACS) Consortium, which was produced in 2007 in response to Computing Curricula 2001, puts a course titled "Discrete Structures and Functional Programming" in the introductory sequence [4].

While many texts exist either on discrete mathematics or functional programming, not many are available for teaching the two together. Doets and van Eijck [5] and O'Donnell, Hall, and Page [10] have texts that use Haskell to illustrate discrete mathematics. Fenton and Dubinsky have a text that similarly uses ISETL [16]. Moreover, the author of this article has a forthcoming text that completely integrates discrete mathematics and functional programming, using Standard ML.

5. Implementing Discrete Mathematics and Functional Programming

In this section we list some suggestions in implementing the approach advocated in this paper. We provide a sketch of an outline for such a course and report on our experience in teaching a course that follows this program.

5.1 Course outline

Discrete mathematics courses, even those intended for computer science students, vary greatly in what topics are covered and in what order. Should the course start with symbolic logic since logic is the most fundamental science, or should "raw material" like sets or integers be introduced first? Should the students' first experience with proofs be on sets or integers, or a combination of the two? Should the chapters on relations and functions be ordered from general to specific (relations first, then functions) or specific to general (functions first, then relations)? Should graphs and relations be introduced together or separately? Should induction be introduced early as a basic proving tool or late as an advanced proof technique?

We believe that the DMFP approach is not tied to any particular ordering of the material. In the list below we describe the points of contact between the discrete math topics and the functional programming topics, but there are few hard dependencies between items in the list.

Sets. Functional programming makes heavy use of lists, and even though lists are ordered and sets are unordered, it is natural to introduce lists along side of sets as a way to model them in a programming language. Functions on lists model operations on sets. Sets and types also illuminate each other, and this point in the course is an opportune time to introduce simple user-defined types, such as SML's datatype construct (type in F# and OCaml). Tuple types are introduced to illustrate Cartesian products.

Symbolic logic. Boolean values and operations naturally model ideas from symbolic logic. Functions that return boolean values represent predicates. Whether the course begins with sets or with logic, once the students have seen both concepts, then multiple quantification can be used in and illustrated by algorithms. For example, an exercise asking the students to write a function that takes a list of integers and determines whether it contains an item that is the divisor of all the others requires the students to nest a universally quantified question inside of an existentially quantified question.

Proofs. Instructors may find that the portion of the course that introduces proofs has the fewest natural ties to programming. With a little effort, however, the course can show students how algorithms give insights into theorems and their proofs and that mathematical results and their proofs sometimes provide algorithms. As an example of the former, students can write a function that computes a powerset of a set and then experiment with sets of several sizes. The observation that the size of the power set doubles as the size of the original set grows leads to the theorem $|\mathscr{P}(A)| = 2^{|A|}$. Moreover, the algorithm itself suggests an outline for the proof. In the other direction, the Euclidean algorithm and the division algorithm grow naturally out a theorem about greatest common divisors and the quotient-remainder theorem, respectively.

Induction. Induction is one of the clearest places in the semester where functional programming ties in. If induction is introduced later in the semester, then by that time students already have experience thinking recursively, so proofs by induction will not seem as foreign to the students as is often the case. Structural induction and recursively defined types should be taught together, and students will find that proofs of structural induction will look very similar to functions on recursive types. Moreover, if structural induction is taught before mathematical induction, then an implementation of whole numbers using the Peano axioms makes the transition from structural induction to mathematical induction seamless. Moreover, proofs of algorithm correctness give a concrete motivation for mathematical induction.

Relations. Relations provide an opportunity to illustrate the trade-offs between different ways to represent or store information. Relations can be represented on a computer in at least three ways: as predicates (functions), as sets of pairs (lists of tuples), or as matrices. The students' experience in programming earlier in the semester also makes it easier to talk about applications of relations to different areas of computing, such as databases.

Functions. One goal of studying functions in a discrete math course is for the students to understand functions as mathematical objects. This is the time in the semester to talk about functions as first class values. This opens the way for introducing several idioms in functional programming, some of which have convenient ties to ideas in the study of functions. For example, the use of map is an illustration of the image of a function.

Cardinality and computability. Some of the deeper results of set theory provide the background for big ideas in the theory of computation. For example, Russell's paradox (there can be no set of all sets), countability (when cardinality is extended to infinite sets, reals are a higher order infinity than integers), and computability (the Halting Problem is not computable in known models of computation) form a triad of special topics.

Graphs. In a DMFP course, the section on graphs presents both the theoretical aspects of graph theory (the handshake theorem, isomorphisms) and the practical side (algorithms for searches, spanning trees, and shortest paths). The course could also explore the trade-offs of different ways to represent graphs on a computer.

The course should also include excursions into larger programming examples that exercise students' functional programming skills, illuminate the mathematical topics, and generally excite the students about the field. Obvious examples include a system for parsing and transforming text, an automatic theorem prover, and applications in game theory.

The combined experience in programming and discrete math provides the foundation for other and more advanced topics, especially if the course is spread through two semesters. Many discrete math courses have units on number theory, combinatorics, and discrete probability, and some explore mathematical structures such as boolean algebras, lattices, and groups. In any of these cases, the students' experience in programing allows for the inclusion of applications, uses, and illustrations in computing. If the course should include computer science topics such as a survey of automata and formal languages or complexity classes and asymptotic notation, students will have the mathematical background to deal with those ideas rigorously.

5.2 Experience

The author has taught discrete math with a functional programming component (using Standard ML) eight times. In

six of those offerings the programming component has made up at least 40% of the course content and the two topic streams were fully integrated. The course is populated by both math majors and computer science majors, as well as a few students from other programs. The course is required for computer science majors; for math majors, the course is one of four options available for fulfilling a supporting requirement in computing. Students from other programs take the course as pure elective. The computer science majors are freshmen and sophomores, taking the course in parallel with a first, second, or third semester of programming in Java or C. There has been at least one case of a computer science major taking the course as her first course in the program. The math major population in the course is drawn from all class years; almost all of them have little or no programming experience coming into the course.

The math majors naturally are at an advantage over the computer science majors on the mathematical topics, and likewise computer science majors over the math majors on programming topics. However, neither population dominates the other in overall performance over the course of the semester, and top students in the class have come from either major.

Since the course is taught at a small college, the author can observe the long-term result of the course among computer science students by seeing how they put the ideas to use in later courses in the curriculum. In particular, the early exposure to functional programming has made students better prepared for topics in software development, programming languages, and analysis of algorithms. Moreover, the author has observed students expressing long-lasting appreciation for the ML language and for the usefulness of discrete mathematics.

It is harder to observe the long-term benefits of the course among math majors. However, enrollment in the course for the fall 2010 was up 275% over enrollment in fall 2009. (The course is offered only in the fall.) This did not correspond to an increase in enrollment in the computer science program but came primarily from an increase of math majors and nonmajors signing up for the course. Among math majors the increased interest appears in part to be from math majors being advised by upperclassmen and mathematics professors that the course is good preparation for modern algebra (a change in the course meeting time also made it more accessible to math majors than in previous offerings).

6. Conclusions

Computer science, as a quickly-changing and still relatively young field, has resisted standardization of undergraduate curriculum and has seen many pedagogical trends come and go. It is not our present intention to advocate yet another trend but to make the case for a solution to a specific problem in light of the current curricular landscape.

Teaching a course in discrete mathematics and functional programming has the advantage of finding a place for functional programming in an increasingly full curriculum, showing the students a second or third programming paradigm early in their course of study, and making explicit links between ostensibly disparate topics. The approach is particularly appropriate for liberal arts colleges that value integration between fields and where the course can serve several populations of the student body.

References

[1] H. Abelson and G. J. Sussman. *Structure and Interpretation of Computer Programs*. McGraw Hill and the MIT Press, Cambridge, MA, second edition, 1996.

[2] E. Allen, R. Bodik, K. Bruce, K. Fisher, S. Freund, R. Harper, C. Krintz, S. Krishnamurthi, J. Larus, D. Lea, G. Leavens, L. Pollock, S. Reges, M. Rinard, M. Sheldon, F. Turbak, and M. Wand. SIGPLAN programming language curriculum workshop: Discussion summaries and recommendations. *SIGPLAN Not.*, 43(11):6–29, 2008. ISSN 0362-1340. doi: http://doi.acm.org/10.1145/1480828.1480831.

[3] M. W. Bailey. Injecting programming language concepts throughout the curriculum: An inclusive strategy. *SIGPLAN Notices*, 43(11):36–38, 2008. ISSN 0362-1340. doi: http://doi.acm.org/10.1145/1480828.1480835.

[4] L. A. C. S. Consortium. A 2007 model curriculum for a liberal arts degree in computer science. *Journal on Educational Resources in Computing*, 7(2):2, 2007. ISSN 1531-4278. doi: http://doi.acm.org/10.1145/1240200.1240202.

[5] K. Doets and J. vanEijck. *The Haskell Road to Logic, Maths and Programming*. Texts in Computing. King's College Publications, London, 2004.

[6] M. Felleisen, R. B. Findler, M. Flatt, and S. Krishnamurthi. The structure and interpretation of the computer science curriculum. *Journal of Functional Programming*, 14(4):365–378, 2004. ISSN 0956-7968. doi: http://dx.doi.org/10.1017/S0956796804005076.

[7] P. Graham. Revenge of the nerds, May 2002. http://www.paulgraham.com/icad.html.

[8] P. B. Henderson. Functional and declarative languages for learning discrete mathematics. In *The Proceedings of the International Workshop on Functional and Declarative Programming in Education*, 2002. Technical Report No 0210 of the University of Kiel.

[9] P. Norvig. Design patterns in dynamic languages, March 1998. http://norvig.com/design-patterns/.

[10] J. O'Donnell, C. Hall, and R. Page. *Discrete Mathematics Using a Computer*. Springer, London, second edition, 2006.

[11] C. Scharff and A. Wildenberg. Teaching discrete strcutres with SML. In *The Proceedings of the International Workshop on Functional and Declarative Programming in Education*, 2002. Technical Report No 0210 of the University of Kiel.

[12] J. Spolsky. Can your programming language do this? In *Joel on Software* blog, August 2006. http://www.joelonsoftware.com/items/2006/08/01.html.

[13] The Interim Review Task Force. Computer science cirriculum 2008: An interim revision of cs 2001, December 2008. http://www.acm.org//education/curricula/ComputerScience2008.pdf.

[14] The Joint Task Force on Computing Curricula. Computing curricula 2001, December 2001. http://www.acm.org/education/education/education/curric_vols/cc2001.pdf.

[15] R. L. Wainwright. Introducing functional programming in discrete mathematics. In *SIGCSE '92: Proceedings of the twenty-third SIGCSE technical symposium on Computer science education*, pages 147–152, New York, NY, USA, 1992. ACM. ISBN 0-89791-468-6. doi: http://doi.acm.org/10.1145/134510.134540.

[16] E. D. William E Fenton. *Introduction to Discrete Mathematics with ISETL*. Springer, London, 1996.

[17] C.-C. Xing. Enhancing the teaching and learning of functions through functional programming in ml. *Journal of Computer Sciences in Colleges*, 23(4):97–104, April 2008.

Mining Student Capstone Projects with FRASR and ProM

Wouter Poncin   Alexander Serebrenik   Mark van den Brand

Eindhoven University of Technology, Eindhoven, The Netherlands

w.poncin@alumnus.tue.nl, {a.serebrenik, m.g.j.v.d.brand}@tue.nl

Abstract

Capstone projects are commonly carried out at the end of an undergraduate program of study in software engineering or computer science. While traditionally such projects solely focussed on the software product to be developed, in more recent work importance of the development process has been stressed. Currently process quality assessment techniques are limited to review of intermediary artifacts, self- and peer evaluations. We advocate augmenting the assessment by mining software repositories used by the students during the development. We present the assessment methodology and illustrate it by applying to a number of software engineering capstone projects.

Categories and Subject Descriptors   K.3.2 [*Computers and Education*]: Computer and Information Science Education—computer science education; H.2.8 [*Database Management*]: Database applications—data mining

General Terms   Management, Measurement

Keywords   capstone project, mining software repositories, software engineering

1. Introduction

Undergraduate computer science or software engineering curriculum is often crowned by a *capstone project*, providing the students with the opportunity to undertake a significant software engineering project on their own. Recommended by such model curricula as [3, 4], capstone projects build upon the knowledge gained from courses throughout the program, and should includes development of requirements, design, implementation, and quality assurance [3]. While traditionally such projects solely focussed on the software *product* to be developed, in more recent work importance of the development *process* has been stressed [13, 30].

Growing importance of the development process poses new challenges to instructors acting as assessors: quality of the software development process has to be assessed and taken into account while determining the students' grades. The importance of process quality assessment has been recognized, e.g., in [18]. In practice to obtain insights in the development process the assessors resort to evaluation of artifacts produced during the development (e.g., project management plans or requirements specifications), possibly augmented with the self- and peer assessment [5, 19].

To improve on the objectivity of the assessment as well as to provide the learners with prompt feedback, we propose to augment the existing assessment techniques with software repository mining, i.e., analysis of the development process based on repository data. Software repositories such as source-code management systems, document repositories and issue-tracking systems, are commonly seen as a part of the project infrastructure [31], and, hence, are readily available for the analysis. A plentitude of data available in such repositories triggered an extensive research effort on repository mining [6, 12, 14, 24]. Specifically, we suggest applying process mining to analysis of data from multiple software repositories. Process mining [10] has been developed to extract information from event logs produced by an information system, and since then has been demonstrated to be a valuable technique for analyzing business processes in various domains [2, 23]. Moreover, recently it has been successfully applied to analyze and visualize information from multiple software repositories, including version control systems, issue-trackers and mail archives [21].

The main advantage of process mining applied to software repositories is a clear separation between the preprocessing step and the analysis step. The preprocessing step extracts information from software repositories and combines information into an event log, while the analysis step aims at discovering the process structure, reflected in the log, and analyses its correctness or visualizes it. Both steps are supported by tools: FRASR [21] and ProM [10], respectively. Both tools are highly flexible allowing the instructor to answer a multitude of questions pertaining to the software development process, followed by the students.

The remainder of the paper is organized as follows. We start with a brief discussion of the assessment methodology

SPLASH'11 Companion,   October 22–27, 2011, Portland, Oregon, USA.
Copyright © 2011 ACM 978-1-4503-0942-4/11/10... $10.00

proposed and the supporting tools in Section 2. Next in Section 3 we introduce the capstone software engineering project as organized at Eindhoven University of Technology, identify the instructor's questions pertaining to the process assessment and show how these questions can be answered using the methodology proposed. Related work is discussed in Section 4 and, finally, Section 5 concludes the paper.

2. Assessment methodology

Development process quality assessment begins with identifying a process-related *assessment question*. This step is carried out by the instructor depending on the project learning goals associated with the development process. Next, using FRASR, the instructor combines information from different software repositories into one event log, imports the log in ProM and analyzes it using ProM mining and visualization plugins to answer the initial assessment question.

2.1 Event logs

In order to be amenable for process mining, the event logs should conform to the process mining event log meta model[1] shown in Figure 1. An *event log* contains data from a number of *processes* (usually one). Each process has a number of *process instances*, also known as *case instances*, that can be uniquely identified. Furthermore, each process has a number of *activities*, and each process instance—a number of *events*, consisting of an activity being executed at a certain moment in time and associated with certain data.

For instance, a log of an insurance company might contain information about a billing process and a refund process. A refund process has a number of process instances uniquely identified by the claim number. Activities that should be executed in the refund process may include registering the claim, and checking the insurance policy. An example of an event is "On Thursday September 23, 2010 Alice checks the insurance policy of the persons involved in claim 478-12". Process mining aims, therefore, at discovering the information about a process, based on the information about different process instances. The preprocessing step produces a log conforming to the process mining event log meta model. Given such a log, process mining techniques can, for instance, derive abstract representations of the process control flow or detect relations between the individuals involved in the business process and their tasks.

2.2 Preprocessing with FRASR

The preprocessing step commences with *defining data sources*, i.e., providing FRASR with information about software repositories. Data sources can be defined either as a local file or by entering the repository URL and authentication information.

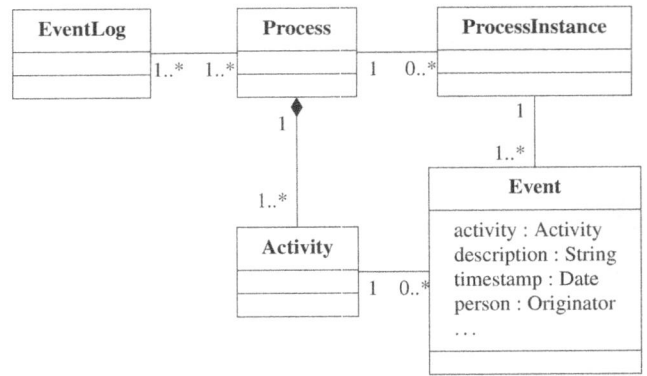

Figure 1. Process mining event log meta model, modified from [9].

Next, the user has to choose the way related events should be associated with each other by means of a *case mapping* and then has to define ways to *extract the events* from the data sources. For instance, one can consider student as a process instance, where the associated events are, e.g., mails sent by the student or file modifications performed by her as recorded in the version control system. Alternatively, one can consider a software component as a process instance, where the associated events are, e.g., bugs or code modifications associated with this component.

Furthermore, FRASR supports *developer matching* definition: indeed, the same student might be using different or multiple user names in different software repositories. Developer matching can be either defined manually by the instructor, or determined using heuristics.

Finally, the combined event log can be exported either as a comma-separated list or in the MXML format, supported by ProM. More information about FRASR can be found in [21].

2.3 Mining with ProM

As opposed to FRASR, ProM does not enforce a well-defined sequence of processing steps. However, it provides the user with more than 170 mining, analysis, monitoring and conversion plugins.

Mining plugins aim at discovering a process model for a given log: e.g., the Alpha algorithm extracts a control flow. Analysis plugins aim at providing insights in correctness or performance of the process reflected in the log. For instance, Dotted Chart Analysis [26] shows a spread of events of an event log over time. Conversion plugins are responsible for transformations between different process model formats, such as BPMN, eEPC and Petri nets, while the monitoring plugins observe the process behavior, detect deviations with respect to the expected behavior, try to diagnose the origin of the problem and to resolve it.

More information about ProM can be found in [10].

---

[1] As process mining terminology was evolving, different papers use different names for notions as process, event, etc. In our choice of names in Figure 1, we follow [21].

3. Capstone project at Eindhoven University of Technology

Capstone software engineering projects have been introduced at Eindhoven University of Technology in 1997/98. Since then hundreds of students have participated in these projects, including the first author. The project aims at familiarization of the students with working in a large nontrivial software project. The capstone projects are carried out by groups of 7–10 third-year undergraduate computer science students developing a software system for real customers. Cooperation with a real customer has been reported to provide the students with an opportunity to increase their occupational identity [17]. Customers involved in capstone project at Eindhoven University of Technology include SMEs and multinationals, research institutions and nonprofit organizations.

During the project the students are assisted by a project manager (a master student), a technical advisor (a member of the academic staff) and the senior management (senior academic staff members). Students are expected to develop a software system following the well-known V software development model and adhering to the guidelines of the European Space Agency [1], i.e., to produce a number of prescribed *management documents*, such as Software Quality Assurance Plan (SQAP), a number of prescribed *product documents*, such as User Requirements Document (URD), a *prototype* and finally an *implementation*. The implementation should be delivered to the customer and accepted/rejected by her based on the original requirements and the corresponding acceptance test plan (ATP).

Every two weeks the project manager and one of the students have an appointment with the senior manager to discuss the project progress, e.g., timeliness of the delivered documents, task distribution balance within the group, adherence of the process followed to the ESA standard and to the V-model. A technical advisor is present during weekly group meetings and provides the group with feedback on the technical quality of the product delivered as well as on adherence of the intermediate product documents to the ESA standard. Should the students fail to meet the expectations of the senior management or of a technical advisor they can decide to intervene and implement a corrective action, e.g., by reassigning the students to different tasks within the group.

Upon the project completion approximately fifteen aspects of the project work are evaluated: the customer evaluates her degree of satisfaction, the technical advisor—quality of the product and of the intermediate product documents, while the senior management assesses the process-related aspects of the project mentioned above. The final grading is done by the senior management.

So far, the only means to verify, e.g., adherence to the ESA standard, required both for the intermediate feedback and for the final assessment, were interviews with the students, project managers and technical advisors augmented by scrutiny of development artifacts submitted by the students. Based on the interviews with the senior management, we have identified three questions to be addressed in this study: prohibition of the prototype reuse, exemplifying adherence of the process followed to the ESA standard, work distribution among the students and adherence to the V-model.

The ESA standard prescribes development of a prototype at the software requirements stage. While prototyping is beneficial when high risk functional, performance or user interface requirements are concerned, it commonly represents only a limited view of the system and often ignores quality, reliability, maintainability and safety requirements. Therefore, the ESA standard explicitly prohibits delivering the prototype as part of an operational system [1]. Hence, the first process-related software engineering question we consider, is *whether the prototype was reused as a part of the final implementation delivered to the customer*.

While software development in the industrial setting usually involves specialized project members, e.g., architects, developers, testers and technical writers, this is not necessarily the case in capstone projects. In fact, one could argue that one of the learning objectives could be that all students should demonstrate their ability to play all aforementioned roles. At Eindhoven University of Technology the decision how each one of the students should contribute to the project is left to the students themselves. Senior management is still, however, interested in obtaining *insights in the work distribution within the group*.

Finally, the students are required to follow a slightly *modified version of the traditional V model*. While in the traditional V model the subsequent software development phase can commence only once the preceding phase has been successfully finished, the modification used for the capstone projects recommends starting the subsequent phase a little bit *before* the deadline of the preceding phase. Senior management motivates this modification by the need to take the students' learning process into account: while experienced engineers are on beforehand aware of the constraints the subsequent phase of the V model imposes on the deliverables of the preceding phase, the students have yet to discover these constraints. If constraints are discovered early enough, i.e., before the completion of the preceding phase, the deliverables of the preceding phase can be easily adapted to meet these constraints. If constraints are, however, discovered once the preceding phase has been completed, any modification of the deliverables would require implementing a change request procedure prescribed by the ESA standard.

Our decision to assess the development process based on software repositories relies on the assumption that all information required for such an assessment is present in the repositories. Validity of the following conclusions can be threatened if this assumption is violated. To ensure the independence of the analysis, it has been carried out by the

Name	Year	#	Customer	Subversion	Additional data sources
I	2005	8	Multinational	2082	none
II	2006	9	SME	1069	none
III	2007	7	Biomedical research institute	1134	none
IV	2008	10	Multinational	2032	234 Trac tickets with 505 modifications/comments, 71 Trac Wiki articles with 178 modifications, 124 mail messages organized in 73 threads
V	2009	7	Nonprofit organization	1574	20 Trac tickets with 51 modifications/comments, 66 Trac Wiki articles with 204 modifications, 204 mail messages organized in 130 threads
VI	2009	8	SME	1553	409 mail messages organized in 218 threads

Table 1. Capstone projects considered

first author supervised by the second author, while detailed information about the projects was available to the third author, who acted as an expert validating the results obtained.

3.1 Projects considered

Table 1 summarizes data of the six capstone projects we consider in our study. For each project we indicate the year when it has been carried out, the number of students involved not including the master student acting as the project manager, type of the customer, number of revisions in the Subversion repository (all projects made use of Subversion repositories) and additional data sources available.

In the remainder of this section we study prototype reuse, developers' roles within the group and adherence to the V-model. For the first study, FRASR had to export data from the software repositories and to create the event log. On a 32bit Windows 7 machine with an Intel Core2 Quad CPU @ 2.40 GHz with 3GB of memory this took between 10 seconds and 4 minutes for the various capstone projects. Since FRASR uses caching, the subsequent studies no longer required exporting data from the repositories, i.e., the existing data had only to be rearranged to create a new log. Time required to rearrange the log was negligibly small.

3.2 Prototype reuse

The ESA standard explicitly prohibits reusing prototype software as a part of the system implementation delivered to the customer: "*Prototypes usually implement high risk functional, performance or user interface requirements and usually ignore quality, reliability, maintainability and safety requirements. Prototype software is therefore 'pre-operational' and should never be delivered as part of an operational system.*" [1]. In order to assess whether the students have followed the ESA prohibition to reuse the prototype as a part of the final implementation, we have considered the information present in the version control system. Each capstone project we have studied had one Subversion repository that contained all files produced for the project. The files contained in the Subversion repository are used as process instances, while the actions performed on them

(addition, modification, deletion and renaming) are used as the events. The developer matching has been constructed manually based on the Software Project Management Plan. The resulting event log has been exported in the MXML format. Next we have imported the log to ProM and using ProM we have filtered out all non-code related files, such as process or product documents. Figure 2 shows the Dotted Chart visualization obtained by ProM for the Project IV data. The files are displayed vertically, sorted by creation time, and colored by 'modification type' (additions are colored blue, modifications—white, deletions—red, and renamings—black). Two distinct triangles can be identified.

Each of those triangles indicates a period in which related files have been modified (added, deleted or renamed). The left triangle ranges from the beginning of the project until halfway the project and the second triangle ranges from halfway the project until the end of the project. As the events in the left triangle end close to the deadline of the software requirements phase, there is an indication that these files belong to the prototype, which should have been developed during this phase [1]. Furthermore, as the prototype files were not modified after the deadline, we see that the prototype files have not been reused during the actual development. It should be noted that one could argue that the final implementation could have been obtained by copying the prototype implementation files to a new folder. This is, however, also not the case in the project on Figure 2: indeed massive file copying would have resulted in a large vertical blue line (similar to the line around 2008-05-20, corresponding to the creation of a development branch).

In four out of five further capstone projects we have analyzed (Table 1), a similar pattern of two triangles has been observed, i.e., these projects conform to the ESA guideline that the prototype may not be reused in the final implementation. These observations were confirmed by the interviews with the group members and project managers. In Project III, however, only one triangle was observed (Figure 3). Presence of one triangle could be interpreted as absence of the prototype, as prototype not being stored in the version control system or as prototype evolving to the final implementa-

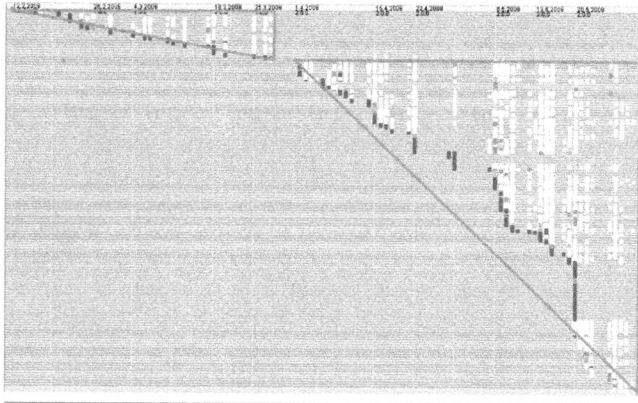

Figure 2. Project IV: the triangle on the top corresponds to the prototype, the triangle on the bottom corresponds to the final implementation.

tion. Since the prototype is supposed to be developed during the software requirements phase, absence of a prototype or prototype being stored outside of the version control system would mean that the triangle should start not earlier than at the architectural design phase. This, however, turned out not to be the case for the student project as the triangle started at the beginning of the project. Hence, in this project the students reused the prototype implementation instead of implementing the functionality from scratch.

Figure 3 suggests, therefore, that should FRASR+ProM have been used during the run of Project III, the senior management or a technical advisor could have intervened in the development process and suggested the students to reconsider the development strategy.

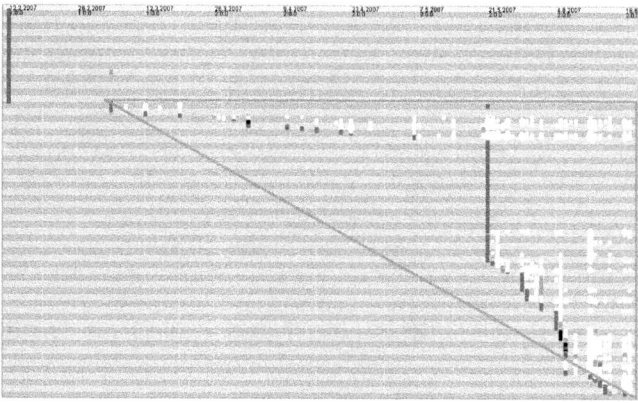

Figure 3. Project III: only one triangle starting at the beginning of the project, i.e., the prototype has been reused in the final implementation.

3.3 Developers' roles

The second question we address pertains to the task distribution balance within a group. Accurate individual assessment of group project participants is a well-known challenge [8, 22]. In this section we study how one can get a

better insight in contributions of individual students using FRASR+ProM. As the case study we have chosen the capstone project with the largest amount of data available, i.e., Project IV. Data sources available for Project IV included the Subversion version control system with 2032 revisions, 234 Trac tickets with 505 modifications/comments, 71 Trac Wiki articles with 178 modifications, and 124 mail messages organized in 73 threads. This project involved eleven students: ten bachelor students acting as software developers and one master student acting as the project manager. While we could have eliminated the project manager *a priori*, we have opted to keep this information as a form of a sanity check. Project manager can be expected to have a very different contribution to the project than the other students, and this role should have been easily identifiable.

In order to check how the work has been developed between the project participants, we have included information from all data sources available. We have categorized all the artifacts such as repository files and mails as being related to one of the documents prescribed by ESA, to the process organization (e.g., meeting minutes), or to the implementation. We no longer distinguish between the prototype and the final implementation. We have also created a separate category "null" for a small number of events that cannot be classified according to the aforementioned categories. From the FRASR perspective the categories are used as process instances, while the actions performed on them (e.g., sending an e-mail) are used as the events. As above, the developer matching has been constructed manually based on the Software Project Management Plan. The resulting event log has been exported in the MXML format and imported to ProM.

For each category and each project member we determine the number of events contributed by the project member to the category. This step has been accomplished by the so called "originator by task" matrix, calculated by ProM and shown in Table 2. Next, for each category we calculate the share of events associated with the specific project member. Based on these shares we have calculated the cosine similarity [25] between the project members, and finally, for each project member we have determined the average similarity with other project members.

The project member most dissimilar to other project members is D (average cosine similarity with other project members is $\simeq 0.0369$). Indeed, the contribution of D is limited to agendas, minutes and Software Project Management Plan. One can conjecture that D was a project manager. This conjecture has indeed been confirmed by the Software Project Management Plan.

The second most dissimilar project member is F (average cosine similarity measure $\simeq 0.0858$). While F contributed to the code, he was the one with the highest share of events pertaining to the Software Verification and Validation Plan and to test plans (ATP, ITP, STP and UTP), i.e., F can be labeled as the "dedicated tester" of the project. We also see that the

Student	Management documents				Req.		Design		Code	Testing plans				Transfer		Process execution				Misc.
	Project Management Plan (SPMP)	Configuration Management Plan (SCMP)	Quality Assurance Plan (SQAP)	Verification and Validation Plan (SVVP)	User Requirements Document (URD)	Software Requirements Document (SRD)	Architectural Design Document (ADD)	Detailed Design Document (DDD)	Code	Unit Testing Plan (UTP)	Integration Testing Plan (ITP)	System Testing Plan (STP)	Acceptance Testing Plan (ATP)	Software Transfer Document (STD)	Software User Manual (SUM)	Agenda	Minutes	Presentation	Process report	null
A	12	2	0	0	5	18	52	0	90	1	0	0	4	1	1	0	13	0	1	4
B	6	11	4	3	25	51	25	2	184	1	0	1	11	5	6	1	28	16	1	21
C	0	0	0	0	9	0	65	1	57	0	0	0	0	0	7	0	0	5	0	10
D	5	0	0	0	0	0	0	0	0	0	0	0	0	0	0	12	1	0	0	4
E	0	0	0	0	1	0	17	1	82	0	0	0	0	0	0	0	0	0	0	8
F	0	0	0	14	1	7	2	0	65	3	3	5	21	6	1	0	0	5	0	8
G	0	0	0	0	10	28	8	5	108	0	0	0	0	0	0	0	0	3	0	8
H	0	0	0	0	1	1	31	6	285	0	0	0	0	2	4	0	0	0	0	14
I	0	0	16	0	8	30	65	2	97	0	0	0	0	9	21	0	0	4	0	25
J	1	23	0	0	11	33	52	2	106	0	0	0	0	7	5	0	0	2	0	4
K	0	0	0	0	1	56	65	6	84	0	0	0	2	1	22	0	3	4	2	34

Table 2. Project IV: activities of different project members. Higher level categories such as "Management documents", "Testing plans" and "Process execution" have been added manually.

developer with the most significant contribution to the implementation is H, who according to the project documents was also responsible for the implementation effort. Furthermore, we see that while all the developers were involved in the architecture design (ADD), the software requirements phase shows a clear distinction between those that have been actively involved (e.g., B and J) and those that have not been (e.g., E and H).

Since one of the aforementioned learning objectives is that all students should demonstrate their ability to play all roles, students focussing on one development role can be considered to be undesirable. As in case of the prototype reuse in Project III (Section 3.2) we observe that should FRASR+ProM have been available during the run of Project IV, the senior management could have considered to intervene and to suggest reassigning student developers to different tasks, e.g., reassigning F to a non-testing task.

3.4 Development model

The prescribed development model for the software engineering projects, is the V development model, in which the phases are executed sequentially. Furthermore, a test plan has to be created for each subsequent phase. As explained above, the capstone projects at Eindhoven University of Technology follow a slightly modified variant of the

V model, allowing a limited overlap between two adjacent phases.

To study the adherence to the modified V model we consider management documents and product documents as process instances. We also introduce a dummy process instance "Code" corresponding to the implementation files: we do not distinguish between the prototype implementation and the final implementation. As events we consider modifications of the corresponding documents, reporting bugs pertaining to them or e-mail communication about them. The developer matching has been constructed manually, using information provided by the software project management plan (prescribed by ESA and available in the Subversion repository). The log obtained with these settings is imported in ProM. Since the management documents do not correspond to a specific development phase of the modified V-model, we filter these process instances and visualize the remaining log using the Dotted Chart visualization. We expect to observe a limited overlap between the series of dots corresponding to adjacent V-model phases.

Figure 4 presents the Dotted Chart visualization obtained for Project IV. For the sake of presentation we have added vertical lines indicating the deadlines stated by the senior management and reflected in the Software Project Management Plan: user requirements phase, software requirements phase, architecture design phase, detailed design and implementation phase, and two acceptance tests. The size of a dot represents the number of events at the corresponding time. As customary in the V-model design phase, documents (e.g., User Requirements Document) are matched with the corresponding test plans (e.g., Acceptance Test Plan). To visualize this matching we use the same color for dots corresponding to the matching documents.

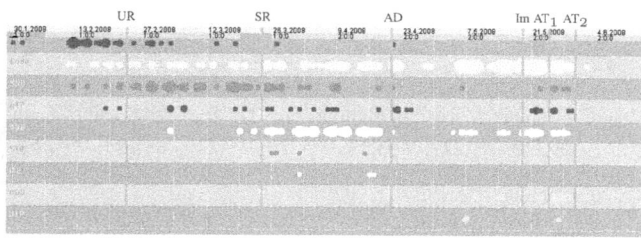

Figure 4. V-model: sequential development with a limited overlap between the phases and early work on the prototype development are clearly visible.

Figure 4 shows a limited overlap between the adjacent phases. However, the activity peaks, visible as constellations of larger dots, indicate sequential development. Furthermore, closer inspection of Figure 4 reveals that not all test plans were developed according to the V-model: for instance, the Acceptance Test Plan should have been created before the deadline of the User Requirements phase, but was developed throughout the entire project. Relatively late events corresponding to the User Requirements Document and Software Requirements Document represent updates of these documents as the result of change requests.

We have repeated this study for five additional software engineering projects listed in Table 1. In Projects I and VI the user requirements and the software requirements phases overlap, in Projects III and V the software requirements and architectural design phases overlap, and in Projects I and V the architectural and detailed design phases overlap. Project II was exceptional since no significant overlap between the phases has been observed. Moreover, in Project III the overlap between the software requirements and architectural design phases covered almost a half of the time allocated for architectural design. If FRASR+ProM chain would have been available at the time, the senior management could have considered an intervention, e.g., to terminate the work on the Software Requirements Document.

4. Related Work

Capstone projects have been extensively studied in the literature on computer science education [5, 13, 19, 30, 31]. While [30] stresses the importance of a software development process in the classroom and [13] assesses the development process while determining the final grade, the only assessment techniques reported in the literature are evaluation of intermediary artifacts and inherently subjective self- and peer evaluations [5, 13, 19].

Quality assessment of software processes has been a subject of an intensive research and standardization effort (see, e.g., [16]). However, even applying software process assessment models adapted for small companies [29] will require unreasonably high assessment effort from the instructor: evaluation durations of one to three weeks are reported in [29]. As an alternative we propose to augment the existing process assessment by mining software repositories.

Repository-based student software development has been studied in [11]. However, when [11] considered only basic commit patterns in individual assignments as registered in one data source (Subversion), our work addresses a much broader spectrum of software engineering questions, data sources and analysis techniques.

Although mining software repositories is an active research area [6, 12, 14], the research achievements have yet to be applied to assess students' performance. When compared to the existing repository mining approaches the added value of the FRASR+ProM combination consists in its versatility: multiple data sources can be efficiently combined in multiple ways to produce a multitude of different event logs (FRASR) that in their turn can be be analyzed by applying a wide palet of successful process mining techniques (ProM).

A complementary group of studies has recently applied process mining techniques in the educational setting [15, 20, 27]. These works, however, focussed on learning aspects independent of the learning subject, such as collaborative writing and assessment by means of on-line tests, while our work specifically targets student software development process in capstone projects. Hence, our work had to address specific challenges absent from the aforementioned studies, such as multiplicity of data sources and ways to identify and group events extracted from these data sources.

Both FRASR and ProM have been subject of earlier publications: [21] and [10], respectively. The focus of this paper is, however, on demonstrating how state-of-the-art repository mining can be applied to support the capstone project assessment, rather than on technical details of the solution.

5. Conclusions

Capstone projects are sometimes considered to be crowning achievements of undergraduate software engineering study, amalgamating the knowledge gained in the preceding courses and superseding them in size, complexity and realness. In this paper we have proposed a novel approach to assessment of the development process component of such projects. The approach borrows from the existing research on mining software repositories and business processes. We have shown that the approach proposed allows the instructor to obtain insights in the development process followed without resorting to self-assessments or peer evaluations.

As *future work* we consider integration of additional software quality assessment tools in preparing intermediate feedback as well as the final evaluation of capstone projects. For instance, while the FRASR+ProM combination can identify separation between the prototype implementation and the final implementation, certain code fragments in the final implementation might have been literally taken from the prototype. To detect this, our approach should be combined with duplication detection techniques [28]. Furthermore, we intend to apply FRASR+ProM to additional projects in the past to create sufficiently large basis for statistical analysis of the way the students carry out the capstone projects. Finally, we plan to conduct a user study, where senior management will be able to give feedback with and without the FRASR+ProM support, and to compare quality of the feedback provided to the students.

References

[1] *ESA Softw. Engineering Standards, ESA PSS-05-0 Issue 2.* February 1991.

[2] Wil M. P. van der Aalst, Hajo A. Reijers, Ton Weijters, Boudewijn F. van Dongen, Aana Karla Alves de Medeiros, Minseok Song, and Eric Verbeek. Business process mining: An industrial application. *Inf. Syst.*, 32(5):713–732, 2007.

[3] ACM and IEEE Computer Society. *Curriculum Guidelines for Undergraduate Degree Programs in Softw. Eng.*, 2004. http://sites.computer.org/ccse/ Visited March 23, 2011.

[4] ACM and IEEE Computer Society. *Computer Science Curriculum 2008: An Interim Revision of CS 2001*, 2008. http://www.acm.org/education/curricula/ComputerScience2008.pdf Visited March 23, 2011.

[5] Nicole Clark, Pamela Davies, and Rebecca Skeers. Self and peer assessment in software engineering projects. In *7th Australasian conference on Computing education*, volume 42 of *ACE '05*, pages 91–100. Australian Computer Society, Inc., 2005.

[6] Davor Čubranić, Gail C. Murphy, Janice Singer, and Kellogg S. Booth. Hipikat: A project memory for software development. *IEEE Trans. Softw. Eng.*, 31(6):446–465, 2005.

[7] Ryan Shaun Joazeiro de Baker, Agathe Merceron, and Philip I. Pavlik, Jr., editors. *Educational Data Mining*, 2010.

[8] Marie Devlin, Sarah Drummond, Chris Philips, and Lindsay Marshall. Improving assessment in software engineering student team projects. In H. White, editor, *9th Annual Conference of the Subject Centre for Information and Computer Sciences*, pages 133–139. Higher Ed. Acad., Subject Centre for ICS, 2008.

[9] Boudewijn F. van Dongen and Wil M. P. van der Aalst. A meta model for process mining data. In *Conf. on Advanced Information Systems Engineering*, volume 161, 2005.

[10] Boudewijn F. van Dongen, Ana Karla Alves de Medeiros, Eric Verbeek, Ton Weijters, and Wil M. P. van der Aalst. The ProM framework: A new era in process mining tool support. In *Int. Conf. on App. and Theory of Petri Nets*, volume 3536 of *Lecture Notes in Computer Science*, pages 444–454. Springer, 2005.

[11] Louis Glassy. Using version control to observe student software development processes. *J. Comp. Small Coll.*, 21:99–106, 2006.

[12] Georigios Gousios and Diomidis Spinellis. Alitheia core: An extensible software quality monitoring platform. *Softw. Eng., Int. Conf. on*, pages 579–582, 2009.

[13] Dennis P. Groth and Matthew P. Hottell. Designing and developing an informatics capstone project course. In *IEEE Conference on Software Engineering Education and Training*, pages 61–68. IEEE, 2006.

[14] Carl Gutwin, Reagan Penner, and Kevin Schneider. Group awareness in distributed software development. In *ACM Conf. on Computer supported cooperative work*, pages 72–81, 2004.

[15] Larry Howard, Julie Johnson, and Carin Neitzel. Examining learner control in a structured inquiry cycle using process mining. In de Baker et al. [7], pages 71–80.

[16] Analia Irigoyen Ferreiro Ferreira, Gleison Santos, Roberta Cerqueira, Mariano Montoni, Ahilton Barreto, Andrea O. Soares Barreto, and Ana Regina Rocha. Applying ISO 9001:2000, MPS.BR and CMMI to achieve software process maturity: BL informatica's pathway. In *IEEE International Conference on Software Engineering*, pages 642–651. IEEE, 2007.

[17] Ville Isomottonen and Tommi Karkkainen. The value of a real customer in a capstone project. In *IEEE Conference on Software Engineering Education and Training*, pages 85–92, april 2008.

[18] Samuel Mann and Lesley Smith. A value proposition model for capstone projects. In *19th Annual Conference of the National Advisory Committee on Computing Qualifications*, pages 175–183. ACM, 2006.

[19] Melody Moore and Colin Potts. Learning by doing: Goals and experiences of two software engineering project courses. In *Softw. Eng. Education*, volume 750 of *Lecture Notes in Computer Science*, pages 151–164. Springer, 1994.

[20] Mykola Pechenizkiy, Nikola Trcka, Ekaterina Vasilyeva, Wil M. P. van der Aalst, and Paul De Bra. Process mining online assessment data. In Tiffany Barnes, Michel C. Desmarais, Cristóbal Romero, and Sebastián Ventura, editors, *Educational Data Mining*, pages 279–288, 2009.

[21] Wouter Poncin, Alexander Serebrenik, and M. G. J. van den Brand. Process mining software repositories. In *European Conf. on Softw. Maintenance and Reeng.*, pages 7–15. IEEE, 2011.

[22] Clive C. H. Rosen. Individual assessment of group projects in software engineering: a facilitated peer assessment approach. In *Conf. on Softw. Eng. Education*, pages 68–77, April 1996.

[23] Anne Rozinat, Ivo S. M. de Jong, Christian W. Günther, and Wil M. P. van der Aalst. Process mining applied to the test process of wafer scanners in ASML. *Trans. Sys. Man Cyber Part C*, 39(4):474–479, 2009.

[24] Vladimir Rubin, Christian W. Günther, Wil M. P. van der Aalst, Ekkart Kindler, Boudewijn F. van Dongen, and Wilhelm Schäfer. Process mining framework for software pro-

cesses. In *Softw. Process Dynamics and Agility*, volume 4470 of *Lecture Notes in Computer Science*, pages 169–181. Springer, 2007.

[25] Gerard Salton and Michael J. McGill. *Introduction to Modern Information Retrieval*. McGraw-Hill, USA, 1986.

[26] Minseok Song and Wil M. P. van der Aalst. Supporting process mining by showing events at a glance. In *Workshop on Information Technologies and Systems*, pages 139–145, 2007.

[27] Vilaythong Southavilay, Kalina Yacef, and Rafael A. Calvo. Process mining to support students' collaborative writing. In de Baker et al. [7], pages 257–266.

[28] Rebecca Tiarks, Rainer Koschke, and Raimar Falke. An assessment of type-3 clones as detected by state-of-the-art tools. In *SCAM*, pages 67–76, 2009.

[29] Sylvie Trudel, Jean-Marc Lavoie, Marie-Claude Paré, and Witold Suryn. PEM: The small company-dedicated software process quality evaluation method combining CMMI^{SM} and ISO/IEC 14598. *Software Quality Journal*, 14:7–23, 2006.

[30] David A. Umphress, T. Dean Hendrix, and James H. Cross. Software process in the classroom: The capstone project experience. *IEEE Software*, 19(5):78–81, 2002.

[31] Hadar Ziv and Sameer Patil. Capstone project: From software engineering to informatics. In *IEEE Conference on Software Engineering Education and Training*, pages 185–188. IEEE, mar 2010.

SPLASH 2011 Experience Reports

Welcome to the SPLASH 2011 Experience Reports track. We think you'll be glad you came.

Experience reports are all about how we create practical software systems that solve real-world problems. Each paper presented here is based on production software in use by real customers. These are systems that have had to face up to the brutal reality of everyday use. My grandfather used to tell me, "Deep learning happens in deep trenches. You dug yourself in, you gotta dig yourself out." These papers are your chance to learn how to avoid the trenches in the first place. Listen to our stories and, hopefully, adapt them to your own environments.

This year we have three sessions that we believe offer something for everybody. The presentations in *"Being a Team"* discuss how the authors were able to effectively find ways to be more productive in working with various groups. Teams have large scope these days. Many are geographically dispersed over large areas. Some are highly focused, consisting of a small group of tight-knit developers. And all have to work within larger teams, composed of members of the organization not traditionally considered part of a development team.

"Making Frameworks" is the coding session. These authors provide you with tips you can take home and apply directly to what you build. Engineering is at best a tricky process, a mixture of both art and science. As practicing developers we know this to be true but don't always get to exercise all aspects of our craft. Come and learn some new insights.

Finally, *"Getting Down to the Bone"*. These papers present glimpses into systems you will be using in the future. Practical for those that need them now. Informative for us all. No rarified atmosphere of pure code for these guys!

And please remember that a large part of Experience is Participation. These authors have submitted their papers because of a desire to share. Actively participate in the Q&A. Hang around afterwards for more penetrating discussion. Then come back next year with your own deep trench learning and tell us how you dug yourself out!

Tim O'Connor
SPLASH 2011 Experience Reports Chair
K12, Inc.

Harnessing Collective Software Development

Luis Artola

Digital Domain
Venice, California, USA
la@luisartola.com

Abstract

Python has become established as the *de facto* scripting language in many industries including the post-production of visual effects. Its shallow learning curve enables a wider range of individuals to produce code much more quickly than before. This often leads to increased code duplication, competing tools and increased maintenance costs. This talk presents an attempt to harness all that coding power in a fast-paced production environment with the intention of increasing code reuse, reducing maintenance costs and improving the quality of the development process and the code itself. It describes philosophy, tools, techniques and challenges of harnessing collective software development in the pursuit of better software.

Categories and Subject Descriptors D.1.0 [*Programming Techniques*]: General; D.2.1 [*Software Engineering*]: Requirements / Specifications—Methodologies; D.2.2 [*Software Engineering*]: Design Tools and Techniques—Modules and interfaces; D.2.3 [*Software Engineering*]: Coding Tools and Techniques—Top-down programming; D.2.8 [*Software Engineering*]: Metrics—Process metrics; D.2.9 [*Software Engineering*]: Management—Cost estimation; D.2.13 [*Software Engineering*]: Reusable Software—Reuse models

General Terms Design, Documentation, Experimentation, Languages, Management, Measurement, Standardization.

Keywords Object-oriented Programming, Procedural Programming, Software Development Methologies, Software Process, Python.

1. Introduction

Collective Software Development takes place in environments where there are multiple simultaneous projects that require development of software tools. Each project has its own team of developers ready to quickly produce code to keep up with demaning schedules. The focus of a project is not the production of software *per se*, but support software is essential for the end result.

Each project has very similar needs, but time pressure tends to inhibit communication and code sharing amongst developers working on similar tools and scripts. This inevitably leads to code duplication and the proliferation of competing similar tools at the end of a few projects. The cost of maintenance and training increases as well. And, the amount of code that is eventually thrown away can be substantial.

Collective development is not the same as collaborative development. The former is normally done by a group that is not working in concert. The latter implies some level of communication and sharing.

The production of visual effects is a perfect example of such environments with an additional twist. Python is widely used in the industry to create supporting software and extend applications. Its ease of use enables people with little or no formal education in software engineering to produce code [4]. This usually results in code that is not easily reusable or maintainable, and is poorly documented.

This paper describes an approach to:

- Bridge the gap from collective to collaborative.
- Add structure to an otherwise disorganized development [6].
- Facilitate capturing and communicating knowledge across time and developers [3].
- Increase code reuse.

2. Methodology

2.1 Traditional scripting

Let's illustrate concepts and approach using an example.

The script in Figure 1 shows what a developer would typically write using only Python to solve a specific problem in production. The code performs a series of steps for taking some digital elements, validating, exporting different file formats, registering files in production tracking systems and cleaning up.

```
def publish():
  elements = getSelectedElements()
  validate()
  paths = getFilePaths()
  exportAnimation( elements, paths )
  exportGeometry( elements, paths )
  exportBoundingBoxes( elements, paths )
  exportThumbnails( elements, paths )
  registerFiles( paths )
  cleanUp()
```

Figure 1. publish.py: A traditional Python script.

There is nothing fundamentally wrong with this approach. But, the reality is that code is never written in a way that lends itself for easy reuse, especially not under time pressure. It is normally a highly cohesive mix of user interface, business logic and data transformation that is not easily modularized. This matters because at the same time a specific department in the production pipeline needs tasks like this to be coded and automated, there are people in other departments with similar needs.

2.2 Dividing and organizing code

This can be improved by following some basic principles to add structure and policies to the code:

1. Programs are **static descriptions** of what needs to happen, instead of actual code that only programmers can read and understand.

2. Every step in that program is **an individual module** that performs one and only one well defined operation, instead of a function in a larger piece of code [5].

3. **Data is separated from logic** and is planned, well-defined and predictable.

A program becomes a tree of connected modules that transform data [4, 5]. We refer to this as the *workflow* approach.

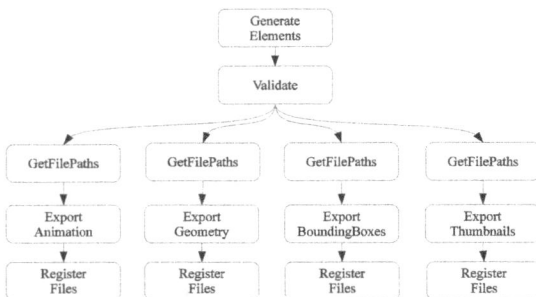

Figure 2. Workflow: A tree of connected modules

Figure 2 represents an alternative structure functionally equivalent to the script in Figure 1. The diagram shows the following elements:

Workflow Static description of connected actions. The entire tree.

Process Sequence of actions in a workflow. Each branch or subtree.

Action A discrete operation on application-specific data. Each node.

```xml
<?xml version="1.0"?>
<workflow>
  <process name="main">
    <action module="GenerateElements"/>
    <action module="Validate"/>
    <process name="ExportAnimation">
      <action module="GetFilePaths"/>
      <action module="ExportAnimation"/>
      <action module="RegisterFiles"/>
    </process>
    <process name="ExportGeometry">
      <action module="GetFilePaths"/>
      <action module="ExportGeometry"/>
      <action module="RegisterFiles"/>
    </process>
    <process name="ExportBoundingBoxes">
      <action module="GetFilePaths"/>
      <action module="ExportBoundingBoxes"/>
      <action module="RegisterFiles"/>
    </process>
    <process name="ExportThumbnails">
      <action module="GetFilePaths"/>
      <action module="ExportThumbnails"/>
      <action module="RegisterFiles"/>
    </process>
  </process>
</workflow>
```

Figure 3. Publish.xml: Workflow equivalent of publish.py

```python
class ExportAnimation( Action ):
  def run( self, data ):
    for element in data[ 'elements' ]:
      # export animation from element
    return data
```

Figure 4. ExportAnimation.py: Python module containing an action.

The workflow in Figure 2 is implemented with the following files:

• Workflow: An XML file that describes the operations to be performed (Figure 3.)

  ▪ Publish.xml

- Actions: A Python module per operation that contains a single Action class. (Figure 4 shows an example action.)
  - GenerateElements.py
  - Validate.py
  - GetFilePaths.py
  - ExportAnimation.py
  - ExportGeometry.py
  - ExportBoundingBoxes.py
  - ExportThumbnails.py
  - RegisterFiles.py

The actual separation of the initial Python script into multiple files can appear as overhead at first glance. However, the code that was originally written as functions inside a monolithic script is now packaged individually in smaller modules. The main function was replaced by an XML description. In terms of lines of code, the overhead is not significant [6]. And, the many benefits that will be explained shortly more than compensate for the added structure.

Even at this early stage, Figure 3 shows evidence of how smaller modules have now better chances of being reused. For example, the `GetFilePaths` and `RegisterFiles` actions are reused four times in the same workflow. And, since it is a standalone module with a very simple and well-defined interface, it has a higher probability of being reused in other workflows.

2.3 Static descriptions and XML

Having a workflow be a static description encoded in XML was somewhat controversial at the beginning. However, it provides many advantages, let's elaborate on some of them:

1. A static description is a contract, not only for the developer and ultimately the programming language, but also enables other, non-programmers and less techical stakeholders to get closer to understanding what a particular workflow in production does.

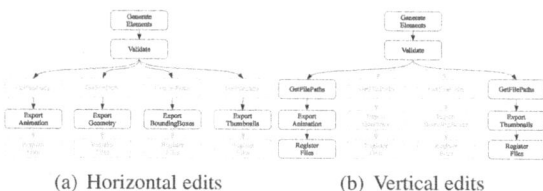

(a) Horizontal edits   (b) Vertical edits

Figure 5. Workflow variations

2. Because the description is expressed in XML, making changes, adapting or quickly responding to changes in production due to external factors becomes *a configuration problem, not a programming task*. Examples include changes in the back-end, temporary disruption of certain services, etc. that should not require modifying the code.

This is particularly valuable in fast-paced production environments where the response time is often times critical. Figure 5 shows variations of the workflow in Figure 2 to disable certain aspects of the workflow by simply removing select actions or entire processes.

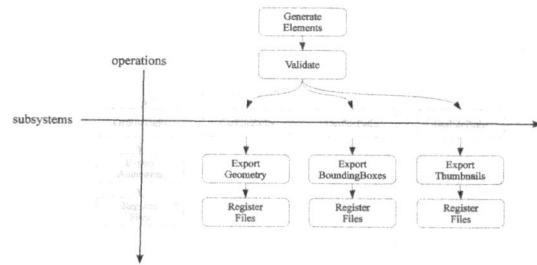

Figure 6. Workflow variations

3. An interesting property discovered after analyzing changes to workflows over time is that vertical edits normally translate to disabling the generation or transformation of certain data that was useful in some projects, but not in others. Horizontal edits normally translate in disabling or changing interaction with support systems. See Figure 6

4. Another important benefit of using XML is that the description of what a program would do becomes a service for a number of consumers. The primary consumer is of course the framework that executes the Python code that is referenced in the XML. But, because actions are very application-specific, XML enables the ability to gather statistics, extracting documentation from modules, etc. *without* having to actually run a live Python session to import modules. In the majority of cases an approach like this would be impractical as many actions would not have all the application-specific Python modules they need to even be imported in the first place.

2.4 Overriding code

Dividing code in workflows and actions is a hybrid of two programming approaches. Workflows are akin to procedural programming albeit at a higher level. Actions are still coded using object-oriented programming. One of the benefits of object-oriented programming is the ability to specialize code and override specific functionality to adapt to the needs of a specific project. Normally, this is accomplished using inheritance. And this is still true for individual actions at the implementation level. The question is how to provide a similar mechanism at the modular level used in the worklfow specification.

There is a simple solution. Use the file system to provide different locations where workflows and actions can be installed. Locations have precedence. When executing a workflow, actions are searched in those locations starting from the one that is *closer* to the user environment. To explain how this is determined, let's look at locations first. There can be four locations on disk for installing workflows and actions:

1. framework

2. shared

3. project

4. user

While it is possible to add an arbitrary number of levels, more than four are not practical in real world use. These levels provide automatic overriding for both workflows and actions. The framework that executes workflows reads the XML and locates actions based on the user environment. The *user* level is closer to the user, *framework* is farther way.

The level to use can be part of the environment, where the tools indicate what is the closest level for that particular execution.

This setup has some interesting properties:

The closer actions and workflows get to the *framework* level, the more stable they are. But, also the harder it is to make changes because they affect many other workflows.

Likewise, the closer they get to the *user* level, the less stable they are. However, the easier it is to make changes and do faster prototyping.

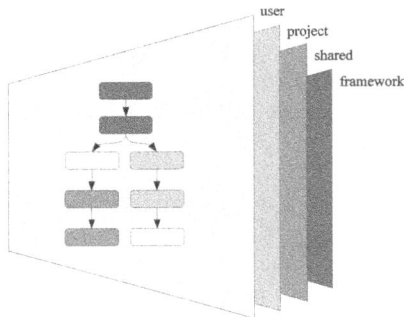

Figure 7. Overriding actions selectively

These levels can be visualized in Figure 7. Because actions and workflows can live at any given level, looking at a workflow definition is like looking through a series of translucent windows. A workflow is a projection of actions from different overriding levels.

Overriding is possible at a very granular level. This flexibility makes it also possible to quickly debug and diagnose problems at specific points in the process. For example, there are situations where a given workflow installed at the project level is failing in a particular action. A developer would simply copy that action to the *user* level and make changes, set breakpoints, etc. for easier troubleshooting.

2.5 Executing workflows

Traditional Python scripts control their internal data structures and can be executed directly from a command interpreter. Workflows on the other hand need a supporting framework for execution. The framework can be very nimble though, at the bare minimum it simply parses the XML file, locates and imports Python modules representing each individual action, and executes them one at a time sequentially passing data from one to another.

Actions are free to modify, append and destroy the data that is flowing through as needed. `Action` is the base class for all actions and has an extremely simplified interface. The only thing required is a method with the following signature: `def run( self, data )`.

Leveraging the highly-dynamic nature of Python when it comes to data types, `data` can be anything and can be transformed [4] as it flows down from action to action. Defining data structures that are simple to understand is one of the most challenging aspects of writing reusable actions. In our experience, all the workflows used a plain dictionary.

The following is a contrived example but representative of real use. Error checking and obvious import statements are intentionally omitted to illustrate how data flows downstream and is used and transformed by each action in turn.

```xml
<?xml version="1.0"?>
<workflow>
  <process name="main">
    <action module="GetElements"/>
    <action module="CreateDirectories"/>
    <action module="WriteContents"/>
  </process>
</workflow>
```

Figure 8. example.wam

```python
class GetElements( Action ):
  def run( self, data ):
    data[ 'elements' ] = [
      dict( name='house' ),
      dict( name='car' ),
      dict( name='trees' ),
    ]
    return data
```

Figure 9. GetElements.py

```python
def CreateDirectories( Action ):
  def run( self, data ):
    for element in data[ 'elements' ]:
      directory = '/elements/' + element.name
      element[ 'directory' ] = directory
      os.mkdir( directory )
    return data
```

Figure 10. CreateDirectories.py

```
class WriteContents( Action ):
  def run( self, data ):
    for element in data[ 'elements' ]:
      file_name = \
        element.directory + '/contents.txt'
      output = open( file_name, 'w' )
      output.write( element.name )
      output.close()
    return data
```

Figure 11. WriteContents.py

The workflow in Figure 8 illustrates how three actions work in concert to create files on disk. The GetElements action listed in Figure 9 gets executed first and seeds the data dictionary with three elements represented by simple dictionaries containing their names. In a real world scenario, an action like this would pull data from a database of some sort, e.g. an asset management or production tracking system.

The data returned by this action is then passed on to the CreateDirectories action listed in Figure 10. This action demonstrates how to use data coming into the action and modifying it for further use downstream. It uses the name key of each element in the elements list to build a directory path on disk. The directory is created and added as a directory key to each element dictionary.

The data is once more passed along to the third action listed in Figure 11, WriteContents. This action iterates over the elements using their name and directory keys to write a simple text file on disk for each element.

The beauty of separating data and logic this way is that other workflows can easily reuse, for example, the CreateDirectories action. The only thing there is to know about that action is that it requires a dictionary-like object to be passed in as the data argument. It also expects data['elements'] to be a list of dictionary-like objects that provide access to a name key. Therefore, there exist implicit connections between modules based on the assumptions they make on each other [5].

This methodology does not enforce any specific data structure to be used in actions. However, the simpler and better documented the data structures and the data that each individual action requires, the easier it would be to reuse them.

3. Metrics, Analysis and Benefits

3.1 Enabling collaboration

This methodology was used in multiple ocassions to scope out a particular problem to solve in production, devise a plan of attack, arrange and connect all the pieces of functionality that would need to be executed, divide the work and have multiple developers simultaneously code portions of

the workflow much faster and with less interdependencies than traditional scripting.

Besides making better use of coding resources simultaneously, it also improves collaboration amongst developers in sucession over time. This is possible because workflows are modular by definition, every developer new to a workflow can contribute more easily because actions are very targeted.

To illustrate this point, a great practical example in our experience was the creation of a workflow to automate the preparation, packaging and delivery of digital assets and related data to outsourcing vendors. From a high level perspective, the problem required coding in the following domains:

- Filtering and coverting elements to make sure that no proprietary elements found their way outside the facility. This required a developer with intimate knowledge of the mayor artistic applications and tools used in production.

- Extracting SQL records from various back-end systems in a way that could be easily processed on another database cluster. This required a developer with database experience.

- Packaging, transferring and bookkeeping in various production tracking systems. This required a developer with knowledge of file system, online file distribution and production tracking systems.

It is easier to find three different developers with experience in one of these areas each than it is to find a single developer that masters them all. This is where enforcing modularity and separation of data from logic really stands out. In this particular case, the workflow was planned to be divided in three sections. Each developer added the necessary actions to the section they owned. This happened incrementally with no impact to other actions in the workflow.

The only thing that developers needed to agree on beforehand was the type and contents of the data that needed to flow from one action to another. In this example the data was decided to be a plain dictionary with the following keys:

- elements: A list of instances of an Element class that had well-known attributes to identify a digital asset tracked in our asset management systems. The absolute minimal was the unique ID.

- source: Name of the facility originating the package.

- destination: Name of the facility receiving the package.

- location: Full-path to the directory where all the actions in the workflow were to write relevant data related to the list of elements.

Besides having better utilization of coding resources and their expertise, it facilitated incremental development and more agile development and test iterations.

After this was implemented, the volume of data that was processed by this workflow grew very rapidly and performance started to suffer. Profiling this code to gather timing statistics and narrowing down the bottleneck was a very straightforward approach if not trivial thanks to its modular implementation.

More importantly, with performance data in hand, it was possible to bring programmers and non-programmers alike to the table in the same room to analyze it in the context of the workflow description. It was discovered that packaging all the files from disk was the action that took the longest depending on the number of elements to process. The solution was to simply remove that one action from the workflow and creating a new workflow with just that one action to execute as a secondary step. This proved that fixing problems and adpating to unforseen issues can be solved as a *configuration* change, not a *programming* task.

3.2 Code reuse

One of the motivations for this methodology was code reuse. After a year of development applying it in various projects we measured how well it fared. The following table shows the number of workflows an actions written for various projects:

Level	Workflows	Actions
shared	94	216
project 1	340	560
project 2	158	264
project 3	94	127
project 4	108	209

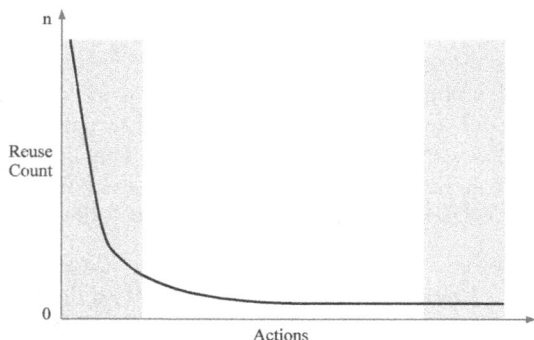

Figure 12. Action reuse pattern

Measuring code reuse required parsing workflows and gathering statistics about what actions were being reused, by which workflows and how often. After normalizing and graphing usage counts, the first intersting discovery was that every project exhibited exactly the same usage pattern: an inverse exponetial as illustrated in Figure 12.

Actions reused the most are on the left and reuse count decreases rapidly as we move on the horizontal axis towards the right. Further scrutiny revealed some interesting properties of this usage pattern. Reuse can be divided in three sections.

The left-most section is a range of high reuse counts. It is not uncommon to find actions reused over 50 times or even 100 times or more by many different workflows. Actions in this range are clearly reusable and should be protected and embraced as the official solution for the particular tasks they solve.

The middle section contains a range of reuse counts that is high enough to indicate that they have some value for a number of workflows, but not high enough to be considered widely useful for a variety of tasks. Actions in this range normally turned out to be very specific to a particular domain in production. One reason could be that the process was only applicable to a very particular artistic need in a project, not easily transferrable to others. Another reason was that such actions were a competing solution to similar other actions that turned out to be favored by other developers and yielded higher reuse - this phenomenon resembles natural selection in software development.

The right-most section is a range of extremely low reuse counts. Normally, there is a tail of actions that only achieve a reuse count of 1. The first impression is that such actions are probably just one-offs that could hardly be reused or not worth trying to. While that was true in some cases, another interesting discovering was that actions in this group turned out to be the one and only way of solving a very particular problem. These actions were prime candidates for protection to prevent competing solutions from sprouting to avoid duplicated efforts and wasted development resources.

Code reuse then is more easily identified with this methodology and it is characterized by those actions within the highest and the lowest reuse count ranges. Considering the lowest count as reusable becomes less counterintuitive by understanding that code reuse has two sides:

- Code that is reused many times by developers in other programs.

- Code that is written once and used many times by different users, as opposed to allowing competing solutions to appear over time instead of maintaining and extending the existing solution.

3.3 Code maturity vs. branching

Once the most reusable actions are identified, the challenge is making sure that they are protected and promoted to a higher level in the hierarchy of modular overriding. That is, moving actions vertically from the *project* level to *shared* and ultimately to the *framework* level. Code maturity can be measured by the transition of any given action to higher levels.

Code maturity is a worthy goal, but in practice, as new projects get started, copy-and-paste is by far the most common form of code reuse. Rather than having code percolate to higher levels, it replicates horizontally to the domain of other projects. Code branching happens on every copy leading eventually to multiple variations of the same action. Over time, it becomes more difficult to keep track and reconcile code differences.

There are many reasons why branching is favored over maturity. It is easier to copy and adapt as needed than it is to spend the time and effort in cleaning up, generalizing and promoting existing code to higher levels so that they can be more widely reused. Time pressure is certainly the number one cause. Human aspects also play an important role. For example, the lack of interest in contributing to build good code legacy. Or, simply avoiding the responsibility inherent to making sure an action promoted to a higher level not only works for the new intended uses, but that it does not break existing workflows depending on it.

While this methodology facilitates code maturity and encourages it, it does not prevent code branching. However, it makes it more manageable. Because workflows can be parsed, it is easy to further analyze the actions they use and perform side by side comparisons with similar code from different projects.

3.4 Breeding grounds

This methodology is particulary suitable for breeding new ideas in faster code-test-retrofit cycles by leveraging the hierarchical module overriding levels. Complete applications can be coded in a modular way with a collection of workflows and actions. The maturity path normally goes from the *user* level to the *project* level. Once the feature set reaches a milestone, workflows can be parsed to locate all of the dependent actions and code can be physically carved out or copied from the different levels into self-contained packages.

3.5 Abstracting process execution.

A wide variety of domain-specific applications used in production come bundled with an embedded Python interpreter for providing scripting support. Applications for modeling, texturing, animation, effects, compositing, lighting, etc. It is very common for tools used in production to have to run certain portions of code within the context of a very specific interpreter. For example, the conversion of a geometry file from one format to another by scripting some commands of a modeling tool.

The `<process/>` tag can be extended with an attribute to indicate what kind of interpreter to use when executing the actions inside it. The framework can handle all the technicalities of executing a subprocess within the context of the given application. For example `<process interpreter="maya"/>`[1].

4. Tool set.

This methodology can be implemented with a simple framework that imposes minimal overhead, both in code footprint

---

[1] Maya is an application commonly used in the Visual Effects industry for various departments including modeling and animation.

and execution time. A minimalistic implementation requires three components:

1. A Python API that provides simple classes that represent the action tree described in XML.

2. A custom Python module importer that can locate modules by name using relative paths that can be found paying attention to the mulitple overriding levels on disk.

3. Optionally, a command-line interface for executing worflows directly from a shell and other utilities.

4.1 Python API

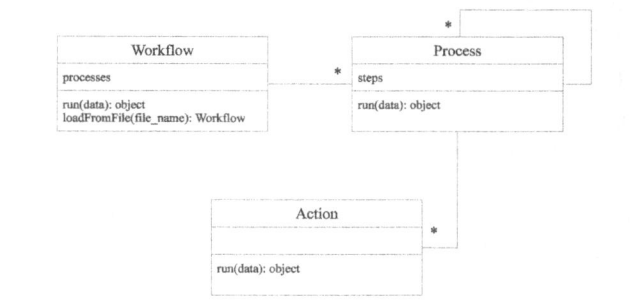

Figure 13. Minimal core components.

Figure 13 shows the minimal core classes required to represent and execute a tree of connected actions described in an XML workflow. `Workflow`, `Process` and `Action` provide an extremely simple interface to execute them by calling `run(data)`, passing along some data from step to step and returning the modified data.

`Workflow.loadFromFile` is a factory method that locates an XML on disk using the overriding levels on disk, parses it and constructs a tree of instances of the core classes. The actual modules that represent each action can be lazily imported and instantiated.

4.2 Module importer

A custom module importer is required for two main reasons.

The first one is that modules can be overriden using the various overriding levels described in section 2.4. The importer would append a relative path to all entries in the system path and try to locate and import the module.

Second, the nature of Python packages does not allow overriding subpackages and submodules of a package that exists in multiple overriding levels. Because folders in the file system are used broadly to classify actions per subsystem, the custom importer locates modules in different relative paths.

4.3 Optional command-line interface.

A very simple interface with commands and subcommands can be optionally written to execute workflows directly from a shell; copy all modules depending on a worflow, inspect, etc. The interface looks something like this:

- `workflow run`: Executes a workflow.

- `workflow stats`: Gathers statistics about action usage, code reuse, etc.

- `workflow diff`: Compares two workflows and their actions side by side.

5. Visualizing code development and evolution.

Every single module used by workflows is stored in its own file and tracked individually in a source control system. This presents very interesting opportunities to have a better insight on various aspects of software development for leaders, managers and software developers alike.

5.1 Statistics

All the action modules were broadly classified in folders named after the subsystem or application they were intended for, e.g. asset management, production tracking, Maya, Houdini[2], Nuke[3], utilities, etc. The following table shows statistics gathered from the Maya folder:

Metric	Value
First checkin	8/25/2009
Last checkin	11/09/2010
Active development time (months)	14.5
Number of files	103
Lines of code (LOC)	15,545
Developers	12
Average LOC per file	150
Average LOC per developer	1,295
Total check-ins	580
Average LOC per check-in	26
Average check-ins per developer	48

An average of 150 lines of code per file turned out to be very reasonable in practice. This is a good indicator that each action module for this system is performing one particular task, as it was intended by design.

Statistics like this can be gathered for all subsystems and plotted in a regular bar chart for comparison. At a glance, such simple graphs and statistics can help answer questions such as: How much effort is really going into extending or supporting any given subsystem? How much developer time is involved? Is more than one developer maintaining the same actions? Are development resources properly utilized? What is the cost of all this development?

5.2 Dependencies and patterns.

Workflows can also be used to detect and visualize dependencies amongst workflows based on what actions are reused and how. Figure 14 shows an extremely small sample of

[2] Houdini is an application used for various three-dimensional visual effects.

[3] Nuke is a high-end non-linear compositing application.

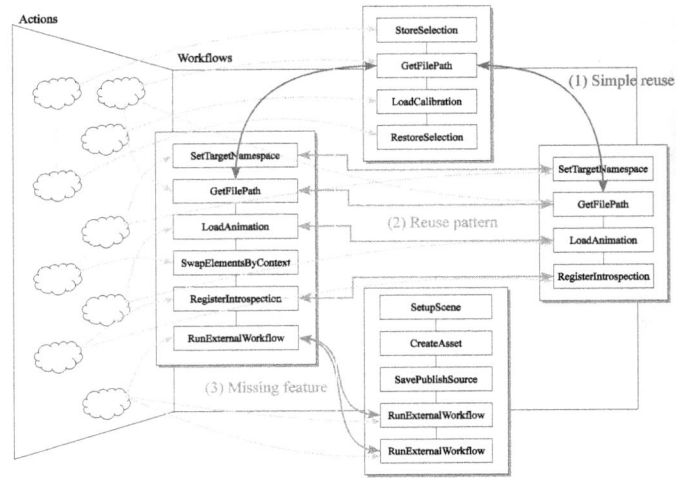

Figure 14. Module reuse, dependencies and common patterns in complex systems.

workflows and the names of their actions. This is remarkably close to the representation of the canonical form of a complex system [1].

Arrows indicate actions that are reused in other workflows. They denote a *reuse dependency* between otherwise independent workflows. There are also three types of dependencies worth noting in Figure 14:

1. Simple action reuse. Provides an indication of what workflows share code without any other specific relationship.

2. Some times, there is a group of actions that appears in exactly or almost exactly the same sequence in other workflows. Cases like this can be refactored to have one workflow simply including the definition of another workflow. As opposed to duplicating the same block of actions from workflow to workflow.

3. Some actions like `RunExternalWorkflow` are normally an indication of some functionality that should be provided natively by the implementation framework. In this particular case, by declaring the exeuction of a block of actions in a detached process execution.

5.3 Code evolution

By inspecting the revision logs of each individual action module in a workflow, it is possible to visualize code evolution in the XML itself and action modules over time.

Figure 15 shows one of the most recent check-ins for a particular workflow. In the upper side, there is time slider that allows to scrub in time from the first check-in to the last. At the chosen time in the slider, each action is represented by a white rectangle that has the following information: its name; a blue progress bar providing a sense as to how quickly the action is maturing and stabilizing; and, a list of

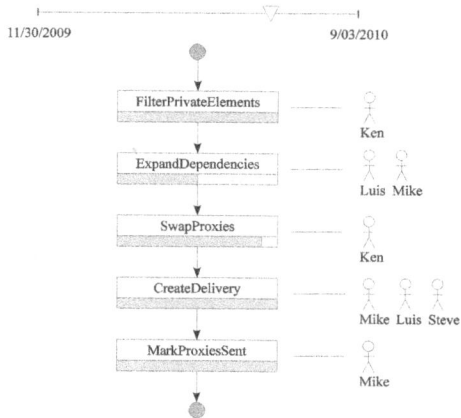

Figure 15. Code evolution time lapse. Later revision.

developers to the right of each action that have performed some modification to it in a previous check-in.

6. Conclusion

Writing code that is simple to understand, reusable and easy to maintain is challenging for individuals, let alone for multiple programmers developing collectively. Time pressure is the most common reason for cutting corners and producing code that is more cohesive than modular.

The workflow approach provides simple guidelines to facilitate writing modular code that separates data from logic to increase the chance of code reuse. This also adds structure that make programs self-documenting.

Additional benefits include the ability to monitor code reuse and patterns at any given time. Highly reusable actions can be identified, improved and promoted to higher levels of visibility in the framework. Code maturity can also be quantified as the amount of code that is promoted to higher levels. And, compared against the amount of code that is reused by branching on copy.

It is easy to keep track of the evolution of each individual module over time by relying on a source control system. The modification logs and people associated with them for every single module can be correlated with other actions in the various workflows to gain interesting insights on development, developer behavior and patterns. The possibilities of data mining are great from a managerial perspective to help better understand how the development effort and resources are begin spent in reality.

Acknowledgments

I would like to thank Brandon Ashworth, Chip Collier, Michael Irani and Mylène Pepe for their contributions to the implementation of the internal framework that enables this software development methodology in various areas of the production pipeline at Digital Domain. Craig Zerouni and Gregory Stoner for their support throughout this project. Jonathan Gerber and Steve Galle for their support in adopting these ideas in a major production. Mattias Bergbom, John Cooper, Amanda Hampton, Takashi Kuribayashi, Michael Morehouse, Antony Serenil, Blake Sloan, Geoff Wedig and many other developers who contributed invaluable feedback by using these ideas, methodology and framework to solve a wide variety of real problems in production. Doug Roble for his advice in preparing this paper. Many thanks to all of you.

References

[1] Grady Booch. Object-oriented Analysis and Design with Applications. Addison-Wesley. Second Edition.1994. pp. 14, 42.

[2] Robert Glass. Facts and Fallacies of Software Engineering, Addison Wesley, 2003, pg 120.

[3] Donald Knuth. "Literate Programming (1984)" in Literate Programming. CSLI, 1992, pg. 99.

[4] Barbara Liskov. OOPSLA Keynote: The Power of Abstraction. Dec 23, 2009 http://www.infoq.com/presentations/liskov-power-of-abstraction.

[5] D.L. Parnas. Information Distribution Aspects of Design Methodology. IFIP Congress, 1971.

[6] Bjarne Stroustrup. The C++ Programming Language, Addison Wesley, 2000, pp. 694, 695.

Virtual Machines with Sharable Operating System

Trieu C. Chieu

IBM T. J. Watson Research Center
19 Skyline Drive
Hawthorne, NY, USA
Email: tchieu@us.ibm.com

Hoi Chan

IBM T. J. Watson Research Center
19 Skyline Drive
Hawthorne, NY, USA
Email: hychan@us.ibm.com

Abstract

Virtualization technologies commonly known as Cloud model enable the execution of multiple virtual machine instances (VMs) with different operating systems (OSs) on the same physical host. Each VM instance functions independently as an isolated system with its own physical resources, OS copy and applications. There is only a limited number of currently available and widely used OSs used by most of the running VM instances; it is wasteful to store all the VM images with virtually the same common OS code. It is also inefficient in terms of performance and system resources utilization to virtually clone the entire image each time a new VM instance is provisioned. In addition, performing OS updates and patches are complicated, tedious and error prone since not only the stored images need to be updated, all the running VM instances must be properly refreshed. More importantly, faster provisioning of VM instances in respond to workload changes is critical to the successful operation of Cloud service providers. In this paper, we show our exploration work to address these performance issues by using a common, sharable operating system approach which provides run-time on-demand operating system components to individual VM instances in Cloud environment. This new approach allows optimized VM image storage, faster VM provisioning and efficient OS updates with minimum interruption.

Categories and Subject Descriptors D.2.13 [**SOFT-WARE ENGINEERING**]: Reusable Software – Reuse models, Reusable software, Rapid prototyping

General Terms Performance, Design, Experimentation, Verification

Keywords Cloud; Virtual machine; Patching; Virtualization; Operating system

1. Introduction

With the widespread adaptation of virtualization technologies and Cloud Computing [1,2,3] services and as Cloud service providers [4] expand in size, the number of VM images, VM instances and physical hosts increases substantially, with resources scattering across multiple locations and even continents [5]. Fast and responsive VM instance provisioning [6], optimal image storage [7] and efficient software updates and patches [8, 9] are the major game-changers in terms of cost, performance and customer satisfaction. VM image storage [10] has been studied extensively, and many researches focus on efficient mechanisms such as removing I/O bottlenecks, fast image retrieval structure and efficient and optimized namespaces, etc. There is little emphasis on actual image size reduction from the point of view of the efficient use of the operating system (OS). As there are only a limited number of currently available and widely used OSs, and with the well-developed virtualization technologies in image management and VM execution, sharing the OS code from a common file system by other VM instances is a real possibility.

The traditional way of provisioning a VM instance requires a copy of the entire VM image which includes the OS, the required applications and configuration files. Faster VM instances provisioning can be achieved by directly reducing the size of the VM image by extracting and sharing common components in the OS. In addition, performing expected and emergency OS updates and patches are complicated, tedious and error prone since not only the stored images need to be updated, all the running VM instances must be properly refreshed. Image storage, provisioning latency and software updates down time and reliability are the major factors which affect user experiences and Cloud service provider profitability. A question that almost every CIO and software architect would ask: How can innovative software techniques be used to enable better user experiences and increased provider profitability in the Cloud setting? To help achieve these objectives, we explore a new approach on the OS level by maintaining a common, sharable central OS image which provides on-demand OS functionalities (components) to individual VM instances dynamically in a Cloud environment. The production VM images will only keep proxies to some common, non-application and non-user specific OS components, OS code will be loaded from the central OS system (disk or cache) to the actual running VM instances on demand, analogous to the dynamic class loading mechanism of the Java Virtual Machine [11]. VM image size will be reduced since only OS component proxies are maintained in the VM images, with user specific configuration and applications, in contrast to the entire OS system. For centralized managed VM instances such as those in a large data center and with the appropriate VM instance management tools, certain OS patches and updates can be performed on the central OS system (and its original VM image) and subsequently, all changes will propagate to all of its associated VM instances after refresh. The VM instances management tools for OS patching and updates on a common shared OS is beyond the scope of this paper and will be addressed in subsequent papers.

The rest of this paper is organized as follows: Section 2 gives an overview of the architecture of a shared OS approach in Cloud setting and describes the OS component sharing mechanism. Section 3 shows an analogous system and possible design and implementation approach using the common Linux file sharing system. Section 4 uses the VMware ESX server, its snapshot management mechanism and APIs as the basis to prove the feasibility and show the increased performance of the proposed shared OS approach in Cloud setting. Section 5 discusses issues related to the shared OS approach and possible future works and Section 6 concludes the paper.

2. Overview of On-Demand OS Components

As we have observed in a typical desktop or laptop computer, its limited main memory does not contain the entire copy of the OS but only the components for the functionalities that are currently or recently used when it runs [12]. OS components for the required functionalities are swapped in as needed and out when done. We apply basically the same principal to the running VM instances in the Cloud setting – common components of the OS are factored out and persistently stored and centrally maintained, these components are swapped in or out by the running VM instances dynamically on an on-demand basis. Since the number of types of common operating systems (e.g. Windows, Linux, UNIX, AIX) used in most of the VM instances is small, and for each of the OSs with the same version and up-to-date service patches, the components are virtually identical. Maintaining a server or file system for the common OS components for each of the common operating systems is relatively manageable with reasonable cost.

Figure 1 shows an overview of a typical Cloud environment with on-demand OS components sharing. In contrast to a classical Cloud setting, it maintains one or more dedicated VMs with an installed OS component server (Figure 2). Or alternatively, the OS components can be stored in a in a common sharable file system and accessed locally (Figure 3).

For simplicity, we will use the common OS server approach in subsequent discussions. The server hosts a collection of common, non-user and non-application specific OS components and will be delivered to any of its clients dynamically upon request (loaded into the client's main memory). For those VM instances that participate in the OS component sharing scheme, a thin version of OS of the required type (Figure 4) and a pointer to the OS server replaces the regular full OS copy. For those VM instances that do not participate in this scheme, it runs normally with the entire regular OS image stored locally.

The thin OS layer includes only the required VM and installed application and user specific components (such as drivers and configuration settings), and a set of proxies

(pointing mechanism) for accessing the shared OS components. The VM instance hosting the OS server behaves as an independent VM instance, with the OS image stored locally. The OS server is highly scalable; instances of the VM with the OS server can be provisioned or removed in respond to workload. (The same holds true for using the file system approach as multiple copies of the OS images can be created on different disks or mounted on remote storage systems).

With the shared OS system, each individual VM image only needs to store the pointers (as part of the configuration parameters), its own applications and data instead of the entire OS copy; as a result, less storage capacity is required. Figure 5 shows the storage view of VM of OS servers and their client VM images. For large scale Cloud operation with thousands of VM images, the savings in storage cost is significant.

Another major potential benefit of the OS sharing system in Cloud is the significant time and reliability improvement in performing software patches and updates. The traditional approach of on-line software OS updates and patches add significant costs to the management of a Cloud environment, since each VM image needs to be powered up and shut down for the updates to be installed. In a control environment where all VM instances are centrally managed, such as data centers, the OS component sharing approach with the appropriate VM instance version management tools, a significant number of OS patches and updates can be performed only on the various OS component servers or file system with a single master image for each of target OS types. Subsequently, all changes will propagate to its entire set of VM instances upon re-start. The time and cost saving in performing regular and emergency updates and patches are substantial, in addition to the increased service reliability by reducing the risk associated with power up and down thousands of VM images while performing the traditional software updates and patches.

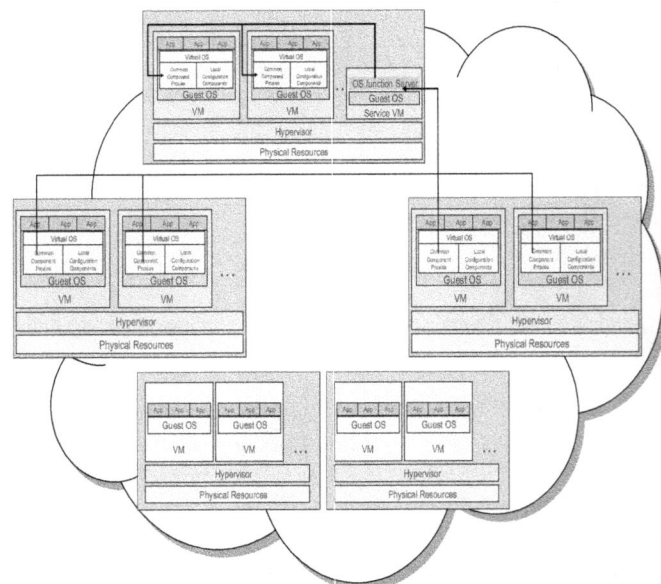

Figure 1. Cloud with VM OS component sharing.

110

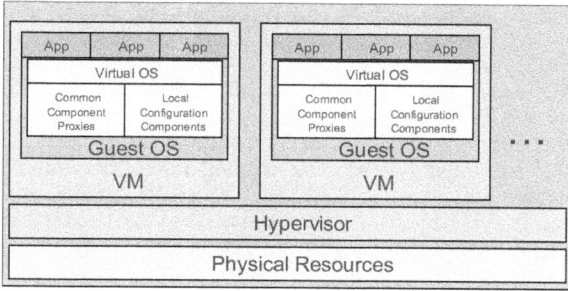

Figure 2. VM with thin virtual OS layer.

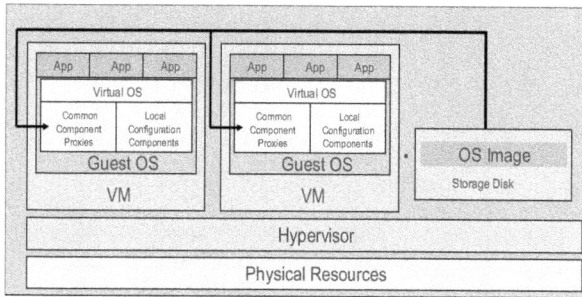

Figure 3. OS components from image storage.

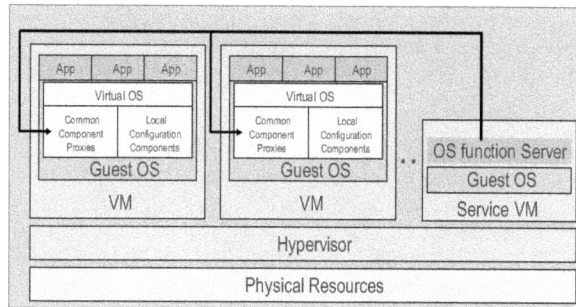

Figure 4. Dedicated VM with OS component server.

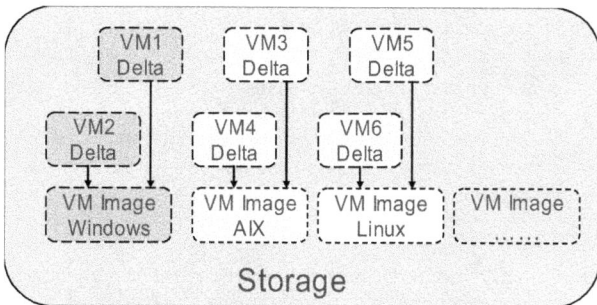

Figure 5. Storage view of master OS VMs.

3. Linux-Based Shared OS

There are numerous ways to design and implement the OS component sharing system, depending on the operating system type. For some OSs, it may not be possible without substantial changes to the OS structure (e.g. Windows), some OSs may have existing infrastructure that can be leveraged to achieve relatively simple design and easy implementation. For simplicity, we use the common Linux file mounting process as an example to show a possible way of how the OS component sharing among VM instances in a Cloud setting can be realized. In a typical Linux OS installation [13], the */boot* directory, which contains files used by the bootstrap loader, LILO and kernel images, along with some necessary modules which are needed during start-up and system initialization, are kept and loaded locally. Others such as */lib/modules* which contain the loadable kernel modules can be loaded on-demand (Figure 6).

File system mounting is a common process in Linux OS that sets up a file system for use by the OS simply by adding the mount information in the */etc/fstab* configuration file [14]. Based on the mounting information entries in this file, file systems are automatically mounted when the system boots. Figure 7 shows an example of the file mount information added to */etc/fstab* configuration file.

A modified Hypervisor keeps a registry of the available OS component sharing servers. At VM instance start-up, the Hypervisor locates the */etc/fstab* configuration file and insert the remote file mounting information to a Hypervisor selected OS component sharing server, making it available to the VM instance's OS after start-up. This change affects only the running VM instance, the original VM image remains unchanged. As far as the users and applications are concerned, all these changes are transparent to them and it looks to them as if they have the full OS and the isolated environment. This example takes advantages of the Linux OS infrastructure and is the simplest, but not necessarily the best way to enable OS components sharing. Recently, there are numerous new ideas and developments in the Linux world (and other OSs) that attempt to provide a more flexible executing environment, which will provide a better foundation for the OS component sharing system. The recent advance of network boot [15] and diskless OS [16] is an example to move away from the traditional OS executing environment to meet the challenges of a new generation of applications and usages. Researchers may look into the Linux initial system boot process [17] and the kernel system for a better and more efficient design and implementation, but this is beyond the scope of this report.

4. Experiment with VMware ESX Server

To prove the feasibility of the OS sharing architecture in a Cloud setting with a typical and widely used virtualization platform, we conducted a serious of experiments on a VMware ESX 4 server [18] hosted on an IBM Blade server (IBM BladeCenter HS22 - 7870 - 4 GB RAM - 2.53 GHz) to simulate the operation of the OS sharing system. The idea is to create multiple snapshots from the original master image and support running independent VM instances from these snapshots.

```
|---root
|---boot
|---lib
      |-----modules
|----
```

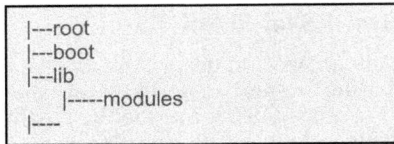

Figure 6. Linux directory structure.

```
// network mount info in /etc/fstab file
9.7.25.123:/vol/shared_lib  /shared  nfs
ro,soft,bg,timeo=3,intr 0 0

//establish symbolic link
ln -s /shared/lib/modules  /lib/modules
```

Figure 7. File mount and symbolic link example.

A master VM image with complete OS, which serves as the repository or master copy for the common sharable OS components is created. We then utilized VMware' Snapshot Manager [19,20] to provide the snapshot and instance creation functions. Although these functions can be performed using the Snapshot Management GUI, our entire process of snapshots and VM instances creation and the subsequent modification in the delta of the children images is done automatically by a script using VMware's published APIs [21].

Figure 8 shows the high-level algorithm to create snapshots and independent VM instances from the master VM image. In the example algorithm, the key idea is the use of VMware ESX server's existing Snapshot Manager to create snapshots and VM instances are supported from these snapshots. Snapshots are utilized by many VMware and third party products and features such as VMware Consolidation Backup, VMware Data Recovery, VMware vCenter and the VMware Infrastructure Client and VMware Lab Manager.

Obviously, the algorithm we developed for the experiment is not the intended use of snapshot mechanism by VMware, but we were able to modify each of the VM instances' configuration parameters (e.g. new IP and host name as in step 6 in Figure 8) in a way that each of the snapshot supported VM instances acts as independent VM instance from the perspective of the users (users can login in simultaneously into each of the created VM instances and communicate among them using their unique assigned IPs and host names). Internally from the Hypervisor, it acts as a typical VM instance created from the snapshot and managed by VMware's snapshot management functions.

Experimental Results:

Running the script produces a set of new snapshots and VM instances, all of these VM instances can be logged in simultaneously with their assigned IP addresses (step 6 of figure 8). Normally, it will take around 15 minutes to provision a VM instance from a VM image of roughly 10G in a typical server. With the automatic fast provisioning script, we were able to provision instances from the 10GB image without copying the entire master image in less than 1-2 minutes per VM instance, including the time to establish network communication, this is significantly less than the amount of time it takes for an instance provisioned in the traditional way from individual full images.

The initial storage of the snapshot and delta image is relatively small, since it only includes the configuration files (*<vm>.vmx*, *<vm>-<number>.vmdk*, *<vm>-<number>-delta.vmdk*, and *<vm>Snapshot <number>.vmsn*). The child *delta.vmdk* file which is initially created with the snapshot is a sparse disk. The virtual disk (delta) contains no data and no OS code in places, and yet is able to be used to provision independently running VM instance, which suggests that the OS code from the master image is used by the VM instances. As the VM instance runs and application data is added (via the COW – copy on write mechanism), it will grow in size up to the full storage size determined initially by the master image.

The purpose of this experiment is to prove indirectly the feasibility and performance of the shared OS approach in Cloud setting using a common and widely used Cloud platform (VMware ESX server) and its supported utilities e.g. the Snapshot Manager, it is by no means the way or the only way to implement the shared OS system. We do not go into the internal memory paging mechanism for snapshot operation of the VMware ESX Server platform and used only the available VMware ESX APIs, as we believe that the implementation of the OS sharing idea in Cloud is platform specific.

This experiment proves that the concept of shared OS in Cloud setting is possible even with the currently available and unmodified virtualization platform. In summary: we have demonstrated the concept of OS sharing by VMs in Cloud setting by a master VM image as the OS repository, and the created snapshot instances as the independent VM instances sharing the OS of the original master VM image. We have also showed that the size of the OS-sharing VM images are reduced, resulting in faster provisioning and reduced storage need.

1.	Create Master Image on VMware ESX Server with fixed IP and embedded host public key (to allow remote login from script without password), this image is immutable
2.	Create child image by cloning only the configuration files(.xmx, .vmdk, .vmxf) from the Master Image, assign new name to the new child image in configuration files and remain pointing to the Master Image's flat vmdk file
3.	Register the child to the ESX Server
4.	Create a snapshot instance from the child image's .vmx file (the cloned and modified configuration file in step 2)
5.	Boot up and log on to child instance using the Master copy's IP, as it still uses the IP of the Master Image
6.	Assign new IP and host name to the child instance, thus the new IP and host name are saved in the delta of the snapshot's image.
7.	Reboot and login to new instance with the new IP established in step 6
8.	Verify communication with the new instance by pinging the new instance using the new IP established
9.	Repeat 2-8 for new instances

Figure 8. Algorithm of creating VM instances with a master VM image in VMware ESX Server.

5. Issues and Future Works

As mentioned in earlier sections, in a large scale Cloud setting, dynamically sharing common components by VM instances is obviously beneficial in terms of image storage, ease of maintenance especially for software updates and patches, reliability and the more efficient use of resources. However, there are numerous issues to be explored before its full benefit and potential can be realized: (1) Not all current OS infrastructures can be adapted for component sharing. (2) This approach deviates from the current common Cloud model in which a VM image other than its own snapshots is completely isolated and self-contained. (3) A new Hypervisor may be needed for real-time instance modification which adds to complexity of the entire approach. (4) Dynamic component loading incurs system overhead which may affect performance especially when the common components swap in/out frequently due to custom applications. (5) Shared component may cause security concerns to some users. (6) Sharing OS components among VM instances represents a small step towards centralized computing, or at the minimum, a hybrid between total independence and centralization, this will cause controversies such as "Is some degree of centralized computing necessary to meet the current and future challenges of Cloud computing model ?". (7) Since running VM instances relies to some extent on external components, it becomes less portable. 8) As the size of the VM instance grows, the OS part of the image becomes relatively less important, and potential benefit of sharing OS in terms of storage and provisioning time decreases, but the potential benefit of more efficient OS patching and updates remain. These issues are very interesting topics, and present themselves uniquely in a Cloud setting.

We have raised the question of the classical arguments of the advantages and disadvantages of centralized vs. distributed computing in a Cloud setting with service providers facing issues on economies of scale and management. Perhaps, a hybrid of centralized and distributed computing approaches will be a viable solution to address some of the Cloud computing issues, all these are interesting questions that may stimulate further research interests. In the future, we will focus on using the Linux OS, study and prototype tools to extract common components from various OSs, and different ways of efficient component sharing in the Cloud setting.

6. Conclusion

In summary, our initial works have showed the concept and an approach to VM instance execution by enabling OS components sharing among VM instances in Cloud environment by sharing the OS of the master VM image. We have demonstrated indirectly this concept in a currently available and widely used commercial virtualization platform by creating and running multiple VM instances from a master VM image. We also explained that this approach benefits the Cloud computing service providers with increased storage efficiency, faster provisioning, efficient and reliable software updates and patches which are among the major pain points affecting customer satisfaction, efficiency and profitability of a Cloud service provider. We also identified some issues and obstacles with

this approach and raised questions on how much centralization is needed to supplement the current Cloud computing management system to fully take advantages of the benefits of Cloud computing model.

References

[1] G. Gruman, "What cloud computing really means", InfoWorld, Jan. 2009.

[2] R. Buyya, Y. S. Chee, and V. Srikumar, "Market-Oriented Cloud Computing: Vision, Hype, and Reality for Delivering IT Services as Computing Utilities", Department of Computer Science and Software Engineering, University of Melbourne, Australia, July 2008, pp.9.

[3] D. Chappell, "A Short Introduction to Cloud Platforms", David Chappell & Associates, August 2008.

[4] Amazon Elastic Compute Cloud (EC2), http://aws.amazon.com/ec2/.

[5] Enterprise Cloud, http://websphere.sys-con.com/node/1017378

[6] J. Zhu, Z. Jiang and Z. Xia, Twinkle: A Fast Resource Provisioning Mechanism for Internet Services To appear in Proc. of IEEE Infocom, April 2011

[7] Virtual Machine Storage, http://www.gluster.com/solutions/usecase/virtualization/

[8] W. Zhou P. Ning, R Wang, Z Zhang, G Ammons and V. Bala, "Always Up-to-date – Scalable Offline Patching of VM Images in a Compute Cloud", ACSAC '10 Dec. 6-10, 2010, Austin, Texas USA

[9] G. Altekar, I. Bagrak, P. Burstein, and A. Schultz.Opus, "online patches and updates for security", In SSYM'05:Proceedings of the 14th conference on USENIX Security Symposium,pages 19–19, Berkeley, CA, USA, 2005. USENIX association.

[10] A.C Amarie, T.V Dinh, G. Antoniu, "Efficient VM Storage for Clouds Based on the High-Throughput BlobSeer BLOB Management System", INRIA Sept 2010, 7434

[11] IBM DeveloperWorks, "Java programming dynamics, Part 1: Java classes and class loading", http://www.ibm.com/developerworks/java/library/j-dyn0429/

[12] Gesellschaft für Mathematik und Datenverarbeitung, "Progress in distributed operating systems and distributed systems management", European Workshop, Berlin, FRG, April 1989 Proceedings

[13] Linux Directory Structure, http://www.comptechdoc.org/os/linux//linux_ugfilestruct.html

[14] File Mounting, http://itc.virginia.edu/desktop/linux/mount.html

[15] Linux Network Boot, http://www.linuxtoday.com/infrastructure/2009051801935OSNT

[16] Linux Remote Booting a Diskless Computer, http://www.comptechdoc.org/os/linux/howtos/Howtoremoteboot//index.html

[17] IBM DeveloperWorks, "Inside the Linux boot process", http://www.ibm.com/developerworks/linux/library/l-linuxboot/

[18] VMware URL: VMware ESXi & ESX Information Center, http://www.vmware.com/products/vsphere/esxi-and-esx/index.html

[19] VMware URL: Snapshot Manager Information, http://www.vmware.com/support/ws55/doc/ws_preserve_sshot_manager.html

[20] VMware Knowledge Base: Working with Snapshots, http://kb.vmware.com/selfservice/microsites/search.do?language=en_US&cmd=displayKC&externalId=1009402

[21] VMware Infrastructure (VI) API Reference Guide, http://www.vmware.com/support/developer

Crossfire - Multiprocess, Cross-Browser, Open-Web Debugging Protocol

Michael G. Collins

IBM Research - Almaden
mcollins@collinsmichaelg.com

John J. Barton

IBM Research - Almaden
johnjbarton@johnjbarton.com

Abstract

We present *Crossfire*, a system and protocol designed to enable debugging of Web pages in another process or machine. Issues specific to any one Web browser are abstracted by the protocol and implementation, allowing a new generation of Open Web development tools to be implemented. We discuss the major refactoring of Firebug, the open source Web debugging tool to use *Crossfire* and the interplay between goals and resources that such an effort requires. In addition to the cross-browser focus of the protocol, we also discuss support for extensions which themselves will be cross-browser and client-server.

Categories and Subject Descriptors D.2.5 [*Software Engineering*]: Testing and Debugging debugging aids, distributed debugging

General Terms Experimentation, Reliability

Keywords Source-Level Debugging, Distributed Debugging, Open Source

1. Introduction

Web Applications continue to grow in size and complexity. The appearance of AJAX, which enabled data to be downloaded by a Web page in the background, started the surge. This led to the emergence of common toolkits and libraries for JavaScript, which drove performance increases in Web Browsers, fueling more growth in client-side Web application development. These improvements, combined with new features available in Web browsers shifted investment from server- to client-side. Recent empirical analysis of representative major Web sites shows program sizes in the range of hundreds of kilobytes of sophisticated code[27].

To develop and maintain these large applications, programmers and designers rely on numerous tools, most notably Web page debuggers. This paper describes *Crossfire*, a protocol and implementation to provide a next generation platform for Web page debuggers: support for cross-browser, remote and mobile development tools. We describe the major re-architecting of the most widely used Web page debugger, Firebug, to use *Crossfire* to support its client-server communications. Our description focuses on practical, state-of-the-art issues in an on-going, fast-moving, open-source project. Thus we cover details of protocol important for implementation and issues of matching resources to goals important for project management: we must deal with both low and high level issues to be successful.

2. Background

To understand the importance and challenges of the *Crossfire* work we start by introducing Firebug. Released by Joe Hewitt in 2006, Firebug was the first integrated Web debugger. Firebug is a runtime debugger: it directly accesses, responds to, and operates on the running Web browser. Rather than separate views of JavaScript, CSS, and HTML, Firebug integrated its views such that interaction with, for example, an HTML element would cause synchronized views of the CSS rules. Rather than static views of browser state, Firebug included dynamics like network traffic analysis and console logging; rather than read-only views, Firebug allowed live edits where possible so developers could try out changes. The resulting tool became very popular with developers and contributing significantly to the growth in Web applications.

The primary implementation of Firebug is a Firefox extension, a supplemental software component that loads into the Firefox Web browser. A secondary implementation with fewer features and, in particular, limited support for JavaScript debugging, called Firebug Lite, works in multiple browsers. The success of Firebug triggered competitive implementations of Web Page debuggers in other browsers, including DragonFly for Opera[20], Web Inspector for Google Chrome and Apple Safari[5], and the developer tools in Microsoft Internet Explorer[12]. Since 2007 Firebug has been developed as an open source project, with seven major releases.

To give a flavor of the kinds of operations Firebug supports, we outline an example more completely described in Ref.[22]. Suppose a developer wants to understand why a block of text in the Web page turned green while the page was loading. They might use the Firebug "inspect" feature, moving their mouse cursor over the green text, causing Firebug to display the corresponding HTML element. They see that the element has a *style* attribute setting the color green. While hovering over the green block of text, the developer clicks down to lock the user interface on the element, then moves to the HTML panel in Firebug and right-clicks on the selected HTML element representation. A menu pops up allowing the developer to select "Break On Attribute Change". When the developer reloads the page, Firebug halts in the JavaScript code panel, on the line where the attribute is changed from red to green.

This example illustrates that we will need to synchronize mouse events on the Web page with the debugger UI, identify HTML element representations rendered in the debugger UI with the elements in the Web page and synchronize DOM mutation event handling wit JavaScript execution. Crossfire is designed to support the kinds of features available in current built-in development tools such as Firebug, while enabling the advantages of a remote debug connection.

3. Design Motivation

Crossfire has three main design goals: multiprocess support, remote and mobile debug, and cross-browser debugging. These closely related goals arose out of an interplay between user benefit and development costs. As an open source project we must work with development resources motivated by goals: no matter how much value Firebug users may receive from a goal, the selection must be limited by the motivation of open source contributors.

Necessity motivated the first *Crossfire* design goal, multiprocess support. Soon after the Google Chrome browser was released, the Firefox team at Mozilla began plans to convert Firefox to a multi-process design. The Google browser uses one controlling process for the application and one process for each Web page. This allows the browser to use the operating system isolation to prevent problems on one page from bringing down the entire application and it allows each page to use a different physical processor on modern multi-core computers [11]. Depending upon the Firefox browser platform changes, a shift to multiprocess could render a single-process Firebug debugger unusable.

As a practical matter we could not wait for the new platform to become available: with only two full-time developers plus a number of dedicated but part-time contributors, and a commitment to continuous compatibility with Firefox we had to begin work immediately to ensure that our small resource could complete the transition in time to remain a viable project.

Therefore we assumed that Firefox would eventually adopt an architecture similar to Google Chrome: a client/server split debugger with a back-end in one process and a front-end in another process. We believe that this assumption is planning for the worst case: converting Firebug to client/server is a multi-person-year effort but likely to work with what ever the Firefox team decides to do.

While necessity forced our action, opportunity followed. The client/server choice, if successful, adds two new dimensions to Firebug for users: remote debug and mobile device debug. We expect the value of these dimensions to grow as more developers work in distributed teams and as mobile plays an increasingly important role in Web application development. In fact this value was recognized by the DragonFly Web debugger for Opera[20] well before the Google Chrome browser.[5] The additional cost of designing for remote and mobile debug on top of a client/server design – primarily mechanisms for specifying the connection addresses – comes with potentially high benefits. Moreover, the benefits align with directions important to the project's primary open source contributors (IBM and Mozilla).

The final goal of cross-browser debugging offers even more benefits to Firebug users. Web application developers by definition target all Web users, but not all Web users are running identical Web platforms. Almost all potential users of a Web site will be running one of few similar but slightly different browsers. The commonality allows Web developers to do most of their work on one browser, then test for differences on other browsers. Of course in the latter case they need to debug the problem on a browser with unfamiliar debugging tools. A common debugging tool across the major browsers would help with this common and significant problem.

The benefit of cross-browser debugging comes at a high cost for the project. Instead of one server and one client, we face at minimum one server for every browser. And for each server we have to deal with both the slight differences in browser implementation of standard Web APIs and potential large differences in how debuggers can connect to the browser.

Unlike commercial or pure research projects, a community-driven open source project like Firebug might balance the cost of implementing cross-browser debugging support by attracting more contributors interested in this particular goal. That is, by adding this costly goal we can attract new contributors, allowing us to create more total value. In particular new contributors from the Orion project[21], joined to create a *Crossfire* server for Microsoft Internet Explorer and from the Eclipse project[10] to create a new *Crossfire* client in Java for connecting to Eclipse. Moreover, a cross-browser client for Web debugging can be largely implemented with

Firebug Lite code, allowing our project to consolidate developer resources around fewer lines of code to maintain.

Our three design goals created constraints for the *Crossfire* implementation. Above we outlined how the multiprocess support lead to a client-server design choice. Support for remote and mobile debug forces isolation of user interface to the client (excepting some small interface for connection specification). The cross-browser goal creates constraints indirectly: to minimize the extra cost of supporting multiple servers we chose to adopt the Google Chrome communications channel (sockets) and wire protocol format (JSON). Neither Firefox nor Internet Explorer had existing servers, so they did not alter our choices. Opera had a server but no one on our open source team planned to work with Opera and the server itself was not open source making implementation more difficult. Since Firebug is already written in JavaScript, JSON format is especially easy to work with and has good performance[25]. For the communications protocol, HTTP would be a better choice for the project: the JavaScript support for HTTP is much better than sockets and HTTP works better in practical remote scenarios through firewalls. However we made the judgment that better socket support was coming in the near future[1], support was adequate now, and lowering cost on a Google Chrome back-end was important. In addition our goals imply that the client and the communication protocol should be built from open Web standards to maximize the reuse across target browsers.

4. Evolution not Revolution

In addition to motivating developers to contribute to *Crossfire*, we also need to motivate users to help us test and refine the system. As a practical project supporting 3 million users, Firebug provides a large base of experienced Web developers working with a broad spectrum of Web technologies. An open source, working, state-of-the-art debugger motivates users to explain problems, create test cases, provide documentation and to help other users with problems that come up. To harness this unusual resource for *Crossfire* we need a plan for incremental refactoring of Firebug to be compatible with *Crossfire*. The refactoring plan needs to provide waypoints for the development and it needs to provide intermediate value to users and/or contributors.

4.1 Inter-application JavaScript Debugging

The first intermediate state for *Crossfire* is shown in Fig.1. In Firefox we implemented a *Crossfire* server limited to support for JavaScript debugging. In Eclipse we implemented a *Crossfire* client. This allows the user interface in Eclipse to control and examine the JavaScript program running in Firefox. A proprietary version of the client shipped in IBM's Rational Application Developer product for two years, then the open source Eclipse team created a new implementation as part of it's JavaScript Developer Tools (JSDT) project[10]. By working towards the Eclipse team's goals of remote

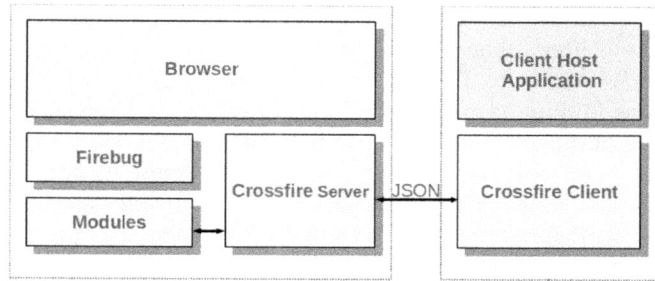

Figure 1. Inter-application JavaScript Debugging *Crossfire* architecture. *Crossfire* versions 0.1 to 0.3 connected to an Eclipse plugin, supporting simple JavaScript debugging

JavaScript debugging, this stage of the work provided valuable implementation experience and engagement with the Eclipse team. This work has been released to users but continues to be improved.

4.2 Intra-browser JavaScript Debugging

The second intermediate state implements the client side of the JavaScript part of *Crossfire* in a Web browser as sketched in Fig. 2. While this diagram seems a bit bizarre, with the

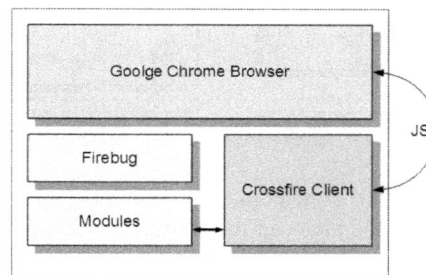

Figure 2. Intra-browser JavaScript Debugging *Crossfire* architecture. *Crossfire* versions 0.4 targets supporting simple JavaScript debugging with the client and server in the same application.

debugger running in and connecting back into the the same browser, this step allows us to add JavaScript debug support to the Firebug Lite implementation in the Google Chrome browser while we simultaneously refactor the Firefox *Crossfire* server to resemble the Google Chrome back end.

The key reason this architecture makes sense is that a large part of the non-JavaScript parts of a Web page debugger uses standard Web APIs. That means that three different applications, Firebug Lite running as co-resident with a Web page, Firebug Lite running as a Google Chrome extension, and the HTML/CSS/Console debug support code in Firebug for Firefox can use identical code in different wrappers. By re-engineering our current somewhat divergent code to group the identical parts we reduce maintenence. By adding JavaScript debugging using the now platform-independent Firefox code to the Firebug for Google Chrome code we add user value: the beginnings of cross browser development. Both efforts contribute to our final goals.

Furthermore, the two JavaScript-only *Crossfire* servers, one for Firefox and one for Google Chrome, will be able to support alternative clients. In particular, the Orion project, a Web based Web-development system, plans to support JavaScript debugging over *Crossfire* on their editor user interface. In return that project is implementing a *Crossfire* server for Internet Explorer, allowing us to cover more than 75% of the browser market with *Crossfire* supported tools. Versions with these features are scheduled to complete in June, 2011.

4.3 Cross-browser Debugging

The final stage completes the transformation of an in-process single-browser Web page debugger to a client-server cross-browser tool as shown in Fig. 3. Conceptually we simply re-

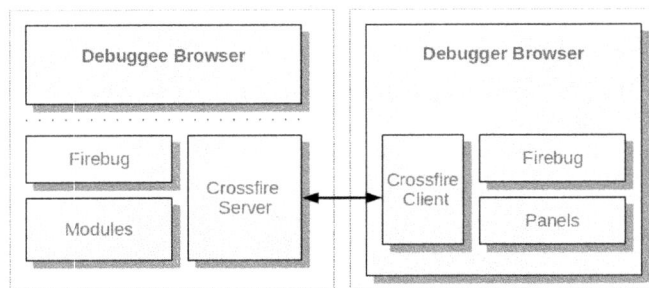

Figure 3. Cross-browser Debugging architecture, proposed.

apply the approach ironed out in the previous step to the rest of the program and arrive at the complete value proposed at the outset. In practice, the concept hides a lot of work. Many lines of code must be carefully divide into two piles and the whole must be made to work again. This work is scheduled to complete in Dec. 2011.

4.4 Modules and Tools Interface

In parallel with the architectural changes outlined above, we also need to make important infrastructure improvements. Two such improvements are of particular interest: conversion of the source code to 'modules' and introduction of a cross-browser JavaScript tools application programming interface (API).

Modules The original Firebug for Firefox and Firebug Lite code used HTML `<script>` tags to load and compile the source. This approach has two major drawbacks: 1) all of the top-level symbols in each file mix with the top-level symbols of any other files loaded in the same scope and 2) the load/compile steps are serialized. The first drawback never affected Firebug code because all of the files encapsulated their symbols in function scope. But the second one means that loading code always causes an upfront overhead to starting the application.

A replacement for `<script>` tag loading will need to support both client and server sides of a refactored Firebug and it must allow us to debug our own code. As in other cases, we also want a solution that avoids additional work by the development team. The solution we adopted was *RequireJS*[23], a form of a module loader inspired by the CommonJS[14] open standards effort. For the client side or Firebug Lite we can use this loader directly once we change our source to its format. For the server side we needed to implement code to read source files within the Firefox platform and to support debugging.

Tools Interface During the transformation from monolithic to client-server application, Firebug needs to operate in both modes. The obvious way to deal with this is to introduce a programming interface between the front and back ends. In Firebug for Firefox, the interface functions call the back end directly; in the intermediate and cross-browser version these functions call the *Crossfire* client API. Similarly in the back end, the multiprocess versions of the interface call the *Crossfire* server. Notice that this interface becomes a natural programming layer for interaction between parts of the debugger. Since *Crossfire* is designed to be cross-browser, with some care in the design, the programming interface we create becomes a general purpose Tools Interface for Open Web development.

The module and Tools Interface infrastructures complement one another. Each logical chunk of the Tools Interface corresponds to the exported symbols from one of the modules and the conditional assembly of the application from modules, to become either in-process or client-server, works by using the module loader to select the appropriate implementations of the interface.

5. Crossfire

The Crossfire protocol is an asynchronous, bi-directional protocol designed to enable the full functionality of the Firebug debugger in a multi-process or remote scenario. Where it was possible, the design of the protocol took cues from existing debug protocols such as DBGP[24], Opera Scope[8], Google's Chrome Dev Tools[4] , as well as common Web technologies (e.g. HTTP, JSON[25]). Certain features unique to Firebug and to debugging code running inside a Web Browser had to be taken into account in the design of the protocol. We give an overview of the protocol and discuss some aspects that are important to its design.

5.1 Overview

Debugging the code that implements a Web page or Web application differs in some significant ways from debugging applications developed for other types of systems. HTML and CSS are used to declaratively specify the structure and style of the user-interface, which is rendered by the Web browser. Developers cannot (easily) debug the rendering code itself. Instead, built-in tools like Firebug allow the developers to interact with the rendering engine by modifying the input and observing the output in real time, via live CSS and DOM editing. JavaScript code on the page can be stepped through when it is executing, however there is no guarantee that any JavaScript code is necessarily running at any given moment. JavaScript code on a Web page can be triggered by timers, user interactions or network events. There is no outermost main or idle loop to return to; when a section of JavaScript code is finished executing, control returns to the Web browser. This confounds attempts at things such as a simple 'halt' command, which is common among debuggers for other systems. The closest analog in Firebug is the *break-on-next* feature.

The Crossfire protocol is heavily event-driven, and requests made via Crossfire are asynchronous. This differs from many other debug protocols which are often synchronous or a combination of synchronous and asynchronous calls. The reasons for this decision stem from the nature of code running in a web page, and the fact that in some scenarios, especially the intermediate scenarios we wished to achieve, we would have a remote client connected to a server which also had a co-resident debug UI (Firebug). In other words, a complete Firebug and Crossfire server implementation would be running in a single Firefox process, and clients could connect to the Crossfire server. The result of this scenario is that clients cannot assume or rely on being the only agent acting on the runtime engine. For instance, a Crossfire client cannot safely assume that the debugger will remain suspended on a line of code until the client issues a request to resume. It is also possible that this action was triggered by the user from another client (in this case it is helpful to think of Firebug's in-process UI as another client to the debugger). However any connected Crossfire client will receive an event whenever the JavaScript debugger suspends or resumes, and should react accordingly.

Implementations of the protocol differ based on whether the implementation is intended to operate as a client or server. A Crossfire server resides in or is connected to the process which is acting as the runtime platform for the Web page, application, or other code which is to be debugged. This is typically a Web Browser, although supporting other runtime environments is envisioned. A Crossfire client connects to a server in order to receive events and issue requests, typically in order to provide a user-interface for debugging, (e.g. GUI or command-line debugger). It is not necessary for the client and server to reside in the same process or even the same host machine.

5.2 Connection and Handshake

To avoid conflicts with existing ports, Crossfire does not specify a standard or well-known port. Port agreement is left up to the user, or the client software must start the server listening on the same port it will attempt to connect to.

The connection protocol is purposefully conventional. The Crossfire server listens for a TCP connection on the specified port (greater than 1024). A client wishing to connect sends the string "CrossfireHandshake" followed by a CRLF (a blank line specified by a carriage-return followed by a line-feed character, as with HTTP). An optional second handshake line may contain a comma-separated list of tool names to be enabled immediately, followed by another CRLF. The server replies with the same handshake string, at which point the connection is established and the client may begin sending requests and receiving events from the server.

5.3 Client/Server Behavior

Once a connection has been established and a successful handshake is completed, the server may begin sending events to the connected client using the same TCP connection used for the handshake. A client may also begin sending requests to the server using the same connection. Clients should not expect the server to respond synchronously to requests or in order. The most common example is a Crossfire server sending one or more events to the client before responding to a client's request, because the events occurred during the time the request was being sent or processed.

5.4 Message Packets

As described above, the packet format follows the design of the Google Chrome browser[13]. A well-formed Crossfire packet contains one or more headers consisting of the header name, followed by a colon (":"), the header value, and terminated by a CRLF. A "Content-Length" header containing the number of characters in the message body is required, and additional headers are allowed.

The message body is separated from the headers by another CRLF blank line. The blank line is followed by a well-formed JSON string. The message must contain a "type" field with the value one of "request", "response", or "event", and a "seq" field which contains the sequence number of the packet. The sequence number of each message should be greater than that of the last message received.

5.5 Contexts

Unlike desktop or server application debuggers, a Web browser typically runs multiple applications or Web pages. A developer is likely to debug one or two of these applications, while the rest are unrelated to the application. The debugger must have a mechanism to focus on the particular page being debugged. Firebug represents an instance of a Web page via an object called a *Context*. The context object allows Firebug's panels and modules to share information about a web page that is being debugged, therefore it has a central role in Firebug's architecture.

Most of the events that occur in a Web browser that are of interest to a debug UI are related to individual pages, and therefore individual Firebug contexts. Examples of context-specific events include loading (or reloading) of a page, loading and compiling a script, errors being generated from an executing script, DOM elements being added or modified, a breakpoint being added to a script, etc.

The Crossfire protocol uses contexts for most requests / events. Crossfire represents a context as a mapping of the unique context ID and the URL of the page. This allows a connected Crossfire client to distinguish between separate loads of the same URL, as is often the case when a developer reloads a page several times in the course of developing or debugging the page. Firebug's TabWatcher component monitors loading and unloading of Firefox windows and tabs. The Crossfire server assigns a unique identifier to each context, and passes this ID as part of most event and response packets.

5.6 Breakpoints

Breakpoint debugging is a standard tool for debugging software at runtime in many languages and environments. The Web Browser environment creates several challenges for designing a remote protocol which supports breakpoint debugging. Firebug also introduces several types of breakpoints which are not present in other environments [22].

Even the simplest case, a JavaScript line breakpoint, has design implications that must be considered. Typically, such a breakpoint is identified by a line number and the URL of the script. However, existing JavaScript debugging APIs such as Firefox's do not contain the concept of Firebug's contexts. Therefore if a user places a breakpoint on line 23 of a URL http://localhost/script.js, then that breakpoint will exist for all occurrences of that URL. This may or may not be what the user actually desires. Considering the increasing use of JavaScript libraries, it is entirely likely that a script from the same URL is loaded into two completely unrelated pages. It is conceivable that a user would wish to debug his or her code and the interaction with the library, without affecting code running in another tab or window.

Crossfire's breakpoint protocol allows breakpoints to be set in one of two ways, either with or without a context ID. If a Crossfire client specifies a context ID along with a request to set a breakpoint, then that breakpoint should be enabled for that location in any existing context, or a future context which is created with the same URL in the same container (i.e. the page is reloaded).

If a client does not specify a context (by passing null as the value of the context ID), then the behavior is to set a breakpoint for the specified location in any future contexts. The intended use case for this behavior is setting a breakpoint in a client UI such as an editor, where the source code location has changed (due to editing), but the changes have not yet been applied to the page in the browser.

More advanced breakpoints, such as the HTML element breakpoints, are supported by specifying that the *location* property of a breakpoint in Crossfire is an arbitrary JSON object. A location object is defined depending on the type of breakpoint. A JavaScript line breakpoint has a location object which consists of a target URL and line number.

Firebug's HTML breakpoints have a location object which consists of an XPath expression that identifies the target element. Eventually other location types may be added, e.g. to support network-related breakpoints such as Firebug's *Break-On-XHR* feature[22].

5.7 Extensibility

One of the goals of Crossfire is to support remote and multi-process versions of Firebug. One of Firebug's features is its ability to be extended, and there are already many existing extensions. Therefore, we have developed what an API for Crossfire, called the *Crossfire Tools API*. The Tools API allows Firebug extension developers a clean and consistent way to access the Crossfire client and/or server connection.

On the server-side, the Tools API allows an extension to send custom events and handle custom requests using Crossfire's connection and transport mechanism. A client extension can listen for these events and respond to the requests. Using this API, it will be possible for Firebug extensions to continue to adapt to architectural changes in future versions of Firebug.

One consequence of this design choice is that the set of possible commands or event names cannot be specified definitively by the protocol. A Crossfire client or server must therefore be able to accept and respond to any well-formed message packet, even if it may not know how to handle a particular command or event type.

6. Implementation

6.1 Crossfire Firefox Extension

The first implementation of the Crossfire protocol is an extension to Firefox and Firebug. Implemented entirely in JavaScript, it uses a modular design to allow us to share code between client and server implementations, as well as cross-browser implementations. The transport layer operates as either a Crossfire client or server; currently the transport operates over TCP sockets. Future support for operating over HTTP and/or WebSockets is planned.

The extension can be started in client or server mode either from the Firefox user interface, or via command-line switches to Firefox. This latter mode of operation allows external tools to launch Firefox and start the Crossfire server listening on a known port so that the external tool may automatically connect back to it.

6.2 Crossfire Tools API

To support extensions, *Crossfire* maintains a registry on both the client and server side as show in Fig. 4. The Crossfire extension also implements an API, called the *Crossfire Tools API* which enables extensibility of the Crossfire system and protocol. Firebug features such as the Console, Inspector, and Net Panel, are implemented as tools using the API, allowing them to be enabled/disabled independently.

A tool can be implemented as a JavaScript file or collection of files that implements the Crossfire Tools API. The tool registers itself with the core Crossfire Module, providing an identification string that is used to identify messages via the 'tool' header. In server operation, the tool is then able to receive notification when a connection is created or when request packets are received. The Tools API allows a tool to access Crossfire's transport layer in order to send events or command responses. Typically, a tool operating within the context of a Crossfire server might register listeners with one or more Firebug modules, in order to dispatch events generated by the module to the remote connection. A tool operating as part of a Crossfire client would process the events sent from the server tool, and update part of the client UI, such as a Firebug panel. The tool could also listen for client events from the UI, and send the appropriate requests to the server, to be handled by the tool's server-side component.

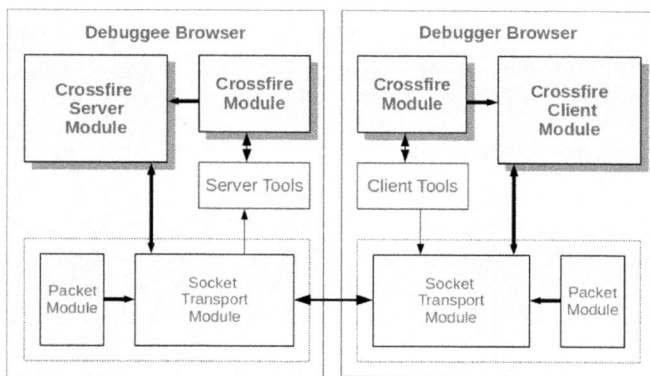

Figure 4. Crossfire Extension Architecture. The Crossfire Module running in both client and server load extension modules which register 'tools', one half in the Server Tools registry and the other half in the Client Tools registry.

7. Related Work

7.1 Multiprocess Web Debug Tools

As we discussed above, Opera's DragonFly[20] implements a complete remote debug solution and Google Chrome's Web Inspector works across processes. These implementations are specific to their host browser.

7.1.1 Weinre

The Weinre (Web Inspector Remote)[26] project implements a partial Web page debugger (no JavaScript debugging) by adding JavaScript code to a Web page in a proxy server much like Firebug Lite. The added code connects back to the proxy which then re-transmits to a third process running the user interface code from WebKit's Web Inspector. The main target for this work is mobile devices. If a *Crossfire* server were implemented in Weinre, the proxy could support connections to *Crossfire* clients.

7.1.2 Eclipse JSDT

The Eclipse JavaScript Development Tools (JSDT) project[10] includes a *Crossfire* client implementation (currently in incubation). This code is written in Java and supports connections to Firebug's server as well as an early implementation of *Crossfire* in Internet Explorer.

7.1.3 Orion

The Orion project[21] aims to create Web development tooling based on Web technologies, and plans to use Firebug and Crossfire as part of their debugging support. Discussions with the Orion team helped inform the design of *Crossfire*.

7.1.4 Cloud 9 IDE

The Cloud 9 IDE[6] supports remote JavaScript debugging (only) from a Web page to Google's V8 engine running in a `Node.js` server.

7.2 Remote Protocols

Many protocols have already been designed for the purposes of remotely debugging an application running in another process, virtual machine, host, etc. The GNU GDB debugger has an associated Remote Serial Protocol (RSP)[7]. While it is the only debugger we know of with its own song [3], it is primarily designed for debugging native code, particularly on embedded systems, and would not be well-suited for use with Firebug. The Java Debug Wire Protocol (JDWP) [2] provides remote debugging of Java Virtual Machines. The protocol supports command and response message pairs similar to Crossfire and other Web debugging protocols. However the design of the protocol, particularly the synchronous aspects, would not work well with Firebug's existing architecture.

7.2.1 DBGp

DBGp[24], is an acronym for Debug Protocol, and was developed for version 2 of the XDebug debugger for the PHP language. Although it was designed not to be language specific, many of the commands are intended to be synchronous, as opposed to the asynchronous nature of Crossfire. DBGp also allows for the debugger engine to send an event to a client via the 'notification' element, with a custom body. However in order to support Firebug, we would need to define the same events defined by Crossfire as DBGp notifications, essentially creating another protocol within the protocol.

7.2.2 Opera Scope Protocol

The Opera browser has a built-in Web development tool called DragonFly, which also supports the Scope remote debug protocol. The Scope protocol[8] supports XML and JSON formats, and features such as JavaScript debugging and remote DOM inspection. It is used to allow the desktop DragonFly client to connect to another Opera browser instance, including mobile versions.

7.2.3 V8 / Chrome Dev Tools Protocol

The V8 protocol[13] is a JSON-based wire protocol for debugging JavaScript programs running within the V8 engine. The Chrome Dev Tools protocol[4] wraps the V8 protocol to provide the additional information needed to debug a Web page running within Google's Chrome browser. The protocol implements JSON messages over TCP/IP sockets, and was the basis for much of the initial work on the Crossfire protocol. However, over the course of developing Crossfire and refactoring of Firebug, it was realized that Crossfire would require more functionality than the Chrome protocols provided.

8. Future Work

8.1 Web Sockets

Implementations of the WebSocket API[1] and protocol[9] standard are beginning to appear in recent versions of several Web Browsers. The WebSocket API allows JavaScript code in a Web page to create a full-duplex socket connection to another host using a lightweight protocol. Using these API's, it may be possible in the future to provide a Firebug front-end (similar to Firebug Lite) and Crossfire client which do not rely on other browser-specific extension APIs.

8.2 Mobile Web Debugging

Mobile devices such as smart phones and tablet computers now include full-featured Web browsers. In contrast to Desktop browsers, which have been adding more tools for developers, mobile browsers do not have the built-in Web development tools. The intuitive reason for this lack of tools is that the form factors of these mobile devices do not lend themselves to software development tasks. In this scenario, the remote debugging solution may be the only viable alternative.

8.3 Multi-user Debugging

The architecture and system we have built thus far has been implemented and demonstrated with a single user in mind, but is not restricted to that. Even in cases with a single user, there could be cases where it is desirable for a Crossfire server to support connections to multiple clients, such has connecting an external IDE while also using Firebug's in-browser UI.

Though the default operating mode of our Crossfire server implementation is to accept incoming connections only on the local host interface, it is possible to connect from a remote host. Since Crossfire should support multiple clients, it is conceivable that multiple users could use separate Crossfire clients connected to the same Web page instance to collaborate on developing or debugging that page. While it is beyond the original goals of the Crossfire project, it would be possible to build on the Crossfire work to add additional features to facilitate this kind of collaborative debugging.

9. Conclusion

Our work thus far has demonstrated that it is possible to incrementally refactor and rearchitect an existing codebase while maintaining the ability to support Firebug's large userbase with releases which are compatible with new releases of Firefox. In addition we have shown it is possible to implement a system for remote debugging similar to existing solutions in other browsers, but using a modular approach that is written purely in JavaScript. The project has been successful in attracting new contributors and new opportunities for Firebug, enabling the project to explore new directions. Continuing this work will provide numerous benefits for Firebug users as well new features that are in demand, while allowing Firebug to adapt to possible future changes in Firefox, and increasing the features offered by Firebug/Firebug Lite in other Web browsers.

Crossfire is an on-going open source project with source[16] and documentation[15] made available as part of the Firebug project, as is Firebug's source[18] and developer documentation. Documentation and downloads for Firebug are also available from the Firebug project's website.[19]

Acknowledgments

As a multi-year open source effort, *Crossfire* results from a broad collaboration and contributions from many individuals. Simon Kaegi from the Orion team lead us towards collaboration with the Orion and Eclipse teams. Darin Wright wrote the initial implementation of the Tools Interface. Grant Gayed and Mike Rennie heavily influenced the *Crossfire* protocol during their implementation of the IE server and Eclipse clients. Pedro Simonetti Garcia, Kevin Dangoor, and Atul Varma provided key insights to the module loading work. Jan 'Honza' Odvarko powers the Firebug project essential to our evolution strategy, especially implementing a test suite critical to maintaining the quality of the waypoint implementations. Steven Roussey helped with an early implementation and feedback on issues it raised.

References

[1] WebSocket API Specification, 2001. `http://dev.w3.org/html5/websockets/`.

[2] *Java Platform Debugger Architecture*, 2004. `http://download.oracle.com/javase/1.5.0/docs/guide/jpda/`.

[3] GDB Song, 2007. `http://www.gnu.org/music/gdb-song.html`.

[4] Google Chrome Dev Tools Protocol, 2009. `http://code.google.com/p/chromedevtools/wiki/ChromeDevToolsProtocol`.

[5] WebKit Web Inspector, 2010. `http://trac.webkit.org/wiki/WebInspector`.

[6] Cloud 9, 2010. `http://cloud9ide.com/`.

[7] *GNU Debugger (GDB) Manual*, 2010. `http://sourceware.org/gdb/current/onlinedocs/gdb/`.

[8] Opera Scope Protocol, 2010. http://dragonfly.opera.com/app/scope-interface/.

[9] WebSocket Protocol, 2010. http://www.whatwg.org/specs/web-socket-protocol/.

[10] Eclipse JSDT, 2011. http://wiki.eclipse.org/JSDT/Debug.

[11] Google Chrome, 2011. http://www.google.com/chrome.

[12] Microsoft Internet Explorer Developer Tools, 2011. http://msdn.microsoft.com/en-us/library/dd565628.

[13] V8 Debug Protocol, 2011. http://code.google.com/p/v8/wiki/DebuggerProtocol.

[14] CommonJS, 2011. http://www.commonjs.org/.

[15] Crossfire online documentation, 2011. http://getfirebug.com/wiki/index.php/Crossfire.

[16] Crossfire source repository, 2011. http://fbug.googlecode.com/svn/extensions/crossfire/branches/.

[17] Firebug developer api documentation, 2011. http://getfirebug.com/developer/api/firebug1.7/.

[18] Firebug source repository, 2011. http://fbug.googlecode.com/svn/branches/.

[19] Firebug website, 2011. http://getfirebug.com.

[20] Opera DragonFly, 2011. http://www.opera.com/dragonfly/.

[21] Orion, 2011. http://www.eclipse.org/orion/.

[22] J. J. Barton and J. Odvarko. Dynamic and graphical web page breakpoints. In *Proceedings of the 19th international conference on World wide web*, WWW '10, pages 81–90, New York, NY, USA, 2010. ACM. ISBN 978-1-60558-799-8. doi: http://doi.acm.org/10.1145/1772690.1772700. URL http://doi.acm.org/10.1145/1772690.1772700.

[23] J. Burke. RequireJS, 2011. http://requirejs.org/.

[24] S. Caraveo and D. Rethans. DBGP, A common debugger protocol for languages and debugger UI communication, Draft 16, 2007. http://www.xdebug.org/docs-dbgp.php.

[25] D. Crockford. JSON, 2006. http://json.org.

[26] P. Mueller. Weinre, 2011. http://pmuellr.github.com/weinre/.

[27] G. Richards, S. Lebresne, B. Burg, and J. Vitek. An analysis of the dynamic behavior of javascript programs. In *Proceedings of the 2010 ACM SIGPLAN conference on Programming language design and implementation*, PLDI '10, pages 1–12, New York, NY, USA, 2010. ACM. ISBN 978-1-4503-0019-3. doi: http://doi.acm.org/10.1145/1806596.1806598. URL http://doi.acm.org/10.1145/1806596.1806598.

Moving Back to Scrum and Scaling to Scrum of Scrums in Less Than One Year

Rafael P. Maranzato

Universo Online S.A.
Dept. of R&D
Sao Paulo, SP, Brazil
rmaranzato@uolinc.com

Marden Neubert

Universo Online S.A.
Dept. of R&D
Sao Paulo, SP, Brazil
mneubert@uolinc.com

Paula Herculano

Universo Online S.A.
Dept. of R&D
Sao Paulo, SP, Brazil
pherculano@uolinc.com

Abstract

We report on the experience of re-introducing Scrum in a project team that had previously failed to adopt that agile method. We explore the reasons we believe that caused the failure and explain how we approached the team to uncover them. Then, we describe our strategy to avoid incurring in those problems again and to take the team to a higher level of productivity, quality and personal satisfaction. We also present the motivation and the actions taken to go further and scale this scenario to multiple feature-oriented teams using Scrum of Scrums. All these changes occurred in less than one year.

Categories and Subject Descriptors K.6.1 [*Project and People Management*]: Management techniques

General Terms Experimentation, Management, Human Factors

Keywords Scrum, agile, scaling Scrum, Scrum of Scrums, experience, cultural change

1. Introduction

This paper is based on our experience in the Research and Development (R&D) department of *Universo Online* (UOL), the largest Internet portal in Brazil. UOL was launched in 1996 as an Internet Service Provider focusing on content providing and basic Internet services, such as chat and e-mail. Most of the projects were small and short lived; services were launched and few of them evolved significantly after that. Around 2006, following the company's IPO in the Brazilian stock market, it expanded its portfolio to offer new services that would be managed by independent business units. Most of those services were meant to compete with incumbent Internet companies in Brazil and included an online marketplace, a price comparison shopping, a sponsored links platform, among many others.

In the Research and Development (R&D) department, significant changes also happened during this period. In the first few years there was no formal process and each team decided how to develop and deliver software to the company. In 2000 we started using the Rational Unified Process (RUP) [3]. At first, we used most of the documents and templates provided by RUP, but along the years we adapted our process and focused only in core artifacts such as Vision and Use Cases [2]. Although we felt that this process was inefficient, until 2006 it was compatible with the type of projects that we were assigned—simple and fixed scope, relatively short duration (at most three months) and no fixed team.

Around 2006 we began to realize that this process was becoming a burden given the new business needs of the company. The newly constituted business units demanded continuous effort in the development and evolution of their software products. Soon the company decided that these products should have fixed teams, but at first, these teams were composed only of Java developers. Other skills necessary to build the software, such as testers, webmasters, data administrators and system administrators, were still allocated by demand from the functional teams they belonged. This situation exacerbated the inefficiency of our process and we began to actively discuss how we should change the way developed software.

In the beginning of 2008, we had come to the conclusion that Scrum [5] was the best choice for our scenario and we started its implementation in three pilot projects. One of the authors had the opportunity to be the first Scrum Master of the company and was involved in two of the pilot projects. One of them was the evolution of a very complex software, an online marketplace for buying and selling products. The other project was creating a new tool for managing complex sets of data and metadata, targeted to internal users. Although these projects were very different in their scope, stage of development and relevance to the company, Scrum proved to be an excellent fit for both.

The third pilot Scrum project was also very ambitious and still different in purpose from the other two: its goal was to rewrite a very large system, replacing an old and limited platform with a new and efficient one, while maintaining all functionalities. However, Scrum was not successfully implemented in this project. Viewed from the outside, the team seemed just not able to make progress. As we later learned, they were lost in pointless technical analyses, endless discussions and personal conflicts. Initially expected to be completed in nine months, the project was already running for almost one and a half years when management concluded that Scrum might be causing the delays. In order to meet a new deadline, they returned to a more traditional project management approach, abandoning Scrum. The project was actually delivered a few months after the new deadline, but not without much distress, extra hours and removed functionalities. After the release one, a group of managers with more experience with Scrum, including two of the authors, was involved in the project and to put the team back on the tracks with Scrum. And in less than one year, we have scaled Scrum in four feature teams. This is the experience that we will describe in this paper.

This paper is organized as follows. Section 2 presents the team in which we based our study and its first experience with Scrum. Section 3 describes how Scrum was reintroduced to this team and the new approaches that we took. Section 4 draws conclusions on our report. Some Scrum terminology can be found in Appendix 5.

2. First Agile Experience

As soon as the company decided to adopt Scrum in early 2008, the next step was to provide training in agile fundamentals for all professionals involved in product development, from software engineers to business specialists. Beside the pilot product teams, we created interest groups gathering Scrum Masters, Product Owners and other technical skills. The new product teams were at the spotlight of the company and Scrum was the most spoken word in the environment. Everyone wanted to learn or teach something. The groups were infected by agile feelings. People did not need to use boring processes and corporate tools anymore. They were allowed to choose the tools they considered appropriate because, after all, the Agile Manifesto said "Individuals and interactions over processes and tools [1].

As we mentioned before, one of the pilot product teams had to rewrite a system built in an old platform. The requirements were well known and there were not many business risks involved, but there were significant technology risks. The team was formed by professionals that had never been in a product team before. Instead, they came from different departments, organized according to their technical skills. This should not be a problem if the involved departments had common goals, but that was not the case. The department managers gave directions to their professionals according to their old way of working, without considering that things had changed. For example, in the old methodology there was a person responsible for testing. With Scrum, there is a testing role inside the team, which could be performed by a test engineer or a software engineer. But this did not sound correct to the functional departments, and they wanted to create rules for their members. For instance, each functional manager involved wanted to define what the concept of *Sprint Done* meant, according to their own criteria.

As we should expect, team members coming from different functional departments did not agree with each other. Each was following a different agenda, according to the objectives of their departments. This led to very long discussions during the sprints, mostly during the *Daily Scrums*, which almost always exceeded the recommended 15 minutes. There were also lots of blaming and unfruitful discussions in Retrospectives. Since people were not aiming at the same target, which should be delivering business value in the form of working software, they could not agree on many topics. One example of disagreement was related to the use of a new technology in the project. One of the functional departments decided that the project was a good opportunity to validate a new technology they wanted to employ in their own projects. Since most of the developers of the team reported to that department, they were instructed to study and use this technology. This decision slowed down the project for about three months. When the Product Owner noticed this and questioned the head of that department, he answered that, according to Scrum, this technology decision was a prerogative of the team, so there was nothing wrong with their choice. After a few months debate, the issue scaled up to the head of R&D and the team was instructed to abort the use of the new technology.

Sprint after sprint, most of the user stories were considered *Not Done*, due to the conflicting definitions that each department had on the concept of *Done*. This would accumulate more work to each subsequent sprint, generally to make adjustments that would not generate value to the end product. As a consequence of all these unsuccessful sprints, the conflicts inside the team were becoming more frequent. Discussions on sprint velocity and the format of meetings were also among the top discussions and disagreements. Surrounding all conflicts, or adding one more, there was the estimated time to accomplish the project, which was uncertain yet. And all of these problems became due to Scrum, so they were considered all *Scrum's fault*. By that time the mindset was: "If we want to deliver this project we should come back to the traditional model because we know we have problems but we deliver projects. And then the decision was made: the team was not required to use Scrum anymore and then could be free again. The release one was delivered but there was a directive to use Scrum again, since it was being successfully used in other teams in the company.

3. Moving Back to Scrum

In the beginning of 2010, before returning to Scrum, we talked a lot with the most experienced people in the team to discover what they were expecting from that return and what important lessons could be learned from the past. After some talks we could see they were very focused on some rules, such as the definition of done, the opposite of Scrum and agile values. At this time, over the regular evolution of the system, there was a business need to integrate that system with other services of the company. We could see that it was a different backlog, and a good approach would be to split the team as we split the product backlog.

To start the process, we reintroduced Scrum to the team focusing on the values, like commitment, transparency, teamwork and so on. and we had to change one important concept of the majority of the team: that it was possible to have more than one team working in the same software components. So, we broke the team and the backlog by feature, creating feature teams [4]. Another important change that we made was to add three new members to the team that had experience in working with Scrum. Besides their technical skills, these three professionals were easygoing people who could aggregate positive attitudes during the sprints.

One important concept that we have emphatized and that continues nowadays is that we could break the backlog into two or more feature teams but everybody were part of one team. No matter what happens, we were one team. It was very important because it is not possible to have team competition, velocity comparison, owner of software components, bugs per team and things that could be harmful to teamwork.

With this preparation, we started these two sprint plannings on the same day and we invited people from the other team to be at the sprint planning, to see what features would be created. We also invited them to the sprint review to share what each team had produced.

We also asked team members to help and participate of some decisions, like suggestion to the backlog (including features to the product and technical improvements), test infrastructure and other question that in the past were concentrated at the management level or with one or two team members - the others were just informed of those decisions, and we think that approach is opposed to agile values, since we need people commitment.

After six months of these two teams running sprints quite well, we could see the good results of creating features teams. At the same time, the results of the business and the increase of revenues and users in the product, made the business owners and the IT management consider creating more teams to focus on specific backlogs. It was good because we could see that our approach was bringing results, but, of course, we also faced some problems.

At this moment, one of the problems was the need of hiring more team members and how to put them in a system that has a lot of business rules and deals with money. We agreed that it would be better to hire good people and wait to start new feature teams instead of just increasing the team members and starting new teams. We also have proposed to transfer people from other teams inside the company because they were used to developing with the company procedures and rules.

As we were hiring, we increased the existent teams before creating the third and the forth one that we have identified as priority. In parallel, we created the backlog for the new feature teams. Another decision that we made was not to start the forth team at the same time as the third one: we knew that we would learn from that division and face some impediments. When we had people and the backlog ready to start, we initiated the third team and we found some issues. The most relevant were:

- Teams per release: we observed that having more than 3 teams per release would be hard to manage considering the number of functionalities, bug fixes and database modifications.

- Merge instead of one build: considering the previous issue, we prefer to maintain two branches of code. One to the teams A & B and other to teams C & D, for example. As A & B deliver, teams C & D merge the code and A & B start a new branch. The opposite occurs when C & D deliver. This example is in Figure 1.

- Sprint length: before starting the third team, we spend 3 weeks in the sprint. We agreed that to add one more week would be easy to fit the sprint length during the days of the week.

- Develop environment: each team needs a proper environment without sharing with another team. The Quality Assurance (QA) environment is unique for all the teams because it reflects the production environment and when features from different teams run in the same build.

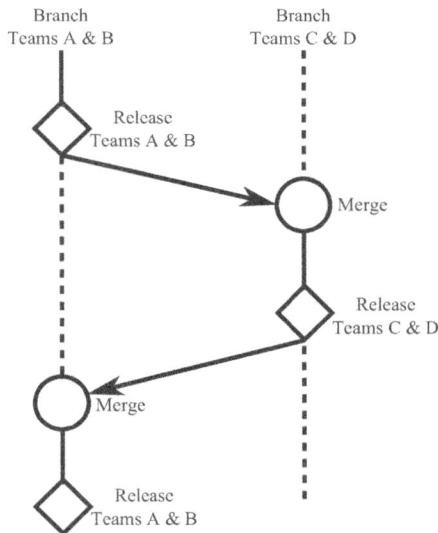

Figure 1. Branches between teams

These impediments and others helped us to understand how to implement a good Scrum of Scrums. We could see it would be very important to improve the communication among ScrumMasters, Product Owners and all the teams. So, as we had some rituals in the Scrum, we added some meetings to the team agenda:

- All Product Owners and ScrumMasters: there is a meeting every week with all Product Owners and ScrumMasters to talk about features that have impact on the other teams or about subjects that are relevant for everyone. We spend around 90 minutes on this meeting.

- Mega Planning: just after we finish the sprint planning of the teams, that is usually every other Monday, we talk to all the team members about the stories that each team has chosen. These meetings are very important because a member of one team can advise or warn the others and people can see the impact of these stories among the teams. It is important to emphasize that we start this meeting talking about the schedule ahead for everyone to know the deadlines and the relevant dates during the sprint. We also address generic topics that are important to most of the team and team members. We spend less than one hour with this meeting.

- Mega Daily: in the weeks when we do not have sprint plannings, there is a meeting that is similar to the Mega Planning. The main difference is that we focus on the status of development of new features and it lasts around 30 minutes.

- Knowledge Sharing: once or twice a month, usually on Fridays, we have some presentations about training or conferences people attend, relevant features or best practices that we consider important for everyone. We also share experiences from some teams to the others.

- Members of new teams: we do not create new teams with new people in the organization. Basically we add new employees into the existent teams and we create new teams with the old ones. It motivates everybody because people know that there will be opportunities of creating and learning new things. It is also important to knowledge sharing.

One example of this meeting during the weekdays is the listed schedule in Table 1. As we can see, we add more points of communication to our Scrum framework. We believe that improving communication and creating these rituals we can synchronize the development of the features in each team with the whole system. We think we can add two more teams to that agenda, but more than that would probably be hard to administrate.

Another issue that we think we could have is that although our mega meetings are productive, it is hard to find rooms that are big enough for everyone. When this happens, we will have to try other approaches like virtual meetings or we may choose teams' representatives to attend these meetings and pass on all the information after the daily Scrum. But we are not comfortable with this situation because we think this is an important channel of communication that we have nowadays, especially with mega plannings and mega dailies.

If the team, in the beginning of this process, was very distrustful about splitting the job into feature teams, nowadays they have learned how to work in this way and are contributing to scale our development process. One example is related to improvements in our development environment and refactorings that are necessary to facilitate working in parallel. It is important to remember that the system was created with a vision of one or two teams working in parallel, but the business is growing fast and we cannot stop the market – we need to keep up with this growing. So, people started to suggest refactoring in components, builds and other things because they are convinced that it is the responsibility of all the feature teams - and they are happy with the results of their work.

After 10 months of returning to Scrum, we checked with our business clients how they evaluated these changes. We did had a meeting - similar with to the Scrum retrospectives - and the balance was very positive: they were satisfied with the feature teams and they asked us how to create more teams, because the backlog is enormous and it is impossible for only one or two teams only to develop it. Another important improvement that we had was in the relationship between the R&D and business people. Before Scrum there was a lot of misunderstands and competition between

Monday	Tuesday	Wednesday	Thursday	Friday
Planning A & B	Mega Planning			Knowledge Sharing
Mega Daily		Review C & D	Release C & D	Retrospective C & D
Planning C & D	Mega Planning			Knowledge Sharing
Mega Daily		Review A & B	Release A & B	Retrospective A & B
Planning A & B	Mega Planning			Knowledge Sharing

Table 1. Basic Schedule

areas. Nowadays this relationship is much more trustful and we are continuing trying to improve it.

As explained before, the relationship between the teams and the environment had an improvement if you compare it to the times without Scrum. We can also observe that the business area is happy with the new methodology. Besides that, we have had an increment in the team velocity.

When we started the second team and split the backlog, we told the teams to create its own velocity and we did the same to the third and fourth ones. After that, we conducted an experiment to compare the story's sizes of teams and we observed that the estimates were very similar among these teams. It can be a coincidence but we believe that is explained because some members worked in two or more teams and probably influenced this fact.

Considering that the estimates are similar, we could see that we have had an improvement in team velocity meanwhile we were adding more members and creating new teams. In Figure 2, we can see that our velocity was growing month by month (line points) and our productivity too (line points per person). There is a peak in October but we consider that an abnormal event because it is out of the trend.

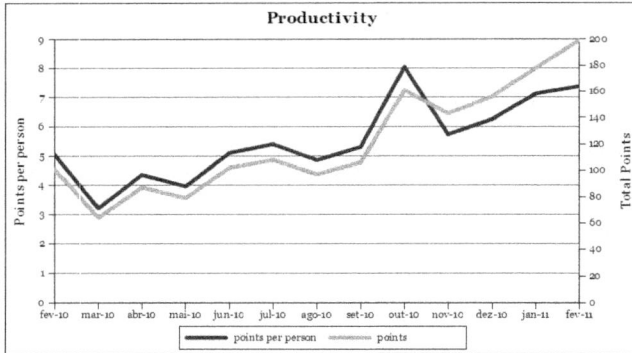

Figure 2. Productivity

As you can see, we have made a lot of modifications with this team in less than one year. Firstly, we had a cultural change while the management and the methodology were modified. Secondly, we changed their vision of the product so that we could have a lot of feature teams but we are just one big team. In addition, we changed the methodology in the product development using Scrum, focusing on values like commitment and transparency. And finally, we scaled Scrum creating more feature teams, using Scrum of Scrums.

Nowadays, our main challenge is to maintain our vision and values meanwhile we continue creating more feature teams. We believe that we will face some problems and issues but we also believe that by using an approach similar to the one that we have used until now we will be able to do that.

4. Conclusion

This paper described how we managed to implement Scrum in a team that had previously failed to adopt the agile culture. We also showed how we were able to scale this team to multiple feature-oriented teams, using Scrum of Scrums. All this transformation was done in less than one year. We found that some key factors for our success were the early identification of the causes of the initial failure of Scrum adoption, the allocation of professionals to Scrum roles according to their abilities and the addition of new professionals with good team skills and experience with Scrum.

Regarding the need for scaling the team, we demonstrated that separating teams by feature was the best decision in order to focus on the main priorities for the evolution of the product and to avoid conflicts in backlog management. We concluded that it is very important to create each new team with at least one professional with good technical skills and knowledge of Scrum, backed-up by an experienced ScrumMaster and a Product Owner. The practices we employed to deal with multiple teams – such as mega plannings and mega dailies – were crucial to keep the information flowing through all teams and maintain the concept that everybody belongs to one big team. Moreover, techniques such as parallel version control, continuous integration and carefully planned deploys were important to keep the quality of the work even with many new members being added in a short period of time.

5. Appendix: Scrum Terminology

This section is based on [6].

- Daily Scrum Meeting: A stand up fifteen-minute daily meeting for each team member to answer three questions:
  1. "What have I done since the last Daily Scrum meeting? (i.e. yesterday)"
  2. "What will I do before the next Daily Scrum meeting? (i.e. today)"
  3. "What prevents me from performing my work as efficiently as possible?"

  The third question refers to the Impediments and it is assigned to the ScrumMaster.

- Impediments: Anything that prevents a team member from performing work as efficiently as possible is an impediment. The ScrumMaster is charged with ensuring impediments get resolved.

- Product Backlog: The product backlog (or "backlog") is the requirements for a system, expressed as a prioritized list of product backlog Items. These included both functional and non-functional customer requirements, as well as technical team-generated requirements. While there are multiple inputs to the product backlog, it is the sole responsibility of the product owner to prioritize the product backlog.

- Product Backlog Item: In Scrum, a product backlog item ("PBI", "backlog item", or "item") is a unit of work small enough to be completed by a team in one Sprint iteration.

Backlog items are decomposed into one or more tasks. Some practitioners represent backlog items into User Stories.

- Product Backlog Item Effort: Some Scrum practitioners estimate the effort of product backlog items in ideal engineering days, but many people prefer less concrete-sounding backlog effort estimation units. Alternative units might include story points, function points, or "t-shirt sizes" (1 for small, 2 for medium, etc.).

- Scrum Roles: There are three essential roles in any Scrum project:

  - Product Owner: A person that represents the customer's interest in backlog prioritization and requirements questions.

  - ScrumMaster: A facilitator for the team and product owner

  - Team: A group of people responsible for constructing and delivering the product. The team members are usually a mixture of software engineers, architects, programmers, analysts, QA experts, testers, UI designers, etc. This is often called "cross-functional project teams".

- Sprint: An iteration of work during which an increment of product functionality is implemented.

- Sprint Backlog: Defines the work for a sprint, represented by the set of tasks that must be completed to achieve the sprint's goals, and selected set of product backlog items.

- Sprint Planning Meeting: The Sprint planning meeting is when team and the Product Owner negociate and agree on what will be delivered in the end of the Sprint.

- Sprint Review Meeting: A Sprint Review is a meeting where the team demonstrates working software corresponding to project backlog items they have completed in a given Sprint.

- Sprint Retrospective Meeting: The Sprint retrospective meeting is when the team discusses what went well and they should keep doing and what to improve in the next Sprint.

- Velocity: The velocity is calculated based on how much product backlog effort a team can handle in one Sprint. This is based on the average of previous Sprints and it should assume that the team composition and the Sprint lenght are kept constant.

Acknowledgments

First of all, we thank the *Phoenix* team, which we analyzed in this report. All team members were completely available to our interviews and provided very sincere and insighful opinions on the project. We also thank Marcio Drumond, head of the Department of R&D, for supporting this research and revising our drafts.

References

[1] K. Beck, M. Beedle, A. van Bennekum, A. Cockburn, W. Cunningham, M. Fowler, J. Grenning, J. Highsmith, A. Hunt, R. Jeffries, J. Kern, B. Marick, R. C. Martin, S. Mellor, K. Schwaber, J. Sutherland, and D. Thomas. Manifesto for agile software development, 2001. URL http://www.agilemanifesto.org/.

[2] M. Fowler and K. Scott. *UML distilled - a brief guide to the Standard Object Modeling Language (2. ed.).* notThenot Addison-Wesley object technology series. Addison-Wesley-Longman, 2000. ISBN 978-0-201-65783-8.

[3] P. Kruchten. *The Rational Unified Process: An Introduction.* Addison-Wesley Longman Publishing Co., Inc., Boston, MA, USA, 3 edition, 2003. ISBN 0321197704.

[4] C. Larman and B. Vodde. *Scaling Lean & Agile Development: Thinking and Organizational Tools for Large-Scale Scrum.* Addison-Wesley Professional, 1 edition, 2008. ISBN 0321480961, 9780321480965.

[5] K. Schwaber and M. Beedle. *Agile Software Development with Scrum.* Prentice Hall PTR, Upper Saddle River, NJ, USA, 1st edition, 2001. ISBN 0130676349.

[6] V. Szalvay. Glossary of scrum terms @online, mar 2007. URL http://www.scrumalliance.org/articles/39-glossary-of-scrum-terms.

A Case Study for Prioritizing Features in Environments with Multiple Stakeholders

Eduardo Cristiano Negrão
Aeronautical Institute of Technology
São José dos Campos, São Paulo – Brazil
eduardocnegrao@gmail.com

Eduardo Martins Guerra
Aeronautical Institute of Technology
São José dos Campos, São Paulo – Brazil
guerraem@gmail.com

Abstract

In corporations where the focus is a very dynamic business inserted in web environments, agile methods can fully meet almost all needs. However, in some particular companies, there are multiple stakeholders, who represent different interests in prioritizing activities. There is, consequently, a heavy challenge to implement agile methodologies which deal with such conflicts in order to prioritize the features of the system. It is important to focus on higher earned value as possible and consider the technical risks exposed by the development team. These barriers often lead these companies to abandon such agile methods, incorporating an approach of a chaotic work environment. This paper proposes an agile technique for prioritizing features in environments with multiple stakeholders and reports a successful experience in its usage.

Categories and Subject Descriptors D.2.9 [**Software Engineering**]: Management – cost estimation, productivity, programming teams, software process models, time estimation.

General Terms Management, Measurement, Experimentation, Human Factors, Theory, Verification.

Keywords Prioritization, Estimating, Planning, Agile, Stakeholders, Conflict of Interests.

1. Context

The software product, which is contextualized in this paper, involves the work of a development team aligned to another team of business analysts. It consists in an e-commerce system focused on health care. It involves the marketing of high cost products of hospitals, such as orthosis, prostheses and other special surgical materials. The application has features to meet the needs of five different actors: hospitals buyers, product suppliers, health plan operators, hospital service providers and system administrators.

The agile methodology used to manage the work is the Scrum [4]. Three developers, a professional in quality assurance and a Scrum Master compose the team that meets the demands of maintenance and evolution of this software.

In this case, the application does not have a single product owner. Actually, it has one person responsible for each area, giving a total of five main stakeholders. All of them participate in the planning meeting in order to prioritize product backlogs and sprint backlogs, bringing demands from customers that they represent. When possible, they have tried to prioritize it within general consensus. However, this reality is often very different: there is a wide disparity of interests, leading to conflicted priorities and increasing the planning efforts.

Some proposals [1] attempt to minimize the planning efforts. However, they do not address all solutions to solve the problems in contexts which involve more than one stakeholder from different business areas and a small development team to attend the needs. This paper documents the adopted solution to define a technique to prioritize software requirements impartially, organizing the product backlog and the sprint backlog, aiming solely at increasing the return on the corporation's investment. This work also describes the search for consolidated existing techniques and how they can be adapted and combined into the given context.

Nowadays, with the high dynamism and diversity of internet businesses, this problem is common and recurrent in such corporations. As a consequence, it is extremely important that studies aimed at mitigating these problems are considered and evolved.

This study documents the solutions adopted to define a technique for prioritizing software requirements in environments with multiple stakeholders by organizing the artifacts in an impartial way for product maintenance planning, in order to maximize the return on the corporation's investment. It also describes the researches performed to go through already established techniques in the market; and how and why they were combined and adapted to suit this context. The proposed technique has been implemented in a real corporate context and its results were collected and then evaluated by means of some established metrics.

2. Major Occurred Problems

As mentioned previously, the company has faced the stake-holders' conflict of interests to prioritize their customers' demands. As a result, this context increases the development team's effort to expose the barriers and technical risks, which are important to maintain a higher quality of the software.

Stakeholders have thus considered abandoning the agile methods, as these had been understood by them as being very inflexible, since they did not allow new business demands to interrupt an iteration in course. But, actually, such demands had often been considered urgent, however, after being developed, these features were never or rarely used. This situation avoids the development of other demands that could be developed primarily to deliver greater earned value to the application, meeting the real needs of a higher number of customers.

Therefore, it has been extremely important to the project's success to define better ways to prioritize features mitigating the risks of building low-value software to the customers and avoiding the abandonment of agile techniques.

3. Initial Approach: Researching Solutions

Given these problems, the major objectives were to define a planning technique to prioritize development features in this complex environment. The approach was to use agile values and techniques in order to decrease those planning efforts and balance the existing technical risks and business interests.

As a research base for studies of existing solutions and for the realization of the tailoring of the existing processes, the book "Agile Estimating and Planning" [1] was used. It proposes the usage of already established techniques in environments that are using agile methodologies. Then, the resulting studies combined those theories with traditional methods of risk management from the Professional Management Body of Knowledge (PMBOK) [3].

Some solutions have been chosen for implementation in the current work, in the use of Scrum. The proposed technique has then been implemented in a real corporate context and the results were collected and evaluated by means of some metrics.

The researched solutions are based on already established techniques in the agile world such as the Relative Weighting, Kano, Theme Screening and Theme Scoring [1].

The Relative Weighting method was chosen as the approach which best fits the solution of the encountered problem.

This method has been adopted because it provides a more efficient way to classify the priorities for each requirement. In this technique, not only the relative benefit of adding that feature is considered, but also how much the product would be hurt if it were not included. To get the complexity of each story [2], story points are estimated by methods such as the planning poker [1].

The Relative Weighting contributed positively to the planning activities, since it reaps the business value and technical costs score in a more democratic approach.

To get the value of each story, it is necessary that the stakeholders score, from 1 to 9, the benefit that it brings, being 1 the story with the lowest benefit and 9 the one with the higher benefit. Then, the story needs to be scored, also

from 1 to 9, to punctuate the penalty a story can bring if it is abandoned. It is given 1 point to the story that brings no penalty and 9 the story that has a higher penalty to be abandoned.

The cost of the software development, in this method, is achieved by reaching a relative measure on how big is each story. The development team uses the estimated size in points, known as Story Points, obtained by methods like the Planning Poker, in which the development team scores the size or the cost of each story according to its technical complexity and importance, a story over another, following the Fibonnacci scale [1].

Given all three scores, then sum up the benefit added to the penalty, resulting in a number known as "Total Value". Having then the total value and the cost of each feature, it is still necessary to obtain another derived value: the percentage that each of these two scores represents on the whole. Finally, to give the value of the priority of each feature, the percentage of each total is divided by the percentage of each corresponding cost [1]. These ideas are better explained in figure 1.

Themes		Relative Benefit	Relative Penalty	Total Value	Value Percent	Estimate	Cost Percent	Priority
	More investment choices	8	6	14	40	64	44	91
	Portfolio rebalancing	9	2	11	31	40	27	115
	Comply with new law	1	9	10	29	42	29	100
Total				35	100	146	100	

Total Value = Relative Benefit + Relative Penalty
Value Percent = Total Value / ∑ (Total Value)
Cost Percent = Estimate / ∑ (Estimate)

© 2003-2008 Mountain Goat Software

Figure 1. Relative Weighting Method [7]

One of the other major approaches researched (though this one comes from projects based on more traditional methods) is the risk management suggested by the Project Management Institute (PMI). With the risks identified, it is possible to classify how they could impact on the organization, being also possible to measure if they would be low, medium or high.

A tool named Probability and Impact Matrix can be used as a concept to represent the analytical structure of risks defined, in which it can view the level of the numbered risks and classify them into four quadrants. As follows, it is viable to get the degree of the possibility that the risk can occur; what impact it could cause if it occurred; which actions should be taken; who would be those responsible for addressing the identified risks and how should it be proceeded to monitor the risk. As a result, it is possible to evaluate whether the project that is being planned is a project of high, medium or low risk and if it is feasible to continue.

The Probability and Impact Matrix and its four quadrants are represented in Figure 2.

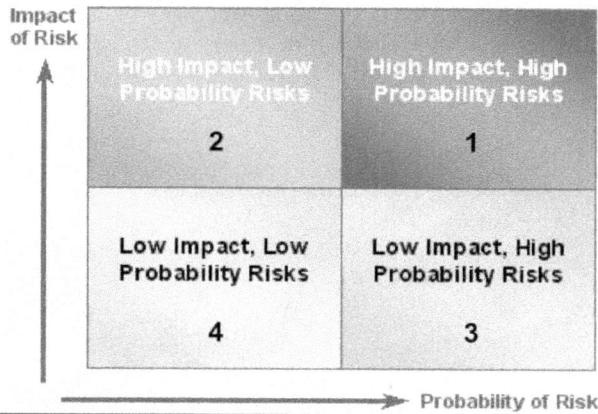

Figure 2. Probability & Impact Matrix *[8]*

The quadrants are classified as follows [3]: (1) High probability of risk that can very aggressively impact the project; (2) Average probability of risk, yet can be very costly to the company and should be monitored routinely; (3) High probability of risks and cause little impact to the company; and (4) Risk of low probability and low impact on the project. As a conclusion of these researches, achieving a mature idea about the use of these techniques to face the existing problems in the corporation, it was necessary to adapt and combine them in order to solve mainly the conflicts of interests. As a result of this, a new process model for agile planning has been created.

4. Proposed Agile Planning Technique: Brew Model

During the implementation of Relative Weighting, some deficiencies have been encountered. In short, the conclusion is that the existing methods aim to prioritize the activities under the business optics at the expense of priorities associated with the technical risks. Consequently, we face situations in which some features should be taken as a technique premise to the other one, but its business assigned value becomes a low priority. Then, it has conflicted desired approaches by the development team with business interests from the stakeholders.

The main original Relative Weighting shortcoming in this context for the desired prioritization based on technical risks is that it proposes the division of the value by the cost (technical complexity), consequently, the higher the complexity, the lower priority has the feature. This factor is contrary to what is stated in the Scrum guide [4]: *"Products are built iteratively using Scrum, wherein each Sprint creates an increment of the product, starting with the most valuable and riskiest"*.

Another factor that has been changed in the proposed technique is the scale 1-9 used to measure the values of the requirement. Since sequence numbers are a bit comparative, the use of a Fibonacci-based scale is more suitable in this situation. This is because with the Fibonacci scale, it is possible to have an increasing range of numbers, which

make each one more comparative with the increase of range of the scale. If a stakeholder, for example, has a User Story scoring 13 and immediately looks to score a second User Story, he compares it to the previous one.

The stakeholder can then have a doubt between punctuating 8 or 13, but seeing that 13 is relatively much larger than 8 and that this feature is not enough to have the same importance as the first, they decide more safely to keep the score 8.

Therefore, in the proposed technique, the scale was defined by the following numbers: 1, 2, 3, 5, 8, 13 and 20. The last number was rounded off in order to fix the end of the scale.

To obtain a form to qualify and justify the technical risks in a principled way, this technique uses a traditional approach, often not considered in agile environments: the Probability & Impact Matrix proposed by PMBOK [3]. This approach offers ways to address the risks much more thoroughly, predicting and assessing impacts at different levels of organization and providing ways to analyze the actions to be taken. A fundamental premise of this approach that fits exactly in the objectives is the fact that Probability & Impact Matrix proposes that the highest risk of technical requirements must be considered first, and precisely driven to the context of these real interests. This approach does not hurt agile principles, since it demonstrates ease of understanding, facility of communication between team members and ease of maintenance.

Then, as a gain from the combination of these practices, the proposed planning technique suggests a visual way to represent and communicate the priorities to all stakeholders named as Attractiveness versus Risks Matrix (Figure 3). It represents the features organized in a table composed of quadrants of risks combined with attractiveness.

Each feature has a location defined by coordinates provided by the business value versus technical risk or cost. Using this matrix, it is possible to achieve a greater transparency in the priority choices.

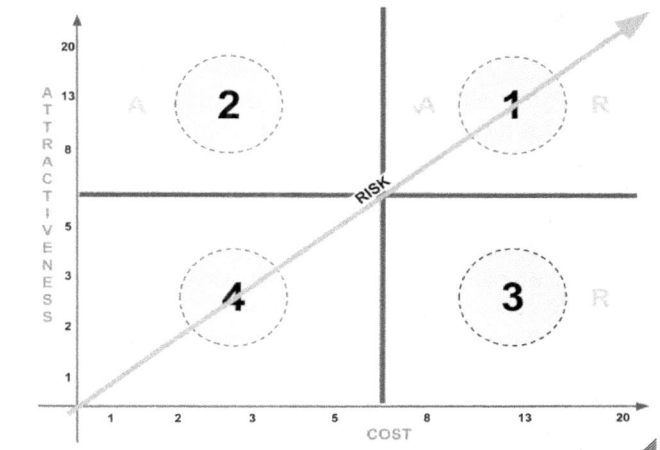

Figure 3. Attractiveness versus Risks Matrix.

This matrix suggests that the more is the earned value (attractiveness) and cost, the higher is the priority. This is because the cost for the development team is also considered based on the risks that each feature can represent to the probability of the non-delivering by its complexity.

The earned value, following the definitions of the Relative Weighting method, consists of two values: benefit and penalty, both at the same scale defined by just an axis, represented by the Attractiveness. It has been proposed accordingly that the result of each value belonging to this axis derived from the arithmetic average of the two scores. Therefore, it is defined:

$$Attractiveness = (benefit + penalty) / 2.$$

As an adaptation based on the ideas of the Probability & Impact Matrix [3], which considers the risks for all aspects of the project, this new matrix has been adopted for only the software requirements in a little different view. For the software development team, the features within the quadrants provide the following vision: (a) Quadrant 1 – A feature in this quadrant is exceedingly complex, it may be such as a definition of an architectural feature or a creation of a new component, for example, being often a basic premise to build the other features. It characterizes a key feature to be implemented, because besides its complexity, it adds higher earned value; (b) Quadrant 2 – A feature in this quadrant is considered as a lower risk, however, it provides a relevant earned value; (c) Quadrant 3 – A feature in this quadrant is often a minor feature that adds a little or irrelevant earned value. It is also complex to implement or has a high risk to the project that should be monitored, prevented or delayed if necessary; (d) Quadrant 4 – A feature in this quadrant is something simple and has low priority, since it causes little impact to the project and also provides the fewest earned value. It should be implemented only when the features of higher value have already been made.

In relation to existing works, this approach provides a more effective way of valuing a requirement according to their degree of risk and the impact that it may cause to the project, also offering subsidies to the design decisions based on its risks. In addition, it becomes a visual tool, which helps the development team to evaluate the risks of each feature and expose these facts to all those involved in a clearer and more honest communication approach. This visual presentation approach to the entire team gives an explanation based on the PMBOK risk management, which also results in more efficient ways to monitor or even mitigate those risks.

So, after the main tools for the processes of prioritization have been defined, the ideas of the model's dynamic were created. Therefore, the proposed approach was called "BREW Model", in which "BREW" stands for "Benefit-Risk Effective Weighting". It also settles the idea from its principle, of "brewing" the processes of prioritization in the context of agile methodologies.

To demonstrate these proposed processes of prioritization by the BREW Model it is necessary to explain them in terms of successive steps. The dynamic is then described in Figure 4.

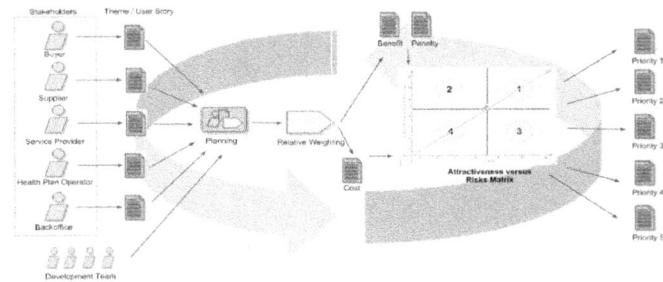

Figure 4. Steps for execution of the BREW Model.

First, the stakeholders bring their features to the planning meetings. This discussion should involve all the stakeholders and the development team. Here, within a consensus, the demands have their benefits and penalties scored, one against the other. In the second part of the meeting, only the development team discusses the complexity of each feature and its corresponding technical risks. Then they place each feature over the Attractiveness versus Risks Matrix, following the values of the scores as coordinates. They obtain the most valuable features, which are farther from the zero axis. So, the development team presents the order of priority to the stakeholders and gives their views on the priorities according to all the concepts of risk analysis.

Finally, all involved in the prioritization process can achieve the understanding about business and technical issues. The communication among them becomes clearer.

5. An Example Of Case Study

This section aims to describe a fictional story about planning to develop features related to an e-commerce platform of electronic sporting goods. The aim here is to illustrate the use of the BREW model in detail to unfold the dynamics of its implementation in a software project.

It is a system developed by a startup, which was released to the market with some features and even a few limitations. It was given only basic functionality which allowed customers to make their purchases with payment by boleto, without the possibility of monitoring the delivery of the products and without an online help chat, features that are considered as essential in a system of that category. The planning to be held, therefore, has the objective of increasing the product with all these features, in the shortest time as possible and ordering activities efficiently and productively to make it more attractive to the market and thus able to keep up with competitors.

The project has three stakeholders, who work directly in researches of new capabilities that may evolve the system to gain market competitiveness and improve relationships with their customers, thus increasing the volume of sales through the site. They will be called here as John, representing the purchase module, Mary, representative of the customer care module and Anthony, representative of the management module in orders and shipping. The development team has two developers, one test analyst and a Scrum Master.

The stakeholders travel throughout the country and take turns in tracking the activities of the development team, serving as the Product Owners of the project. Consequently, it requires that meetings of time-boxes have short duration, so that everyone can be present and thus participate in the defense of their prioritizations.

The company that develops software uses Scrum to manage the development processes. With the imminent need to release a new version of the system with all required increments, a Sprint Planning meeting was scheduled, in which all stakeholders participate in bringing their needs.

As the scope of new valuable features to be released, some requirements have been collected according to the customer's opinion as well as perceived needs through the use of the system. Then the Sprint Planning meeting started. Each stakeholder, therefore, presented their demands through their description of User Stories.

John brought the following stories:
• US01 - "As a buying customer, I want to pay by credit card, so that I can get more speed in my shop";
• US02 – "As a buying customer, I want the appropriated discounts calculated in cash payment by boleto, so that I can get advantages in this kind of payment".

Mary brought a few other needs:
• US03 - "As a buying customer, I want to take my doubts online with an attendant, so that I can solve them quickly and gain more agility in my shop";
• US04 – "As a buying customer, I want to be able to assess each help received by an attendant, so that I can continuously improve the way I met on it".

Anthony also brought his need:
• US05 – "Just like the carrier's delivery, I want to be able to signal the status of shipping for tracking, so that customers can have a schedule for delivery, increasing the reliability for the customer in making requests and the credibility in the transport service".

All these stories here were labeled with the initials "US" (User Story) followed by a sequential number for easy identification of each one along the explanations.

Each stakeholder presented their benefit and penalty and scores according to the degree of importance given to each of their stories and scores based on historical data of past meetings of prioritization. Each score is shown according to Table 1.

Table 1. Scores of benefit and penalty for the case study.

User Story	Benefit	Penalty	Total Value	Value Percent
US01	20	8	28	23
US02	13	8	21	18
US03	13	13	26	22
US04	8	3	11	9
US05	13	20	33	28
TOTAL:	67	52	119	100

The benefit is mainly ruled by the last clause of the sentence of each User Story, because it is where the importance is explained precisely, the reason for the existence of the story. In planning meetings, often in order to enhance the justification, the argument becomes necessary for each stakeholder in order to defend their priorities.

So, John thought about the reasons for the creation US01: "[...] so that I can get more speed and ease in my shop" and he appreciated with the maximum benefit. He thought, therefore, that as he represented the main focus of the system (the purchases), shopping would bring greater sales with more speed and ease.

However, the penalty to abandon this feature for the next iteration would not be severe since it would not prevent the customers from continuing doing their shopping, even though in somehow obsolete ways those were already implemented, such as payment by boleto.

The second story, US02, John relativized in comparison to the first, as being lesser attractive than the payment by credit card. In addition, paying by boleto, customers no longer receive this discount and live well with it. The system could then "survive" for one more iteration without this functionality. So it has the same penalty as the previous one.

Then Mary, considering good service as primordial for an electronic procurement system as it would provide an increase in the purchase volume, judged the benefit of US03 as thirteen, the same as US02, as it would be so attractive to the customer as having payment discounts. The penalty to abandon this feature in the current Sprint, in her view, could further alienate customers and cause some loss of fidelity of regular customers. It would be severe to delay this feature.

The functionality described for US04 would be dependent on the previous one. So, its benefit and penalty were scored based on this premise. It would therefore be a story with less priority.

As previously reported, there are no current features that show the status of deliveries. Therefore, Anthony would like to prioritize his needs considering this. Although it had less priority than the functionality of US01, (payment by credit card) even though, that would be fundamental in this Sprint. The functionality has therefore a maximum penalty if it is abandoned at this moment.

After all the discussion of the scores in the view of business, the meeting assumed a technical focus. The development team then scored the development cost of each feature as follows in Table 2.

Table 2. Scores of cost for the case study.

User Story	Estimate	Cost Percent
US01	13	31
US02	3	7
US03	13	31
US04	5	12
US05	8	19
TOTAL:	42	100

The team judged the functionality of US01 as being of high complexity. The need to implement the communication with the credit card system operators was considered and it would be necessary to study the solution. So this feature presents a high risk of not being completed on time.

The US02 story would be something regarded as simple to develop since it does not incur significant risks. But the US03 functionality has more complexity, so the development team scored with similar cost to the US01 because it would be necessary to implement an online chat with communication via socket technology, which would also be necessary to study.

The feature expressed in the US04 story would be relatively simple to implement, then the cost of taking it was five, with only a little more complexity than US02. And finally, the feature US05 would be a little more complex, since the team took into account the implementation of a service for external access by the carrier. There is therefore a more technological risk from this new form of communication.

After this stage, the development team held all the stories on the Attractiveness versus Risks Matrix and carried out the risk and impact assessment. They analyzed each story to fit in the quadrant that corresponds exactly to the design they had on their corresponding risk to the project. The matrix was then presented to the stakeholders and the necessary technical arguments were exposed.

In order to achieve a better visual differentiation between stories belonging to each one involved, they were represented by different colors as follows in Figure 5.

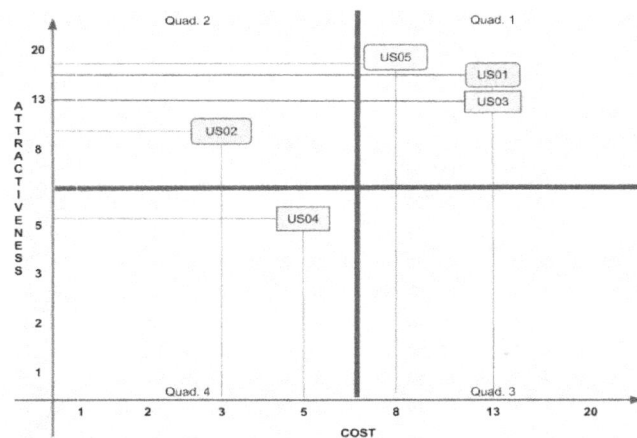

Figure 5. Attractiveness versus Risks Matrix for the case study.

The order prioritized for implementation was as follows: US01, US03, US05, US02 and US04. It may be noticed that the risks related to the development of technologies that make use of new communication protocols have been prioritized. Therefore, it can be developed to the components that can be reused by subsequent other features.

Thus, the system is componentized, achieving increased productivity and quality in software development with this emerging architecture, giving conditions to meet other demands with greater agility.

The original Relative Weighting approach, compared to this method, if applied in this project, would have a totally different order as shown in Table 3.

Table 3. Application of the case study in the relative weighting approach.

User Story	Benefit	Penalty	Total Value	Value Percent	Estimate	Cost Percent	Priority
US01	20	8	28	23	13	31	76
US02	13	8	21	18	3	7	247
US03	13	13	26	22	13	31	71
US04	8	3	11	9	5	12	78
US05	13	20	33	28	8	19	146
TOTAL:	67	52	119	100	42	100	617

The resulting order, considering the highest score to the lowest, would therefore be: US02, US05, US04, US01 and US03. It becomes clear that priorities with lower risk and technological complexity would be of higher priority such as the story US02, as it would not add anything innovative on the technical point of view. In addition, some demands that were the premise for the creation of others, for example, the US03 and US04 stories, had their priorities reversed.

6. Evaluation To Adopting The New Model

In order to measure the effort spent in the prioritizing processes, it has been necessary to apply some methods that would provide an efficient way to compare and know if a proposed solution would be effective. A plan has been made to define the required period to apply the validation. The main objective of this period was to collect a body of consistent data for evaluation. Then, a necessary interval of time involving a Planning Meeting and a number of Sprints that would be sufficient for its completion were defined.

The evaluation of the existing scenario occurred in two perspectives: qualitative and quantitative. It is because analyzing qualitatively makes it possible to analyze the degree of satisfaction of the stakeholders in maintaining the existing prioritization processes. Analyzing quantitatively is a way of getting the performance of this approach in the time-boxes meetings as an essential indicator to get concrete data to demonstrate the existing communication problems. So there were two tests to reach the necessary conclusions about the low quality of the implemented model: under different views; and collecting the key points, the focus to apply the improvements.

In order to implement all the proposed assessment in a qualitative view, a questionnaire containing some objective questions to the stakeholders was created.

The questions were initially asked to analyze the entire period that had preceded the implementation of an improvement.

It had been planned to analyze them again a second time after a new implementation, seeking to analyze the results obtained by the stakeholders in the prioritization processes intended to evaluate the evolution of this view with the implementation of the new model. All data was analyzed using the method of the Grounded Theory (GT).

GT is a both qualitatively and quantitatively technique suitable for studying human behavior and organizational culture [5], so the choice to use it as a basis for analyzing the results of this study. GT is aimed at generating explanations for the actions of individuals, focusing on why and how certain groups interact with other groups in specific situations, according to a context delimited from the reality experienced by these groups. So, the questions answered by the stakeholders were analyzed by this theory. This technique in software engineering areas is even scarcer, however, there are successful experiments in software engineering, which also use it, such as investigations of the practice of software process improvement in the Irish industry [6].

The defined period for observation and analysis of the actual situation without a consistent method of prioritizing in fact lasted for a Release Planning Meeting and two Sprint Planning Meetings, a sufficient number of Sprints to deliver this release. The duration of each meeting and each demand prioritized were registered, and after that, the questionnaire was applied and answered by all of the five stakeholders.

The qualitative conclusion of the evaluation this time was that the main problem appointed was caused by the great effort found to prioritize features, often caused by difficulty in executing prioritizing, combined to the fact of not having a concrete method on how to do it. The lack of transparency demonstrated by the software development team to represent their difficulties was also one of the problems.

The quantitative evaluation showed the following results as demonstrated by Table 4.

Table 4. Metrics before implementation of the new method.

Previous Situation - Without Methods			
Release Planning			
	Quantity of Themes	Total Time Duration (hours)	Avg. Duration Per Theme (hours)
	3	05:05	01:41
Sprint Planning			
	Quantity of User Stories	Total Time Duration (hours)	Avg. Duration Per User Story (mins)
First Meeting	4	01:43	25.75
Second Meeting	3	02:20	46.6
	Final Avg. Duration Per User Story (mins):		36.18

7. Use Of The Brew Model And Results Assessment

In the first meeting, the Release Planning, it was necessary to explain how the new method works in terms of steps, to start the process of implementing it. This explanation took about twenty minutes and then the whole dynamic was put in place to prioritize the themes brought up to this discussion. There were many questions over the use of this process still they were promptly answered. The theme that had a higher earned value in the view of all stakeholders and that also had a higher technological risk to the system in the view of the development team was prioritized. The data for the duration of the meeting was properly collected.

With the theme properly prioritized, it was necessary to start planning the execution of the order of their coding features, at the level of their User Stories, from the first Sprint Planning meeting. Then, the proper benefit and penalty punctuations of each started being scored and put on the Attractiveness versus Risks Matrix. Nevertheless, the conclusion that some priorities did not match the real need for this first delivery was reached, which resulted in the prioritization of too complex items. The team would stand to deliver a unique User Story for this Sprint and that this would not bring any earned value in a business view. The stakeholders then disagreed with this approach for this kind of meeting.

They came to the conclusion that in this particular case, the approach of the Relative Weighting would be better. So, that was used and the team finally managed to reach a proper prioritization, with three User Stories prioritized, two less complex than the others that would add good earned value of business and a third more complex that would bring good benefits to the system, mitigating some architectural risks.

The second Sprint Planning Meeting has already occurred with the process model adapted to the reality of the company, with the deficiencies corrected. Then all the scores were submitted to the Relative Weighting approach and the User Stories were properly prioritized. An important fact to notice this time was that the stakeholders were concerned about bringing the new demands now properly punctuated. This fact showed that the use of a concrete technique to enable them to have ways to prioritize and justify their priorities had good motivational effects. There were five User Stories involved in this discussion for prioritizing.

There was a third Sprint Planning Meeting for this release. The results of prioritizing were better than the previous discussions and the meeting lasted for less time. The understanding of the method sounded clearer and its adoption was consolidated. The total of this release was then delivered and the time was once more registered.

Then, it was time to make a new qualitative evaluation and compare both results, before and after this approach, in order to get the performance at the quantitative metrics realized and the level of adherence to the method, at the qualitative evaluation. The same questionnaire used at the prior time to the use of the technique was applied, this time, to review the new processes in place. Then it was employed to qualitative analysis, using the method of Grounded Theory again, on the responses collected.

The analysis of the answers post-of the questionnaire after the implementation of BREW Model revealed a quite positive result. As responses to the questionnaire, there were citations indicating that the model provided simple demands and necessary effort, which brought good results to the team. It was concluded as a consensus that there was a significant decrease in the process of prioritizing efforts to the implementation of the new technique.

For the quantitative analysis, a decrease in the time for each story or theme means that the team communication has been improved and the number of conflicts was decreased. The results for this new metric, after the use of the technique, are in the table 5.

Table 5. Metrics after the implementation of the new method.

Subsequent Situation - With BREW Model		
Release Planning		
Quantity of Themes	Total Time Duration (hours)	Avg. Duration Per Theme (hours)
3	03:20	01:06
Sprint Planning		
Quantity of User Stories	Total Time Duration (hours)	Avg. Duration Per User Story (mins)
First Meeting — 3	01:47	36
Second Meeting — 5	00:33	6.6
Third Meeting — 2	00:22	11
Final Avg. Duration Per User Story (mins):		17.87

So, for the Release Planning meeting, the total time spent compared to the previous meeting without the technique was approximately 47% lower. It can be concluded that the method, combined to the motivation provided to stakeholders in bringing their demands has already punctuated to this meeting, has brought more efficiency to this process. For the Sprint Planning meeting there was an average reduction of about 51% at the time of prioritization for each User Story.

This fact is evidence that the use of the suggested model reached the desired improvement and efficiency for the prioritization. Therefore, it shows that the conflicts of interests have been mitigated.

In conclusion, the evaluation evidenced some positive results in the use of the proposed technique. As a result, the evaluation pointed out that the conflict of interests and the time spent with prioritization discussions was drastically reduced, giving more time to refine the solution and to keep the team motivated within the agile approach.

8. Important Improvements

As previously reported, some improvements resulting from real use of the BREW Model could be applied to refine the technique according to the perceptions of those involved.

This gain is presented as something significant to the continuous improvement of its processes. So with this reformulation of the process model, figure 6 shows the optimized version of its details, presenting the model with different execution steps under each of the meetings that it applies to.

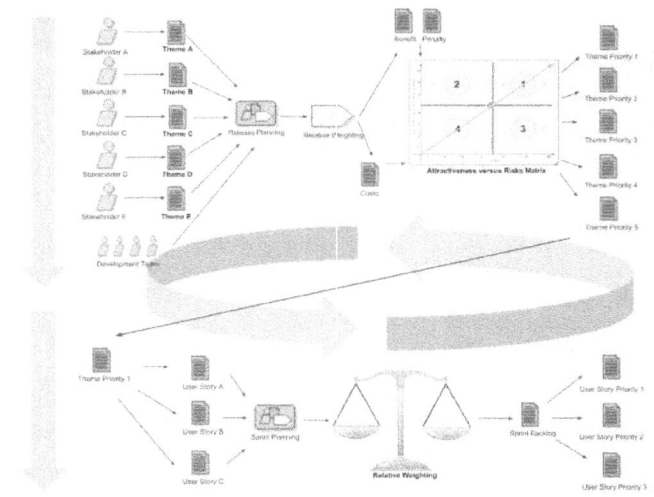

Figure 6. Steps for execution of the improved BREW model

Now, this methodology basically proposes an execution of two different ways into two time-boxes: the Release Planning Meeting and the Sprint Planning Meeting. For the Release Planning, it is proposed to use the Attractiveness versus Risks Matrix to prioritize the themes. After that, for the Sprint Planning corresponding to such theme, it is used the complete and original Relative Weighting method to prioritize the User Stories from that theme.

Therefore, in the first meeting, it is possible and necessary to prioritize the themes (group of related User Stories) according with their degrees of risk, and after that, in order to maximize the productivity for the main User Stories, in the second meeting, the Relative Weighting model may be used, prioritizing the most important one to the business and the simplest to develop.

So, in the first part of the prioritization processes, for the Release Planning, the analysis is less detailed in order to consider a greater quantity of demands. The second part, for the Sprint Planning processes, presents a deeper detailed approach in order to analyze the importance of each feature in its particularities.

9. Conclusion

This paper discusses planning activities in the context of agile software development, especially in scenarios where there are multiple stakeholders involved. Activities intrinsic to this approach are related to estimation and prioritization of work, which require inspection and adaptation depending on the context or environment where the agile methodology is implemented. Therefore, it proposes some adaptation and combination on consolidated theories, to tailor the processes used to achieve full compliance within a dynamic environment with multiple stakeholders. As a result, the proposed model solves conflicts of interest between them, evidenced by the reduction of the time duration of the planning meetings.

The original creation of this work is a compilation of studies that have already been consolidated, combined with ideas and principles suggested as ideas resulting of researches. As a result, the elaboration of new concepts involved solutions that have not been covered in its fullness yet, such as the effective resolution of interests in environments whose product focuses on various areas of business and a more transparent risk management to everyone involved. It already incorporates the best-known approaches both in agile methodologies and traditional approaches.

The main contribution of this work is the proposed BREW Model practices, that aims to decrease the conflict of interests in a common environment found nowadays at the corporations: teams of business analysts with different interests in the same application. This approach was applied in a real project and the assessment techniques used indicates that it was able to reduce the team conflicts and increased their communication, resulting in a decrease of the prioritization efforts.

Another contribution is the proposed way for the presentation of risks to the whole team, since the classification of risks in the Attractiveness versus Risks Matrix provides a more visible and understandable view of them to everyone involved. The compilation of all these studies resulted in a model known as BREW Model, which achieves improvements in the prioritization techniques to a specific environment that is commonly found nowadays.

Aiming to know if the proposed approach achieves its goals, assessment techniques were used intending to measure the stakeholders degree of satisfaction, its ease of use in the planning meetings and whether there was a performance optimization in the planning activities.

The first evaluation was based on questionnaires that were distributed to the stakeholders before and after its implementation in order to analyze impacts of the new approach. These reports were submitted to a qualitative assessment technique known as Grounded Theory [5].

A parallel evaluation approach used metrics based on the time measurement for the prioritization activities. These metrics assess the time spent in planning meetings and the time used for priority discussion in between them. The goal was to verify if the proposed technique directed the discussions and increased the consensus among the stakeholders.

In conclusion, the evaluation evidenced some positive results in the use of the proposed technique. As a result, the evaluation pointed out that the conflicts of interest and the time spent with prioritization discussions were drastically reduced, giving more time to refine the solution and to keep the team motivated within the agile approach.

Many current efforts are aimed to improve planning in agile projects, but there is still too much to be explored in this wide area. Therefore, this study contributes to software engineering, intending to advance the existing studies and expand the horizon of other forms of improvement about agile methodologies, without ruling out major contributions that have been offered by more traditional approaches.

References

[1] COHN, Mike. "Agile Estimating and Planning", Addison Wesley, TBD.

[2] COHN, Mike. "User Stories Applied", Addison Wesley, 2004.

[3] PMBOK. "A Guide to the Project Management Body of Knowledge", 2004.

[4] SCRUM GUIDE. "Scrum Guide", Ken Schwaber and Jeff Sutherland. Scrum.org. 2009. http://www.scrum.org/scrumguides. Retrieved 2010-02-03.

[5] GROUNDED THEORY. "What is Grounded Theory?", Jillian Rhine. 2009. http://www.groundedtheory.com/what-is-gt.aspx. Visited in 2010-10-15.

[6] COLEMAN, G.; O'Cconnor, R. 2007. "Using grounded theory to understand software process improvement: A study of Irish software product companies, Information and Software Technology". Journal of Information and Software Technology, v. 49, n. 6, p. 654-667, jun.

[7] COHN, Mike. "Prioritizing Your Product Backlog Presentation". 2009. http://www.mountaingoatsoftware.com/system/presentation/file/101/ Cohn_NDC09_Prioritizing.pdf?1267636319. Retrieved 2011-02-05.

[8] JISC infoNet, "A JISC Advance service". 2009. http://www.jiscinfonet.ac.uk/InfoKits/infokit-related-files/riskmatrixpic/view. Visited in 2011-06-22.

Classifiers: A Simple Framework for Accelerating Application Development

David Raal

Occam Software
Vancouver, BC Canada
davidraal@yahoo.com

Abstract

Software applications need an approach for providing simple, configurable, persistent value sets. Large applications can require dozens of these value sets for drop downs, radio selections, menus, object attributes and business logic. A common framework which solves this problem can be widely leveraged across many applications, reducing code complexity and improving application configurability and maintainability. A framework, based on classification schemes containing a set of classifiers, and is persistent, elegantly solves this problem. Practical experience with the framework on several projects has proven that it is easily adopted by application development teams. The framework was widely used and significantly reduced code size and complexity, reducing risk and project schedules.

Categories and Subject Descriptors   D.2.1.1 [Software Architectures]: Patterns

General Terms   Design

Keywords   Classifier, framework, value sets, code re-use

1.   Introduction

Designing a large application with hundreds of web pages/screens can require the definition, storage, and management of dozens (if not hundreds) of value sets. Each drop down, radio selection and check box, and many object fields require a well defined set of values. For an application which persists its state in an RDBMS, these value sets need additional characteristics than simple enumerations:

- Temporal attributes (lists change over time and may need to be historically accurate)

- Persistence (code changes should not be required in an application to expire or modify a simple value, database updates should be used)

- Configurable Ordering (capabilities to order lists alphabetically or through database configuration are very useful)

- Configurable set members based on business needs (e.g. organization/role specificity)

Currently available to address this type of programming requirement (in Java and C#) is the enum. Although the Java enum is quite powerful in jdk 1.5, it falls short in several areas:

- Is not persistent and requires coding to change values (configuration through a database is not possible, although an enum value can be persisted)

- Is not effective dated and cannot be expired through database configuration

- Cannot be specialized for an organization/role through database configuration

To address these shortcomings, a framework based around the concept of a scheme with a set of contained classifiers was designed and implemented.

2.   Background

The initial notion of classifiers and schemes was provided to me by Chip Morris [1] of Ariel Partners in 2003. Chip had no implementation or concrete details to offer, so I started work on a design that evolved over many months on a large J2EE web application I was working on as an Architect. This initial implementation was widely adopted and had great success on the project, although it was somewhat over-designed and complex. The design (outlined here) was simplified for a subsequent small web application I built and proved to be easier to manage and implement.

3.   Classifiers and Schemes

A simple object oriented framework based on a classification scheme which contains a set of classifiers provides the basis for this framework. These objects can provide the backbone for many core value sets in an application. One construct with a few simple classes and an associated set of database tables is sufficient to implement the framework. Applications can make extensive use of the framework to reduce code and centralize the configuration and management of drop downs, radio selections, enumerated lists, and object attributes (e.g. state, status). Classification schemes need to be available through an easily accessible service within the application. Once they are retrieved from the database and cached, they can be quickly accessed and reused due to their (mostly) static nature. As classifiers and schemes are data driven, yet have well-known IDs that do not change over time, they can play the role of both a constant with an associated display value and a dynamically configured value set. This flexibility has proven to be extremely useful in practice.

The classification scheme entity has the following design characteristics:

- A well defined identity (Name and ID)
- A description as well as a name
- Immutable id (once created and referenced in the database)
- A public interface to access the classifiers contained in the scheme
- Methods to retrieve Classifier sets (retrieve all, retrieve by effective date and/or organizationId)
- Methods to add and remove classifiers

The classifier entity has the following design characteristics:

- Ownership by a classification scheme
- Contains staticName, name and description fields
- staticName is useful when maintaining persisted classifiers so they can be easily recognized in the database tables. The name attribute is visibly displayed to end users and may be altered over time
- Well known identity (ID or scheme + staticName)
- Classifier ID and scheme ID are immutable once they have been created and referenced in the database
- Temporal attributes (effectiveDate and expirationDate)
- Can be specialized for different businesses/organizations via an organization ID

The SchemeGroup entity has the following design characteristics:

- A well defined identity (Name and ID)
- A description as well as a name
- Immutable ids (once created and referenced in the database)
- Contains a list of Schemes for the scheme group
- A public interface to access the list of schemes contained in the scheme group

3.1 Managing the data

The management of the scheme and classifier IDs in the database is of critical importance to ensuring this framework is easy to adopt and implement. One of the most important benefits of Classifiers and Schemes is that they are data driven via database table records. However, successful adoption of the framework is easier to achieve if there are simple processes for managing the database records. Experience has shown that the following rules greatly simplify management of this framework (and data) and its integration into applications:

- Scheme IDs are sequenced numbers starting at 1 and going forwards. They may be loosely grouped by ID (e.g. All menu schemes are between 150 and 170, object status schemes are 200 to 300, report schemes are 300 to 350).
- Classifier IDs are a sequenced group starting with the schemeID multiplied by 1,000 (e.g. Scheme 102 has classifierIDs starting with 102,000; 102,001 ...). This enables simple administration of classifier and scheme-IDs in the database. It is highly unlikely that a scheme will need more than 1000 classifiers. If this should occur, classifiers may not be a good fit for this value set.
- Commonly referenced schemes and classifiers should have their IDs declared as constants in the application for quick reference. This supports rapid lookup and retrieval of schemes and classifiers from the application service which provides them.

3.2 Example Interfaces

There are 5 important classes/interfaces that must be implemented to support this framework:

- ClassificationScheme (or Scheme) - container for a set of classifiers
- Classifier - represents a single unique value in a set
- SchemeGroup - represents a collection of related schemes configured in the database
- ClassifieriersSvc - application svc used to retrieve classifiers, schemes and scheme groups from the database. Should encapsulate some caching mechanism.
- Classified - an interface any class can implement to support being classified (has been tagged with one or more classifiers)

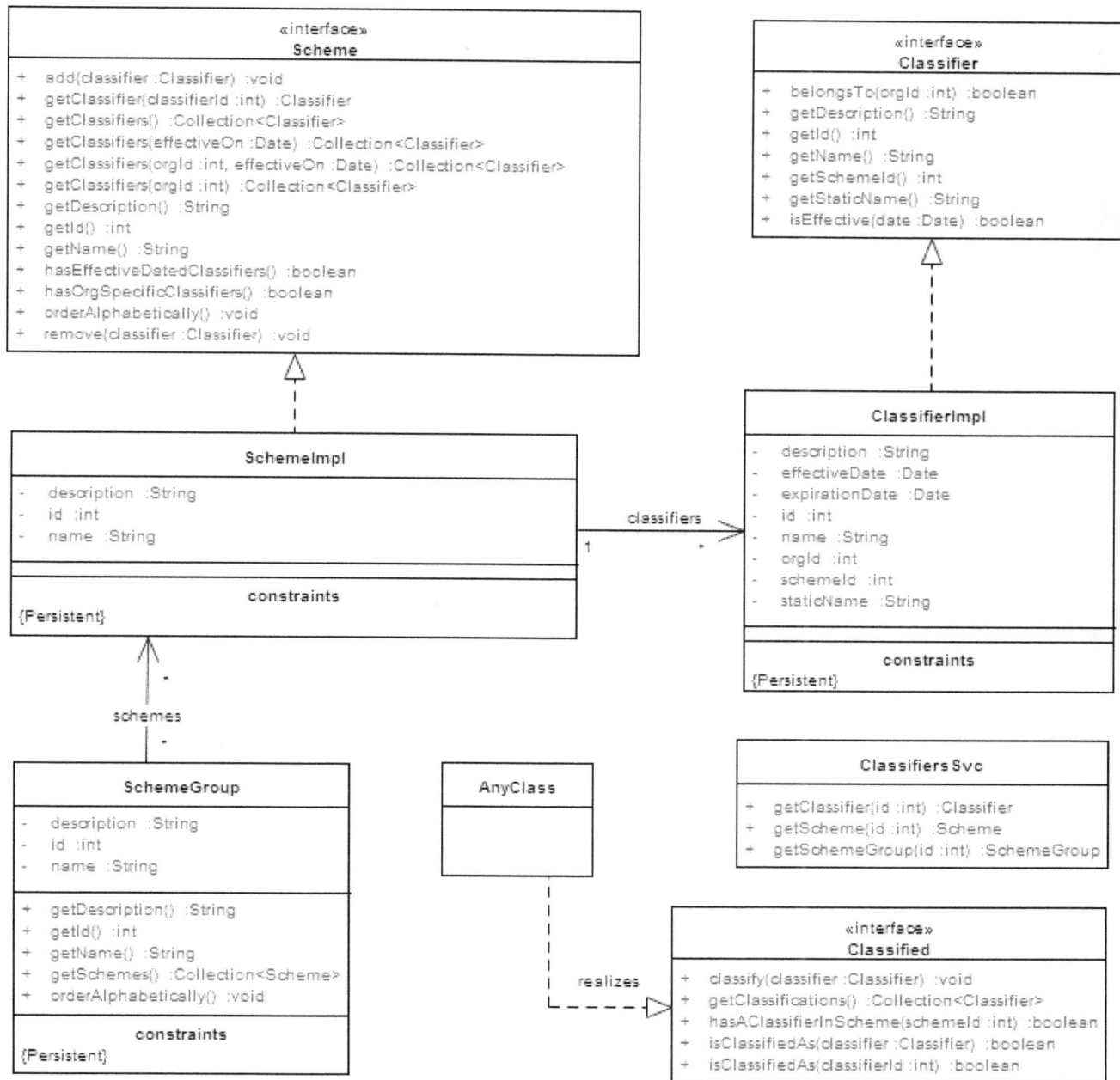

Figure 1. Class diagram: Classifiers and Schemes

```
public class ClassifiersSvc {
    public Classifier getClassifier(int id);
    public Scheme getScheme(int id);
    public SchemeGroup getSchemeGroup(int id);
}
```

Figure 2. ClassifiersSvc interface example

```
public interface Classifier {
   public String getName();
   public String getStaticName();
   public String getDescription();
   public int getId();
   public int getSchemeId();
   public boolean isEffective(Date d);
   public boolan belongsTo(long orgId);
}
```
Figure 3. Classifier interface example

```
public interface SchemeGroup {
   public Collection <Scheme> getSchemes();
   public String getName();
   public String getDescription();
   public int getId();
}
```
Figure 4. SchemeGroup interface example

```
public interface Scheme{
   public String getName();
   public String getDescription();
   public int getId();
   public Collection <Classifier> getClassifiers();
   // effective on this date
   public Collection <Classifier> getClassifiers(Date d);
   // belongs to this org
   public Collection <Classifier> getClassifiers(int orgId);
   // effective on this date and belongs to this org
   public Collection <Classifier> getClassifiers(int orgId, Date d);
   public void add(Classifier cl);
   public void remove(Classifier cl);
   public void orderAlphabetically();
   public Classifier getClassifier(int ID);
}
```
Figure 5. Scheme interface example

```
public interface Classified {
   public void classify (Classifier cl) throws InvalidClassificationException;
   public boolean isClassifiedAs(Classifier cl);
   public boolean isClassifiedAs(int classifierId);
   public boolean hasAClassifierInScheme(int schemeId);
   public Collection<Classifier> getClassifiers();
}
```
Figure 6. Classified interface example

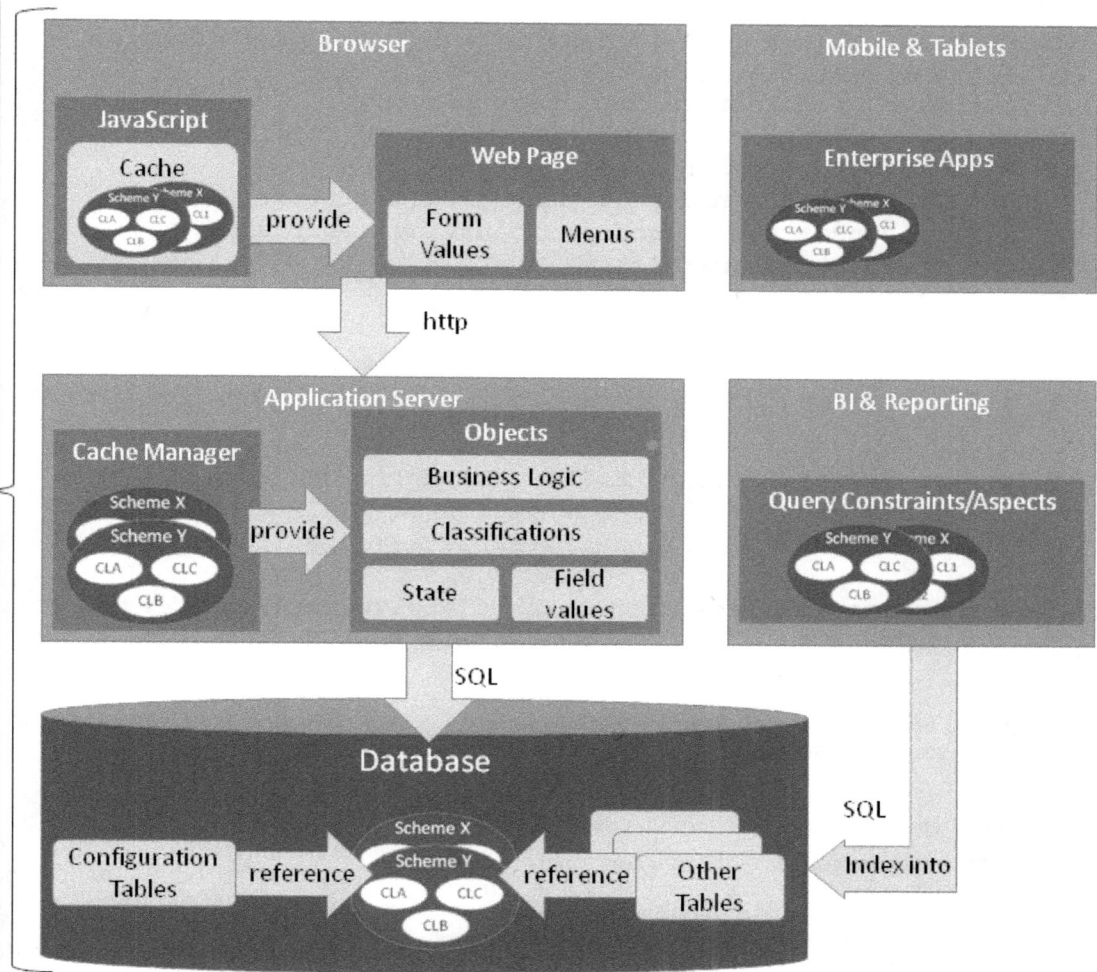

Figure 7. Broad usage of classifiers pattern

4. Extending the usage pattern

Classifiers and schemes can have a broader reach of duties than UI drop downs and lists and bounded object values. Once they become accepted and widely used, they can fill other roles in an application and can be extended across all layers and tiers of IT applications (web applications, business intelligence, server code, browser code). The simplicity of the framework is a key factor in its rapid adoption on IT projects. Figure 7 shows how classifiers and schemes become integrated into tiered IT applications.

4.1 Using classifiers in business logic

Classifiers can also be used in complex processing and logic flows. When a business object implements a Classifiable interface, has fields that contain classifiers or extends a Classifiable abstract base class, the business object can now be analyzed and processed in useful and complex ways.

Objects which are classifiable can be used to help implement complex rules. A rules engine is a good candidate for working on objects which have been classified. Complex logical expressions can be built around classified objects. This simple interface can easily be supported by many different business objects. The results of rules processing and calculations can be re-applied to objects as further classifications. In this approach, multi-pass processing can be used to layer classifications on business objects for sophisticated rules and processing requirements.

For example, most applications require some form of menus for navigation. These may be links in a web page or drop down menus in a desktop or more sophisticated web application. Classifiers and schemes are an excellent fit for creating these menus and applying business logic to them to refine the menus based on entitlements. First, a scheme group is retrieved which contains all of the schemes and classifiers for an applications drop down menus (configured in the database). Then, each scheme is cloned (for a user) and has classifiers removed if they are not authorized for that menu item (simple role-based configuration in the database). Additional menu items for specialized roles can be layered on top of the basic authorization. Finally, the scheme group is checked to see if there are any schemes that have no classifiers. If so, then the scheme is removed from the group. Once the scheme group has been cloned and narrowed for authorized menu items, a simple factory class can render the scheme group as HTML, JavaScript, etc. for display within the browser. Pseudo code for this would look like:

```
SchemeGroup menus = ClassifiersSvc.getSchemeGroup(MENUS_ID);
Collection<Classifier> authorizedClassifiers =
   configSvc.getAuthorizedMenuItems(person);
SchemeGroup myMenus = menus.clone();
for (Scheme menu : myMenus.getSchemes()) {
   for (Classifier menuItem : menu.getClassifiers() {
      if (!authorizedClassifiers.contains(menuItem) {
         menu.remove(menuItem);
      }
   }
}
// If there are other business rules for menu items, they can
// be subsequently applied in a second pass. e.g. Add central
// admin menu items if a person has special status.
if (person.isClassifiedAs(CENTRAL_ADMIN)){
   Scheme adminScheme = myMenus.getScheme(ADMIN_SCHEME_ID);
   adminScheme.addClassifier(ClassifiersSvc.getClassifier(
                           CHANGE_PASSWORD_MENU_ITEM_ID));
   adminScheme.addClassifier(ClassifiersSvc.getClassifier(
                           DEACTIVATE_PERSON_MENU_ITEM_ID));
}
```

Figure 8. Example code for classifier and scheme customizations based on a users role

4.2 Classifiers can help define domain constraints

If a system has a complex set of domain constraints related to classifications, classifiers and related meta data can be used to define and enforce these constraints. If a user interface were built to manage the schemes, classifiers and constraints, an application could be easily configured to implement these constraints at the application level. Consider the following examples of classification constraints that can be built into an application with this approach:

- A Person must be classified with at least one ROLE classifier and must have one and only one STATUS classifier

- A person cannot be classified as both an EMPLOYEE and a CONTRACTOR

- A person classified as a CONTRACTOR cannot also have a status of MATERNITY_LEAVE

4.3 Synergy with configurability and Business Intelligence

An application built using classifiers also benefits from synergy with configurability and business intelligence. Classifiers can be easily referenced in data-driven configurations and will have referential integrity in the database through foreign key mappings. Only one mechanism is required to access, update and store Classifier based configurations resulting in a small easy to maintain code base. For example, classifier configurations can be used to configure a time and attendance application to allow one organization to support CASH AND COMP time selections for Overtime requests and another organization to support only

COMP time for Overtime requests. Pseudo code would look like:

```
orgAConfigModel.addAllowedOTType(CASH);
orgAConfigModel.addAllowedOTType(COMP);
persist(orgAConfigModel);

orgBConfigModel.addAllowedOTTYpe(COMP);
persist(orgBConfigModel);
```

Similar benefits exist for business intelligence. When data is "tagged" with classifiers, it populates the database with precise well known information that makes it easier to build accurate reports and analytics. Once reports users and developers become familiar with the classifiers and schemes that database entities are populated with, information analysis and reporting becomes more accurate. The number of free form text fields are reduced and information becomes more consistent with well defined value sets.

5. Benefits

After having applied this pattern to both a large enterprise application and a small web application, the following benefits were realized:

- Significant reduction in code size and complexity for user interfaces as one simple set of classes supplies a large portion of the UI selection data.

- Reduction in number of tables and table complexity as all drop downs, lists, value sets, selections etc. are stored in one set of database tables

- Improvements in application performance as the Classification Schemes are cached in memory and are very fast to retrieve

- Ease of configurability due to the simple storage in a set of tables. Classifiers can be added and expired easily with simple database scripts. Often, no code changes are required.

- Dramatic code simplification throughout the application code base due to the breadth of the implementation which uses classifiers. The UI, business objects, configuration engine and the rules engine all make extensive use of classifiers.

- Rapid acceptance and usage by developers. The Classifier pattern was well documented and extensively used throughout the code base. It is a very simple concept and easy to adopt. This makes the adoption rate by new developers very high and productivity gains are quickly realized.

6. Problems/pitfalls

Classifiers and schemes are a very useful framework which can be widely applied to many applications. However, their use (like all design patterns) must be carefully applied to avoid issues or problems. For example:

- Classifiers should not replace all occurrences of enums. When enums reside purely in the programming realm and are not based on persistent values or referenced in persistent configurations, they can be an excellent implementation choice.

- Classifiers and schemes must be carefully managed across various environments and deployment stages to ensure correctness and consistency. This is critical to prevent database integrity issues or runtime failures as the code evolves with the persistent classifiers.

- For dynamically growing schemes (classifiers are added via data loads or external interfaces), there are additional complexities in key management. The classifier IDs do not have to be contiguous if they are dynamically created during run-time they just need to within the set range for the scheme. e.g. For a schemeID =105, the classifiers IDs must be within 105,000 and 105,999. However, once a classifier has been stored and referenced, its ID cannot change. If it needs to be retired, its status can be set to inactive and/or its expirationDate can be set to the appropriate value.

7. Looking forward

Taking the Classifier/Scheme framework to the next level could involve the following:

- Building a UI framework to manage the creation and configuration of Classifiers across one or multiple projects. This framework would be able to generate SQL scripts to deploy changes to classifiers and schemes across environments.

- Building a rules framework to enter and apply constraints on business objects based on their classifications and persist those rules

- Extending the database schema and object model to support internationalization of classifiers and schemes

8. References

Dr. Walter G. "Chip" Morris, formerly of Ariel Partners

A Regression Testing Framework for Financial Time-Series Databases

An Effective Combination of FitNesse, Scala, and KDB/Q

Roberto Salama

Morgan Stanley
Roberto.Salama@morganstanley.com

Abstract

In this paper we present the testing framework built during the development of Morgan Stanley's next generation enterprise-wide time-series database, *Horizon*. Horizon replaces two separate time-series data containers: one houses a-periodic tick by tick data originating from real-time feeds and the other houses periodic data received from vendors at regular intervals. Both of these data sets, although disparate in nature, are now managed through the same system, and the original containers, both traditional row-ordered relational databases are now being retired. One of the biggest challenges the team faced was how to migrate data and functionality from systems with a long history into new containers while guaranteeing the same data quality and accuracy.

Categories and Subject Descriptors D.2.4 [**Software/Program Verification**]: Validation. D.2.9 [**Testing and Debugging**]: Software Quality Assurance.

General Terms Languages, Reliability, Verification.

Keywords Functional Programming, Test Driven Development, Financial Time-Series Databases, Asynchronous actor-based concurrent programming, FitNesse, Scala, KDB/Q,

1. Introduction

A time-series is essentially a table where its primary key consists of a date and at least one other identifier (i.e. a stock ticker) along with observations which happened at the same time (for example, bid and ask, or open, high, low, close, ask, bid, and volume). Moreover, financial time-series, once stored, are typically not modified. Corrections made to already recorded data are handled by storing the correction records as new events and linking the correction event with the corrected event in a manner that we can query *as-of* a particular date. Our implementation is a fairly standard bi-temporal database similar to the ones in [1] and [2].

Time series databases are typically very large and grow very fast. We expect ours to grow to the peta-byte range within the next couple of years. With this footprint and growth profile, the existing containers, both relational, row-oriented databases were unable to keep up with the current volume let alone with projected volumes. In order to achieve this type of scalability it was necessary to switch to a column-oriented database. Refer to [3] for a comparison of both approaches.

We chose the KDB+ database from Kx. KDB+ is a column-oriented database with a single data format for real-time and historical formats providing a unified environment for handling all types of time-series data. It is programmed through its scripting language Q, a vector-based functional language, provides users with a powerful environment for querying data and applying transformations through anonymous functions, lambdas. KDB+ is able to handle millions of records per second, billions per day accumulated in in-memory databases, and, trillions of historical records stored in databases on disk. [3]. Q is a vector processing language which is well suited for performing complex calculations quickly on large volumes of data [5]. The following are some of the virtues of Q:

- In memory database (RDB) with a persistent backing. store (HDB).
- Stronly typed, dynamically checked interpreted interpreted language allows for rapid prototyping.
- Table oriented supporting a rich SQL dialect
- Fixed set of datatypes: scalar including date, datetime, minute, second, and time; list; dictionary; and table.
- Support for IPC, both asynchronous and synchronous.

Divided into two parallel development streams, we iteratively developed different components of the Horizon plant. The *container* group focused on developing the core infrastructure, the various processes that are required to run the plant, and the management system around KDB, while the *content* group focused on developing the data readers, formatters, and data schemas for both the real-time (in-memory, RDB) and historical databases (on disk, HDB) as well as the transformation layer that stores the contents of the RDB into its corresponding HDB.

Tight development iterations required that we address testing fairly early in the process. It was clear that a waterfall development methodology where developers first develop the code then QA tests and often integrates, was not going to work. The intricacies of the different time series, related schemas, and type of queries was business knowledge that our QA team did not

Fixture	Constructor Args			
name	pass?	msgs	eval	pass
SIMPLE	=2	ResultsSimple	1+0	{[x] x}
DOTZ	true	ResultsDotZ	(.z.N;.z.i;.z.K)	{[y] all ({-16h~type x};{x>0};{x=2.6}) @@' y}
CALFILL	true	ResultsCalFll	.hz.heval\".hz.calFill[`f`ed`ff,2010.04.01 2010.04.24].da.getOSTSData`dname`tname`id s`cnames`ed`edi(`de;`da_price;`IBM;`rawtp`id`v d;2010.04.01;2010.04.24)	{not[null exec first rawtp from x where vd=2010.04.02]&17=count x}

Figure 1. Example FitNesse Table.

have, Therefore it was critical that we adopt a more test driven development approach whereby developers write tests for the components they are working on, and the system evolves in parallel to an evolving set of regression tests. To do so, we needed a framework that would allow a developer to manage tests akin to writing code.

2. Testing Frameworks

We searched for a test framework that would execute tests written in Q by developers. The tests, typically but not limited to query statements, retrieve data from Horizon, and use, dynamically injected functions also written by developers to determine whether a test passed or not. We also required that that it be straight forward to manipulate comparison results in order to facilitate analysis of large data sets whilst identifying mismatches.

We started using an internally developed, Perl based testing infrastructure but quickly found ourselves writing too much Perl code to manage test hierarchies as well as marshaling data to and from Q.

We also considered Cucumber, a Behavior Driven Development framework which allows users to describe how software should behave. It uses a Domain Specific Language which serves as documentation, automated test, and development aid all rolled into one format [7]. Unfortunately, having to learn another language that wrapped our Q-based query statements and functions was going to take too long.

We settled on FitNesse [8]. FitNesse is a wiki, a known paradigm among developers. As a software testing tool, FitNesse empowers developers to collaboratively define tests as web pages containing tables of inputs and expected outputs. As a web server, FitNesse packages up the data from wiki tables into objects, executes the underlying code, and returns actual values which FitNesse then uses to compare to the expected values specified in the tables. Cells in the table are displayed in red if their content does not match the expected value, and green otherwise. The code that executes with data from a wiki table is called a *fixture*. FitNesse provides a rich set of standard fixtures which can be extended by developers.

3. The Horizon FitNesse Framework

By extending FitNeses fixtures we provided developers with a testing environment where they can dynamically inject test and pass criteria functions, both implemented as Q anonymous functions. The fixtures we wrote extend from the standard *DecisionTable* fixture. A fixture spawns off a Q process, marshals data from the wiki table into the Q process via KDB's Java interface, executes the anonymous functions, first the test itself, *eval*, then the *pass* function with results from *eval*, compositionally as:

$$passLambda(testLambda(inputs)),$$

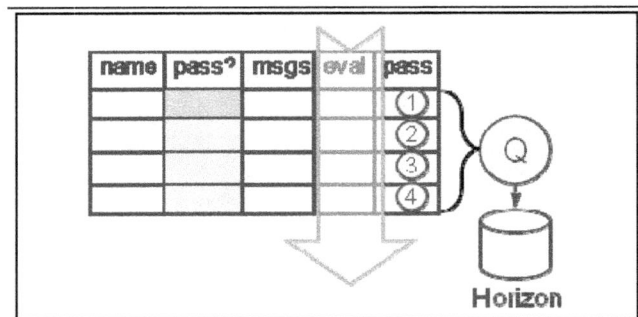

Figure 2. Dynamic Output Fixture Scala Code.

vd	id	op	vss	adv21
2011.02.23	VOD.L	[176.5, 178.1813]	[83226795, 101751172]	[70622091, 71504204]
2011.02.24	VOD.L	[173.4, 173.4]	[74559045, 74559045]	[67993092, 68875205]
2011.02.25	VOD.L	[172.3, 172.3]	[61039111, 61039111]	[68185910, 69068023]

Figure 3. Example Rendered Comparison Table.

Figure 1 shows an example wiki table consisting of three tests after they have executed. The first test failed ($2 \neq 1+0$), whereas both the second and third tests passed. In the first test, SIMPLE, the lambdas, *1+0* and *{[x] x}* (the identity function) are sent to the spawned Q process. It executes *1+0* composed with the identity function. The result, *1* is returned to the fixture, and since that does not match the expected value, *2*, the *pass?* cell is colored red. The second tests evaluates the values of 3 KDB variables. Its *pass* functions tests all values and returns true or false; the *pass?* is colored accordingly. The third function is a query against the Horizon database using the *getOSTSData[]* function for a given date range and passing the resulting time series to a *calendar fill* function. The pass function then looks for a specific condition in the returned data, and in this case, returns *true*. In these test, intermediate results are stored in an adjunct wiki page specified in the *msgs* column. As shown in Figure 2, this fixture, executes each row in the wiki table individually as a single test. State between execution can be preserved in the Q process allowing us chain tests in a single table.

The rest of this paper details the other fixtures we implemented in order to execute larger regressions suites created along two dimensions:

- Number of tickers, grouping of tickers, and date range
- Number of columns (i.e. open, high, low, close, volume)

3.1 Actor Fixture

Retiring a legacy database with millions of time series requires a mechanism with which we can readily compare result sets from both databases. To achieve this, we implemented a fixture which sends queries to each database in parallel and creates views on the result sets enabling us to visually analyze data mismatches. We implemented this fixture in Scala leveraging its actor-based concurrency model actor framework [9].

The actor fixture, creates a preset number of actors, one for each row in the table. Each actor spawns a q process, and each q process maintains its own connections to the databases. Each actor executes two queries, one on the legacy database and the other on on Horizon. The result sets are then aggregated into a *comparison table* where each cell is a pair of values, one value from the legacy database, the other from Horizon. We then extract a *truth table* by applying a user defined compare function across the comparison table. This table records *true* where the values of both databases match, and a *false* where they do not. This truth table is used for computing the percentage of cells that matched. Since the tables can be quite large, we also use the truth table to prune the comparison table by row and column in order to zoom in on mismatched cells. In the *mismatches* table only sections of the comparison table where there is at least one row or one column that had a mismatch are shown. Lastly, we use the truth table to generate the HTML *results* table where cells that did not match are shown in red and cells that matched in green. Figure 3 shows a much reduced results table. Figure 4 shows the Fixture's architecture.

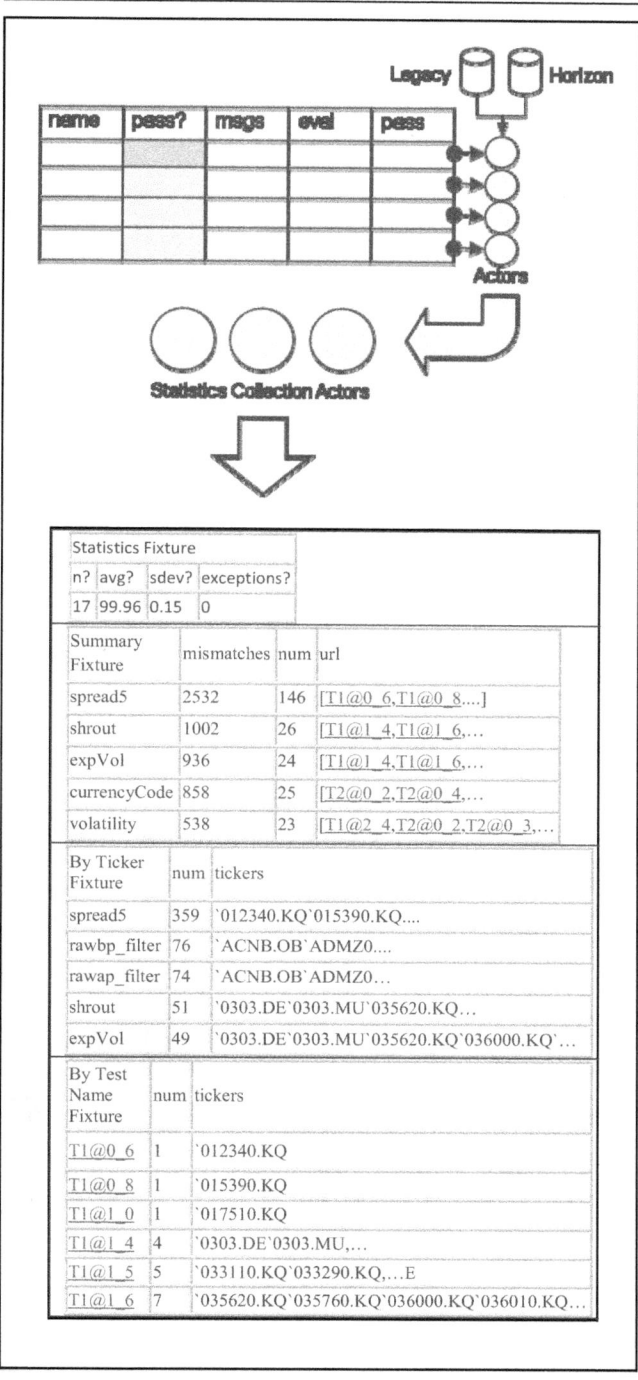

Figure 4. Horizon Actor Fixture Architecture.

We leveraged Q's powerful vector processing language for all table manipulations. For example,

cmpTbl: t,''u

creates the comparison table from tables *t* and *u*. A comparison table is a table joined by primary key where each cell consists of a pair of values. Figure 5 shows two tables, *t* and *u* and their comparison table, **cmpTbl**. The following statement shows the

comparison function, **cmp**, applied to the non-primary key cells of the comparison table in order to derive the truth table, ***truthTbl***.

$$\textbf{truthTbl}: ?[cmpTbl;();0b;f!(each;\{\textbf{cmp}\ x\}),/: f:cols\ value\ cmpTbl]$$

Exploiting Q's functional nature, we define a function lookup dictionary (*sp*) by type:

```
-9| {1e-5>abs x-y}
-6| {x=y}
```

The key -9 holds the comparison function for doubles, and the key -6 holds the comparison functon for integers. For brevity, the other scalar types are not shown, The comparison function is defined as:

$$\textbf{cmp}:\{all\ (first\ x)\ \{sp[type\ x].\ (x;y)\}\}/: x\}$$

This function looks up the actual compare function by the type of the first argument and applies that function to its arguments returning *true* or *false* (0 or 1).

t				u		
vd	*tp*	*vss*		*vd*	*tp*	*vss*
4/14/2010	131.25	2018700		*4/14/2010*	131.35	2018700
4/15/2010	130.□9	1688100		*4/15/2010*	130.89	1688100
4/16/2010	13□.63	3163900		*4/16/2010*	130.63	3163800
4/19/2010	132.23	2195400		*4/19/2010*	132.23	2195400
4/20/2010	129.69	3605000		*4/20/2010*	129.69	3605000
4/□1/2010	128.99	1952600		*4/21/2010*	128.99	1952800
4/22/201	129.13	1720400		*4/22/2010*	129.23	1720400

cmpTbl		
vd	*tp*	*vss*
4/14/2010	131.25 131.35	2018700 2018700
4/15/2010	130.89 130.89	1688100 1688100
4/16/2010	130.63 130.63	3163900 3163800
4/19/2010	132.23 132.23	2195400 2195400
4/20/2010	129.69 129.69	3605000 3605000
4/21/2010	128.99 128.99	1952600 1952800
4/22/2010	129.13 129.23	1720400 1720400

truthTbl		
vd	*tp*	*vss*
4/14/2010	0	1
4/15/2010	1	1
4/16/2010	1	1
4/19/2010	1	1
4/20/2010	1	1
4/21/2010	1	0
4/22/2010	1	1

htmlTbl		
vd	*tp*	*vss*
4/14/2010	131.25 131.35	2018700 2018700
4/15/2010	130.89 130.89	1688100 1688100
4/16/2010	130.63 130.63	3163900 3163900
4/19/2010	132.23 132.23	2195400 2195400
4/20/2010	129.69 129.69	3605000 3605000
4/21/2010	128.99 128.99	1952600 1952800
4/22/2010	129.13 129.13	1720400 1720400

Figure 5. Making a comparison table.

Generating HTML is implemented as a table join between the comparison table and the truth table applying an anonymous function that looks at the bit in the truth table to pick the HTML CSS style to apply the cell. Figure 5 shows the resulting html table. These tables make it easier to spot patterns of mismatches..

Aggregating the truth tables across all tests provides us with a macro view of where there are problems. As shown in Figure 3, the *Statistics Fixture* shows us the average number of cells that were correct in the entire suite. The *Summary Fixture* shows us the number of mismatches by column. In this example, the column, *spread5* has the largest number of breaks. The url on the right enables us to navigate to tests which have a *spread5* mismatch. The *By Ticker Fixture* shows us which tickers have had mismatches by column. This is useful for identifying patterns in the breaks due to loading issues in the back-end. Lastly, the *By Test Name Fixture* provides a way to navigate from a ticker to its test result. This is useful when trying to identify a particular ticker in a result set where the ticker might be one of 50 tickers in the query.

Mismatches gleaned from the individual truth tables sent by each row actor (refer to Figure 3) are asynchronously sent to the *Statistics Collection Actors*. These in turn organize this data by the appropriate dimension, and at the end of a test run, produce the summary tables tables shown in Figure 4.

We use this fixture to execute test sets in the 10,000 ticker range and a yearly date range and vary the columns included in the test in order to narrow down problems.

3.2 Dynamic Input Fixture

As some of the columns involve calculations, we can use the column information to drive another set of tests. In this manner, we automatically stream column names and tickers to other test sets which, depending on the column, query the database for underlying columns that make up that calculation. In this case, a test suite dynamically prepares input for another test suite where the output stream of a test becomes the input stream of another.

We also leverage this fixture to run larger data sets on the order of 200,000 tickers using a Scala stream from which groups of tickers are read and concurrently processed by row actors. A typical 200,000 ticker test suite takes on the order of 3 hours to execute. Often times the tickers set is extracted from the database via a regular fixture which then streams the tickers into the Dynamic Input Fixture.

3.3 Dynamic Output Fixture

This fixture enables us to move all the fixture functionality into Q. It has an *eval*, but no pass function. Rather, execution of the *eval* function must return a table with one Boolean column named *pass?* The fixture uses this column to paint the cell red or green. This fixture is implemented by extending FitNesse's *TableTable* fixture and implementing a *doTable* method. This method takes and returns list of list of strings. As shown in the Scala code in Figure 7, the input cells are used to construct a Q dictionary which is passed into Q. Q executes the *eval* function and returns a column ordered table. This table is then formatted as a wiki table in Scala and returned as a list of list of string to be rendered by FitNesse. Figure 6 shows an example where the lambda function in the *func* column creates a table of random values including the Boolean column, *pass?*.

Dynamic Output Fixture	qa	userfunc.q	
func	n	sd	
{[n;sd] ((3#cols t),`$"pass?") xcol t:([] dt:sd + til n; k:n?`3; v:n?100.; p:rand each n#0b)}	5	2011.01.01	
dt	k	v	pass?
2011-01-01	afe	3.42	false
2011-01-02	gad	88.72	true
2011-01-03	fje	17.60	true
2011-01-04	ipo	98.31	false
2011-01-05	doh	76.63	false

Figure 6. Example Dynamic Output Fixture.

4. Future Work

Currently the entire testing infrastructure runs on one 32 core machine with 256 Gb of memory. Although we create hundreds of actors in a test run, scaling out by core, even larger speedups could be achieved by distributing the test runs across multiple machines scaling out by machine. We have started to experiment with Akka [10] and GridGain[11] distribution mechanisms in order to achieve this level of parallelism.

5. Conclusion

We presented a testing framework made possible by leveraging several technologies, FitNesse was chosen for its ease of use as a test development front end platform, Scala addressed the scalability factor through its actor concurrency model enabling us to execute large number of queries in parallel., Finally Q, a vector oriented functional programming language, was leveraged for its versatile table manipulation. Q is also the native scripting language in Horizon.

With this infrastructure in place, we have been able to introduce testing at the beginning of every project. As we migrate query sets into the new database, our methodology is to create a few test pages with varying number of tickers, typically 10,000 to prove out that the queries are matching the legacy database on a limited set of columns. We then iteratively grow the test suites in both dimensions (tickers and columns) until we have a good enough confidence level, typically > 99%. We know that we will never match 100% as we have, using this methodology, already discovered inconsistencies in the legacy database.

```
package com.ms.horizon.fitnesse.fixtures

import kx.K;
import kx.Dumper;

class DynamicOutputFixture(env: String, script: String)
extends HorizonBaseFixture with FixtureTrait {
    implicit def boolToInt(b:Boolean) : Int = if (b) 1 else 0
    val fmt = Map[String, (Any) => String]("pass?" -> ((x:Any) =>
List("fail","pass")(x.asInstanceOf[Boolean])+":"+x)).withDefaultValue((x:Object) => "report:"+x)

    def doTable(ts: java.util.List[java.util.List[java.lang.String]]) :
        java.util.List[java.util.List[java.lang.String]] = {
        val rows = List.range(0, ts.size()).map((i) =>
            List.fromArray(ts.get(i).toArray).asInstanceOf[List[String]].toArray)
        val (argNames, args) = (rows(0), rows(1))
        val d = new K.Dict(argNames, args map (_.toCharArray))  // toCharArray -> Q sees args as strings

        val f = callQ(d).toTable
        val p = (f.fields zip f.data) map {case(x,y) => y map (fmt(x)(_))} transpose
        val h = List(argNames, args, f.fields) map (_ map (fmt("D")(_)))
        val r = (h ::: p.toList)
        val ret = java.util.Arrays.asList(r.map((x) => java.util.Arrays.asList(x.toArray: _*)): _*)
        ret
    }

    def callQ(dict: K.Dict) : K.Flip = {
        try {
            val hrz = HorizonConnectionFactory.getInstance().create("M", env, script)
            logger.debug("Executing: " + dict)
            val o = hrz.execute("executeUserFunc", dict)
            hrz.exit()
            o.asInstanceOf[K.Flip]
        } catch {
            case e =>
                logger.error("callQ", e)
                throw e
        }
    }
}
```

Figure 7. Dynamic Output Scala code

References

[1] Bela Stantic, Sankalp. Khanna, and John Thornton (2004), An Efficient Method for Indexing Now-relative Bitemporal Data, in Proceeding of the 15th Australasian Database conference (ADC2004), Denidin, New Zealand

[2] Christian S. Jensen, Richard T. Snodgrass (1999), Temporal Data Management, IEEE Transactions on Knowledge and Data Engineering

[3] Daniel J. Abadi, Samuel R. Madden, and Nabil Hachem [2008], Column-Stores vs. Row-Stores: How Different Are They Really? Proceedings of SIGMOD.

[4] Kx Systems White Paper, http://kx.com/papers/Kdb+_Whitepaper-2010-1005.pdf

[5] Jeffrey Borror (2008), Q for Mortals – A tutorial in Q Programming. ISBN 1434829014

[6] Kdb+ Database and Language Primer, Dennis Shasha (2005), http://kx.com/q/d/primer.htm

[7] Cucumber Behavioral Driven Development: http://cukes.info

[8] FitNesse : http://fitnesse.org

[9] Scala Actors – A Short Tutorial: http://www.scala-lang.org/node/242

[10] Akka: http://akka.io/

[11] GridGain: http://www.gridgain.com

Coping with Distance: An Empirical Study of Communication on the Jazz Platform

Renuka Sindhgatta

IBM Research - India
Bangalore, India
renuka.sr@in.ibm.com

Bikram Sengupta

IBM Research - India
Bangalore, India
bsengupt@in.ibm.com

Subhajit Datta

IBM Research - India
Bangalore, India
subhajit.datta@in.ibm.com

Abstract

Global software development - which is characterized by teams separated by physical distance and/or time-zone differences - has traditionally posed significant communication challenges. Often these have caused delays in completing tasks, or created misalignment across sites leading to rework. In recent years, however, a new breed of development environments with rich collaboration features have emerged to facilitate cross-site work in distributed projects. In this paper we revisit the question "does distance matter?" in the context of IBM Jazz Platform – a state-of-the-art collaborative development environment. We study the ecosystem of a large distributed team of around 300 members across 35 physical locations, which uses the Jazz platform for agile development. Our results indicate that while there is a delay in communication due to geographic separation, teams try to reduce the impact of delays by having a large percentage of work distributed within same/few time zones and working beyond regular office hours to interact with distributed teams. We observe different communication patterns depending on the roles of the team members, with component leads and project managers having a significantly higher overhead than development team members. We discuss the practical implications of our findings in terms of some best practices that can help lessen the impact of distance.

Categories and Subject Descriptors D.2.7 [**Software Engineering**]: Distribution, Maintenance and Enhancement.

General Terms Measurement, Human Factors.

Keywords Communication,Distributed Development,Delay

1. Introduction

Distribution of team members across several locations is now common in software development projects. Indeed, many of the benefits of global software development – such as availability of a large skill pool, access to emerging markets, cost arbitrage etc. - are leveraged out of this very distribution. But along with these benefits, distributed development also brings several challenges [11]. Many of the difficulties that arise in practice can be traced to inadequate communication and lack of awareness between team-members, separated by distance and time-zone differences. Early evidence had shown that these communication gaps frequently lead to inefficient information flows, delays in completing tasks, misalignment and rework [5, 12].

These challenges were an important trigger for a new breed of Collaborative Development Environments (CDEs) that have emerged in the last few years. CDEs are meant to provide a "virtual space wherein all the stakeholders of the project – even if distributed by time or distance – may negotiate, brainstorm, discuss, share knowledge, and generally labor together to carry out some task, most often to create an executable deliverable and its supporting artifacts" [13]. For example, the IBM Jazz platform1 facilitates distributed development in significant ways; it offers mechanisms to discuss and track units of work as they are acted upon by developers who may not have any face-to-face contact. The IBM Rational Team Concert2 based on the Jazz platform, is now widely used by distributed teams to coordinate development work. The success of CDEs have led some to pose the question: "Does Distance Still Matter?" [8]. Indeed, how the distributed development teams of today use CDEs to communicate across sites and

---

[1] http://www-01.ibm.com/software/rational/jazz/

[2] http://www-01.ibm.com/software/awdtools/rtc/

time-zones, is an interesting topic of research, which has motivated us to undertake the study reported in this paper.

The "distributed" in distributed software development has several dimensions. As Gumm [1] has pointed out, physical distribution, organizational distribution, temporal distribution, and distribution among stakeholder groups all play significant roles in a distributed development project. Physical distribution is a characteristic of distributed people across different offices, cities or countries. Temporal distribution refers to work-hour synchronicity or the time during which team members are available for real-time interactions. Different types of stakeholders groups exist in each project – managers, testers, developers, etc., each with different perceptions and responsibilities about a project. Organizational distribution refers to distribution of the team across organizations. Out of these dimensions, physical and temporal distribution are closely linked to one another, and by far the most ubiquitous in global software development. In this paper we focus on the interplay of these dimensions as they introduce delays in project communication and require teams to devise mechanisms to cope with such delay. We also explore the relation between the roles of developers and their position in the network of interactions. As the subject of our study, we have selected a large, globally distributed project in IBM that has been developing a product on the IBM Jazz platform for a number of years. The contributions of our work can be summarized as:

- We explore the origins of delay in project communication in terms of lack of work-hour synchronicity across different locations.
- We examine how teams try to minimize the effects of delay through pragmatic distribution of work and flexible working hours.
- We use constructs from social network analysis to understand how developer roles relate to interaction.

Our study was guided by a series of questions related to communication patterns in global software development, which we introduce next in Section 2. The following section describes the project under study and the key terms associated with it. Section 4 provides a detailed report on the findings from our study in relation to the questions. In Section 5, we discuss the practical implications of our findings in terms of best practices that can help lessen the impact of distance. Related work is described in Section 6, while Section 7 concludes the paper.

2. Study Questions

Our study questions center on three of the four key dimensions of distribution [1] – physical, temporal, stakeholder groups. As the development was done within IBM, we did not look into the fourth dimension of distribution that oc-

curs across organizations. These questions are introduced below.

Q1: Does lack of work-hour synchronicity across different sites introduce delay in project communication?
Previous studies indicate that the distribution of work across multiple-sites hinders informal communication among developers who need to work together [5]. Synchronous communication becomes less common due to time zone and language barriers. We evaluate the extent of delay in communication caused due to distribution across geographic locations. This question relates to the temporal dimension of distribution.

Q2: How do distributed teams cope with communication delays?
Synchronous communication is hindered by physical location of teams. Assigning work to different work sites in a manner that minimizes the need for multi-site communication has been recommended by earlier studies [4]. We examine the distribution of work and communication (occurring in the context of work) across teams. This question relates to physical dimension of distribution.

Q3: Do the roles of team members' influence their communication behavior and their social networks?
Stakeholder groups play a key role in project communication. Team leads, testers, developers have different responsibilities and perceptions about the software being developed [2]. This question relates to the impact of distribution on different stakeholders.

3. Project Background

This section introduces the project under study, describes the collaborative development environment used in the project and explains the key terms associated with the study.

3.1 Project and Environment Overiew

The project under study has been developing a software product on the Jazz platform for more than 3 years using Java and JavaScript programming languages. The project team comprises close to 300 developers and component leads, spread over 35 locations and 19 time zones. The team members belong to multiple functional areas of the product being developed.

The project uses IBM Rational Team Concert (RTC) as the development platform. IBM RTC provides mechanisms for creating and managing a Scrum-based project. In IBM RTC, a project area that refers to a project can be created. Users and their specific roles can be defined. Sprints with their time lines can be recorded. A product backlog is associated to a project area and further a sprint backlog for each sprint can defined. The sprint or product backlog is a set of work items. A work item is a unit of work. Work items can be of different types – plan, user story, task, defect, enhancement, test case, etc.

Each work item consists of a set of basic attributes that are useful for tracking it; these include, name, unique identifier (ID), description, iteration it has been planned for, creator (name of the team member who created the work item), owner (name of the team member who is responsible for successfully completing the work item), creation date, closure date and priority. The code changes made against each work item can be committed into the version repository as change sets.

Discussions between team members are recorded into the tool and associated with the work item as comments. Each team has daily meetings within the site. There is a weekly team meeting that includes multiple sites for each functional area. While team members may use face to face (when possible) and telephonic meetings to coordinate work, they generally record most of the important communication along with the work item to enable other team members from different sites in understanding the context of the work item.

3.2 Key Terms and Definitions

This section briefly explains all the terms used in the context of the project and our study.

Team Area: The project consists of 35 functional areas called team area. Each team area primarily represents a component or a module of the system. There are a few team areas representing project management based activities such as build and release of the system, user documentation and testing

Work Item: A work item represents a single unit of work. There can be different types of work items. In the context of our study, we focus on task, defect and enhancement work items which represent the development or build activities. A work item is associated to a team area.

Comments/Discussion: All interactions in the project are in the context of the development activities or work items. Hence, any team member can add comments to the work item. Each comment has the discussion text, the name of the team member and the date and time of its creation stored along with the work item.

Site (City, Country, and Time Zone): Site represents the physical location of the work place of team members. The city, country and time zone of each site are identified for each team member. This information is available in the people management system within IBM.

Overlap Time: Overlap time represents the time period when team members are available in the context of their working hours. In our study, 9 AM – 6 PM is considered as the regular work hour window. Hence, two team members working in the same time zone have a 9 hour overlap time as they are available for synchronous communication for all the 9 hours of work hour window.

Comment Response time: We use the assumption as conceptualized by Wolf et al [8]. Considering that a comment thread on a work item represents a conversation about the work item, a comment is assumed to be a reply to the previously created comment. We measure the intervals between the creation times of successive comments, and consider this as the Response Time of the second comment with respect to the first.

Work Item Response Time: The Response time for a work item is the time interval between the first and the last created comments for a work item.

Team Roles: Team members play different roles in project development. A *contributor* to a team area owns work items and develops the system. A *component lead* is a scrum master responsible for defining the sprint back log, reviewing the architecture of the component and assigning the work items to the contributors of the team area (which may include the lead herself). The *project management committee* is responsible for the project-wide coordination that includes iteration planning and release of the entire system.

4. Data Analysis and Results

In this section we describe the data analysis methods and findings in relation to each of our questions. For our study, we evaluate the release of the software system spanning over 16 months with 10,967 work items. There were 4311 work items having *at least* two distinct users making comments, and these are the work items we selected for studying communication patterns. Of the 300 team members,

Table 1 Comment Response Time based on the Overlap Working hours of the team members in discussion

	Maximum Response time of 5 days					
Overlap working hours across time zones	# of conversations (pairs of comments)	% of conversations	25 PERCENTILE (HRS)	MEDIAN (HRS)	MEAN (HRS)	75 PERCENTILE (HRS)
0-1 hrs	2354	14.54%	2.23	8.18	14.75	16.70
2-3 hrs	1772	10.95%	0.50	3.44	10.37	12.69
5-6 hrs	1275	7.88%	0.67	2.76	11.69	14.82
7-8 hrs	1454	8.98%	0.40	1.37	9.11	9.13
9 hrs	9334	57.66%	0.43	1.73	10.20	12.18

there were 200 developers who had contributed to source code changes for the release under study. The remaining team members were testers, system administrators, user assistance experts and the project management team or developers contributed to a different release of the system. Note that there are over 6000 work items that either had no discussions, or had comments from only one user. This is not surprising since many work items may not require coordination across multiple developers (for example, a work item may only depend on other work items owned by the same developer.) Also, several defect work items are related, or are duplicates, and only one may be taken up for discussion.

We now discuss our findings for the first question.

Q1. Does lack of work-hour synchronicity across different sites introduce delay in project communication?

To examine the impact of time synchronicity - or the lack of it - on communication delays, we compute the response times for pairs of sequential comments that have been exchanged between any two team members in the context of a work item. We categorize the response times by time synchronicity of the team members – the overlap work time of the team members. Table 1 shows the mean, median, lower and upper quartile measures of the response time. On manual analysis of comments on work items and their responses, we realized that there are mainly two types of exchanges that occur. The first type is ad-hoc communication that occurs to clarify the details of work, handle exceptions, correct mistakes etc. where typically synchronous response is expected. It is here that the time-zone differences have the potential to cause significant delays. We limit the maximum response time for ad-hoc communication to 5 days considering the possibility of holidays and weekends. The second type is planned communication, where a longer timeframe (e.g. several days to few weeks) is needed to provide a response, often on the completion of work or update of status. For such exchanges, time-zone differences are unlikely to make any significant difference.

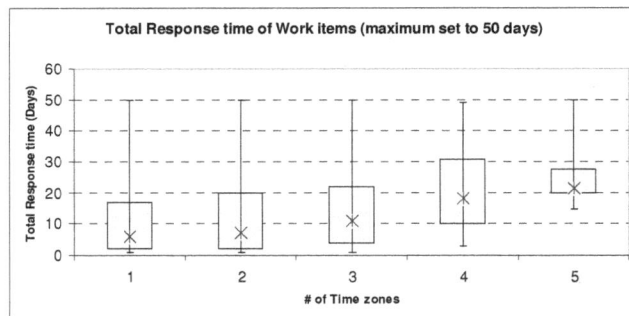

Figure 1 Box plot of the work item response times categorized by the number of sites involved in the work item communication

Hence, we focused primarily on the analysis of ad-hoc communication. With reference to Table 1, the median response times vary from 1-2 hours (when there is significant overlap in working hours) to over 8 hours, when the overlap is minimal (0-1 hour). We also notice that with a small increase in overlap (2-3 hours), the delay in response comes down appreciably. Finally, it is interesting to note that the response times for cases where there is full synchronicity (9 hours overlap), is higher than that for 7-8 hours overlap. We hypothesize that this may be due to the fact that people in the same time-zone are more likely to have other means of communication (e.g. face-to-face, telephone etc), through which an initial response may be provided before formally updating the discussion thread to inform other team members.

We also compute the total response time for each work item. We limit the maximum response time to 50 days as the largest iteration during our study was 50 days long, and we wanted to focus on communication that is relevant for a specific iteration. Figure 1 shows the box plots of the total response time of all work items categorized by number of time zones. The horizontal cross in the middle shows the median value. The bottom/top line of the box shows the 25th/75th percentile. The box shows where 50% of the data lie. The whiskers show the minimum and maximum response time values. We see that with an increase in the number of time-zones from where users communicate on a work item, there is a steady increase in the total response time.

To address Q1 in summary, we may say that response times are impacted by geographic distance, measured in terms of the time synchronicity of the interacting team members. The response time to work item comments is high when the work hours between the team members do not overlap. Even a small window of overlap time reduces the response times considerably. Finally, more is the number of time-zones that need to be involved in discussing a work item, the higher is the total response time.

Q2. How do distributed teams cope with communication delays?

Given that time-zone differences can cause significant delays, a natural question to ask is how distributed teams cope with the challenge. From Table 1, we see that ~58% of comments/responses happen within the same time-zone. This suggests that the distribution of work may have been done in a manner that localizes dependencies to the extent possible, and this is what we decided to explore in more depth. At the same time, ~25% of communication exchanges happen between time-zones with little overlap in working hours (0-3 hours). Given this, we wanted to explore if global development calls for "stretchable" working hours, where team members frequently communicate beyond regular hours to stay in sync with remote colleagues.

To examine the extent of distribution of interactions across sites, we identify the city, country and the time zone of the team members involved in the communication. Figure 2(a) shows the box plots containing the number of work items with discussions spanning across cities, countries and time zones. As the plots indicate, 75% of the work items have communication spanning within 2 cities, countries and time zones. We also found that 99% of the work items have discussions restricted to within 3 time-zones. Thus, localization of dependencies seems to have been a guiding principle in work allocation. The maximum number of distributed team members involved in discussions is in 9 cities across 6 time zones.

As discussions on a work item are primarily by team members belonging to the team area of the work item, we also evaluate the distribution of team areas across sites. The box plots in Figure 2(b) shows that 75% of teams lie within 4 cities and 3 countries or time zones. We found a team having maximum distribution of developers across 10 cities. The team was dealing with user documentation of the software being developed hence was divided across all the major cities where the software was being developed.

However, even the distribution of a team area across 3 time-zones seemed to be on the high side, as far as localization of work is considered. Hence, for each team, we

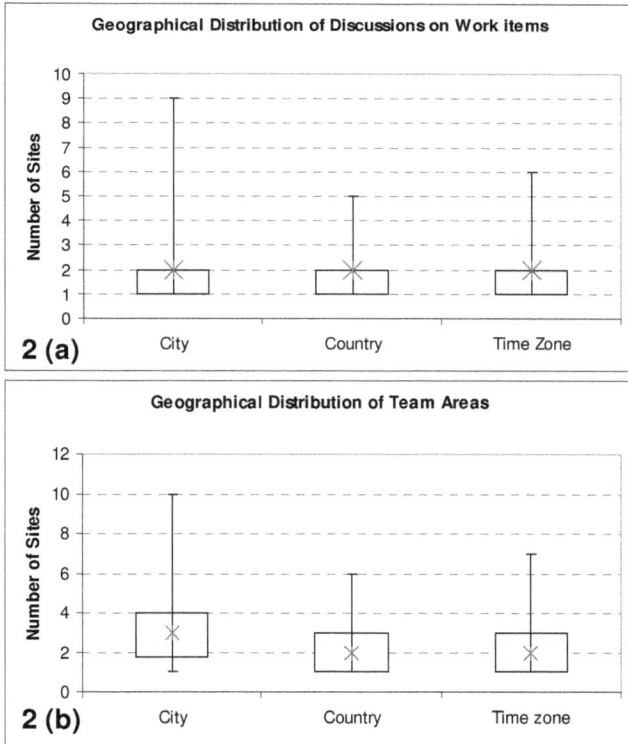

next reviewed the relative percentage of team members across the different time-zones. This is shown in Figure 3, for some of the largest team areas. It is clearly evident that while a team may span several time-zones, the large majority of the team members reside in the same time-zone or at most in two time-zones. For example, while team area 1 is distributed over 4 time-zones, 75% of the team is in the

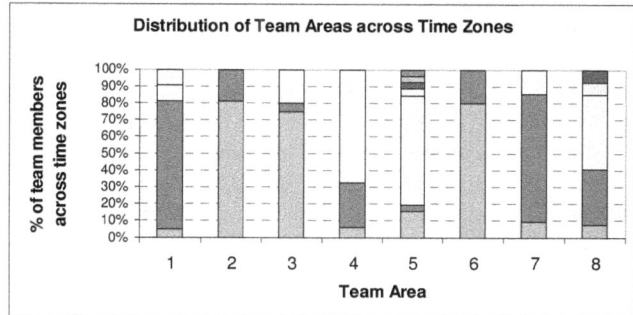

Figure 3 Percentage of team members across time zones for large team areas

same time-zone, and a similar trend is observed for the other team areas as well. Hence, there seems to have been a conscious effort towards localizing teams, so that most of the team-members who need to work together may enjoy the benefits of time synchronicity.

Finally, we report on the other mechanism used to deal with the lack of time synchronicity – increasing "virtual" synchronicity by communicating with remote colleagues outside of regular office hours. For each team member, we identify when the comment was made by him/her (the local time based on the time zone of the team member's work location). Figure 4 shows the percentage of discussions that occur through the day aggregated for all the discussions in the release. As we can see, the number of discussions increases sharply with the start of regular working hours in the morning; it then reduces around lunch time, before increasing again in the afternoon, peaking close to the end of regular office hours (probably to sync up with colleagues before closure) and then trails off.

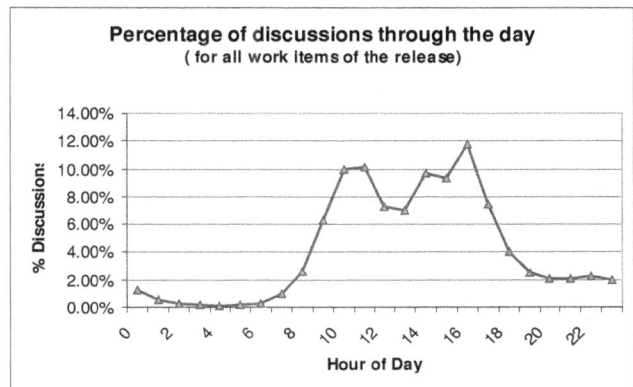

2 (a)

2 (b)

Figure 2 Box plot of (a) geographical distribution of users discussing on work items (b) geographical distribution of team areas

Figure 4. Percentage of Discussion through the day

Table 2 Percentage of discussions made by members with different roles

Role	Members	Comments	Median (# of comments per member)	Mean (# of comments per member)
Contributor	174 (68%)	15462 (42%)	28	88.86
Component Lead	62 (24%)	16115 (44%)	96.5	259.92
Project Management Committee	20 (7%)	5323 (14%)	146	266.15

However, a steady stream of discussions is sustained through the evening extending till almost midnight or even beyond, as team members seek to stretch the time synchronicity with remote sites. Overall around 20% of the discussions happen out of work-hours (6 PM to 9 AM),

Thus the second question can be answered as: A distributed project can cope with distance by restricting its functional teams within a few sites/time-zones, with a large majority of team members residing in the same time-zone. The team members also spend a considerable amount of time out of office hours to co-ordinate with team members across time zones.

Q3. Do the roles of team members influence their communication behavior and their social network?

Our final question seeks to explore the impact of team roles on communication. First, we look at the distribution of discussions against work items across each of the roles contributor, component lead and project manager. We considered only roles related to the development of the system – we have not considered tester, administrators, etc. Table 2 shows the percentage of team members belonging to different roles and the percentage of discussions they have contributed. It is clear that component leads have a significantly higher communication overhead compared to contributors, and project managers need to communicate even more. A component lead contributes to a large number of discussions as (s)he is responsible for several coordination activities – reviewing architecture of the component, defining sprint backlog, reviewing the work items and assigning them to the team. Project managers have an even wider span of responsibility, as they need to ensure project wide coordination, as well as engage in iteration planning and project releases on a large scale. We also discovered that higher coordination responsibilities also lead to a higher percentage of communication beyond office hours. For example, component leads have 25% of their communication beyond office hours, compared to 17% for contributors.

To understand the impact of roles on the collaboration structures in a project, we constructed a communication-based social network that includes all team members and their communication. We create a network of developers who have commented on work items. With reference to Figure 5, each vertex of talk network is a developer and an edge exists between two developers if both of them have commented on at least one work item. In the rare instance of the owner of a work item has not having commented on the work item, (s)he is also connected by edges to all others who have commented on the work item. Talk network

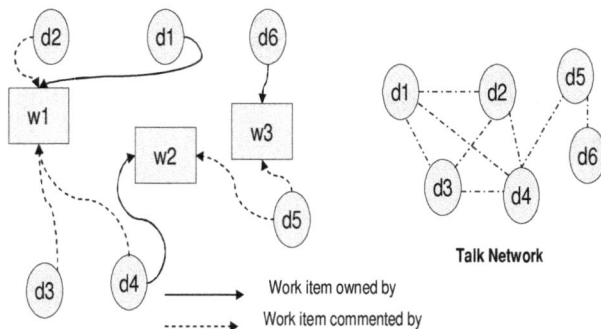

Figure 5 Communication based Talk Network

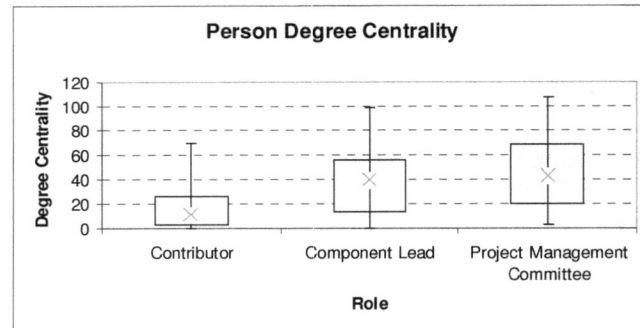

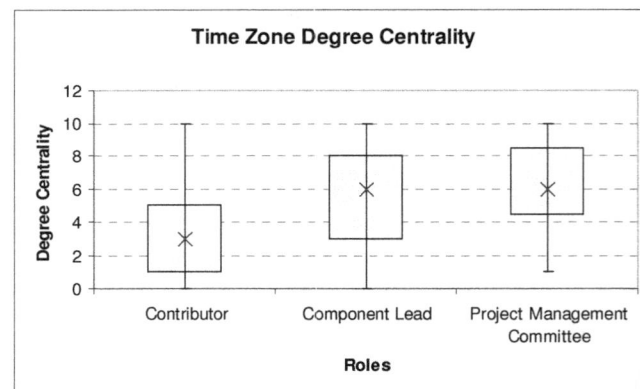

Figure 6 Person degree centrality, Time zone degree centrality of team members with different roles

is generated for the set of developers who own at least one work item. In Figure 5 edges exist between d1, d2, d3 and d4 as d1 is the owner of work item w1 and d2, d3, and d4 have commented on w1; similarly for edges between d4 and d5 as well as d5 and d6. We have made the links between vertices non-directional. We investigate a key measures used to understand the communication structures across roles.

Degree centrality: In a network, degree centrality of a vertex is its degree, sometimes expressed as a ratio with the highest possible degree in the network [10]. In our context, degree centrality of a developer indicates the number of other developers (s)he is collaborating with.

The box plot of Person degree centrality of different roles in Figure 6 shows a high median (40) for Component Leads and Project Management Committee (PMC) as compared to Contributors (12). A component lead interacts with several people for all the coordination activities related to his/her team area. We compute the degree centrality index based on the time zone of team members in the network to identify the communication needs of different roles across time zone. With reference to figure 6, 75% of contributors have communication spanning within 3 time zones, while for component leads and project management committee members, this can go up to 8 time zones.

We conclude that the role of a team member has a significant influence on his/her collaboration patterns.

5. Discussions

While quantitative analysis of communication data (as reported above) has helped provide clear answers to our study questions, it is pertinent to ask what implications all of this has for the successful governance of a globally distributed project. Below, we summarize some of the key insights that can be gleaned from the results of our study.

- Communication delays due to distance are a reality – hence this needs to be accounted for during estimation, project planning and work distribution in global projects.
- Even a 2-3 hour overlap in working hours can significantly reduce delays between dependent sites. Without this, however, the response time grows sharply and can extend over working days.
- In general, more the number of sites (time-zones) that need to collaborate on a task, larger will be the delays. Hence, it is advisable to localize component ownership as far as practicable.
- Team members on global projects are likely to spend a significant amount of time beyond regular office hours communicating with remote colleagues. This calls for providing more flexibility in their working environment.

- The coordination responsibilities of component leads (and management staff) make them the focal point of many communication links, generally extending across a number of sites and time-zones (thereby, also cultures). Thus, together with technical acumen, component leads need to possess strong social skills to ensure smooth collaboration across sites.

6. Related Work

As mentioned, a significant body of research has been reported around the general theme of distributed software development. In a pioneering study Herbsleb and Grinter highlighted the "extraordinary communication and coordination problems" faced by distributed development teams [4]. They advocated modular design to address some of these problems, but pointed out that modular design by itself may not be sufficient to avoid the ill-effects of distance. In a subsequent paper, Herbsleb and Mockus analyze information from source code change management and survey of development team members to report a key finding: distributed work items take more than twice the amount to time to be completed vis-a-vis similar items with entirely collocated work [5]. The detrimental effect of distance on work completion time has also been corroborated in other studies [3]. Taweel et al. identify the factors of better management of communication, knowledge and co-ordination across distributed teams for leveraging the full potential of distributed software development [7]. Hinds and McGrath report results from the correlation study of 33 research and development teams to conclude that an informal hierarchical structure facilitated coordination in distributed teams, even as collocated teams communicate more smoothly in flatter organizational structure [6].

Collaboration in Jazz development using constructs of social network analysis have been studied at depth in [8] and [9] . In [8], the Wolf et al. examine the communication structure of a distributed, project-wide Jazz team – in the context of their larger research question, "does distance still matter?" – and conclude that redundant communication ties exist across project participants located in different geographies; and barring the measures group degree centralization and group betweenness centralization, significant differences do not exist in other measures between communication structures of co-located and multi-site Jazz teams. The authors consider the response time of a work item as the average of time interval between each pair of comment in the comment thread. Considering the average of time intervals between pairs of comments for a work item obscures the impact of physical and temporal distance as a there could be a high proportion of comments in a comment thread for a work item occurring within the same time zone or the same site. In [9] the authors report results at predicting build failures using a Bayesian classifier model trained by social network metrics from the respective communication network of developers around successful and failed build in the past.

7. Conclusions

In this paper, we have reported on a study of communication characteristics of team members in a large, globally distributed software development project that uses the IBM Jazz platform. Our results indicate that while there is a delay in communication due to geographic separation, teams try to reduce the impact of delays by having a large percentage of work distributed within same/few time zones and stretching beyond regular work hours to interact with distributed teams. In general, component leads and project managers were found to have a significantly higher communication overhead than development team members. We discuss the practical implications of our findings in terms of some best practices that can help lessen the impact of distance. In future, we would like to leverage our findings to develop quantitative models of communication and delays in a distributed project that can aid project planning and estimation.

References

[1] D. C. Gumm. Distribution dimensions in software development projects: a taxonomy. IEEE Software, 23(5):45–51, 2006.

[2] J.R. Evaristo and R. Scudder, Geographically Distributed Project Teams: A Dimensional Analysis, Proc. 33rd Hawaii Int'l Conf. System Sciences (HICSS 00), IEEE CS Press, 2000, pp. 7052–7063.

[3] Ehrlich, K., Valetto, G., and Helander, M. Seeing inside: Using social network analysis to understand patterns of collaboration and coordination in global software teams. In Proceedings of the International Conference on Global Software Engineering (Washington, DC, USA, 2007), ICGSE '07, IEEE Computer Society, pp. 297–298.

[4] Herbsleb, J. D., and Grinter, R. E. Architectures, coordination, and distance: Conway's law and beyond. IEEE Softw. 16, 5 (1999), 63–70.

[5] Herbsleb, J. D., and Mockus, A. An empirical study of speed and communication in globally distributed software development. IEEE Trans. Softw. Eng. 29 (June 2003), 481–494.

[6] Hinds, P., and McGrath, C. Structures that work: social structure, work structure and coordination ease in geographically distributed teams. In Proceedings of the 2006 20th anniversary conference on Computer supported cooperative work (Banff, Alberta, Canada, 2006), ACM, pp. 343–352.

[7] Taweel, A., Delaney, B., Arvanitis, T., and Zhao, L. Communication, knowledge and co-ordination management in globally distributed software development: Informed by a scientific software engineering case study. In Global Software Engineering, 2009. ICGSE 2009. Fourth IEEE International Conference on (2009), pp. 370–375.

[8] Wolf, T., Nguyen, T., and Damian, D. Does distance still matter? Softw. Process 13, 6 (2008), 493–510.

[9] Wolf, T., Schroter, A., Damian, D., and Nguyen, T. Predicting build failures using social network analysis on developer communication. In Proceedings of the 31st International Conference on Software Engineering (2009), IEEE Computer Society, pp. 1–11.

[10] De Nooy, W., Mrvar, A., and Batagelj, V. Exploratory Social Network Analysis with Pajek. Cambridge University Press, Jan. 2005

[11] Sengupta, B., Chandra, S., and Sinha, V. A Research Agenda for Distributed Software Development. In Proceedings of International Conference on Software Engineering (ICSE), 2006, pp 731-740.

[12] Herbsleb, J.D. and Moitra, D. Global Software Development. IEEE Software, March-April 2001, pp 16-20

[13] Booch, G. and Brown, A. Collaborative Development Environments. Aadvances in Computers, Vol. 59, Academic Press, August 2003.

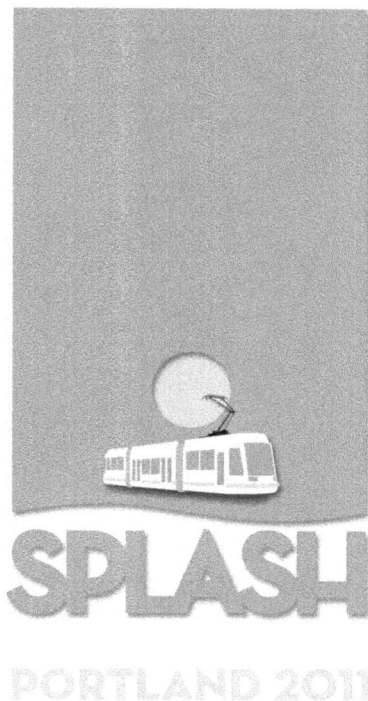

SPLASH 2011 Panel Chair's Welcome

Welcome to SPLASH 2011!

Panels are an opportunity for learning and engaging in dialog, in an informal environment. Each panel member contributes a unique perspective on a topic, and then you have the opportunity to ask questions and contribute new ideas.

As I look at the Panels that we have scheduled, I am confident that we will provide both educational and entertaining experiences. Each focuses on a timely, relevant, and important topic:

- **Going Green with Refactoring: Sustaining the "World Wide Virtual Machine"**: What exciting advances have been made in refactoring strategies and tools to help sustain rapid growth of system scale and scope?

- **Language-based Security as Extreme Modularity**: How can programming language design help us write abstractions robust against malice and accident, at little cost to expressiveness?

- **Multicore, Manycore, and Cloud Computing**: Is a new programming language paradigm required? Does the arrival of multicore, manycore, and cloud computing mean that we need new languages with new programming paradigms, and if so, what should these new languages look like?

- **Industry-Academic Research Partnerships in the Age of Big Data and Global Computing Networks**: Research partnerships between industry and academia are grown through relationships, a desire for innovation, and opportunities for sponsorship. Can we improve research engagement strategies?

I would like to thank all of the panel conveners:

Daniel Weinreb
SPLASH 2011 Panel Chair
Google, Inc.
dlw@google.com

Steven Fraser	**Mark S. Miller**	**S. Tucker Taft**
Director	Research Scientist	CTO
Cisco Systems, Inc.	*Goole Research*	*SofCheck, Inc.*
sdfraser@acm.org	erights@google.com	stt@sofcheck.com

Panel
Multicore, Manycore, and Cloud Computing: Is a New Programming Language Paradigm Required?

S. Tucker Taft

SofCheck, Inc.

Burlington, MA

stt@sofcheck.com

Joshua Bloch

Google, Inc.

josh@bloch.us

Robert Bocchino

Institute for Software Research
Carnegie Mellon University

rbocchin@cs.cmu.edu

Sebastian Burckhardt

Microsoft Research
Redmond, WA

sburckha@microsoft.com

Hassan Chafi

Oracle Labs and
Pervasive Parallelism
Laboratory
Stanford University

hchafi@stanford.edu

Russ Cox

Google, Inc.

rsc@google.com

Benedict Gaster

AMD, Inc.

benedict.gaster@amd.com

Guy Steele

Oracle Research

guy.steele@oracle.com

David Ungar

IBM Research

davidungar@ibm.com

Abstract

Most of the mainstream programming languages in use today originated in the 70s and 80s. Even the scripting languages in growing use today tend to be based on paradigms established twenty years ago. Does the arrival of multicore, manycore, and cloud computing mean that we need to establish a new set of programming languages with new paradigms, or should we focus on adding more parallel programming features to our existing programming languages?

Consistent with the SPLASH theme of the *Internet as the world-wide Virtual Machine*, and the *Onward!* theme focused on the future of *Software Language Design*, this panel will discuss the role that programming languages should play in this new distributed, highly parallel computing milieu. Do we need new languages with new programming paradigms, and if so, what should these new languages look like?

Categories and Subject Descriptors D.1.3 [**Programming Techniques**]: Concurrent Programming – distributed programming, parallel programming; D.3.2 [**Programming Languages**]: Language Classifications -- concurrent, distributed, and parallel languages; D.3.3 [**Programming Languages**]: Language Constructs and Features – concurrent programming structures.

General Terms Algorithms, Performance, Languages,.

Keywords multicore programming; manycore programming; cloud computing; new programming paradigms.

1. Introduction

Over the past decade, there have been various approaches to addressing the challenge represented by the explosion in parallel and distributed systems. In the programming language world, two fundamentally different approaches have been taken, namely designing new languages specifically adapted to this new challenge, versus extending existing languages with new parallel or distributed programming features. On this panel we have aficionados of both approaches, sometimes residing within the same person.

New languages of interest to this panel include Clojure, Go, Fortress, ParaSail, and Scala. Each of these languages incorporates one or more fundamentally new programming paradigms intended to address the challenges of parallel or distributed programming. Extensions of existing languages of interest to this panel include Cilk+, CUDA, Deterministic Parallel Java (DPJ), MPI, and OpenCL. These languages start from an existing language, typically C, C++, or Java, and then add in additional libraries and/or language features that add capabilities without restricting the use of the existing language features.

This panel will discuss the merits and costs associated with these two approaches to addressing the parallel and distributed computing environment challenge, and provide specific examples of how these distinct approaches can help the programmer navigate this new sea of possibilities.

2. Panel Members

2.1 S. Tucker Taft *(panel organizer)*

S. TUCKER TAFT is Founder and CTO of SofCheck, Inc., a company devoted to providing tools and technologies for helping to improve software quality and increase programmer productivity. From 1990 to 1995, Mr. Taft served as the lead designer of the Ada 95 programming language. In 2001, he led the architecture and development effort of the J2EE-based Mass.gov portal for the Commonwealth of Massachusetts. In 2002, Mr. Taft founded SofCheck. From 2001 to the present, Mr. Taft has been a member of the ISO Rapporteur Group that developed Ada 2005, and more recently is finalizing Ada 2012. In September 2009 Mr. Taft embarked on the design of ParaSail, Parallel Specification and Implementation Language, a new language that marries pervasive parallelism with formal methods.

New languages with new paradigms are critical to meeting the challenge of multicore and manycore computing. Programmers using existing languages are already nearing the limit of what they can manage in the way of complexity. Adding in the need to take full advantage of the exponentially increasing number of processors per chip, without new programming paradigms, will likely push past what most software development organizations can handle. Developing large software systems will take longer and longer, and may never reach the level of quality and stability required for the given application domain.

ParaSail represents an attempt to create a new language with relatively familiar syntax and semantics, but with some critical differences in terms of control structuring (the language has a pervasively parallel execution model), data structuring (no pointers, global variables, or aliasing), and error checking (all error checking is performed at compile-time, including all race-condition checking, uninitialized or null data reference, array index out-of-bounds, numeric overflow, etc.). Formal annotations, such as preconditions, postconditions, and invariants, are woven into the core syntax and enforced at compile time. Initial experience with this combination shows the language to have a profound effect on the parallelism and robustness of the code, while still being straightforward for existing programmers to learn and to use effectively.

2.2 Josh Bloch

JOSH BLOCH is Chief Java Architect at Google, author of the bestselling, Jolt Award-winning "Effective Java" (Addison-Wesley, 2001; Second Edition, 2008), and coauthor of "Java Puzzlers: Traps, Pitfalls, and Corner Cases" (Addison-Wesley, 2005) and "Java Conurrency in Practice" (Addison-Wesley, 2006). He was previously a Distinguished Engineer at Sun Microsystems, where he led the design and implementation of numerous Java platform features including the Java Collections Framework and JDK 5.0 language enhancements. He holds a Ph.D. from CMU and a B.S. from Columbia.

In a recent Wall Street Journal article entitled "Why Software Is Eating The World," Marc Andreessen said: "All of the technology required to transform industries through software finally works and can be widely delivered at global scale." I agree, but I would add: "so long as programmers are willing to hold their noses and assemble an odd assortment of barely-functional software with duct tape and baling wire." So the question is, will we improve on this state of affairs, or will worse-is-better design (as described by Dick Gabriel) carry the day?

The rise of multicore processors and cloud computing certainly does present a great opportunity for language and library designers. We've had a string of modest successes, such as Doug Lea's java.util.concurrent, and Jeff Dean and Sanjay Ghemawat's MapReduce. These systems solve real problems and make the world a better place. Can we do better? Is there a great new paradigm waiting to be discovered, or do pragmatic concerns favor evolutionary approaches? Others have opined that such a paradigm already exists (Actors, Transactional Memory, and Functional Programming come to mind). While these paradigms all have their uses, I'm reasonably certain that none of them are the silver bullet for making use of the new generation of multicore hardware.

So where is this all leading? In the words of the Magic 8-Ball, "the future is cloudy." Yes, the opportunity for a distinctly better new platform aimed squarely at cloud computing and multicore hardware is staring us in the face. But the inertia of existing platforms has never been greater. If I had to place my bets, I'd guess we're stuck with evolutionary improvements for the next decade, with the possibly of something fundamentally new and different thereafter. But I've never been all that good at prognosticating.

2.3 Robert Bocchino

ROBERT BOCCHINO is a Postdoctoral Associate at Carnegie Mellon University. His research interests lie in programming language design, type theory, formal verification, and concurrency. Robert completed his Ph.D. at the University of Illinois at Urbana-Champaign in fall 2010. His dissertation described a Java-based object-oriented parallel language called Deterministic Parallel Java (DPJ). DPJ uses a novel effect system to (1) guarantee that parallel programs execute deterministically unless nondeterminism is explicitly requested; (2) ensure that any nondeterminism is subject to strong safety guarantees, including freedom from data races; and (3) check that uses of object-oriented parallel frameworks are safe. At CMU, Robert is working with Jonathan Aldrich on the Plaid programming language and on designing and verifying high-level abstractions that make it easy for programmers to write correct and efficient parallel code.

Writing correct and efficient parallel or distributed code is hard. So the increasing prevalence of parallel and cloud computing poses challenges for both programmer productivity and code quality. I believe that the most important way to meet these challenges is to develop good abstractions. Ideally, a programmer working in a particular domain should use domain-specific abstractions, with the details of parallel correctness and efficiency hidden in the implementation. That way, a parallelism expert can write and tune the implementation, with most programmers just interacting with the API. Most programmers should not be writing low-level code with threads, locks, and communication primitives, though such code might be hidden in the implementation.

In my view, once we get the abstractions right, whether we present them as a new language or as an extension of an existing language is a secondary consideration. Modern languages like C++, Java, and C# have sufficiently powerful type systems that these kinds of abstractions can be presented as libraries or frameworks. New languages can have significant benefits: their design can draw on both new ideas in language design and experience with features that worked well or didn't in previous languages. And a special-purpose language may be able to express programming concepts more cleanly or efficiently than a library or framework. Where the investment in tool chain infrastructure is warranted, new languages can be developed. But the most important thing is to get the abstractions right.

2.4 Sebastian Burckhardt

SEBASTIAN BURCKHARDT was born and raised in Basel, Switzerland, and studied Mathematics at the local University. During an exchange year at Brandeis University, he discovered his affinity to Computer Science and immigrated to the United States, where he completed a second Master's degree. After a few years of industry experience at IBM, he returned to academia and earned his PhD in Computer Science at the University of Pennsylvania. For the past 4 years, he has worked as a researcher at Microsoft Research in Redmond. His research interests revolve around the general problem of programming concurrent, parallel, and distributed systems conveniently, efficiently, and correctly. More specific interests include memory consistency models, concurrency testing, self-adjusting computation, and the concurrent revisions programming model.

In my opinion, the biggest challenge and opportunity for PL research today is to discover understandable, robust, and efficient abstractions that empower programmers to work seamlessly with shared state in a world where concurrency, parallelism, and distribution are omnipresent. On multicores, we need programming languages to rise to an abstraction level where correctness issues (such as atomicity violations, data races, and deadlocks) and performance concerns (such as scheduling) are no longer nasty surprises, but become transparent properties of a program. In browser or mobile applications, we want languages to support the illusion of a consistent, persistent, global, shared state; specifically, we need abstractions that reduce the amount of explicit copying and conflict management by the programmer, but do so without introducing expensive scalability bottlenecks.

In either case, the question of whether we need a new language or extend existing languages is somewhat secondary. Once we find the right abstractions, they can provide tremendous value, whether they be delivered as libraries, language extensions, or domain-specific languages.

2.5 Hassan Chafi

HASSAN CHAFI is a research manager at Oracle Labs leading a couple of projects in the area of heterogeneous computing. Hassan is in the final stages of pursuing a PhD degree at Stanford University. He is being advised by Kunle Olukotun. Some of Hassan's initial work at Stanford included implementing a profiling environment for programs using Transactional Memory and implementing a scalable version of the Transactional Coherence and Consistency (TCC) protocol. After taking a leave of absence during which he founded GenieTown, a start-up with the goal of creating an online marketplace for local services he returned to Stanford to join the newly formed Pervasive Parallelism Laboratory (PPL). At PPL, Hassan has been leading a team of talented graduate students working on building Delite, an open-source infrastructure to support the implementation and execution of performance oriented DSLs.

A Domain-Specific Approach to Multicore, Manycore and Cloud Computing: Ideally a parallel programming language should provide generality, high productivity, and produce high-performance binaries that take advantage of all the hardware resources available in a given platform. Unfortunately, no such language currently exists and some of these goals seem to be conflicting. Most successful languages usually focus on only two of the aforementioned goals. For example C/C++ and Java are high performance and general, but not highly productive. Python and Ruby are highly productive and general but suffer from poor performance.

We propose focusing on high productivity and performance by foregoing generality. This can be achieved via the use of Domain-Specific Languages (DSLs). There are already a few examples of successful DSLs in widespread use (SQL, OpenGL, Matlab). DSLs have a long history of increasing programmer productivity by providing extremely high-level, in a sense "ideal", abstractions tailored to a particular domain. DSLs are usually declarative in nature which leads to programs that express intent as opposed to implementation details. Such details are best left to a compiler. Since the programs are expressed at a very high level, a DSL compiler can generate different concrete implementations suited to the various execution environments (Multicore, GPU, Cluster or a hybrid). The Pervasive Parallelism Laboratory (PPL) at Stanford has been working diligently on lowering the bar for the implementation and adoption of such performance oriented DSLs. We will be presenting some of the insights uncovered so far by the PPL and discuss the big challenges that remain to be solved.

2.6 Russ Cox

RUSS COX worked on the open source releases of Plan 9 from Bell Labs and wrote the search engine for the Online Encyclopedia of Integer Sequences before joining Google. At Google, he led the design and implementation of Google Code Search, a regular expression-based search engine for public source code, and has for the last three years worked on Go. He holds bachelor's and master's degrees in computer science from Harvard University and a Ph.D. in computer science from M.I.T.

The paradigms needed to address the challenges of multicore, manycore, and cloud computing are not new, but neither are they embodied in the mainstream programming languages used today. The most widespread paradigm for multicore computing today is threads sharing memory and synchronizing with mutexes and condition variables. Programmers who can write correct, scalable programs with these primitives are the exception, not the rule.

The Go programming language (golang.org) turns to an alternate approach, shared memory coordinated by message passing in the style of Hoare's CSP. That is, instead of communicating by sharing memory, Go programs share memory by communicating. We have found that programmers new to concurrent and parallel programming are much more likely to write correct programs when reasoning about communication instead of synchronization. This explicit focus on communication also generalizes well to thinking about the cloud.

2.7 Benedict Gaster

BENEDICT GASTER is an architect at AMD, where he is working on programing models for heterogeneous APUs containing multicore and manycore architectures. He has a PhD in computer science for his work on type systems for records and variants.

The move towards Multicore, Manycore, and even more recently Cloud Computing has again pushed the envelope in computer science for the development of new programming languages and paradigms but is this really what's needed? There are too many programing languages to mention, each of which have their advantages and disadvantages, but many of them lack concurrency abstractions and ones that do have them often emit a strong model for reasoning about communication and shared access to data. The last few years have seen an effort to define stronger memory models for shared memory programming with respect to data race free (DRF) programs, c.f. Java and C++11, and with this direction comes hope. Not because DRF shared memory programming is necessarily the final answer but because it looks beyond a particular programming language or paradigm and instead tries to address the fundamentals of building software for Multicore and Manycore machines, by providing a clear semantics for when and how data can be shared with others.

2.8 Guy Steele

GUY STEELE has spent most of his career as a slacker, only managing to accomplish:
- Contributions to and illustrations for *The Hacker's Dictionary*
- Design of the original Emacs command set
- The first port of TeX
- *C: A Reference Manual* (with Sam Harbison) and standards committee work for C
- *Common Lisp: The Language* which became the ANSI standard for Common Lisp
- Definition of the Scheme dialect of Lisp (with Gerald Sussman)
- The "Lambda Papers" (with Gerald Sussman)

- *The_High Performance Fortran Handbook* (with Koelbel, Loveman, Schreiber, and Zosel) and standards committee work for Fortran and High Performance Fortran
- *The Java Language Specification*
- Project editor for the first ECMAScript standard (aka Javascript)
- Currently working on Fortress, a growable parallel language that integrates object-oriented and mathematical notation

(Bio by Alex Miller, slightly updated to give credit where it's due, this sentence being one example.)

Not only is a new programming language paradigm required, but in fact more than one is required.

If we consider the famous "Fallacies of Distributed Computing" (enumerated by Peter Deutsch, with input from Bill Joy, Tom Lyon, and James Gosling — see http://en.wikipedia.org/wiki/Fallacies_of_Distributed_Com puting) we see that both multicore applications and cloud applications need to take their principles into account in ways that existing popular languages do not—but we also see that there are tradeoffs, and principles that are less important for multicore computing become much more important for cloud computing. These tradeoffs have implications for language design.

In addition, we argue that existing language designs encourage programming strategies that are inherently too difficult to parallelize automatically; new language designs need to encourage the expression of divide-and-conquer algorithms rather than algorithms that rely on iterative accumulation of results.

2.9 David Ungar

DAVID UNGAR is an out-of-the-box thinker who enjoys the challenge of building computer software systems that work like magic and fit a user's mind like a glove. He received the 2009 Dahl-Nygaard award for outstanding career contributions in the field of object-orientation, and was honored as an ACM Fellow in 2010. Three of his papers have been honored by the Association for Computing Machinery for lasting impact over ten to twenty-four years: for the design of the prototype-based Self language, dynamic optimization techniques, and the application of cartoon animation ideas to user interfaces. He enjoys a position at IBM

Research, where he is taking on a new challenge: investigating how application programmers can exploit manycore systems, and testing those ideas to see if they can help with large-scale data analysis.

In the not-too-distant future, manycore microprocessors will become commonplace: every (non-hand-held) computer's CPU chip will contain 1,000 fairly homogeneous cores. Such a system will not be programmed like the cloud, or even a cluster because communication will be much faster relative to computation. Nor will it be programmed like today's multicore processors because the illusion of instant memory coherency will have been dispelled by both the physical limitations imposed by the 1,000-way fan-in to the memory system, and the comparatively long physical lengths of the inter- vs. intra-core connections. When this future arrives we will have to change our very model of computation.

If we cannot skirt Amdahl's Law, the last 900 cores will do us no good whatsoever. What does this mean? We cannot afford even tiny amounts of serialization. Locks?! Even lock-free algorithms will not be parallel enough. They rely on instructions that require communication and synchronization between cores' caches. We need to develop a body of knowledge around computing without any synchronization whatsoever.

In our Renaissance project at IBM, Vrije, and Portland State, (http://soft.vub.ac.be/~smarr/renaissance/) we are investigating what we call "anti-lock," "race-and-repair," or "end-to-end nondeterministic" computing. When we give up synchronization, we of necessity give up determinism. (In fact, there seems to be a fundamental tradeoff between determinism and performance, but that's another topic.) The obstacle we shall have to overcome, if we are to successfully program manycore systems, is our cherished assumption that we write programs that always get the exactly right answers. This assumption is deeply embedded in how we think about programming. The folks who build web search engines already understand, but for the rest of us, to quote Firesign Theatre: **Everything You Know Is Wrong!**

Ungar will be expanding on this topic in an invited talk at the Dynamic Languages Symposium 2011 co-located with the SPLASH 2011 conference.

Panel

Going Green with Refactoring:
Sustaining the "World Wide Virtual Machine"

Steven Fraser

Cisco Research Center
San Jose
sdfraser@acm.org

Emerson Murphy-Hill

North Carolina State University
Raleigh
emerson@csc.ncsu.edu

Werner Wild

University of Innsbruck
Innsbruck
werner.wild@unibz.it

Joseph Yoder

The Refactory
Urbana-Champaign
joe@refactory.com

Bo Q. Zhu

Pattern Insight
Mountain View
bo.zhu@patterninsight.com

Abstract

This year's SPLASH theme is the "Internet as a World-Wide Virtual Machine" to highlight the challenges of continuous system growth, multi-site development, big data, with millions of interacting users and devices. This panel will discuss how refactoring systems can enable them to "go green" by reducing power consumption, increasing simplicity of interface, and/or extending system longevity in a world of constantly changing technology.

Categories and Subject Descriptors
K.0 Computing Milieux

General Terms   Design, Experimentation, Standardization

Keywords   Innovation, creativity, refactoring

1. Steven Fraser

STEVEN FRASER joined the Cisco Research Center as Director in July 2007 with responsibilities for fostering university research collaborations, managing PhD recruiting, and technology transfer. Prior to joining Cisco Research, Steven was a Senior Staff member of Qualcomm's Learning Center in San Diego, leading software learning programs and creating the corporation's internal technical conference (QTech Forum). Steven held a variety of technology strategy roles at BNR (Bell-Northern Research) and Nortel including: Process Architect, Senior Manager (Disruptive Technology and Global External Research), and

Advisor (Design Process Engineering). In 1994 he spent a year as a Visiting Scientist at the Software Engineering Institute (SEI) collaborating with the "Application of Software Models" project on the development of team-based domain analysis (software reuse) techniques. Fraser has organized multiple conference panels and was the Corporate Support Chair for OOPSLA'08 and OOPSLA'09. He was the Tutorial Chair for XP2008 and the Tutorial Co-Chair for ICSE'09. Fraser holds a doctorate in EE from McGill University in Montréal – and is a senior member of both the ACM and the IEEE.

2. Emerson Murphy-Hill

EMERSON MURPHY-HILL is an assistant professor at North Carolina State University. By conducting formative studies, building tools based on the findings, and then evaluating the effect that those tools have on software developers' work, his research aims to bridge the gap between the capabilities of tools and how software developers actually use them. He received his Ph.D. from Portland State University in 2009 and his B.S. from The Evergreen State College in 2001.

Emerson's research suggests that refactoring is a common practice among software developers, and that the types of refactorings that developers perform are also the types of refactorings that modern development environments offer. Although new kinds of refactoring tools may support developers in making new types of program transformations, this research suggests that developers are currently well supported by the existing tools.

Nonetheless, Emerson's research also suggests that existing refactoring tools are also underused -- perhaps 90% of refactorings that developers could do with modern refactoring tools are instead done manually. This is a problem because refactorings done by hand can be more error prone and slower than those done with tools. One significant challenge, then, is to make refactoring tools that developers use frequently. Emerson believes this problem can be solved by improving the usability and discoverability of existing tools.

3. Werner Wild

WERNER WILD studied Computer Science and Mathematics at the University of Innsbruck and currently teaches at the Free University of Bolzano, the University of Innsbruck and the Management Center Innsbruck. Previous assignments include UNESCO, NIO Goa, ISS The Hague, UBS Switzerland, SwissRe Zurich, Joanneum Research Graz and others. His involvement with computers started 1972; he developed virtual machines, compilers, medical and financial applications, and is involved in the latest (agile) trends in Software Engineering. He is an organizer of workshops at international conferences, publishes together with Barbara Weber and is an elected official to the Austrian Chamber of Commerce in the Tyrol, identifying and tackling the challenges ahead of the Austrian IT industry. He loves to fly airplanes and holds a Commercial Pilot License in the US, including a current Instrument Rating.

Going "Green" is about sustainable solutions, from CSR (Corporate Social Responsibility) on the company level all the way down to the development of products consuming less energy per value unit delivered over the full product life cycle. This includes resources used during the development process, in the working product and when decommissioning. With the already hitting tidal wave of mobile devices the good old skills of considering code size and execution speed come to the forefront of desperately looked after skills, together with the new focus on reducing power consumption to extend useful battery life. In general, we fail as Computer Science educators to inspire the next generation of developers about the sustainability of their software and hardly any new engineer knows about the impact of a chosen implementation on maximum power used, life cycle energy consumption and its long term maintainability. However, teaching Refactoring for all kinds of "-ilities" (testability, changeability, scalability, ...) extends the students' mental software development model and gives them critical skills and tools needed to attack the issues mentioned above, right during development, not as an afterthought!

4. Joseph Yoder

JOSEPH YODER is a founder and principal of The Refactory, Inc., a company focused on software architecture, design, implementation, consulting and mentoring on all facets of software development. Joseph is an international speaker and pattern author, long standing member of the ACM, and the President of The Hillside Group, a, a group dedicated to improving the quality of software development. Joseph specializes in Architecture, Analysis and Design, C#, Java, Smalltalk, Patterns, Agile Methods,

Adaptable Systems, Refactoring, Reuse, and Frameworks. Joe is the author of many patterns, including being an author of the Big Ball of Mud pattern, which illuminates many fallacies in the approach to software architecture. Joe currently resides in Urbana, Illinois. He teaches Agile Methods, Design Patterns, Object Design, Refactoring, and Testing in industrial settings and mentors many developers on these concepts. He currently oversees a team of developers who have constructed many systems based on enterprise architecture in the .NET environment. Other projects involve working in both the Java and .NET environments deploying Domain-Specific Languages for clients.

Joe presents tutorials and talks, arranges workshops, and organizes leading technical conferences held throughout the world, including international conferences such as Agile, Agile Portugal, Encontro Ágil in Brazil, AOSD, CBSoft, JAOO, QCon, PLoP, AsianPLoP, SugarLoafPLoP in Brazil, OOPSLA, ECOOP, SATURN, and SPLASH. Joe thinks software is still too hard to change. He wants do something about this and believes that with good patterns and by putting the ability to change software into the hands of the people with the knowledge to change it seems to be on promising avenue to solve this problem.

Refactoring is a discipline approach to improve the overall design of the code. Refactoring is the process of changing software without altering its external behavior. Refactoring is usually done to make the code easier to extend or maintain and is done in the content of adding features to the software. A lot of small steps are taken to make the code better. Regression tests are critical to insure that the restructuring of the code did not break anything.

Refactoring software to make it maintainable and extendable has become a recognized best practice and has been accepted and incorporated into many Agile practices such as Scrum, TDD and XP. However, there are still many problems with the practice of refactoring. Quite often any type of redesign or evolution of code is considered "refactoring" the code.

Additionally there are many refactoring obstacles even in accepted Agile practices such as a rush to the next iteration and to add the next feature. It is important to support refactorings and include them as part of the regular development process as a lot of little steps before the code evolves to a state where refactoring can become more difficult. Knowing how and when to refactor is key towards being successful and also to reap the true benefits of keeping your code clean.

5. Bo Q. Zhu

BO Q. ZHU is Co-Founder and VP of Products at Pattern Insight. Bo is responsible for all products at Pattern Insight, from strategic planning to execution, through the entire product lifecycle. Pattern Insight is a VC backed enterprise software company that has developed a powerful data mining technology for analysis of source code to improve software quality, increase development productivity, and reduce product cycle time. Code Insight, the company's flagship product, is currently used on tens of billions of lines of critical source code in industry leading companies such as Cisco, Qualcomm, Motorola, and Juniper. Bo obtained his Ph.D. in Computer Science from the University of Illinois at Urbana-Champaign. His interests lie in system research including using data mining with static code analysis to improve system reliability and manageability. His has published pioneering research papers in the top conferences such as SOSP and SIGMOD and holds several patents. He obtained his M.S. and B.S. in Computer Science from Nanjing University, China and previously worked at IBM Almaden Research Center and China's National Laboratory of New Software Technology.

Code reuse is a standard practice in modern software development. Practiced most commonly in the form of copy-paste programming, it has an inevitable side effect: Code bloat. Bloated code leads to poor code quality, increased software maintenance costs, as well as increased power drain on batteries in devices. In the mobile industry in particular, device vendors have launched initiatives to pragmatically refactor codebases in an effort to combat quality problems and increase battery life. Step 1 in such refactoring processes is to accurately and efficiently identify candidate code clones. However, this is not an easy job. Studies show that 67% of code clones are not exact copies – with code often modified after reuse. Variable names are altered and statements are added deleted or modified. And this is not a matter of open source being the culprit: commercial code is as prone to this problem as open source. By combining data mining with static code analysis, Pattern Insight's Clone Detection solution quickly detects cloned patterns in code, even when code has been modified after reuse. It is fast, able to detect a greater quantity of clones than any other method (due to its fuzzy match capability), and easy to use. Our technology is used by the companies like Motorola and Qualcomm, that power a vast array of Android devices, to improve code quality, reduce bloat and maintenance and help make the world a bit more "green".

Panel

Industry-Academic Research Partnerships

Steven Fraser

Director
Cisco Research Center
Cisco Systems, San Jose
sdfraser@acm.org

Judith Bishop

Director
Microsoft Research
Redmond
jbishop@microsoft.com@acm.org

Rajarshi Rajarshi

Senior Staff Engineer, Manager
Qualcomm Corporate R&D
Silicon Valley
rajarshi@qualcomm.com

Dennis Mancl

Distinguished Member of Technical Staff
Alcatel-Lucent, Murray Hill
Dennis.Mancl@alcatel-lucent.com

J. Christopher Ramming

Director
Intel Labs Academic Research Office
Santa Clara
james.c.ramming@intel.com

Salvador Rivas

Director
Corporate and Foundation Relations
Henry Samueli School of Engineering
UCLA
srivas@support.ucla.edu

Abstract

Research partnerships between industry and academia are grown through relationships, a desire for innovation, and opportunities for sponsorship. Relationships mature through the mobility (virtual or otherwise) of academics, graduates, and seasoned industry professionals. From an industry perspective, innovation is driven by a need to grow product portfolios, market share and rejuvenate the corporate talent pool. Academics may be more motivated by the search for knowledge, the desire to publish, and the need to move education yardsticks by keeping curriculum relevant and mentoring top students. Research in an industry context ranges from in-house "labs" to a hybrid combination of company acquisitions and – or university partnerships. Tech talks, facilitated workshops, forums, sabbaticals, internships, grants, equipment donations, and corporate philanthropy – not to mention active engagement between researchers are all part of the mix. Panelists will discuss and debate the merits various of research engagement strategies.

Categories and Subject Descriptors
K.0 Computing Milieux

General Terms   Management, Design, Economics, Experimentation, Standardization, Legal Aspects.

Keywords   Innovation, creativity, industry partnerships, research

1. Steven Fraser

STEVEN FRASER joined the Cisco Research Center as Director in July 2007 with responsibilities for fostering university research collaborations, managing PhD recruiting, and technology transfer. Prior to joining Cisco Research, Steven was a Senior Staff member of Qualcomm's Learning Center in San Diego, leading software learning programs and creating the corporation's internal technical conference (QTech Forum). Steven held a variety of technology strategy roles at BNR and Nortel including: Process Architect, Senior Manager (Disruptive Technology and Global External Research), and Advisor (Design Process Engineering). In 1994 he spent a year as a Visiting Scientist at the Software Engineering Institute (SEI) collaborating with the "Application of

Software Models" project on the development of team-based domain analysis (software reuse) techniques. Fraser has organized multiple conference panels and was the Corporate Support Chair for OOPSLA'08 and OOPSLA'09. He was the Tutorial Chair for XP2008 and the Tutorial Co-Chair for ICSE'09. Fraser holds a doctorate in EE from McGill University in Montréal – and is a senior member of both the ACM and the IEEE.

Academic-Industry research partnerships face challenges in a variety of areas:

- Time scales - in industry these are often measured by fiscal quarters in contrast to academic generations measured in 3-5 annual cycles of graduate students
- Continuity of funding (both corporate and academic) - which may include gifts, fellowships, contracts, equipment donations, consortia fees, and/or goods and services-in-kind.
- Leveraging innovation to create value - through technology transfer of publications and intellectual property
- Attracting and retaining top talent – in both academic and industry milieus
- Geography – taking collaboration from a physical world to a virtual world has created challenges in "information overload" with many partnerships deserving our attention yet competing for resources

We plan to have a panel that will bring together interesting perspectives on university-industry research partnerships and foster both debate and convergence.

2. Judith Bishop

JUDITH BISHOP is Director of Computer Science at Microsoft Research. Her role is to create strong links between Microsoft's research groups and universities globally, through encouraging projects, supporting conferences and engaging directly in research. Her expertise is in programming languages and distributed systems, with a strong practical bias and an interest in compilers and design patterns. She initiated the Software Innovation Foundation (SEIF) and is currently working on a new way of running programs in browsers (especially F#).

Judith received her PhD from the University of Southampton and was previously in academia, having been a professor at the Universities of Witwatersrand and Pretoria, with visiting positions in the UK, Germany, Canada, Italy and the USA. She is currently an Honorary Professor at the University of Cape Town. Judith serves frequently on editorial, program and award committees, and has received numerous awards and distinctions.

In any collaboration, an important measure of success is that each player comes out with more than they put in. This effect can only occur through the ingredient of active collaboration between the industry partners and the academics. Achieving the goal of active collaboration brings with it challenges. Within industry, we have security and IP concerns which conflict directly with the openness and identical IP concerns of universities these days. Students who take internships might find it hard to break off from their graduate work, despite the prestige of the position, and the university itself loses the student for three months with no recompense. Grants are a minefield for both sides because of the concern to maximize return on investment and to minimize overheads. Unrestricted gifts do not enable the industry partner to set milestones or any kind of report back requirement, but contracts require the academic to pay sometimes very heavy overheads. Conference sponsorships are easy to give, but to send personnel to the conference to engage with academics is becoming increasingly expensive. Finally, when giving company money away, one would like to think that the company's hardware or software is going to be used, but this desire cannot always be stated as a requirement.

Thus industry is taking a long hard look at the kinds of engagements that do work and where and how to target their outreach budget. I'll describe some of the Outreach programs from Microsoft Research and pinpoint why some of these have adopted new methods to make them more effective. These include dramatically increasing person-to-person contact, visits, and conference attendance, being more careful in screening requests for funding in terms of return on investment for the company and tapping into the wide open pool of talent by running competitions. I'll also mention how we measure success, and why innovation is such a key factor in all we do.

3. Rajarshi Gupta

RAJARSHI GUPTA is a Senior Staff Engineer and Manager at Qualcomm Corporate R&D (CRD), which he joined in July 2005. He began working on interference management for femto cells, and the 4G LTE project, where he was the SON (self organizing networks) lead and also a delegate to 3GPP RAN3. In August 2008, Rajarshi moved to the Bay Area R&D (BARD) lab in Silicon Valley, where he is currently an engineering lead on the Indoor Positioning project. Rajarshi loves to work on innovative and unsolved problems, and is the author of over 100 filed patents. Rajarshi also heads the University Relations program for BARD, as part of which he started the Qualcomm Innovation Fellowship. Prior to joining Qualcomm, Rajarshi completed his M.S. and PhD in EECS at UC Berkeley, having worked for a start-up in between the two degrees.

The Qualcomm Innovation Fellowship (QInF) was created to encourage innovative thinking and creativity in graduate students. It reflects Qualcomm Corporate R&D's (CRD) motto of "Innovate, Execute, Partner". Unique among many fellowships, QInF asks PhD students to get together in teams of two (partner) and make a proposal of the work (innovate), that is recommended by one/two advisors. The winning team then receives the Fellowship, at which point they work in close collaboration with a Qualcomm mentor to bring their innovative ideas to fruition (execute).

The fellowship started in 2009 as an experiment in two schools – Berkeley and Stanford. The excellent response and participation from the academic community has encouraged us to expand this to 11 schools across USA. In 2011, we received 146 proposals, which were reviewed by 100+ researchers within Qualcomm. The 33 finalists teams were then invited to one of 3 CRD labs across USA to present their proposal before the judges. 8 teams were picked as winners and are now beginning their Fellowship.

By soliciting innovation proposals, we are able to encourage the students to pursue the research problems that they are excited about, while allowing both the mentor and the advisor to guide them towards their goal. The collaborative model of assigning a mentor to each team has been a key reason for success in the eyes of the students. We have a lot of respect for the innovative ideas emanating out of the schools, and QInF has enabled us to learn about exciting new avenues for research.

4. Dennis Mancl

DENNIS MANCL is a Distinguished Member of Technical Staff at Alcatel-Lucent in Murray Hill, NJ. His interests range from software requirements practices to legacy code transformation techniques. He has worked 30 years in many roles in the technology transfer process: research, internal tools and consulting organizations, an internal training organization, and partnering with external companies.

One problem with industry-academic research partnerships: they are often narrowly focused on research areas that are less likely to produce a real paradigm shift. There are some new innovative ideas that are "easy to launch" as a new product, such as web apps, open-source toolkits, and other products that are centered around new innovative algorithms but in relatively conventional packaging. The most creative and different new ideas are the most difficult for established industry product groups to embrace. It is already difficult for most product development groups to accept an "escaped from the lab" product idea from an internal corporate research organization, it is doubly difficult to build on the work of graduate students in a corporate environment. On the other hand, if a partnership is done right, there are plenty of benefits going in both directions. In particular, both sides of an industry-academic partnership will usually bring in useful ideas about how to convert an innovation into a marketable product.

5. Chris Ramming

CHRIS RAMMING is the director of Intel Labs' Academic Research Office (ARO). Chris joined Intel in November of 2008 to create a new model of academic research with an emphasis on strategic impact. His experience also includes a 4-year term of service as a program manager in DARPA's Strategic Technology Office. In that role, he was responsible for designing and managing R&D programs to create and exploit high-risk/high-payoff technology opportunities with special emphasis on new approaches to mobile ad-hoc networking. Prior to joining DARPA, the bulk of Chris' career was with AT&T/Bell Labs Research where he focused on telecommunications-related software, services, and languages. Chris has a background in computer science with degrees from Yale and UNC Chapel Hill.

Intel deeply values academic collaboration and has a long history of experimentation and innovation in its approach to open collaborative models ranging from small grants to strategic programs to large centers. Our research initiatives cover a spectrum of time horizons and goals ranging from short-range product-related innovations to long-range transformative breakthroughs. The collaboration model for these academic partnerships extends from the hands-off to the highly engaged. At the same time we support academic engagements with many motivations other than pure research, ranging from hiring pipelines to technology dissemination to technological literacy to entrepreneurship. I hope to illustrate some of the more interesting points in our current spectrum, and will discuss the idea that having a multiplicity of models and organizational interfaces can lead to a more robust, productive, and valuable connection between industry and academia than any single, potentially brittle, one-size-fits-all model. I will hope to initiate discussion and feedback that can be used as we continue to innovate in our approaches.

6. Salvador Rivas

SALVADOR RIVAS is responsible for developing a comprehensive and mutually beneficial relationships with corporate and foundation partners to provide benefits to industry, plus support the priority needs of the School, its departments, centers, faculty, students, and programs. He brings a strong background in university administration and finance. He has held a number of administrative positions in student and academic affairs in higher education. Before joining UCLA he was a researcher at the University of Southern California. Salvador Rivas received his B.A. from California Polytechnic State University (San Luis Obispo), his M.A. from the University of San Diego, and his doctorate from the University of Southern California.

Posters & ACM Student Research Competition Co-Chairs' Welcome

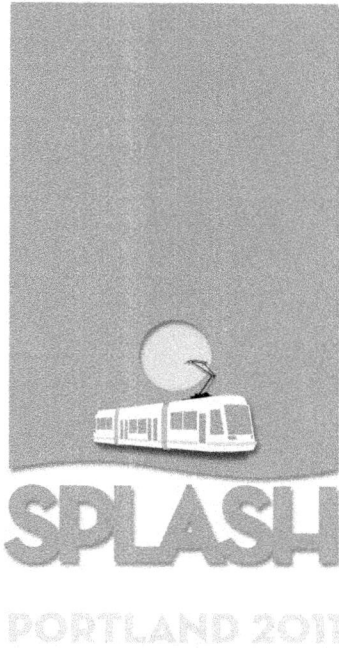

SPLASH Posters provide an excellent forum for authors to present their work in an informal and interactive setting. Posters are ideal to showcase speculative, late-breaking results or to introduce interesting, innovative work. Posters sessions are highly interactive. They allow authors and interested participants to connect to each other and to engage in discussions about the work presented. Posters provide authors with a unique opportunity to draw attention to their work during the conference. Authors in other SPLASH technical tracks therefore are strongly encouraged to complement their submission with a poster about their work.

After its remarkable success in previous years, SPLASH is again hosting an ACM SIGPLAN Student Research Competition. The competition, sponsored by Microsoft Research, is an internationally recognized venue that enables undergraduate and graduate students to experience the research world, share their research results with other students and SPLASH attendees, and compete for prizes. The ACM SIGPLAN Student Research Competition shares the Poster session's goal to facilitate students' interaction with researchers and industry practitioners, providing both sides with the opportunity to learn about ongoing research. Additionally, the ACM SIGPLAN Student Research Competition affords students with experience in both formal presentations and evaluations.

On the following pages, you will find the SPLASH Poster and ACM SIGPLAN Student Research Competition abstracts that cover an interesting mix of topics from the domains of systems, applications, and programming languages. It is worth noting that students participating in the ACM SIGPLAN Student Research Competition submit their abstract as sole author. You can use the abstracts to receive a brief introduction to posters from both the SPLASH Posters and ACM SIGPLAN Student Research Competition on display during the poster session, or to find further information about the authors and their work. The ACM SIGPLAN Student Research Competition abstracts can also be used to get a general overview of what the student will be presenting during their formal presentation at the second round of the competition.

At this time, we would like to take the opportunity to thank everyone who has participated in making SPLASH Posters and the ACM SIGPLAN Student Research Competition a success. In particular, we would like to acknowledge the contributions of the SPLASH Poster and ACM SIGPLAN Student Research Competition Program Committee members. The reviews helped considerably in selecting the most worthy submissions and providing valuable feedback to the authors. Finally, we would also like to acknowledge Microsoft Research for sponsoring the ACM SIGPLAN Student Research Competition.

We look forward to seeing you in Portland, Oregon at SPLASH.

Eli Tilevich & Sushil Bajracharya
SPLASH 2011 Posters and SRC Co-Chairs
Virginia Tech & Black Duck Software Inc.
tilevich@cs.vt.edu & bajracharya@gmail.com

The Ink Language Meta-Metamodel for Adaptive Object-Model Frameworks *

[Extended Abstract]

Eli Acherkan[1,2]   Atzmon Hen-Tov[2]

[2]Pontis Ltd.
Glil Yam 46905, Israel
{eliac8,atzmon.hentov}@gmail.com

David H. Lorenz[1]   Lior Schachter[1]

[1]Open University of Israel
1 University Rd., Raanana 43107 Israel
lorenz@openu.ac.il, liorsav@gmail.com

Abstract

We present a meta-metamodel for implementing AOM systems in two languages collaboratively: Ink for structure and Java for behavior. Using two languages rather than one facilitates a style of programming that imposes a strict separation of structure and behavior.

Categories and Subject Descriptors   D.1.5 [*Programming Techniques*]: Object-oriented Programming; D.3.3 [*Programming Languages*]: Language Constructs and Features—Frameworks.

General Terms   Design, Languages.

Keywords   Adaptive-object model (AOM), Mirrors, Type Object.

1. Introduction

We present a new approach to implementing AOM systems. In this approach, two languages are used in the implementation collaboratively:

- *A language for describing structure:* The structure of the system and static configuration is expressed in a new type-safe dynamic Smalltalk-like language, named Ink [5]. Ink can dynamically change the class structure at runtime.

- *A language for describing behavior:* The behavior of the system is expressed in a statically typed OO language, namely, Java.

---

* This research was supported in part by the *Israel Science Foundation (ISF)* under grant No. 926/08.

Using two languages rather than one facilitates a style of programming that imposes a strict separation of structure and behavior. At runtime the Ink VM uses dependency injection to configure the behavior instances with the corresponding Ink instances.

2. The Ink Meta-Metamodel

Ink is class-based and supports explicit metaclasses [3]. The Ink meta-metamodel is a 4 meta-level system similar to that of MetaclassTalk [2] with some additional concepts borrowed from the MOF. Figure 1 depicts the basic classes and relationships within the Ink meta-metamodel.

InkObject   The InkObject class is the root of the Ink inheritance hierarchy. It is an instance of the metaclass InkClass. Every object in Ink is an indirect instance of InkObject, which defines the basic structure of all objects (except primitives) in the Ink language. An Ink object may provide property values for the properties defined in its class. The type of each property value must conform to the type declared by the property definition in the class.

Generally, the definition of an addressable object (one that is not contained within another object) must specify a unique ID. Each Ink object belongs to a class, e.g., the definition of an object O_2 in Ink must indicate the object's class C_2. Ink supports object inheritance. An object O_2 of class C_2 may indicate a super-object O_1 of class C_1 (which O_2 is said to extend), provided that C_2 is a descendant of C_1. By extending O_1, O_2 inherits all the property values of O_1, and may override them. A property value can be either a primitive (string, integer, date, etc.), a complex (e.g., another Ink object), or a collection of primitives or Ink objects. Object inheritance is applied recursively on the entire objects graph. An object O_4 contained within O_2 inherits all the property values of O_3 contained within O_1, and may override them.

InkClass   InkClass is the root of the metaclass hierarchy. InkClass is an instance of InkClass (itself) and extends InkType (which extends InkObject). Every class (and metaclass) in Ink is an instance of InkClass or one

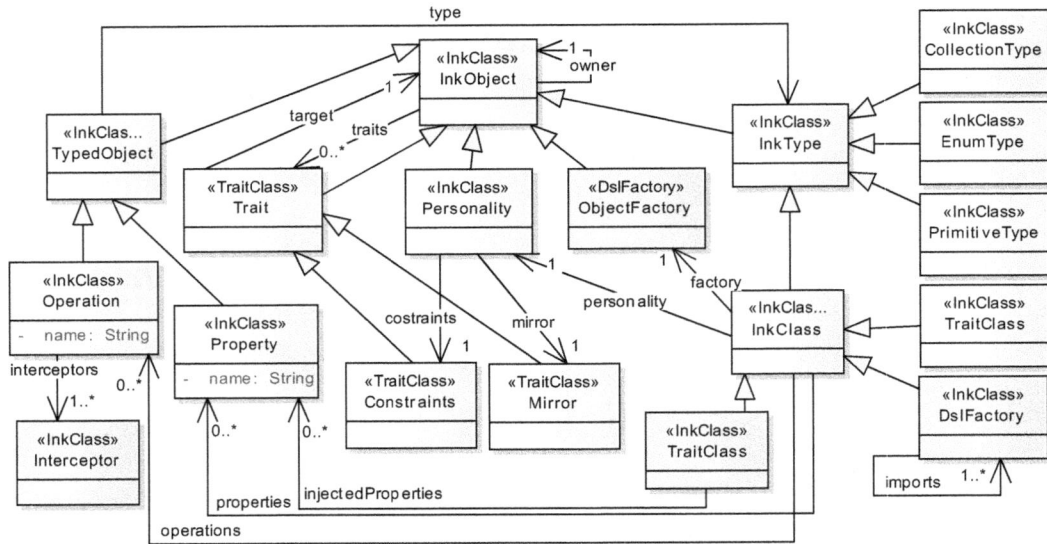

Figure 1. The Ink language meta-metamodel.

of its subclasses, and extends `InkObject` or one of its subclasses. An explicit metaclass in Ink is a class that extends `InkClass`. Class inheritance in Ink is essentially object inheritance applied to classes. Like objects, classes may refine the type of an inherited property definition (in a covariant manner).

Properties A property in Ink is a first class object and can be extended by programmers. `Property` is an instance of `InkClass` and extends `TypedObject`. `InkClass` defines the `properties` property, which is a list of `Property`'s. This list determines the structure of objects, by specifying the name and type of the property as well as other metadata and constraints. A class may define a property as either mandatory or optional. An instance is valid if all mandatory properties have values. A subclass of `Property` may expresses application-specific constraints that will be applied to the assigned value.

Operations `Operation` is an instance of `InkClass` and extends `TypedObject`. An operation corresponds to a method, and is used to control its execution. The execution is controlled via before/after interceptors (e.g., for security, transaction control, SLA and other crosscutting concerns). `Operations` can also be used as hook points to dynamically incorporate behavioral changes to an AOM model [1].

Traits Ink supports traits [4] through the `Personality` class, of which each property value is a `Trait` instance. The `Trait` class is an instance of the `TraitClass` metaclass, which extends `InkClass`. A trait is a kind of `InkObject` with a target property. The target of a trait is another `InkObject`.

A trait is typically used to handle crosscutting (technical or business domain) concerns that are not handled in the target. A trait may add properties to its target, which

are injected to the target's class and thus change the target class's structure (`injectedProperties` in Figure 1). Consequently, instances of the target class will have to supply values to these properties, and the trait behavior can adapt its execution accordingly.

A metaclass may add new traits by overriding the personality property definition in `InkClass` and providing a subclass of `Personality` as the personality property type.

3. Conclusion

Ink enables a two languages approach to building AOM application with a strict separation of structure and behavior. Ink is being developed as an open-source project [5].

References

[1] E. Acherkan, A. Hen-Tov, L. Schachter, D. H. Lorenz, R. Wirfs-Brock, and J. Yoder. Dynamic hook points. In *Proceedings of the 2nd Asian Conference on Pattern Languages of Programs (AsianPLoP '11)*, Tokyo, Japan, Oct. 5-7 2011. ACM. To appear.

[2] N. Bouraqadi. Safe metaclass composition using mixin-based inheritance. *Computer Languages, Systems & Structures*, 30 (1-2):49–61, 2004.

[3] J. Briot and P. Cointe. Programming with explicit metaclasses in Smalltalk-80. *ACM SIGPLAN Notices*, 24(10):419–431, 1989.

[4] G. Curry, L. Baer, D. Lipkie, and B. Lee. Traits: An approach to multiple inheritance subclassing. *SIGOA Newsletter*, 3(1 and 2):1–9, June 1982. ACM-SIGOA Conference on Office Automation Systems, Philadelphia, Penn.

[5] Ink. The Ink project. Software Engineering Research Lab, The Open University of Israel, 2010. http://code.google.com/a/eclipselabs.org/p/ink/.

Plaid: A Permission-Based Programming Language *

Jonathan Aldrich[†]   Robert Bocchino[†]   Ronald Garcia[†]   Mark Hahnenberg[†]   Manuel Mohr[†*]
Karl Naden[†]   Darpan Saini[†]   Sven Stork[†]   Joshua Sunshine[†]   Éric Tanter[‡]   Roger Wolff[†]

[†]School of Computer Science, Carnegie Mellon University   [*]Karlsruhe Institute of Technology
[‡]PLEIAD Lab, Computer Science Dept (DCC), University of Chile
jonathan.aldrich@cs.cmu.edu (contact author)

Abstract

Access permissions (permissions for short) are a lightweight way to specify how an object may be aliased and whether aliases allow mutation. Prior work has demonstrated the value of permissions for addressing many software engineering concerns, including information hiding, protocol checking, concurrency, security, and memory management.

We propose a *permission-based programming language*: that is, a language whose object model, type system, and runtime are all co-designed with permissions in mind. The key elements of such a language are (1) an object model in which the structure of an object can change over time; (2) a type system that tracks changing structure in addition to addressing concerns such as those listed above; and (3) a runtime system that dynamically checks permission assertions and leverages permissions to parallelize code. We sketch the design of the permission-based programming language Plaid and argue that the approach promises significant software engineering benefits.

Categories and Subject Descriptors D.2.10 [*Software Engineering*]: Design—Representation; D.3.3 [*Programming Languages*]: Language Constructs and Features—Permissions

General Terms Design, Documentation, Human Factors, Languages, Performance, Reliability, Security, Theory, Verification

Keywords types, permissions, programming languages

1. Introduction

Access permissions (permissions for short) are annotations on pointer variables such as `unique` or `immutable` that specify how an object may be aliased and which aliases may read or write the object [3]. Permissions have been used to support encapsulation, protocol checking, and safe concurrency, among other applications. However, prior permission systems have been specialized to address particular concerns. Prior systems also lack key features that make modern type systems practical, such as the ability to carry out dynamic checks (typically as casts) when static checking is overly conservative.

In this poster, we present the concept of a *permission-based programming language*: that is, a language whose object model, type system, and runtime are all co-designed with permissions in mind [1]. In such a language, every pointer variable is associated not just with a type describing the object pointed to, but a permission describing aliasing, mutability, and other aspects of how the object may be used.

Such a language generalizes existing specialized permission systems, providing a single set of permissions that can check multiple software engineering concerns in a unified way. A language-based approach can also go beyond mere checking, to enable completely new capabilities in the runtime system and object model of the language.

For example, just as the runtime system of an object-oriented language tracks the types of objects, the runtime system in a permission-based language can track permissions. Thus, if a programmer has a pointer with a `shared` permission (indicating aliases to the pointer are possible) and casts it to `unique` (indicating there are no aliases to the pointer), the runtime system will allow the cast to succeed only if there are no other pointers to that object. The runtime system can also execute different operations concurrently whenever permissions show that the operations are independent.

Permissions also support interesting new object models—for example, the ability to change the interface, representation, and behavior of an existing object at run time, as in typestate-oriented programming [2]. Permission-based languages thus enable new design and modeling capabilities, verification of diverse properties, and a level of practicality that prior permissions systems have lacked.

2. A Permission-Based Language

First-Class States in Plaid. We are developing a new permission-based programming language called Plaid. Plaid's permissions allow it to support *typestate-oriented*

* Partially funded by Fondecyt project 1110051, NSF grant CCF-0811592, CI Fellows grant #0937060 from NSF to CRA, and CMU—Portugal grant CMU-PT/SE/0038/2008.

```
1    state Buffer comprises EmptyBuffer, FullBuffer { }
2
3    state EmptyBuffer case of Buffer {
4       method void put(unique Element ≫ none e) [EmptyBuffer ≫ FullBuffer] {
5          this ← FullBuffer { elem = e };
6       }
7    }
8
9    state FullBuffer case of Buffer {
10      requires unique Element elem;
11      method unique Element get() [FullBuffer ≫ EmptyBuffer] {
12         val e = elem;
13         this ← EmptyBuffer { };
14         e;
15      }
16   }
```

Figure 1. A buffer implementation in Plaid.

programming [2], a new programming paradigm that extends object-oriented programming with first-class states. Rather than be a member of a fixed class, each object has a *typestate* that can change as the program runs. Unlike prior approaches to typestate based on static analysis, Plaid's first-class states define not just an interface but also representation and behavior.

As an example, consider the Buffer implementation in Figure 1. The Buffer state is abstract; the **comprises** clause ensures that every Buffer is either an EmptyBuffer or a FullBuffer. EmptyBuffer has an operation put. In the implementation of put (line 5), the left arrow is a *state change operation* that causes the object **this** to transition to the FullBuffer state. The FullBuffer state requires a field elem, and so when we transition from EmptyBuffer to FullBuffer we must provide a value for this field. FullBuffer has a single operation get, which reads the value in elem and returns it, after changing receiver object back to the EmptyBuffer state.

Note that the implementation in Figure 1 is clearer and less error-prone than an equivalent Java implementation. Since Java does not support states explicitly, a single Buffer class would need to support both get and put methods, and a runtime check would be needed against the possibility of calling get on an empty buffer. Such checks are often omitted in practice either by accident or because they are costly. Furthermore, in Java the element field must contain some sentinel value (e.g., null) when the buffer is empty, and if this value is not correctly associated with the state of the buffer, then an error (e.g., a null pointer exception) may result. In contrast, Plaid's explicit support for states means that methods and fields are present only in the states where they make sense. If the programmer uses the states incorrectly, then the system automatically generates a meaningful error message. For example, it might say that get has been called on an EmptyBuffer.

Typechecking State Change. Plaid tracks the state of each object flow-sensitively. Each method declares how it changes the state of the receiver (and of each argument, if relevant), using the ≫ notation to distinguish the pre-state from the post-state. For example, the signature of put (line 4) declares that the receiver's state changes from EmptyBuffer to FullBuffer.

Permission-based Types. Unrestricted aliasing makes tracking states very difficult, because changing the state of one variable can cause others to change in hidden ways. To address this issue, our permission system expresses whether and how aliases can exist. For example, **unique** means that we have the only reference to an object, while **shared** means that there may be other aliases. A **unique** permission can be converted into an **immutable** permission (destroying the original **unique**), which allows other aliases but ensures that the object cannot be modified through them.

In Figure 1, the argument to put is **unique** and is in the Element state. When the method returns, however, no permission to that element is returned to the caller, because we have created a **unique** field reference to that element in the FullBuffer state, and returning a permission to the caller would violate the uniqueness invariant. That is, the caller may still have a reference, but it does not have permission to use it. This is indicated with the **none** permission.

Permissions default to **unique** for mutable states; for example, the state transition of the receiver of put is really [unique EmptyBuffer ≫ unique FullBuffer]. We also allow the declaration of **immutable** states, which means the default permission for objects of that state is **immutable**. This allows programs without aliasing, or purely functional programs without mutation, to be expressed without any additional permission annotation overhead.

Concurrency by Default. Plaid's permissions not only help track state, they also allow the natural concurrent execution of programs [4]. If we have a function fill that fills a buffer, we can create two **unique** buffers and if we call

```
fill(buf1); fill(buf2); combine(buf1, buf2);
```

then the Plaid compiler will automatically execute the two calls to fill in parallel, since they operate on different state. The compiler will wait until both fills are complete before calling combine as this requires the same resources as fill. Plaid's permissions can also support safe non-deterministic concurrency when needed [4].

References

[1] J. Aldrich et al. Permission-based programming languages. In *ICSE (NIER track)*, 2011.

[2] J. Aldrich, J. Sunshine, D. Saini, and Z. Sparks. Typestate-Oriented Programming. In *Onward!*, 2009.

[3] J. Boyland, J. Noble, and W. Retert. Capabilities for sharing: A generalization of uniqueness and read-only. In *ECOOP*, 2001.

[4] S. Stork, P. Marques, and J. Aldrich. Concurrency by Default: Using Permissions to Express Dataflow in Stateful Programs. In *Onward!*, 2009.

The Design and Implementation of the Habanero-Java Parallel Programming Language

Zoran Budimlić   Vincent Cavé   Raghavan Raman   Jun Shirako

Sağnak Taşırlar   Jisheng Zhao   Vivek Sarkar

Department of Computer Science, Rice University

{zoran, vcave, raghav, shirako, sagnak, jz10, vsarkar}@rice.edu

Categories and Subject Descriptors D.1.3 [*Concurrent Programming*]

General Terms Languages

Keywords Language, Parallel Programming, Habanero-Java

Abstract

The Habanero-Java language extends sequential Java with a simple but powerful set of constructs for multicore parallelism. Its implementation includes a compiler that generates standard Java class-files, a runtime system that builds on the `java.util.concurrent` library, an IDE (DrHJ) that extends DrJava, and a new data-race detection tool.

1. Habanero-Java Language

The Habanero-Java (HJ) language [1] was developed at Rice University during 2007-2010 as a pedagogic extension to the original Java-based definition of the X10 language [2][1]. In addition to its use as a research language in the Rice Habanero Multicore Software research project [5], HJ is used in a new sophomore-level course on "Fundamentals of Parallel Programming" (COMP 322 [3]) which has become a required course for all Computer Science majors at Rice. The code generated by the HJ compiler consists of Java class-files that can be executed on any standard JVM.

The HJ extensions to Java are primarily focused on task parallelism. Similar extensions to C and Scala are being pursued in the Habanero C and Habanero Scala projects at Rice. A brief summary of the most commonly-used HJ constructs is included below. A number of recent papers have demonstrated that HJ programs can achieve comparable or superior performance to programs written using standard Java Concurrency features.

1) async: Async is a construct for creating a new asynchronous task. The statement `async ⟨stmt⟩` causes the parent task to create a new child task to execute ⟨stmt⟩ (logically) in parallel with the parent task.

HJ also includes support for *async* tasks with return values in the form of *futures*. The statement, "`final future<T> f =`

---

[1] See http://x10-lang.org for the latest version of X10.

`async<T> Expr;`" creates a new child task to evaluate `Expr` that is ready to execute immediately. In this case, `f` contains a "future handle" to the newly created task and the operation `f.get()` (also known as a *force* operation) can be performed to obtain the result of the future task. If the future task has not completed as yet, the task performing the `f.get()` operation blocks until the result of `Expr` becomes available. *Data-driven futures* [8] extend futures by adding an *await* clause that specifies a set of future values that need to be available before the *async* task can be scheduled.

2) finish: The statement `finish ⟨stmt⟩` causes the parent task to execute ⟨stmt⟩ and then wait until all sub-tasks created within ⟨stmt⟩ have terminated (including transitively spawned tasks). Operationally, each statement executed in an HJ task has a unique *Immediately Enclosing Finish* (IEF) statement instance [7].

3) isolated: The *isolated* construct enables execution of a statement in isolation (mutual exclusion) relative to all other instances of isolated statements. The statement `isolated ⟨Stmt⟩` executes ⟨Stmt⟩ in isolation with respect to other *isolated* statements. Certain patterns of `isolated` statements can be replaced by semantically equivalent calls to `java.util.concurrent` (`j.u.c.`) libraries for atomic variables and concurrent collections. A new scalable implementation for HJ's isolated construct is described in [6].

4) phasers: The *phaser* construct [7] integrates collective and point-to-point synchronization by giving each task the option of registering with a phaser in *signal-only/wait-only* mode for producer/consumer synchronization or *signal-wait* mode for barrier synchronization[2]. These properties, along with the generality of *dynamic parallelism*, *phase-ordering* and *deadlock-freedom* safety properties, distinguish phasers from synchronization constructs in past work including barriers and X10's clocks [2]. In general, a task may be registered on multiple phasers, and a phaser may have multiple tasks registered on it.

5) forall: The statement `forall (point p : R) S` supports parallel iteration over all the points in region `R` by launching each iteration as a separate *async*, and including an implicit *finish* to wait for all of the spawned asyncs to terminate. A *point* is an element of an n-dimensional Cartesian space ($n \geq 1$) with integer-valued coordinates. A *region* is a set of points, and can be used to specify an array allocation or an iteration range as in the case of *async*.

Each dynamic instance of a `forall` statement includes an implicit phaser object (let us call it `ph`) that is set up so that all iterations in the `forall` are registered on `ph` in *signal-wait* mode.

6) places: The *place* construct in HJ provides a way for the programmer to specify affinity among async tasks. A place is an abstraction for a set of worker threads. When an HJ program is launched with the command, "`hj -places p:w`", a total of $p \times w$

SPLASH'11 Companion, October 22–27, 2011, Portland, Oregon, USA.
ACM 978-1-4503-0940-0/11/10.

[2] The latest release of `j.u.c` in Java 7 includes Phaser synchronizer objects, which are derived in part from the phaser construct in HJ.

worker threads are created with p places and w workers per place. The number of places remains fixed during program execution. However, the management of individual worker threads within a place is not visible to an HJ program, giving the runtime system the freedom to create additional worker threads in a place, if needed, after starting with w workers per place.

The main benefit of use $p > 1$ places is that an optional `at` clause can be specified on an async statement or expression of the form, "`async at`(*place-expr*) ...", where *place-expr* is a place-valued expression. This clause dictates that the child async task can only be executed by a worker thread at the specified place. Data locality can be controlled by assigning two tasks with the same data affinity to execute in the same place.

2. Habanero-Java Implementation

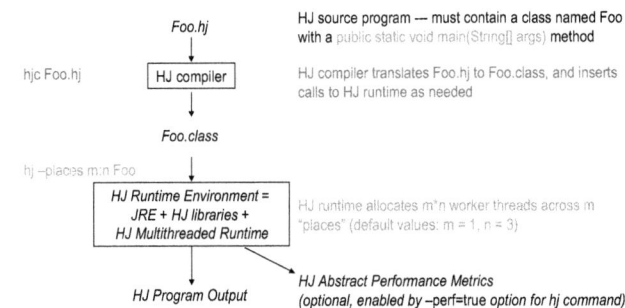

Figure 1. Habanero-Java (HJ) Compilation and Execution Environment

Figure 1 summarizes the compilation and execution environment for HJ programs. It is similar to that for Java programs. HJ programs are stored in files with a `.hj` extension, and the `hjc` command is used to compile an HJ program. An HJ program, Foo.hj, must contain a class named Foo with a `main()` method. The `hj` command is used to execute an HJ program after it has been compiled. Program execution begins with a single task at the start of the `main()` method.

2.1 The Habanero-Java Compiler

The Habanero-Java compiler (hjc) is written in Java and is composed of two major components — the Polyglot-based front-end which parses HJ source code to create an abstract syntax tree (AST), and the Soot-based back-end which analyzes, optimizes and transforms a Jimple-based intermediate representation, followed by class file generation. Jimple is a typed 3-address intermediate representation available in Soot that is more convenient to use than bytecode. Another advantage of transforming Jimple (compared to source code) is the ability to generate goto's and labels, which is required to support the work-stealing schedulers used for HJ.

The front-end is mostly responsible for enforcing the various programming rules of HJ. For instance, it checks that local variables accessed by a child task are not written to. Once a program has successfully pass both the syntactic and semantic analysis, the Polyglot AST is transformed into the Jimple IR and handed to the Soot backend. The Jimple IR is extended to a parallel intermediate representation (PIR) which features new Jimple IR nodes to represent HJ constructs. The backend then gradually applies a series of transformations to go from the high-level PIR to lower-level representations.

2.2 The Habanero-Java Runtime System

The HJ runtime provides support for implementing HJ's parallel constructs. It is also responsible for executing and orchestrating the creation, scheduling and execution of tasks. The core of the runtime provides support for the finish/async model which track s the parent-child relationship between finish scopes and their async tasks. Extensions such as phasers also need runtime support to maintain data structures and keep track of synchronization status.

The HJ runtime supports both work-sharing and work-stealing scheduling mechanisms [4]. The work-sharing scheduler relies on a single work queue, whereas the work-stealing scheduler includes a distributed deque implementation. The decision of which mechanism to use must currently be made at compile time. While the work-stealing scheduler is more efficient than the work-sharing scheduler, it currently only supports a subset of HJ constructs (async, finish, isolated).

2.3 Interactions with the Environment

The HJ runtime can interact with the host system in various ways. First, an HJ program can call native code through the `extern` interface. This enables the use of highly optimized native libraries as well as invocation of GPU kernels from HJ programs. Second, the user can tune the HJ runtime deployment using the `-places` option and the embedded thread-binding mechanism. These deployment options allow to better tailor the runtime execution to the host system parameters (number of available cores, cache and memory hierarchy).

The `extern` keyword, introduced in X10 1.5, is related to the Java native keyword. In HJ, the programmer just has to declare a method to be extern in an HJ file and implement the native method using regular native types in a C file. All the necessary casting from the Java type system to the native type system is handled by stub code that is generated by the HJ compiler, without requiring the HJ programmer to learn JNI. Another feature unique to HJ is that *array views* can be used as parameters to extern methods.

The combination of array-views and extern makes the switch from a classical native code implementation to a GPU implementation seamless. The programmer only need to replace the native implementation by the GPU implementation and compile a new version of the native shared library. The subsequent execution of the HJ program will then perform calls to the GPU through the extern interface.

References

[1] Vincent Cavé, Jisheng Zhao, Jun Shirako, and Vivek Sarkar. Habanero-Java: the New Adventures of Old X10. In *PPPJ'11: Proceedings of 9th International Conference on the Principles and Practice of Programming in Java*, 2011.

[2] P. Charles et al. X10: an object-oriented approach to non-uniform cluster computing. In *OOPSLA'05 Onward! track*, pages 519–538, New York, NY, USA, 2005.

[3] COMP 322: Fundamentals of Parallel Programming. https://wiki.rice.edu/confluence/display/PARPROG/COMP322.

[4] Yi Guo, Jisheng Zhao, Vincent Cavé, and Vivek Sarkar. SLAW: a Scalable Locality-aware Adaptive Work-stealing scheduler. In *IPDPS '10*, Apr 2010.

[5] Habanero Multicore Software Research Project web page. http://habanero.rice.edu.

[6] Roberto Lublinerman, Jisheng Zhao, Zoran Budimlic, Swarat Chaudhuri, and Vivek Sarkar. Delegated isolation. In *Proceedings of OOPSLA '11*, October 2011.

[7] J. Shirako et al. Phasers: a unified deadlock-free construct for collective and point-to-point synchronization. In *Proceedings of ICS '08*, pages 277–288, New York, NY, USA, 2008. ACM.

[8] Sagnak Tasirlar and Vivek Sarkar. Data-driven tasks and their implementation. In *Proceedings of ICPP'11*, September 2011.

[9] R. Vallée-Rai et al. Soot - a Java Optimization Framework. In *Proceedings of CASCON 1999*, pages 125–135, 1999.

SugarJ: Library-based Language Extensibility

Sebastian Erdweg* Lennart C. L. Kats† Tillmann Rendel*
Christian Kästner* Klaus Ostermann* Eelco Visser†

* University of Marburg
† Delft University of Technology

Abstract

SugarJ is a Java-based programming language that provides extensible surface syntax, static analyses, and IDE support. SugarJ extensions are organized as libraries; conventional import statements suffice to activate and compose language extensions. We illustrate how programmers can use SugarJ to modularly extend Java's syntax, semantic analyses and IDE support.

Categories and Subject Descriptors D.3.2 [*Language Classifications*]: Extensible languages; D.2.13 [*Reusable Software*]

General Terms Languages

Keywords language extensibility, library, DSL embedding, language workbench

1. Introduction

With embedded domain-specific languages (DSLs) and language-oriented programming [1, 6], two core requirements arise: Languages have to be extensible and language extensions need to compose easily. Programmers require language extensibility to break up the ties to a single (typically general-purpose) programming language and to benefit from all aspects of embedded DSLs (for instance, domain-specific syntax or IDE support). Furthermore, since software projects touch upon multiple domains, it is essential to support composing DSLs for the common case of conflict-free language composition. For example, it should be possible to extend Java with SQL, XML or regular expressions with regard to their concrete syntax, IDE support (e.g., code completion), static analyses (e.g., XML Schema validation), and so forth. It should be simple for programmers to use any combination of such language extensions within a single source file.

To address these goals, we propose to organize and implement language extensions as libraries in the object language itself. In contrast to conventional libraries, *language libraries* do not export functionality and data structures but rather stipulate an augmentation of the object language. Due to our library-based design, a programmer can easily activate and compose language extensions by simply importing the corresponding language libraries; no external configuration or reasoning is necessary to understand a given source file. Furthermore, programmers can readily implement a language extension themselves by writing a language library; no additional tools but the object language compiler are required. Lastly, language libraries inherit the self-applicability property from conventional libraries, that is, language extensions can be used for developing language extensions: domain syntax, IDE support and static analyses for the definition of syntactic extensions, IDE extensions, static analyses, and so forth.

We have developed an extension of Java—called *SugarJ*—which demonstrates the feasibility of our library-based approach for extending a language [4]. SugarJ supports the definition of syntactic sugar within libraries, where each syntactic sugar extends the grammar of the object language and specifies a transformation—called desugaring—from the extended syntax into the base syntax. Programmers can activate and compose (domain-specific) syntax extensions through simple import statements that bring the corresponding libraries into scope. Technically, we support library-based syntax extensions through an incremental parsing process that parses a file one top-level entry at a time and adapts its own grammar as it goes along. The finally resulting abstract syntax tree is desugared using all desugarings in scope.

For example, consider the illustration of a SugarJ source file in Figure 1, where we extended the base language with syntax for XML through an import of the xml.Sugar library. In our embedding, we compose the grammar of XML with SugarJ's base grammar, so that SugarJ parses XML documents as part of the surrounding Java syntax. Furthermore, the xml.Sugar library declares a desugaring of XML to Java, which SugarJ applies after parsing. Programmers can easily compose the XML embedding with other syntactic extensions such as SQL or regular expressions by adding more import statements.

As the screenshot furthermore highlights, we generalize our library-based extensibility mechanism towards IDEs [2]. Accordingly, we promote to organize and implement IDE extensions within libraries of the object language, so that simple import statements suffice to activate and compose editor services of several DSLs. In the example above, we import the xml.Editor library and the Book schema to bring syntax coloring and code completion for XML into scope. Such editor services compose with editor services for Java because each one only affects those fragments of the syntax tree that correspond to Java *or* XML, respectively. We have implemented a prototypical extensible IDE—called *Sugarclipse*—based on the Spoofax language workbench [5] and its support for the declarative configuration and dynamic reloading of editors. Sugarclipse provides editor services on a file-by-file basis, according to the libraries in scope.

In summary, SugarJ is a lightweight and scalable alternative to model-driven language workbenches: it is lightweight because it is purely textual and aligns with the host language's module system; it is scalable because DSLs and their code generators can easily be combined and composed.

SPLASH'11 Companion, October 22–27, 2011, Portland, Oregon, USA.
ACM 978-1-4503-0940-0/11/10.

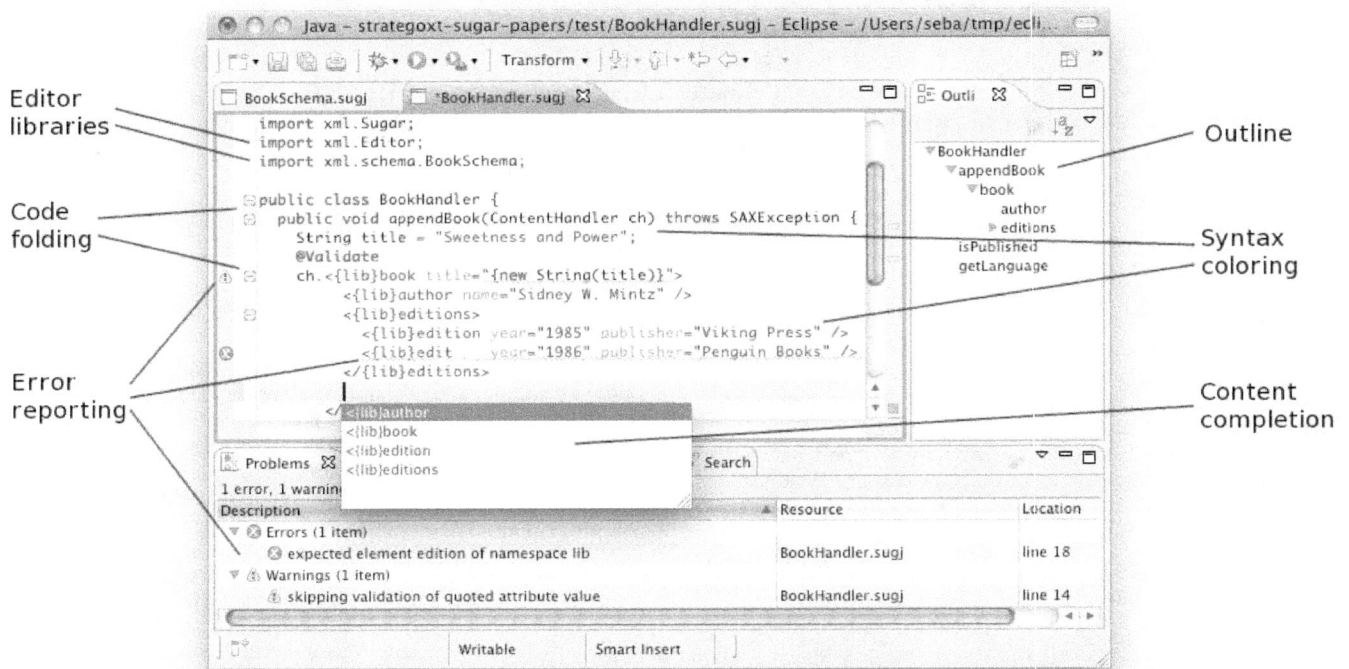

Figure 1. SugarJ extended with support for XML processing: The library xml.Sugar provides an integration of XML syntax, xml.Editor provides XML IDE support (e.g., code coloring, folding and outlining), and xml.schema.BookSchema integrates XML validation and auto-completion rules derived from an XML schema.

SugarJ is an open source project; its compiler, Eclipse plugin and case studies are publicly available at http://sugarj.org.

A slightly altered version of this text has been published as a demonstration proposal at the same conference [3].

Acknowledgments

This work is supported in part by the European Research Council, grant No. 203099, and NWO/EW Open Competition project 612.063.512, *TFA: Transformations for Abstractions*.

References

[1] S. Dmitriev. Language oriented programming: The next programming paradigm. Available at http://www.jetbrains.com/mps/docs/Language_Oriented_Programming.pdf., 2004.

[2] S. Erdweg, L. C. L. Kats, T. Rendel, C. Kästner, K. Ostermann, and E. Visser. Growing a language environment with editor libraries. In *Proceedings of Conference on Generative Programming and Component Engineering (GPCE)*. ACM, 2011.

[3] S. Erdweg, L. C. L. Kats, T. Rendel, C. Kästner, K. Ostermann, and E. Visser. Library-based model-driven software development with SugarJ. In *Companion to Conference on Object-Oriented Programming, Systems, Languages, and Applications (OOPSLA)*. ACM, 2011.

[4] S. Erdweg, T. Rendel, C. Kästner, and K. Ostermann. SugarJ: Library-based syntactic language extensibility. In *Proceedings of Conference on Object-Oriented Programming, Systems, Languages, and Applications (OOPSLA)*. ACM, 2011.

[5] L. C. L. Kats and E. Visser. The Spoofax language workbench: Rules for declarative specification of languages and IDEs. In *Proceedings of Conference on Object-Oriented Programming, Systems, Languages, and Applications (OOPSLA)*, pages 444–463. ACM, 2010.

[6] M. P. Ward. Language-oriented programming. *Software – Concepts and Tools*, 15:147–161, 1995.

Refactoring towards the Good Parts of JavaScript

Asger Feldthaus *

Aarhus University

asf@cs.au.dk

Todd Millstein †

University of California,
Los Angeles

todd@cs.ucla.edu

Anders Møller *

Aarhus University

amoeller@cs.au.dk

Max Schäfer

University of Oxford

max.schaefer@cs.ox.ac.uk

Frank Tip

IBM Research

ftip@us.ibm.com

Abstract

JavaScript is one of the most widely used programming languages of the present day. While its flexibility is treasured by proponents, its lack of language support for encapsulation is an obstacle to writing maintainable programs. We propose refactorings for improving modularity, and discuss challenges arising in their implementation.

Categories and Subject Descriptors D.2.7 [*Distribution, Maintenance, and Enhancement*]: Restructuring, reverse engineering, and reengineering

General Terms Languages

1. Introduction

Recent years have witnessed a resurgence of dynamic programming languages, such as JavaScript and PHP, which eschew the focus on static typing and modularity constructs of languages like Java, promising less development overhead and powerful dynamic techniques. The domain of web programming, in particular, is dominated by such languages.

While these features help with rapidly writing new code, they often become a liability once programs grow beyond a certain size, and can be an obstacle to reusability and integration. Modern textbooks on JavaScript hence put particular emphasis on programming patterns and idioms that can be used to modularize and structure code, advocating the use of what a popular textbook terms the "good parts" of the

language [1]. Additionally, the new ECMAScript 5 standard for JavaScript provides for a so-called *strict mode* that disallows the use of some problematic language constructs, and restricts the use of others [2].

The experience of the ill-fated ECMAScript 4 effort has shown that major changes or additions to the language are unlikely to happen in the near future. Instead, programmers have to be persuaded to migrate their programs to safe sublanguages or employ recommended idioms and patterns to make up for missing language features where possible.

However, doing this by hand can be a difficult task that may involve changing many different parts of the program and reasoning carefully about aliasing patterns and side effects. Hence programmers would benefit from having tool support for performing such refactorings.

A refactoring tool for a language like JavaScript can assist with enforcing best practices, eliminating uses of problematic language features, and enabling programs to make use of higher-level frameworks and domain specific languages. Refactoring can thus play an active role in mitigating deficiencies of the refactored language and raising the level of abstraction at which a programmer can work.

2. Modularization Refactorings

This section briefly introduces two modularization refactorings for JavaScript that refactor towards patterns recommended in the literature [1]. More detailed specifications of these refactorings can be found in the companion paper [3].

The ENCAPSULATE PROPERTY refactoring encapsulates a property of an object, rerouting all accesses to the property through accessor methods.

An example application of this refactoring is shown in Fig. 1. The original program, shown on the left, defines a constructor function Rect. When invoked on a newly created object, this function initializes properties width and height of the object to the values passed in parameters w and h. On line 5, the function's prototype property is assigned an object literal containing a method area that will be available on all objects constructed using Rect. Finally, a new Rect

---

* Supported by The Danish Research Council for Technology and Production, grant no. 09-064210.

† Supported by the US National Science Foundation, award CCF-0545850.

SPLASH'11 Companion, October 22–27, 2011, Portland, Oregon, USA.
ACM 978-1-4503-0940-0/11/10.

```
 1  function Rect(w, h) {           13  function Rect(w, h) {
 2    this.width = w;               14    var width = w;
 3    this.height = h;              15    this.height = h;
 4  }                               16    this.getWidth = function()
 5  Rect.prototype = {              17    {
 6    area: function() {            18      return width;
 7      return this.width           19    };
 8           *this.height;          20  }
 9    } };                          21  Rect.prototype = {
10                                  22    area: function() {
11  r = new Rect(23, 42);           23      return this.getWidth()
12  alert(r.width);                 24           *this.height;
                                    25    } };
                                    26
                                    27  r = new Rect(23, 42);
                                    28  alert(r.getWidth());

         (a)                                (b)
```

Figure 1. Using ENCAPSULATE PROPERTY to turn property `width` into a local variable of the constructor `Rect`.

object is constructed on line 11, and the value of its `width` property displayed using an alert dialog.

Since JavaScript has no access control for properties, the properties `width` and `height` of a `Rect` object can be freely read, written or even deleted by any code that has a reference to it. The ENCAPSULATE PROPERTY refactoring makes it possible to restrict access to a property by a well-known technique shown in the refactored program on the right, where changes have been highlighted.

The former property `width` has now been turned into a local variable of the constructor function and is thus no longer accessible from outside `Rect`. To compensate, the refactoring adds an accessor method `getWidth` that returns the value of `width`. Former read accesses to the property `width` on lines 23 and 28 have to be adjusted to use the method instead. If there had been a write access, the refactoring would additionally have introduced a setter method `setWidth`.

Thus, while the transformation from a property to a local variable looks innocuous enough, it necessitates global adjustments that are non-trivial to perform by hand. In addition, the refactoring will have to check several preconditions to ensure that this transformation is behavior-preserving. For instance, there cannot already be a method `getWidth`, and the program cannot use the reflective features of JavaScript to access properties of `Rect` objects [3].

This is a typical example how a refactoring (ENCAPSULATE PROPERTY) emulates a missing language feature (access control) by making a workaround easily available.

Another, similar example is the refactoring EXTRACT MODULE: JavaScript provides no modularity constructs, which often leads to a proliferation of global definitions, making programs brittle and hard to integrate. Utilizing a well-known module pattern [1], this refactoring packs global definitions into a record with a shared scope provided by a closure, and adjusts their uses all over the program. Again, a refactoring makes up for a missing language feature by facilitating the use of a workaround.

3. Challenges

Carefully specifying and implementing refactorings is a challenging task even for statically typed languages like Java, and it is considerably more difficult for JavaScript.

Consider, for instance, the ENCAPSULATE PROPERTY refactoring. After transforming the given property into a local variable, we have to determine which property accesses need updating. This is tricky, since properties are not declared in JavaScript but are created upon first write. Clearly, a form of static analysis is needed to (conservatively) determine whether two property accesses can potentially refer to the same property at runtime.

Static analysis of JavaScript is a fairly new, but quite active field of research. In order to prevent prematurely committing ourselves to one particular analysis technique, we have instead defined an abstract interface between the analysis engine and the refactoring specifications, consisting of a set of queries that the analysis has to implement.

We have specified and implemented the refactorings RENAME, ENCAPSULATE PROPERTY and EXTRACT MODULE in terms of this interface, using a custom pointer analysis to implement the queries. The implementation, including an integration into Eclipse as a plugin, is available online at `www.brics.dk/jsrefactor`.

The dynamic features of JavaScript are particularly difficult to handle. Our specifications conservatively handle reflective features such as `for-in` loops and computed property names: renaming a property that could be accessed reflectively is forbidden. However, `eval` and equivalent constructs are not handled at all; instead, we emit a warning about possible unsoundness if a use of `eval` is detected.

4. Conclusions

We have argued for the use of tool-supported refactoring for JavaScript to enable programmers to restructure their programs and make use of patterns and best practices. We have described two examples of such refactorings that can be used to improve program modularity, and we have discussed some of the challenges arising in their implementation.

We believe our approach points the way to a powerful new usage of automated refactorings as a proxy for language extension. While JavaScript lacks some commonly desired modularity and encapsulation mechanisms, with appropriate refactoring support developers can effectively add these mechanisms to the language and reliably use them in programs. In a sense, refactoring towards the "good parts" contributes to building a better JavaScript language.

References

[1] D. Crockford. *JavaScript: The Good Parts*. O'Reilly, 2008.

[2] ECMA. ECMAScript Language Specification, 5th edition, 2009. ECMA-262.

[3] A. Feldthaus, T. Millstein, A. Møller, M. Schäfer, and F. Tip. Tool-supported Refactoring for JavaScript. In *OOPSLA*, 2011.

Smaller Footprint for Java Collections

Joseph (Yossi) Gil

The Technion
yogi@cs.technion.ac.il

Yuval Shimron

The Technion
shimro@cs.technion.ac.il

Abstract

Bloat, specifically, containers's bloat is a potential JAVA *performance bottleneck. We identify five memory compaction techniques that can be used to reduce the footprint of the small objects that make containers. Using these techniques, we describe methods for more efficient encoding of some JRE's ubiquitous data structures. For* HashMap *and* HashSet *the fused hashing encoding method, reduces memory overhead by 20%–45% on a 32-bit environment and 45%–65% on a 64-bit environment. This encoding guarantees these figures as lower bound regardless of the distribution of keys in hash buckets. A more opportunistic squashed hashing encoding method, achieves expected savings of 25%–70% on a 32-bit environment and 30%–75% on a 64-bit environments. For* TreeMap *and* TreeSet *we employ these five techniques, and capitalizing further on the special properties of the red-black balanced tree, we can reduce the overhead of tree nodes by 43%–55% on a 32-bit environment and 59%–61% on a 64-bit environment.*

Categories and Subject Descriptors   D.1.0 [*Software*]: Programming Techniques—General

General Terms   Design, Performance

Keywords   Software, Bloat, Java, Memory Compaction, HashMap, TreeMap

1. Background

JAVA and the underlying virtual machine provide software engineers with a programming environment which abstracts over many hardware specific technicalities. The *runtime* cost of this abstraction is offset by modern compiler technologies. However, *memory* cost is not an easy target for automatic optimization. With the ever increasing use of JAVA for implementing servers and other large scale applications, indications are increasing that the openhanded manner of using memory, which is so easy to resort in JAVA, leads to memory bloat, with negative impacts on time performance, scalability and usability [2].

This work is concerned with what might be called "container bloat", which is believed to be one of the primary contributors to memory bloat. [1] Previous work on the container bloat problem

---

[1] Consider, e.g., Mitchell & Sevitsky's example of a large online store application consuming $2.87 \cdot 10^9$ bytes, 42% of which are dedicated to class HashMap (OOPSLA'07 presentation).

included methods for detecting suboptimal use of containers [4] or recommendations on better choice of containers based on dynamic profiling [3]. Our line of work is different in that we propose more compact containers. Much in the line of work of Kawachiya, Kazunori and Onodera [1] which directly attacks bloat due to the String class, our work focuses on space optimization of collection classes, concentrating on HashMap, HashSet, TreeMap and TreeSet classes.

We emphasize that our work does not propose a different and supposedly better algorithmic method for organizing these collections, e.g., by using open-addressing or prime-sized tables for hashing, prime-sized or the use of AVL trees instead of red-black tree for balanced binary search trees. Research on this has its place, but our interest here is in the question of whether given data and data structures can be *encoded* more efficiently. After all, whatever method a data structure is organized in, there could be room for encoding it more efficiently, just as subjecting a super fast algorithm to automatic optimization could improve it better.

For this reason, we insist on full compatibility with the existing implementations, including e.g., preserving the order of the keys in HashMap, and the tree topology of TreeMap. Unlike Kawachiya et. al's work, we do not rely on changes to the JVM—the optimization techniques we describe here can be employed by application programmers not only to collections, but to any user defined data structure. We believe that the techniques we identify and the detailed case studies in employing these for current JAVA collections could pave the way to a future in which automatic tools would aid and even take control of exercising these.

2. Memory Compaction Techniques

We describe a tool chest consisting of five memory compaction techniques, which can be used to reduce the footprint of the small Entry objects that make the HashMap and TreeMap containers: null pointer elimination, boolean elimination, object fusion, field pull-up and field consolidation. The techniques can be applied independently, but they become more effective if used wisely together, often with attention to the memory model and to issues such as memory alignment:

1. *Null pointer elimination.* Say a class C defines an *immutable* pointer field p which happens to be **null** in many of C's instances. Then, this pointer can be eliminated from C by replacing the data member p with a non-**final** method p() which returns **null**. This method is overridden in a class C_p inheriting from C, to return then value of a data member p defined in C_p. Objects with **null** values of p are instantiated from C; all other objects instantiate C_p.

2. *Boolean elimination.* A boolean field in a class C can be emulated by classes C_t (corresponding to **true** value of the field) and C_f (corresponding to **false**), both inheriting from C. Note that both null-pointer elimination and boolean elimination

SPLASH'11 Companion,   October 22–27, 2011, Portland, Oregon, USA.
ACM 978-1-4503-0940-0/11/10.

move data from an object into its header, which encodes its runtime type. Both however are applicable mostly if class C does not have other subclasses. Mutable fields may also benefit from these techniques if it makes sense to recreate the instances of C should the eliminated field change its value.

3. *Object fusion.* Say that a class C defines an ownership pointer in field of type C', then all fields of class C' can be inlined into class C, eliminating the $C \to C'$ pointer, the header of the C' object, and the back pointer $C' \to C$ if it exists. It is often useful to combine fusion with null-pointer elimination, moving the fields of C' into C, only if the pointer to the owned object is not **null**.

Before describing the remaining two techniques, a brief reminder of JAVA's object model is in place: Unlike C++, all objects in JAVA contain an object header which encodes a pointer to a dynamic dispatch table together with synchronization, garbage collection, and other bits of information. In the HotSpot implementation of the JVM, this header spans 8 bytes on HotSpot32, and 16 bytes on HotSpot64. In addition, all objects and sub-objects are aligned on an 8-bytes boundary. [2] [3]

Together, the header and alignment may lead to significant bloat, attributed to what the literature calls small objects. Class Boolean *for example, occupies 16 bytes on HotSpot32 (8 for header, one for the* value *field, and 7 for alignment.), even though only one bit is required for representing its content. Applying boolean elimination to* Boolean *could have halved its footprint. Alignment issues give good reasons for applying the space compaction techniques together. Applying null pointer elimination to class* HashMap.Entry *would not decrease its size (on HotSpot32); one must remove yet another field to reach the minimal saving quantum of 8 bytes per entry.*

We propose two additional techniques for dealing with waste due to alignment:

4. *Field pull-up.* Say that a class C' inherits from a class C, and that class C's layout is not fully occupied due to alignment. Then, fields of class C' could be pre-defined in class C, avoiding alignment waste in C', in which the C' sub-object is aligned, just as the entire object C. We employ field pull up mostly for smaller fields, typically byte sized.

5. *Field Consolidation.* Yet another technique for avoiding waste due to alignment is by consolidation: a field which incurs alignment cost in a large number of object, is consolidated into an array with entries for each of these objects. Of course, consolidation is only effective if there the appropriate array index for each object is easy to determine.

3.   Reducing the Footprint of Java Collections

Demonstrating these techniques we describe *fused hashing*, a re-implementation of HashMap and HashSet, which reduces memory overhead by 20%–40% on a 32-bit environment and 45%–65% on a 64-bit environment, and *squashed hashing*, an even more more opportunistic implementation, which gives rise to 25%–70% savings on a 32-bit environment, and 30%–70% savings on a 64-bit environment. These savings are achieved mainly by

1. fusing together the nodes of the linked list comprising a bucket of the hash table,

2. eliminating the trailing **null** pointer,

3. applying field-pull up for storing lists of various sizes more compactly, and

4. storing singleton buckets, which form the majority of the buckets, in consolidated form (squashed-hashing only).

In employing the compaction techniques for TreeMap and TreeSet which revolve around the classical red-black balanced binary search tree, we give an implementation which uses the following facts:

1. 9% of all nodes have two leaf children;

2. 14% of all nodes have precisely one child which is a leaf;

3. 43% of all nodes are leaves.

Each of these cases (which together, excluding overlaps, account for the majority of the tree nodes), calls for immediate application of fusion (of the node with its children, or the leaf with its parent), whereby saving both down- and up- pointers, along with null pointer elimination.

Further analysis shows that we can also eliminate the **boolean** field used for marking node colors, e.g., if a node has one leaf child, then the node must be black, and its child must be red. Tree operations are naturally slowed-down (searches by 2%, insertions by about 20%, etc.), but we obtain memory overhead savings ranging between 43% (for TreeMap on 32 bit environment) to 61% (for TreeSet on 64 bit environment).

References

[1] K. Kawachiya, K. Ogata, and T. Onodera. Analysis and reduction of memory inefficiencies in Java strings. In G. E. Harris, editor, *Proc. of the 23rd Ann. Conf. on OO Prog. Sys., Lang., & Appl. (OOPSLA'08)*, Nashville, Tennessee, Oct.19-23 2008. ACM.

[2] N. Mitchell, E. Schonberg, and G. Sevitsky. Four trends leading to Java runtime bloat. *IEEE Software*, 27(1), 2010.

[3] O. Shacham, M. Vechev, and E. Yahav. Chameleon: Adaptive selection of collections. In *Proc. of the Conference on Programming Language Design and Implementation (PLDI'09)*, Dublin, Ireland, June 15-20 2009. ACM Press.

[4] G. Xu and A. Rountev. Detecting inefficiently-used containers to avoid bloat. In *Proc. of the Conference on Programming Language Design and Implementation (PLDI'10)*, Toronto, Canada, June 5-10 2010. ACM Press.

---

[2] http://kohlerm.blogspot.com/2008/12/
how-much-memory-is-used-by-my-java.html

[3] http://www.javamex.com/tutorials/memory/object_memory_
usage.shtml

CREST: Principled Foundations for Decentralized Systems

Michael Gorlick   Kyle Strasser   Alegria Baquero   Richard N. Taylor

University of California, Irvine

mgorlick@acm.org   kstrasse@uci.edu   abaquero@uci.edu   taylor@ics.uci.edu

Abstract

CREST is an architectural style for decentralized, flexible, and secure open and adaptive systems. Adopting the bilateral transfer of computation as the fundamental medium of exchange among peers, CREST reduces content to a side-effect of computational exchange. We discuss the style's constraints, its anticipated benefits, and the implementation mechanisms.

Categories and Subject Descriptors   D.2.11 [*Software Engineering*]: Software Architectures

General Terms   Design

Keywords   Mobile code, decentralization, web services

1. Introduction

Emerging web architectures are constantly stretching the boundaries of REST [6]—the architectural style underlying the evolution, performance, and scaling of the web. Prior work [3, 4] analyzed the dissonance between unforeseen web technology such as Ajax and mashups, and REST-based services and applications. Resolving the discrepancies between REST prescriptions and web architecture as practiced lead to a novel generalization of REST where computations displaced content as the fundamental unit of exchange among web elements.

Experimentation with a first generation testbed led to a model of *computational exchange* as the foundation for a new generation of decentralized, autonomous, self-governing applications where independent and physically distributed agencies collaborate by exchanging computations rather than content. Decentralization allows multiple parties to both offer and request customized services that serve their individual purposes and interests. In our vision of the future, systems will be dominated by peer-to-peer architectures and asynchronous interactions where high availability, resilience, adaptation, and dynamic extensibility will be principal drivers.

In this context we present CREST [3, 4], an architectural style for decentralized, adaptive and secure collaboration that embraces computation exchange as the engine of application state evolution and transfer. Our hypothesis is twofold: first, the CREST architectural style is a model for secure, decentralized applications offering customization, interface uniformity, dynamic adaptation, component autonomy, and flexibility, and second, the infrastructure required for CREST cleanly supports a broad variety of attractive, decentralized, but collaborative architectures.

2. Research Goals

Our goals include: (a) defining a model of architectures supporting networks of decentralized, dynamic, and adaptive applications, including a set of stylistic principles guiding application design [3, 4], a set of mechanisms derived from these principles, and a set of scenarios illustrating CREST's benefits in example application domains; (b) building an infrastructure for computation exchange that includes a compiler for a specialized mobile code language; an implementation of URLs as capabilities; peer-specific binding environments and environment sculpting; and an application network protocol supporting computation exchange; and (c) demonstrating sample CREST applications in the domains of awareness, collaboration, commerce, and gaming—each exhibiting various combinations of dynamic, reconfigurable, and decentralized behaviors.

3. The CREST Architectural Style

An architectural style is a named collection of architectural design decisions that apply to a particular development context, constrain the design space, and promote beneficial properties in a software system [13]. The CREST architectural style adheres to the following principles: (a) all computations are named by Capability URLs (CURLs), which provide authority-to-execute semantics; (b) all computations are mobile, reified as continuations, closures, and binding environments; (c) all computations are conducted within CURL-specific execution environments that explicitly confer capability; and (d) the interpretation of computations is CURL-specific.

4. Features and Infrastructure

Our CREST testbed reflects the principles enumerated above. Previous versions [3, 4] implemented a subset of the CREST principles as early validation of our ideas. Our most recent infrastructure implements the following core mechanisms: (a) each computation is an actor [1] where message-passing and actor spawning (both local and remote) are core operations; (b) actors are organized into hierarchical *clans*. Each actor is a member of exactly one clan and each clan is governed by a distinguished actor, the *chieftain*. Clans occupy an *island*, a single address space named by a unique IP address/port pair; (c) CURLs are self-certifying [9] and signed, and may contain computations and arbitrary metadata including embedded predicates and contracts that are checked when a message directed at the CURL is processed; (d) deserialization, recompilation, and execution of closures, continuations, and binding environments takes place in a clan-specific sandbox and binding environment. A sandbox regulates an actor's consumption of fungible resources (processor cycles, network bandwidth, and memory) while a binding environment dictates the capability conveyed to an actor; (e) actors may derive new binding environments from old, termed *environment sculpting*, to apply to their own computations or the computations they receive from others; and (f) computations are exchanged via a peer-to-peer asynchronous messaging protocol with a simple structure and provision for arbitrary metadata.

These mechanisms also provide capability-based security [10]. Actors gain capabilities by receiving a binding environment at start-up time, obtaining a CURL in a message or, transitively, receiving a message containing a CURL naming another actor with distinct capabilities. Conversely, capabilities are regulated by by restricting the binding environments with which new actors are spawned, restricting the generation of CURLs (since CURLs are the capability to communicate), or restricting the communications of an actor.

Our exchanged computations are written in a mobile code language, Motile, a purely functional dialect of Scheme specifically designed as a mobile code language amenable to network serialization and subsequent recompilation into the execution environment of a receiving island.

Actors, each executing a Motile closure or continuation, communicate with one another only by sending messages, even if the actors occupy the same address space. Since Motile is a single-assignment language with only purely functional data structures [11], there is no mutable shared memory by which Motile actors can exchange out-of-band information: consequently, intra- and inter-island actor behaviors are functionally identical. Motile is one of the few languages where binding environments are a fundamental data type that may be directly manipulated—notably, as an evaluation context for closures and continuations. Our prototype CREST islands exchange and execute 4000–5000 closures/second.

5. Related Work

CREST draws upon Internet-scale architectures including the web, [6], peer-to-peer, and event-based integration [13]. Its security model draws upon the Object Capability Model [10] and relies on self-certification [9] and sandboxing. The CREST computation exchange implements a combination of remote evaluation [12] and code-on-demand [7] mobile code, while supporting isolated message-passing [1]. Motile draws upon prior work in closure compilation [5] and first-class binding environments [8], while its primitives are inspired by Erlang [2].

Acknowledgments

This work was supported by the National Science Foundation under Grant Numbers 0917129 and 0820222.

References

[1] G. Agha. *Actors: A Model of Concurrent Computation in Distributed Systems.* MIT Press, 1986.

[2] J. Armstrong. *Programming Erlang: Software for a Concurrent World.* Pragmatic Bookshelf, 2007.

[3] J. R. Erenkrantz. *Computational REST: A New Model for Decentralized, Internet-Scale Applications.* PhD thesis, University of California, Irvine, 2009.

[4] J. R. Erenkrantz, M. Gorlick, G. Suryanarayana, and R. N. Taylor. From representations to computations: the evolution of web architectures. In *Proceedings of the ACM SIGSOFT symposium on The foundations of software engineering*, pages 255–264, Dubrovnik, Croatia, 2007.

[5] M. Feeley and G. LaPlame. Using closures for code generation. *Journal of Computer Languages*, 12(1):47–66, 1987.

[6] R. T. Fielding and R. N. Taylor. Principled design of the modern web architecture. In *22nd International Conference on Software Engineering*, pages 407–416, Limerick, Ireland, 2000.

[7] A. Fuggetta, G. P. Picco, and G. Vigna. Understanding code mobility. *IEEE Transactions on Software Engineering*, 24(5):342–361, 1998.

[8] S. Jagannathan. Metalevel building blocks for modular systems. *ACM Transactions on Programming Languages and Systems*, 16:456–492, 1994.

[9] D. Mazières. *Self-certifying file system.* PhD thesis, Massachusetts Institute of Technology, Cambridge, 2000.

[10] M. S. Miller. *Robust Composition: Towards a Unified Approach to Access Control and Concurrency Control.* PhD thesis, John Hopkins University, Baltimore, Maryland, 2006.

[11] C. Okasaki *Purely Functional Data Structures*, Cambridge University Press, 1998.

[12] J. W. Stamos. *Remote Evaluation.* PhD thesis, Massachusetts Inst. Technology, Cambridge, 1986.

[13] R. N. Taylor, N. Medvidovic, and E. M. Dashofy. *Software Architecture: Foundations, Theory, and Practice.* John Wiley & Sons, 2010.

McLAB: Enabling Programming Language, Compiler and Software Engineering Research for MATLAB

Laurie Hendren, Jesse Doherty, Anton Dubrau, Rahul Garg, Nurudeen Lameed,
Soroush Radpour, Amina Aslam, Toheed Aslam, Andrew Casey, Maxime Chevalier Boisvert,
Jun Li, Clark Verbrugge, and Olivier Savary Belanger

McGill University
http://www.sable.mcgill.ca/mclab
{hendren, jdoher1, adubra, garg, nlamee, sradpo, aaslam1, taslam, acasey, mcheva, jli127, clump, osavary}@cs.mcgill.ca

Abstract

MATLAB is a popular language for scientific computation, used by millions of students, scientists and engineers world-wide. The MCLAB project aims to provide an open source compiler and virtual machine infrastructure to enable programming language, compiler and software engineering researchers to work in this important area.

Categories and Subject Descriptors D.3.4 [*Processors*]: Compilers

General Terms Experimentation, Languages, Performance

1. Introduction

MATLAB®[1] is currently one of the most popular languages for scientific and numerical computing. Although a huge number of users program with MATLAB, programming language, compiler and software engineering research for MATLAB has not been as well developed as for other mainstream programming languages. This is at least partly due to a lack of clear specifications and publicly-available infrastructures. The MCLAB project aims to provide an open source infrastructure to enable the research community to make important contributions which can help engineers and scientists build more robust and more efficient MATLAB programs.

MCLAB consists of: (1) an extensible front-end to parse MATLAB and to enable compositional definitions of extensions to MATLAB; (2) an analysis framework which supports both a high-level and lower-level IR and a framework for defining new flow analyses; and (3) back-ends to support both static compilation to FORTRAN90 and dynamic compilation in a Virtual Machine with a JIT. In the remainder of this paper, we elaborate on the structure of MCLAB, provide some details for each major component, and summarize our current and future directions.

---

[1] MATLAB is a registered trademark of The Mathworks, Inc. (www.mathworks.com/products/matlab/).

2. Components of MCLAB

Figure 1 shows the overall structure of MCLAB. The framework is composed of well-defined sub-pieces — different researchers may be interested in different parts. For example, a researcher interested in developing a new MATLAB programming language extension may only be interested in the front-end, whereas someone interested in developing a new dynamic optimization would be most interested in the VM. All components are implemented in Java, with the exception of the VM which is implemented in C++.

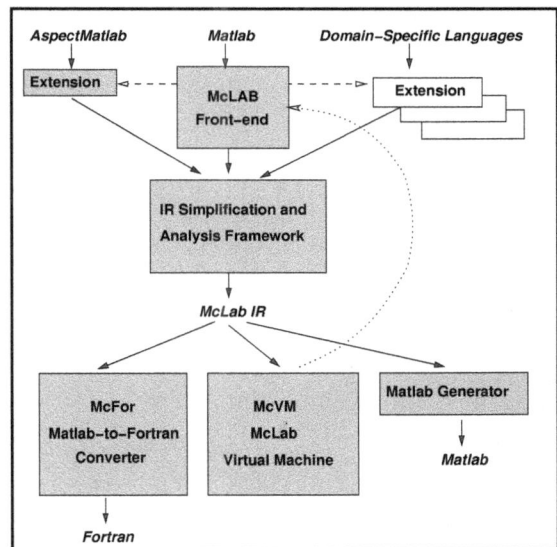

Figure 1. Structure of MCLAB

2.1 Front-end

The front-end has been designed to be modular and extensible. The core front-end is built using: (1) a modular lexer tool that we developed which is called MetaLexer[2]; (2) Beaver, a LALR Parser Generator [1]; and (3) JastAdd[5], a modular and extensible meta-compilation system that supports Reference Attribute Grammars.

Since MATLAB has been designed to be convenient for scientists, there are several syntactic features which are actually quite hard to express using a clean LALR grammar. For example, the **end** keyword is sometimes optional, the newline character sometimes has meaning (to indicate the start of a new row of a matrix), and the separator of array elements can be either a space or a comma. Thus, in order to define a grammar that is easy to extend we defined a cleaner, but more restricted, grammar that we call Natlab. The front-end includes a tool that converts a regular MATLAB program into an equivalent cleaned-up Natlab version. This approach isolates the syntactic idiosyncrasies to the MATLAB-to-Natlab translator.

One of the central goals of MCLAB is to provide a system in which it is easy to implement both general-purpose and domain-specific language extensions. We have used MCLAB to implement one such new extension called ASPECTMATLAB, an aspect-oriented extension to MATLAB [9]. ASPECTMATLAB brings aspect-oriented programming to the scientific programming community. It is designed to be simple to use and understand and it is also focused towards the needs of the numerical programming domain by providing loop-level extensions apart from more classical aspects provided in other languages. We have already demonstrated the utility of ASPECTMATLAB in writing aspects which provide better insight to the programmer about performance and correctness of the program.

2.2 Analysis Framework

The front-end produces a high-level AST which we call McAST. The analysis framework works on both this high-level IR, as well as on the lower-level McLAST. The analysis framework includes a suite of simplification transformations to transform McAST to McLAST. The framework also provides support for several kinds of intra-procedural analyses including a very basic depth-first traversal, as well as more complex structure-based traversals with built-in fixed-point iterations to support both forward and backward flow-sensitive analyses.

The MCLAB user can use the analysis framework to quickly implement new analyses, to add new simplifications, or to implement new traversal mechanisms. Some analyses, such as our *kind analysis*[4] must be done on the higher-level McAST[2], whereas other analyses are better suited to the lower-level McLAST.

We are using the analysis framework to develop a suite of refactoring transformations for MATLAB, as well developing an inter-procedural framework and call-graph constructor.

2.3 Back-ends

MCLAB provides two different back-ends: McFor[8], a static MATLAB-to-Fortran compiler; and (2) McVM[3], a virtual machine with a JIT compiler. Interestingly, the McFor component of MCLAB is the one which is currently attracting the most interest from scientists and engineers. It appears that many MATLAB users wish to automatically translate all, or part of, their MATLAB code into Fortran. In contrast, McVM is probably of most interest to compiler researchers, as it provides a test-bed for new ideas in dynamic compilation of MATLAB.

2.3.1 McFor

Our first version of McFor[8] supported a modest subset of MATLAB. Our experiences with this version convinced us that the translation could be done, and that both good performance and reasonable readability of the generated code could be achieved. Focusing on a subset of MATLAB with fewer dynamic features allows more aggressive static analyses like type inference and can thus produce highly-optimized Fortran code. This allows tapping into the high performance of existing advanced Fortran compilers.

Although MATLAB has too many dynamic features to allow for the full MATLAB language to be compiled efficiently to a static language like Fortran, we are now working on a second version of McFor, pushing the envelope and attempting to handle as much of the language as possible. This effort is leading us to understand more about the tradeoffs between static and dynamic languages and is leading to an interesting subset of MATLAB that can be effectively automatically translated to Fortran.

2.3.2 McVM

McVM is an high-performance virtual machine for the MATLAB programming language. It includes a generic interpreter and a type-specialization-based JIT compiler. The JIT is based on LLVM[7]. McVM performs a range of classical optimizations and some more advanced dynamic optimizations, including advanced type-inference optimization to achieve high performance.

MATLAB poses many new challenges in VM implementation and we continue to develop new sets of analysis and optimization techniques to increase performance. One such challenge was minimizing copies that are required to support MATLAB's call-by-value semantics[6].

Apart from the optimizations mentioned, we are also exploring the adaptation of techniques such as on-stack replacement for application in McVM, and we have also started a research project to extend McVM to generate code for multi-core CPUs and GPUs.

3. Conclusions

MCLAB provides an extensible toolkit for compiler construction for MATLAB. The framework has been designed to be both modular and extensible, and it builds upon many other excellent compiler tools such as MetaLexer, Beaver, JastAdd and LLVM.

The research community has not focused very heavily on MATLAB in the past, and it is our hope that our MCLAB tools will provide a framework for other research teams to make progress on developing new language extensions, new static and dynamic compiler techniques, and new software engineering tools for MATLAB. We also hope that the actual compilers, VMs and tools produced using MCLAB will be useful for the end-user scientists and engineers by providing new language abstractions, better performance, and better software development tools.

References

[1] Beaver - a LALR parser generator. http://beaver.sourceforge.net.

[2] A. Casey and L. Hendren. MetaLexer: A modular lexical specification language. In *AOSD*, pages 7–18, 2011.

[3] M. Chevalier-Boisvert, L. Hendren, and C. Verbrugge. Optimizing MATLAB through just-in-time specialization. In *International Conference on Compiler Construction*, pages 46–65, March 2010.

[4] J. Doherty, L. Hendren, and S. Radpour. Kind analysis for MATLAB. In *OOPSLA*, 2011.

[5] T. Ekman and G. Hedin. The JastAdd system – modular extensible compiler construction. *Science of Computer Programming*, 69(1-3):14–26, 2007.

[6] N. Lameed and L. Hendren. Staged static techniques to efficiently implement array copy semantics in a MATLAB JIT compiler. In *CC*, pages 22–41, 2011.

[7] C. Lattner and V. Adve. LLVM: a compilation framework for lifelong program analysis and transformation. In *CGO*, pages 75–88, 2004.

[8] J. Li. McFor: A MATLAB to FORTRAN 95 compiler. Master's thesis, McGill University, August 2009.

[9] A. D. Toheed Aslam, Jesse Doherty and L. Hendren. AspectMatlab: An aspect-oriented scientific programming language. In *AOSD*, pages 181–192, March 2010.

---

[2] Kind analysis determines whether an identifier refers to a named function or a variable. This information is necessary for the simplifications to produce more specialized nodes in the lower-level McLAST.

Babylscript: Multilingual JavaScript

Ming-Yee Iu

babylscript@babylscript.com

Abstract

Babylscript is a multilingual version of JavaScript. It has different language modes in which keywords, objects, and functions are translated to non-English languages. Babylscript uses separate tokenizers for each language and extends JavaScript's object model by allowing properties to have multiple names, so objects expose different interfaces for different languages.

Categories and Subject Descriptors   D.3.3 [*Programming Languages*]: Language Constructs and Features–Classes and objects

General Terms   Design, Human Factors, Languages

Keywords   JavaScript, internationalization

1. Introduction

Most programming languages are biased towards a certain vocabulary, usually American English. Keywords are in English, objects are given English names, and methods are given English descriptions. The dominance of English in programming languages provides many benefits to the programmer community. With a common language, professional programmers form a single community that can share code and ideas. This dominance does lead to many peculiar effects though. In non-English countries, students cannot learn about programming until they learn English first. Office workers cannot write macros or scripts to automate their daily work without developing a proficiency in English first. Non-English programmers are often forced to write their code in English if they want their code to be used by others.

Although a programming language may have different language versions, such as French, Spanish, and English versions, these different versions are often mutually incompatible. Code that uses French keywords and functions cannot be used with an English compiler, for example. As such, these different language versions have small user communities, resulting in less documentation, fewer libraries, and slower evolution.

Babylscript is a multilingual version of JavaScript. It is an open source project available at http://www.babylscript.com. It is based on the premise that for a programming language to be multilingual it is not sufficient to simply provide translations of some keywords and function names. In a proper multilingual programming language, awareness of multiple languages must be integrated into the syntax and semantics of the language. Instead of separate incompatible language versions, Babylscript offers a single multi-

```
// English code
var win = new Window();
win.setText("Hello", Color.RED);

// French code
---fr---
win.écrireTexte(«Allô», Couleur.ROUGE);
```

Figure 1. When programming in English, Babylscript objects export an English API; when programming in French, the same objects export a French API

lingual version into which different non-English programmer communities can pool their resources.

Although Babylscript extends JavaScript to support many different languages at the same time, one can write programs in a single language without being aware of Babylscript's support for other languages. Babylscript has different language modes. When using a French language mode, for example, all keywords, function names, and objects are in French. When Babylscript is used in the English language mode, all keywords and objects are in English, so Babylscript behaves like normal JavaScript. A programmer can write normal JavaScript code in the English language mode without any awareness of the multilingual features of Babylscript.

These language modes are not isolated silos. Programmers can switch language modes in the middle of their code, meaning that programs can be composed of a mix of different languages. Objects created in one language mode can be used by code in a different language mode. For example, a function can be defined in a Chinese language mode and then be called by code in an Arabic language mode. A Spanish programmer can take a code snippet from an English programming forum, and paste it into their Spanish code.

In JavaScript, the global scope, methods, and fields are represented as properties. A property is a data value with an associated name. Babylscript extends properties by allowing multiple names to be bound to a data value. In different language modes, different sets of names can be used to access properties. In this way, programmers can create their own libraries that have translated function and object names for different languages (Figure 1).

2. Design

The underlying basis for the design of Babylscript is the observation that punctuation and mathematical notation are fairly consistent among current natural languages. Since JavaScript's syntax makes heavy use of punctuation and mathematical notation, its syntax does not need to be significantly changed for different language modes. In Babylscript, the same grammar is used for all the different language modes, but the individual tokens for keywords and operations can differ. Similarly, the same functions, objects, and methods are used for all language modes, but the names given to these constructs can differ from language mode to language mode.

SPLASH'11 Companion,   October 22–27, 2011, Portland, Oregon, USA.
ACM 978-1-4503-0940-0/11/10.

```
// Create a property with a default name
var obj = new Object();
obj['property'] = 5;

// Create a French translated name
obj['fr':'propriété'] = 'property';

---fr---
// Both default and translated names are valid
assert(obj.property == obj.propriété);
```

Figure 2. Properties can be referred to using their default name or translated name

Babylscript initially defaults to using an English language mode where keywords and library APIs are in English. To change language modes, programmers write three minus signs, the language code for the desired language mode, and then another three minus signs. For example, `---fr---` is used to switch into a French language mode. Once in a different language mode, all keywords and other symbols are translated into the given language. The command for switching language modes is always the same in all modes, so that programmers can always switch to their desired language mode without knowing the current language context.

To support having translated APIs for libraries in different language modes, Babylscript extends the object model of JavaScript. In JavaScript, objects can be viewed as associative arrays in which names are mapped to data. A data value and its associated name is called a property. In Babylscript, the name given to a property is called a *default name*. In addition to a default name, Babylscript allows properties to have multiple *translated names*. A property can have a different translated name for each of Babylscript's supported language modes. When in a certain language mode, programmers can access properties using the corresponding translated name, if one is available, or the default name (Figure 2). Translated names allow libraries to have different API translations for different language modes yet provide a reasonable fallback if no translations are provided. Since JavaScript stores global variables and functions as properties of a global "object," global variables automatically gain support for having translated names.

Babylscript also extends JavaScript's model for prototype inheritance to handle translated names. Translations can be specified in a parent object where they will be inherited by child objects. Child objects can also override the translations of their parent objects.

3. Implementation

Babylscript is implemented as a modification to the Mozilla Rhino JavaScript interpreter [1]. Since Babylscript uses the same grammar for all the different language modes, there is a single parser, bytecode generator, and bytecode interpreter for all languages. Each language mode does have a separate tokenizer for identifying keywords and other tokens though.

Since the access of the properties of an object is dependent on the language mode, the Babylscript compiler must track the language context of all operations. It does this by adding language tags to all structures passed between stages of the compiler. Figure 3 shows an example of how existing JavaScript tokens, parse trees, and bytecodes are extended with language tags.

During tokenization, the Babylscript tokenizers translate keywords into a canonical form (i.e. English) while leaving identifiers unchanged. The tokenizers also tag all tokens with the current language. These tags are propagated through the compiler chain. Since JavaScript names are resolved at runtime, the interpreter needs the tags to look-up the correct table of translated names of an object.

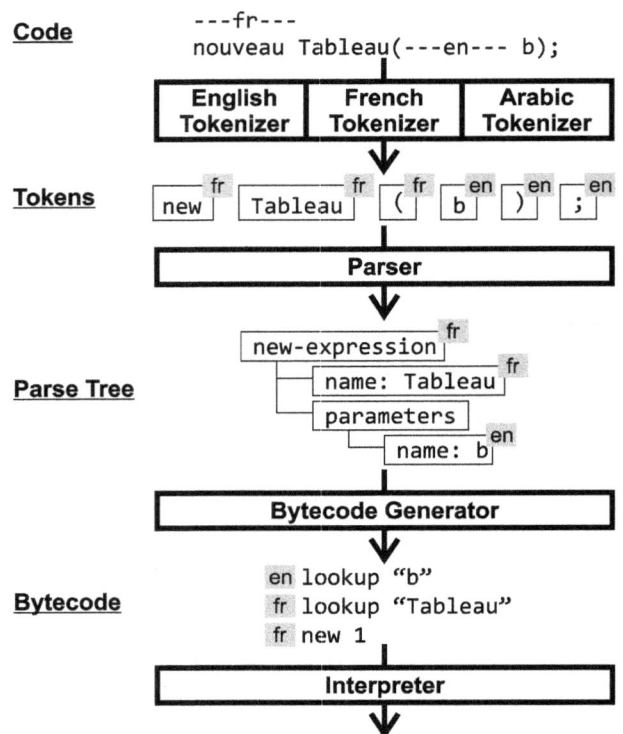

Figure 3. Babylscript modifies a standard JavaScript engine by supporting different tokenizers for different language modes and by extending different stages of the compiler with tags describing the language

The interpreter also has new instructions for setting and modifying translations of properties.

Babylscript provides translations of JavaScript's standard library for different languages. JavaScript's standard library is quite small compared to other languages, making this translation task fairly straight-forward. Unfortunately, JavaScript's standard library is also very US-centric, and Babylscript does not modify the libraries to properly support international number and date formats.

4. Conclusion

Babylscript is a multilingual version of JavaScript. It demonstrates that it is possible to design a language that supports the mixing of code written in different languages. Within each language mode, a programmer can write code using their own native languages without being aware of Babylscript's support for other languages. But programmers may unknowingly be using libraries written in a different language, and their code can, in turn, be used by code written in yet another different language.

In the future, some of the ideas behind Babylscript could be applied to statically typed languages like Java. The extra type information could potentially allow for more complex language models, improved performance from resolving translated names statically, and automated translation of program code between languages.

References

[1] Mozilla. Rhino: JavaScript for Java. http://www.mozilla.org/rhino/ [accessed 2011-06-08].

A Case Study of Language Oriented Programming with Cedalion *

[Extended Abstract]

David H. Lorenz   Boaz Rosenan

Open University of Israel,
1 University Rd., P.O.Box 808, Raanana 43107 Israel
lorenz@openu.ac.il   brosenan@cslab.openu.ac.il

Abstract

Cedalion is an LOP language designed for hosting internal DSLs while providing projectional editing. We present a case study where Cedalion was used to help colleagues in the field of Biology design a DNA microarray for a protein-binding assay.

Categories and Subject Descriptors   D.2.6 [*Software Engineering*]: Programming Environments—Programmer workbench; D.3.2 [*Programming Languages*]: Language Classifications—Specialized application languages.

General Terms   Design, Languages.

Keywords   Language-oriented programming (LOP), Language workbenches, Domain-specific languages (DSLs).

1. Introduction

Language Oriented Programming (LOP) [3, 4, 7] is, at least by name, a relatively new software development paradigm. In contrast to traditional paradigms, where software is designed to match a designated programming language, in LOP the language is designed to match the software it is intended to express. This is done by defining, implementing and using domain-specific languages (DSLs) as the main method of software development.

This approach has several advantages. By tailoring DSLs to the software's problem domain, the implementation of the software becomes very concise, ideally, very close to the software specifications. LOP can increase code reuse significantly [6] by capturing the complexity of implementing high-level concepts inside the DSL implementations. This is increased when LOP is implemented by using multiple, interoperable DSLs to implement software.

To enjoy the benefits of LOP, a few challenges need to be met. First, the implementation of LOP must be made cost-effective. Traditionally, the implementation of DSLs is considered to be hard, and when provided they often come with no tooling to support them, thus harming productivity. Second, DSL interoperability is often not easy to achieve. Some techniques such as the use of XML or Lisp macros, address the first two challenges. However, they pose restrictions on the DSL's syntax and sometimes semantics. To properly use LOP we would like to define DSLs with nearly no syntactic nor semantic restrictions. Traditional techniques generally do not provide answers to all three challenges.

Recent work in the field introduced *language workbenches*. These are integrated development environments (IDEs) for defining, implementing and using DSLs. By Fowler's definition [4], language workbenches are meant to target external DSLs, addressing some of their limitations by providing some internal DSL features to them. They allow interoperability by providing a common representation for all DSLs. This common representation allows them to apply LOP on itself, thus providing DSLs for language definition and implementation tasks, thus making LOP more cost-effective.

2. The Cedalion Approach

In our work, we take an alternative approach. Instead of starting with external DSLs and bringing them closer to internal DSLs, we take internal DSLs and bring them closer to external DSLs. Our programming language, Cedalion [5], is designed to be a host for internal DSLs.

Cedalion is a logic programming language, based on Prolog, and thus can host internal DSLs just like Prolog. Unlike Prolog, however, Cedalion uses projectional editing as an alternative to parsing. This removes any syntactic limitations

* This research was supported in part by the *Israel Science Foundation (ISF)* under grant No. 926/08.

from DSLs, and supports syntactic interoperability, i.e., the ability for code in one DSL to be embedded in code in another DSL. Projectional editing works even if a combination of DSLs results in an ambiguous syntax. Disambiguation is done when editing, by selecting the desired language construct from a list.

Another difference is the fact that Cedalion is statically typed. Static typing allows DSLs to express and enforce validity rules. It is also used by Cedalion's projectional editor to guide users in writing valid code to begin with. If the rules enforced by the type system are not powerful enough or if the error messages produced by the type system are not informative enough, DSL designers can define custom *checkers*, predicates that relate DSL code to error messages. Cedalion's type system is implemented in Cedalion, using checkers. Users are free to implement their own, to define DSL-specific validity rules.

Cedalion is implemented as an open-source project [2]. Its implementation consists of the language itself, implemented in Prolog and Cedalion, and its projectional editor (the Cedalion Workbench), implemented in Java over Eclipse.

3. Case Study: Bioinformatics

To validate our work we conducted a case study where Cedalion was used to help colleagues in the field of Biology. In this case study, Cedalion provided a DSL-based solution to a study of the binding properties of a protein named p53 with DNA [1].

One of the methods in this study is the use of a *Protein Binding Microarray (PBM)*. This is a special kind of *DNA microarray*, a chip containing microscopic wells, each containing a different DNA sequence, with multiple instances in each well (a PBM is a microarray dedicated to binding proteins to DNA sequences). This method allows tens of thousands of DNA sequences to be tested in a single experiment. The microarray can be customized for the needs of a particular experiment. However, doing so requires providing the chip's manufacturer a list of 10^5 DNA sequences. This list has to be considered carefully, as the number of possible sequences is often much bigger then the number of wells on the chip.

In previous experiments, our colleagues used a Java program of about 500 lines of code to prepare such a list, based on logic associated with a previous hypothesis. This logic was expressed using imperative Java code, and there was no easy way to tell that the sequence list it produced was indeed based on the intended logic.

We proposed doing this with Cedalion. We took an LOP approach to this problem, by first defining a DSL that would best express a microarray design. Then we implemented it to provide the list of sequences. In our analysis, we found that a more general DSL, one for expressing sets of DNA sequences, would do most of the work, as the microarray con-

tains several such sets, each with different properties. This more general DSL can also be used for other Bioinformatics tasks such as expressing search patterns for chromosomal searches. The implementation of this DSL is able to list the members of a particular set, and test whether a sequence is a member of a set. Then we added microarray-specific capabilities, such as the ability to decimate the list in a uniform way, to allow samples to be specified. Together, they allows our colleagues to express their particular experiment relatively quickly, and upload the list of sequences to the manufacturer's website.

4. Conclusion

Our work introduces a novel approach to LOP and an alternative to language workbenches. In contrast to language workbenches, we take internal DSLs and provide them with language workbench features, to make them closer to external DSLs. Cedalion is a proof of concept implementation of this approach. As evidence that this approach provides a viable alternative to language workbenches, with some trade-offs, we conducted a case study examining the usage of Cedalion in solving a real life problem.

During this process, our colleagues changed their design twice. Making the changes in the DSL was straightforward and was done quickly. Computation time (the time it took the Cedalion program to come up with the list) was much higher than with the Java program (a few minutes compared with a few seconds), but still within reason.

References

[1] I. Beno, K. Rosenthal, M. Levitine, L. Shaulov, and T. E. Haran. Sequence-dependent cooperative binding of p53 to DNA targets and its relationship to the structural properties of the DNA targets. *Nucleic Acids Research*, 39(5):1919–1932, Mar. 2011.

[2] Cedalion. The Cedalion project homepage. Software Engineering Research Lab, The Open University of Israel, 2010. http://cedalion.sourceforge.net.

[3] S. Dmitriev. Language oriented programming: The next programming paradigm. *JetBrains onBoard*, 1(2), Nov. 2004.

[4] M. Fowler. Language workbenches: The killer-app for domain specific languages, June 2005. http://www.martinfowler.com/articles/languageWorkbench.html.

[5] D. H. Lorenz and B. Rosenan. Cedalion: A language for language oriented programming. In *Proceedings of the ACM International Conference on Systems, Programming Languages, and Applications: Software for Humanity (SPLASH'11)*, Portland, Oregon, USA, Oct. 2011. ACM.

[6] D. H. Lorenz and B. Rosenan. Code reuse with language oriented programming. In *Proceedings of the 12th International Conference on Software Reuse (ICSR12)*, number 6727 in Lecture Notes in Computer Science, pages 165–180, Pohang, Korea, June 13-17 2011. Springer Verlag.

[7] M. P. Ward. Language-oriented programming. *Software-Concepts and Tools*, 15(4):147–161, 1994.

Learning CUDA: Lab Exercises and Experiences, Part 2

Christopher T. Mitchell   Jens Mache

Lewis & Clark College
Portland, OR 97219, USA
{chrism, jmache}@lclark.edu

Karen L. Karavanic

Portland State University
Portland, OR 97207-0751, USA
karavan@cs.pdx.edu

Abstract

The rise of multi-core computer hardware has introduced new urgency to learning parallel programming. In this presentation, we again focus on CUDA exercises suitable for undergraduate students. Trying to appeal to a wide audience of today's learners, we have developed a "Game of Life" exercise and an introductory CUDA summary. We discuss our classroom-test of the exercise, our experiences, and our lessons learned.

Categories and Subject Descriptors D.1.3 [*Software*]: Programming Technique—Concurrent Programming; K.3.2 [*Computer and Information Science Education*]: Computer Science

General Terms Algorithms, Design, Human Factors, Languages, Measurement, Performance

Keywords parallel computing, GPGPU, CUDA, computer science education

1. Introduction

The rise of multi-core computer hardware has introduced new urgency to learning parallel programming, and CUDA is a well-known approach to general-purpose computing on graphics processing units (GPGPU). Although a typical CPU today has two, four or six cores, today's graphics cards can already have hundreds of cores.

Existing learning materials for parallel programming focus on scientific computing. Many of the applications presented in current textbooks include: matrix operations, numerical integration, finite element computations, and FFTs.

This focused set of applications is insufficient for two reasons: it is not representative of the broad range of applications that must soon be implemented in parallel, and the importance of these applications is only clear to students with a background in scientific computing.

Thus, there is a need for more widely-accessible examples that demonstrate the diverse applicability of parallel programming and motivate a broader group of students. To help accomplish this, we began developing a "Game of Life" exercise and a website that would help students quickly become familiar with important CUDA concepts.

2. Pieces of the Puzzle

While learning CUDA, we identified essential concepts necessary for understanding how CUDA applications are designed. We wanted to impress these concepts on students so that they would have a cohesive (though not necessarily detailed) mental model of how a CUDA application works. The hope is that from this model, students will be better able to internalize the details learned from other, more detailed, sources. We produced an informational web-page and a related lab exercise to teach and affirm these concepts [2].

The first concept involves understanding the differences between a CPU and a GPU — the differences in processor design encourage radically different ways of composing a program to solve a problem. Understanding the architecture of a GPU can help illuminate the rationale behind some of the ideas found in CUDA. The other pieces that we discuss in our webpage are:

- running a kernel on the GPU
- executing many copies of the kernel in configurable grids.
- the idea of being able to execute many distinct iterations of certain loops simultaneously by using `blockIdx` and `threadIdx`.
- allocating and copying to and from device memory

Each of these concepts are relevant to all but the most trivial CUDA programs, and having a grasp on them should make understanding CUDA source code and other materials much easier.

SPLASH'11 Companion,   October 22–27, 2011, Portland, Oregon, USA.
ACM 978-1-4503-0940-0/11/10.

2.1 Game of Life Exercise

The undergraduate students who helped write part one of this series [3] worked through four labs associated with the book "Programming Massively Parallel Processors: A Hands-on Approach" [5]. The students reported that many of the labs rewarded student effort only with simple pass/ fail messages and that these textual messages were not very engaging or motivating. Students wished that their efforts could be met with a more rewarding outcome such as a visual. For a more engaging and visual lab, we explored the idea of using Conway's Game of Life.

We realized that instructing students to port a CPU-only version of the Game of Life to CUDA would serve well to reinforce the essential concepts that we identified. We settled on a prompt that offered no guidance and only explained that the student should get practice "putting all of the CUDA pieces together" by converting a serial Game of Life implementation into a CUDA one. This would require students synthesize what they have learned from other resources.

Our first attempt at developing the CPU-only code and the CUDA-enabled solution used the console for output. Because both versions were being bottlenecked by the slow console output, discerning a speed difference between the two was impossible. We took issue with this because without a perceptible speed difference, students would not get feedback demonstrating that their CUDA port had any benefit over the CPU-only version. To rectify this, we augmented the program with Xlib to draw the board in a window with one pixel per cell. With 1000×1000 sized boards, the speed increase that CUDA enables is easily observable, even on machines with fast CPUs.

3. Evaluation

We evaluated the Game of Life exercise with students enrolled in a 2011 summer Special Topics course at Portland State University titled "General Purpose GPU Computing" (GPGPUC). The course was open to senior undergraduates and graduate students, and covered both GPU hardware and CUDA. Because the exercise was added after the course was designed and already underway, we added it as an extra credit exercise, with the credit contingent upon the students' completion of a short survey. Student preparation prior to completing the exercise included readings from the CUDA C Programming Guide [1], the first three articles in the Dr. Dobbs series [4], and several recent research papers. They had completed two short programming assignments: the first one was designed to familiarize them with the CUDA environment and course machines; the second one required them to implement a simple matrix-vector multiplication in C, Pthreads, OpenMP, and CUDA. They were partway through more complex group programming projects using CUDA at the time they completed the extra credit exercise. Ultimately, eight students provided feedback.

Several respondents mentioned difficulty using tiling (described in Chapter 4 of [5]) to accommodate a Game of Life board with more cells than the maximal number of threads that can be in a single block. This was not an intended sticking point of the exercise and suggests that tiling (especially given it's general utility and ubiquity) should be introduced by our summary website.

We had anticipated that the exercise would take one or two hours to complete. The seven students who answered the question "Approximately, how many hours did you spend on the exercise?" answered with 1, 2, 3, 4, 4, 5, and 5 hours. A few students reported that the bulk of their time was spent on things related to tiling. Other students wished that they were able to use the CUDA debugger, but their environment did not readily support using it.

Students found the exercise to be interesting (4 vs. 0), worthwhile (6 vs. 0) and helpful for understanding course materials (5 vs. 1). Some felt that the Game of Life was a compelling problem for parallel computing (3 vs. 1). Four of the eight students thought that the exercise was slightly difficult while three found it to be slightly easy. Two students found our summary website to be sufficient for helping them understand the exercise, and three found our website insufficient; the rest felt neutral, indicating room for improvement.

Acknowledgments

We would like to thank David Bunde for discussions, and Julian Dale for his role in creating the exercise and website. This material is based upon work supported by the National Science Foundation under grant 1044932, by the John S. Rogers Science Research Program at Lewis & Clark College, by NSF award 1044973, and by a PSU Miller Foundation Sustainability Grant.

References

[1] NVIDIA CUDA C programming guide. http://developer.download.nvidia.com/compute/DevZone/docs/html/C/doc/CUDA_C_Programming_Guide.pdf.

[2] http://www.lclark.edu/~jmache/CUDA/.

[3] N. Anderson, J. Mache, and W. Watson. Learning CUDA: Lab exercises and experiences. SPLASH '10, pages 183–188, New York, NY, USA, 2010. ACM. ISBN 978-1-4503-0240-1. doi: http://doi.acm.org/10.1145/1869542.1869571.

[4] R. Farber. CUDA, supercomputing for the masses: Part 1. http://www.drdobbs.com/high-performance-computing/207200659, 2008.

[5] D. B. Kirk and W.-m. W. Hwu. *Programming massively parallel processors: a hands-on approach.* Morgan Kaufmann Publishers, Burlington, MA, 2010. ISBN 0123814723.

A Comparative Study of Parallel Sort Algorithms

Davide Pasetto

IBM Dublin Research Lab, Dublin, Ireland
pasetto_davide@ie.ibm.com

Albert Akhriev

IBM Dublin Research Lab, Dublin, Ireland
albert_akhriev@ie.ibm.com

Abstract

In this paper we examine the performance of parallel sorting algorithms on modern multi-core hardware. Several general-purpose methods, with particular interest in sorting of database records and huge arrays, are evaluated and a brief analysis is provided.

Categories and Subject Descriptors F.2.2 [*Analysis of Algorithms and Problem Complexity*]: Nonnumerical Algorithms and Problems — parallel sorting

General Terms Algorithms, Performance

Keywords parallel sorting, sorting throughput, scalability

1. Outline of the work

Sorting is undoubtedly one of the most valuable algorithms in computer science. Recently, many parallel sorting methods have been proposed. However, despite the number of publications it is still difficult to decide which method best suits specific requirements. The lack of comparative studies has driven our interest to hardware-friendly sorting algorithms. In this research we try to shed some light on hardware specific restrictions that can make an algorithm to perform poorly even though it is theoretically efficient.

This study focuses on general-purpose sorting of huge arrays. The data-specific algorithms have been abandoned because usually an application does not know the data type in advance. A few *unstable* sorting methods, which well fit the modern SMP architectures, were carefully selected. Our choice is based on criticism found in other papers, inspection of available implementation code and intensive experimentation. Each method has $O((N/P) \log N)$ time complexity, where N is the size of input array, and P is the number of threads. The selected methods and their abbreviations are:

1) **STL.** The sort algorithm from the GNU C++ STL is used as a reference method and as a back-end for all other parallel methods. It is well designed from algorithmic and cache-usage perspectives.
2) **EM.** Edahiro's Mapsort [1] is based of the fast parallel partition procedure that splits the whole array into a number of pieces, each independently sorted by a thread using STL sort. Advantages: EM makes only two passes over the input data and moves each item only once from the input to the output array. Shortcomings: EM requires an output array and copies items to the random positions in the output array, using the memory bandwidth ineffectively.
3) **MS.** The parallel Mergesort with exact partition is based on the article [4] and popularized by developers of the GNU Multi-Core

STL [2]. Advantages: most operations are cache-optimal since they read/write data in sequence maximizing the use of hardware prefetching; minimal synchronization overhead and good scalability. Shortcomings: MS requires a separate output array.
4) **TZ.** Tsigas-Zhang's Parallel Quicksort proposed in [3] is a fine-grain, block-based parallel extension to the classical quicksort algorithm. Advantages: in-place sorting; the parallel partition procedure compares/copies/swaps most of the elements only few times. Shortcomings: synchronization overhead might be high.
5) **TZJL.** A job-list extension to the previous method that divides the whole sorting job into a number of smaller jobs and pushes them into a list of pending jobs. Any free thread executes the first available job; this technique improves workload balancing.
6) **AQ.** Alternative Quicksort modifies the parallel partition procedure. At first, each thread splits its own sub-range against a pivot element, then all threads together split the whole range against the pivot in block-wise fashion, where block size can exceed L1 cache.

We have designed TZJL and AQ as the natural extensions to the quicksort method. The goal was to alleviate synchronization overhead and memory access bottleneck.

We have investigated several sorting scenarios like direct sorting, sorting by pointers, sorting by means of intermediate key-pointer array, etc. We were also experimenting with different data types – integers, floats and 100-byte records ordered by 10-byte keys. For the sake of space, results for direct sorting of arrays of 100-byte records will be only reported, which is our main interest here. Direct sorting implements the usual scenario when elements of array are swapped directly over the course of computation. Some methods require the output buffer while others sort in-place. The very brief summary for other sorting scenarios is that sorting by pointers is slower [5] and sorting via intermediate key-pointer array may be sometimes faster than the direct sorting.

The two machines used in experiments (Core i7 architecture):
Nehalem: Xeon 5550, 2.67 GHz, 4 cores/8 threads, 3-channel memory controller, 6 Gb of memory, Linux 64-bit.
Westmere: Xeon 5670, 2.93 GHz, 6 cores/12 threads, 3-ch. mem. controller, **dual-socket** board (24 threads), 24 Gb, Linux 64-bit.

Four series of experiments have been conducted to investigate the following characteristics of the parallel sorting methods:
1) **Sorting throughput** in bytes per second that exposes the actual algorithm performance as a function of array size in elements.
2) **Scalability**, which measures the sorting throughput as a function of the number of software threads fixing the input array size.
3) **CPU affinity** influence. Two runs have been made on "Westmere" using only 12 hardware threads via affinity mask control. The first run disabled one socket, i.e. 12 threads and the cache memory of one CPU were used. The second run enabled 6 threads on both sockets, i.e. the caches of both CPUs were used. As expected, the *throughput ratio*: (one socket throughput)/(dual socket throughput) of the second run is smaller on *large* arrays despite synchronization overhead through the QPI connection.

SPLASH'11 Companion, October 22–27, 2011, Portland, Oregon, USA.
ACM 978-1-4503-0940-0/11/10.

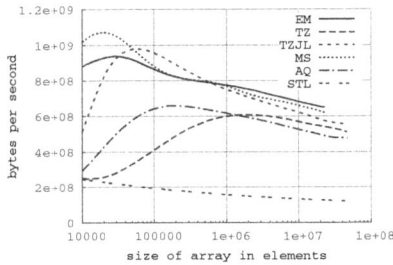

Nehalem. Sorting of 100-byte records by different methods. Sorting throughput is defined in bytes per second as a function of array size in elements.

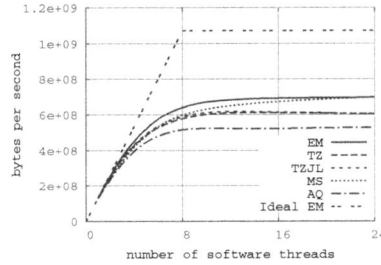

Nehalem. Scalability in the number of threads on a random array of 10^7 100-byte records. "Ideal" curve extrapolates the single-thread performance up to the number of *hardware* threads.

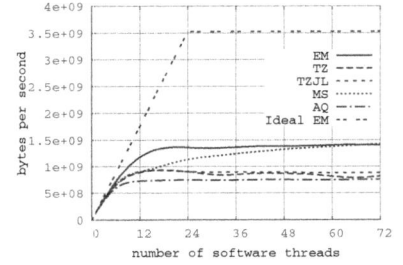

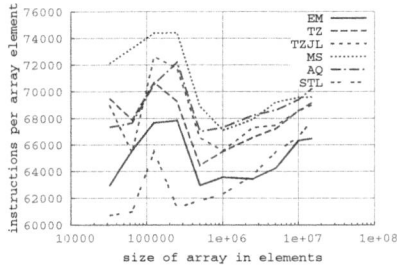

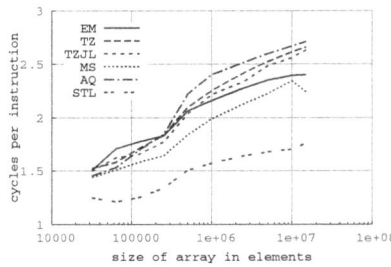

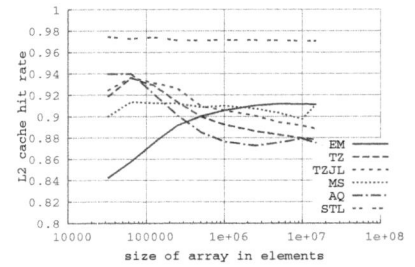

Westmere. Scalability in the number of threads on a random array of 10^7 100-byte records. "Ideal" curve extrapolates the single-thread performance up to the number of *hardware* threads.

Nehalem. Performance metrics as the functions of array size in elements, where array element is a 100-byte record. *Left*, the number of instructions per element. *Middle*, the number of clock cycles per instruction. *Right*, L2 cache hit rate.

4) **Micro-architecture** analysis. The Intel Core i7 architecture is *in theory* able to execute multiple instructions per clock cycle, if implementation does not exhibit too many resource lockups inside the instruction scheduling logic. Statistics collected by `OProfile` shows the number of instructions required per input element as well as the clock cycles per instruction measured for each algorithm.

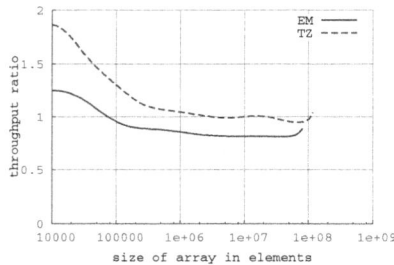

Westmere. CPU affinity test. Throughput *ratio* between using a single socket and dual sockets as a function of array size in elements, where array element is a 100-byte record.

Several observations can be made from presented diagrams. First, in-place methods TZ, TZJL and AQ demonstrate poor performance comparing to the single-threaded STL when sort small arrays (less than 100,000 elements), see the sorting throughput diagram for Nehalem. More attention should be paid to alleviate synchronization overhead, which is the main reason here.

Second, some algorithms can be slightly accelerated, if the number of *software* threads is larger than the number of available *hardware* CPU threads regardless of contention, see the scalability diagrams. The phenomenon can be explained by gradual improvement of workload balance as the number of software threads increases. There is room for further refining of sort algorithms.

Third, the scalability diagrams also make clear that achievable scalability is far below the "ideal" one. The powerful dual-socket Westmere system (24 threads) is only twice as fast than Nehalem one (8 threads). To avoid excessive inter-socket communications, the possible remedy is to divide an array into two halves on early stage and then sort both sub-arrays separately on each CPU socket.

Fourth, the figures reveal that no algorithm is able to achieve even one clock per instruction. Sorting is heavily data intensive. It requires constant load and store of words through the memory hierarchy. Modern CPUs are capable of executing several instruction per cycle only when data come mostly from registers or L1 cache.

The contribution of this paper is twofold. It gives an insight into typical problems arising from hardware limitations and presents improvements of in-place quicksort method (TZJL and AQ). We would recommend MS method, if double buffer is not a concern, and TZJL as in-place one. The full paper can be found at: https://researcher.ibm.com/researcher/view.php?person=ie-pasetto_davide, https://researcher.ibm.com/researcher/view.php?person=ie-albert_akhriev.

References

[1] M. Edahiro. Parallelizing fundamental algorithms such as sorting on multi-core processors for EDA acceleration. In *Proc. of the Asia and South Pacific Design Automation Conf.*, pages 230–233, Japan, 2009.

[2] J. Singler, P. Sanders, and F. Putze. MCSTL: The Multi-core Standard Template Library. *Lect. Notes in Comp. Science*, 4641: 682–694, 2007.

[3] P. Tsigas and Y. Zhang. A Simple, Fast Parallel Implementation of Quicksort and its Performance Evaluation on SUN Enterprise 10000. In *Proceedings of the 11th Euromicro Conference on Parallel Distributed and Network based Processing*, pages 372–384, 2003.

[4] P. Varman, S. Scheufler, B. Iyer, and G. Ricard. Merging multiple lists on hierarchical-memory multiprocessors. *Journal of Parallel and Distributed Computing*, 12 (2): 171–177, 1991.

[5] C. Wu, G. Kandiraju, and P. Pattnaik. Analysis of High-Performance Sorting Algorithms on AIX for Mainframe Operation Offload. In *Proc. of the International Computer Symposium*, 2008.

Observationally Cooperative Multithreading *

Christopher A. Stone   Melissa E. O'Neill   The OCM Team

Computer Science Department
Harvey Mudd College
{stone,oneill,ocm}@cs.hmc.edu

Abstract

Observationally Cooperative Multithreading (OCM) is a new approach to shared-memory parallelism. It addresses a key problem of mainstream concurrency control mechanisms—they can be prohibitively hard to reason about and debug. Programmers using OCM simply write code as if they were using the cooperative multithreading model (CM) for uniprocessors. The underlying OCM implementation then optimizes execution—running threads in parallel when possible—in such a way that the results are consistent with CM. In addition to providing easier reasoning and debugging, OCM is also highly adaptable in terms of its underlying concurrency-control mechanism. Programmers using OCM have the capability to take a finished program and choose the strategy (e.g., locks or transactions) that provides optimal performance.

Categories and Subject Descriptors D.1.3 [*Programming Techniques*]: Concurrent Programming—Parallel programming; D.3.2 [*Programming Languages*]: Language Classifications—Concurrent, distributed, and parallel languages

General Terms Languages, Performance

Keywords Observationally cooperative multithreading, cooperative multithreading, transactional memory, lock inference, parallel model, parallel debugging.

1. Introduction

Parallel programming is notoriously difficult; it is hard to predict all ways in which threads may interact. Synchronization code to manage these interactions can be complex and error-prone. And when bugs inevitably arise, hard-to-reproduce race conditions make debugging more difficult than in sequential code. Although there has been valuable progress in making parallel programming more accessible, popular models for parallelism are still difficult for many programmers to use effectively [3].

Inspired by Cooperative Multithreading (CM) for uniprocessors, where threads run one at a time and continue until they explicitly yield control, we propose a new model for parallel programming. *Observationally Cooperative Multithreading* (OCM) offers

- Simple semantics and syntax, taken from CM;
- Parallel execution, taking advantage of modern hardware;
- Implementation flexibility, allowing a variety of contention management methods (e.g., transactional memory, lock inference);
- Serializability, simplifying debugging and reasoning.

OCM is not an implementation mechanism, but rather an abstraction for programmers. The observable behavior of programs is consistent with execution on a uniprocessor with cooperative multithreading, even if behind the scenes threads are running simultaneously or preempting one another.

Designed to emphasize correctness over raw performance, OCM may not be suitable for all multithreaded applications. But just as many systems use garbage collection and runtime bounds checking rather than manual memory management and unsafe array accesses, we feel that there is a place for systems like OCM that provide an easier and safer path into parallel programming. And, as with garbage collection and bounds checking, there is wide scope for interesting research and design work to decrease runtime overhead.

2. Observationally Cooperative Multithreading

As with CM, under the OCM model the programmer simply specifies locations in their code where it is safe for a thread to yield control; the syntax for an OCM program is the same as for a CM program. For example, the following "banking" example of concurrent account transfers is valid in CM and in OCM.

```
# repeatedly move $5          # repeatedly move $10
while acct[x] >= 5:           while acct[i] >= 10:
    acct[x] = acct[x] - 5         acct[i] = acct[i] - 10
    acct[y] = acct[y] + 5         acct[j] = acct[j] + 10
    yield                         yield
```

Unlike CM, OCM is a model for *parallel* computation. A system implementing the OCM model is free to run programs in parallel, provided that the observable behavior (final results, I/O, etc.) of a program is consistent with a possible execution under some (nonpreemptive, uniprocessor) CM model. We call this requirement *CM serializability*, and it is the fundamental property of OCM.

In the above code example, CM (and hence OCM) guarantees the the comparison and updates in each interation execute atomically.[1] The two loops can execute simultaneously if x and y are disjoint from i and j. Otherwise, the loops must be interleaved. Either way produces results consistent with CM.

---

* This material is based upon work supported by the National Science Foundation under Grant No. CCF-0917345. Any opinions, findings, and conclusions or recommendations expressed in this material are those of the authors and do not necessarily reflect the views of the National Science Foundation.

[1] Obtaining equivalent behavior with block-structured `atomic` blocks would be much more awkward.

3. Implementations

Any means to execute code consistent with CM is a valid OCM implementation. We have developed several different implementations, which are available for download at http://ocm-model.org. In creating these implementations, we show that a variety of implementation strategies for OCM are feasible. Doing so also allows us to compare the tradeoffs of these different implementation strategies.

Undoubtedly the simplest implementation of the OCM model is traditional uniprocessor CM (or, for a parallel implementation, a single global lock on the CPU). Although it does not exploit multiple cores, it has value as a baseline. An OCM implementation that exploits multiple cores should outperform CM in general, but CM may be best in specific cases (e.g., for programs with massive thread contention, or on a uniprocessor machine).

3.1 Nontrivial Lock-Based Implementations

We have developed a proof-of-concept lock-based OCM implementation as an extension to the Lua scripting language. This extension is a dynamic library loaded by the Lua interpreter, so it cannot perform static analysis to obtain the information needed for correct locking. Access to shared data is therefore mediated solely through "proxy objects" obtained through the OCM library—threads are otherwise completely separate. Because the system knows that a thread can only access shared data through proxies, and the system knows which threads are holding which proxies, the OCM scheduler can acquire and release all necessary locks on behalf of threads.

We have also implemented lock-based OCM in the form of a source-to-source translator for C with the addition of `yield` and `spawn` statements. The translator does dataflow analysis to conservatively determine which variables may be accessed in the future following each `yield` statement—those are the variables that `yield` needs to lock. This information is then used to insert calls to locking and unlocking functions using Pthreads in the necessary locations. Any `spawn` or `yield` statements are replaced with calls to library functions.

3.2 STM-based Implementations

The OCM model also permits implementations based on software transactional memory (STM), whereby all reads and writes of shared data are routed through an STM system. Each `yield` statement ends the current transaction and begins a new one, so that changes made by the current thread become visible to others.

As when investigating lock-based implementations, we began with a proof-of-concept modification to Lua. In this case, we implemented the OCM system by requiring the Lua interpreter to use the TinySTM library when accessing memory.

We have also created an STM-based OCM implementation as a C++ library using Pthreads. This library allows the programmer to indicate that certain variables are shared, which causes all accesses to those variables to be routed through the STM library. Because transactions may begin and end in different lexical scopes, our system saves and restores stack frames as necessary. Our library approach requires no changes to the underlying language, relying instead on C++ language features (overloading, templates, etc.) to make access to shared data feel natural.

4. Debugging and Performance Profiling

Although OCM dramatically reduces the potential for race conditions and deadlock compared to, say, explicit locking, it does not eliminate them.

Fortunately, reproducing bugs is far easier in OCM than in many other models, because every program execution has at least one corresponding execution under CM. If an OCM system wishes to allow reproducible debugging, it simply has to record a corresponding serial execution for that program. With that *serialization trace*, it is possible to rerun the program serially following that trace and thereby reproduce the exact sequence of interleavings that trigger the bug.

5. Conclusions and Future Work

OCM is a promising solution for shared-memory program development. It retains many of the benefits of currently existing concurrency-control systems, while mitigating their complexity. It allows the programmer to focus on the logic of the program instead of the subtleties of parallelism.

Because OCM does not require a specific implementation, an application can be written according to the OCM model and use whichever implementation is best suited for it.

To promote the broad adoption of OCM, others could implement OCM using their own concurrency-control schemes. We also hope that educators see the value in using OCM as a "kinder, gentler" form of multicore parallelism, even if they later introduce other models, like locks or transactions. In fact, OCM can serve as a springboard for subject; synchronization primitives are easy to write in OCM (e.g., `semWait(`i`)` is `while (`i` > 0) yield; `$--i$ and `semSignal(`i`)` is $++i$), and discussions of efficient OCM implementations naturally lead to topics like transactions. We hope that our available implementations and further examples of OCM in use will provide a good starting point for these efforts.

In addition, OCM needs benchmarks that can be used to assess the performance of different concurrency control techniques and of the OCM approach as a whole. We are currently adapting the benchmarking suites STAMP and PARSEC to OCM and writing a series of examples from *The Little Book of Semaphores* [2] using OCM. We are investigating how OCM scales to larger applications, and which debugging and profiling tools prove most valuable.

6. Related Work

As a parallel model, OCM intersects with a significant portion of prior work on parallelism and concurrency. OCM is particularly closely related to Automatic Mutual Exclusion [1] where all code is atomic unless marked unsynchronized (an empty unsynchronized block corresponds to `yield`), and to work by Yi et al. [4] that explains lock-based code in terms of cooperative multithreading.

Acknowledgments

The undergraduate OCM Team included Bartholomew Broad, Kwang Ketcham, Samuel Just, Alejandro Lopez-Lago, and Joshua Peraza (2009); Sonja Bohr, Adam Cozzette, Joe DeBlasio, Julia Matsieva, Stuart Pernsteiner, and Ari Schumer (2010); and Xiaofan Fang, Sean Laguna, Stephen Levine, Jordan Librande, Stuart Pernsteiner, and Mary Rachel Stimson (2011).

References

[1] M. Abadi, A. Birrell, T. Harris, and M. Isard. Semantics of transactional memory and automatic mutual exclusion. In *POPL '08*, pages 63–74, 2008.

[2] A. B. Downey. *The Little Book of Semaphores*. Green Tea Press, 2nd edition, 2008.

[3] C. J. Rossbach, O. S. Hofmann, and E. Witchel. Is transactional programming actually easier? In *PPoPP '10*, pages 47–56, 2010.

[4] J. Yi, C. Sadowski, and C. Flanagan. Cooperative reasoning for preemptive execution. In *PPoPP '11*, pages 147–156, 2011.

Automatic Protocol-Conformance Recommendations

Ernesto J. Alfonso

Carnegie Mellon University

ealfonso@andrew.cmu.edu

Abstract

Misuse of reusable components in software is common. Systems of software analysis based on formal specifications provide a mechanism for automatically detecting non-conformance to protocols. The focus of this research is to automatically generate task-specific user recommendations for correcting misuse of arbitrary protocols using results from software analysis systems.

Categories and Subject Descriptors D.2.4 [*Software Engineering*]: Software/Program Verification

General Terms Verification

Keywords protocol, automatic fix, suggestions, error message generation, predicate logic, specifications

1. Introduction

As the utility of a reusable software artifact increases, so does the complexity of its public interface and usage protocols. This often leads to errors of misuse at the points of contact of reusable artifacts with their users. In order to explicitly enforce proper usage protocols, formal specifications of reusable components may be used by software analysis systems in order to automatically verify conformance to these protocols. However, upon discovery of a misuse, any user feedback provided directly by such systems must be in terms of the protocol specification, which is unusable to the user who is not already an expert in the protocol. The contribution of this research is a system which automatically generates task-specific, user level recommendations for correcting misuse of protocols, based on results from analysis mechanisms with formal specifications.

2. Motivating Example

Consider the following example of a protocol misuse,

Listing 1. Misuse of the iterator protocol

```
1
2  public Object clumsyPoll(Queue queue) {
3    Iterator iter = queue.iter();
4    Object o = null;
5    if (iter.hasNext())
6      o = iter.next();
7      iter.remove();
8    return o;
9  }
```

Listing 2. Current feedback from Fusion

```
1  Broken constraint: Removable(iter)
```

Currently, the formally specified iterator protocol along with the Fusion[1] program analysis provide the feedback in listing 2 in response to the protocol misuse in listing 1 (i.e. Iterator.next must be called before Iterator.remove). Despite listing 2 being a relatively intuitive error message, which might serve a user already familiar with the very simple protocol, this type of error still refers to the internal representation of Fusion and the Iterator specification implementation, and in general does not provide any direction towards fixing the problem. Note also, whereas the example in listing 1 is intentionally simple, real life examples of misuse tend to be more involved.

Our goal is to provide task-specific recommendations which the user can understand, such as the following suggestions independently addressing the misuse in listing 1:

- Move call to "iter.remove()" to line 7 within if-block starting at line 5.

- Remove the method call to "iter.remove()" on line 7

- Call "iter.next()" before line 7

Approach

Consider,

- An analysis system which relies on a formal specification language (e.g. Fusion and its spec. language)

- A reusable component which usage protocol is specified for the above system (e.g. Iterator)

- A user program U which uses the reusable component improperly, breaking specification C (e.g. U, C are listings 1, 2 resp.)

Our goal is to produce a small set of recommendations to fix U's misuse of the protocol of the reusable component. For a given analysis system, we must define the following two functions, A, H:

- A such that $A(U, C)$ is a finite set of close alternatives to U which do not break C. A member of $A(U, C)$ is a program which results from a small modification to U and is possibly within protocol.

- H such that if X is a set of alternatives to U correcting C (e.g. $X = A(U, C)$), then $H(X) : X \Rightarrow \mathbb{N}$ is a heuristic which sorts alternatives according to their likelihood of being correct. The benchmark correct alternative(s) is defined to be what a human expert would suggest to correct the broken spec. C.

The final result to the user is the top k alternatives from $H(A(U, C))$. The capabilities of A and H will depend directly upon the analysis system used.

Generating Fusion Suggestions

Fusion provides an expressive specification language to encode arbitrary software protocols, and we define A and H within the context of this analysis system. A brief overview of the system's analysis approach is provided.

Fusion's specification language is based on a first order logic over *relationships*, which are protocol abstractions that indicate meaningful associations between objects upon specific protocol operations. A protocol specification for Fusion defines pre and post conditions upon specific protocol operations, in the form of predicate logic over relationships. By keeping track of the state of relationships throughout the program, Fusion reports a broken specification, along with the offending operation, whenever the precondition is false for that operation.

Given a reusable component which implements a Fusion specification, and a user program U which uses that component, breaking a specification C, we now define A and H.

- $A(U, C)$.
  Define $C(R : RELATIONSHIP \rightarrow \{T, F\}) = TRUE \iff$ the relationships which are T (present) in R satisfy the precondition for C, and let R be the relationships T at the point where C is broken.
  Let $P = \{R\prime | C(R\prime) = true \land \forall R\prime\prime.diff(R, R\prime\prime) \subsetneq diff(R, R\prime) \rightarrow C(R\prime\prime) = false\}$, where $diff(A, B) = \{r | A(r) \neq B(r)\}$.
  Hence, of all classes of maps which satisfy constraint C, only the representative which incurs the fewest number of changes from R is in P.
  Define $f(r)$, where
  $f : (RELATIONSHIP \times TRUE, FALSE) \rightarrow MODIFICATION = \{INSERT \cup CREATE\_BRANCH \cup DELETE \cup MOVE \cup \{NONE\}\}$, to be the set of source code modifications that under any precondition of any col-

laboration constraint have the effect of negating r (union-ed with a no-action option), and let $F(\{r_1 \ldots r_k\}) = f(r_0) \times \ldots f(r_k)$. Hence, F takes a set of relationships which must be negated, and returns all possible combinations of modifications that might have the effect of negating every relationship in the input.
  Then $A(U, C) = \bigcup_{P_i \in P} F(P_i) \cap$ SATISFY_C.
  Hence, $A(U, C)$ is simply the set of all modifications which do result in constraint C being satisfied.

- $H(X)$ The sorting function assigns a score based mainly on whether the alternative does in fact satisfy the constraint C and whether a new broken constraint is introduced, although the types of source code modifications used are also considered.

3. Evaluation

Our system was tested on 23 self contained excerpts of misuse of the file IO, iterator, and asp.net protocols. The following criteria was used to asses the performance of the system's fixes on each misuse example: "expert" if the fix matches the human expert's; "correct" if the fix is within protocol but does not match the human expert's; "wrong" if the fix is not within protocol. A test is judged with the highest grade which appears at least once within the top 3 suggestions. Out of all 23 examples, 14 were judged "expert", 7 were judged "correct" and 2 were judged "wrong".

4. Future Work

Eventually, H could be improved into a learning algorithm based on feedback of human experts over time, providing an indicator of the level of confidence on the correctness for each recommendation.

5. Related Work

[2] focuses on automatically correcting type errors in a program by analyzing similar programs which type-check. This work focuses on type-checking and not on arbitrary protocol conformance, and their approach uses a less focused search than the one described here in order to find feasible alternatives. ERL [3] describes a way to improve auto-generated error messages from a failing logical predicate by concentrating only on the failing atomic predicates. This work does not provide recommendations for fixing errors.

References

[1] C. Jaspan and J. Aldrich. Checking framework interactions with relationships. In Proceedings of the 23rd European Conference on Object-Oriented Programming (ECOOP 2009)

[2] B. S. Lerner, M. Flower, D. Grossman, Searching for type-error in Programming language design and implementation, 2007

[3] Ciera Jaspan, Trisha Quan, and Jonathan Aldrich. Error Reporting Logic, in the Proceedings of the Conference on Automated Software Engineering, L'Aquila, Italy, 2008.

Efficient Implementation of the Plaid Language

Sarah Chasins

Swarthmore College, Carnegie Mellon University

schasi1@cs.swarthmore.edu, schasins@andrew.cmu.edu

Abstract

The Plaid language introduces native support for state abstractions and state change. While efficient language implementation typically relies on stable object members, state change alters members at runtime. We built a JavaScript compilation target with a novel state representation, which enables fast member access. Cross-language performance comparisons are used for evaluation.

Categories and Subject Descriptors D.3.4 [*Programming Languages*]: Optimization

General Terms Languages

Keywords Plaid, states, state change

1. State-Based Languages

Consider a simple file object. When it is open, it has read and close methods. When it is closed, it can only be opened. In essence, this single file object has the methods of two distinct classes during these different phases of its use. Yet in typical object-oriented languages, this state information is never directly expressed.

The Plaid language introduces a model in which object state is made explicit[2] [4]. The practice of maintaining implicit state information is pervasive in program design, whether in the case of a simple file or in objects composed of six states simultaneously, or even nested states. By introducing abstract states and explicit state change, Plaid makes these transitions salient to users, facilitating code that depicts object structure more clearly. Without the need to write one's own state checks, code is neater and more compact. Further, where programmers forget to write state checks, the runtime can indicate that a member is unavailable, rather than permit continued execution and possible data corruption.

In Listing 1, simple Plaid code lays out the design of a File state. OpenFile and ClosedFile are substates of

SPLASH'11 Companion, October 22–27, 2011, Portland, Oregon, USA.
ACM 978-1-4503-0940-0/11/10.

File; method close uses the <- operator to cleanly transition between them. Though state check elimination may seem trivial in the case of a file with two states, the advantages are clear in the context of a more complex state space.

```
1   state File {
2      val filename; }
3   state OpenFile case of File {
4      val filePtr;
5      method read() {}
6      method close() { this <- ClosedFile;} }
7   state ClosedFile case of File {
8      method open() { this <- OpenFile;} }
```

Listing 1. Plaid declaration of File state and two substates.

2. Implementation

While maintaining state and permitting state change is excellent from the perspective of a programmer, the challenges for implementation are significant. A Java implementation of Plaid has already been created. However, it relies heavily on inefficient reflection. At runtime, every representation of a Plaid object contains a map of members, and each member is itself an object. Method calls require finding the member in the map, and then calling a method on the member object, which is essentially a container for the body of the function. Performance is unsurprisingly slow.

In formulating a new implementation, JavaScript was a natural target for compilation. As a prototype-based language with first-class objects, it shares some features with Plaid that make translation from one to the other clear and intuitive. Given the language's current ubiquity on the web, a JavaScript implementation of Plaid should be useful, and given the carefully optimized virtual machines, a JavaScript implementation should be fast.

The central design question at this juncture was the matter of how to represent a Plaid object in JavaScript, taking into account the conflicting demands of member usage and state transitions. Efficient member access requires that all methods and fields be part of a single Javascript object. However, efficient state change would most naturally be implemented by storing members in multiple objects. With only naive solutions in mind, decreased efficiency in one realm seems bound to accompany improved efficiency in the other.

An intuitive representation entails maintaining a JavaScript object for each state and substate: one for File, another for

OpenFile, another for ClosedFile. Pointers to the states that currently compose the Plaid object would render state change a simple process. However, consider that a file will commonly be opened once, read many times, and closed once. It is easy to bring to mind many such examples, and it is a rare program that will require more state transitions than method calls or field reads. This being the case, it is essential that member access be fast.

The need for fast method calls and field lookup motivates an alternative approach, one that places members at the level of the JavaScript instance object. That is, any member of a Plaid object must be a member of the JavaScript object that represents it. If JavaScript object f represents a File in the OpenFile state, a call to read should produce the code f.read() at runtime, rather than trigger a search through File and OpenFile objects. However, with this accomplished, how can state change be enacted? When one case of state is removed and another added, how is the runtime to identify the appropriate modifications?

Maintaining a metadata field within JavaScript representations of Plaid objects yielded a solution. A tree details all current states, the members associated with them, and their relationships to each other. State change entails a traversal of the current and target trees – in accordance with Plaid semantics [4] – to identify members to be altered. With JavaScript's first-class treatment of objects, it is trivial to update members. If f is an object, the code delete f.close removes member close. The code f[open]=fileOpen sets the open member of f to fileOpen, whether it is a variable or a function. With member revisions completed, a metadata update completes the process.

3. Preliminary Results

To evaluate the performance of this implementation, we translated the Splay and Richards benchmarks from the V8 JavaScript benchmark suite[1] into Plaid. These Plaid benchmarks were compiled to JavaScript, after which the resultant code was timed alongside the original V8 JavaScript versions, the results of which appear in the first two charts of Figure 1. These preliminary results – produced with a still non-optimizing compiler – reveal a range of slowdowns, from a 158.4% increase in Splay running time, to a 768.8% increase in Richards running time.

Even with the current naive compilation strategy, the JavaScript compiler far surpasses the performance of the pre-existing Java compiler, as is evident in the third chart in Figure 1. Our implementation produces code that runs in 2.1% the amount of time required by the compiled Java code, with an average running time of 76,279.4 milliseconds for the Java Richards, and an average running time of 1,566.5 for the JavaScript Richards. As planned optimizations move forward, the performance of the JavaScript compiler should compare even more favorably.

[1] http://v8.googlecode.com/svn/data/benchmarks/v6/run.html

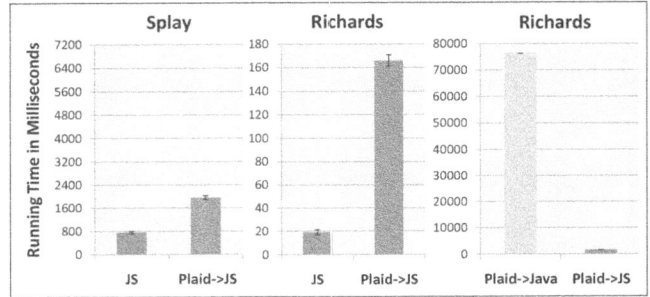

Figure 1. Average running times and the standard deviations appear above. To compare JS to compiled JS, each benchmark was run 500 times in SpiderMonkey. To compare compiled Java to compiled JS, each benchmark was run 100 times within a loop.

4. Contribution

Substantial work has gone into optimizing compilation for dynamically typed languages, and early Scheme [1] and Self [3] innovations continue to furnish valuable insights. As languages like Python and Ruby meet with steadily greater success, the importance of such work is only growing. It is in developing state change that Plaid introduces a new challenge for implementation, one that has not yet been addressed in the field. If this research successfully optimizes state change, it will be the first implementation to do so. This will be an important step in establishing state-based languages' usefulness for practical purposes, and in making state abstraction a viable option for language users and designers.

5. Future Work

There remain many pressing questions on the topic of how to efficiently compile a language that supports state change. This research will go on to investigate further refinements of the JavaScript implementation. However, additional future work will center on implementations for target languages without prototype support – for instance, a traditional object-oriented language like Java. With classes able to inherit members from only a single superclass, how can a Plaid state be created as a composition of two other states? How can states be allowed to transition, and their members with them? While slow solutions come readily to mind, efficient ones do not. These and many other questions will provide fertile ground for continued research.

References

[1] N. Adams, D. Kranz, R. Kelsey, J. Rees, P. Hudak, and J. Philbin, *ORBIT: an optimizing compiler for scheme*, In *Proc. Symposium on Compiler Construction*, 1986.

[2] J. Aldrich, J. Sunshine, D. Saini, and Z. Sparks, *Typestate-oriented Programming*, In *Proc. Onward*, 2009.

[3] C. Chambers and D. Ungar, *Making pure object-oriented languages practical*, In *Proc. OOPSLA*, 1991.

[4] J. Sunshine, K. Naden, S. Stork, J. Aldrich, and E. Tanter, *First-Class State Change in Plaid*, In *Proc. OOPSLA*, 2011.

Creating Domain-Specific Modeling Languages Using a By-Demonstration Technique

Hyun Cho

University of Alabama
Department of Computer Science
Box 870290, Tuscaloosa, AL, U.S.A.
hcho7@ua.edu

Abstract

Domain-Specific Modeling Languages (DSMLs) have been widely used in several domains (e.g., finance, combat simulation, and image manipulation) because they have been shown to improve productivity and quality by reducing the gap between domain abstractions and computational expression within specific domains. DSMLs are often designed by iterating complex and mundane language creation tasks that requires domain knowledge and language development expertise. To tackle the challenges of DSML development, this poster abstract outlines a new approach for specifying and generating the abstract and concrete syntax of a DSML based on user demonstration. The goal of the research is to develop the underlying science and tool support to enable end-users to assist in designing a DSML for their domain, while minimizing the typical mundane tasks of DSML development involving many accidental complexities.

Categories and Subject Descriptors D.3.3 [**Programming Languages**]: Language Constructs and Features – abstract data types, Frameworks.

General Terms Design, Economics, Reliability, Languages.

Keywords Domain-Specific Modeling Language; By-Demonstration; Flexible Modeling Tools

1. Dscription of Purpose

Domain-Specific Modeling Languages (DSMLs) are languages that support encapsulation and abstraction of a particular domain. Due to tailored notations for the domain, they offer substantial benefits such as rich expressiveness and shortened learning curves for non computer scientists who need to express some computational task in a specific domain [7].

As an example, consider report designers for embedded devices, who do not have language development expertise, but would benefit from a domain-specific language to capture the diagrams that they currently draw informally. The formats of reports slightly vary according to the characteristics of embedded devices and customer requirements, but much of the reports are common. The job responsibility of these designers is to customize report formats for each embedded device and link each data field with predefined APIs. However, it may be challenging for them to implement quality report formatting because report formats may be hard-coded with a specific programming language. Therefore, the report designers may desire a DSML that can customize a report format through a WYSIWYG editor. In general, at least two experts (domain expert and language development expert) collaborate when creating a new DSML because learning language development techniques in a short time is difficult for domain experts who do not have language development expertise and hiring experts that have both domain and language development expertise may be challenging. Moreover, the complexity of the DSML development process makes DSML development tedious, error-prone and time-consuming. The purpose of the research described in this poster abstract is to provide a framework that assists domain experts, who have domain knowledge but do not have language development expertise, in building their own DSMLs.

2. Goals of the Research

Like other languages, a DSML consists of three main components; abstract syntax, concrete syntax, and semantics. The components are developed by iterating over complex language creation tasks until the language meets the needed requirements and/or reaches desired quality. To develop a DSML, the requirements of a problem domain are captured, and then the concrete syntax is defined by domain experts and language development experts. Based on the concrete syntax definition, language development experts define the abstract syntax (often represented as a metamodel). In addition, the semantics of a DSML is associated to the abstract syntax. Finally, domain experts and language development experts collaborate to verify the correctness of the DSML. As described, DSML development requires language development expertise as well as domain knowledge so that domain experts who do not have language development expertise may face several challenges if they try to develop their own DSMLs [2].

The main goal of the research described in this abstract is to build a framework that assists domain experts (who do not have language development expertise) in developing their own DSMLs. From the DSML development process, automated and systematic approaches for defining a DSML grammar (both concrete and abstract syntax) and its semantics are crucial toward resolving the challenges of DSML development. Thus, the research aims to simplify and automate DSML development by (1) capturing concrete syntax as end-users demonstrate their domain through modeling, (2) inferring abstract syntax from concrete syntax and model instances, and (3) associating semantics to abstract syntax.

3. Technical Approach

In this section, we describe the technical approach that is being pursued in this research. The overall process for developing a new DSML is represented by a framework for creating modeling languages that is shown in Figure 1.

DSML development begins with domain experts drawing their domain models with domain-specific notations in a modeling canvas of the framework. While domain experts demonstrate domain notions, the actions of these experts are recorded and analyzed to a candidate concrete syntax.

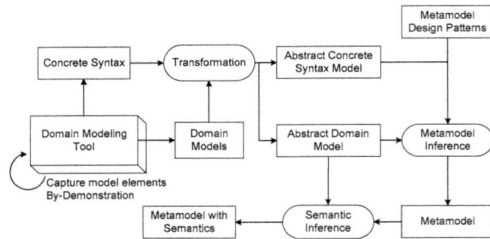

Figure 1. Framework for DSML

To infer the abstract syntax, the concrete syntax and domain models are transformed into a graph representation after the concrete syntax is identified. The inference process induces abstract syntax in the form of a metamodel by comparing abstract models of the concrete syntax and the domain models with patterns representing common metamodel idioms. Metamodel design patterns represent a set of training data that are passed on to an abstract syntax inference engine. The framework completes its process by inducing and associating relevant static semantics to the inferred metamodel.

3.1 Technical Challenges and Solutions

In this section, we identify major technical challenges that this research encountered. We describe the challenges and our solutions below.

- *Concrete syntax definition*: Concrete syntax represents the visual representation of a DSML through a set of domain notations and their relations. In our approach, candidate concrete syntax is automatically captured when domain experts demonstrate domain concepts using the notation of a specific domain. In order to capture the concrete syntax, we adopt a by-demonstration technique, which is similar to earlier work on Program By Example (PbE) or Query By Example (QBE) [4][8]. However, maintaining an optimized sequence of actions (i.e., pruning unnecessary actions) while preserving the demonstrator's intent is challenging.

- *Abstract syntax inference*: Inferring abstract syntax is a special case of inductive learning. This step aims to generate abstract syntax (i.e., metamodel for a DSML) by applying machine learning algorithms to concrete syntax and domain models, which are created in a previous by-demonstration step of the process. To induce abstract syntax, many approaches have been proposed, such as Bayesian learning [1], hill climbing [3], genetic programming [5], and graph [6]. In our research, we

adopt a graph-based approach to leverage the benefits of graphs (e.g., analysis of structural and dynamic properties, design for verification, and model transformation).

- *Semantics inference*: Inferring semantics is emerging as the most challenging area of the research because specifying semantics in a formal way is difficult even for language development experts. Currently, the framework can infer some static constraints from model instances. To infer constraints, the semantic inference engine generates a model instances by traversing graph representation and obtaining feedback about positive and negative sample instances.

4. Current status and Future Work

A prototype has been developed with Microsoft Visio to understand the feasibility of the approach. The prototype was implemented with an understanding that Visio provides various predefined shapes that support the creation and definition of user-specific shapes. In this sense, a Visio template has a correspondence to the metamodel of a DSML. The prototype implementation focused on (1) the identification of concrete syntax, (2) creation of a Visio template, and (3) the identification of rules between shapes as a part of an initial static semantics.

Although we believe that the prototype demonstrates the feasibility of a "by-demonstration" approach for creating a DSML semi-automatically, the prototype is difficult to extend the functionality because Visio provides a limited set of APIs. Thus, we are working on extensions to the framework that can be applicable to other programming environments.

Acknowledgments

This work is supported by NSF CAREER award CCF-1052616.

References

[1] Chen, S. F. 1995. Bayesian grammar induction for language modeling. *In Proceedings of the 33rd annual meeting on Association for Computational Linguistics (ACL '95)*, Stroudsburg, PA, USA, 228-235.

[2] Cho, H., Sun, Y., Gray, J., & White, J. 2011. Key Challenges for Modeling Language Creation By Demonstration, *ICSE 2011 Workshop on Flexible Modeling Tools*, Honolulu HI, May 2011.

[3] Cook, C. M., Rosenfeld, A., & Aronson, A. R. 1976. Grammatical inference by Hill Climbing. *Information Science*. vol. 10, no. 2, 59-80.

[4] Cypher, A., Halbert, D. C., Kurlander, D., Lieberman, H., Maulsby, D., Myers, B. A., & Turransky, A. (Eds.). 1993. *Watch what I do: Programming by Demonstration*. MIT Press, Cambridge, MA, USA.

[5] Dupont, P. 1994. Regular Grammatical Inference from Positive and Negative Samples by Genetic Search: The GIG method. *Proceedings of the 2nd International Colloquium on Grammatical Inference and Applications*, ICGI'94, LNAI, vol. 862, 236-245.

[6] Jonyer, I., Holder, L. B., Cook, D. J. 2004. Mdl-based context-free graph grammar induction and applications. *International Journal on Artificial Intelligence Tools (IJAIT)*, vol. 13, no. 1, 65-79.

[7] Kelly, S. & Tolvanen. 2008. *Domain-Specific Modeling: Enabling Full Code Generation*. Wiley-IEEE Computer Society Press.

[8] Zloof, M. M. 1975. Query-by-example: the invocation and definition of tables and forms. *In Proceedings of the 1st International Conference on Very Large Data Bases (VLDB '75)*. ACM, New York, NY, USA.

Safira: A Tool for Evaluating Behavior Preservation

Melina Mongiovi

Department of Computing Systems, Federal University of Campina Grande
{melina@copin.ufcg.edu.br}

Abstract

We propose a tool (Safira) capable of determining if a transformation is behavior preserving through test generation for entities impacted by transformation. We use Safira to evaluate mutation testing and refactoring tools. We have detected 17 bugs in MuJava, and 27 bugs in refactorings implemented by Eclipse and JRRT.

Categories and Subject Descriptors   D.2.2 [*Software Engineering*]: Tools and Techniques

General Terms   Reliability, Design

Keywords   Refactoring, Testing

1. Introduction

Evaluating whether a program transformation is behavior preserving is required in several tasks, such as refactoring and mutation testing. In refactoring activities, tools are required to ensure that a transformation preserves behavior. On the other hand, mutation testing tools must introduce behavior changes on to programs. Every transformation must contain a set of conditions stating when behavior must be preserved. However, it is not an easy task to formally establish conditions for Java on account of its non-trivial semantics. For this reason, a number of refactoring and mutation testing tools are likely to present bugs.

Some approaches [3, 9] have formally established a number of refactoring conditions for a subset of Java. Steimann and Thies [9] have formally specified a set of refactoring conditions related to Java visibility. However, these conditions are not proven sound with respect to a formal semantics. In fact, it represents a challenge to formally propose sound refactoring [4]. A similar problem happens in the mutation testing area. Some approaches have suggested ways to avoid certain kinds of *equivalent mutants* — a mutant that is functionally equivalent to the original program. Based on previous work [9], Steimann and Thies have proposed an approach to generate mutants based on negating the conditions required for a refactoring [10]. Schuler and Zeller [5] have proposed an approach to detect equivalent mutants based on changes in test coverage. However, a simpler, safer and more practical approach to evaluate whether a transformation preserves behavior is required.

We propose a tool, called Safira, to evaluate whether a transformation is behavior preserving. This tool generates a test suite focusing on exercising only the entities impacted by a transforma-

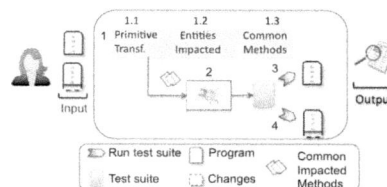

Figure 1. Safira architecture

tion. Safira yields a test case whenever it detects a behavior change. We propose an approach to evaluate mutation testing tools based on Safira and on a Java program generator (JDolly [8]). We use it to evaluate 11 mutations of MuJava [6] and found 17 bugs in all of them. We have also used Safira and JDolly to test refactoring implementations following a previous approach [8]. We found 27 bugs in refactorings implemented by Eclipse and JRRT [3].

2. Safira

The major steps performed by Safira are explained as follows: Firstly, the original (source) and the modified (target) programs are passed as parameters by developers. The change impact analyzer checks both the original and modified programs (Step 1), beginning by decomposing the transformation into primitive ones (Step 1.1). Secondly, for each primitive transformation, Safira identifies the entities impacted by it (Step 1.2). Finally, Safira identifies a set of methods in common that exercises, directly or indirectly, impacted entities (Step 1.3). A method in common must have the same signature in the source and target programs. After this a test suite is generated only for the identified methods (Step 2). The tests are then executed on the source (Step 3) and on the target programs (Step 4). Safira reveals a set of tests that passes on source program but fails on target program. If this set is empty, the developer increases confidence that the transformation has not introduced behavior changes. Otherwise, test cases show behavior changes. Our approach is illustrated in Figure 1.

In order to identify the entities impacted by a transformation, we decompose a transformation into primitive ones by following a similar approach as the one used by Chianti [2]. The set of entities impacted by the transformation encompasses the union of the entities impacted by each primitive transformation. We have considered nine primitive transformations: add and remove an empty class, add and remove an empty method, add and remove a field, add and remove extends and modify a method body. We have formalized the set of impacted methods and constructors for each primitive transformation. Safira uses Randoop [1] to automatically generate unit tests. Randoop, randomly, generates a test suite for the classes and methods received as parameters within a time limit specified by the developer. Randoop executes the program to receive a feedback gathered from executing test inputs as they are created, to avoid generating redundant and illegal inputs. It creates

Table 1. Results of the MuJava evaluation using Safira and JDolly

MuJava Evaluation					
Mut. Typ	Mut.	Equiv. Mut.	Bugs	1st Bug (s)	Time (s)
AOIU	227	1 (0.44%)	1	1040	1338
ISD	101	2 (1%)	2	337	1969
AOIS	454	57 (12%)	1	1070	9727
OMR	185	31 (16%)	2	34	2000
IHD	58	25 (43%)	2	16	1227
OMD	100	56 (56%)	1	27	1580
IOR	69	66 (95%)	2	40	2857
IHI	100	38 (38%)	2	23	2652
IOD	21	12 (61%)	1	6	196
JID	195	63 (32%)	2	35	5870
JSI	100	100 (100%)	1	26	109

method sequences incrementally, by randomly selecting a method call to apply and selecting arguments from previously constructed sequences. Each sequence is executed and checked against a set of contracts.

3. Evaluation

We used Safira to assess mutation testing tools (Section 3.1) and refactoring engines (Section 3.2).

3.1 Mutation Testing

Mutation testing can help developers to evaluate their test suite. It consists of introducing defects on to the code in order to modify its behavior. If a test suite fails to detect behavior change, it needs to be improved. There are a number of mutation testing tools, such as MuJava [6]. However, these tools may generate equivalent mutants. Then when a test suite does not kill a mutant, developers do not know whether the problem resides in their test suite or it is an equivalent mutant. We can use Safira in the program and on its mutant. If Safira does not detect any behavior changes, developers improve confidence that it is an equivalent mutant. However, if it finds a behavior change, Safira yields a test case by means of which developers can improve their test suite.

Testing mutation testing tools is nontrivial, since one needs structurally complex inputs such as programs. Moreover, an oracle is required to determine whether a transformation is behavior preserving. We propose an approach to test mutation testing tools based on Safira. To begin with, a number of programs are generated by JDolly, a Java program generator which, exhaustively, generates programs up to a given scope. It specifies a subset of Java metamodel in Alloy, a formal specification language. JDolly receives, as input, a scope (the maximum number of packages, classes, fields, and methods that a program must have), and the additional constraints. For every program generated, we use MuJava to generate mutants. Finally, Safira evaluates whether each mutant is functionally different from the original program.

For each mutation, we generated 100 programs using JDolly. We evaluated 11 mutations of MuJava and tested all of them by using a scope up to 4. For instance, our approach found 25 equivalent mutants for the IHD mutation. Some of them are related to the same bug. We manually analyzed them and classified in 2 distinct bugs. The first equivalent mutant was detected in 16 seconds. We found 17 bugs in 11 mutations.

3.2 Refactoring

Safira was also used in the refactoring context to assist developers in refactoring activities. We implemented an Eclipse plug-in — the user selects a refactoring to apply. Then the plug-in reports whether the transformation preserves behavior or not. Soares et al. [8] proposed an approach based on JDolly and SafeRefactor [7] to test

refactoring tools. They found a number of bugs in refactoring implementations of Eclipse and JRRT. We used their approach, but we replaced SafeRefactor for Safira. The impact analysis performed by Safira allows to generate tests guided by the change impact. We evaluate the results comparing our approach with theirs in terms of time consuming, test suite and correctness. We evaluated 10 kinds of refactorings. We detected 27 bugs related to behavioral changes.

4. Conclusion

Safira found a number of bugs in refactoring and mutation testing tools. To understand inheritance, this/super, package, accessibility modifiers and other Java constructs in isolation may be simple. However, when they are taken together, the task becomes nontrivial. So, it is difficult to propose all the conditions required by a transformation to preserve behavior, considering the whole scope of Java language. For example, a simple transformation, changing the access modifier, may have an impact on a number of Java constructs [9].

Steimann and Thies [9] formalized some refactoring conditions to change visibility. By negating some conditions, they proposed an approach to generate mutants [10]. However, they did not formally prove the conditions were correct. It is not simple to formally specify such conditions. Javalanche has identified a number of program invariants. If a mutation does not violate these invariants, then they are more likely to be equivalent mutants [5]. The tool implements four mutations. When Safira detects some behavior change, it yields a test case different from all previous approaches. Our technique is simple, and can be used to evaluate any kind of mutations. It can also be useful for testing tools.

Schäfer et al. [3] formally specified a number of refactorings and implemented them in JRRT, which outperformed Eclipse in terms of correctness. However, we have identified a number of bugs in JRRT. They already fixed some of the bugs found by us. SafeRefactor [7] has also identified the same bugs which were detected in Eclipse and JRRT. However, we have reduced the test suite and the total analysis time in 74% and 30%, respectively, on account of our change impact analyzer. Moreover, Safira is less dependent on the time limit used to generate tests. As future work, we intend to evaluate other refactoring and mutations testing tools.

References

[1] C. Pacheco, S. K. Lahiri, M. D. Ernst, and T. Ball. Feedback-directed random test generation. In *ICSE*, pages 75–84, 2007.

[2] X. Ren, B. G. Ryder, M. Stoerzer, and F. Tip. Chianti: a change impact analysis tool for java programs. In *ICSE*, pages 664–665, 2005.

[3] M. Schäfer and O. de Moor. Specifying and implementing refactorings. In *OOPSLA*, pages 286–301, 2010.

[4] M. Schäfer, T. Ekman, and O. de Moor. Challenge proposal: Verification of refactorings. In *PLPV*, pages 67–72, 2009.

[5] D. Schuler and A. Zeller. (Un-)Covering equivalent mutants. In *ICST*, pages 45–54, 2010.

[6] Y. seung Ma, J. Offutt, and Y. R. Kwon. MuJava: an automated class mutation system. *Software Testing, Verification and Reliability*, 15: 97–133, 2005.

[7] G. Soares, R. Gheyi, D. Serey, and T. Massoni. Making program refactoring safer. *IEEE Software*, 27:52–57, 2010.

[8] G. Soares, M. Mongiovi, and R. Gheyi. Identifying too strong conditions in refactoring implementations. In *ICSM*, 2011. To appear.

[9] F. Steimann and A. Thies. From public to private to absent: Refactoring java programs under constrained accessibility. In *ECOOP*, pages 419–443, 2009.

[10] F. Steimann and A. Thies. From behaviour preservation to behaviour modification: constraint-based mutant generation. In *ICSE*, pages 425–434, 2010.

Misfits in Abstractions: Towards User-centered Design in Domain-specific Languages for End-user Programming

Hiroki Nishino

NUS Graduate School for Integrative Sciences and Engineering, National University of Singapore

G0901876@nus.edu.sg

Abstract

In this paper, we discuss user-centered design of end-user programming languages with an example of computer music language. We describe an approach to analyze the misfits between the users' conceptualization and the programming language design in an existing usability problem with a focus on the abstraction layers both in conceptualization and language. When an entity in the users' conceptualization involved in problem-solving has no counterpart in a DSL, this can appear as a usability problem. Analysis of such a misfit caused by inappropriate abstraction in DSL design can contribute to better usability in end-user programming.

Categories and Subject Descriptors   H.5.2 [**User Interfaces**]: User-centered design

General Terms   Design, Human Factors, Languages.

Keywords   user-centered design; end-user programming; domain-specific language; computer music

1. Introduction

While end-user programming is becoming more popular, it is still largely unexplored in regards to how the usability of domain-specific languages (DSLs) for end-users can be improved with the perspective of user-centered design in mind. In this paper, we discuss this issue with a focus on abstraction. We propose a user-centered approach that starts from the analysis of a concrete instance of a usability problem in programming, with consideration the good fit/misfits between the users' conceptualization and the language design.

While abstraction is considered to play a significant role in software design, it is also considered that inappropriate abstraction can result in significant usability problems [1]. We extend such a view to discuss the design of DSLs for end-users. A DSL can involve many layers of abstraction. When some detail in the lower layer is made inaccessible from the higher layer, this can be a source of potential usability problems; If a certain entity or operation in the users' conceptualization that is involved in problem-solving has no accessible counterpart in a programming language because of inappropriate abstraction, such a situation can appear as a significant usability problem. The assessment of such misfits between the users' conceptualization and the language design can contribute to improve usability of DSLs so that users can facilitate their programming activity, making the best of their expertise knowledge for problem-solving.

2. Related Work

Blackwell discusses how inappropriate abstraction in software design can cause serious usability problems in [1].

Lee argues that *"the core abstraction of computing needs to be rethought to incorporate the essential properties of the physi-*

cal systems, most particularly the passage of time" in [6]. Though Lee's argument has a focus on 'time' in a computer system, yet it suggests that inappropriate abstraction in the abstraction layers of computing can cause a significant problem in the higher layers.

Blandford and her colleagues discuss their CASSM approach to evaluate usability by the goodness of fit between the users' conceptualization of a system and the actual implementation as the source of usability problems [3]. The approach *"focuses on concepts rather than tasks or processes"* and is considered to *"reveal potential problems of a semantic type that are not revealed by existing HCI approaches'* [4]. Such an analysis of misfits would also be appropriate for DSL design, since the tasks that the users want to achieve and the processes how they work can vary a lot and are considerably unforeseeable at the time when a programming language is being designed.

3. Misfits in Abstractions

In programming activity, programmers are considered to *"use knowledge from at least two domains, the application (or problem) domain and the computing domain, between which they establish a mapping"*[5, p22]. In this perspective, a DSL should be designed to facilitate such a mapping between these two domains for better usability in programming activity and any design that might cause difficulty in such mapping should be avoided.

The three views in the previous section suggest a perspective to assess such usability problems in DSL design when discussed altogether; (a) the abstraction layers in a DSL design can make some entity in the lower-layers less accessible or inaccessible. (b) Yet, the counterpart of this entity in problem domain may be involved in problem solving activity. (c) Mapping between the problem domain and the computing domain is made harder by the DSL design. (d) Such a situation appears as a usability problem caused by inappropriate abstraction in the DSL design.

Then, the analysis of the entities in the users' conceptualization of the problems and their expertise knowledge can help in avoiding inappropriate abstraction in a DSL design, and also assessing the existing usability problems. In the next section, we experimentally analyze a concrete example of usability problem in computer music programming in the view above.

4. Experimental Analysis and Proposed Design

In this section, we analyze a usability problem example of *single sample feedback* in *SuperCollider*[1], one of computer music languages widely used by computer musicians. Feedback loop with single sample is required even for a basic digital signal-processing task such as one-pole filter (Figure 1).

$$out(i) = (1 - abs(c)) * in(i) + c * out(i-1)$$

where $out(i)$ is the current output sample
$in(i)$ is the current input sample
$out(i-1)$ is the last output sample
c is the given filter coefficient.

Figure 1. One-pole filter algorithm

Many computer music environments compute signals in blocks of samples, not sample-by-sample for performance efficiency. This makes a feedback loop within the period smaller than the block size difficult or impossible in some environments; instead, most environments offer built-in objects for DSP algorithms that involve such a feedback loop. *SuperCollider* offers a built-in one-pole filter object written in C++ as in Figure 2 below.

```
01:{
02:var insig;
03:insig = WhiteNoise.ar(1);
04:OnePole.ar(insig * 0.5, -0.95);
05:}.play;
```

Figure 2. a built-in object of one-pole filter in *SuperCollider*

Such a solution to provide built-in objects does not contribute to improve the usability in end-user programming when the users' intention in programming is in '*exploratory design*' or '*exploratory understanding*' [2]; What users need is not one-pole filter itself, but to quickly experiment the related algorithms. Built-in objects won't be helpful for such a programming activity.

```
01:{
02://blksize is the signal block size for 1 dsp cycle
03:var blksize = Server.local.options.blockSize;
04:var coef    = -0.95;
05:var obuf    = LocalBuf(blksize);
06:var ibuf    = LocalBuf(blksize);
07:var in, out, lastout, insig;
09://write input (white noise) to the buffer
10:insig = WhiteNoise.ar(1);
11:insig = insig * 0.5;
12:BufWr.ar(insig, ibuf, Phasor.ar(0,1,0,blksize));
13://access each sample via built-in objects.
14:blksize.do {
15:    arg i; //the loop index.
16:    in = BufRd.kr(1, ibuf, i);
17:    out = ((1- abs(coef) * in)) + (coef * lastout);
18:    BufWr.kr(out, obuf, i);
19:    lastout = out;
20:};
21://recover a sample block from the buffer
22:BufRd.ar(1, obuf, Phasor.ar(0,1,0,blksize));
23:}.play
```

Figure 3. implementing one-pole filter only in *SuperCollider*

Yet, it is still possible to implement one-pole filter only in *SuperCollider* as in Figure 3. The strategy is to write the signal blocks once into buffers, where each sample can be accessible via some built-in objects. How can we assess this usability problem in perspective of misfits in abstractions? Two entities, *out* and *in*, in Figure 1 correspond to signal input/output. Also in Figure 3, there exist two entities (*insig* and *obuf*) that correspond to signal input/output as well. There is a certain fit between Figure 1 and Figure 2 for signal input/ouput. However, while each sample in output/input signals is also accessible as *out(i)*, *out(i-1)*, *in(i)* in Figure 1, *SuperCollider* offers no counterpart for such an direct access to a single sample in its design. As a result, the code in Figure 3 shows the usability problem of *viscosity* (resistance to change) [2] when the sample-level access is required; even when a sample-level access is required for some programming tasks, a user must read/write the signal via built-in objects.

This *viscosity* is caused by the lack of accessibility to each sample in blocks, which is abstracted at the lower level in language design. If so, recovering accessibility to each sample in blocks should contribute solving this usability problem. Figure 4 below is our proposed design for this problem. Each sample in a signal block or a *LocadBuf* is made accessible by an index value.

```
01:{
02://blksize is the signal block size for 1 dsp cycle
03:var blksize = Server.local.options.blockSize;
04:var coef    = -0.95;
05:var obuf    = LocalBuf(blksize);
06:var lastout, insig;
07://write input (white noise) to the buffer
08:insig = WhiteNoise.ar(1);
09:insig = insig * 0.5;
10://access each sample directly
11:blksize.do {
12:    arg i; //the loop index.
13:    obuf[i]=((1-abs(coef)*insig[i]))+(coef*lastout);
14:    lastout = obuf[i];
15:};
16://recover a sample block from the buffer
17:BufRd.ar(1, obuf, Phasor.ar(0,1,0,blksize));
18:}.play
```

Figure 4. proposed design for better fits

out(i) in Figure 1 and obuf[i] in Figure 4 are not completely the same; *out* is a stream of digital signal and *out(i)* stands for the sample at the current time, whereas 'obuf' in Figure 4 is a buffer and obuf[i] is the sample at the index *i* in the buffer. Yet, there is a better fit than the code in Figure 3, where there is no counterpart entity to *out(i)* and built-in objects must be used for sample-level access. By not abstracting away the direct access to each sample, *viscosity* shown in Figure 3 is also amended to a certain degree.

5. Conclusion

Programming activity involves the knowledge of both the problem domain and computing domain. It is important to facilitate the mapping between these two domains for better usability in domain-specific languages for end-users. While the users' conceptualization in the problem domain sometimes appears to be organized hierarchically or made of several abstraction layers and it may seem appropriate to abstract away some low-level entities in DSL design, for certain type of programming tasks, end-users need to manipulate some lower-level entity in the problem domain directly, or several entities in different abstraction levels at the same time. Inappropriate abstraction in the computing domain can cause a serious usability problem in such a situation. The analysis to asses the appropriateness of fit between the users' conceptualization and language design would help avoiding inappropriate abstraction in DSL for better usability in end-user programming.

References

[1] Blackwell, A.F. et al. *The Abstract is 'an Enemy': An Alternative Perspective to Computational Thinking, Proc of PPIG08* (2008)

[2] Blackwell, A.F. & Green, T.R.G. *Notational Systems – the Cognitive Dimensions of Notation Frameworks, HCI Models, Theories and Frameworks: Toward a Multidisciplinary Science, pp103-104,* Morgan Kaufmann (2003)

[3] Blandford, A et al. *Evaluating system utility and conceptual fit using CASSM.* Intl Jrnl of Human-Computer Studies, Vol. 66(6), (2008)

[4] Blandford, A & Green, T.R.G. *From tasks to conceptual structures: misfit analysis,* In Proc. IHM-HCI2001 Vol. 2. (2001)

[5] Détienne, F. *Software Design –Cognitive Aspects,* Springer Verlag (2001).

[6] Lee, E. *Computing Needs Time,* Communications of the ACM, 52(5), (2009)

[1] http://www.audiosynth.com

[2] While line 10 in Figure 3 actually assigns an instance of a WhiteNoise object to *insig* in *SuperCollider*, it can be treated virtually as a signal output as in line 11; doubling amplitude can be written as '*insig= insig*2*'

Coarse-Grain Speculation for Emerging Processors

Hari K. Pyla

Virginia Polytechnic Institute and State University

harip@cs.vt.edu

Categories and Subject Descriptors D.1.3 [*Programming Techniques*]: Concurrent Programming—Parallel programming; D.3.3 [*Programming Languages*]: Language Constructs and Features—Concurrent programming structures

General Terms Algorithms, Design, Languages, Measurement and Performance

Keywords Speculative Parallelism, Coarse-grain Speculation, Program Analysis, Concurrent Programming and Runtime Systems

1. Research Problem

The impending multi/many-core processor revolution requires that programmers leverage explicit concurrency to improve performance. Unfortunately, a large body of applications/algorithms are inherently hard to parallelize due to execution order constraints imposed by data and control dependencies or being sensitive to their input data and not scale perfectly, leaving several cores idle. *The goal of this research is to enable such applications leverage multi/many-cores efficiently to improve their performance.*

2. Motivation

The important application domain that will benefit from our approach are multiple equivalent algorithms whose performance differ depending on input data. For example, graph coloring is widely used in domains such as job scheduling, bandwidth allocation, pattern matching, and compiler optimization (register allocation). Existing approaches to this problem rely on probabilistic and meta-heuristic techniques, whose performance varies widely with the input parameters such as the graph's topology and number of colors. In addition to input sensitivity, graph coloring algorithms are hard to parallelize due to inherent data dependencies.

As another example, consider partial differential equations (PDEs) solvers in large scale simulations for computational science and engineering applications such as fluid dynamics, weather and climate modeling, structural analysis, and computational geosciences. The large, sparse linear systems of algebraic equations use preconditioned iterative methods, whose performance varies widely from problem to problem, even for related problem sequences (e.g., discrete time steps in a time-dependent simulation). Unfortunately, the best iterative method is not known a priori.

Yet another example are combinatorial problems including sorting, searching, permutations and partitions with well-known theoretical algorithmic bounds, but whose runtime depends on a variety of factors,s including the amount of input data (algorithmic bounds assume asymptotic behavior), the sortedness of the input data, and cache locality of the implementation [1].

3. Approach

This work equips programmers with a powerful tool for exploiting parallelism by means of *coarse-grain speculation*. Speculative execution at coarse granularities (e.g., codeblocks, methods, algorithms) offers a promising programming model for exploiting parallelism for many hard-to-parallelize applications.

Our programming model can express computation at any granularity, so that any application unit can be executed speculatively. Although the idea of coarse-grain "speculative execution" is relatively straightforward, its efficient implementation is strewn with challenges. Shared memory parallel programs are difficult to implement correctly, and so is detecting concurrency bugs (e.g., data races, deadlocks, order violations, atomicity violations) [5]. Hence, the programmer must not be burdened with using the low level threading primitives to create speculative control flows, manage rollbacks, and recover in the event of mis-speculations.

We present a simple speculative programming framework, Anumita (*guess* in Sanskrit), in which coarse-grain speculative code blocks execute concurrently, but the results from only a single speculation modify the program state. Anumita is implemented as a shared library that exposes APIs for common type-unsafe languages including C, C++ and Fortran. Its runtime system transparently (a) creates, instan-

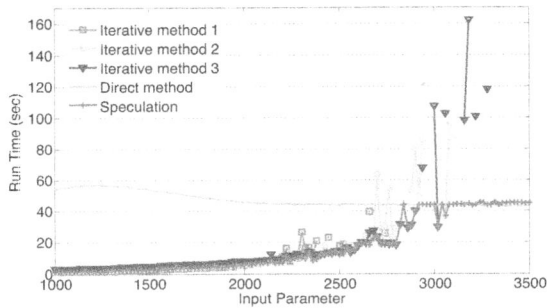

Figure 1. PDE solvers (iterative and direct); Y-axis: time-to-solution; X-axis: input parameter. Anumita consistently matches the fastest method for each problem.

tiates, and destroys speculative control flows, (b) performs name-space isolation, (c) tracks data accesses for each speculation, (d) commits the memory updates of successful speculations, and (e) recovers from memory side-effects of any mis-predictions.

Anumita associates each speculation flow's (e.g., an instance of a code block or a function) memory accesses in a speculation composition (loosely, a collection of possible code blocks that execute concurrently) and localizes them, isolating speculation flows through privatization of address space. Ultimately, a single speculation flow within a composition is allowed to modify the program state. We present well-defined semantics that ensures program correctness for propagating the memory updates. Anumita supports a wide range of applications by providing expressive evaluation criteria for speculative execution that go beyond *time to solution* to include arbitrary *quality of solution* criteria. Anumita simplifies speculative parallelism and relieves the programmer from the subtleties of concurrent programming.

Using Anumita requires minimal modifications (8-10 lines on average) to application source code. Additionally, the speculation-aware runtime manages memory and collects garbage from failed speculations. In the context of high-performance computing, with the prevalent OpenMP threading model, Anumita naturally extends speculation to an OpenMP context through a pragma.

4. Background and Related Work

Speculative execution is used in a variety of contexts to improve performance, including low level fine-grain speculation in hardware and compilation (e.g., branch prediction, prefetching). Software transaction systems rely on optimistic concurrency. In contrast to existing systems [1–4] Anumita neither relies on value speculation nor employs optimistic concurrency to achieve parallelism. It does not require annotating any variables nor rely on binary instrumentation or collect traces. Anumita introduces the notion of a non-deterministic choice operator to imperative programming.

5. Experimental Results

We evaluated Anumati using three real applications: a multi-algorithmic PDE solving framework, a graph (vertex) coloring problem, and a suite of sorting algorithms. Our experimental results indicate that Anumita is capable of significantly improving the performance of hard-to-parallelize and input sensitive applications by leveraging speculative parallelism. For instance, for the PDE solver (Figure 1) the speedup ranged from 0.84-36.19, for the graph coloring problem it ranged from 0.95-7.33, and for the sort benchmark it ranged from 0.84-62.95. With Anumita, it is possible to obtain the best solution among multiple heuristics. In some cases of heuristics failing to arrive at a solution, speculation guaranteed not only a solution but also the one that is nearly as fast as the fastest alternative. We are currently working on improving the performance of Anumita through program analysis and provide support for I/O.

6. Contributions

We presented Anumita, a language-independent runtime system for exploiting coarse-grain speculative parallelism in hard to parallelize and/or highly input sensitive applications *–an increasingly important problem in this multi/many-core era*. Our goal is to make speculation a first class parallelization method in such applications. Our research efforts aim at helping adapt and sustain the increasing core counts.

Additionally, Anumita's language transparency and simplicity, will relieve the programmer from the subtleties of concurrent programming and help enable its use with a wide variety of programming languages including C, C++ and Fortran. To our knowledge, Anumita is the first system to provide support for exploiting coarse-grain speculative parallelism in OpenMP based applications. Finally, using real applications we show how our proposed programming constructs achieve significant speedup without sacrificing performance, portability and usability.

References

[1] J. Ansel, C. Chan, Y. L. Wong, M. Olszewski, Q. Zhao, A. Edelman, and S. Amarasinghe. PetaBricks: A Language and Compiler for Algorithmic Choice. In *PLDI '09*, pages 38–49, 2009.

[2] E. D. Berger, T. Yang, T. Liu, and G. Novark. Grace: Safe Multithreaded Programming for C/C++. In *OOPSLA '09*, pages 81–96. ACM, 2009.

[3] C. Ding, X. Shen, K. Kelsey, C. Tice, R. Huang, and C. Zhang. Software Behavior Oriented Parallelization. In *PLDI '07*, volume 42, pages 223–234.

[4] P. Prabhu, G. Ramalingam, and K. Vaswani. Safe Programmable Speculative Parallelism. In *PLDI '10*, volume 45, pages 50–61, 2010.

[5] W. Zhang, C. Sun, and S. Lu. Conmem: Detecting Severe Concurrency Bugs Through an Effect-oriented Approach. In *ASPLOS '10*, spages 179–192, 2010.

Exploring Developer's Tool Path

Jelena Vlasenko

Free University of Bolzano/Bozen

Piazza Domenicani – Domenikanerplatz, 3 I – 39100 Bolzano – Bozen, Italy
+39 0471 016138
Jelena.Vlasenko@stud-inf.unibz.it

Abstract

In this study we introduce the concept of "cycle" in daily work of software developers. A cycle is occurs when a developer working on a tool switches to another tool, or also to more, and eventually goes back to the first tool. Using the concept of cycle we explore how the developers distribute their time and navigate among different tools during their work. Analysing the cycles can be beneficial for identifying effective strategies for improvement both of the development processes and of how computers (and their tools) are designed and used.

The approach has been validated on data collected non-invasively from team of professional developers for 10 months.

Categories and Subject Descriptors

D.2.9 [Software Engineering]: Management – *productivity, programming teams*

General Terms

Management, Measurement, Human Factors.

Keywords

Cycles of work, non-invasive data collection, tool usage

1. The Research Problem and Motivation

Despite almost 50 years of studies, it is still mostly unclear how people develop software, especially how they interact with each other and with computers to achieve the desired results. Such understanding would enable the definition of very effective strategies for improvement, both of the development processes and of how computers, and tools within computers, are designed and used. In particular, it is still mostly unknown how people use tools to work on their tasks. We know only that people tend to use classes of tools for specific tasks: say, they typically use IDE (Visual Studio, Eclipse, ...) for development, Word Processors (Microsoft Word, OpenOffice, ...) for text processing, etc. Still, we do not know what they exactly do with their tools – for instance, they could do some editing of C code with OpenOffice just because they have OpenOffice open and they would not like to launch an IDE. Moreover, developers tend to use multiple different tools to achieve desired results. For instance, often while developing the code they use both the IDE and the browser: they use the IDE to write and test the code and the browser to gather information. Still, very limited research has been done so far on

how multiple tools cooperate together to achieve specific goals. This problem contains **two** very important aspects. The **first** is on how data are collected on tool usage, so that it is possible to determine exactly which tool a developer is using at a given time. This has been addressed using tools like PROM [1]. PROM is a tool that runs on a background on a developer's machine and collects data about his/her activities. The main advantage of PROM is that the developer does not even perceive that his/her activities are being recorded. Thus, using PROM for data collection allows to obtain the data that represent developer's real activities in real working environment. The **second** aspect is how to structure the data on tool usage. This problem has been approached recently with L-Graphs [2, 5]. An L-Graph is a directed, labeled graph containing information on individual tool usage and on the transitions between tools. However, L-Graphs do not represent in details how different tools are used together to perform tasks. Such information is especially important to establish process improvement initiatives and to design more effective tools.

This paper is organized as follows. In Section 2 we present some of the existing work done in this area; Section 3 describes the proposed approach; Section 4 discussed the results we have obtained so far; Section 5 draws some conclusions and outlines the future research we plan to do in this area.

2. Background and Related Work

Very limited research has been published on how developers use tools. Most of the existing works focus on identifying purposes and drawbacks of the tools aiming to propose substitutes or enhanced versions of these tools. For example, [4] investigates which features are the most used and best implemented in the installed CASE tools. It has been found that developers are not satisfied with the existing CASE tools and most of the advanced features are not used. Furthermore, in [3] authors aim to identify how to improve the tools that are used by developers to increase productivity. It has been identified that there is a need for a tool that would help to explore existing software. Still, it has not been studied yet how the different tools are used together and how they interact. The idea proposed in [5] approaches this problem. In [5] authors focus on time distribution, frequencies of switching between tools, and average time to stay in a tool before switching. L-Graphs are used to visualize these variables. This idea has been applied in [2]. The results indicate that the developers doing Pair Programming are more focused on directly productive activities than the developers working alone.

3. Approach and Uniqueness

In this study we introduce a definition of a cycle and show some preliminary results. A cycle is defined as follows: assuming that a developer is working a tool A, a cycle occurs when he/she switches to a tool B and possibly to other tool, and eventually returns to A. The number of steps involved in the cycle is called the size of the cycle: if a user starts in A, then switches to B, and then goes back to A, then the size of the cycle is 2. Cycles could be of any size: between two usages of the same tool there can be any number of other tools usages. However, the meaningfulness of a cycle is only when we can assume that there is a cause in the use of the original tool that triggers the move to other tools and eventually the come back. In this work we introduce a concept of a cycle and show some preliminary results. In the future work we want to keep a track of history: we want to identify if a developer works on a task T in a tool A, then he switches to a tool B to continue working on the task T, and then goes back to the tool A to continue working on the same task. Analyzing cycles could help to understand better how different people develop software, how they organize their working process, and how to improve it [7]. One of the improvement proposals could be the following: if there is a very strong connection between tools it might be useful to ingrate them so that developers would not loose time and focus when switching. Another possible benefit of studying cycles is to it identify those cycles when developers are unproductive and to understand the reasons why it so.

4. Results and Contributions

The data for this study have been collected from a team of professional software developers working in a IT department of a large Italian manufacturing company which prefers to remain anonymous. The dataset represents a time frame of 10 months: October 2007 – July 2008. The team is composed of 17 developers all with more than 15 years of experience. In our previous work [5] we found that during this period the developers were using 26 distinct tools and that 80% of the total time was devoted to the following 9 tools: Visual Studio, Browser, Outlook, Word, Excel, Microsoft Management Console, Microsoft Messenger, Remote Desktop, and Windows Explorer. In this study we are interested only in these 9 most time consuming tools.

To compute cycles, we extracted switching sequences in a time-based order. Each record in the sequence consists of two parameters: a tool itself and the time spent in this tool before switching to another one. Then we calculated all the possible

cycles of size 2. We got 72 cycles. For these cycles we computed the following 3 parameters: percentage of time (represented by y-axis in Figure 1) developers spent in each cycle, percentage of cycles (represented by y-axis in Figure 1), and average time (AVG in the Figure 1) developers spent in a cycle. Percentage of time spent in a cycle, total number of cycles, and average time spent in a cycle were computed with respect to the whole time frame. We found that in the given time frame the developers spent more time in the cycles where Visual Studio was involved either as a starting or as a middle tool. Figure 1 represents 9 most time-consuming cycles. Other cycles consume less than 3% of the total time. The obtained results indicate that the most time consuming cycles are those where are involved the following 3 tools: Visual Studio, Browser, and Outlook. From the developers we know that they receive their requirements via Outlook what explains a very strong connection between email client and Outlook [6]. Furthermore, we noticed that the developers spend a lot of time switching from Visual Studio to Browser and back. We assume that the reason why the developers spend so much time in this cycle is because Browser is a source of knowledge and is essential for their daily work.

5. Conclusions and Future Work

In this study we introduced an idea of a cycle in daily work of software developers. A cycle is a unit of work when a developer goes to one tool, then starts switching between other tools, and eventually returns to the starting tool. The obtained results indicate that the developers spend a notable part of their time in those cycles where are involved the following 3 tools: Visual Studio, Browser, and Outlook. The idea proposed in this study helps to understand better how people use tools when developing software. In future work we want to expand the idea of a cycle and to consider also task history when switching between tools: i.e. we want to identify which tools developers use to work on particular tasks. This information could be helpful to improve software development process. It would be possible to identify the tools that are mainly distractive – when developers start switching between tools and loose focus, and the tools that really needed for work purposes and how to improve them to facilitate the process.

6. References

[1] Abrahamsson, P., Moser, R., Pedrycz, W., Sillitti, A., Succi, G. Effort Prediction in Iterative Software Development Processes – Incremental Versus Global Prediction Models. In Proceedings of ESEM2007, Madrid, Spain, 2007

[2] Fronza, I., Sillitti, A., Succi, G., Vlasenko, J. Does Pair Programming Increase Developers' Attention? In Proceedings of ESEC/FSE2011, Szeged, Hungary, September 2011

[3] Lethbridge, T.C. and Singer, J., "Understanding Software Maintenance Tools: Some Empirical Research," In Workshop on Empirical Studies of Software Maintenance, pp 157-162, 1997

[4] Maccari, A., Riva, C., and Maccari F., "On CASE tool usage at Nokia," In Proceedings of ASE2002, pp 59-68, 2002

[5] Sillitti, A., Succi, G, Vlasenko, J. 2011. Toward a better understanding of tool usage. In Proceedings of ICSE2011, Honolulu, Hawaii, May 2011

[6] Sillitti, A., Ceschi, M., Russo, B., Succi, G., Managing uncertainty in requirements: a survey in documentation-driven and agile companies. In Proceedings of ESEM2005, Como, Italy, 2005

[7] Succi, G., Pedrycz, W., Liu, E., Yip, J. Package-oriented software engineering: a generic architecture. IT Professional, 3(2), pp 29 – 36, 2002

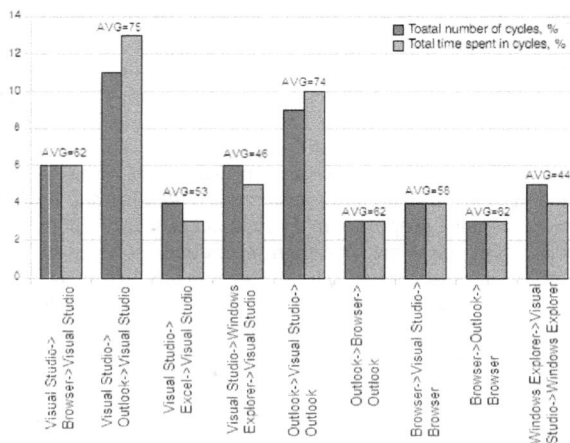

Figure 1: Cycles in daily work of software developers

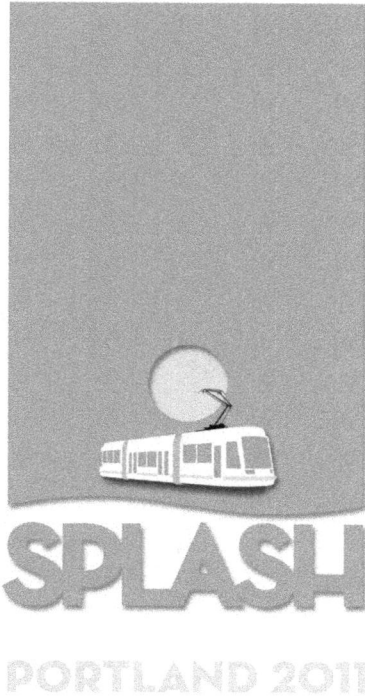

SPLASH 2011
Wavefront Chair's Welcome

This is the first year for Wavefront, a new component of SPLASH. Wavefront was created to provide a forum for reporting on innovative work that occurs in the gap between academic computer science research and everyday software engineering. The Wavefront is about the systems that innovative software developers are creating and deploying today.

In defining Wavefront, we wanted to make sure that its submission process was approachable to practicing software professionals who were unfamiliar with the process of creating and submitting a refereed conference paper. To this end we solicited submission of both complete papers and of extended abstracts for paper proposals. Program committee members shepherded the authors of accepted proposals as they prepared their final conference papers.

Both full papers and extended abstract proposals were evaluated by the program committee based upon the following criteria:

- Novelty: The paper presents new applications, system architectures, software designs, user interfaces, development tools, or implementation techniques.
- Interest: The paper addresses a significant and immediate problem or opportunity. The results in the paper have potential for immediate impact on state-of-the art software development projects.
- Evidence: The paper presents implemented designs, system case studies, or intriguing observations. Preference will be given to papers based upon deployed systems.
- Clarity: The paper is clearly written and understandable by practicing software developers. However, shepherding will be available for papers that present good ideas but need help in their presentation.

The Wavefront committee received a total of twelve submissions, six full papers and six extended abstract proposals. Of these, six papers were accepted including three paper proposals requiring shepherding. In addition, two Wavefront submissions were accepted as SPLASH Experience Reports.

Thank you to all the authors, reviewers, and shepherds who contributed to this first Wave program.

Allen Wirfs-Brock
SPLASH 2011 Wavefront Program Chair
Mozilla Corporation

The JavaScript World Domination Plan at 16 Years

Brendan Eich
Mozilla Foundation
USA
brendan@mozilla.com

Abstract

The title says it all.

Categories and Subject Descriptors
D 1.5 [**Object Oriented Programming**]

General Terms   Design, Languages

Keywords   *JavaScript*

1.   Biography

Brendan Eich is CTO of Mozilla and widely recognized for his enduring contributions to the Internet revolution. In 1995, Eich invented JavaScript (ECMAScript), the Internet's most widely used programming language. He also co-founded the mozilla.org project in 1998, serving as chief architect. Eich helped launch the award winning Firefox Web browser in November 2004 and Thunderbird e-mail client in December 2004. Today, Eich's central focus is guiding the future technical work to keep Mozilla vital and competitive. In the greater Web community, Eich remains dedicated to driving innovation in Internet technology with his work in JavaScript and with the Mozilla platform.

In August 2005, Eich became CTO of Mozilla. He has also been a board member of the Mozilla Foundation since its inception in 2003. He holds a bachelor of science in math and computer science from Santa Clara University and a master of science in computer science from the University of Illinois. Eich and his wife have four children.

Improving User Experience by Infusing Web Technologies into Desktops

Jonathan Bardin   Philippe Lalanda

Laboratoire d'Informatique de Grenoble &
Université de Grenoble
Grenoble, France
{firstname.lastname}@imag.fr

Clément Escoffier   Alice Murphy

akquinet AG
Berlin, Germany
{firstname.lastname}@akquinet.de

Abstract

Modern applications are able to adapt their architecture dynamically in order to tackle requirements, correctives and context changes. Such dynamism is often an echo of complexity and is not well supported by traditional client and user software stacks making complex the design, implementation and maintenance of the end user interface. Meanwhile, the web has seen the emergence of user interface technologies (e.g. HTML5, CSS3, JavaScript) widely adopted by developers to create highly flexible user interfaces. However, such clients are intrinsically bound to run on a web browser which is out of the control of the application.

In this paper, we present ChameRIA, an application framework where a browser engine is reified as a component within the framework, thus allowing for better control over the rendering engine. We describe how we preserve a clear separation of concerns between the user interface and the application logic while maintaining coherence between them. We discuss how ChameRIA has been successfully used in two projects: a DRM document reader and a valve control application.

Categories and Subject Descriptors   D.2.11 [*Software Engineering*]: Software Architectures—Languages,Patterns

General Terms   Design, Experimentation, Reliability

Keywords   Runtime software evolution, components, service, OSGi, JavaScript

1. Introduction

Nowadays, application availability is critical, not just in high-risk spheres like the financial and aerospace industries, but also in everyday applications such as operating systems and Internet services. Indeed, as already noted by Oreizy at the end of the 90s [25]:

> "Continuous availability is a critical requirement for an important class of software systems."

However, software must also adapt and evolve over its lifetime. Software engineering research has highlighted the importance of taking these evolutions into account in the software life-cycle. Although these types of changes are familiar to developers and architects, it is also increasingly necessary to accommodate them later in the life-cycle. It is therefore imperative to emphasize approaches that allow us to address the issues while minimizing the downtime of the application in other words, to be able to apply changes during execution [20][5].

In prior work, we and others have proposed service-oriented component approach to supporting application changes during execution [24][6][19][9]. Such approach allows us to designed and developed extensible applications capable of change during execution [4]. Unfortunately, this extremely dynamic resource availability is not well-supported by traditional client and user interface software stacks. Desktop user interface technologies such as Swing, SWT and QT all have severe limitations. Swing and QT pose too many difficulties in terms of threading, are not modular, and are not easily adaptable. SWT, while modular, requires manual object deallocation which is delicate for the developer and can hurt extensibility [12].

Despite the usefulness of those user interface technologies, such concerns make their cohabitation with the application logic in a same dynamic framework deeply critical. Indeed, dynamic frameworks (e.g. OSGi) are based on dynamic loading/linking language capabilities. Applications evolves at run-time thanks to the dynamic loading and unloading of modules. If the complexity associated with the dynamic loading of modules is hidden from developers thanks to the framework, the intrinsic problematic persists.

Each modification within the application logic potentially impacts the user interface and reciprocally. This underlying behavior implies that each unintended behavior within the user interface modules can result in memory leaks and incoherent states in the long-run as well as the crash of the whole application. In OSGi those problematics are linked to the manipulation of distinct java ClassLoader for each module of the application, manipulation which can result in linking errors during the execution and in the apparition of dangling objects within the framework [13] (i.e. Stale Reference [1] in OSGi). This question of isolation make the usage of classic desktop user interface technologies potentially harmful for dynamic applications.

The web, meanwhile, has seen the emergence of user interface technologies such as HTML5, CSS3 and JavaScript. These have been widely adopted by developers to create highly flexible user interfaces. The recent adoption of the web-socket makes it possible to push asynchronous changes to the client. Furthermore, recent browser evolution allows for the isolation of web programs instances from each other, thus improving stability and performance [30][11]. Nevertheless, such clients are intrinsically bounded to run on a browser engine which is out of the control of the application. This restriction could lead to a lack of reliability and convenience (no file association, device access) for the user [2][18].

In this work, our goal is to take the best in terms of dynamism of both world, the OSGi platform and the browser client technologies. That is, we are able to provide an homogeneous framework for the design and runtime management of rich client applications. We thus propose ChamRIA an application framework which target the development of dynamic application and their user interface. We present a new software stack and its architecture were the user interface is fully developed in web technologies and run on an rendering engine while the application logic is fully developed in java and run on an OSGi platform, thus isolated from the user interface runtime. To better control the browser engine, we present how we have integrated the browser within the framework thus allowing to easily create and configure a browser window following a factory pattern. We discussed how using a service-oriented component programming model in both the development of the web user interface and the application logic helps to tackled down the problematic induced by the dynamism of the application and the runtime heterogeneity.

The rest of this paper is organized as follows. The next section gives a brief background on OSGI. We then present the ChameRIA approach and show how it allows for the creation of dynamic applications (from the application logic to the user interface) in section 3. In section 4, we describe the framework implementations and how to create an application on top of this framework. The section 5 describes how a ChameRIA application is able to evolve at runtime. We introduce two projects: a DRM document reader and a valve control application which have been developed on top of ChamRIA in section 6. In section 7, we consider the limitations and dissonances of our approach, along with different application domain. Finally, we discuss related work in section 8 and conclude in section 9.

2. OSGi

OSGi (formerly known as Open Services Gateway Initiative) is both a component-based platform and a service platform for the Java programming language. OSGi aims to facilitate the modularization of Java applications as well as their interoperability. The OSGi framework can be divided into three distinct layers:

Module layer: This layer allows for the division of a Java application into modules. An OSGi unit of modularization is called a *bundle*. Bundles address some of the weaknesses of Java's deployment model; a bundle extends the Java Archive files (JAR) with a special *manifest*. The manifest is used to specify static information about the bundle, such as the Java packages shared or required by the bundles. The module layer needs those information in order to install correctly and activate a bundle within the framework. In OSGi, bundles are the only entities for deploying Java-based applications.

Life cycle layer: The life cycle layer defines a runtime model for bundles. This model specify how bundles are started, stopped, installed, updated and uninstalled. Fundamentally, the life-cyle layer provides an API to control the bundles. This API covers the installation, starting, stopping, updating, uninstalation as well as the monitoring of bundles. This layer depends on the module layer.

Service layer: The service layer is the heart of dynamism in OSGi. It allows for the creation of component depending on services rather that other components. This enable a concise model built on interface based programming. Bundles developers are able to bind to services only using their interface specification. Services are not a component model but enable a true component model by reifing the coupling between components [17].

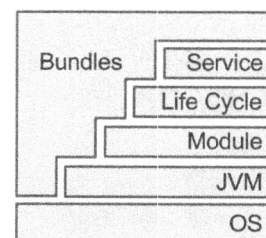

Figure 1. OSGi layers.

3. ChameRIA

3.1 Motivation

The OSGi Service layer allows for a smooth functional coupling between bundles. Unfortunately, in practice, bundles are tightly coupled via their packages. This coupling can result in complex problems such as dangling objects and linkage exceptions during the execution, especially when bundles are installed, updated or uninstalled. One common way to address this problem in OSGi is to extract interface packages in specific bundles containing only the application service interface package. In that way consumer and producer bundles are not coupled together via their interface packages since it is contained in an independent bundle. Such bundles can thus be updated independently from one and other, the dynamism being handled by the Service layer. However, such a process is not always possible, and in practice most of bundles don't even use the service layer (figure 2). Developing a rich client interface in OSGi means wrapping existing java UI libraries into one or several bundles. This operation is laborious, especially if we want to introduce the notion of service into such library in order to use the OSGi Service layer, that is to say, to be able to update the application at runtime.

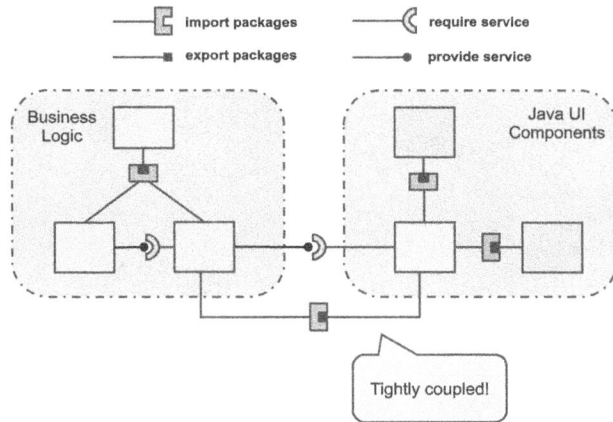

Figure 2. Rich client application.

In order to address this problem and thus to be able to create rich dynamic client applications we propose to use web technologies as a means to develop the dynamic application User Interface (UI). In contrast to classic Java UI technologies, web technologies can easily handle the notion of consuming a service. Furthermore, running UI components in a browser engine allows to fully isolate them from the application logic components, thus avoiding packages coupling between them (figure 3).

3.2 Concepts

The key concept behind ChameRIA is to merge web technologies into the OSGi world (figure 4). ChameRIA is both

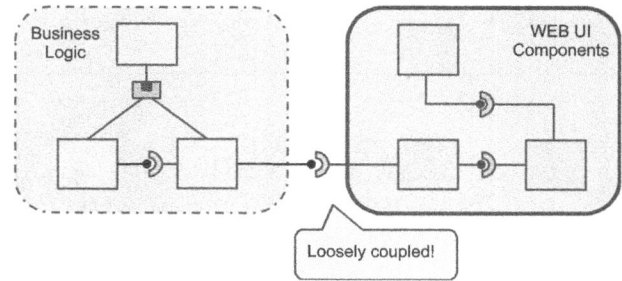

Figure 3. ChameRIA rich client application.

a service-oriented component framework and a web browser (engine supplied by WebKit [35]). The seamless integration of the web browser within the modular platform allows the application's user interface to be built as a web application, while the business part is done in Java.

Furthermore, ChameRIA follows the service-oriented component principles [6]:

1. A service is a provided functionality.

2. A service is characterized by a service contract (i.e. service specification). The contract describes some combination of the service's syntax, behavior, semantics and dependencies on other services.

3. A component implements a contract. In this way, a component provides a service.

4. The service-oriented interaction pattern is used to resolve service dependencies at runtime.

5. Compositions are described in terms of contracts.

6. Contracts are the basis for substitutability. A component can be substituted for another if it implements the same contract.

By following these rules, ChameRIA enables strong support for dynamic availability of services. Indeed, substitutability is encouraged since the compositions are described in terms of specification rather than a specific implementation. Another important principle is the service-oriented interaction pattern which enables the resolution of all service dependencies at runtime.

In conformance with these principles, the WebKit browser component is reified within the framework as a component (figure 4). This component allows the browser view to be created following the factory pattern [28]. It is fundamental to note that while this service provides the functionalities to manipulate the appearance and the behavior of the browser itself, it does not actually construct the web pages. Indeed, the main goal is to use the afore-mentioned web technologies (such as HTML5, CSS3 and JavaScript) in order to develop the user interface.

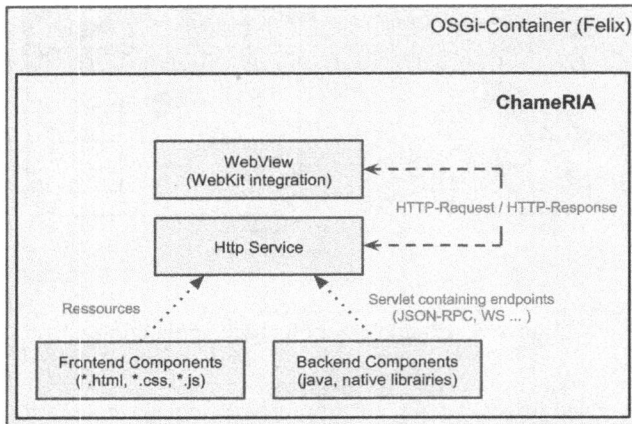

Figure 4. ChameRIA architecture overview.

While the integration of the browser engine within the framework is essential, a clear separation between the Application logic and the interface (web client) allows for a simpler and more efficient development model. Such separation of concerns is achieved by following the client-server style [3] (figure 5). Indeed, by moving all of the user interface functionality into the client, the application logic and the user interface can evolve independently.

This separation can be defined with three simple principles:

1. All communication between the server and client is contract-based and done through the use of virtual objects (e.g. JSON-RPC proxies, REST virtual resources).

2. No part of the web client should be evoked, generated or templated from the server-side. This rules out in-line conditional HTML in JSP, ASP, PHP etc.

3. The server will only implement the business logic.

In order to respect these principles, communications between the application logic (server) and the web user interface (client) are assured by service remote proxies (figure 5). Basically, each service of the server which is required to be invoked from the client is automatically exported through an endpoint. The client is notified and a proxy providing the service contract within the client is dynamically created and made available. Thanks to the service-oriented pattern which enables the resolution of all service dependencies at runtime, the coherence between the web user interface and the application logic is maintained. Indeed, in this way, the proxy service availability within the client is mapped on the service availability within the server. This runtime adaptation can be summed up in five steps:

1. The framework is notified of the availability of a service within the server.

2. If the service must be available within the client an endpoint is created.

3. The client is notified of the endpoint availability through the publication of the contract.

4. A proxy is created which provides the service contract and delegates to the endpoint.

5. If the service is no longer available, the client is notified, the proxy is destroyed along with the endpoint. Thus, the coherence between the server and the client is maintained.

4. Drilling Down

4.1 Browser Integration

The ChameRIA browser is based on the WebKit project. The integration of the browser consist of two modules: the ChameRIA launcher and the *WebViewFactory* component.

First, the Chameria launcher is a wrapper around the webkit gui and the osgi framework. It allows to start the browser engine and the osgi framework as a monolithic application. Secondly, the *WebViewFactory*; each instance of this component receives a configuration, create a browser windows and provides a *BrowserService* through which we can change several property of the web view. Those properties include the window: URL, size, full-screen mode, context menu and the menu bar.

A simple configuration of a *WebView* is the following:

```
#url to load
url = http://localhost:8080/web/index.html

#menu bar
menu.bar = true

#size
resizable = true
fullscreen = false
scrollbar.horizontal=ScrollBarAsNeeded
scrollbar.vertical=ScrollBarAsNeeded

#features
download=false
print=false

# no context menu
# to change before releasing
context.menu=true
inspector=true

#disable local storage
storage=false

application.name=chameria

width= 1200
```

WebView instance configuration.

4.2 The Communication Machine

Both, the application logic and the web user interface are designed and implemented on top of a service-oriented component framework. This particularity allows for a smooth functional cohesion between server and client components. However, both framework are running on two separate run-time machine. Additionally, the application logic is implemented

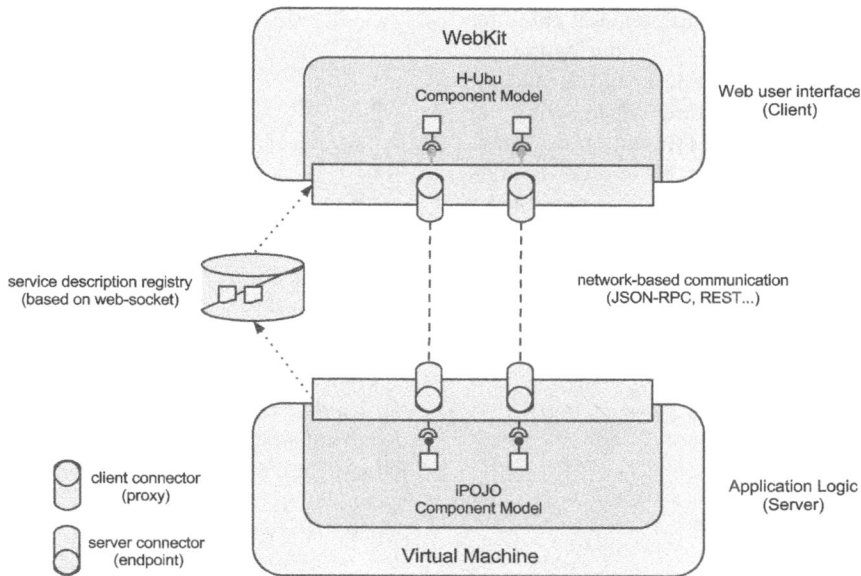

Figure 5. ChameRIA detailed architecture.

in Java while the logic part of the web user interface is implemented in JavaScript.

We addressed those problems via the automatic creation of virtual objects (i.e. proxies). In order to make available a service from the server within the client we define a filter. Each service matching this filter are tracked during the execution. When such service is available on the server, an endpoint is created. Once the endpoint has been successfully created, the contract is published through a network registry. Eventually, the client is notified of the endpoint availability; then a proxy which provides the same contract and delegates to the endpoint is instantiated within the client.

This process is hidden from the applications developers. Programmers are able to access to a remote service in the same way that a local one. The distributed nature of a service is transparent. This notion of transparency has been deeply encouraged in loosely coupled distributed systems [33] [15]. However, such a centralized view of the system must not be the only tool available for programmers. Actually, problems of centralized systems are subsumed by those inherent in distributed systems; it would be illusory and counterproductive to handle a distributed systems exclusively as a centralized system. Especially for aspects such as performance and fault tolerance [36] [8].

We avoid 6 of the 8 fallacies of distributed computing by using remote communication between two virtual machines which are actually running on the same physical machine (i.e. the desktop). This singularity means that we can legitimately assume that: the network is reliable, latency is zero, the network is secure, bandwidth is infinite, transport cost

is zero and the network is homogeneous. The fact that the topology does not change is questionable but can be modelled by service availability. The last common assumption is that there is only one administrator. In our approach, both the web user interface and the application logic can be administrated separately.

In order to ease the administration of the services which are distributed, we have introduce introspection mechanisms and a declarative way to configure the distributed aspect of the application. A specific API enables to know at runtime if a service have an endpoint or if it is provided through a proxy, as well as the endpoint metadata such as the underlying communication protocol and the endpoint address.

The following configuration file specifies that an endpoint must be created for each instance providing an *HelloService* service, the endpoint must be invokable using JSON-RPC protocol.

```
{
  "machine" : {
    "id" : "server",
    "host" : "localhost",

    "connection" : [
      "out" : {
        "service_filter" : "(objectClass=acme.HelloService)",
        "protocol" : [ "jsonrpc" ]
      }
    ]
  }
}
```

Communication configuration.

The configuration example shows that the application logic machine (i.e. OSGi & iPOJO, discussed in the next section) provides HelloServices service through the JSON-

RPC protocol. The configuration is interpreted at runtime, that is to say that changing the configuration during the execution comes to modify this configuration file. Basically, both runtimes are modelled as meta-component sharing the same network registry. We discuss in the section 6 of how we can use our communication framework in order to construct network based applications and how it is possible to address the remaining fallacies of distributed computing, as well as limitations of this approach.

This program show how to use the *HelloService* which runs on the server from the client.

```
..
var jsonrpc = new JSONRpcClient("/JSON−RPC");
var greeting = jsonrpc.helloService.hello("Dave");
$('#greeting').text(greeting);
..
```

HelloService client proxy.

4.3 Building the Application Logic

ChameRIA has been implemented on top of iPOJO. iPOJO is a service-oriented component runtime which eases the development of applications on top of OSGi [1].One main concern with OSGi is that the Service model leaves service dependency management as a manual task for component developers. iPOJO uses inversion of control in order to wrap your plain old Java object within a container. The container handles all service-oriented interactions (e.g. service publication, service object creation, service requirement and selection).

Developing an iPOJO component is as straightforward as creating a Java class. POJO classes are manipulated (via byte-code injection) to become iPOJO component. This bytecode injection process is done at compilation time and allows to easily create a bundle containing an iPOJO component and its specification.Thus, bundles are used as a deployment unit and, thanks to the OSGi module layer, as a mean to resolve packages dependencies. Once a bundle has been deployed and started, iPOJO handle the service dependency management, linking component together thanks to the component specification which has been generated at compilation time and which contains its provided and required services. Additionally, iPOJO provides extension mechanisms known as *handlers* which allows a container to support several non-functional aspects such as security, persistence, scheduling and so on; each handler managing one non-functional property.

The following class realizes a simple iPOJO component which implements the Hello contract.

```
@Component(name="acme.hello.component")
@Instanciate(name="helloService") //default instance
@Provides //Provide HelloService
public class MyComponent implements HelloService{

    @Requires(optional=true) //require a Log Service
    private LogService logger;
```

```
    public String hello(String name){
        return "Hello "+name+" !";
    }

    @Validate //on validation callback
    private void start(){
        logger.log(INFO,"HelloService started.");
    }

    @InValidate //on invalidation callback
    private void stop(){
        logger.log(INFO,"HelloService stopped");
    }
}
```

A simple iPOJO component

Annotations can be replaced by a special file called *metadata.xml*, both are parsed during compilation time in order to manipulate the class and to add the iPOJO component specification to the bundle manifest. The component specification contains its service requirements (*@Requires*), capabilities(*@Provides*) and life-cycle callback (*@Validate*,*@InValidate*).

4.4 Building the Web User Interface

Recently, JavaScript has become mainstream and is used by the majority of web-app stacks. A number of frameworks and libraries such as DOJO and JQuery have been proposed in order to simplify coding. However, such libraries do not help with structuring the code. With the growth of complexity of our user interface, we identified a stringent requirement for a component model structuring our JavaScript code.

We defined a component model named H-Ubu, supporting:

1. component definition : the code is organized into components

2. component injections : components can be injected in other components

3. contract-based interactions : components implement and use contracts (i.e. interfaces)

4. synchronous and asynchronous component communication : components can interact using method calls and events

5. architecture description : the application is composed by registering components and binding them

6. component configuration : components can be configured

7. test : components are testable !

8. component separations: components are developed in separate files, the application code is more scalable.

To start with an example, the following programme shows how to compose an application with H-Ubu:

```
<script src="http://../jquery−latest.js"></script>
<script src="hubu.js"></script>
<script src="backendComponent.js"></script>
<script src="frontendComponent.js"></script>

<!−− The contracts −−>
```

230

```
<script src="UserServiceContract.js"></script>

<script type="text/javascript">

  $(document).ready(function(){
    // Component registrations
    hub
    .registerComponent(backendComponent(), {
      component_name: 'user'
    })
    .registerComponent(frontendComponent(), {
      loginId : '#login',
      logoutId : '#logout',
      statusId : '#status',
      component_name: 'frontend'
    })
    // Declare a binding
    .bind({
        component: 'user',
        to:'frontend',
        into: 'bind', // method called on 'to'
        contract: UserServiceContract // The interface
    })
    // Start the app
    .start();
  });

</script>
```

A simple composition in H-Ubu

The first thing is to import the H-Ubu library, and other dependencies (e.g JQuery), then the component, and finally the contract. In our example, we assume that the contract is implemented by the back-end component. When the page is loaded, we register our components on a special H-Ubu object : hub. This is the *nerve* of the application. As you can see, components receive configurations. The front-end component also receives the HTML *ids* to manipulate the page indirectly. The bind method allows injection of the back-end component into the front-end component. Notice that the binding specifies the contract to use for this interaction. Finally, we start the hub, i.e. the application.

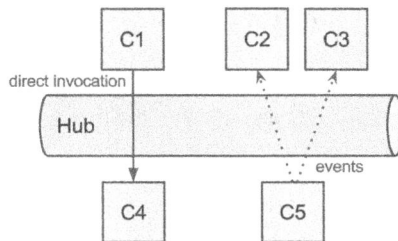

Figure 6. H-Ubu concepts.

In order to improve the modularity we proposed that each component must be define in one JavaScript file. Our web user interface can thus be realized as an assemblage of components. It also becomes easier to follow an MVC pattern [29]. *Controllers* component can easily be bind with *Models* component in order to manipulate the *Views* (HTML DOM). In our approach, Model components are the proxies of some applications logic services. An other aspect of H-Ubu component is the notion of scope. Components supports private and public members; the contracts making ob-

vious the public member of there code. Once a component has been bind to another component, it can invoke the injected component only through its contract. Actually, H-Ubu injects a proxy in order to ensure that only the contract methods are used. Component also support testing. Each component can be tested separately but it is also possible to perform integration test by assembling the component which are required to be tested.

4.5 Web Code Integration

The *HttpService* which is part of the OSGi specification allows bundles in the OSGi framework to register resources to be accessed via HTTP. Practically, the web resources (JavaScript, HTML, PNG, CSS files and so on) are included in the bundle resource. Then the developer must implement a *BundleActivator* as a mean to get the *HttpService* in order to register the resources on the embedded web server providing the *HttpService*. This approach caused us two complication during the development of our applications. The first one was that the graphic artist and web developer in charge of creating the web user interfaces had no experienced with OSGi. Ideally, they should not need deep knowledge of OSGi, particularly not the graphic designer. The second one is that it is deeply annoying to have to repack and then update the bundle containing the web code in order to test the result between each modification.

These two inconvenience led us to the creation of a specific component called: *WebExposer*. This simple component use the *HttpService* in order to publish the content of a local folder. Each resource request on the HTTP server are delegated to the file system. Thanks to that component, web developers are able to test their applications without having to handle OSGi and just have to refresh their browser in order to access to the last version.

Once the web user interface has been fully developed and tested by the web developers and graphic artists, it can be packaged in several bundles (e.g. one bundle by H-Ubu components plus one containing styles and images). Thus allowing to manage the Web User Interface (WUI) components as OSGi bundles during the execution.

5. Coping With Runtime Change

Because we use bundles as deployment units, most runtime change are triggered by adding, removing or updating application bundles. Actually, the OSGi module layer (see 2) provides an API through which we can add, remove or update bundles at runtime. Thanks to these facilities we are able to add new functionalities, remove obsolete ones or update parts of the application during the execution without impacting the availability of the whole application. For example, updating a bundle containing a WUI component will not impact the business logic of the application or even other parts of the WUI. However, this is fully true if and only if bundles are loosely coupled. Indeed, if two bundles are tightly coupled together, updating one of them will require restarting the other; this restart is triggered by refreshing the bundles packages. The process of uninstalling and updating bundles along with the need to refresh packages when bundles are tightly coupled is detailed in [31].

5.1 Changing ChameRIA Bundles at Runtime

A ChameRIA application is made of four different types of bundles:

- **BC** bundles. These bundles contain the iPOJO components (i.e. the business logic components described in section 4.3).

- **SC** bundles. These bundles act as service contracts containers, in OSGI a service contract is a Java interface class.

- **WC** bundles. These bundles contain the H-Ubu components (i.e. the web user interface components described in section 4.4).

- **WV** bundles. These bundles contain web view resources (i.e. HTML, CSS, Images). These resources are manipulated by the H-Ubu components.

Figure 7 shows how these types of bundles are coupled together. BC bundles can be loosely coupled together through service dependencies. Similarly, WC bundles can also be coupled among themselves, but distinctly, they can also be coupled to BC bundles. Tight coupling occurs with bundles providing the service specification (SC). Indeed the bundles which contain a service implementation (i.e. BC & WC) need to be updated along with the service specification if it changes. Finally the WC bundles can also depend on the content of Web view bundles (e.g HTML DOM objects reference).

In regards to the level of coupling, the worst runtime change is a modification to service specifications. Such modifications can impact both the application logic and the web user interface through respectively BC and WC bundles. With the exception of this particular case, both the appli-

cation logic and the web user interface can evolve independently from the rest of the application.

6. Experience

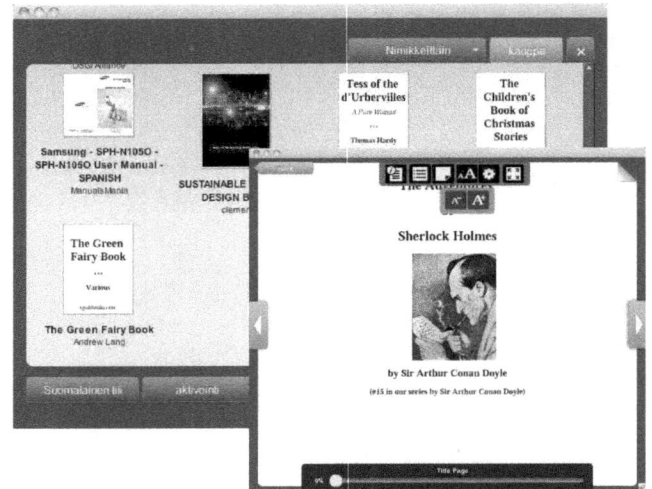

Figure 8. DRM document reader user interface.

ChameRIA has been successfully used in several projects. Two of them are presented in this paper. The first was the design and implementation of a Digital Rights Management(DRM) document reader targeting net-books and tablet PCs (figure 8). The complexity of the user interface in addition to the constraints raised by the use of a DRM native library and the need for file association was addressed by ChameRIA. Indeed, control over the WebKit within the application logic allowed us to handle file association and DRM management. Furthermore, the complexity of the user interface was tackled by the use of web interface technologies which were separated from the application logic.

The second project was a Valve control application (figure 9). In this application, the back-end was required to interact with the serial bus in order to control the valve. The front-end was essentially an administration interface. One requirement was the generation and display of graphs.

7. Discussion

The main constraint introduced by the ChameRIA approach is the requirement to follow a service-oriented component model both in the back-end and front-end parts of the application. This constraint is fundamental to our approach. It forces developers to consider the dynamic nature of services (availability change at runtime) and hence to construct applications which are intrinsically resilient to change in the execution environment. Moreover, following this model does not impact the choice of the underlying language/runtime. We have shown with H-Ubu that the implementation

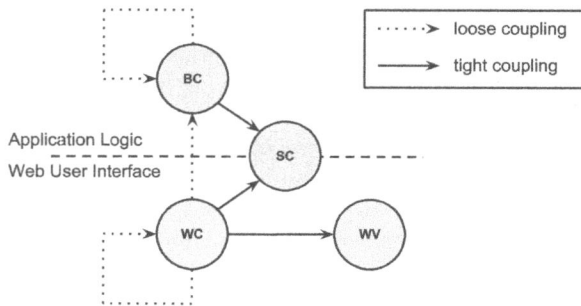

Figure 7. Coupling among ChameRIA application bundles.

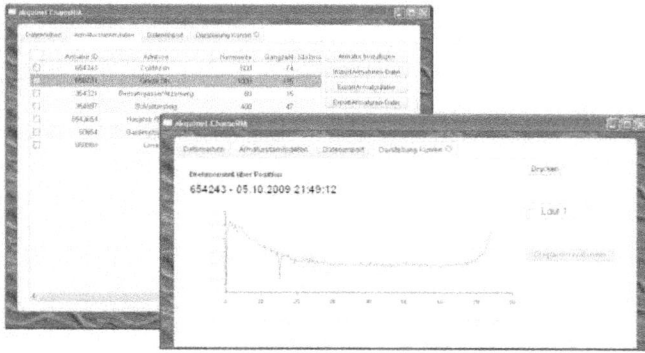

Figure 9. Valve control user interface.

of such a model was relatively straightforward (H-Ubu is about 1000 line of code), not to mention similar component models such as Scala components and COM+.

We have presented in section 4.2 the underlying communication framework of ChameRIA. This framework allows for transparent communication between the browser and the OSGi platform through the dynamic generation of endpoints and proxies. This framework can also be used in order to construct loosely coupled distributed applications. It is straightforward to run the web part of the application on a remote browser rather than the ChameRIA one. Furthermore it is also possible to use the framework as a means to communicate with several OSGi gateways or with remote applications through WebServices or following the REST architectural style.

Nevertheless, despite the fact that the service-oriented component model allows us to reflect change in the network through service availability, this is not sufficient as a means to conceive reliable distributed applications. One work around is to implement *distribution aware* components between business components and the distributed services. Those components handling distribution problematic such as latency or serialization but keeping advantage of being decoupled from the communication protocols and the network topology. Indeed, those concerns are handled by the communication framework. The main constraint imposed by the communication framework is to have at least one common network registry for the machines that need to communicate together.

8. Related Works

Dynamic software update: Several research projects from different domains address the challenges of runtime updates (e.g. [26] [21]). Dynamic software updating (DSU) techniques [14] focus on compiler based approaches to support runtime upgrades. The Ginseng project [23] is a DSU implementation for C that allows updating software during the execution, the update consists in applying a patch. It generates

most of the patch and allows to apply it on-line thanks to runtime support which ensures type-safety and up to date data. The Jvolve project [32] is a DSU-enhanced Java VM, it supports method body updates along with class updates (adding, removing or changing the type of fields and methods). In contrast to these approaches, our system has been designed in order to upgrade individual components in a component-based system. This allows us to independently upgrade each component of the application and fits in with architecture-based approaches such as [16] [34] and [19] [24]. Hence, our work is closer to a runtime software adaptation framework as envisioned in [25].

Browser integration: Browser integration: Similarly to our approach, the SWT Browser widget [7] binds a native browser engine (e.g WebKit) allowing to add HTML viewing capabilities to an SWT application. Hence, developers are able to control the browser through the eclipse runtime. The eclipse runtime [10] is also built in top of the OSGi framework. The main distinction with our approach is that the eclipse runtime does not take advantage of the service layer as a means to support runtime change. This results in modular but tightly coupled applications which do not easily support runtime changes because each individual change can potentially bring down the whole application.

Service-oriented front-end architecture: Service-Oriented Front-End Architecture: The Thin Server Architecture (TSA) Working Group proposed an architectural style where all presentation layer logic is moved from the server to JavaScript logic on the client (i.e Web Browser) [27]. Thus allowing server-side components to be concerned only with business logic. One example of a framework following the TSA principles is the JavaScriptMVC [22] framework. Despite the fact that TSA has been designed for network based client server applications, the principles behind it seem to fit very well with the ChameRIA approach. We believe that the application logic model of ChameRIA along with its communication machine would allow to develop, fairly easily, server-side components as described in TSA.

9. Conclusion

The emergence of applications that have to cope with new requirements, changing context and corrective changes during execution raises new challenges. User interface developers of such applications have to deal with both traditional user interface technologies and modular frameworks (e.g OSGi) in order to build user interfaces. This raises two important problems: the first is that the use of traditional user interface technologies which have not been designed to deal with dynamic business logic is an important source of difficulties for reliability; the second problem is the requirement for user interface developer to be able to manipulate the underlying runtime framework technologies.

In this paper we have shown that following a service-oriented component model while using web technologies makes possible the conception and execution of dynamic desktop applications where both the application logic and the user interface can evolve at runtime. The main advantages of our approach is that the user interface developers are not required to have knowledge about the business logic framework and thus can construct the whole user interface by manipulating only web technologies. We then present the ChameRIA framework which is an implementation of our approach along with two service oriented component frameworks which ease the conception and implementation of both the business logic and the web user interface. We presents two industrial projects were ChameRIA have been successfully used.

Availability

The ChameRIA source code is available for download at `https://github.com/akquinet/ChameRIA`. The H-Ubu component model for JavaScript is hosted on `http://akquinet.github.com/hubu`.

Acknowledgments

This work builds upon the OW2 Chameleon project, accessible at `http://chameleon.ow2.org`. We would like to specifically acknowledge our shepherd Allen Wirfs-Brock along with Walter Rudametkin, Issac Noe Garcia and Kiev Gama for helpful comments on this paper.

References

[1] O. Alliance. Osgi service platform core specification release 4, May 2007. `http://www.osgi.org/Specifications/HomePage`.

[2] C. Anderson and M. Wolff. The web is dead. long live the internet. Wired, August 2010. `http://www.wired.com/magazine/2010/08/ff_webrip`.

[3] G. R. Andrews. Paradigms for process interaction in distributed programs. *ACM Comput. Surv.*, 23:49–90, March 1991. ISSN 0360-0300.

[4] J. Bardin, P. Lalanda, and C. Escoffier. Towards an automatic integration of heterogeneous services and devices. *Asia-Pacific Conference on Services Computing*, 0:171–178, 2010.

[5] L. Baresi and C. Ghezzi. The disappearing boundary between development-time and run-time. In *FoSER'10*, pages 17–22, 2010.

[6] H. Cervantes and R. Hall. A Framework for Constructing Adaptive Component-based Applications: Concepts and Experiences. In *CBSE*, pages 130–137. Springer, May 2004. ISBN 3-540-21998-6.

[7] C. Cornu. Viewing html pages with swt browser widget, August 2004. `http://www.eclipse.org/articles/Article-SWT-browser-widget/browser.html`.

[8] P. Deutsch and J. Gosling. The eight fallacies of distributed computing. James Gosling: on the Java Road, 1997. `http://blogs.oracle.com/jag/resource/Fallacies.html`.

[9] C. Escoffier and R. Hall. Dynamically Adaptable Applications with iPOJO Service Components. In *Software Composition*, pages 113–128. Springer, March 2007. ISBN 978-3-540-77350-4.

[10] E. Foundation. Component oriented development and assembly (coda) with equinox, March 2008. `http://www.eclipse.org/eclipsert/whitepaper/20080310_equinox.pdf`.

[11] M. Foundation. Electrolysis. Mozilla Wiki, April 2011. `https://wiki.mozilla.org/Electrolysis`.

[12] W. Foundation. Standard widget toolkit, 2011. `http://en.wikipedia.org/wiki/Standard_Widget_Toolkit`.

[13] K. Gama and D. Donsez. A survey on approaches for addressing dependability attributes in the osgi service platform. *SIGSOFT Softw. Eng. Notes*, 35:1–8, May 2010. ISSN 0163-5948.

[14] M. Hicks, J. T. Moore, and S. Nettles. Dynamic software updating. *SIGPLAN Not.*, 36:13–23, May 2001. ISSN 0362-1340.

[15] ISO/IEC. Information technology - open distributed processing - reference model: Overview, December 1998. International Standard ISO/IEC 10746-1.

[16] J. Kramer and J. Magee. Dynamic configuration for distributed systems. *IEEE Trans. Softw. Eng.*, 11:424–436, April 1985. ISSN 0098-5589.

[17] P. Kriens. Scala components vs osgi. OSGi Alliance Blog, July 2010. `http://www.osgi.org/blog/2010/07/scala-components-vs-osgi.html`.

[18] G. Lawton. New ways to build rich internet applications. *Computer*, 41:10–12, August 2008. ISSN 0018-9162.

[19] M. Léger, T. Ledoux, and T. Coupaye. Reliable dynamic reconfigurations in the fractal component model. In *Proceedings of the 6th international workshop on Adaptive and reflective middleware.*, ARM '07, pages 3:1–3:6, New York, NY, USA, 2007. ACM. ISBN 978-1-59593-931-9.

[20] M. Lehman and L. Belady. *Program Evolution: Processes of Software Change*. Academic Press, 1985. ISBN 0-12-442440-6.

[21] K. Makris and R. A. Bazzi. Immediate multi-threaded dynamic software updates using stack reconstruction. In *Proceedings of the 2009 conference on USENIX Annual technical conference*, USENIX'09, pages 31–31, Berkeley, CA, USA, 2009. USENIX Association.

[22] J. B. Meyer and B. Moschel. Javascriptmvc 3.0, 2010. `http://javascriptmvc.com/`.

[23] I. Neamtiu, M. Hicks, G. Stoyle, and M. Oriol. Practical dynamic software updating for c. *SIGPLAN Not.*, 41:72–83, June 2006. ISSN 0362-1340.

[24] M. Odersky and M. Zenger. Scalable component abstractions. In *OOPSLA*, 2005.

[25] P. Oreizy, N. Medvidovic, and R. N. Taylor. Architecture-based runtime software evolution. In *Proceedings of the 20th international conference on Software engineering*, ICSE '98, pages 177–186, Washington, DC, USA, 1998. IEEE Computer Society. ISBN 0-8186-8368-6.

[26] A. Orso, A. Rao, and M. Harrold. A technique for dynamic updating of java software. *Software Maintenance, IEEE International Conference on*, 0:0649, 2002.

[27] G. Prasad, R. Taneja, and T. Vikrant. Life above the service tier, October 2007.

[28] W. Pree. *Design Patterns for Object-Oriented Software Development*. Addison Wesley Longman, 1st edition, 1995. ISBN 0201422948.

[29] T. Reenskaug and A. Goldberg. Models-views-controllers. Xerox PARC report, December 1979. `http://heim.ifi.uio.no/~trygver/themes/mvc/mvc-index.html`.

[30] C. Reis and S. D. Gribble. Isolating web programs in modern browser architectures. In *Proceedings of the 4th ACM European conference on Computer systems*, EuroSys '09, pages 219–232, New York, NY, USA, 2009. ACM. ISBN 978-1-60558-482-9.

[31] J. S. Rellermeyer, M. Duller, and G. Alonso. Consistently applying updates to compositions of distributed osgi modules. In *Proceedings of the 1st International Workshop on Hot Topics in Software Upgrades*, HotSWUp '08, pages 9:1–9:5, New York, NY, USA, 2008. ACM. ISBN 978-1-60558-304-4.

[32] S. Subramanian, M. Hicks, and K. S. McKinley. Dynamic software updates: a vm-centric approach. *SIGPLAN Not.*, 44: 1–12, June 2009. ISSN 0362-1340.

[33] A. S. Tanenbaum and M. v. Steen. *Distributed Systems: Principles and Paradigms (2nd Edition)*. Prentice-Hall, Inc., Upper Saddle River, NJ, USA, 2006. ISBN 0132392275.

[34] R. N. Taylor, N. Medvidovic, K. M. Anderson, E. J. Whitehead, Jr., and J. E. Robbins. A component and message-based architectural style for gui software. In *Proceedings of the 17th international conference on Software engineering*, ICSE '95, pages 295–304, New York, NY, USA, 1995. ACM. ISBN 0-89791-708-1.

[35] W. Team. The webkit open source project, 2011. `https://www.webkit.org`.

[36] J. Waldo, W. Geoff, A. Wollrath, and S. C. Kendall. A note on distributed computing. Sun Microsystems, Inc, 1994.

To Inclusive Design Through Contextually Extended IoC

Infusion IoC, a JavaScript Library and Mentality for Scalable Development of Accessible and Maintainable Systems

Antranig Basman

Fluid Project, OCAD University, Toronto, Canada
antranig.basman@colorado.edu

Clayton Lewis   Colin Clark

University of Colorado, Boulder/Fluid Project
clayton.lewis@colorado.edu/cclark@ocad.ca

Abstract

Using current software development techniques, code and designs are often unmaintainable from the point of inception. Code is brittle and hard to refactor, hard to press to new purposes, and hard to understand. Here we present a system aimed at creating a model for *scalable development*, addressing this and several other critical problems in software construction. Such an aim is far from new, and has resembled the aims of each generation of software methodologists over the last 50 years. It deserves comment why these aims have so signally failed to be achieved, and we will present arguments as to why the combination of techniques explained here could expect to lead to novel results.

Software products of today are notoriously unadaptable. An application which meets need A generally cannot be extended to meet apparently very similar need A' without something resembling "software engineering". Applications present users with a "take it or leave it" proposition — if the software doesn't happen to meet a user's needs or preferences, there's no way to change it without writing more code, which is out of reach for most users. Indeed, software regularly fails to be easily adaptable to meet the needs of users with differing needs, such as in the case of accessibility. These "precarious values" — accessibility and usability with different devices, languages, and personal needs — are typically left until the end or ignored, and represent a significant expense in traditional approaches to software development. Often these needs are met by developing a largely unrelated version of the application, requiring maintenance of additional, separate code bases.

Our aim is to enable *Inclusive Design*[3], whose objective is to satisfy the needs and desires of the broadest range of users possible. Every designer sets out with this objective to a certain extent, but as well as limitations of intent, there are also strong limitations placed by the technology and economics of software development. Due to the poor scaling characteristics of current techniques, even meeting one set of relatively inflexible needs can be an expensive undertaking, especially over the long term.

To address these problems of adaptability, we present a model for software construction, together with a base library, Fluid Infusion, implemented in the JavaScript language. Fluid Infusion implements an *Inversion of Control* model, Infusion IoC, which features a notion of *context* as the basis for adaptability, resolved in a scope modelled in terms of a data structure, a *component tree* expressing the computation to be performed. In the Context-Oriented Programming community[7], this model of scoping is known as *structural scoping*. We will also work with a model of *transparent state* in which all modifiable state of interest to users is held in publicly visible locations, indexed by path strings. This model for state is isomorphic to that modeled by JSON[6], a well-known state model derived from, but not limited to, the JavaScript language. Instantiation in the model is handled by an *Inversion of Control* system extended from the model of similar system such as the Spring Framework or Pico first developed in the Java language.

We relate such systems to goal-directed resolution systems such as Prolog, and show that they have beneficial properties such as *homoiconicity*[2] which have not been seen in a strong or widespread form since the days of LISP. We exhibit some cases to show how the framework enables, through a simple declarative syntax, types of adaptation and composition that are hard or impossible using traditional models of polymorphism. We also relate Infusion IoC to other software methodologies such as *Aspect-Oriented Programming* and *Context-Oriented Programming* which have been found to greatly increase flexibility and expressiveness of designs. We conclude with some remarks on the applicability of the system to the parallelisation of irregular algorithms, and its relationship to upcoming developments in the ECMAScript 6 language specification.

General Terms   Algorithms, Design, Human Factors, Languages

Categories and Subject Descriptors D.1.2 [*Software*]: Programming Techniques—Automatic Programming; D.3.3 [*Software*]: Programming Languages—Polymorphism; E.2 [*Data*]: Data Storage Representations—Object Representation

Keywords JavaScript, Inversion of Control, Transparent State, Accessibility, JSON, Context-oriented Programming

1. The Development and Need for Inversion of Control systems

The core of the system described here is an "Inversion of Control" system implemented in the JavaScript language. It constructs applications from trees of components expressed declaratively in JSON notation. Whilst the primary use of the system is in assembling user interface markup and operating logic for HTML web applications, these ideas can be adapted to other domains, illuminating broad issues of software construction. We begin by examining the history and motivation of similar systems, the relationship of our IoC system to other models of software construction, and then finish by describing some current applications, and planned future work.

1.1 The Crucial Nature of Dependency Structure in Software

In a pioneering work, John Lakos[1] identified the patterns of *dependency* of parts of a software system on other parts as key determinants of software quality. In his conception, a piece of code A has "knowledge of" or "dependency on" another, B, if names in B appear in A. To mark our technical uses of these concepts, we will qualify them by referring to "L-dependency" or equivalently "L-knowledge". In the C++ language in which Lakos was working, there are various gradations of this knowledge, for example, whether the knowledge about B was sufficient to affect the memory layout of objects allocated in A, or merely required the compiler to have visibility of B names when compiling A code. Although the details differ, the core of this formulation is invariant across essentially all programming languages.

Lakos argued that code in a "dependency-correct" system should form a *directed acyclic graph* (DAG), when expressed in terms of the logical units into which it was divided and the L-dependencies among them. In the C++ language, these logical units were often classes, although he noted that this kind of boundary could be drawn at any level in a system.

Lakos observed that there were many significant consequences of constructing bodies of code with inappropriately arranged L-dependency, following on from his initial effort to control escalating build times in complex systems. Highly interdependent code was harder to understand, harder to test and maintain, and most importantly to our domain of endusers, tended to be extremely brittle over time. Such code imposes unexpectedly huge development costs in responding to seemingly innocuous feature requests.

1.1.1 Evaluating Physical Design Quality Through Dependence Graphs

L-dependency problems are easiest to see in cyclic cases, for example, when some part A of a system depends on part B, but part B also depends on A. Consider the problem of testing this system. One would like to find an order of testing for the parts of the system, such that all the parts that A (say) depends on have been tested before testing A. But when there is a cycle in the L-dependency structure, there just is no such order: in the example, B has to be tested before A, but A has to be tested before B.

Even when there are no L-dependency cycles, systems still differ in important ways, reflected in their L-dependency structure. Figure 1 contrasts a few different cases of dependency geometry. Each component is labelled with its **level number**, which is the count of all components (including itself) which have L-dependence on that component. At the left is a cyclic structure of the sort we just described. In the centre is shown a system whose dependence graph forms a balanced binary tree, representing a typical reasonably-well factored system. At the right is a system with a horizontal graph, composed of components which have no mutual L-dependency.

Lakos proposed a measurement of "quality" of such a dependence graph, which is the sum of all level numbers in the graph, known as the **cumulative component dependency** (CCD). This measure can be used to compare the quality of the dependence structure of graphs involving the same number of components. Lakos observes that arrangements showing lower CCD numbers are associated with beneficial properties of many kinds. These arrangements correspond to applications which are easier to test, easier to refactor, faster to build, and which offer better opportunities for reuse. We will further observe that CCD numbers that do not ultimately scale linearly in the number of code units form an ultimate barrier to scalable design and ensure that the design will come to be dominated by *accidental complexity* (section 3.3.2).

1.1.2 Consequences of Improving Dependence Structure in Static Languages

As it turns out, the problem raised by Lakos' recommendations on the organisation of dependencies cannot be fully resolved in C++, or other static languages, at all. We will consider a typical case, of a design where the majority of dependence arcs are caused by L-knowledge resulting from an *aggregation* relationship — in classical object-oriented terms, where, for example, object A **has-a** object B. Consider a hypothetical DAG of dependency-correct code, organised into units of these classes. Take two of these elements, A and B — in terms of C++, aggregation-derived L-knowledge of class A about class B, would translate into a requirement for

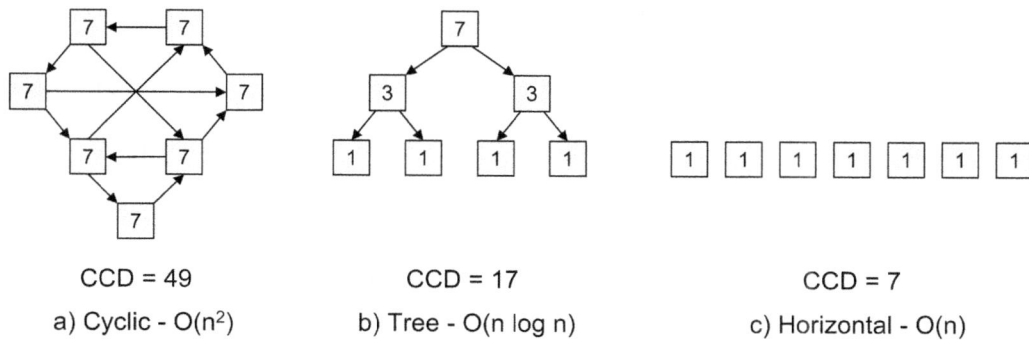

CCD = 49   CCD = 17   CCD = 7

a) Cyclic - $O(n^2)$ b) Tree - $O(n \log n)$ c) Horizontal - $O(n)$

Figure 1: Comparison of Dependence Structures with Different Geometries for 7 components (following Lakos[1], pp.194-195)

objects of class A to bear responsibility for construction of objects of class B, and not vice versa. This knowledge may be pushed into a common ancestor, C — but wherever it resides, this constructional knowledge cumulates towards the root of the tree, creating a *brittle base* to the overall design.

1.1.3   Elaboration of the "brittle base" problem

The "brittle base" issue we described is best seen as a *dynamic* issue, affecting the quality of a design over its entire trajectory from design through to maintenance. At any particular point in time, the naive method of propagating dependencies from place to place across a design with n logical units would require the instantiation in the design of $O(n)$ types with $O(n^2)$ overall information content in order to express the (cumulative) signature contracts between each pair of nodes joined by arcs in the tree. These types express the signatures of callbacks, travelling in the "upward" direction from a point in the tree where a dependency is generated, and the signatures of constructors, travelling in the "downward" direction down to where a dependency is used.

Faced with this unacceptable proliferation of types, a skilled designer will apply judgement to the overall design and attempt to consolidate dependencies and their points of generation into *equivalence classes* of units which may be treated as equivalent ("is-a") with respect to their dependency transfer characteristics. Whilst they may be to some extent "Procrustean" (having unused arguments in some cases, or failing to transfer required ones) these solutions may be of good quality at a particular point in the design trajectory.

A problem occurs when during the "maintenance" phase of the design, (or more accurately, simply its "period of use"), an unexpected user requirement perturbs the situation by requiring an extra dependency transfer. The equivalence mapping previously computed by the designer then is no longer ideal. The design progressively strains under this failure, perhaps even leading to the rejection of such requirements as uneconomic. When the costs are finally paid, the new ideal division of signatures into equivalence classes may not be closely related to the old, leading to large change

costs proportional to the entire size of the design. This is an important source of non-linear scaling of engineering costs with respect to requirements.

1.1.4   Attempted solutions lead back to the core issue

Common attempted solutions to this kind of issue in non-dynamic languages involve constructional *design patterns*, usually factories. These impose two kinds of penalties. Firstly, the family of products from the factory need to have a common signature, a serious restriction. Secondly, whilst *some* type information may be erased at this polymorphic boundary, remanent type information still naturally cumulates upwards in the DAG of knowledge in a way that prevents scaling. In the next section we will explain how a certain kind of framework, known as an *Inversion of Control* system, can resolve these kinds of issues, given a sufficiently dynamic base language.

1.2   Inversion of Control Systems

The Java language is not particularly dynamic, but enjoys enough of this quality through its reflection system and the possibility for bytecode manipulation that some workable solutions to the fragile base problem emerged, generically described as "Inversion of Control" (IoC). Martin Fowler outlines some of the variants of IoC framework in [4]; popular frameworks in Java include Pico, Avalon, and currently most popularly the Spring framework[20].

The defining activity of such an IoC system, specifically named by Fowler as **dependency injection** is as follows: If an object of class A needs an object of another class B at construction time, rather than A's code calling a constructor for B, A's need for a B is registered in some kind of declarative format with the IoC system. The IoC system then **injects** an instance of B into the object that needs it. The "inversion" is that "asking for an object" is replaced by "being given an object". The operation of such a system relies intrinsically on dynamic properties of the target language. In fact, rather than "constructing itself" as is the case in static languages, the entire tree containing A, B and all neighbouring dependencies is constructed by the framework, informing the target code of lifecycle points in a model similar to that of event-driven frameworks. The IoC framework, in this model, takes the place of the brittle constructional code otherwise placed in class A or some higher point of dependency.

Users of these frameworks get increased agility in the face of end-user requests and variability in environment. That is, important environmental decisions (in the concrete terms of workaday developers, issues such as transaction management, database dialect, message resolution etc.) are taken out of the code and replaced by declarative configuration.

As well as resolving the "brittle base" problem, IoC frameworks improve the L-dependence structure of a design in a number of ways. Firstly, a choice may be made not to support designs with cyclic dependencies (use of Infusion IoC mandates and assists this, whilst it is a configuration option available with Spring IoC). Secondly, the facilities of the IoC system may flatten the dependence graph of a design by removing a number of arcs, which represent dependencies that would otherwise be manifest in the application design but instead are subsumed into basic framework facilities. More powerful IoC frameworks can remove progressively more dependence arcs from the application design, depending on their idiom and capabilities.

1.2.1 Conclusions for scaling of design costs

We have identified two important routes through which traditional design methods fail to allow the costs of a design to scale linearly with the number of "function points" addressed by the design. Firstly, the brittle base problem which is resolved by essentially all IoC systems. Secondly, the tendency of Lakos CCD numbers calculated from the physical design structure to scale faster than linearly. This second point can only be addressed by methodologies which allow the physical design structure to be improved whilst still expressing the same design. For this second point we will return in section 4.1.2 to show how the Infusion IoC system can remove a large number of dependence arrows from a physical design map which corresponded to cases of aggregation and inheritance in a traditional object-oriented (OO) design. Before then, we will consider in section 3.3 the implications of these kinds of superlinear scaling for the scale of economic benefits that could be realised through different choices of methodologies.

1.3 Limitations and Extensions to the IoC model

A significant lack in existing IoC systems is a suitably flexible concept of *context*. To a Java IoC system, the context is a static piece of configuration (or associated runtime structure) known as a **container**. A configuration file is entered into the system as a global specification and if users or developers require changes in resolution based on recognition of a new context or requirement, they need to change the file. Even organising such files hierarchically does not permit decisions to be made based on dynamic considerations.

But we can extend the notion of IoC to allow contexts as well as tasks to shape what a system will do.

The Fluid IoC system supervises the matching of names of functions to implementations. What we speak of as a **function name** is more generalised than the traditional notion of a "function" in that it does not necessarily correspond to a function as implemented directly in the programming language. All names of such functions could, however, if registered globally serve as "function names" if required. Instead a "function name" corresponds to the notion of a "task to be performed" in the world of a user. There are generally different classes of "users", operating at different levels in a the tower of abstractions, where the definition of a task at the level of one user, say an end user, decomposes it into subtasks that make sense only to a user at another level, say an application designer.

An implementation provider — and even unrelated third parties — can provide a set of directives to the IoC system, which specify under which conditions a given implementation is an appropriate one to deliver to an end user. These directives are named **demands blocks**, matching conditions which are represented by supplying one or more **context names**. These names are also simple strings, like function names.

The power of the system to proceed in a contextually aware way is significantly enhanced by allowing the names of *products* of the system to serve as names of *contexts* guiding the construction of future products. Some names may serve as both function names and context names. The name of a user interface widget, for example, may be used sometimes to specify needed functionality, and sometimes to specify a context in which a subsidiary widget might be embedded.

2. Relation to other Programming Paradigms

2.1 Link to Goal-Directed Programming

One way of understanding the cascade of instantiations performed by an IoC system in pursuit of constructing a particular component, is as related to the *resolution* process performed by knowledge-oriented systems such as Prolog. Prolog casts knowledge in the from of **relations**, connecting one term with another. The input from the user proceeds "forwards" in their world, expressing the dependence of one proposition (or alternatively seen, "goal") on another. Each rule of this kind is entered into a database of such rules progressively, building up an unbounded network linking these propositions. A run of the system takes the form of requesting the status of a particular proposition — execution then cascades "backwards" (in the view of the developer) through the set of dependent rules until an answer can be determined.

Recursive resolution of dependent components by an IoC system can be seen as a model of a similar process as the cascade of Prolog relation resolution. Important differences are that whilst this IoC system currently operates no form of "backtracking"; on the other hand, we add a concept of **context** to the resolution system. Absence of contextual awareness was historically a weakness of Prolog, which, for example, provided no straightforward means for dealing with situations which changed over time.

2.2 Link to Aspect-Oriented Programming

A popular approach for dealing what it terms "cross-cutting aspects of a design" which has grown up alongside and in some cases intertwined with the use of IoC is known as "Aspect-Oriented Programming" (AOP). In this model, the implementation domain of a codebase is stratified, forming a higher "meta-level" of design comprising units of code (in a related, but usually distinct syntax) which consists of directives which *advise* the operation of the remaining base level of code which can then usually enjoy some kind of simplified implementation.

AOP systems are often extremely powerful, and have the ability to issue *advice* which modifies the execution of the base code at the level of individual method calls or property access — either modifying these operations or replacing them entirely. The points where an AOP advice matches or "joins" a design are indivually named *join points*, described by a specification or query known as a *pointcut*. Pointcut expressions take quite low-level forms, usually expressed in a dialect reminiscent of regular expressions. With the data-hiding mentality which goes together with object-orientation (OO), AOP pointcuts usually have quite limited insight into the contextual situation which has been matched. As a result of the very local oversight of the pointcut matching and advice process, AOP designs can become very hard to understand without custom tools.

The execution modification effected at an AOP join point may be considered as a kind of **dispatch**. A more familiar kind of function dispatch is the resolution from the name of a polymorphic function in an OO hierarchy onto a particular implementation held in a derived class. Infusion IoC also implements a form of dispatch by following rules held in declarative structures known as **demands blocks** (see section4.2). Common across all situations is the progress from a specification of an operation to be performed in the form of a *name* to a particular concrete implementation to be used in a particular context.

Infusion IoC has a similar kind of power of dispatch to traditional AOP, since the set of dispatch rules is always *open* and *external* to the body of code being advised. However, compared to AOP, it is at the same time limited in its scope for matching, as it is broadened in its ability to interpret context. A Infusion demands block can only act at points in a design where the IoC system is already instantiating a subcomponent in the tree, or else where the user has explicitly requested its operation (e.g. by means of a suitably declared event or method). However, when it does act, the dispatch modification may make use of the same contextual resolution system which guided its own matching, to stably dis-

cover relevant pieces of state over the entire component tree in scope, rather than just those located close to the join point site as in traditional AOP. This tradeoff of increased formality of matching against increased contextual understanding should produce designs which are much easier to understand as a whole, although we still anticipate a very important role for assistive tools.

2.3 Relation to Context-Oriented Programming

A relatively recent innovation, aimed at precisely the weakness of traditional goal-directed languages that we identified in section 2.1, is that of **Context-Oriented Programming** (COP) [7]. COP can also be seen as a related development to AOP of the previous section, as well as an outgrowth of OOP. In the original formulation of the authors, code held within standard methods in an OO hierarchy is enhanced by definitions of **partial methods** which are aggregated in groups known as **layers**. At the time of execution of the enhanced method, one or more of these layers may be active, leading to a modification of the base method by partial methods held in the active layers. A partial method differs from a standard method in that it contains a control flow point at which it may defer to the original method — this control flow point is named by the COP authors as `proceed`. The layering of a partial method onto a standard method (or stack of other partial methods) can thus be seen in AOP terms as an *around advice* — when a layer containing such a partial method is activated, it *advises* the base method, wrapping it in the control flow held in the partial method. [9] contains more detailed comparison and contrast of COP with AOP.

Since awareness of context is one of the crucial ways in which our system differs from many previous systems, it is relevant to examine common ground between our system and COP, and also ways in which it differs.

2.3.1 COP Layering with OOP — Portability Profile

COP is explicitly founded upon OOP, since the mechanism of a layer, once activated, is to effect *behavioural modification* by advising the workflow of methods in their position in an OO hierarchy. For this reason, COP can be effectively ported to a wide variety of standard OO languages, such as Smalltalk, Java, Python, etc. — [8] contains a survey of such ports extant at 2009. On the other hand, the Infusion IoC system presented here is not based on OO, and relies strongly on base language features which allow manipulation of state held as recursive literals of the language. As a result our system could only easily be ported to languages without a fundamental OO representation and with support for such literals such as LISP and JavaScript.

2.3.2 COP scoping rules

COP presents a number of routes for determining when layers should be activated — [8] mentions a few, such as *thread-local* and *global* which are supported by our system, and some which are not, such as *dynamic extent*-based (block plus call stack-scoped) activation. However, the essential and most fundamental mode of activation of contexts in our system is one which the COP authors, as well as ourselves, name *structural scoping*. Structural scoping is described in the COP literature at [9]. Since COP is not cast in terms of structures but instead in terms of objects, structural scoping is presented as an extension to the COP activation model for use in a particular domain (a graphical graph editing application, *Morphic*) with activation in practice honoured through dynamic extents in an adaptation library.

Since our system organises code units ("components") into a directly–addressed transparent state structure (section 4.3), the primary and natural means of context scoping is structural, with the global and dynamic methods held as secondary. The scoping rules are treated in detail in section 4.1.3.

2.3.3 Implicit formation of layers

Whilst a layer in COP is built up as a self-contained, named unit, the units of context which are activated in our system are built up implicitly through open aggregation. The "layer" which is active for a particular dispatch in Infusion IoC is composed just out of those *demands blocks* (see section 4.2) which match the names which can be found in the portion of the structure holding the dispatch site which is in scope. Thus our system remains always open for modification by third parties, without requiring access either to a particular layer definition which is in effect, or access to the call stack below the point at which dispatch is to be modified.

3. Context of the Solution

3.1 Domain of Validity

It is useful to try to draw out the domain of software tasks for which this approach may be relevant, against a background of tasks for which it may be less helpful. There is a traditional dichotomy drawn between problems which could be named as "deep" — those limited by problem complexity, such as design of a compiler, operating system or database, and others which could be termed "broad" — those limited by problem change and definition, such as the interfaces and implementations of user-facing systems on the web and elsewhere. The system described here is most applicable to the latter type of problem.

However, this dichotomy itself deserves some comment. Software engineers, and computer scientists, as they are for the most part working surrounded by their peers, tend to arrive at a disproportionate focus on the former, "deep" category of problem, the form of problem which they create for themselves and each other. This leads to an exaggerated focus both on the particular kinds of difficulties which these problems pose, and also on their real value in the world. The overwhelming majority of consumers for software artifacts are not programmers — consisting in the most part of normal human beings wanting some work done — this

work in the most part of some orderly and idiomatic access to some form of shared state in the world. It is actually the norm, rather than the anomaly which software professionals can sometimes take it, for problem definitions to be vague, constantly shifting, and even to themselves comprise a huge domain of variation with respect to the "market" — the full variation of human requirements within the scope of Inclusive Design. We contend that this self-focus by the community has led to the prevalence of and disproportionate value attached to approaches such as the "data hiding" strand of the object-oriented philosophy which are actively counter-productive when applied to the vast majority of programming tasks as laid out in our presentation of this dichotomy. Below (in section 4.3) we will explain how the antithesis of this approach, which we name *transparent state*, is crucial to our formulation of IoC and also to addressing these kinds of tasks in general.

3.2 Existing Configurable Systems

It is worth examining the most configurable kinds of systems which the industry has so far produced, and explain the kinds of variation which we aspire to express, and why they are essential to any conception of Inclusive Design, beyond the traditional conception of "accessibility".

Some highly configurable products are intricate desktop applications, such as Microsoft's Visual Studio or IBM's Eclipse, aimed at developers, and Microsoft Word, a word processing application ostensibly aimed at normal human beings. These offer configurations including the following kinds:

- Configuration of keyboard bindings used to invoke functions of the application

- Reorganisation and customization of "toolbars" holding icons invoking application functions

- Alteration of layout and positioning of panes holding working documents, indexes of these documents, menus and toolbars

- Installation and configuration of "plugins" offering extensions to the application's function (for example, the ability to work with different kinds of document, or integrate with a particular kind of remote service)

- Others

Whilst this is a form of "high water-mark" in terms of configurable systems, it falls short of what is required for Inclusive Design. There it is essential that very many aspects of an application be modifiable to meet diverse user needs. For example, users with low vision will require quite large type fonts, and may require unusual color contrast; users who do not read well may benefit from rarely used content or controls being suppressed or moved to subsidiary screens. In general, Inclusive Design requires that, as much as possible, all aspects of a user interface be subject to configuration.

In addition to these drawbacks to configuration systems, the reach of the system itself falls short. Here are some kinds of configuration which are desirable, and also capable of expression in a system such as Infusion IoC:

- Replacing application-wide, a control with a particular function by one with the same data binding function but different presentation and mode of operation — for example, a numeric bounded range presented with spin buttons replaced by a linear slider

- Changing interaction idioms over domains with a particular geometry — for example, items displayed in a linear list which are navigable by means of arrow keys might be customized to allow navigation to wrap from the top to the bottom of the list, or else to "stick" at the extremes of the list

- Reformulating the workflow of portions of an application so that multiple controls displayed in a single, complex dialog are replaced by a linear sequence of simpler steps

The customization we are seeking also aims at some broader values —

- To make it as easy as possible to transport customisations from one environment or "application" to another whilst preserving as much semantic meaning and function as possible[1]

- To allow as much customisation as possible to proceed by *direct manipulation in context* — that is, by a modal interaction or otherwise — to allow the customization of a UI element to be achievable by an operation directly performed on the element itself, rather than in a distant and separately developed part of the UI

- To achieve this level of configurability with no extra effort on the part of developers — that is, without requiring them to plan up front for the specific axes of configurability which the resulting application offers[2]

These broader values are still distant, but we believe they are only achievable through development organised on the principles we have described for our system, relying on some key choices:

- Expression of customization as well as application structure in a declarative form based on transparent state — for which a good model is the state-based JSON dialect of JavaScript, highly amenable to transformation and transmission

---

[1] This goal is a key goal of one of the major partners of the Fluid Project, the **Global Public Inclusive Infrastructure** (GPII)[15] which aims to deliver universal accessibility (and hence universal customization) for all applications, mediated by means of globally available personal profiles held in a cloud-based system

[2] This is a goal specifically defeated by "object-oriented" methodologies which typically cast amenability to a particular form of configuration in terms of derivation from a previously formulated *interface* or *base class*. New such axes cannot be introduced without rewriting existing code.

- Interpretation of customization as well as application structure in a *context-aware* semantic — where each configuration item is not only *context-aware* but also *context-forming* — that is, forming a context guiding the interpretation of further items.

The conjunction of *customization* with *application structure* in these two goals suggests, as we believe, that a further key element in achieving the goals is the specification of what we call application structure *in the same terms as* those we cast what we have called customization. This conjunction has been seen already in configuration-based IoC systems such as Spring and Guice, but so far only in thin layers representing the outermost and grossest layers of application function (and hence those of less immediate interest to end users) and not in a suitably context-aware way.

3.3 Scale of Potential Benefits

A landmark paper assessing the scale of benefits that might be expected from a new programming methodology or technology was Brooks' "No Silver Bullet" [11] of 1986. In it he makes the crucial distinction between **essential complexity** (the complexity inherent in the specification of a particular task to be met by software) and **accidental complexity** (the complexity which the methods and technologies used in the solution add to the task). Through various considerations, Brooks concludes that it is unreasonable to expect more than one order of magnitude in efficiency improvements through a change in methodology. We consider through arguments here that his conclusions are pessimistic and we should expect that very much greater improvements are possible.

3.3.1 Broadening of the field and redundancy

The number of practicing software engineers may have exploded more than 100-fold since the 1980s when Brooks was writing. The paradox of this huge explosion of the discipline is that rather than driving the satisfaction of differing needs, (the "one size fits one" of Inclusive Design), the average software practitioner finds him/herself mostly involved in makework, integration tasks, or duplicating numerous small pieces of work that have already been performed by his/her peers. This is nowhere more true than in the field of web applications, where millions of apparently very similar widgets and interactions are backed by thousands of different hand-crafted workflows written in standard procedural logic.

The natural economics of the field will gradually improve this situation over time, as standard frameworks and technologies such as jQuery and HTML5 displace their competitors, but this does not obviate the fact that this massive redundancy of effort harbours the possibility for great increases in efficiency — at least an order of magnitude through this cause alone.

One reason Brooks may fail to consider the power of the redundancy argument is that at the time of writing, the majority of the work done in the field was still of the type categorised as "deep" in section 3.1. That is, this was specialised work in the construction of artefacts such as operating systems, IC design, compilers, and numerical algorithms primarily of interest to computer scientists. Because of more tightly defined requirements, and greater variation in delivery environments, less of the redundancy across projects of this kind is likely to result in realisable savings.

3.3.2 Order of essential complexity argument

Brooks accepts that the methods of his day (including the then still nascent object orientation) imply a superlinear scaling of problem complexity with respect to problem size. However, without good reason, he ascribes all of this superlinear scaling to the domain of "essential complexity" rather than "accidental complexity" — to quote, *"Many of the classic problems of developing software products derive from this essential complexity and its nonlinear increases with size."*. He makes no references to superlinear scaling deriving from accidental complexity but instead seems to treat accidental causes as operating simply through proportional effects. In our section 1.2.1 considering the effects of dependency in software design, we have presented several causes through which superlinear accidental complexity is certain, using current methods in software technology, and we are aware of many more. Until the field as a whole has identified and removed *all* perceptible causes of superlinear accidental complexity, Brooks' assertion that the success of software engineering is limited by essentials is not tenable. So far, arguments in the literature that make direct quantitative assertions about the order of accidental complexity which could be expected from following a particular software model or methodology are not common.

4. How Infusion IoC is Used

The configuration for our IoC system is issued in two kinds of JSON structures, known as **defaults** and **demands blocks**. This configuration is *static*, in that it is issued directly upon loading of the containing JavaScript files, and does not change over the lifetime of the application. A different value for defaults/demands constitutes a different version of the application or framework in question. Defaults and demands blocks are governed by a well-defined grammar, although at various points in the "syntax", the content is unconstrained, to allow arbitrary application structure to be expressed. The named units of composition described by the grammar are named "components" although these need not correspond to the traditional concept of a "UI component" or "widget".

The examples presented here show the syntax supported by the version 1.4 release of Fluid Infusion, of September 2011. Since the Infusion IoC system is still under development, future versions of Infusion will feature different support, although the basic syntax presented here is expected to remain essentially stable.

```
fluid.defaults("fluid.uploader.multiFileUploader", {
    gradeNames: "fluid.viewComponent",
    queueSettings: {
        fileSizeLimit: 20480,
    },
    ...
    components: {
        strategy: {
            type: "fluid.uploader.progressiveStrategy"
        },

        fileQueueView: {
            type: "fluid.uploader.fileQueueView",
            options: {
                model: "{multiFileUploader}.queue.files",
                uploaderContainer: "{multiFileUploader}.container"
            }
        },
    ...
    }
}
```

Figure 2: Sample of a defaults block

4.1 Defaults and Components

A **defaults block** sets up a default set of options for a component, as well as defining its immediate composition structure in terms of subcomponents and other non-component material. A run of the IoC system may be triggered by a call to a concrete JavaScript function which directly or indirectly instantiates one or more components in accordance with this configuration, creating a *component tree*. Components are *instances*, analogous to object instances in an OO system but differing in a number of ways. Points of similarity are that components are packages of related data and functions (*methods*) — differences are that components are considered freely addressable as JSON structures, and are not derived from either classes (in the OO sense) or a prototype hierarchy (in the JavaScript sense).

Some roles for components in our system are as follows:

- A generalised "unit of computational work"
- An actual "widget on the screen"
- The result of a decision about an implementation strategy
- A context for further such decisions
- A named unit of scoping where state may be looked up

Figure 2 shows part of the defaults structure for a component `fluid.uploader.multiFileUploader` implementing the UI of a progressively enhanceable Uploader widget. Parts of the configuration similar in nature to that shown are omitted with ellipses. Note that the names of components are qualified names held in a (single) global namespace. Whilst this top-level component is a *view component* in the MVC sense, subcomponents further down the tree will in general have more abstract functions and not be bound to the view.

4.1.1 Grades

Firstly, the component announces its **grade** — grades are forms of *types* but a specific conception based around *com-*

position of JSON documents rather than having a focus on runtime data structure or substitutability as in OO. This composition is operated by **merging** the contents of multiple documents which are given the semantics of *aligned state*. This is a natural operation on the JSON model of state, as canonically implemented by standard utilities such as `jquery.extend()`. This is closely related to our conception of *transparent state* discussed in section 4.3, and consequences of this alignment are discussed further in 4.3.3.

The primary purposes of Infusion Grades are to i) fix the signature of the component's creator function, and ii) to set up any special semantics to be applied when building up component specification through merging of JSON structures. This latter amounts to a light *schema* applied to the JSON structure of the component's options which is otherwise free-form (e.g. in this case, the `queueSettings` section). There are currently only 5 grades built in as primitives the Infusion system itself, named `littleComponent`, `modelComponent`, `eventedComponent`, `viewComponent` and `rendererComponent`, although in fact any component may act as a grade through its `defaults` structure.

In this way, we create a model for **types as documents** which is crucial to the reduction of all application structure to a declarative form. New types can be created by simply supplying new documents to the system, and the effect of *combining types*, often so problematic in the OO world as an unclear pattern of *multiple inheritance* can simply be understood in terms of *combining documents*. The way is paved for end users to engineer the effect of creating their own "types" using straightforward authoring tools, bypassing the traditional "gatekeepers of state", the developers.

4.1.2 Subcomponents

The view in Figure 2 shows 2 subcomponents configured for the top-level component, which are named `strategy` and `fileQueueView`. When the component is instantiated, the subcomponents will be constructed by the system and assigned as top-level members of the overall component with these names. An important aspect of this aggregation system is that, since the subcomponents are resolved and instantiated by the framework, there is no necessary induction of L-dependency (see section 1.1) of a supercomponent on a subcomponent by this form of "has-a" relationship as there is in classical OO systems. In classical OO, this dependency is induced by constructional responsibility for the subcomponent by the supercomponent, which here is absent. Indeed, third parties may freely contribute additional subcomponents, or modify or resolve away the subcomponents drawn up in defaults blocks, without necessarily disturbing the operation of the supercomponent, as we will show in section 4.2 on *demands blocks*.

The subcomponents here are described by **type names** — these are **function names** in the same space as the supercomponent name `"fluid.uploader.multiFileUploader"`. Note that these **need not** correspond to the names of actual functions globally registered into the system. In this case, `"fluid.uploader.fileQueueView"` does indeed correspond to such a concrete function, whereas `"fluid.uploader.progressiveStrategy"` does not. The latter name is supplied as a function name which will enter **function resolution** as described in section 4.2. This contrast may be compared to the contrast between *interface names* and *concrete class names* in a classical OO system, in that the latter are expected to be directly instantiated, and the former are not — the situation is not directly analogous since in Infusion IoC there is no necessarily induced "is-a" relationship between a function name entering resolution and the concretely resolved name used for instantiation. This is a consequence of the fact mentioned in the previous paragraph, that a subcomponent need not, and in most cases does not, impose any direct contract on its supercomponent.

The typical absence of this upward contract in component hierarchies driven by Infusion IoC is one of the crucial ways in which our system improves the L-dependence structure of a design. By removing these "dependence arcs" from the graph, its geometry is pushed further towards the right-hand end of the diagram in Figure 1, representing designs with a flatter, more scalable dependence structure.

4.1.3 Context Expressions and Scoping

The subcomponent `fileQueueView` which is more concretely defined in Figure 2 includes some configuration using a special syntax, e.g. the string `"{multiFileUploader}.container"`. This type of expression is used extensively within IoC, referred to as **contextualised EL expression** or **path expression**[3]. The initial section within braces refers to the name of a **context**, actually resolving onto a particular component in the tree that will instantiate, and the remainder of the expression is interpreted as a path within that component.

A component can be matched via the *context* portion of such an expression through a few routes. In the current system, a component, once instantiated in a component tree, gives rise to either two or three *context names* which can match against such a name within braces, e.g. `multiFileUploader` in this case. Considering as an example, the context names formed by the subcomponent `fileQueueView` above are as follows:

- The fully qualified name of the concrete component as instantiated (in the above case, `fluid.uploader.fileQueueView`)
- The final segment of the fully qualified name (e.g. `fileQueueView`)
- The subcomponent's name within its parent, if any (in this case, *also* `fileQueueView`).

---

[3] The use of *expression* here is slightly misleading since in fact no expression elements (operators, variables, etc.) are permitted in these strings. The usage of "expression" has been inherited from other environments, such as JSPs, ASPs, etc. where a full *expression language* was provided for such string-encoded value references.

Such context names are considered *in scope* from a site of resolution, for example, the instantiating `fileQueueView` component above, if they match a component which is either an ancestor (container) of the component holding the resolution site, or if they are a sibling of such a component. Therefore, in the simple case above showing just three components, *every* component in the tree is a potential site which may match the context name `multiFileUploader` demanded from the configuration of `fileQueueView` — although this name in practice clearly matches the root component. Figure 3 shows the components in scope in a more general case — the most darkly shaded component, numbered 0, is the resolution site and the component currently being instantiated by the system, and the more lightly shaded components, with higher numbers, are the components which are considered in scope for forming context names, with the number indicating the priority order. Components with lower numbers will "hide" scopes formed by components with higher numbers, as in the traditional rules for operating nested scopes in programming languages.

4.2 Demands Blocks

Function names such as `fluid.uploader.progressive Strategy` and `fluid.uploader.fileQueueView` that appear as subcomponent type names in Figure 2 ultimately give rise to concrete function invocations by the Infusion IoC system. The crucial capability of the system to meet the kinds of configuration needs we described in section 3.2 is achieved through the **function resolution** process — the designation of the particular function invocation required, as appearing in subcomponent definitions and in several other places in the framework is *transformed* by the intercession of rules which transform the function invocation from one form into another. This transformation is specified by issuing JSON structures known as "demands blocks", a partner to the defaults blocks of the previous sections.

Whereas defaults blocks specify the basic skeleton of the component tree, demands blocks intercede in a *context–aware way* to transform the elements of this skeleton to meet the particular needs of the user in a particular context. This intercession is the analogous of the *advice* action of Aspect-Oriented Programming that we considered in section 2.2.

4.2.1 Simple Use of a Demands Block

A very simple example of a demands block is shown in figure 4. This shows an "advice" applied to the subcomponent `strategy` of type `fluid.uploader.progressiveStrategy` that we saw in diagram 2. The function `fluid.demands` takes three arguments:

demandedName — a string, the original function name demanded by the configuration site being resolved

contextNames — a string or array of strings, the *context names* which must be visible for this demands block to

be activated in order to resolve the demanded function names

disposition — a JSON structure describing the resolution to be performed ("advice") — as well as resolving the demanded function name, this may also describe rules for transforming the function arguments.

In this case, the disposition simply replaces the demanded function name (which as we mentioned in section 4.1.2 in fact had no implementation) with another. In a context where the context name `fluid.uploader.html5` can be seen, this demands block directs that the function name `fluid.uploader.html5Strategy` be used in place of the original name `fluid.uploader.progressiveStrategy`. The rules for scoping are the same as those shown for *value resolution* in Figure 3 — components which do not fall in the numbered, lightly shaded region of the component tree relative to the resolution site are not considered for the purposes of forming contexts for function resolution by demands blocks.

```
fluid.demands("fluid.uploader.progressiveStrategy",
              "fluid.uploader.html5", {
    funcName: "fluid.uploader.html5Strategy"
});
```

Figure 4: A simple demands block

4.2.2 A More Complex Demands Block

As well as the ability to redirect the dispatch of the required function name held in the demands block, the arguments to the function call may also be freely interspersed, replaced, or merged with material drawn from elsewhere in the tree.

```
fluid.demands("fluid.uploader.local", "fluid.uploader.html5Strategy", {
    funcName: "fluid.uploader.html5Strategy.local",
    args: [
        "{multiFileUploader}.queue",
        "{html5Strategy}.options.legacyBrowserFileLimit",
        "{options}"
    ]
});
```

Figure 5: Sample of a demands block

In Figure 5, the *disposition* entry now contains an entry `args` in addition to `funcName`. This block directs that in addition to resolving the demanded function name onto a particular concrete implementation `fluid.uploader.html5Strategy.local`, its argument list is also to be replaced. The syntax used for argument lists, in addition to allowing literal JavaScript constants, also allows any combination of values using the *value resolution syntax* that we saw in section 4.1, using the same resolution rules.

This adds a new capability to programming. Facing a function with a signature actually unknown to the calling site, three argument values are "fished" out of the environment, the structural scopes surrounding the call site, in order to meet its contract. This adds a capability for loose coupling

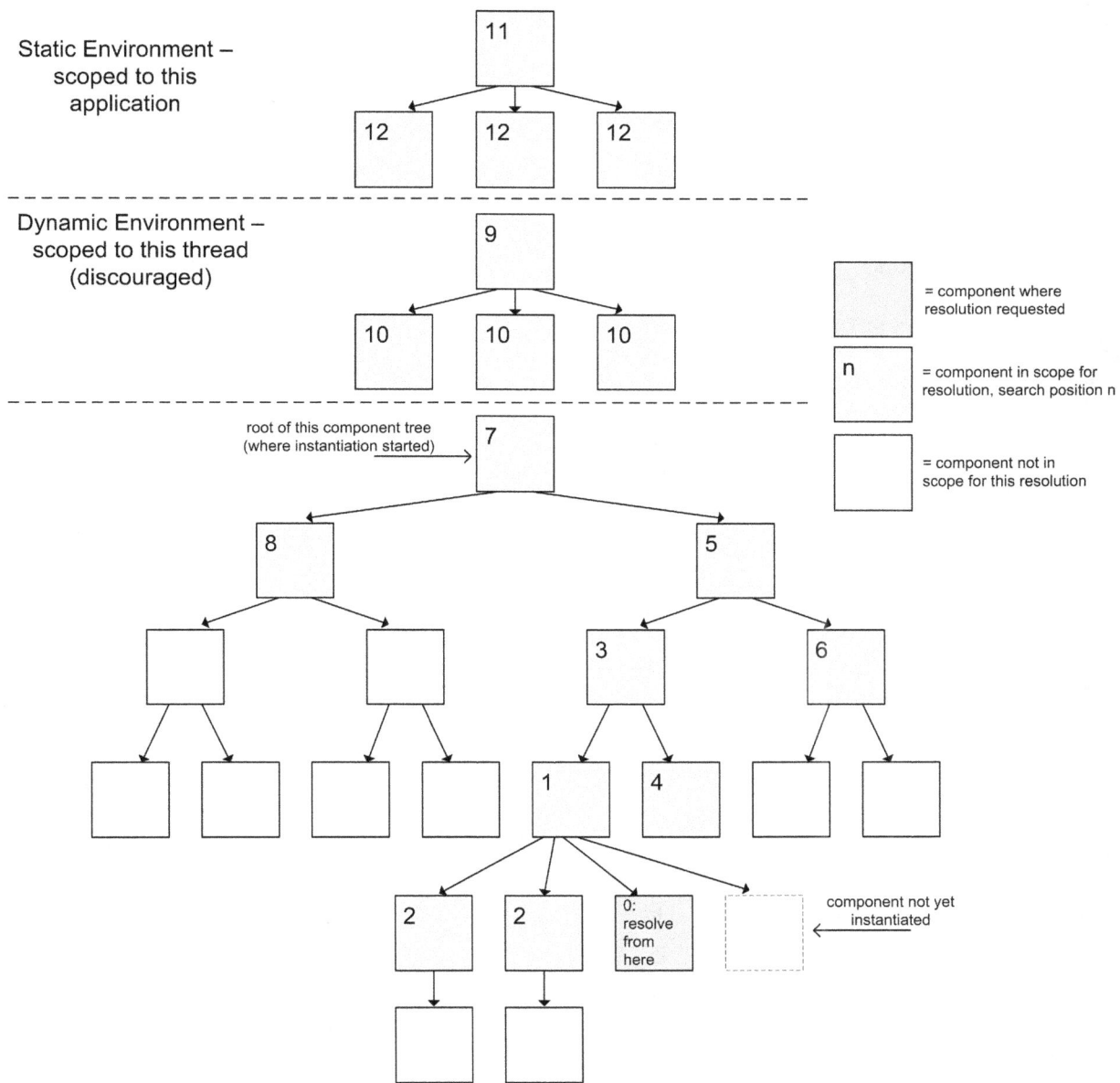

Figure 3: Scope Visibility and Priority for Context Resolution

that was not previously available — a completely unrelated third party may now intercede between any function call site, and any other function implementation site, and cause the caller and callee to be conformed together, irrespective of any mismatch between the actual function name *as well as any mismatch in the function signature*.

This ability to "fish" such values in order to meet unanticipated (by either the caller or callee) function contracts requires a different model for how state is made available in a program design. In particular, it argues against the "data hiding" paradigm that is recommended by object-orientation. In the next section, we will see how the antithesis to this approach, one that we name the use of *transparent state*, can

be made the basis of a workable progamming model, whilst still meeting the goals which originally seemed to motivate the use of data hiding.

4.3 The ChangeApplier and the conception of *transparent state*

It is a key requirement to operate demands blocks, that the component tree is defined in terms of what we call **transparent state**. The meaning of this is something similar to the prescription of *RESTfulness*[16] for web applications — that the state of the system is indexed by path-segmented strings in a public and stable namespace. This feature arises simply and naturally when JSON-encoded data is accessed from the JavaScript language, but tends to be obscured when the traditional recommendations in favour of data hiding are followed.

4.3.1 The "State API"

One way of viewing the adoption of transparent state, is in terms of a "moral API" which is considered to be always in operation when state is being addressed. We use the locution "moral API" here since in contrast to traditional formulations of an API, the most important aspect which is fixed by the standardisation is not the names and signatures appearing in the API, but the underlying semantic. We present a few embodiments of such an API in the wider world, as well as a few which appear in Infusion's API, but note that the commitment to transparent state means that there is wide latitude in the specifics of the API. As long as an API provides appropriate access to some body of underlying state, it is always possible to provide adaptors that allow code that uses any one applicable API to operate with whatever API is actually provided. In the middle maturity of the Infusion system, the use of any explicit API in code will disappear, to be replaced by a declarative syntax, and in the full maturity, the syntax itself will disappear to be replaced by graphical or other tools for direct manipulation of the application.

In terms of our analogy with the HTTP REST verbs, which in the HTTP protocol are named POST, GET, PUT, and DELETE, the members of this API can be considered as representatives of the CRUD (Create, Read, Update, Delete) paradigm, originally proposed by James Martin[17] as an approach towards the management of persistent state. The extra element which REST adds to the original conception of CRUD is the insistence that the data items addressed by the state operations are indexed by stable, public, path-segmented strings.

We argue that this idiom is appropriate for the management of all mutable state (and access to immutable state) *within* an application, rather than just operated across process or machine boundaries as part of the original conception of CRUD/REST. Certainly, the JavaScript language, by providing the native idiom for addressing freely-formed JSON structures as a language primitive, makes this conception extremely natural — the path-segmented stable strings we mentioned are simply the natural member access operators provided by the language.

Using this *RESTful* approach to *all* application state, however, implies that all of this state be made available *"as if"* represented by a single, giant lazily loaded JSON structure. Whilst future developments in the JavaScript language (proxies, arriving in ECMAScript Harmony[13]) do promise to make this a practical possibility, the constraints of the current JavaScript language imply that access to state which is *not* directly embodied by a concrete and directly available JSON structure of the right kind needs to be mediated by the use of an old-fashioned API.

Such APIs are present in Fluid Infusion, as part of a package of data binding primitives in the core framework as well as a particular implementation known as the **ChangeApplier** which mediates mutation of state. Figure 6 shows the equivalence between actions performed directly in the core language, the ChangeApplier, and HTTP REST as a point of comparison.

4.3.2 Addressing the goals which appeared to motivate data hiding

Data access policies We argue that adoption of the transparent state model makes many of the goals which appeared to motivate data hiding, paradoxically, *easier* rather than harder to meet. An interesting representative of these goals is secured access to data. Many applications operate a *security model*, defining rules and predicates which specify which users of the application should be permitted to read, modify, or perform other operations with respect to which data that the application manages.

A very popular framework for managing such security assertions is *Spring Security*[21], a subproject of the Spring IoC framework mentioned earlier as the foremost popular embodiment of IoC ideas in the Java community. Spring Security gains a great measure of its power through reducing security assertions about access of principals to data and implementations to a declarative form — just the same reduction that motivates our own work. However, the power of Spring Security and similar frameworks to express policy is seriously hampered by a necessary lack of insight into the *identity of data* which is a consequence of the OO model.

An example where transparent state aids access policy Here is a real-world example of a desired security policy that arose in the context of work on one of our partner projects, the CollectionSpace Project[14]. This project operates a relational model, connecting together data seen as *records* connected by *relations*. The required security policy expressed that permission for a principal to modify the relation between two records should be derived from the permission held on the records which it related. Specifically, a principal should only have permission to modify a relation between two records if they already held permission to modify the contents of both records separately.

It's clear that without a stable and global identity (expressed, preferably, as a simply-structured string) addressing each record in the system, it is impossible for such a security policy to be expressed in any declarative form — and since Spring Security and suchlike frameworks have no place for such an addressing scheme, they cannot express such a policy at all. This requires such a policy to fall back to non-declarative schemes and be expressed literally in application code, therefore putting it out of reach of end users of the system to inspect and modify.

This example shows a case where the adoption of a transparent state scheme positively assists rather than hinders the

	JavaScript native	Infusion API	HTTP REST
Read	`var x = root.path1.path2;`	`var x = accessor.get(root, "path1.path2")`	`GET root/path1/path2`
Write	`root.path1.path2 = "value";`	`accessor.set(root, "path1.path2", "value")` **OR** `applier.fireChangeRequest({type: "ADD", path: "path1.path2", value: "value"})`	`PUT root/path1/path2 value`
Delete	`delete root.path1.path2;`	`applier.fireChangeRequest({type: "DELETE", path: "path1.path2"})`	`DELETE root/path1/path2`

Figure 6: Comparison of syntaxes for direct access to mapped state

expression of policies controlling capabilities by users of a system to access or modify state.

Maintaining invariants and Serialization   Another important category of goals motivating data hiding is maintaining **data integrity**. Often, state comes together with a set of *invariants* or *validation rules* which must be checked and maintained whenever state modification is attempted. In the OO paradigm, these invariants are traditionally maintained by logic embedded in application code packaged as *methods* (private or public) of the objects holding the state to which the invariant refers.

Having such rules locked up in application code carries similar risks to those just mentioned. A particular difficulty this creates is providing the application function of *serialization* — taking the set of application state and writing it to a serial form such a disk file or network stream, or this process in reverse. Serialization in an OO system always meets the design risk represented by the packaging ensuring an object's invariant protection as a direct part of the object's own API. During the deserialization process, this protection must be "somehow" suspended, this "somehow" being directly at odds with the OO philosophy. As the object tree is built up in memory, it is quite likely that the invariants protecting validity of the state will be violated at intermediate points where the object tree is incomplete — especially if these invariants relate to relations amongst objects. In semi-dynamic environments such as Java, object serialization needs to be a specialised platform/language facility, and is often hard to control. In static languages such as C++, serialization poses a double burden on developers — having designed an object hierarchy once, a separate design effort needs to be mounted to serialize it.

Invariants through ChangeApplier guards   A system which separates state from behaviour, as we recommend, deals with such issues trivially — state serialization and deserialization are performed directly by the primitives provided by the base language, e.g. in JavaScript, the `JSON.stringify` and `JSON.parse`. Alternative serializations are also trivial, either through transforming the JSON tree, or by using the iteration primitives of the language to drive an alternative serialization. The capability to ensure invariants (or not, depending on whether they are required) is mediated by mechanisms held in the *State API* we described earlier. In particular, the machinery held within the *ChangeApplier* allows the registration of **guards**, listeners to the **change events** passing through the system attempting to honour the modification of state requested by the user. If an event violates the invariant embodied in a guard, it is *vetoed* — the event is discarded and the state modification does not occur.

The configuration of guards is defined in a further document, itself following the transparent state model, aligned with the primitive state. This document defines, or can be directly derived from a *schema* for the primary state. This continuation of the "types as documents" model which we touched on in section 4.1.1 on *grades* continues to put power in the hands of users to prescribe behaviour by modifying documents, rather than enfranchising developers by putting power in the hands of authors of application code.

Transactionality   A closely related issue to maintaining of invariants for data integrity, is the requirement for *transactional updates* to state. In a system with transactional updates, it is not possible to observe the effects of partially updated state during a long sequence of coordinated updates — instead, outside the transaction, the updates appear to be applied atomically. This is the kind of issue that is not typically handled at the language level in an OO system, but instead arises as part of a particular object-relational mapping (ORM) technology which maps the state of objects in a running system onto persistent state held in some form of database layer.

By adopting a transparent state model, in conjunction with "change application" machinery such as the ChangeApplier, transactional semantics can be supplied in a standard way for in-memory objects, matching the semantics of their persistent analogues in the database layer. In figure 6, the argument to the method `fireChangeRequest` can be seen to be a piece of transparent state in itself — in fact, a *change request object* which is the natural form of entries in system following the transaction log pattern. The implementation of the ChangeApplier is capable of applying grouping to this stream of events, ensuring that units of change represented by a group forming a transaction are either seen to be applied completely (atomically) or not at all, in the case of a guard (invariant) failure or other error.

4.3.3 New capabilities through transparent, mapped state

The transparency provided by stable addressing of state allows more powerful reorganisations of data and the operations performed on it. Examples include the *bidirectional programming* framework of Pierce et al.[18], in which state is "lensed" through information–preserving transformations. The greatest difficulty with these schemes in practice is the *alignment* of this state before and after the transformation — a transparent state model performs this alignment intrinsically and naturally. Another example is work involving parallelisation of irregular algorithms[19]. An important prerequisite for this kind of task transformation is that units of work are divided up into stably named elements embedded in a graph, without *distant side-effects*. This is just the partitioning of work units presented by the IoC component tree and its indexing model.

4.3.4 Transparency applied to component trees

Since component trees are not in general considered mutable, this potential for global reference raises few problems during the instantiation process itself. The parts of the component trees which hold state which is considered mutable after instantiation are designated as **models** and access to them is mediated by a companion component known as a **change applier**. This, whilst preserving the transparency of addressing through path strings, restores these virtues which are intended to be achieved through encapsulation and data hiding in the object–oriented model — atomicity of update, consistency through verification of invariants, and a publish/subscribe model for notification of changes. A feature known as **proxies** which is upcoming in the ECMAScript 6 specification[13] will enable this package of guarded access to be applied to state accessed through the natural semantics of the language.

5. Case Studies in Implementation

5.1 Case study — Progressively enhanced Uploader component

Whilst the Infusion IoC system to some extent allows us to get beyond traditional conceptions of "component–oriented" or "object–oriented" applications, it is an important stepping–stone in providing value to both users and developers of the system alike to develop packages of functionality that fill well-defined, though flexible functions. This

flexibility is also a stepping-stone to meeting the fuller goals of Inclusive Design.

5.1.1 Goals for the Uploader Widget

An application that we have worked on recently and present here is that of a Uploader "widget". This widget assists users to select one or more files from their local filesystem, and to supervise the process, with feedback, of transmitting them via HTTP to a web server. This implementation is a challenge due to the broad range of technologies potentially available in the browser environment to meet this need, stretching from the very latest versions of HTML5 interactions delivered in this year's Firefox 4 browser, back to the extremely basic support for uploading single files provided by HTML 4 in the 1990s. A crucial goal of the uploader is to provide a single, concrete entry point to the developer/integrator, whilst automatically sensing the capabilities of the environment, registering the user's preferences and selecting an appropriate implementation strategy in a transparent way, in accordance with the goals of progressive enhancement.

Whilst the Uploader presents a straightforward and stable entry point to users as a simple function call, under the surface it uses IoC to intelligently adapt to the combination of the capabilities of the user's browser and their expressed preferences. At the same time, this implementation can be extended to deal with unanticipated technologies and environments, without modification of either the implementation or user code. These requirements of adaptibility to both context and preferences are a proxy for the wider goals of Inclusive Design in more ambitious problems.

5.1.2 From the integrator's point of view

In its simplest possible form, the widget can be used as shown in Figure 7 (assuming inclusion of appropriate Fluid and jQuery[22] JavaScript files).

```
<html>
  ....
    <form method="post" enctype="multipart/form-data"
          class="myUploader">
        <input name="fileData" type="file" />
        <input type="submit" value="Save"/>
    </form>
    <script type="text/javascript">
        fluid.uploader(".myUploader");
    </script>
</html>
```

Figure 7: Sample instantiation of an uploader component

In this simple form, a call to a concretely named JavaScript function is targeted at a block of markup holding a standard (HTML4-style) file upload form. Since no further configuration is supplied, the IoC machinery behind the function call will detect whether a Flash version 9, Flash version 10, HTML5 (Firefox 3.6-style) or Binary XHR-compliant HTML5 style (Firefox 4 or Chrome) uploader is the most appropriate form, inject appropriate markup, and construct a suitable implementation. Should none of these choices be workable, or if JavaScript is not enabled in the browser, the markup will be left as it is and still provide basic functionality for selecting and uploading a file.

5.1.3 Benefits provided by Infusion IoC

The variant enriched implementations all present a common interface, allowing selection of multiple files, feedback of individual and overall progress as well as pausing or cancellation of operations. Due to the power of IoC, this implementation code, as well as several other sections of the implementation are reused across the variants as "invariant sections" of the component tree. Even this relatively compact problem would have been hard to address through standard "object–oriented" techniques — assembling a class hierarchy mapping this area would have run into two principal hazards:

Firstly, the pattern of code reuse, with multiple, mutually–overlapping pieces of implementation shared between the configurations would have been hard to map onto a traditional inheritance hierarchy. Even were this done, it would be hard to be assured that in the face of future variation, the mapping would remain stable. In Infusion's IoC implementation, since essentially all implementation which is in code is packaged in a form equivalent to that of **free**, context-less functions, it is easy to be assured that it can be recomposed by means of demands blocks into a new and suitable arrangement where implementation can be common.

Secondly, the simple point of entry in terms of a stable, context-less function `fluid.uploader` would have been harder to achieve. Given the delivered implementation is polymorphically variable, this would either have required concrete type-names to be mentioned in a "constructor", or the use of some suitable "factory method" on an already existing source of implementations... whose construction would represent the same problem, pushed back one level.

Say that, for example, despite the now obsolescence of Google's "Gears" technology for native browser functions, a user wanted to extend this Uploader implementation set to support it. This could be done without modification of either the user entry point `fluid.uploader` or the implementation files. In fact, all the demands blocks and implementation functions required for, say Gears, or some unanticipated future technology could be scoped to a JavaScript file which is not even delivered to users with user agents not supporting this technology. This kind of "file inclusion-based polymorphism" is hard to package with object–oriented techniques where constructors delivering implementations typically need to appear within the delivering code.

5.1.4 Use of demands blocks in Uploader implementation

Figure 8 shows schematically the structure of some of the demands blocks implementing the Uploader widget. Each arrow linked with a circle along its length represents a *contextual resolution* — a choice made by the instantiation system based on the context provided by constructions which have already concluded. At the top of the diagram are raw **context tags** decoded by a direct inspection of the capabilities of the user agent — `fluid.browser.supportsBinaryXHR`, etc. Below this level in the tree is the point at which user configured material may be used to guide resolution, for a particular instantiation of the uploader, onto a particular strategy to be used. In the absence of this, the default demands structure will proceed by a default algorithm onto the uploader strategy tags, `fluid.uploader.html5` etc. Below this level, the resolution continues to cascade onto particular elements of the uploader implementation, guided by the strategy tags. At each level of demands resolution, there is scope for further demands blocks contributed at the user's request, or an integrator or other party, to intercede, or in AOP terminology to "advise" the construction of subcomponents, by fetching data or implementation sourced from other parts of the uploader's tree — or even, from other parts of a wider component tree. Whilst the uploader is packaged in such a way that it is usable by standard JavaScript citizens as a simple function call, the full power of the IoC system together with the uploader is only realised when the entire implementation of an application is delivered as a single, giant interconnected series of demands blocks — with demands resolution given the power to roam freely and fetch contextualised data to be delivered anywhere within or among elements which would formerly have been seen to be opaque, monolithic "components".

Whilst Figure 8 resembles a standard UML diagram in some respects, the meaning is somewhat different. This diagram shows a schematic for data structures which *might* exist in certain histories of the system, rather than those which will or do exist, statically. It is this contextual awareness at each point of the system that allows it to be easily extended for new cases, with instantiation guided along new paths, made visible by new demands blocks being brought into scope.

5.2 Wider case study - The CollectionSpace Collections Management System

The CollectionSpace project[14], led by the Museum of the Moving Image in New York, is producing collections management software for the use of museum curators and other staff. The project is using the current version of the Infusion IoC system, as described here. This project is proving an excellent ground for exploring the benefits in adaptible and declarative software that the IoC approach can offer. The user interface for this application consists of few but very detailed pages, containing many hundreds of widgets, reflecting the level of detail of the specialised knowledge operated in the domain of exhibit curation. As suggested in the previous section, the entire UI for this application is implemented as a giant, single-rooted tree of components gov-

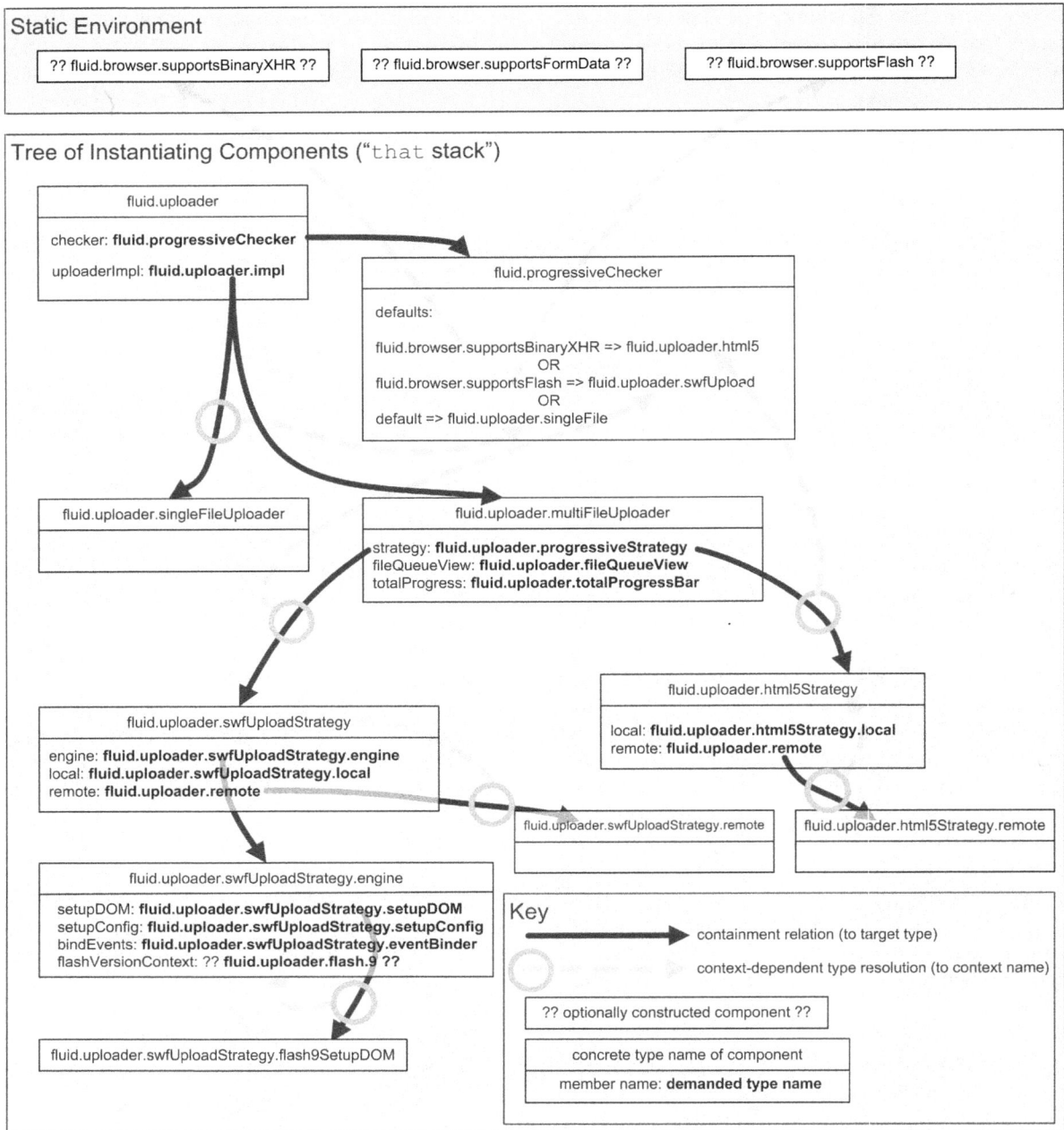

Static Environment

?? fluid.browser.supportsBinaryXHR ??   ?? fluid.browser.supportsFormData ??   ?? fluid.browser.supportsFlash ??

Tree of Instantiating Components ("`that` stack")

fluid.uploader

checker: **fluid.progressiveChecker**

uploaderImpl: **fluid.uploader.impl**

fluid.progressiveChecker

defaults:

fluid.browser.supportsBinaryXHR => fluid.uploader.html5
OR
fluid.browser.supportsFlash => fluid.uploader.swfUpload
OR
default => fluid.uploader.singleFile

fluid.uploader.singleFileUploader

fluid.uploader.multiFileUploader

strategy: **fluid.uploader.progressiveStrategy**
fileQueueView: **fluid.uploader.fileQueueView**
totalProgress: **fluid.uploader.totalProgressBar**

fluid.uploader.html5Strategy

local: **fluid.uploader.html5Strategy.local**
remote: **fluid.uploader.remote**

fluid.uploader.swfUploadStrategy

engine: **fluid.uploader.swfUploadStrategy.engine**
local: **fluid.uploader.swfUploadStrategy.local**
remote: **fluid.uploader.remote**

fluid.uploader.swfUploadStrategy.remote

fluid.uploader.html5Strategy.remote

fluid.uploader.swfUploadStrategy.engine

setupDOM: **fluid.uploader.swfUploadStrategy.setupDOM**
setupConfig: **fluid.uploader.swfUploadStrategy.setupConfig**
bindEvents: **fluid.uploader.swfUploadStrategy.eventBinder**
flashVersionContext: ?? **fluid.uploader.flash.9** ??

Key

containment relation (to target type)

context-dependent type resolution (to context name)

?? optionally constructed component ??

concrete type name of component

member name: **demanded type name**

fluid.uploader.swfUploadStrategy.flash9SetupDOM

Figure 8: Illustration of component tree instantiation for Uploader widget

erned by the underlying graph of demands blocks. This tree comprises components such as the Uploader and numerous others, instantiated by IoC. One immediate benefit of this approach for users is the easy adaptibility of the interface in a schema-driven way. Rather than relying on development support to orchestrate changes required by local institutions which may have very widely differing requirements, these can instead be enacted by editing simply-structured JSON files or in many cases can be inferred automatically from a description of the application's schema.

Component markup, similar to component state, is not locked up in implementation files but "out in the open" in unpolluted and standard HTML files, reskinning of the application similarly can be performed without development support, using standard HTML editing tools. These kinds of reskinning comprise, but go beyond that possible through simple CSS effects. Directly editing HTML enables widespread reorganisation of the layout and content of the markup operated either by individual components or entire pages. This composition of markup is performed by the **Fluid Renderer**, an engine described in more detail in the online references for the Fluid Framework.

6. Status and Trajectory of the Implementation

The Fluid group are currently working towards the 1.4 release of the Infusion system, which is targetted for September 2011. This will be the first public release in which the described implementation of the IoC system (as well as the Uploader widget and other components not described here) will be available. This release is considered to be in a "sneak peek" mode where API and concepts are not fully stabilised. Although several of Fluid's production-ready components are implemented in terms of this system already, the IoC system and framework itself are not yet considered to have reached a production-worthy condition in terms of stable use by general users. Readers are invited to come along and inspect our progress, and even join in, at our github repository held at `https://github.com/fluid-project/infusion`. Overall documentation for the Infusion system, including the IoC implementation, is held at `http://wiki.fluidproject.org/display/fluid/Infusion+Documentation`. Future versions of Infusion are roadmapped at `http://wiki.fluidproject.org/display/fluid/Fluid+Community+Roadmaps` — we will continue to stabilise and expand the capabilities of the IoC system as well as evolving previously implemented components to defer to it more for implementation. A crucially important, but still very early–stage work package involves our server-side implementation, Fluid **Kettle**, an IoC-driven JavaScript implementation based on the rapidly developing `Node.js` framework based on an asynchronous I/O model. A back-end based on Apache's CouchDB persistence technology using JavaScript as a query language will enable a homogeneous development model operating JavaScript at all tiers of the web application, which is hoped to bring developments of lowered barrier to entry by new developers as well as increased mobility of code and implementation algorithms between the layers.

6.1 Directions for the System

We identify two important future directions and roles for the system, continuing from our discussion of Brooks[11], which identifies a number of technical developments which might have the potential to increase the efficiency of development (see section 3.3).

6.1.1 Graphical tools and environments

The categories of *graphical programming* and *environments and tools* which Brooks identifies as crucial are ones which a constant motivation during the development of the system has been to facilitate. We expect work in them to be very fruitful. Brooks criticises the potential of graphical programming on two grounds which might remain relevant today — firstly that "flowcharts" are a poor abstraction of software structure, and secondly that superimpositions of multiple views of a program's structure are unlikely to arrive at a properly synoptic view of its function, as one might expect from the correspondence between a VLSI chip's geometric structure and its function.

We argue that the way software is designed must be modified, precisely to bring about such a correspondence between structure and function. Such structure must be built around the **data** which is being manipulated on behalf of the user, as well as the direct **interface** itself which is presented to manipulate this data. Rather than an abstract flowchart showing a sequence of operations expected to be performed by the machine, the user interface itself should be the focus of operations exposed to the user in expressing their intentions. Until the rules by which the user interface is constructed are specified in a declarative form open to interpretation by the system itself, rather than in opaque code only interpretable to a compiler, the *adaptible interface* required by Inclusive Design cannot be constructed (section 6.1.3).

Similarly, organising parts of this adaptible interface directly around the sources, transformation steps, and sinks governing the user's data, brings this most vital part of the system close to its constituency of users, rather than deliberately setting out in the opposite direction as modern recommendations on *data hiding* propose. Structuring computation around data in publically named, structured units (section 4.3) also promotes free restructuring of the actual algorithms which operate on it, making it easier to exploit variable availability of computing resources (for example, variable numbers of processors, or variable availability of computing power at different nodes of a client-server architecture).

6.1.2 "Automatic" programming and expert systems

Brooks defines automatic programming as "generation of a program for solving a problem from a statement of the problem specifications". He cites Parnas [12] who reinterprets this goal as follows: *"In short, automatic programming always has been a euphemism for programming with a higher-level language than was presently available to the programmer."* Higher-level languages to date have been constructed in two directions. Firstly, "bottom-up", building on the base of lower-level languages in the directions developers consider desirable to increase their expressiveness - for example, the construction of languages such as C++ and Java from the base of C. Secondly, "top-down", deriving from an analysis of natural languages and vocabularies of users the kinds of computer languages their requirements might intelligibly expressed in — this motivated the construction of the so-called "fourth-generation languages" (4GLs) such as MAPPER, Clipper, LiveCode, R and S.

Bottom-up language developments often fail to successfully deliver more end user needs per quantum of developer effort, and are usually focussed towards needs in the developer's domain. Top-down language developments can be very successful within particular domains, but fail to build bridges *downwards* into the world of underlying developers, by creating an impenetrable **abstraction boundary** at the level of the 4GL language syntax. Only by building a "harmonious tower of abstractions" as we allude to in section 6.1.3 can we assist both kinds of community to cooperate harmoniously on the same design, and gain the scalability benefits needed to escape Brooks' curse. By building our system out of the JSON configuration naturally made available by builtin features of the JavaScript language, we avoid creating an impenetrable abstraction boundary of this kind, a boundary on either side of which the stakeholders speak mutually unintelligible languages.

We have described the similarities between the IoC resolution process and the "goal-directed" behaviour of inference engines such as those used in some expert systems (section 2.1). We aim towards a system whereby the "statement of problem specifications" should simply be **identified with** the "program for solving a problem".

6.1.3 The Crucial Important of Homoiconicity

Many of the benefits of Infusion IoC can be interpreted from the viewpoint of seeing its JSON dialect composed of defaults and demands blocks as a *Domain-Specific Language* (DSL) [5] enjoying a crucial property known as *homoiconicity*[2]. Homoiconicity is a property of some programming languages, in which the primary representation of programs is also a conveniently expressed data structure of the language. This property makes it extremely easy to produce tools which **transform** "programs" written in this language into other forms, as well as tools which enable graphical presentation and development of the program by developers and end users.

It is a crucial requirement of the goals of Inclusive Design that bridges can be built between the worlds of software professionals and users. Homoiconic characteristics of the base language are essential to allow a bidirectional transfer of artefacts between developers and end users who work with the finished product — and allow these users to work from effects they see in the finished product back to their causes and thus conform them to their requirements. Without the transparency allowed by this bidirectional transfer, inclusive design becomes uneconomic, since each adaptation of the software must be pursued by *ad hoc* development.

In practice, the transfer from the world of software professionals to end users involves a tower of increasing levels of abstraction. In order for this transfer to be economical, the transfers should not be "mutually blind" but allow some form of harmonised understanding of the transferred abstraction — that is, there should at no level in the system be an impenetrable abstraction boundary, through which the transfer of artefacts involves a complete loss of meaning. Homoiconicity of the base system is essential to such a "harmonious tower of abstractions", stretching from the low levels out into the world of users. Previous similar systems cast as DSLs, "Fourth-generation languages" (4GLs), or code generators (see section 6.1.2) have failed to ensure this harmonious tower by introducing an impenetrable abstraction boundary represented by a language syntax.

7. Conclusion

We have made a case arguing that the longevity of application code, as well as the reach of its design space, is greatly increased by reducing as much of its volume as possible to a declarative form. A promising model for such a form are the JSON blocks we have described here, forming the demands and defaults blocks interpreted by the IoC-driven component system. We presented the feature of *homoiconicity* enjoyed by such code, expressed as natural data structures of the underlying JavaScript language, as one of the crucial enablers of the application flexibility and scalable development required for Inclusive Design.

As platforms and technologies change, new demands blocks can weave together with the old to meet new needs, without fragility in existing implementations. Should JavaScript and the web themselves cease to become current, this declarative form is easier to mechanically transform (following the mentality of LISP "macros") into forthcoming idioms, than implementations specified in imperative, sequential code. Such code that *is* written is packaged in global functions which are more or less "free", maximising the chance that it can be reused in fresh contexts without the worry of assumptions embodied in hazardous shared state such as that found in base classes or object instances. Finally, where expectations and contracts do change over time, old implementations may be adapted to new clients, and vice versa, by the interposition of suitable demands blocks, providing the appearance of new contracts for old.

References

[1] Lakos, J.: Large-Scale C++ Software Design, 1996, Addison-Wesley Professional

[2] McIlroy, D.: Macro Instruction Extensions of Compiler Languages, 1960, Communications of the ACM, Volume 3 Issue 4

[3] Chapter 15: "Everyday Inclusive Design", N. Warburton, *in* Inclusive Design: Design for the Whole Population: Edited by Clarkson, J. et al, Springer (2003)

[4] Fowler, M.: Inversion of Control Containers and the Dependency Injection pattern, http://martinfowler.com/articles/injection.html

[5] Fowler, M., Parsons, P: Domain-Specific Languages, Addison-Wesley, 2010

[6] Douglas Crockford — The JSON Saga: http://developer.yahoo.com/yui/theater/video.php?v=crockford-json

[7] Pascal Costanza, Robert Hirschfeld: Language Constructs for Context-oriented Programming: an Overview of ContextL, in:

DLS'05: Proceedings of the 2005 Symposium on Dynamic Languages, ACM, New York, NY, USA, 2005, pp. 110.

[8] Malte Appeltauer, et al.: A Comparison of Context-oriented Programming Languages. In Proceedings of the Workshop on Context-oriented Programming (COP) 2009 Genoa, Italy, July 7, 2009

[9] J. Lincke, et al.: An Open Implementation for Context-oriented Layer Composition in ContextJS, Science of Computer Programming (2010), doi:10.1016/j.scico.2010.11.013

[10] A. J. Albrecht: "Measuring Application Development Productivity," Proceedings of the Joint SHARE, GUIDE, and IBM Application Development Symposium, Monterey, California, October 1417, IBM Corporation (1979), pp. 8392.

[11] Brooks, Fred P.: "No Silver Bullet — Essence and Accident in Software Engineering". Proceedings of the IFIP Tenth World Computing Conference (1986): 10691076.

[12] D.L. Parnas: "Designing Software for Ease of Extension and Contraction," IEEE Transactions on Software Engineering, Vol. 5, No. 2, March 1979, pp. 128-38.

[13] ECMAScript 6 Proxy proposal: `http://wiki.ecmascript.org/doku.php?id=harmony:proxies`

[14] The CollectionSpace Project: `http://www.collectionspace.org/`

[15] The Global Public Inclusive Infrastructure `http://www.gpii.org/`

[16] Fielding, R.T.: Architectural Styles and the Design of Network-based Software Architectures, Doctoral dissertation (2000), University of California, Irvine

[17] Martin, J: Managing the Data-base Environment, Prentice-Hall, 1983

[18] Pierce, B.C.: Foundations for Bidirectional Programming, or: How To Build a Bidirectional Programming Language, June 2009. Keynote address at International Conference on Model Transformation (ICMT).

[19] Kulkarni, M., Carribault, P., Pingali, K., Ramanarayanan, G., Walter, B., Bala, K., Chew, L.P.: Scheduling Strategies for Optimistic Parallel Execution of Irregular Programs, SPAA '08 Proceedings of the Twentieth Annual Symposium on Parallelism in Algorithms and Architectures

[20] The Spring Framework, `http://www.springsource.org/about`

[21] The Spring Security Framework, `http://static.springsource.org/spring-security/site/index.html`

[22] The jQuery Framework, `http://jquery.com`

Strict Serializability is Harmless: A New Architecture for Enterprise Applications

Sérgio Miguel Fernandes   João Cachopo

INESC-ID Lisboa / Instituto Superior Técnico, Technical University of Lisbon
{Sergio.Fernandes,Joao.Cachopo}@ist.utl.pt

Abstract

Despite many evolutions in the software architecture of enterprise applications, one thing has remained the same over the years: They still use a relational database both for data persistence and transactional support. We argue that such design, once justified by hardware limitations, endured mostly for legacy reasons and is no longer adequate for a significant portion of modern applications running in a new generation of multicore machines with very large memories.

We propose a new architecture for enterprise applications that uses a Software Transactional Memory for transactional support at the application server tier, thereby shifting the responsibility of transaction control from the database to the application server. The database tier remains in our architecture with the sole purpose of ensuring the durability of data.

With this change we are able to provide strictly serializable transaction semantics, and we do so with increased performance. Thus, we claim that strict serializability is harmless, in the sense that programmers no longer have to trade correctness for performance for a significant class of applications. We have been using this new architecture since 2005 in the development of real-world complex object-oriented applications, and we present statistical data collected over several years about the workload patterns of these applications, revealing a surprisingly low rate of write transactions.

Categories and Subject Descriptors   D.2.11 [*Software Engineering*]: Software Architectures

General Terms   Design, Performance

Keywords   Enterprise Application Architecture, Software Transactional Memory, Strict Serializability, Persistence, Transactions, Object-Oriented Programming, Rich-Domain Applications, Fénix Framework

1. Introduction

The adoption of multicore architectures as the only way to increase the computational power of new generations of hardware spurred intense research on *Software Transactional Memory* (STM), leading to many advances in this area over the last eight years (for an actual and comprehensive description of the research made on STMs, see [19]).

STMs bring into the realm of programming languages, the age-old notion of transactions, well known in the area of *Database Management Systems* (DBMSs). STMs, however, are not concerned with the *durability* property of ACID, and, because of this, most, if not all, of the STMs' design decisions and implementations have little in common with their counterparts of the database world [14]: Unlike DBMSs, modern STMs are designed to scale well to machines with many cores, to provide strong correctness guarantees such as opacity [18], and to ensure nonblocking progress conditions such as lock freedom [15].

And yet, surprisingly, all of these great advances in the area of STMs have been mostly ignored by one of the communities that could benefit the most from them: The community of enterprise application development. In this paper, we show that there is much to gain by merging these two areas, namely, both in terms of development effort and of performance.

We propose a new architecture for enterprise applications that uses an STM, rather than a DBMS, to ensure the transactional semantics for its business operations. Because STMs do not guarantee the durability of the data, we show how to extend the STM to collaborate with a persistent storage system to ensure that the application's data are safely stored.

We claim, and provide evidence, that this new architecture is not only much better to develop many of today's complex, rich enterprise applications, but is also better suited to use the new generation of machines with many cores and very large memories that are increasingly running the application-server tiers of those applications.

Both this architecture and its implementation were developed over the last six years alongside the development of a real-world complex application—the FénixEDU[1] web application—and have been driving the execution of that application in a demanding production environment since 2005. In 2008, the FénixEDU web application went through a major refactoring to separate the infrastructure code from the rest of the application code, resulting in the initial version of the Fénix Framework—a Java framework to develop applications that need a transactional and persistent domain model, and that implements our proposed STM-based architecture.[2]

1.1 Main contributions

The main contributions of this paper are threefold.

First, we propose an architecture that is especially suited for the development of many of today's object-oriented enterprise applications, providing not only strictly serializable semantics to the applications' business transactions, but also improved performance over traditional implementations. Serializability alone requires that transactions be ordered as if they had executed sequentially. Strict serializability is an additional requirement on top of serializability: It imposes that transactions be serialized without reversing the order of temporally nonoverlapping transactions [24]. Intuitively, programmers can think of strictly serializable transactions as transactions that are serialized in an instant within the real-time interval in which they executed. Regarding performance, our tests show an increase of throughput in the TPC-W benchmark, for a variety of workloads and cluster configurations, up to 23.7 times, having the best results in the read-intensive workloads.

Second, we describe the key elements of an implementation of this architecture in a Java-based framework—the Fénix Framework: We describe how to extend the commit algorithm of the STM that we use to ensure the durability of the application's data; we describe the life cycle of a persistent domain object; and we describe how we use a shared, global identity map to keep domain objects in memory and preserve their identity across transactions and threads. We describe, also, the mechanisms used to allow the simultaneous existence of more than one application server accessing the same data, while still ensuring strict-serializable consistency guarantees for all the transactions running across all of the application servers.

Third, and finally, we present statistical data about the workload patterns of two real-world enterprise applications. These results were collected over an extended period of several years, with varying usage patterns, and we claim that they are an important contribution for at least two reasons. First, they provide support to the common belief (but rarely confirmed with real data) that enterprise applications have a very high read/write ratio: In both cases, the number of write transactions are, on average, only 2% of the total number of

transactions, peaking below 10% for short periods of write-intensive activity. These numbers are, actually, well below the numbers that are typically observed in benchmarks such as TPC-W. Second, these results confirm our claim that strict serializability is harmless for (at least some) enterprise applications: The rate of conflicts among write transactions is almost negligible for these applications, averaging less than 0.2% of the total number of write transactions (meaning that they represent less than 0.004% of the total number of transactions).

The remainder of this paper is organized as follows. In Section 2 we argue why a new architecture for enterprise applications is needed: We believe that historical reasons have led to some limitations in the programming model, namely with regard to transactional semantics. We discuss those limitations and how they affect programmers and software development. Then, in Section 3 we describe the STM-based architecture that we propose and discuss some of its implementation details. Next, in Section 4, we describe a real-world case of a large application, as well as a smaller-sized application, both developed with this architecture. Additionally, we provide a performance comparison between two implementations of the TPC-W benchmark, one using a traditional approach and another using our architecture. We discuss related work in Section 5 and conclude in Section 6.

2. Why We Need a New Architecture

Over the last 30 years, the development of enterprise applications has evolved, influenced by diverse factors such as the changes in hardware, or the changes in the users' expectations about how applications should behave. Often, these changes had a reflection in the architecture of applications. Still, one thing has remained the same for most applications: The underlying DBMS provides not only persistence but also the transactional semantics on which application developers rely for programming business transactions.

Unfortunately, this means that developers are limited to the isolation levels provided by the underlying DBMS, which often does not provide serializability—a correctness property for concurrent transactions that is crucial to ensure the integrity of the applications' data.

Historically, DBMSs weakened the isolation level of transactions as a trade-off between correctness and performance, which resulted in the generally accepted idea that serializability is incompatible with performance. This line of reasoning is clearly illustrated by the following passage from Martin Fowler's well-known book on patterns of enterprise application architecture [16]:

> To be sure of correctness you should always use the serializable isolation level. The problem is that choosing serializable really messes up the liveness of a system, so much so that you often have to reduce serializability in order to increase throughput. You have to

[1] http://fenix-ashes.ist.utl.pt/

[2] http://fenix-ashes.ist.utl.pt/trac/fenix-framework

decide what risks you want take and make your own trade-off of errors versus performance.

You don't have to use the same isolation level for all transactions, so you should look at each transaction and decide how to balance liveness versus correctness for it.

Even though this book is from 2002, we believe that it still represents faithfully the actual state of the practice in the development of most enterprise applications. One of the problems, thus, is that the use of weaker transactional semantics burdens developers with additional, nontrivial development effort. We shall return to this problem in greater detail later in this section. Before that, however, we provide a brief historical overview of the development of client/server applications and relate it to the *status quo* of complex enterprise object-oriented application development.

2.1 The Shift From a 2-tier to a 3-tier Architecture

A core component of most modern enterprise applications is a DBMS, and its use in such applications goes a long way back. The first enterprise applications were 2-tiered—that is, they had a simple client/server architecture. The clients made their requests directly to the database server, which in turn executed the requested operations and gave back the results. This architecture was adequate in a scenario where all the clients were on a trusted network and most of the computational power resided on a big server. In this architecture, transactional control was placed in the (only) obvious location: The database server. Each client request would perform within a database transaction, and the server ensured the ACID properties. Database servers were expensive and they had to cope with a growing usage demand. Eventually, different semantics for the ACID properties appeared, which relaxed some of the properties (e.g., isolation), mostly for performance reasons. As client machines became more and more powerful, more computation could be performed on the client side, which would also take part in ensuring data consistency. Business logic consistency started to get more complex than simple low-level consistency checking (e.g., referential integrity), including complex high-level consistency (e.g., a list can only contain odd numbers). Often, in this architecture the business logic code was intertwined with the user interface code.

With the growth of the internet and the World Wide Web, a new architecture emerged. As organizations felt the need to interconnect their systems, the 2-tiered architecture no longer served their purposes. There were several reasons for this, including the systems' security and network bandwidth. The clients (now including systems in diverse geographical locations and outside the control of the intranet) were no longer trusted. The number of clients grew. The available bandwidth was far less than it was previously available on the intranet, such that sending large volumes of data, as the result of a database query, was no longer viable. This led to a 3-tiered architecture on which the server side was decomposed in two tiers: One for the application server and another for the database server. The database server was still responsible for the data persistence and ensuring transactional access. The application server was responsible for executing the complex business logic and interfacing with the clients, which would provide the user interface. This new architecture presented two main advantages over the previous: (1) the information was kept safe within the intranet and it was only accessed directly by a trusted system; and (2) large queries could be obtained and processed on the server-side before sending the results over the internet to the clients. Notably, relaxed transactional semantics was kept in place, because database performance was still an important aspect in this architecture.

As the internet grew, another revolution was taking place in the software development area: Object-oriented programming languages became mainstream and started to be used commonly in the development of large server-side applications. Characteristics such as component modularization, ease of reuse, data encapsulation, and abstraction, helped developers control the growing complexity of their applications. The adoption of *Object-Oriented Programming* (OOP), however, created a mismatch between the persistent representation of data and their in-memory representation, known as the object-relational impedance mismatch [21]. The development of *Object-Relational Mapping* (ORM) tools was the industry's answer to handle this mismatch. The purpose of an ORM tool is to take care of the data mapping between the object-oriented model and the relational model. Whereas, in part, these tools simplified the programmers' coding efforts, they also created some difficulties of their own, such as the maintenance of O/R-mapping metadata, and the varied semantics implied by object caching, lazy loading, and support for *ad hoc* queries. Additionally, different ORMs provided different semantics. Yet, the features provided by ORM tools kept depending on transactional support that was still under the responsibility of the underlying DBMS, which, in turn, still offered different flavors for ACID semantics, but none included support for strict serializability [24]. In fact, the isolation guarantees provided by databases have, for long, been a matter of confusion and discussion [2].

The natural evolution in software and hardware has led us to the current state, in which many developers depend on a 3-tiered architecture, develop application servers using an object-oriented paradigm, and rely on a relational DBMS for persistence. There are of course some exceptions to this, most notably in emerging large distributed systems, which may use different programming models [11] or different storage mechanisms [4] with different consistency models [26, 29]. These very large-scale distributed systems fit in a class of their own and, for the time being, are not the target of our study.

We concentrate on the development of complex object-oriented applications that require transactional support and data persistence. By complex, we mean applications that have a rich domain structure with many relationships among the classes, as well as business logic with nontrivial rules (but not typically a massive volume of data to process). Moreover, we assume that these applications have many more read-only than write business transactions, typically in the rate of 10 to 1 or more.

For these applications, we identify two problems with current implementations of the typical 3-tier architecture: One is the difficulty in ensuring consistency; the other is the reduced performance of the application server in the processing of complex operations. We address each problem in the following two subsections.

2.2 Consistency Problems

If given the possibility, it seems clear that every programmer would prefer to have no less than strict-serializability semantics when programming concurrent transactional operations that manipulate the state of the domain objects in their code. Having such guarantee shields programmers from concurrency hazards, and allows them to write cleaner and simpler code.

To illustrate this point consider the following example: Imagine a multi-player game where players can concurrently move their pieces in a map from one point to another with the restriction that after each movement is performed no player can be in the immediate vicinity of another player. Now consider the starting scenario depicted in Figure 1, which shows part of the map containing two players, P1 and P2.

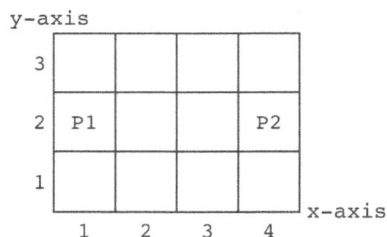

Figure 1. Two players occupying nonadjacent positions on a map.

Suppose that, concurrently, P1 will attempt to move one position to the right and P2 will attempt to move one position to the left. Only one move can succeed, because otherwise the two players would be left next to each other. A typical implementation of the moveTo operation could be similar to the pseudocode presented in Figure 2. The programmer checks that both the target position and its surroundings are available and, if that is the case, updates the position of the player on the map.

This code looks quite trivial and, when several moves are executed concurrently, each within its own transaction, the

```
class Player {
  void moveTo(int x, int y) {
    if (cell(x,y).available(this) &&
        cell(x+1,y).available(this) &&
        cell(x-1,y).available(this) &&
        cell(x,y+1).available(this) &&
        cell(x,y-1).available(this)) {
      this.currentCell().clear();
      cell(x,y).set(this);
    } else {
      throw Exception("Move not allowed");
    }
  }
}

class Cell {
  boolean available(Player p) {
    return this.isEmpty() || this.holdsPlayer(p);
  }
}
```

Figure 2. The moveTo operation checks the surroundings to ensure that the move is allowed and writes to the destination.

programmer might expect the application to work just fine—that is, after each transaction finishes, the moved player should be in a location that does not contain any adjoining players, thus maintaining the domain consistent. Sadly, this may not be the case if transactions are executed with the isolation level provided by most of today's mainstream databases, which ensure at most snapshot isolation. Under snapshot isolation a transaction may commit even if the values that were read changed in the meanwhile, as long as concurrent writes do not intersect. In this example, if transaction T1 executes P1.move(2,2) and transaction T2 executes P2.move(3,2), then Figure 3 presents the points in the read set and write set of each transaction with regard to map coordinates.

Tx	Read set	Write set
T1	(2,2), (3,2), (1,2), (2,3), (2,1)	(1,2), (2,2)
T2	(3,2), (4,2), (2,2), (3,3), (3,1)	(4,2), (3,2)

Figure 3. T1 and T2 write to adjacent places concurrently. Write sets do not intersect.

Note that write sets do not intersect, and as such, snapshot isolation will allow both transactions to commit, leading to an inconsistent domain state. This problem is well known by the name of *write skew* [12]. Yet, without changing the database concurrency control mechanisms, the current solution is to put in the programmer's shoulders the responsibility for forcefully creating a conflict between the two transactions. In this case, that may be accomplished by calling clear() for all of the surrounding positions, thus causing an intersection in the write sets [8]. This is definitely something undesirable from the programmer's perspective, and very much error-prone in complex applications where the potential conflicts might not be easily identified, as they may occur due to the interaction of many functionalities.

2.3 Performance Problems

So, why do not current transactional implementations change to support strict serializability? Probably, because of the generalized idea that providing strict serializability necessarily imposes unacceptable performance penalties. Such may actually be true for today's standard architectures, which ultimately rely on the DBMS for transactional support.

When ORMs were not in use or applications had simple domain models, it was common for programmers to implement a complex database query to return exactly the results sought. Generally, this meant that very few database round trips (often just one) were enough to process each unit of work requested by the client. Most of the business logic computation was embedded on the database query and handled by the DBMS. For an application with a typical 3-tier architecture, where the communication latency between the client and the server is measured in hundreds of milliseconds and the communication latency between the application server and the database takes fewer than 10ms, the time spent with the database query is almost negligible from the client's perspective.

Today, however, programmers can execute complex computations that require reading into main memory many of the application's objects. The use of ORMs and object-oriented programming facilitates and promotes object navigation instead of the creation of custom queries. This type of programming greatly increases the number of database round trips required to answer to a client's request, with negative influence on performance. If instead of one database round trip, the business transaction has to perform tens to hundreds of round trips in sequence, then the accumulated latency of all of those round trips largely exceeds the typical latency between the client and the server.

Trying to alleviate this problem, ORMs cache data on the application server tier, but still they depend on the underlying database to provide the transactional semantics. Unfortunately, developers of ORM tools have followed suit with databases in terms of the transactional properties provided to the application programmer. In fact, the use of application tier caches may further weaken the consistency semantics of the database by inadvertently providing inconsistent reads (served from the cache) within a transaction, as discussed in [25].

3. An STM-based Architecture for Enterprise Applications

The core idea in our architecture is to shift the responsibility for transactional control: It no longer lies on the persistence tier and it is shifted to the application server tier. We use an STM—more specifically the *JVSTM*[3]—to provide in-memory transactional support directly in the application server tier.

[3] http://web.ist.utl.pt/joao.cachopo/jvstm/

The design of the JVSTM evolved alongside the development of the architecture that we describe in this paper, and it was heavily influenced by the observation and development of real-world, domain-intensive web applications [5]. Often, these applications have rich and complex domains, both structurally and behaviorally, leading to very large transactions, but having also a very high read/write ratio (as we shall see later, but see also [5, 9] for more real-world numbers).

The new architecture that we present maintains the typical 3-tier layout, but uses the persistence tier only to ensure the *durability* property of ACID. Atomicity, consistency, and isolation are ensured at the application server tier. Conceptually, any type of storage (such as relational, column-oriented, or key-value) can be used in the persistence tier, but our initial choice was to use a relational database. We had several reasons for this decision. First, relational databases are a reliable technology for data storage. Second, they are still the mainstream backend used in many enterprise applications, as was the case of the FénixEDU web application, which had its data stored in a relational database and there were also other applications that queried the database (in read-only mode) to obtain data for several other systems, mostly for statistics. So, by using the relational model for persistence, we could migrate the FénixEDU application to the new architecture while maintaining compatibility with other legacy applications. Third, relational databases already support some level of transactional support, which enables us to simplify the commit algorithm in our solution. We have developed implementations of this architecture that run on top of other backends, namely using BerkeleyDB, HBase, and Infinispan, but in this paper we describe only the implementation that uses a relational database for the persistence tier.

The general idea is that we extend the JVSTM to make it persistent. Yet, this seemingly simple task poses several new issues. In the next subsection we provide an introduction to JVSTM and describe some of its implementation details that are relevant to the following subsections. In the remaining subsections we describe some of the most important aspects of the Fénix Framework, which implements the infrastructure that provides enterprise applications the support for performing transactional operations on shared persistent objects. We begin under the assumption that there is only one application server running. Then, in Section 3.6 we detail the changes required for this implementation to work in a clustered environment.

3.1 Brief Introduction to JVSTM

JVSTM is a Java library that implements a word-based, multi-version STM that ensures strict serializability for all of its committed transactions. Actually, JVSTM provides the even stronger correctness guarantee of *opacity* [18], which ensures that noncommitted transactions always see a consistent state of the data.

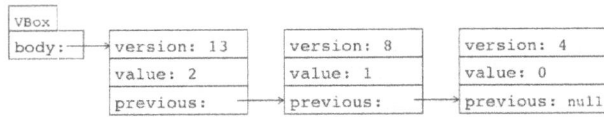

Figure 4. A transactional counter and its versions. From the programmer's perspective, the VBox has only one value at any given time.

JVSTM uses *Versioned Boxes* [7] to implement transactional locations in memory. A versioned box (VBox) holds a sequence of entries (body), each containing a value and a version. Each of the history's entries corresponds to a write made to the VBox by a successfully committed transaction. When such a writing transaction commits, it advances a global version clock and uses the new clock value to tag each of the new bodies that it creates. JVSTM's commit algorithm always keeps the sequence ordered, with the most recent committed value immediately accessible.

Figure 4 shows an example of a transactional memory location for an integer that models a counter. In the example shown, the counter has been set to zero by the transaction that committed version 4, and incremented by the transactions that committed versions 8 and 13. From the programmer's perspective there is a single memory location of the type VBox<Integer> that can be accessed via get() and put() methods.

A transaction reads values in a version that corresponds to the most recent version that existed when the transaction began. Thus, reads are always consistent and read-only transactions never conflict with any other, being serialized in the instant they begin as if they had atomically executed in that instant. Read-write transactions (write transactions for short), on the other hand, may conflict among them, and they require validation at commit-time to ensure that all values read during a transaction are still consistent when they try to commit—that is, values have not been changed in the meanwhile by another concurrent transaction. One of the distinctive features of the JVSTM is that read-only transactions have very low overheads and they are lock-free [15].[4]

3.2 Transactional Domain Objects

An object-oriented enterprise application represents and manipulates its persistent data as a graph of *Domain Objects* (DOs): Each DO represents an entity of the application's domain and its connections to other DOs represent relationships that it has with those DOs; we call this graph of DOs a *domain model*. In an object-oriented application, DOs are instances of some of the application's *domain classes*, and they contain a set of fields that hold the state of the object. Moreover, relationships are represented either by references to other objects or collections of objects, depending

on the multiplicity of the relationship. Naturally, both the DOs' state and their relationships may change over time, as a result of the application's operations, which execute concurrently by reading and changing the domain model.

Thus, as DOs are mutable and shared, they need to be transactional. As we saw before, JVSTM provides us already with transactional memory locations—the versioned boxes—but we need to have transactional DOs instead. To create transactional DOs, we wrap all of the mutable state of the domain model with versioned boxes, which, themselves, may contain only immutable objects. So, if, for instance, we have a DO representing a person with a name and this name may change, we will use a versioned box to hold the person's name and we will keep this box within the instance of the class Person that corresponds to our DO.

To implement this approach correctly, all of the fields of a domain class must be final and their types must be either VBox or an immutable type (such as String, Integer, or any of the Java's primitive types). The contents of each VBox, on the other hand, must always be an instance of an immutable type. Note that all of the types corresponding to domain classes are immutable types also, and so we may have boxes that contain DOs.

The key result of following these rules is that DOs are now transactionally safe: DOs may be shared among all of the concurrent threads running JVSTM transactions within the application, thereby ensuring a strictly serializable semantics for all of the application's business transactions. Moreover, as we shall see in the following section, having transactional DOs will allow us to reduce both the execution time and the memory consumption of the application.

A potential problem with our approach, however, is that the implementation of domain classes that strictly adhere to the above rules is error prone, if done manually by programmers. This problem is avoided in our approach by providing a domain-specific language [17] to describe the structural aspects of a domain model—the *Domain Modeling Language* (DML) [5, 6]. DML has a programmer-friendly, Java-like syntax to describe entity types, their attributes, and relationships among them. So, a programmer using the Fénix Framework creates the application's domain model using DML, and then the DML compiler automatically generates the source code corresponding to the structural aspects of the domain classes; the behavioral code is separately developed in plain Java by the programmer.

Besides simplifying the task of implementing the domain classes, this approach based on code generation has another important benefit: It allows us to change, and eventually fine tune, the layout of DOs. For instance, in Figure 5, we show an example of two possible layouts for an hypothetical domain class Person. In the first layout, all of the DO's attributes are kept in a single versioned box, whereas in the second layout there is one versioned box per attribute. This versatility enables adaptive designs that take into account

---

[4] In fact, apart from the creation of a new transaction instance, read-only transactions run entirely wait-free [20].

262

```
                // using one versioned box per object
class Person {
  final VBox<Person_State> state = new VBox<Person_State>();

  private class Person_State {
    String firstName;
    String lastName;
    Address contact;
  }

  String getFirstName() {
    return this.state.get().firstName;
  }

  void setFirstName(String firstName) {
    Person_State newState = this.state.get().clone();

    newState.firstName = firstName;
    this.state.put(newState);
  }
  [...]
}


                // using one versioned box per attribute
class Person {
  final VBox<String> firstName = new VBox<String>();
  final VBox<String> lastName = new VBox<String>();
  final VBox<Address> contact = new VBox<Address>();

  String getFirstName() {
    return this.firstName.get();
  }

  void setFirstName(String firstName) {
    this.firstName.put(firstName);
  }
  [...]
}
```

Figure 5. Two possible memory layouts for the same persistent data. Also shown are the generated `get` and `set` operations for the `firstName` attribute, in both cases.

application-specific characteristics regarding how domain data are accessed. Objects that are seldom modified can have their entire state in a single versioned box, which reduces memory usage. Objects with high contention can benefit from having one versioned box per attribute, which will reduce the number of conflicts between transactions that manipulate different attributes of the same objects.

3.3 The Domain Object Cache: Domain Objects Have Identity

In complex object-oriented applications where business transactions have to traverse deep graphs of objects, the resulting database round trips typically incur into an unacceptable performance cost. Reducing the number of database round trips, becomes, thus, essential for performance. We address this problem in the Fénix Framework, by using a global *Domain Object Cache*, shared by all threads, which maintains DOs in memory for as long as possible. The key idea is that read-only transactions should access the database only when DOs are not available in memory, which should not happen often if most of the application's data fit in memory. The goal is that, once loaded, DOs will remain in memory until the Java garbage collector needs space that it can

not find in any other way. Only in that case, may DOs be removed from the cache and garbage collected (provided that they are not in use by any transaction). In our current implementation, we rely on Java's `SoftReferences` for this behavior.

One of the results of using this approach for applications whose entire persistent data fit in memory is that, after warming up, the application server will never access the database for read-only transactions.[5]

The implementation of the Domain Object Cache follows the Identity Map architectural pattern [16]. We use only one instance of the Domain Object Cache per instance of the application server. Thus, the Domain Object Cache is shared among all threads (and, consequently, among all transactions) that execute in the application server. Notice that this domain object caching behavior is very different from that provided by most, if not all, of the current ORM implementations. All ORMs that we know of ensure transaction isolation by delivering different copies of the same object to different transactions. In such implementations, new objects are constantly allocated and deallocated, as more transactions execute. This happens, regardless of whether the object came from the database anew or was read from some second-level in-memory cache. The Domain Object Cache of our architecture ensures that, at any given time, the same persistent object is represented by at most one (reachable) instance in memory. As we saw before, DOs can be shared among all transactions because they are transactionally safe. Thus, unlike what happens with ORMs, in our approach the memory required to hold DOs does not depend on the number of concurrently running transactions.

Each entry in the Domain Object Cache maps an object's unique identifier (*OID*) to a reference to the object itself. The OID is assigned automatically by the framework, ensuring its uniqueness, when a domain object is created and remains unchanged thereafter. The reference to the object is a Java `SoftReference`, which allows for cached objects that are no longer referenced elsewhere to be garbage collected when their memory is necessary, but will keep objects in memory while they fit.

The *lookup* and *cache* operations are performed automatically by the infrastructure's implementation during an object's lifecycle. When a new object is allocated it is automatically cached before being made available to the application. This is so, regardless of whether the object is a new instance or an already existing object being materialized from persistence. Next, we detail the object allocation mechanism.

3.4 Domain Object Allocation and Loading

An application's DO is allocated either when the program creates a new instance, or when an existing DO that is not in main memory is requested by its OID.

---

[5] There is an exception to this rule when multiple application servers share the same database. This is discussed further ahead in Section 3.6.

In the first case we simply cache the new instance before returning it to the application, as we already mentioned. Even if the transaction in which the DO was created aborts, there is no problem in having cached it, because OIDs are unique and therefore the DO may linger in cache for a while until it is eventually garbage collected: Its cache entry will never conflict with another.

In the second case, when an existing DO is requested by its OID, we perform a cache lookup. If the DO is found, then it is simply returned. Otherwise, we allocate the DO, put it in the cache, and return it to the application.

In Java, object allocation is tightly coupled with object instantiation. To implement our allocation mechanism we perform bytecode rewriting in all DO classes to inject a special constructor that is used exclusively by the framework whenever an object needs to be materialized in memory.[6]

This allocation mechanism completely avoids database access. Such is possible because the OID encodes information about the DO's concrete class, which enables us to allocate a DO of the correct class without knowing the value of its fields yet. Only if the application later requests the value of any of the DO's fields, will a load from the database be triggered. This corresponds to the *Lazy Load pattern using ghosts* [16]. Each ghost is not a proxy: It is the object itself. The difference is that its state is not yet known, because all of its versioned boxes are created and set to a special empty value (a NOT_LOADED flag). When any value of its attributes is actually accessed, the transactional system identifies the special flag and triggers a database load of the missing value. So, using ghosts maintains the Domain Object Cache's property that, at any given time, the same persistent object is represented by at most one (reachable) instance in memory.

The difficulty with lazy loading the contents of a DO lies in the fact that the in-memory representation of the attributes is versioned (recall that all mutable state is kept in versioned boxes), whereas the persistent representation in the relational database stores only the most recent committed state for any datum.[7] So, we need to ensure than when a running transaction, for example T1, lazily reads a value from the database, it will see a consistent value, and not some other value that another committed transaction may have written after T1 had started. We solve this by (1) opening a database transaction in the beginning of the application server's memory transaction, (2) keeping it open for the duration of the memory transaction, and (3) requiring that the underlying database supports *snapshot isolation* [2], which is common nowadays. With this we ensure that when the application needs to load additional information from per-

sistence it will always see a consistent snapshot corresponding to the most recent version that existed when the transaction started. The most straightforward implementation of this strategy requires a database transaction for every memory transaction. This need can be greatly reduced in two ways: One is to share database transactions among all memory transactions that start in the same version. This is possible because the database transaction is only used to read data. Writes are performed in a separate database transaction during the commit of the memory transaction (cf. Section 3.5). The other way is to not always start a database transaction in the beginning of the memory transaction. If it is likely that all the required information is already loaded in memory, then database access is really not needed. In the event that a memory transaction needs something from the database and no database transaction has been open yet, it is enough to restart the memory transaction, and this time to open a database transaction in the beginning: Using this strategy can pay off when most of the database fits into main memory, and the probability of a missed datum is low. We are currently not using any of these techniques, and we chose to open a database transaction for every memory transaction.

Generically, this mechanism allows us to materialize in memory any object given its OID without having to load it from the database. A typical use case in an object-oriented application is to load some *root* object and then navigate through the object graph by reading the objects' attributes. This way, objects are allocated in memory as soon as they are referenced, but their contents are only loaded from persistence when they are accessed for the first time. Moreover, if different paths in the object graph lead to the same object, they will actually lead to the same instance, not to another copy. This is true regardless of the thread from which the object is accessed.

3.5 Persisting Domain Objects

The JVSTM deals with all the in-memory transactional support: It provides atomicity and isolation with strict-serializability semantics, but it does not provide any form of data persistence. It follows a *redo log* model for STMs [19], which means that it keeps the write set in a transaction-local context, and it applies changes to the corresponding shared transactional locations only during the commit operation if the transaction is valid to commit. A transaction T is valid to commit if its read set does not intersect with the write set of any other transaction that committed meanwhile (between the instant T starts and the instant T commits).

Therefore we need to ensure that the commit of a valid transaction is both persisted and made visible in shared memory, atomically. The transactional API provided to the programmer overrides the commit operation from the JVSTM to add the required behavior.

Figure 6 presents the commit algorithm for write transactions (the commit of read-only transactions simply returns). Committing a transaction is composed of three stages: Read

---

[6] The main reason to inject this constructor, instead of generating it in the source code, is to ensure that it will not include any instance initialization code that the programmer may have added to the class.

[7] Of course that this mismatch could easily be solved by storing all the versions in the database, but that would go against the previous design decision to use the typical relational data structure, and would consequently break compatibility with legacy applications that queried the database.

```
class Transaction {
  void commit() {
    GLOBAL_LOCK.lock();
    try {
      if (validate()) { // throws exception if validation fails
        int newVersion = globalClock + 1;
        persistChanges();
        writeBackToMemory(newVersion);
        globalClock = newVersion;
      }
    } finally {
      GLOBAL_LOCK.unlock();
    }
  }

  void persistChanges() {
    // The database transaction provides write atomicity
    beginNewDBTx();
    writeBackToDB();
    commitDBTx();
  }
}
```

Figure 6. We extend the `commit` operation of the JVSTM to write the changes to persistence, after validating the transaction in memory.

set validation, writing back changes to shared locations, and publishing changes globally. The global lock provides mutual exclusion among all committing write transactions, which trivially ensures atomicity between validating the read set (line 5) and writing back the write set (line 8). Also, the version number is provided by a unique global version clock that only changes inside the critical region. In the commit algorithm of the JVSTM the linearization point occurs when the global clock is updated (line 9). In this new version of the commit algorithm, however, the effects of the commit are visible as soon as the `persistChanges` finishes. After that point, the changes made by the transaction are seen by other transactions that start henceforth, because they open a connection to the database and read the most recent state.

The shaded code in line 7 extends the JVSTM's commit with an additional step that sends changes to the persistence tier. The order of invocation of the `persistChanges` operation is critical to ensure the required transactional behavior: It is performed after the transaction has been validated by the STM, and before actually making the changes visible in memory. The former ensures that the state to persist is consistent, and the latter ensures that a possible failure in the `persistChanges` operation occurs before modifying any shared memory. Because writing to persistence is performed within the global commit lock, a database transaction never conflicts. If the database write fails for some catastrophic reason (such as loosing connection to the database), then the transaction is aborted in memory. We do not depend on the database transactional semantics for any transaction to succeed. However, it is necessary that the `persistChanges` operation performs an atomic write to the database, to account for any catastrophic crash of the application server during the write to persistence. If this happens, then when the application server restarts it will see a consistent state, either

before or after the current commit operation. Again, after persisting changes, the remainder of the commit algorithm can only fail for catastrophic reasons (such as running out of memory), in which case the application server's restart will certainly see the current transaction as committed in the persistence.

When committing a memory transaction, a database transaction is already undergoing, because, as we mentioned in Section 3.4, such is used to ensure consistent reads from the database. For that reason, the `beginNewDBTx` operation will relinquish any database transaction that may be in use and will create a new transaction to write the changes. Therefore the only database transactions that update the contents of the database are always created inside the global commit lock.

3.6 Clustered Environment

Up until this point we have presented the architecture under the assumption that there is only one instance of the application server running. Multicore computers with large amounts of available memory are becoming mainstream and they are the natural target hardware for applications developed with the architecture that we propose: (1) The typical workloads are highly parallel, which benefit from the increasing number of cores, and (2) having lots of memory enables the program to keep most, if not all, of its data in memory, thus reducing the number of database roundtrips. However, even when a single computer built with this commodity hardware is enough to run the entire application server with good performance, there are other reasons for deploying in a clustered application server environment, for example to enable fault-tolerance, or even to enable live hardware upgrades. In this subsection we present the additional changes to the current infrastructure to support more than one application server.

To support multiple application servers we need a mechanism that enables the servers to synchronize their changes, namely updates to the global clock and to the application's shared state. We decided to use the persistence tier to communicate the state synchronization information between the application servers. This was a relatively straightforward decision given that the communication mechanisms between the application and persistence tiers already existed.

As we have previously shown, state changes occur only during the commit of write transactions. The commits are already ordered within one application server because of the global (per application server) commit lock. Additionally, the `commit` operation needs to provide ordering between two concurrent commits from different servers, and to write a *change log* that can be used by the other servers to update their state. Each change log associates the commit version with the identification of the versioned boxes that have changed in that version. The change log is similar to a write set, except that it does not actually contain the values written, only the identification of the versioned boxes where they were written, along with the version number. Figure 7 shows

```
1   class Transaction {
2     void persistChanges() {
3       beginNewDBTx();
4       boolean dbCommit = false;
5       try {
6         if (updateFromChangeLogs(true)) {
7           validate();
8         }
9         writeBackToDB();
10        writeChangeLog();
11        commitDBTx();
12        dbCommit = true;
13      } finally {
14        if ( ! dbCommit) {
15          abortDBTx();
16          throw CommitException;
17        }
18      }
19    }
20
21    boolean updateFromChangeLogs(boolean needLock) {
22      if (needLock) {
23        SELECT ... FOR UPDATE
24      } else {
25        SELECT ...
26      }
27      // process result-set and return whether state changed
28    }
29  }
```

Figure 7. The `persistChanges` operation ensures cluster-wide serialization by relying on a database lock and validating changes against the most recent committed state.

the `persistChanges` operation with the required modifications.

After beginning a new database transaction the application server starts by requesting an update to its state (line 6). The `updateFromChangeLogs` queries the infrastructural table that holds the change logs. The `needLock` flag set to `true` causes the execution of a *SELECT ... FOR UPDATE* SQL query. Given that every committing transaction performs the same database request, this query effectively obtains a cluster-wide lock, and establishes the necessary total order for all commits. The lock is held until the database transaction finishes. The result of the query is the list of change logs. Next, these changes are applied in memory: For each committed transaction, a new version is added to the corresponding versioned boxes, setting the new value with the special `NOT_LOADED` flag. By doing so, rather than loading the most recent value of every versioned box that has changed, we avoid additional database queries within the critical region. In fact, these values may never be needed in this application server, but if they are, when a transaction needs them, the normal database load will be triggered, as discussed in Section 3.4. Finally, the `updateFromChangeLogs` returns an indication of whether it performed any state changes. If so, then the transactional system now needs to revalidate the memory transaction, because the previous validation (Figure 6, line 5) was performed in an earlier state. For code correction, it would be enough to perform validation only once, after checking the database for any updates. However, database access is much more expensive than in-memory validation, so the first validation allows for quick early conflict detec-

tion and, thus, can avoid the cost of a database access for a transaction that is found to be already invalid with the existing in-memory state.

Next, the commit proceeds as before, writing back the changes of the current transaction. Additionally, it writes the change log for the current transaction. When the database transaction commits, changes will be visible to other application servers. As before, if something fails (noncatastrophically) during the `commit` and before the database transaction commits, the system will abort the transaction. After the database commit, the only possible causes for failure are considered catastrophic for the application server, and when it restarts it will view the transaction as committed.

Even though state changes only occur during a commit, their occurrence must be taken into account also during the start of a new transaction. In a clustered environment, every new transaction must check the change log for possible updates from other servers. This is required to ensure that future database reads are consistent with the global version clock that the application server keeps. Recall that we do not store versions in the database. So, when a new memory transaction begins and opens a database transaction (to ensure consistent reads during loads from the database), it will see the most recent committed data. Thus, it needs to update the state in memory from the change log; otherwise it would load data with the wrong version.

There is yet another important reason to update from the change log in the beginning of every transaction: To ensure strict serializability for the clustered system. As an example, suppose that in a cluster of two application servers, a client application performs an **update** request (R1) to an application server (AS1), which is **observed** to have been completed **before** another client application executes another request (R2) to the other application server (AS2). We can ensure that the execution of R2 will already see the effects of R1, because the update from the change log in the beginning of the second transaction will necessarily occur after the database commit of the first transaction. Figure 8 presents the regular `begin` operation extended to invoke `updateFromChangeLogs`. The difference in this invocation from the one performed inside the `commit` is that it sets the `needLock` flag to `false`: It does not need to acquire the cluster-wide lock, because it will only read from the change log. However, because reading the change log may lead to updates in DOs, these updates need to acquire the same lock as the commit (Figure 6, line 3).

4. Evaluation

Since its extraction from the FénixEDU web application, the Fénix Framework has been used to develop several other real-world applications, but FénixEDU is still the largest application that we know of that uses the approach that we propose in this paper.

```
1  class Transaction {
2    void begin() {
3      beginNewDBTx();
4      updateFromChangeLogs(false);
5      // rest of normal begin
6    }
7  }
```

Figure 8. The beginning of a transaction in a clustered environment, not only opens a database transaction to ensure snapshot isolation for loading, but it also updates the application server's state with the most recent commits.

In the following subsection we present some of the statistical data collected over the last years both for FénixEDU and for •IST (read as "dot IST"), which is another real-world web application that started to be developed with the Fénix Framework in 2008. These statistical data allow us to analyze the typical workload of these applications, which, as we shall see, have very high read/write ratios and a remarkably low rate of conflicts. The goals of this initial evaluation subsection are twofold. First, it allows us to show that it is feasible to ensure strict serializability for all business transactions without incurring into many conflicts, which could lead to poor performance of the system. Second, it provides us with extensive data regarding workload patterns for two, independently developed, real-world complex web applications, adding real evidence to the general belief that such applications have many more reads than writes.

To evaluate the performance benefits of our architecture, however, these real-world applications are not the best fit. Even though performance problems in the FénixEDU application were one of the primary reasons for developing this architecture, we do not have quantitative measurements of the performance benefits of the new architecture for FénixEDU: We have only anecdotal evidence from its users that the performance of the application increased significantly once the new architecture was adopted, even though the load of the system increased steadily overtime and the hardware remained the same.

Unfortunately, as in most real-world scenarios, it is overly complex and expensive to reimplement these applications with a traditional architecture, so that we could compare the two alternatives. Instead, we chose a standard JDBC-based implementation of a widely known application server benchmark, the TPC-W, and reimplemented it using the Fénix Framework. In subsection 4.2 we use the two implementations of this benchmark to do a more thorough performance evaluation of our architecture.

4.1 Workload Patterns of Real-world Applications using the Fénix Framework

FénixEDU is a large web application deployed as part of an academic information system for Higher Education developed at *Instituto Superior Técnico* (IST), the largest school of engineering in Lisbon, Portugal. IST is home to more than 6,000 undergraduate students (BSc), 4,000 graduate

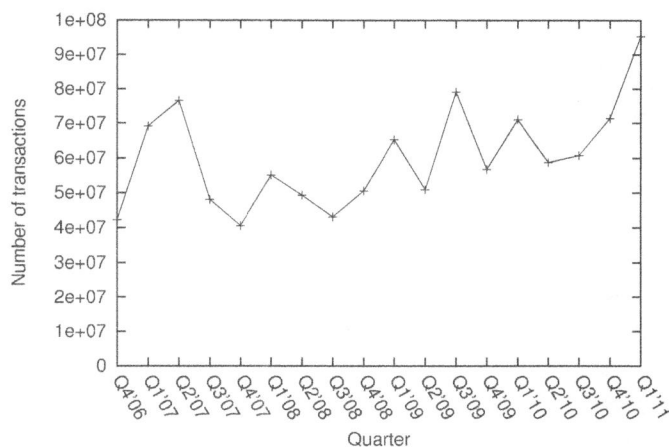

Figure 9. Total number of transactions per quarter in FénixEDU.

students (MSc and PhD), and around 1,100 faculty members and researchers. FénixEDU supports the majority of IST's web-based functionalities for the entire school ranging from courses and academic management to administrative support, scientific support, and admissions. The functionalities it provides can be as simple as logging a summary for a class or as complex as generating and validating timetables for the entire school.

The development of FénixEDU begun in 2002, following the at-the-time best practices of software development and engineering: It was based on a traditional web application architecture. Following a rapid evolution of its feature set, with an ever increasing number of users, in late 2003 the application started to have not only performance problems, but was also facing development problems due to the complexity of the programing model, which was compounded by the pressure put on developers to make the application perform better. These problems urged an architectural shift to the architecture that we described in this paper.

Since September 2005, the application has been running with this new architecture, which has since then been extracted into the Fénix Framework. Currently, the FénixEDU web application contains approximately 1.2 million lines of code, over 8,000 classes, of which more than 1,200 represent domain entities described in the DML. It has over 3,600 different web pages for user interaction. Every 5 minutes, FénixEDU logs statistics about its operation. It is by far the largest application using the Fénix Framework, and the one from which we have collected the most statistical data.

Figure 9 shows the evolution in the total number of transactions processed per quarter since the last quarter of 2006. Overall, the number of transactions has been increasing, which we can relate to the continuous increase in the functionalities provided by the system to its users. The fluctuations occur mostly because users' activity is not constant

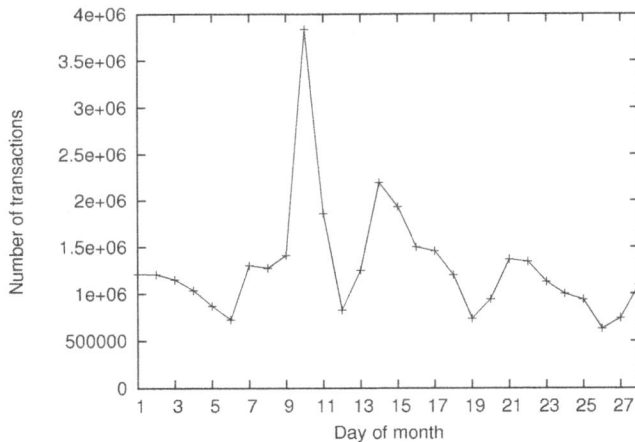

Figure 10. Daily number of transactions in FénixEDU during February 2011.

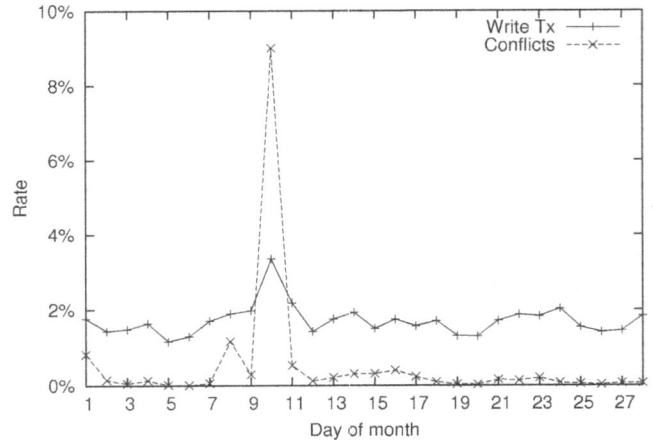

Figure 11. Daily rate of writes and conflicts in FénixEDU during February 2011.

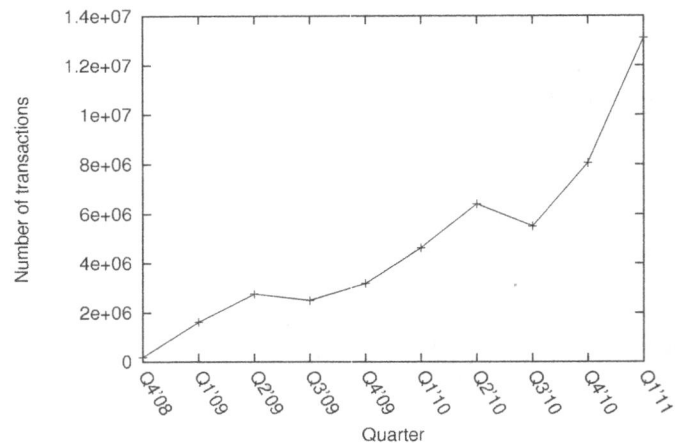

Figure 12. Total number of transactions per quarter in •IST.

over the year. For example, during vacation periods, activity drops considerably.

FénixEDU processes a daily average of 1 million transactions during work days. The peak usage of the system occurs twice a year, when the enrollment period for the next semester opens, at which time nearly 10,000 students hit the system at the same time. Figure 10 shows one such peak during last February. During the entire day of February 10, 2011, the system processed 3.7 million transactions. However, enrollments only started at 6:00 P.M. and in the following 60 minutes the system processed 1.1 million transactions, which amounts to a peak of more than 300 transactions per second.

In Figure 11 we present the daily rate of write transactions and conflicts, also for February 2011. Notice that under normal load, over 98% of the total number of transactions processed by the system are read-only transactions, and of the remaining 2% (the write transactions) there are on average less than 0.2% restarts due to a conflict. At peak times, the rate of write transactions goes up, but still remains under 4% and the conflicts rise to about 9% (of the write transactions).

Note, however, that this throughput is not limited by the hardware, but merely reflects the demand made to the system by its users. In fact, all this is run on a cluster of two machines (for fault-tolerance) equipped with 2 quad-core CPUs and 32GB of RAM each that are under-used. Data loaded in memory usually take approximately 6GB, whereas the relational database size (measured by MySQL) is under 20GB. This shows that it is possible to deploy a real-world application running under strict-serializability semantics without a negative effect on performance. We believe that these characteristics of the FénixEDU web application are not uncommon, and that, in fact, are representative of a large fraction of modern enterprise applications, for which our new architecture provides a very good fit.

More recently, in mid 2008, IST begun the development of another web application, named •IST. The goal of this new web application is to support many of IST's workflow processes. It includes the management of several administrative tasks, such as acquisition processes, travel authorizations, administrative staff evaluation, internal staff transfers, and document management, among others. It is dedicated to support the work of faculty members, researchers, and administrative staff. Because it does not include the students, its user base is much smaller than FénixEDU's, but is used in a more regular fashion by its users.

In Figure 13 we show the evolution in the total number of transactions processed per quarter, since the initial deployment of this application. As we collected statistical data for the entire lifetime of this application, we may see a steady increase of the application's usage, since its early beta stages in the last quarter of 2008, when both few processes were supported and few users were using the application. Since then, the application has been opened to its entire user base

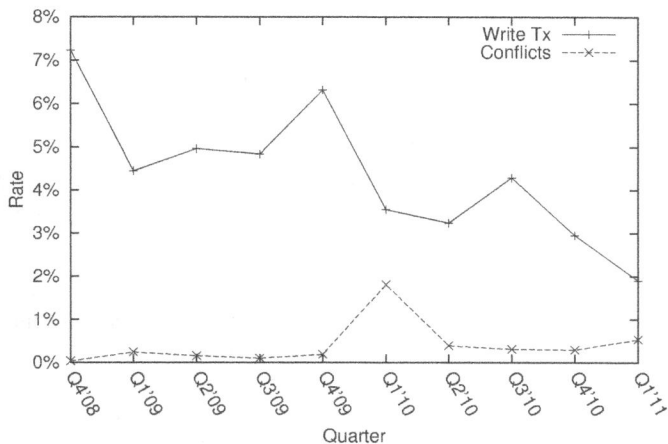

Figure 13. Quarterly rate of writes and conflicts in •IST.

and has also included many more features, leading to a significantly higher number of transactions processed in recent quarters. It is expected that this growth may continue for a while as new features are added. However, it may eventually reach a plateau, because of the limited number of users.

Unlike the FénixEDU, the •IST does not have any publicly accessible web pages, other than the login page. The functionalities it provides tend to increase the number of write transactions, because many of the operations provided to the users involve the execution of workflow steps that cause changes to the application state. Figure 13 presents the rate of write transactions and conflicts in this application, and provides some insightful information. First, we confirm that, as expected, the percentage of write transactions is higher than in FénixEDU. However, it shows a tendency towards decreasing. In fact, the absolute number of write transactions per quarter (not shown in the plots) has been increasing, but so has the number of read-only transactions. And the latter, have increased much more. We believe that this is a natural consequence of having more data available in the system, because more users access the system to check the status of the workflows in which they take part. So, in fact we draw a very interesting conclusion from this observation, and it reinforces our belief that, in this kind of applications, the reads largely outnumber the writes. Even when a web application is more geared towards operations that involve having its users making changes to the application's data, as in •IST, their users tend to execute many more of the read operations. Finally, despite the higher rate of writes, the conflicts remain close to zero. The abnormal spike in the first quarter of 2010 is due to the execution of large migration scripts that executed scattered throughout the weeks and often conflicted with users's activities. Nevertheless, it represents a very low percentage of the write transaction.

4.2 Performance Comparison with a Standard JDBC Architecture

The TPC-W is a benchmark created by the *Transaction Processing Performance Council* (TPC) [8]. It implements a web commerce application for an online bookstore. It has the typical 3-tiered architecture, where the clients (a set of emulated web browsers) access a web server to browse and buy books. The state of the application is stored persistently in a relational database. The TPC-W has already been discontinued by the TPC, but nevertheless it still provides a simulation of the class of applications that we are interested in. Moreover, there was already an open-source implementation available [9] in Java that we could immediately use.

We started from the JDBC-based implementation and modified it to implement our architecture. The detailed changes are documented online [10], together with instructions for running both implementations. In short, we defined the object-oriented domain model of the application using the DML, and then implemented the functionalities that corresponded to the SQL queries found in the original version. The browser emulator for the client remained unchanged, as we completely reused the presentation layer of the application server (developed using Java Servlets).

The primary performance metric of the TPC-W measures throughput as the number of *Web Interactions Per Second* (WIPS). Each successful request/response interaction between the client and the server counts as one web interaction, so the higher the WIPS the better the performance.

We compared the average WIPS obtained by the two implementations of TPC-W (FF-based and JDBC-based) in different scenarios. We used two interaction mixes from the TPC-W specification: The *browsing mix*, and the *shopping mix*. The former mix performs browsing (read-only) operations approximately 95% of the time, whereas the latter performs browsing only for 80% of the time. The rest of the time the clients perform shopping requests that execute write transactions. Besides the mixes specified by the TPC, we created a mix of our own, which consisted of 100% browsing interactions (*read-only mix*). Despite not representing the common case, this scenario is relevant to us, because it exercises the best possible throughput for our architecture, given that it minimizes the required database round trips.

Our architecture was designed to work best on a single application server with many cores and large memory heaps. So, the first group of tests were performed running a single application server in a machine with a NUMA architecture, built from four AMD Opteron 6168 processors. Each processor contains 12 cores, thus totaling 48 cores. The system had 128GB of RAM, more than enough to keep data from all processes (clients, application server and database) loaded

---

[8] http://www.tpc.org

[9] http://tpcw.deadpixel.de/

[10] http://www.esw.inesc-id.pt/permalinks/
fenix-framework-tpcw

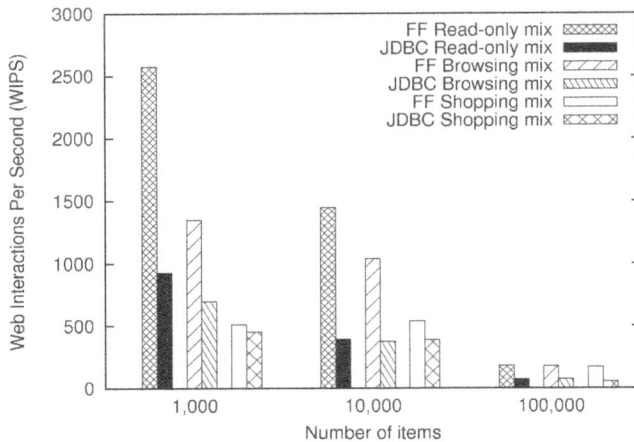

Figure 14. Throughput for a single application server, with 10 concurrent clients, varying the number of items in the database. Our implementation consistently shows a higher throughput.

Mix	WIPS	
	FF	JDBC
Read-only	1904.00	159.68
Browsing	659.77	151.71
Shopping	341.58	279.29

Table 1. Absolute WIPS for 10 clients. The baseline values for our implementation already start atop of the values for the original implementation.

in main memory. The largest amount of memory ever required by the application server, for a single test case, never exceeded 15GB. We tested using Java 6 with HotSpot(TM) 64-Bit Server VM (19.1-b02). The database was MySQL 5.1 and the application server was installed as a web application on Apache Tomcat 6.

For the first test the database was populated with three different data sets of 1,000, 10,000, and 100,000 books, respectively. The WIPS we obtained for all the configurations tested are shown in Figure 14. These are the average WIPS achieved when running with 10 clients that concurrently perform requests to the application server. Each client performed its own requests sequentially, with each request being performed immediately after receiving the server's response (client's configuration parameter THINK_TIME = 0). This value does not simulate the interaction patterns of real users, which always spend some time between consecutive interactions, but our goal was to produce an uninterrupted flow of requests to stress test the application server, and measure how many WIPS it could process under the given load.

The implementation based on the Fénix Framework shows a higher throughput than the JDBC-based implementation for all tests. It shows on average 2.4 times more WIPS, and up to 3.7 times more in the case of the read-only workload for 10,000 items. These results clearly show that it is possible to provide the programmer with strict-serializability semantics and an increased application performance.

Despite these good results, we believe that they could be even better, because in our version of the TPC-W with the Fénix Framework, we tried to do the most straightforward implementation that closely mimicked the original domain structure and SQL queries. In doing so, we have often produced an implementation that is not optimized. As an example, consider the operation that lists the best sell-

ers. This operation requires looking at the 3333 most recent orders. To speed up this web interaction we could have easily maintained a list with the most recent orders, but we did not. Instead, we iterated through the list of all orders every time to produce the list of most recent orders. Note that the original SQL query (...WHERE orders.o_id > (SELECT MAX(o_id)-3333 FROM orders)...) performs much quicker, because the o_id column is the primary key, thus indexed. This kind of optimization is tempting for at least two reasons. First, it is trivial to implement. Second, it is something that a programmer of an object-oriented application would probably do, given the requirement to compute the best sellers. Arguably, we could have made an implementation that would be even faster than it already is, if we had built the application's domain model from scratch, rather than adapted the SQL-based implementation.

We identify two reasons for our current performance gains. One reason has to do with the reduction in database queries: Once loaded from the database, data remain in the application server's memory for as long as possible, whereas in the original implementation every client request requires at least one database query to get the information needed. The other reason is that, in our transactional system, read-only transactions run completely unaffected by other transactions.[11] Being the majority of operations read-only and given that the entire database fits into main memory, most of the requests can be answered much faster in our implementation.

In the next set of tests we intended to measure how the two implementations scale for an increasing number of clients. We populated the database with 1,000 books and 172,800 clients,[12] and tested the application with the number of concurrent clients ranging from 10 to 60 in increments of 10 clients per test. Recall that the hardware provides 48 cores. The work performed by the clients is almost negligible. Most of the computation time is spent either in the application server or in the database processes.

Figure 15 shows the speed-up obtained for 20 to 60 clients. We calculated the speed-up taking as the baseline the WIPS obtained with 10 clients for each test scenario, which are shown in Table 1. Notice that the absolute WIPS

---

[11] Write transactions contend for the global commit lock, during the commit phase only.

[12] According to the TPC-W specification, the database must be populated with $2880 \times c$ clients in order to use up to c concurrent clients.

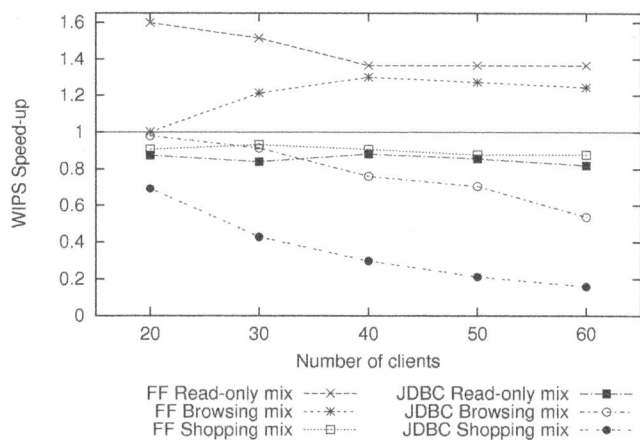

Figure 15. Speed-up for a single application server and a varying number of concurrent clients. The baseline is the throughput for 10 clients.

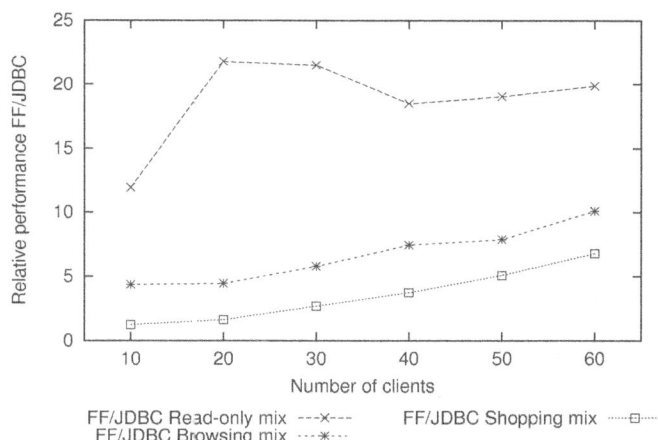

Figure 16. Performance of the FF-based implementation relative to the JDBC-based version.

shown in this table are fewer than those shown in Figure 14 for 1,000 books, because for this test the database had to be populated to accommodate up to 60 concurrent clients, which increased the database size and, consequently, the time per request, thus lowering throughput.

From Figure 15 it is clear that our solution makes better use of the available hardware parallelism: For the read-only and shopping mixes, throughput increases when compared to the baseline. It stabilizes around 1.4 even tough the read-only mix is capable of up to 1.6 for 20 clients. For the shopping mix it does not improve, but at least it does not worsen like the JDBC-based implementation does. The original version never improves: It remains close to 1 for the read-only mix, and it deteriorates a lot for the other two mixes, most notably for the shopping mix, going down to less than 0.2 of its baseline value.

Considering data from Table 1, again we can see that our solution outperforms the original implementation. This is even more so as the number of clients increases and the values for speed-up grow apart between the two implementations. In Figure 16 we present the performance of the FF-based implementation relative to the JDBC-based implementation. As expected, the relative performance increases with the percentage of read operations. Once more, this is due to the reduction in the cost of database access, especially for read-only transactions. Also, the relative improvement is much higher than in the first test, because the database size is much larger, and so we gain by having all of the data in memory.

Note however, that in our single-server tests we did not take advantage of knowing that there was only one application server running and, therefore, the framework still opened a database connection in the beginning of every memory transaction, as presented in Section 3.6. Nevertheless, in this configuration, the `updateFromChangeLogs`

method always returns an empty change log, because the only application server running will, necessarily, be up to date. This means that we could increase even further the performance when running in a single application server environment. In Figure 17, we present this gain for the extreme case of running a read-only mix. Here the application server takes advantage of knowing that it is running a single instance, and it only opens a database connection whenever it needs to load missing data into main memory. During the initial warm-up period, all data eventually becomes loaded and no further database access is needed at all. In this case, we can see that the application is capable of using all of the available hardware parallelism, as the WIPS increase up to the point where the clients reach the number of available cores. This is due to the use of JVSTM, in which read-only transactions do not entail any blocking synchronization whatsoever. If we had kept object versions in persistent storage, then we could also have tested the other mixes with this approach. Unfortunately, the current database structure only keeps the latest version, forcing us to open a database connection at the beginning of each transaction, to ensure consistent reads of any values that may be missing in memory. Finally, Figure 17 corroborates an important underlying assumption in our architecture: Database access takes a heavy toll on the performance of the application server. By reducing this cost, our approach is already capable of greatly increasing throughput, when compared to the original implementation. However, there is still much to gain, if we can further reduce the number of accesses to the database.

Our architecture is better suited for a single application server, running on hardware with many cores and large heaps because, in clustered environments, write transactions cause the invalidation of cache entries in the other application servers, which in turn forces their reloading from the database. Still, it was designed to support multiple application servers sharing the same database. So, we performed

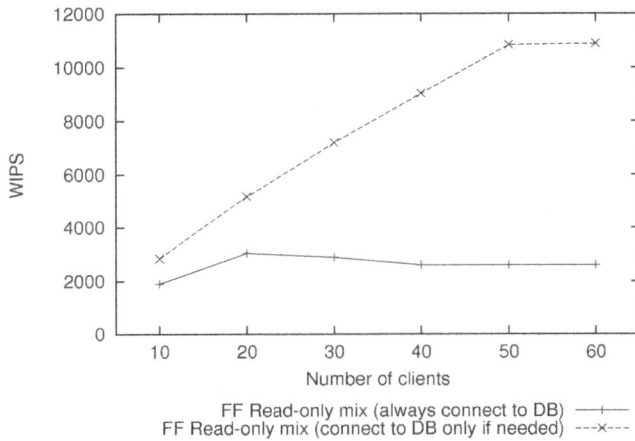

Figure 17. The added cost of database access is clearly seem when comparing two read-only mixes that only differ in whether a database connection is always established at the start of processing a memory transaction.

another test to measure the throughput that could be achieved by increasing the number of application servers for a fixed number of clients. For this final test we used a cluster of ten machines, all connected to the same local network through a 100Mbps switch. Each machine had 2 quad-core Intel Xeon E5506 processors and 8GB of RAM. The versions of Java, MySQL and Tomcat were the same as before. The database was setup in one machine, the clients' simulator in another, and we deployed from one to eight application servers, each in its own machine. The database was populated to support 40 concurrent clients. The clients' simulator always executed 40 clients evenly distributed across the deployed servers. For example, when running a single application server all the 40 clients were directed to that server, whereas when running eight application servers 5 clients were directed at each server.

Figure 18 shows the results obtained. We decided to display the read-only mix in a separate plot, because the WIPS of the FF-based implementation are so much higher than all others that showing them together would make the information harder to read. In the read-only mix, the application servers' caches are never invalidated, because of the absence of writes. For this reason, the throughput increases much more than for other scenarios, as each server is almost independent from the others. The only common aspect is that they all contact the same database.

Considering the other mixes, there is a special condition that occurs in the FF-based implementation for one application server, which causes the WIPS to be close to zero. Here is what happens: The data from the database fits entirely in the application server's memory, taking around 70% of the available memory. Because of the transactional system's infrastructure, update operations take up additional memory in the application server, mostly due to the keeping of

multiple versions that may still be needed for some transaction running in an older version. As memory fills up, the garbage collector starts working hard to remove unreachable objects, which include older versions and may include evicting entries from the object cache. Without special tuning of the Java's garbage collector for this particular workload, the default implementation often performs full garbage collections. Once this occurs the whole system degrades. This combination of events leads to a throughput close to zero, as the application server spends most of its time running single-threaded full garbage collections. In the single server scenario, the given rate of write operations combined with memory and garbage collector limitations caused a huge slowdown. In such cases, our implementation will underperform, unless some tuning is applied.

As we split this load by two servers the problem goes away, and we outperform the original implementation, once more. However, the relative performance increase for two or more servers is less noticeable than in the previous single-server tests, because while on the one hand the increase in the number of application servers leads to an increase in parallel processing, on the other hand it also leads to an increase in the number of cache invalidations of each server due to writes by the other servers.

The WIPS for the JDBC-based implementation barely change for any number of servers, in each of the three mixes. In this implementation, most of what the application servers do for each request depends on a database transaction. Adding more servers does not reduce the constant load of 40 concurrent clients requesting database transactions. Thus, we might expect that increasing the number of cores in the database machine would naturally lead to an increase in the system's performance, but that is not necessarily true. If that was the case, then in Figure 15 we should also see some improvement in the JDBC-based implementation as we increase the number of clients, because the machine has 48 cores. In fact, despite the underlying architecture of relational databases having been developed many years ago, their scalability is still a matter of recent discussion [28]. To this contributes the fact that database architectures originated long before computers with many cores became commodity hardware. Despite their long-time focus on efficiently handling multiple concurrent requests, database architectures have also been faced with limited hardware parallelism, which reduces transactions' simultaneous access to its database's internal structures. It has been shown [22] that popular open-source database implementations fail to take advantage of multicore architectures, and simply do not scale as expected.

5. Related Work

Snapshot isolation was first defined in [2]. Today, most database vendors support snapshot isolation as the strongest isolation level (confusingly, also known as serializable in

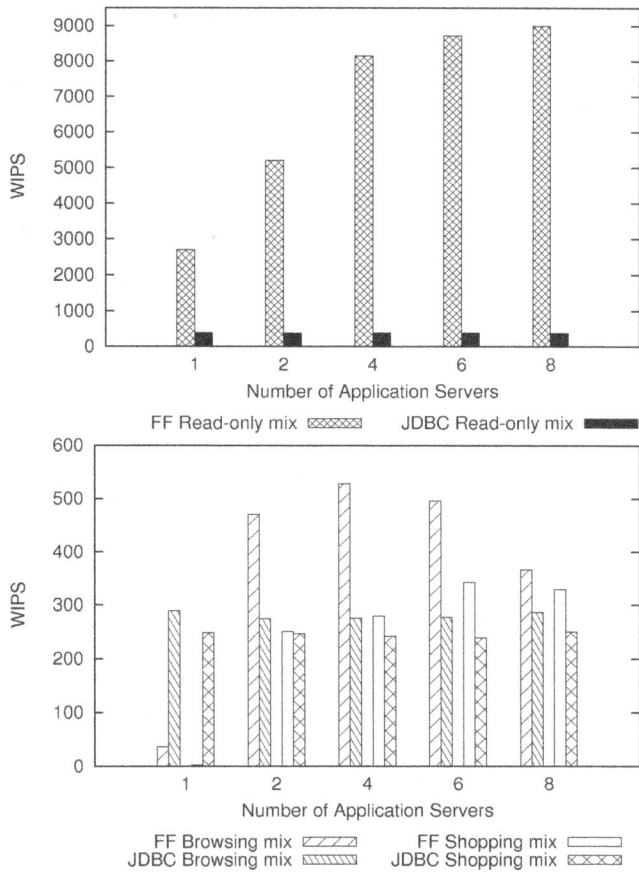

Figure 18. Throughput in a clustered environment for 40 clients evenly split across the servers.

some database implementations), which, despite exhibiting none of the anomalies that the SQL standard prohibits, is not serializable. Since the broad adoption of this isolation level by database implementations, other researchers have cataloged the weaknesses present in this isolation level [12].

In [13] the authors propose a theory to identify when non-serializable executions of applications can occur under snapshot isolation, which has been used to manually demonstrate that some programs may safely run under snapshot isolation without exhibiting any anomalies. This is done, by analyzing possible interferences between concurrent transactions. Additionally, the authors also propose ways to eliminate the identified interferences, but at the cost of manually modifying the program logic of these applications to make it serializable.

Later work [1], has demonstrated that the risks involved in using weaker consistency semantics often do not pay off for the absence of serializability. The effort of ensuring safe executions under snapshot isolation is high, and in many applications the performance penalty for running with full serialization guarantees is low, when compared to the risks

of data corruption because of concurrency bugs due to the absence of strong consistency guarantees.

In another work [23] the authors propose an automated tool to detect the snapshot isolation anomalies, but to ensure full coverage, they incur in false positives. Also, computing the minimum set of conflicting transaction pairs that require modification is a NP-Hard problem. Regardless, modifying the program code to eliminate the conflicts is still a manual task.

An alternative to changing program code is to change the transactional engine to ensure strict serializability. This is proposed in [8]. The authors describe an algorithm that provides serializability, while showing, in most cases, a performance similar to the one obtained when running with just snapshot isolation. This work, albeit different from ours, provides evidence that serializability does not incur necessarily in performance problems.

Yet another approach to ensuring program correctness is presented in [3], which defines a new correctness criteria—semantic correctness—that is weaker than serializability, and describes the conditions in which executions preserve given integrity constraints for each isolation level.

Neither of the previously mentioned approaches reduces the number of database queries. Such requires caching on the application server. In [25], the authors present a versioned object cache for J2EE that reduces the number of database accesses and provides snapshot isolation on top of a relational database that must also provide snapshot isolation. They also describe a vertical replication model where each node in the cluster is built from a relational database and a J2EE application server. Their object cache allows for a reduction in the number of database requests, just like ours, but there are other important differences. Most notably, they do not ensure object identity: When an object is modified a new copy is created, which does not allow for object reference comparison. In our implementation, a single object instance is shared among all transactions. Additionally, our transactional system only blocks during the commit of a write transaction whereas they require locking for each object update operation. Most importantly, we ensure strict serializability across the cluster whereas their implementation ensures only snapshot isolation. The focus of their work is on availability and scalability, which led to an architecture of one database per application server, with the cache updates being sent over a dedicated group communication system. However, there is no protocol for dynamically adding a new node to the cluster, which would require database state synchronization to keep up with the rest of the system. In our solution, there is a single point of access to the database—which can be replicated internally—and the cache in each application server is updated from the database, allowing for adding and removing application servers on-the-fly.

Initially, our work concentrated mainly on improving performance for applications running on single computers with many cores. The performance improvements attained in the clustered environment are, in a sense, a by-product of this architecture, which we believe can be even further improved by taking into account the specificities of a distributed system in the design of the system. The work reported in [10, 27], which extends the JVSTM design with scalable and fault-tolerant distributed transactional memory algorithms, is a step in that direction. This work concentrates only on the distribution aspects and, like [25], builds on a group communication system between the nodes, currently implementing only a single entry point to the persistence tier.

6. Conclusion

In this paper we have described a new architecture for the development of enterprise applications, which is based on shifting transaction control from the database to the application server tier. This architectural change was made possible by developments both in hardware as well as software that did not exist when relational databases became widely adopted, thus biasing development towards current architectures. In hardware, the change was enabled by the development of machines with many cores and large memory heaps. In software, STM technology has enabled us to think in terms of transactions managed by the application server and also to a change in the way persistent application objects are managed in main memory.

Some observations led to this change. For one, programmers are often burdened with additional programming efforts because of limitations in the transactional semantics provided by existing systems. By providing strict serializability the programming of concurrent operations becomes simpler and less prone to error. Another problem is related to the cost of database access in current enterprise applications. Often these applications are feature-rich with complex domain and business logic that is implemented in object-oriented applications. These cause several round trips to the persistence tier to transactionally manipulate persistent application data. Often, simply the execution of a read-only operation can trigger several round trips to the persistence tier. The accumulated latency of this communication is no longer negligible and is perceived by the client of the service. Shifting transaction control to the application tier can reduce the need for these accesses with a significant reduction in the time it takes to answer a client's request.

The architecture that we presented is designed to make good use of the improved computational capacity of single application servers running on hardware with many cores and large memory heaps. It excels when applied to object-oriented enterprise applications that have complex object structures and exhibit many concurrent accesses with a high read/write ratio. Based on the evidence that we collected over the past six years, during which we employed this architecture to several applications and collected statistics about their workload patterns, we believe that many of today's mainstream web applications have these same characteristics. Thus, we claim that our architecture is a better solution for many, if not most, of the modern enterprise applications.

It is not a panacea, however, and, as such, is not exempt of problems. For instance, even though our implementation works in clustered environments, it suffers from cache invalidations in scenarios where the rate of write operations is higher. Looking ahead, it is our intention to continue to work in the development of this architecture, trying to broaden the scenarios in which it can be applied to increase application performance and safety, namely in write-heavy scenarios and in continued reduction of the database access costs.

Acknowledgments

The work described in this paper would not have been possible without the contribution of many people that have been involved in some way or another with the development of the Fénix Framework and of the FénixEDU system. These include the excellent development and systems' administration teams at CIIST, and the members of the Software Engineering Group at INESC-ID.

Also, this work was partially supported by FCT, both via INESC-ID multiannual funding through the PIDDAC Program funds and via the Pastramy project (under contract number PTDC/EIA/72405/2006), and, more recently, by the Cloud-TM project, which is co-financed by the European Commission through the contract number 257784.

References

[1] M. Alomari, M. Cahill, A. Fekete, and U. Rohm. The cost of serializability on platforms that use snapshot isolation. In *Proceedings of the 2008 IEEE 24th International Conference on Data Engineering (ICDE '08)*, pages 576–585, Cancun, Mexico, 2008. IEEE Computer Society.

[2] H. Berenson, P. Bernstein, J. Gray, J. Melton, E. O'Neil, and P. O'Neil. A critique of ANSI SQL isolation levels. In *Proceedings of the 1995 ACM SIGMOD International Conference on Management of Data (SIGMOD '95)*, pages 1–10, San Jose, CA, USA, 1995. ACM.

[3] A. Bernstein, P. Lewis, and S. Lu. Semantic conditions for correctness at different isolation levels. In *Proceedings of the 16th International Conference on Data Engineering (ICDE '00)*, pages 57–66, San Diego, CA, USA, 2000.

[4] M. Brantner, D. Florescu, D. Graf, D. Kossmann, and T. Kraska. Building a database on S3. In *Proceedings of the 2008 ACM SIGMOD International Conference on Management of Data (SIGMOD '08)*, pages 251–264, Vancouver, Canada, 2008. ACM.

[5] J. Cachopo. *Development of Rich Domain Models with Atomic Actions*. PhD thesis, Instituto Superior Técnico/Universidade Técnica de Lisboa, Sept. 2007.

[6] J. Cachopo and A. Rito-Silva. Combining software transactional memory with a domain modeling language to simplify web application development. In *Proceedings of the 6th inter-*

national conference on Web engineering (ICWE '06), pages 297–304, Palo Alto, CA, USA, 2006. ACM.

[7] J. Cachopo and A. Rito-Silva. Versioned boxes as the basis for memory transactions. *Science of Computer Programming*, 63(2):172–185, Dec. 2006. doi: 10.1016/j.scico.2006.05.009.

[8] M. J. Cahill, U. Röhm, and A. D. Fekete. Serializable isolation for snapshot databases. *ACM Transactions on Database Systems*, 34(4):20:1–20:42, Dec. 2009. doi: 10.1145/1620585. 1620587.

[9] N. Carvalho, J. Cachopo, L. Rodrigues, and A. R. Silva. Versioned transactional shared memory for the FénixEDU web application. In *Proceedings of the 2nd Workshop on Dependable Distributed Data Management (WDDDM '08)*, pages 15–18, Glasgow, Scotland, 2008. ACM.

[10] M. Couceiro, P. Romano, N. Carvalho, and L. Rodrigues. D2STM: Dependable distributed software transactional memory. In *Proceedings of the 15th IEEE Pacific Rim International Symposium on Dependable Computing (PRDC '09)*, pages 307–313, Shanghai, China, Nov. 2009.

[11] J. Dean and S. Ghemawat. MapReduce: Simplified data processing on large clusters. *Communications of the ACM*, 51(1): 107–113, Jan. 2008. doi: 10.1145/1327452.1327492.

[12] A. Fekete, E. O'Neil, and P. O'Neil. A read-only transaction anomaly under snapshot isolation. *ACM SIGMOD Record*, 33 (3):12–14, Sept. 2004. doi: 10.1145/1031570.1031573.

[13] A. Fekete, D. Liarokapis, E. O'Neil, P. O'Neil, and D. Shasha. Making snapshot isolation serializable. *ACM Transactions on Database Systems*, 30(2):492–528, June 2005. doi: 10.1145/ 1071610.1071615.

[14] P. Felber, C. Fetzer, R. Guerraoui, and T. Harris. Transactions are back—but are they the same? *ACM SIGACT News*, 39(1): 48–58, Mar. 2008. ISSN 0163-5700. doi: 10.1145/1360443. 1360456.

[15] S. M. Fernandes and J. Cachopo. Lock-free and scalable multi-version software transactional memory. In *Proceedings of the 16th ACM symposium on Principles and Practice of Parallel Programming (PPoPP '11)*, pages 179–188, San Antonio, TX, USA, 2011. ACM.

[16] M. Fowler. *Patterns of Enterprise Application Architecture*. Addison-Wesley Professional, Boston, MA, USA, 2002.

[17] M. Fowler. *Domain-Specific Languages*. Addison-Wesley Professional, 1st edition, 2010.

[18] R. Guerraoui and M. Kapalka. On the correctness of transactional memory. In *Proceedings of the 13th ACM SIGPLAN Symposium on Principles and Practice of Parallel Programming (PPoPP '08)*, pages 175–184, Salt Lake City, UT, USA, 2008. ACM. ISBN 978-1-59593-795-7. doi: http://doi.acm. org/10.1145/1345206.1345233.

[19] T. Harris, J. R. Larus, and R. Rajwar. *Transactional Memory, 2nd edition*. Synthesis Lectures on Computer Architecture. Morgan & Claypool Publishers, 2010.

[20] M. Herlihy. Wait-free synchronization. *ACM Transactions on Programming Languages and Systems*, 13(1):124–149, Jan. 1991. doi: 10.1145/114005.102808.

[21] C. Ireland, D. Bowers, M. Newton, and K. Waugh. A classification of object-relational impedance mismatch. In *Proceedings of the 1st International Conference on Advances in Databases, Knowledge, and Data Applications (DBKDA '09)*, pages 36–43, Cancun, Mexico, Mar. 2009.

[22] R. Johnson, I. Pandis, N. Hardavellas, A. Ailamaki, and B. Falsafi. Shore-MT: A scalable storage manager for the multicore era. In *Proceedings of the 12th International Conference on Extending Database Technology: Advances in Database Technology (EDBT '09)*, pages 24–35, Saint Petersburg, Russia, 2009. ACM.

[23] S. Jorwekar, A. Fekete, K. Ramamritham, and S. Sudarshan. Automating the detection of snapshot isolation anomalies. In *Proceedings of the 33rd International Conference on Very Large Data Bases (VLDB '07)*, pages 1263–1274, Vienna, Austria, 2007. VLDB Endowment.

[24] C. H. Papadimitriou. The serializability of concurrent database updates. *Journal of the ACM*, 26(4):631–653, Oct. 1979. doi: 10.1145/322154.322158.

[25] F. Perez-Sorrosal, M. Patiño-Martinez, R. Jimenez-Peris, and K. Bettina. Consistent and scalable cache replication for multi-tier J2EE applications. In *Proceedings of the 8th ACM/IFIP/USENIX International Conference on Middleware (Middleware '07)*, pages 328–347, Newport Beach, CA, USA, 2007. Springer-Verlag.

[26] D. Pritchett. BASE: An acid alternative. *Queue*, 6(3):48–55, May 2008. doi: 10.1145/1394127.1394128.

[27] P. Romano, N. Carvalho, M. Couceiro, L. Rodrigues, and J. Cachopo. Towards the integration of distributed transactional memories in application servers' clusters. In *The Third International Workshop on Advanced Architectures and Algorithms for Internet DElivery and Applications (AAA-IDEA '09)*, Las Palmas, Gran Canaria, Nov. 2009. ICST, Springer.

[28] M. Stonebraker and R. Cattell. 10 rules for scalable performance in 'simple operation' datastores. *Communications of the ACM*, 54(6):72–80, June 2011. doi: 10.1145/1953122. 1953144.

[29] W. Vogels. Eventually consistent. *Communications of the ACM*, 52(1):40–44, Jan. 2009. doi: 10.1145/1435417. 1435432.

Naming Anonymous JavaScript Functions

Salman Mirghasemi

École Polytechnique Fédérale de
Lausanne(EPFL)

salman.mirghasemi@epfl.ch

John J. Barton *

IBM Research - Almaden
bartonjj@us.ibm.com

Claude Petitpierre

École Polytechnique Fédérale de
Lausanne(EPFL)

claude.petitpierre@epfl.ch

Abstract

JavaScript developers create programs by calling functions and they use functions to construct objects. JavaScript development tools need to report to developers about those functions and constructors, for example in debugger callstacks and in object representations. However, most functions are anonymous: developers need not to specify names for functions. Based on our analysis of ten large, widely used JavaScript projects, less than 7% of JavaScript functions are named by developers. After studying examples from these JavaScript projects, we propose *Static Function-Object Consumption*, a principled, automated approach based on local source code analysis for providing names to nameless JavaScript functions. We applied our approach to 90000 anonymous functions that appeared in the analyzed JavaScript projects. The approach is successful in naming more than 99% (91% are unique within their file) of anonymous functions while the average length of function names is kept less than 37 characters.

Categories and Subject Descriptors D.2.5 [*Testing and Debugging*]: Debugging aids; D.2.6 [*Programming Environments*]: Integrated environments

General Terms Algorithms, Human Factors, Languages

Keywords JavaScript, Anonymous Function, Debugger

1. Introduction

The unique and important role of JavaScript in web programming is undeniable. Along with the wave of "Web 2.0," JavaScript has become the inevitable part of almost every modern web site[1]. It is very likely that JavaScript keeps this crucial role for the next few years or even the next decade. Due to the growth of demands for more comprehensive user interfaces, the size and the complexity of web applications are increasing. Moreover, JavaScript is also becoming a general-purpose computing platform [17] for office applications [14, 15], browsers [9, 10], program development environments [13], and even server-side applications [5, 18].

To cope with these large and sophisticated systems, JavaScript developers turn to development tools. One prime example is a runtime debugger: The developer can halt a running program and examine the program state and execution call stack. All of these tools need to express program artifacts in a compact way that the developer can understand. For example, the debugger must present the execution call stack so the developer can understand which functions are currently active. Obviously, a particularly good compact representation would be a name given by the developer in the source code. However, the JavaScript language does not require names for many program artifacts, and, as we shall see, nameless or anonymous artifacts are more common than named ones. Anonymous artifacts prevent tools from communicating effectively with developers.

Among program artifacts, functions are central to understanding a JavaScript program. In addition to their role in the execution stack, they are first-class objects that are used for different purposes by developers; they may be used as an object constructor, a closure scope (module), or even passed as an argument in a function call. These functions can be defined and created without a name or identifier.

In this paper, we analyze 10 large, well-known projects. We show that within these projects, less than 7% of the function bodies are named. We analyze the syntactic constructs surrounding these function bodies and rationalize how developers think about the bodies in relation to the structure of the code.

We propose an automated approach based on extracted data from the source code for naming JavaScript functions. The candidate function names can be used in debuggers for

---

* The author's current affiliation is: Google, Inc, Mountain View, CA, johnjbarton@google.com.

---

[1] As an evidence, JavaScript is used in all the Web's 100 most popular sites [16].

Project	Ver.	Description	Total	Named
Closure	r683	Google Web Library	9195	208(2%)
DoJo	1.5	JavaScript Toolkit	18676	2810(15%)
ExtJS	3.3.1	JavaScript Framework	37717	1184(3%)
Firebug	1.7	Web Development Tool	3424	406(11%)
jQuery	1.4.4	JavaScript Library	422	23(5%)
MochiKit	1.4.2	JavaScript Library	1866	37(1%)
MooTools	1.3	JavaScript Framework	625	7(1%)
Prototype	1.7	JavaScript Framework	645	203(31%)
Scriptaculous	1.9	JavaScript Library	1092	208(19%)
YUI	3.3	Yahoo UI Library	22346	922(4%)
All		All Projects	96008	6008(6.3%)

Table 1. The total number of functions and the number of named (and percent named) functions in ten large JavaScript projects. See appendix 1 for the project citations.

```
 9  var main = function() {          // main
10    var foo = new Foo(
11      function(){                  // main/foo<
12        this.welcome = "Hi!";
13      });
14    var bar = new Bar("GoodBye.");
15    alert(foo.welcome);
16    alert(bar.message);
17  };
18  var Foo = function(){             // Foo<
19    var instances;
20    return function(initializer){   // Foo
21      instances++;
22      initializer.apply(this);
23    }
24  }();
25  var Baz = Bar = function(msg){    // Bar
26    this.message = msg;
27  }
```

Figure 1. An excerpt of a JavaScript code illustrating anonymous functions. The comments give the results from Sec. 5 and these are discussed in Sec. 5.5

more descriptive object summaries and call-stack views, or in integration with proposed JavaScript typing systems for providing modern editing features in development environments.

2. The Anonymous Function Problem

A JavaScript function can be defined with the `function` definition or the `Function` constructor (i.e., `new Function(args, source)`) [7]. The `function` definition can appear in a function declaration, function expression, or function statement. Of these forms, only the function declaration requires a function name and the `Function` constructor has no mechanism to name the function. In other words, JavaScript developers can define functions with or without function names.

If you are unfamiliar with JavaScript or other functional programming languages, you might imagine that developers would naturally select the form with names, simply as an organizational tool. However this is not the case. Functions in JavaScript are first-class objects. They can be assigned to any variable or object property, or passed as an argument to a function. Consequently JavaScript programmers can use these other constructs to organize their thinking about the program, without the use of function names.

So what do JavaScript developers do in practice? To get empirical evidence we analyzed the source code of ten well-known JavaScript projects[2]. For every project, the total number of functions and the number of functions with an identifier are shown in Table 1. The average ratio of named functions to all functions is less then 7 percent and, excepting one project, *Prototype*, the ratio does not exceed 13 percent. Among all functions only a very limited number of them (116 functions) are defined by the `Function` constructor. Our analysis does not include the functions defined dynamically by `eval` function or `new Function()`; these cases would only make the ratio even smaller. Therefore, we

conclude that a large proportion of JavaScript functions are anonymous.

To understand the consequences of anonymous functions on development tools we will focus on one example, the impact on debuggers. Two main issues appear in debuggers due to the lack of function name. First, the object constructor name, which can facilitate understanding the object value, is not available in the object summary. Second, the call-stack view is usually full of *anonymous* functions and therefore much less informative. We discuss these issues in the next two subsections.

2.1 Missed Constructor Name in Object Summary

JavaScript does not support classes, but objects can be created by constructors (`new` followed by a function call). A constructor is a regular JavaScript function. Once the `new` keyword is evaluated, an empty object, with the constructor prototype as its prototype, is created, then the new object is bound to `this` and the constructor is called. The role of constructor is to initialize the empty object. Unlike class-based object-oriented languages, the structure of the object may change during the object's lifetime [17]. Nevertheless, the constructor can still be useful in classifying the object most of the time. Debuggers employ this fact and display the constructor name in the object summary to facilitate the developer's understanding.

Figure 1 shows an excerpt of a JavaScript program we use to illustrate this issue. We set a breakpoint on line 15 and examine the runtime elements at this breakpoint by two JavaScript debuggers, Google Chrome and Firebug (Figure 2). Two objects assigned to variables `foo` and `bar` are constructed by two different constructors: `Foo` and `Bar`.

The Google Chrome debugger shows the general class of `Object` for `foo` and the `Baz.Bar` class for `bar` in their summaries. The first class is very general and the second

---

[2] We did not perform any preprocess to exclude third-party or repeated files in the provided source code bundles.

```
▼ Local                                    ⊞ this        Window JSFunction_Names.html
   ▶ bar: Baz.Bar                          ⊞ bar         Object { message="GoodBye." }
   ▶ foo: Object                           ⊞ foo         Object { welcome="Hi!" }
   ▶ this: DOMWindow                          toString   function()
 ▶ Global                  DOMWindow       ⊞ [object Window]   Window JSFunction_Names.html
```

(a) Google Chrome Debugger   (b) Firebug

Figure 2. The screenshot of variables view of Google Chrome and Firebug JavaScript debuggers paused on a breakpoint at line 15 of the program shown in Figure 1. The content of these views is discussed in Sec. 2.1

one is misleading. The developer has to expand the object nodes to recognize their similarities and differences.

Firebug classifies both objects in the general Object class, but includes some of the object properties in the summary. These additional properties may give a hint to the developer about the object structures. Foo and Bar definitions at lines 20 and 25 explain the debuggers' behavior: the function statements has no explicit name (identifier), therefore debuggers considered them as anonymous functions or they infer a misleading name.

2.2 Anonymous Function Names in Call-stack View

The second problem is the call-stack. To illustrate this, we pause the program (Figure 1) at line 12 by a breakpoint. Figure 3 shows how the program call-stack is displayed in Google Chrome debugger and Firebug. The differences in the number of frames and line numbers between two call-stacks are due to dissimilar event handling implementations in the underlying platforms. Among the three top functions in the call stack, Google Chrome shows only the name of the third one down, function (main), correctly. For the second frame from the top (marked as line 22), it shows anonymous, and for the top frame (marked at line 12), it gives a wrong name, foo. Firebug performs better by guessing two function names correctly, but it still fails in one case. It shows main as the name of the function on the top frame (marked at line 12) but this is the name of another function (the enclosing function at line 9). In these cases, the information provided by the debugger is useless and the developer has to locate the function source to understand or recall the function behavior.

3. Automated Function Naming

The anonymous functions problem is discussed in several articles and forums on the Web [6, 20]. Different solutions have been proposed and discussed by practitioners. A basic solution is a mechanism for naming functions by developers without affecting the variables in scopes. For example, a new property (e.g., *displayName*) in the function object can be used for storing the function name, or the function name can be defined by an annotation. Although these solutions may help, they require extra work from developers, the displayName value can become out of sync with the meaning

of the code over time, the annotation may be incorrectly recognized in programs that use the same property name for another purpose, and maintenance of the debugger becomes more difficult once the call-stack names can be overridden by user code.

We instead propose an automated approach for naming anonymous functions by analyzing the source code. Before getting into explaining the algorithm details we discuss the rationale behind some of decisions we made in this approach.

3.1 What Should Be Named?

A statement defining a function creates a new Function object. The definition may be evaluated multiple times, and depending on the times a function definition is evaluated, zero to many Function objects can be created from the same definition. Two function objects which are created from the same function body may have different object properties added at runtime. They may also have different enclosing scopes and therefore different behaviors. Thus our first question: do we try to name the Function objects or the source that defines them?

For the common cases, the different Function objects are bound to one or more properties of objects. The names of these properties inform the developer about the role of the function in the actions of the object. To determine the actions of the functions in turn, the developer must read the function source (or perhaps its documentation). Our function names serve to recall or summarize that source or documentation for the developer. Therefore we seek to name the source, the content between the curly braces known as the *Function-Body* in the standard[7].

After reflection the reader may be puzzled by the preceding claim. On the one hand we claim that the function object instance may be bound to properties in multiple objects and those property names are not helpful for naming. On the other hand we will shortly introduce an algorithm that uses a property name (in part) to name a *FunctionBody*. Ultimately we are relying on a subtle characteristic of JavaScript programming: the first binding of a *Function* to an object property differs from all other bindings because it is located in text near the *FunctionBody* and thus developers associate this first binding with the meaning of the *FunctionBody*.

foo	JSfunction_names.html:12
(anonymous function)	JSfunction_names.html:22
main	JSfunction_names.html:10
(anonymous function)	JSfunction_names.html:34
onclick	JSfunction_names.html:35

(a) Google Chrome Debugger

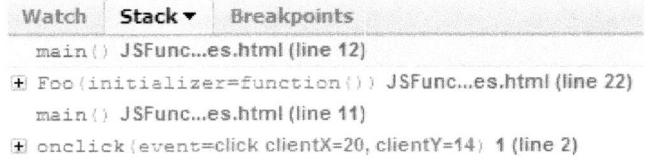

| Watch | **Stack** ▾ | Breakpoints |

```
main() JSFunc...es.html (line 12)
⊞ Foo(initializer=function()) JSFunc...es.html (line 22)
main() JSFunc...es.html (line 11)
⊞ onclick(event=click clientX=20, clientY=14) 1 (line 2)
```

(b) Firebug

Figure 3. The screenshot of call-stack view of Google Chrome and Firebug JavaScript debuggers paused on a breakpoint at line 15 of the program shown in Figure 1. The contents of these views are discussed in Sec. 2.2

3.2 What Makes a Good Function Name?

A function name is basically used to assist the developer to recall or understand the function behavior. For a developer who is already familiar with the function, it works more like an identifier. However, this identifier should be easily recognized by the developer. For example, a naive proposal for the function name is a combination of the function file name and its first line number. Although it may work as an identifier, it does not assist the developer to recall or understand the function behavior.

On the other hand, for a developer who does not know the function, a function name should explain the function behavior, or an abstraction of the function behavior, or why/where the function is used/defined (e.g., to create the object *foo*). A function name must not be so long that it can not be displayed or read by the developer. For example, the entire function body source code explains the function behavior well, however it is not an appropriate function name.

3.3 Context, Package and Function Names

JavaScript does not support a standard packaging mechanism to be used for modular programming. Scripts are loaded from different files and executed within the same or different global objects. Developers usually use objects at the top level to encapsulate objects, properties and functions from a framework or library. The same mechanism is reused for defining subpackages. As the project size and the number of functions increases, the short function name will not be enough for recognizing the function. The developer also wants the class or the module that contains the function. In addition to the package name, knowing the context (the enclosing function body) that contains the function can help in better understanding the function behavior.

4. Building Up Intuition by Example

We know that we face an ill-defined task: we are after all attempting to create short useful names for nameless functions. We have to create salient information from source code: we anticipate that removing characters will be our biggest challenge. To create an algorithm we decided to study the spectrum of examples from our 10 large collections of functions. We want to see what kinds of cases are

important and what aspects of these cases help us identify functions. For this purpose we created 12 categories of function body expressions shown in Table 2 and we categorized all of the nameless functions from the 10 JavaScript projects into one of these 12 cases, giving the numerical results in Table 3.

			Description	Code
1	The function object	is assigned to a(n) object property through	property of a new object in an object literal.	{ ..., foo: function(){...}, ...}
2			new array index in an array literal.	[..., function(){...}, ...]
3			direct access by a property identifier.	bar*.foo = function(){...}
4			hashmap access by a string.	bar*["foo"] = function(){...}
5			hashmap access by a variable name.	bar*[foo] = function(){...}
6			hashmap access by a JavaScript expression.	bar*[foo*] = function(){...}
7		array index.		foo*[0] = function(){...}
8		variable.		foo = function(){...}
9		is directly called.		function(){...}()
10		property is accessed.		function(){...}.foo
11		is returned from a function call.		{... return function(){...}}
12		is passed as an argument to a function.		foo*(..., function(){}, ...)

Table 2. Different cases of anonymous function object creation and usage in JavaScript. Identifiers with a star in the table can be expressions as well as simple identifiers; we explain how we reduce expressions to pseudo-identifier in 5.3.

280

	1	2	3	4	5	6	7	8	9	10	11	12
Closure	23(0.3%)	0	8466(94%)	3	4	0	0	67(0.7%)	16(0.2%)	0	43(0.5%)	365(4%)
DOJO	9601(61%)	7	1765(11%)	21	24	2	1	1151(7%)	476(3%)	2	175(1%)	2641(17%)
ExtJS	30221(83%)	0	1476(4%)	3	40	9	0	859(2%)	788(2%)	180	517(1%)	2439(7%)
Firebug	2296(76%)	0	539(18%)	1	2	0	0	17(0.4%)	7(0.2%)	2	6(0.2%)	148(5%)
jQuery	233(58%)	0	34(9%)	0	10	2	0	24(6%)	10(2%)	0	0	86(21%)
MochiKit	1080(59%)	10	385(21%)	0	4	0	0	110(6%)	18(1%)	0	41(2%)	181(10%)
MooTools	339(55%)	0	79(13%)	0	4	3	0	53(9%)	21(3%)	20	14(2%)	85(13%)
Prototype	265(60%)	0	28(6%)	0	0	1	0	25(6%)	44(10%)	1	8(2%)	70(16%)
Scriptaculous	564(64%)	0	75(8%)	0	2	2	0	27(3%)	45(5%)	21	9(1%)	139(15%)
YUI	14154(66%)	7	1721(8%)	0	90	0	0	1181(6%)	172(1%)	0	95(0.5%)	4004(19%)
All	58776(65%)	24	14568(16%)	28	180	19	1	3514(4%)	1597(2%)	226	908(1%)	10072(11%)

Table 3. The number of nameless functions in each category defined in table 2.

Then we examine each of these cases to think about how we want the functions named. We will skip over the nesting of function scopes in the analysis to avoid taking on too much at one time; we return to this aspect at the end of this section.

4.1 Case 1: Object Property Initializer

This case usually appears when developers try to group a set of functions in a new object. A common case is grouping a set of functions in the `prototype` property of the constructor. This structure resembles the class structure in traditional object-oriented languages. When a new object is created by the constructor, the new object also inherits all functions defined in the constructor's prototype. This structure is also used when the owner object is a shared object with a set of utility functions.

The majority of nameless functions (more than 65%) in almost all studied projects (except Closure), are defined in object literals. This case seems particularly simple: the property name makes a good name for the function body. But what logic are we implicitly applying here? Our reasoning: the developer-invented property name has high information content, it is textually close to the function body, and the function object created by the function body initializes to the property. These observations guide us in more complex cases.

4.2 Case 2: Entry in an Array Literal

Contrary to the previous case the appearance of this case is very limited. It usually appears in initializations or when an array of functions are passed as an argument. Among all projects only three have instances of nameless functions defined in this way. For example array argument to `Event._attach` in this example from YUI [3]:

```
_attach: function (el, notifier, delegate) {
  if (Y.DOM.isWindow(el)) {
    return Event._attach([type, function (e) {
      notifier.fire(e);
    }, el]);
  }
}
```

The developer will probably think of the array entry as one item in a collection passed to `Event._attach`. In general we shall want to name these kinds of functions by the destiny of the containing array.

4.3 Case 3: Property Assignment With Property Identifier

This case is the second most common case in the studied projects. Here, we can see why the Closure project is different from other projects in the first case. About 94% of nameless functions in this project are defined in this way. It seems that the Closure developers follow an internal standard for function objects creation and usage.

Following the model from Case 1, we think a good name would combine the object name with the property identifier. The complication in this case comes from the object name: in general the object reference can be a computed expression [4]. Here is a simple example from the Closure project:

```
this.eventPool_.createObject = function () {
  return new goog.debug.Trace_.Event_();
};
```

In general, the expression can be long and complex: to create a useful name we need to focus on developer-invented identifiers in the expression and work to keep the total number of characters small. For example, `this.` add no information to the name since we cannot know the value of `this` while parsing.

4.4 Case 4: Property Assignment With Property Name String

In JavaScript, objects are like hashmaps and their properties can also be accessed by a string specified in the brackets after the object. Semantically this is the same as the previous case and we see few instances of this form of function object assignment. The string inside the brackets can be considered a property identifier for naming.

---

[3] The example is nested in more function definitions we do not show here.

[4] This comment applies to all of the cases in table 2 marked with an asterisk on the expression identifier

4.5 Case 5: Property Assignment With Property Name Variable

Object member names can be variable references that get converted to strings at runtime: this is syntactically similar to Case 4, but we cannot (usually) statically compute the string to use as a property identifier. The usage of this case is also limited. This form usually appears when the same function body is assigned to different properties in a loop. For example see the inner function in Fig. 4. The variable name in the cases we examined was a generic name like o or item. Unlike the previous two cases, we do not have a specific property name. Nevertheless identifying the function body using the assignment target with the variable name as the property name follows the reasoning used for the simple cases.

```
jQuery.each("ajaxStart ajaxStop ajaxComplete ajaxError"
  .split(" "), function( i, o ) {
    jQuery.fn[o] = function( f ) {
      return this.bind(o, f);
    };
});
```

Figure 4. An example of a function (the inner definition) assigned to a hashmap using a variable name (row 5 in Table 2) and an example of functions passed as arguments to a function (row 11 in Table 2). The function is from the jQuery library but simplified to fit on the page.

4.6 Case 6: Property Assignment With Property Name Expressions

Object member names can be expressions that get converted to strings at runtime: this is more general than case 5. A common case of expression in this case is a conditional expression, e.g., condition?"prop1":"prop2", where the property that we assign the function to depends upon runtime values. Another kind of example of computed names comes from the Prototype project (reformatted to fit in the page):

```
function define(D) {
  if (!element) element = getRootElement();
  property[D] = 'client' + D;
  viewport['get' + D] = function() {
    return element[property[D]]
  };
  return viewport['get' + D]();
}
```

The word get is concatenated with the toString() value of the argument D at runtime to create the property name. Unlike Case 5, the property name expression need not be a simple developer-invented identifier. In this example, viewport[getD] could be a good name, but in general we will need to process the expression to balance length with information.

Notice that from the programming language point of view, Cases 3 through 6 are all special cases of Case 6. After all we are just selecting an object property in all of these cases. But from a naming point of view these cases present different challenges and the more complex cases will make our necessary tradeoffs more costly.

4.7 Case 7: Assignment to an Element of an Array

We only observed one instance of this form in the studied projects. The numerical index should clearly be part of the name; the array name may be an expression that we have to analyze to create name.

4.8 Case 8: Assignment to a Variable

This case is widely used and we expect developers would expect the function body to get the name of the variable. As the function objects' bodies are immutable, it is very likely that a function object which is assigned to a variable, is used with the same variable name in the function scope and its internal scopes. There are cases in which a variable name is used temporarily, as the function is passed to another function or assigned to an object property. However, in most cases the variable name works well as the function name.

4.9 Case 9: Anonymous Functions Immediately Called

Calling function objects just after their creations is a common pattern in JavaScript. For example see the assignment to Y.ClassNameManager in Fig. 5 (the function is called at the bottom of the example).

```
Y.ClassNameManager = function () {
  var sPrefix = CONFIG[CLASS_NAME_PREFIX],
  sDelimiter = CONFIG[CLASS_NAME_DELIMITER];
  return {
    getClassName: Y.cached(function () {
      var args = Y.Array(arguments);
      if (args[args.length-1] !== true) {
        args.unshift(sPrefix);
      } else {
        args.pop();
      }
      return args.join(sDelimiter);
    })
  };
}();
```

Figure 5. An example the YUI project of function bodies from cases 9 (the outer function) and 12 (the argument to Y.cached) from Table 2

If the called-function is assigned to a variable or object property, then we have a version of one of the other cases in Table 2. The difference here is that we can tell from static analysis that the assignment will use the return value of the function, not the function object itself. But for naming purposes the key information will be the assignment target.

If the function call has no result, it means that the function performs one task (e.g., initialization of some values in the outer scope for later use). In this case we cannot use the assignment target idea from Case 1, but the source proximity and the developer-invented names concepts point to using interior identifiers in a name. To avoid confusing the developer by using the same name for the outer and interior functions, we will need some way to signify that the name we create in this way is for an immediately called function.

4.10 Case 10: Function Property is Accessed

In this unusual case a property of the function is accessed directly from the function body. This case usually happens when one of the predefined functions (i.e., `call`, `apply`, `bind`) or added functions to the `Function` prototype is called. Here is an example, from ExtJS, reformatted for display here:

```
setVisible : function(v, a, d, c, e){
  if(v){
    this.showAction();
  }
  if(a && v){
    var cb = function(){
      this.sync(true);
        if(c){
          c();
        }
    }.createDelegate(this);
  }
  // .....
}
```

The inner function body is not used directly, but the result of `createDelegate` is assigned to `cb`. The most valuable information here is the variable name `cb`, followed by the `createDelegate` function name. This example also illustrates that automatic naming could have an effect on developers coding style: giving a longer name for `cb` would give better names in development tools but currently developers have limited expectations that tools will show such information.

4.11 Case 11: Returned From a Function Call

In this case the function body appears in a return statement of another function body. Although this category only includes 2% of nameless functions, proper naming of functions in this class is important. Many constructors are built using this form and therefore the names of these functions appear in object summaries. Clearly the name of these returned functions is almost the same as the name of the functions that define them. For example, in Fig. 6 a developer might pick names like `registerWinOnIE` and `registerWinNotOnIE` for the functions returned by the Dojo function `registerWin`.

4.12 Case 12: Function Passed as an Argument

Numbers in table 3 show that creating and passing functions as arguments is very common in JavaScript. For example, see Fig. 4. The calling function and the other arguments look helpful, to the extent that they have identifiers invented by the developer. As in this example, we see that the calling function, `jQuery.each()`, can be generic so it provides less valuable information, but the arguments in that example are highly specific to the function body. Fig. 5 shows different example, where the function called (`Y.Cached()`) seems much less important for naming the function than the

```
registerWin: function(targetWindow, effectiveNode){
  ...
  if(doc){
   if(dojo.isIE){
    ....
    return function(){
     doc.detachEvent('onmousedown', mousedownListener);
     doc.detachEvent('onactivate', activateListener);
     doc.detachEvent('ondeactivate', deactivateListener);
     doc = null;
    };
   }else{
    ....
    return function(){
     doc.removeEventListener(
              'mousedown', mousedownListener, true);
     doc.removeEventListener('focus', focusListener, true);
     doc.removeEventListener('blur', blurListener, true);
     doc = null;
    };
}}}.
```

Figure 6. An example of a function body in a return statement, case 11 of Table 2 adapted from the Dojo project code

property that we initialize with the result of calling the function. This important case will stress any naming algorithm: we somehow have to summarize the function call – which itself may be an expression – and the other arguments – any or all of which may be expressions.

4.13 Results of Studying Examples

We reached two main conclusions from studying the way anonymous functions are used in the source of the 10 projects we examined. First, we want to try to find the name of the initializer or assignment target that will receive the function object created from a function body. JavaScript programmers are creating anonymous functions but they are loading them into object references and the expressions that result in those references have informative identifiers inside. Second, these expressions that we focus on may often be simple identifiers, but if they are not we will need to analyze the source code of these expressions to extract meaningful summaries. This summary has to balance information against length.

Overlaying our analysis above is hierarchy: any of the cases can be nested in function scopes. Obviously this hierarchy must be represented in our names. Algorithmically this is straight forward recursion. But from the name usability point of view, deep hierarchy means long names, exactly the problem we want to avoid. Fortunately developers are well trained in dealing with this kind of problem and we anticipate that hierarchical names can be shown to users in progressive depth depending on the particular needs in the user interface.

5. Static Function Object Consumption

Using our analysis we have created a preliminary automatic naming solution. The three parts of our solution match three observations for our study. First we apply *(Static) Func-*

tion Object Consumption, which tracks the function object created from a function body to where the object is 'consumed', for example by assignment to or initialization of an object property, variable reference, or function argument. The "static" qualifier just indicates that we will only use a parser. Second, we reduce complex expressions to pseudo-identifiers focusing on developer-invented names. Third we apply our approach hierarchically to deal with nested function bodies.

We will describe the details in the next sections. In constructing names we realized one additional aspect: as we move from simple object property names to more complex examples, the path of the object consumption is an added bit of information helpful in naming. Thus we add some symbols to guide the developer to the function body in complex cases: in this way the extra information does not take a lot of space and it can be ignored by developers who have not yet learned about its significance. We describe these symbols in Sec. 5.4.

5.1 Consumption Summary Algorithm

We parse the JavaScript and search the resulting syntax tree for function body nodes. For each function body, we apply the algorithm outlined in Algorithm 1. The basic idea (the `while` loop) is to walk the syntax tree from the body up through parent nodes until we hit a node that is not a JavaScript expression. For each node we create an entry in a list and record in it information about the relationship between the node and its parent. We'll use this relationship information in Sec. 5.4. Then for each node we record developer-invented identifiers related to the destiny of the function object created from the body as outlined in Table 4. For the first and third rows of the table we record the information recursively; for the second row, assignment node, we record the information after the loop terminates. The algorithm ends when we reach a node which is an assignment or a statement which does not return any value (i.e., the node is not an expression). The algorithm result is an *object consumption summary*, a list of collected data at every visited parent node of the function body.

The algorithm uses three subroutines: `getNextNode`, `nameExpression`, and `argSummary`. The `getNextNode` routine normally returns `n.parent`, but we also use this point in the algorithm to handle an important special case, function bodies inside of *immediate functions* typically used for modularity or scoping in JavaScript. We discuss this case in Sec. 5.2. The remaining two subroutines construct a pseudo-identifier from the expression as described in 5.3; they return their argument if it is simply an identifier.

5.2 Consumption by Immediate Functions

JavaScript developers use function scope to dynamically create functions with shared but private state. In this pattern, an enclosing function contains a number of function and object definitions and it is called immediately after it is

---

Algorithm 1 Compute Object Consumption Summary for Function Body Nodes

---

Input: Function Body Node n in Abstract Syntax Tree
Output: Object Consumption Summary

> $List\ summary = new\ List()$
> **while** $n.parent$ is an expression **do**
> > $dataItem = new\ DataItem()$
> > **if** n value is same as $n.parent$ value **then**
> > > $dataItem.isSameAs = true$
> > **else if** n value is a property of $n.parent$ value **then**
> > > $dataItem.isPartOf = true$
> > **else**
> > > $dataItem.isContributesTo = true$
> > **end if**
> > **if** $n.parent$ is a function call and n is an argument **then**
> > > $dataItem.isFunctionCall = true$
> > > $dataItem.id = nameExpression(n.parent)$
> > > $dataItem.hint = argSummary(n.parent)$
> > **else if** $n.parent$ is an object literal and n is its expression **then**
> > > $dataItem.isObjLiteral = true$
> > > $dataItem.id = n.parent$ property name
> > **end if**
> > $summary.add(dataItem)$
> > $n = getNextNode(n)$
> **end while**
> **if** $n.parent$ is an assignment **then**
> > $dataItem = new\ DataItem()$
> > $dataItem.isAssignment = true$
> > $dataItem.id = nameExpression(n.parent)$
> > $summary.add(dataItem)$
> **end if**
> **return** $summary$

---

defined. We call these functions *immediate functions*. For an example, see line 10 of the Figure 1 which is enclosed in the function on line 9. If the developer returns a function from this outer, immediate function, we want to follow the returned object to where it is consumed.

To keep our core algorithm simple we handle these returns from immediate functions as a special case. At the end of each loop in Algorithm 1 at the point marked `getNextNode()` we check to see if the parent is a `return` node. If not we return the parent node and the loop continues. If we have a `return` node, we look to the parent of the `return` node to see if it is a `function` node with a parent call node (either directly with () or via `apply()` or `call()`). If so, we know we are returning a function object from an immediate function. We return the parent of the immediate function, effectively skipping the intermediate nodes so that the name will reflect the consumption of the return value into the destination of the immediate function.

		Description	Code
1	*The parent node*	is an object literal.	{ ..., foo: expr }
2		is a function call.	foo*(..., expr, ...)
3		is an assignment.	foo* = expr

Table 4. Nodes produce identifiers in the function object consumption summary. Identifiers with a star in the table can be expressions as well as simple identifiers; we explain how we reduce expressions to pseudo-identifier in 5.3.

Description	Pattern	Name
Primitive	value	value.toString()
Variable	id	id
GetProp	e.id	Name(e).id
GetElem	e1[e2]	Name(e1)+[+Name(e2)+]
Operation	e1 op e2	Name(e1)+op+Name(e2)
Condition	cond?e1:e2	Name(e1)+:+Name(e2)

Table 5. JavaScript Expression Reduction to a Name. Expressions which match an entry in the pattern column are converted as shown in the Name column. Here e indicates an expression, `id` indicates an identifier, + means string concatenation and `Name()` means we apply the pattern matching recursively.

5.3 Expression Reductions

In simple cases the syntax tree node will have an identifier we can use as part of our name. In more complex cases an expression will be written in place of an identifier. We reduce these expressions to pseudo-identifiers (i.e. not necessarily a valid JavaScript identifier) that resembles the expression. This work is done during the Object Consumption Summary algorithm in the functions described here:

Identifiers for Function Arguments Search for all literal string nodes in other arguments and concatenated them by "-", dropping characters beyond 10. (This work is on in Algorithm 1 in `argSummary`).

Identifiers for Assignments and Function calls This function gets called for nodes resulting from the last 2 rows of Table 4. The expressions here will evaluate to a writable or readable address, so we want to extract the most specific developer-invented identifiers from the expression. Thus we apply the rules from Table 5, which starts from the right hand side of the expression; we skip any JavaScript keywords like `this` or `prototype`. We also skip any pattern which does not match (e.g., a function call). (This work is on in Algorithm 1 in `nameExpressions`.)

Obviously these rules are heuristic and can be improved through experience and interaction with developers. We are attempting to balance information content with length. Large complex expressions will give pseudo-identifiers which are complex, but with some identifiable parts adequate for developer recognition and search.

5.4 Conversion to a Name

At this stage of the algorithm we have a list of identifiers with attributes which we want to concatenate to create a name.

First we drop function-call identifiers if we have anything else to use for a name. The function-call identifiers typically tell us about a transformation of the function body before it is assigned to an object property or variable. The transformation may be used many places in the code, while the assignment target is typically an identifier defined by the developer for a specific section of source code. See, for example, function on line 14 and the function call on line 13 in

the Figure 1. Specifically we drop identifiers from row 2 of table 4 in any case where we have identifiers from rows 1 or 3. The outer function in Fig. 4 illustrates the opposite case, where we do not drop function-call identifier.

Second we concatenate the identifiers with a symbol between each parent and child showing the relationship. As shown in Algorithm 1, if the parent expression is an array or object literal then the identifier will be marked as *isPartOf* and we insert a dot character. If the identifier was marked as *isContributesTo* we insert a left angle bracket. An identifier marked *isSameAs* is skipped over because we already have identifier information for it. An identifier marked *isAssignment* suppresses any other marks to signify the importance of the assigned-to identifier. Because some entries on the object consumption list are empty strings we may have duplicate symbols. Any duplicates are replaced by a single symbol. The result contains identifiers (i.e., variable and property names) and strings available in the source code plus some explanatory tokens. It compactly explains the function object creation, consumption and assignment.

The particular symbols we use may be refined with more experience in how developers respond to them. Our intuition is that these extra symbols need to be visually compact because their purpose is to adjust the developers expectation for the identifier. For example, the function on line 11 of Fig. 1 is named `main/foo<` but the developer may only key on the word `foo` to recall the function body.

The name built by the above process does not contain any information about enclosing scopes. We call it *local name*. We get the function *full name* (that is a local name qualified by its position in the scope hierarchy) by adding the enclosing function full-name with a slash before the local-name, recursing through enclosing scopes. This full-name is the function body name.

5.5 Examples

To further explain our approach we now apply it to the JavaScript code presented in Figure 1. We can recognize five function bodies in the code, none of them has a name.

The first function on line 9 is assigned to the variable `main`. The parent node for the function body in the syntax tree will be an assignment, so in Algorithm 1 we skip the `while` loop and compute the `nameExpression` as `main`. Ultimately this becomes the name of the function.

The second function on line 11 is nested in the first one. It is passed as an argument to a constructor call on line 10 and the resulting object is assigned to `foo`. In Algorithm 1 we create two entries in the consumption summary, one for the function call with identifier `Foo` and one for the assignment with identifier `foo`. The first one gets marked with `isContributesTo`. Following the logic in Sec. 5.4, we drop the function call identifier but mark the name with < for contributes-to. The resulting local name is `foo<` and the full name includes the enclosing function name: `main/foo<`.

The third function on line 18 is called immediately after definition, on line 24. This means the function body in the syntax tree will have a parent from the immediate call and then the assignment parent node; the call does not give us an identifier but it does give a consumption summary entry with `isContributesTo`. The name becomes `Foo<`.

The fourth function on line 20 is returned by `Foo<`. After the first pass through the `while` loop in Algorithm 1 we enter `getNextNode` and trigger the code described in Sec. 5.2. This will cause us to walk up the syntax tree to find the assignment target for the outer function. We end up with name `Foo`. Because do not process the intermediate nodes in the `while` loop we do not mark the name with contributes-to and we do not record that the function is nested. Of course the function body is nested, but it is bound to an un-nested variable. To keep the name compact we choose not to encode this complex information. Rather we stick to the simple picture that the function 'is' `Foo`. If the developer wants to know more they can look up `Foo` to see the construction and nesting.

The fifth function on line 25 is assigned to two variables. This example illustrates that we stop processing in Algorithm 1 as soon as we hit the first assignment, giving the name `Bar`. This aligns with our observation that the visually closest identifier is the best choice.

Finally, Table 6 gives the names of functions from examples discussed in 4.

Example Code	Static Function-Object Consumption Full Name
Sec. 4.2 outer	YUI.add(event-focus)/_attach
Sec. 4.2 inner	YUI.add(event-focus)/_attach/Event._attach()
Sec. 4.3	eventPool._createObject
Fig. 4 outer	jQuery.each(ajaxStart)
Fig. 4 inner	jQuery.each(ajaxStart)/jQuery.fn[o]
Sec. 4.6	define/viewport[get+D]
Fig. 5 outer	YUI.add(classnamem)/Y.ClassNameManager<
Fig. 5 inner	YUI.add(classnamem)/Y.ClassNameManager.getClassName<
Sec. 4.10 inner	setVisible/cb<
Fig. 6 inner	registerWin/

Table 6. Results from applying the approach in Sec. 5 to the examples in the paper at the point given in the first column. Full names are listed, even in cases where our example code omitted the enclosing function scope.

6. Evaluation

In Table 7 we compared our results to Firebug's naming output for each of the 10 projects used previously and listed in Appendix 1. Firebug does not use a parser for naming functions. It instead employs a number of regular expressions and apply them on a few lines around the function definition to obtain a name (a function called `guessFunctionName()`). Although this approach is not reliable and may provide wrong names for some functions, it infers acceptable names in many simple cases. About 10 percent (the second column) of anonymous functions still remained nameless in Firebug (in addition, some named functions may be quite incorrect because of the simple algorithm). The third column shows that more than 98 percent of anonymous functions have a FOC-defined local name. By adding the enclosing function names, this number increases to more than 99 percent for FOC-Full(the fourth column). Based on our observations, most functions remaining anonymous in FOC-Full are top level *immediate* functions which are usually used for creating a local scope for a set of variables.

The "Duplicates By" columns show the number of functions which get a name which is also assigned to another function(s) for Firebug, FOC-Local and FOC-Full. The number shows that Firebug assigns duplicate names to about 47 percent of anonymous functions. The first reason behind this huge number is that Firebug relies on regular expressions instead of abstract syntax tree for locating names. The second reason is that Firebug does not analyze the function object flow but tries to construct the name from the identifiers close to function definition. The second column shows that FOC-Local gives much less duplicates (13%) comparing to Firebug. This means that local names are sufficient for recognizing functions within a file, which is helpful because they have shorter length than full names. The third column says that less than 9 percent of anonymous functions get duplicated names by full names. Based on our observations, many of duplicates in projects such as DOJO, ExtJS and YUI come from test files. In a test file the same use case is repeated with different data and therefore the same function names appear several times. In projects like JQuery, Prototype, MooTools the conditional statements are the main source of duplicates. These libraries usually check against different environment properties (e.g., browser) to load the appropriate function.

The last two columns show the average and longest function name lengths (in characters) for both short and full names. The average length is at most 37 characters. The last column shows that only 3 percent of functions get local names longer than 50 characters or full names longer than 80 characters. Again, based on our observations a main source of long names are deep nested functions which mostly appear in test files.

Project	Anonymous Functions By				Duplicates by			Local/Full Length		
	Developer	Firebug	FOC-Local	FOC-Full	Firebug	FOC-Local	FOC-Full	Average	Longest	>50/>80
Closure	8987	312(3%)	51	10	662(7%)	211(2%)	103(1%)	33/35	76/101	471/30
DoJo	15866	3362(21%)	528	390	3325(21%)	2993(19%)	2287(14%)	24/36	81/162	680/765
ExtJS	36533	1543(4%)	631	231	23777(65%)	3737(10%)	2342(7%)	22/25	65/91	177/2
Firebug	3018	167(5%)	14	10	481(16%)	85(3%)	32(1%)	27/36	70/140	76/18
jQuery	399	95(24%)	9	8	162(40%)	97(24%)	56(14%)	14/18	50/65	0/0
MochiKit	1829	202(11%)	59	16	491(27%)	314(17%)	191(10%)	17/22	49/80	0/0
MooTools	618	121(19%)	30	18	272(44%)	158(26%)	138(22%)	12/14	36/73	0/0
Prototype	442	125(28%)	24	19	154(35%)	70(16%)	70(16%)	21/25	55/88	5/1
Scriptaculous	884	195(22%)	25	19	306(36%)	131(19%)	86(9%)	21/27	55/132	7/5
YUI	21424	3317(15%)	212	15	10073(47%)	3558(17%)	2205(10%)	16/37	114/145	223/292
All	90000	9439(10%)	1583(2%)	736(1%)	39703(44%)	11354(13%)	7510(8%)	N/A	N/A	1639/1113 (3%)

Table 7. Results of Function Object Consumption. The rows are the projects listed in Appendix 1. The first column contains the number of anonymous functions in each project. The second column shows the number of functions Firebug could not name. The third column contains the number of functions nameless after applying the static Function Object Consumption (FOC) algorithm; and the fourth column is the number of functions the FOC leaves without a name even from enclosing scopes. The next three columns give the number of times a Firebug, FOC-Local, and FOC-Full function name appears twice in a file, respectively. The last three columns contain the length information. Every cell has two entries divided by a slash, the first is the local name and the second is the full name. The eighth and ninth columns give the average and longest name character counts respectively. The last columns shows the number of functions with local names greater then 50 characters in length separated by a slash from the number of functions wit full names with length greater than 80 characters.

7. Discussion

Overall the Function-Object Consumption approach dramatically reduces the number of functions that a development tool cannot name for a developer. By looking at the examples and comparing the algorithms, the names selected by FOC will be the same as the one's selected by Firebug's `guessFunctionName()` when that function gives reasonable results. In other cases FOC will give a more useful name including many cases where the current Firebug approach fails.

There is room for improvements. The heuristic elements of the naming solution need to be tuned based on more experience. Given that our goals trade precision for rapid recognition, our names are not unique. We also leave some cases anonymous which need further investigation.

A complete naming solution will need to consider some additional issues. The user interface that shows names typically has limited space and even our efforts to create short names may be adequate. Often the hierarchy can help: we can show the trailing entry in a slash delimited list and the trailing entry in a dot delimited list with mouse-over expansion to bring up an overlay line with more of the full name displayed. Some JavaScript libraries have a regular pattern or specific re-naming registration system (see for example the ExtJS ClassManager[8]). A naming solution should recognize these patterns or systems. Similarly JavaScript libraries might support the `.displayName` to provide custom names where the developer overhead to introduce and maintain the extra field is justified by the wide spread use of the library.

8. Related Work

To best of our knowledge, this paper is the first study in naming anonymous functions in JavaScript. However, there have been a few studies on the JavaScript programs behavior. In a recent work, Richards et al. conducted a study on dynamic behavior of JavaScript programs [17]. Although their study contains some aspects of JavaScript function objects creation and usage, such as the number of different call sites and arities in function calls, it does not provide any data about anonymous functions.

We previously mentioned four JavaScript naming approaches: Zaytsev advocates expanded use of names in function expressions[20], support for `displayName` in debuggers has been requested[6], the Firebug Regular expressions, and the Google Chrome debugger's function name 'inference'[4]. The last one appears to be a parser based approach with goals similar to the ad-hoc Firebug regular expressions: look for identifiers preceding anonymous function bodies.

Høst and Østvold [12] attempted to find and fix inappropriate function names in Java programs. Their approach employs rules extracted from a large corpus of Java projects to recognize buggy names. To fix a name, a list of candidate names are constructed and ranked, the name with the highest rank is proposed for the replacement. This approach assumes that the function is already named and constructs the names based on the function internal structure. In contrast, our approach construct the function name by analyzing the function context.

Caprile and Tonella [3], analyze the structure of function identifiers in C programs. The identifiers are decomposed into fragments that are then classified into seven lexical categories. The structure of the function identifiers are further described by a hand-crafted grammar.

The result of our work can be improved and impact other aspects of JavaScript programming if a stronger typing system is employed. A few static typing systems have been proposed for JavaScript [1, 2, 11, 19]. These approaches discover the type of values and object structures for a variable by statically analyzing the source code and possible program control flows lead to the variable assignment. The discovered facts about variable types are not only useful for catching errors but to assist developers in code comprehension. Nevertheless, none of the mentioned approaches provided effective means for sharing this information with the developer. Our approach can help in this regard by assigning names to nameless elements.

9. Conclusion

Our contributions in this paper include an empirical study of the extent of anonymous functions in JavaScript libraries, categorization of those functions to understand the potential for automatic naming, a practical algorithm based on the empirical study, and its evaluation. We believe our result can be applied directly in existing JavaScript development tools to give immediate benefit to developers and provides a basis for future improvements.

A. JavaScript Projects Analyzed for Function Names

Closure Closure Library, r683, Google Code,
http://code.google.com/p/closure-library

Dojo Dojo JavaScript Toolkit, version 1.5,
http://dojotoolkit.org

ExtJS JavaScript Framework, version 3.3.1
http://www.sencha.com/products/extjs

Firebug Web Page Debugger, version 1.7
http://code.google.com/p/fbug

jQuery JavaScript Library, version 1.4.4
http://jquery.com

MochiKit version 1.4.2
http://mochi.github.com/mochikit

MooTools JavaScript Framework, version 1.3
http://mootools.net

Prototype JavaScript Framework, version 1.7
http://www.prototypejs.org

Scriptaculous JavaScript Library, version 1.9
http://script.aculo.us

YUI Library, Yahoo, Inc., version 3.3
http://developer.yahoo.com/yui

References

[1] C. Anderson, P. Giannini, and S. Drossopoulou. Towards Type Inference for JavaScript. In *Proceedings of the 19th European conference on Object-Oriented Programming(ECOOP)*, July, 2005.

[2] C. Anderson and P. Giannini. Type checking for javascript. *Electr. Notes Theor. Comput. Sci.*, 138(2), 2005.

[3] B. Caprile and P. Tonella. Nomen est omen: Analyzing the language of function identifiers. In *Proceedings of the 6th working conference on Reverse Engineering(WCRE)*, October, 1999.

[4] V8 Google FuncNameInferrer. http://v8.googlecode.com/svn/trunk/src/func-name-inferrer.h

[5] Common JS. http://www.commonjs.org

[6] Add prettyName/displayName support to Profiler output and Stacks. *Firebug Bug Repository*, http://code.google.com/p/fbug/issues/detail?id=1811

[7] ECMA International. *ECMA-262: ECMAScript Language Specification*, ECMA (European Association for Standardizing Information and Communication Systems), Geneva, Switzerland, third edition, December 1999.

[8] Jacky Nguyen. *Ext.ClassManager*. http://docs.sencha.com/ext-js/4-0/#/api/Ext.ClassManager

[9] Firefox Add-ons. https://addons.mozilla.org/en-US/developers/docs/getting-started.

[10] Google Chrome Extensions. http://code.google.com/chrome/extensions.

[11] P. Heidegger and P. Thiemann. Recency types for dynamically-typed, object-based languages. In *Proceedings of Foundations of Object Oriented Languages (FOOL)*, 2009.

[12] E. W. Høst and B. M. Østvold. Debugging Method Names. In *Proceedings of the 23rd European conference on Object-Oriented Programming(ECOOP)*, July, 2009.

[13] D. Ingalls, K. Palacz, S. Uhler and A. Taivalsaari. The lively kernel a self-supporting system on a web page. In *Self-Sustaining Systems*, 2008.

[14] JScript development in Microsoft Office 11. http://msdn.microsoft.com/en-us/library/aa202668(office.11).aspx

[15] JavaScript development in OpenOffice. http://framework.openoffice.org/scripting/release-0.2/javascript-devguide.html

[16] G. Richards, C. Hammer, B. Burg and J. Vitek. The eval that men do. In *Proceedings of the 25th European conference on Object-Oriented Programming(ECOOP)*, July, 2011.

[17] G. Richards, S. Lebresne, B. Burg and J. Vitek. An analysis of the dynamic behavior of JavaScript programs. In *Proceedings of the 2010 ACM SIGPLAN conference on Programming language design and implementation(PLDI)*, June, 2010.

[18] Server-Side JavaScript Reference v1.2. http://research.nihonsoft.org/javascript/ServerReferenceJS12.

[19] P. Thiemann. Towards a type system for analyzing JavaScript programs. In *Proceedings of European Symposium on Programming (ESOP)*, 2005.

[20] J. Zaytsev. Named function expressions demystified. http://kangax.github.com/nfe, June, 2010.

A Framework for Analyzing Programs Written in Proprietary Languages

V. Krishna Nandivada[1]   Mangala Gowri Nanda[1]   Pankaj Dhoolia[1]   Diptikalyan Saha[1]

Anjan Nandy[2]   Anup K Ghosh[2]

IBM Research - India[1], IBM GBS - India[2]

{nvkrishna, mgowri, pdhoolia, diptsaha, anjan.nandy, anup.ghosh}@in.ibm.com

Abstract

There are several commercial products that use proprietary languages, which typically look like a wrapper around (some proprietary extension of) the standard SQL language. Examples of these languages include ABAP, Informix, XBase++, SQR and so on. These application are difficult to analyze not only because it is hard to model the semantics of the underlying database systems but also because of the lack of standard tools for analysis. One naive way to analyse such programs is to collect dynamic trace using proprietary debuggers and run the analyses on the trace. However, this form of dynamic trace collection can be a severe performance bottleneck. In this paper, we present our experience with building a framework to help in efficient program analysis in the context of ticket resolution for ABAP programs.

In our framework, we first translate the given ABAP programs to semantically equivalent annotated Java programs. These Java programs are then executed to generate the required dynamic trace. Our framework allows the plugging of off-the-shelf static analysis tools (applied on the Java programs) and dynamic trace analysis tools (on the generated trace) and maps the results from these analysis tools back to the original ABAP programs. One novel aspect of our framework is that it admits incomplete ABAP grammar, which is an important aspect when dealing with proprietary languages where the grammar may not be publicly available. We have used our framework on several benchmarks to validate the translation, and establish the efficiency and the utility of our instrumented Java code along with the collected trace.

Categories and Subject Descriptors: D.3.4 [**Processors**] Debuggers, Code generation
General Terms: Verification, Experimentation, Languages
Keywords: error recovery, source to source translation

1. Introduction

Ticket resolution is an important part of a service organization. In a typical context, a client discovers a bug in the field, which needs to be resolved as fast as possible. For the scope of this paper, we assume the code and not the database to be source of the bug; this is reasonable, because the same database typically feeds into several other applications that do work properly.

Working with proprietary code in an proprietary environment, in an industrial settings brings in interesting set of challenges: a) hard to reproduce the bug outside the client execution environment, b) the original code writer may not be the debugger of the code. This problem gets compounded when the number of available program analysis tools (proprietary or otherwise) for that language are limited. In this paper, we discuss our experience with bug resolution in the context of a proprietary language ABAP. However, the techniques and methodologies developed here can be applied to other languages with a similar purpose (database access and report generation).

A naive way of analyzing these programs is to analyze the trace of the faulty program, obtained via running it through a proprietary debugger inside an automated script that collect a trace of the values of all variables at all program points. Unfortunately, this can be a major performance hurdle; for instance, such a trace collection for a small ABAP program, that otherwise runs well under 60 seconds, takes more 20-30 minutes. It may also be noted that, in general the approach of (automated) instrumentation of the ABAP source programs to collect the trace is not a feasible option, as executing a modified version of the source program is typically not permitted by the clients.

In this paper, we present a scheme to overcome these hurdles. Our solution works in three steps
1. We first do a semantics preserving translation of the input ABAP program to Java. We generate the Java code with built-in instrumentation, so that it outputs a trace when it is executed; this helps in overcoming the performance issues discussed above.
2. In the second step we execute the Java program with the

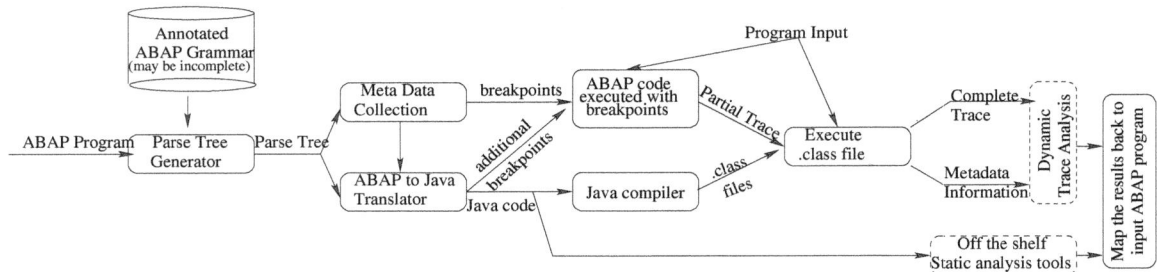

Figure 1. The block diagram for our ABAP program analysis framework

given input and collect a trace dump of the execution.

3. Our proposed framework allows plug-and-play of standard off-the-shelf static analysis techniques on the Java code and fault localization techniques on the generated trace, whose results are mapped back to the input ABAP program.

One main feature of our framework is that it decouples the source language of the input program from the actual analysis, thereby opening the doors for using arbitrary analysis tools on programs written in proprietary languages.

Translating programs written in languages like ABAP to a general purpose language like Java comes with its own set of challenges, such as development of the grammar from the scratch from language manuals, and implementation of complex database operations in the target language. To overcome these hurdles we present a scheme that a) results in the generation of correct trace even in the absence of complete grammar, and b) emulates physical database operations by gathering the results of the database operations in the proprietary debugger and plugging them back in the Java program[1]. Since we are using the debugger to extract information only about very specific commands, the process continues to be comparatively efficient. We present a specialized ABAP parser that helps identifying the statements and the corresponding defined variables requiring debugger-based trace collection. Note that, unlike the code in three address code form [2], identifying the *uses* and *defs* is non-trivial in the context of programs with database statements.

Figure 1 shows the overall block diagram of our analysis framework. Given an ABAP program, and possibly incomplete ABAP grammar, we first generate the parse tree. The parse tree generator can handle cases where valid ABAP statements are not parsed because of the incomplete nature of the available ABAP grammar. The parse tree is used to generate metadata such as data structures, type information of the required underlying system libraries, line number information for the different database related operations (to be used for setting breakpoints later), and use-def annotations on the variables used in the statements, by using our annotated ABAP grammar. Our ABAP to Java translator uses the parse tree and the data structure information from the metadata to generate equivalent Java code, and some additional

breakpoints for collecting use-def information for statements that could not be translated during the translation phase. We execute the ABAP code in the debugger and collect partial trace for the breakpoints set in the previous steps. We use the generated partial trace and class files from the Java files to execute the program and generate the complete trace, which is then fed to the plugged in dynamic trace analysis tool (shown in a dashed box) such as the one by Saha et al [14]. Similarly, the geneated Java code can be fed to a plugged-in static analysis tool (also shown in a dashed box) such as Findbugs [8]. Finally, the inferences derived from the analyses are mapped back to the input ABAP programs.

The contributions of this paper are given below.

• We present a framework for program translation in the presence of incomplete grammar rules.

• We present a grammar annotation based scheme to obtain the used and defined variables for each statement. Compared to the standard techniques where the task of generating use-def information is relegated to the semantic translation phase [2], our scheme considerably reduces the development time and bugs in the process.

• A fail proof translation of ABAP code to annotated Java: We present a scheme for ABAP to Java translation which ensures that the translation rules are written in an incremental fashion for different grammar production rules, such that, unhandled grammar productions do not lead to incorrect translation.

• We let plug-and-play of off-the-shelf static and dynamic analysis tools (for Java programs) to analyze ABAP code.

• To argue about the applicability of our framework, besides plugging-in different existing tools, we have developed a new pattern-check based analysis to reason about both "good" and "bad" patterns in ABAP programs and have successfully applied it on many existing real world programs.

Organization: We present an overview of ABAP commands that are relevant to this paper in Section 2. We discuss our grammar annotation and exception handling schemes in Section 3. Challenges and details about our ABAP to Java translation are presented in Section 4. Our pattern-check based analysis is discussed in Section 5. Details of the overall framework is presented in Section 6, and that of the implementation in Section 7. We present an evaluation of our framework in Section 8 and conclude in Section 9.

---

[1] ABAP allows the programs to read and update the physical screen, which can be seen as a database table with some additional attributes.

Related Work

We are not aware of any past works, that create a translation and analysis bridge between different programming languages. We instead present related work aligned to different components of our framework.

Program Translation for reverse engineering

Source-to-source program translation approaches in support of reverse engineering and migration, may largely be classified into -

• *Translation via Transliteration and Refinement* [6, 20]: Translators in this class - first transliterate a source program into a target language on a line by line basis, by translating each line in isolation; and then apply various refinements to improve the target program produced.

• *Translation via abstraction and re-implementation* [7, 18]: In this approach the source program is first analyzed to obtain an abstract description of the computation being performed. The program is then re-implemented in the target language based on the abstract description.

These techniques do not support incremental evolution of the translator itself.In the context of evolving tools, where their coverage of the language increases in an incremental fashion, unexpected errors may be thrown when they encounter un-handled instructions. Our generic translation error handling strategy is able to meaningfully continue in the presence of translation exceptions, while ensuring trace semantics preserving translation.

Parser Error Recovery

A large body of work [1, 4, 9, 13, 17] has looked at the area of handling syntax errors and recovery in language translation systems by automatic correction of missing, or erroneous tokens. These techniques focus on continuation of the parsing process in the presence of errors to list all the possible errors. Our framework addresses the challenge of producing a trace semantic preserving translation in the presence of incomplete grammar. This, goes beyond the artificial addition of missing, or deletion of not comprehended tokens, or just continuing after the first error to locate other errors.

Pattern Analysis

There are a number of pattern detection tools, such as Find-Bugs [8], SPLINT [5], Flawfinder [19], MOPS [3] and so on. The analyses performed by these tools are static in nature, and suffer from the common drawback of generating false positives. In our framework we use pattern analysis tool on dynamic traces, and as a result false positives due to infeasibility of path is removed. Further, unlike the above tools that only encode patterns for 'bad' behavior, we allow encoding of both 'good' and 'bad' behavior. Further, we admit complex patterns (going beyond simple regular expressions) involving data flow relations between variables. This leads to a significant reduction in false positives. We use an Extended Finite State Automata (EFSA) to specify the desired properties (by extending the specification language of Sekar et al [16]) to describe and check good and bad behavior.

2. Background

In this section, we will be presenting a subset of ABAP language constructs relevant to this paper. Details can be found in the ABAP language reference manual [10].

SELECT <fields> FROM tab INTO itab WHERE <cond>.   projects selected columns from a physical or internal table to an internal (in-memory) table in the program
SORT itab BY <keys> [ASCENDING|DESCENDING].   sorts the internal table on the keys
DELETE FROM tab WHERE <cond>.   deletes rows that satisfy the condition
LOOP AT itab INTO rec WHERE <cond>. <loop-body> ENDLOOP.   executes the instructions in loop body for each record in the table.
AT NEW fld. <at-body> ENDAT / (AT END fld. <at-body> ENDAT)   Occurs inside a loop over the records of a table. Equivalent to an if-statement, whose predicate evaluates to true, if the current record is (not) *fresh* with respect to the *criterion* fields therein; starting from the first field of the record to till fld.
READ itab INTO rec WHERE <cond>.   selects a row from table based on the WHERE clause. If more than one row matches, the last row is returned
WRITE <vars>.   prints the specified variables

Figure 2. Basic ABAP syntax

Figure 2 presents a subset of ABAP statements for the database related operations. While the actual ABAP language commands are more involved and have many variations, for the sake of presentation in this paper, we restrict ourselves to this subset. Each command in ABAP terminates with '.' (dot). Fields of a record are dereferenced by using the operator '−'.

```
1    SELECT uid name price FROM dbtab INTO itab.
2    SELECT uid discount FROM dbftab INTO ftab.
3    SORT itab BY uid DESCENDING.
4    LOOP AT itab INTO wa WHERE price > 0.
5      AT NEW uid.
6        sum = 0.0;
7      ENDAT.
8      sum = sum + wa−price;
9      READ ftab INTO fa WHERE uid = wa−uid.
10     IF NOT IS INITIAL fa.
11       sum = sum − fa−discount.
12     ENDIF.
13     AT END uid.
14       WRITE fa−name, sum.
15     ENDAT.
16   ENDLOOP.
```

Figure 3. Sample ABAP program

To help understand the ABAP syntax, in Figure 3, we show an example ABAP program processing item discounts. It first reads uid, name, and price from a physical table into an internal table itab. It then reads the discount information from another physical database and stores relevant information into another internal table ftab. It then sorts the item table (itab) and iterates over it. For each *fresh* record wa, it initializes the variable sum to 0. The report then adds the price of that item to sum, reads the discount information and subtracts the discount from the sum. Finally, the report prints to the screen the name of the item and the total cost (after discount), once for each unique item.

3. ABAP Grammar for Java translation

Program analysis tools for domain specific complex programming languages face two main challenges. First one is that of parsing and translating the complete program (irrespective of availability of the complete grammar). The second one (important for dynamic trace analysis) is that for each statement the trace must include the variables used and defined in that statement. In the context of traditional compilers that deal with some form of three address codes, identifying the variables used and the variables defined in a statement is trivial. However, in a language like ABAP which includes many macro-level statements (that update multiple variables present at different positions in the statement), identifying the use-def variables is a challenge. In this section, we present our approach to solve these problems.

3.1 Exception Handling in Grammar

Unavailability of complete grammar forms a major hurdle in building program analysis tools. Most of the language documentation is available in the reference manual. However, this tends to become incomplete [11] as the language evolves in various versions of the software; our experience was similar. While grammar inference techniques such as [15] can be used to fix the grammar automatically to some extent, the completeness of the grammar obtained is guaranteed to be limited by the sample set used to learn the grammar. Thus for an unknown program which has no syntactic errors, the existing grammar may be incomplete to parse the program.

As shown in Figure 1, parsing a given program and generating the parse tree is the first step of our framework, which makes the absence of complete grammar a severe impediment. In this paper, we present an exception handling strategy to overcome the above problems.

Given a program, the parse-tree-generator has a preprocessing stage to collect all the included files, and parse each file. If the file is not parsed, then an exception handling strategy is invoked. The main goal of the exception handling strategy is to determine the statements (ending with '.' (dot)) in the file that are responsible for the unsuccessful parsing, and subsequently replace each such statement with a new type of statement, called `parser-error` statement that has the variables of the original statement. We explain our exception handling strategy by the help of an example.

Consider the example program given in Figure 3. Say two of the syntactic constructs, DESCENDING at Line 3 and WHERE clause at Line 4 are not handled by the grammar. Here SORT is a *simple* statement and LOOP is a *compound* statement. This program will fail to parse. We first extract each simple statement (Lines 1, 2, 3, 6, 8, 9, 11, 14), and try to parse them. Only SORT statement will fail to parse. We replace the sort statement by the statement '`parser_error itab, f1.`', by collecting all the terminals and removing the keywords SORT, BY and DESCENDING. The grammar is augmented to parse the `parse_error` statement:

```
parse_error_stmt: parse_error pe_clause? DOT ;
pe_clause: id (COMMA! id)* ;
```

The terminal id represents an identifier and ';' (semicolon) is used to terminate a rule.

After this change, the file is parsed again, and we still encounter a parser failure which is due to the compound statement LOOP. Since, all the simple statements of the loop body are parsing successfully, the loop statement is determined as the cause of the parser failure. Subsequently, its header at Line 4 is replaced by a statement '`loop_parser_error itab, wa, f2.`'. by collecting all potential variables. To be able to parse such a statement, the grammar for the particular compound statement is augmented. For instance, the modified rule for parsing the loop_statement is given below, which leads to successful parsing:

```
loop_stmt: loop_header statement+ endloop
         | loop_error statement+ endloop ;
endloop: ENDLOOP DOT ;
loop_header: LOOP AT id INTO id WHERE expr DOT ;
loop_error: LOOP_PARSER_ERROR pe_clause DOT ;
```

While the modification of the program allows it to be parsed, it does not assist the Java code generation, as the semantics of the underlying statement is still unknown. We use a process of *state synchronization* during the translation to help generate correct trace (c.f. Section 4.3).

Limitations

If a statement is not parsed by our grammar, and it is not a recognized compound statement by the grammar, then we assume it to be a simple statement, and accordingly generates the `parse_error` statement. While in general this assumption can lead to incorrect code generation, in practise we have found our strategy to be quite sound because our initial grammar did take into account all the compound statements and all the observed parse errors were coming from either missing variations for a known statement or an unknown simple statement.

3.2 Use-Def Generation

Unlike programs in imperative languages, it is not always straightforward to infer the set of defined and used variables in 4GL languages like ABAP. Thus to generate a trace in these declarative programs, trace generation algorithm needs to know the exact set of variables defined and used in each statement. In this section we present a simple yet effective way to infer the used and defined variables in each statement.

There are essentially two tasks in finding use/def information for each statement, finding all variables in the statement, and determine whether they are used or defined. Below we describe an easy yet effective process to obtain such information specifically in the context of large grammars. Our methodology is dependent on the rewrite rules which are used to modify the AST in ANTLR ([13]) grammars.

We represent the ABAP grammar in ANTLR grammar format, in Extended Backus Naur Form (EBNF) form.

ANTLR provides rewrite rules to construct Abstract Syntax Tree (AST) generated by parsing. Typical rewriting syn-

```
sort_stmt: SORT itab  sort_by_cl? sort_option? DOT
      -> ^(SORT itab sort_by_cl? sort_option? DOT)
itab: id -> ^(USEDEF id);
sort_by_cl: BY sort_by_item -> ^(BY sort_by_item)
sort_by_item: id -> ^(USE id);
sort_option:  DESCENDING |  ASCENDING;
```

Figure 4. Grammar for the SORT statement.

tax includes ^ to specify a node as parent node. For example, for this rewrite rule: '$x : yz \rightarrow \, ^\wedge(yz)$', rewriting makes the token accepted by y as the root node, and the token accepted by z as its child node in the AST. The main usefulness of rewrite rules is the ease of traversal of the AST.

The use-def information of all statements are maintained by annotating the grammar. The annotations are determined by manually identifying the variable part of each statement, and then annotating *each occurrence* of a variable with its *ud-type*. The ud-type for a variable can either be USE, DEF, or USEDEF, to denote used, defined or used+defined nature of the variable, respectively. The annotations are made using rewrite rules in such a way that the generated AST satisfies the following invariant: *Every node corresponding to the variable of a statement appears as a leaf node of the AST, and its immediate parent node is one of the ud-type nodes (USE/DEF/USEDEF).* An example rewrite grammar for the SORT statement (Figure 2), is presented in Figure 4.

The main advantage of this technique is that the grammar rewriting followed by a general traversal is considerably easier than developing AST traversal for each possible variation in the AST generated for each statement. Further, this technique is arguably easier to maintain as the new variations in the language constructs are simple to understand.

These use-def annotations can be used by the Java translator to emit code to output the defined and used variables during the final trace collection. Another use of these annotations is found in generating code in the presence of different incompletenesses in the grammar and the translator (discussed in Section 4.3).

4. ABAP to Java translation

Translating ABAP programs to Java programs can pose interesting challenges because of the loose nature of the ABAP language semantics; for instance, it is legal to assign a string to an integer variable (provided the string contains an integer) and vice versa, so a straightforward translation would lead to uncompilable Java code. In this section, we discuss some of the challenges and our proposed solutions.

We first note that a full fledged translation would be quite challenging for the following reasons: (a) It would require implementation of a complex runtime and library implementing all the abstractions of database related activities. (b) It can be challenging to execute all the database related commands and queries more efficiently than a commercial package like SAP. (c) the issues relating to incomplete grammar and incremental development of the translator make the

```
class BaseStruct {
   public Vector<String> names;
   ... }
class record1 extends BaseStruct{
  String fld1; String fld2;
  public record1(){
     names.add("fld1"); names.add("fld2");...}
  public String getValue(int index){
     if (index < 0) return null;
     return getValue(names.elementAt(index)); }
  public String getValue(String fldName){
     if ("fld1".equals(fldName)) return fld1;
     if ("fld2".equals(fldName)) return fld2; }...}
```

Figure 5. Code generated for a structure `record1` with two String fields `fld1` and `fld2`.

problem much harder. We now present the details of our ABAP to Java translation scheme that tries alleviate some of these problems.

4.1 Data Structures Design

The ABAP to Java translation has two aspects to it: generated Java code and the underlying libraries. We first present the architecture of our generated Java programs, and discuss some interesting aspects of the underlying libraries in the later part of the section. For each ABAP program, we generate a corresponding Java class. As discussed in in Section 2, in ABAP programs many commands update global variables (such as `sy_subrc`). We first create a base class `BaseABAP` which acts as the parent class for each of the generated Java class; `BaseABAP` contains declarations for the global variables, and wrappers for the different scalar types required by the ABAP programs.

In this section, we discuss the internal representation of the variables and data structures used in our generated Java programs. We organize this discussion by separating the discussion on scalars and non scalar variables.

Scalar variables In ABAP, every variable (scalar or otherwise) has five attributes: *name*, *type*, *length*, *padding-character*, and optionally the *decimal precision* for floating point numbers. These details are used in the Java program to a) serialize the contained value of a scalar, and b) compare with other scalar variables by comparing the serialized strings. The serialization of a value of a variable outputs a string of size *length*. If the actual number of characters required to represent the value are more than *length* then value is truncated, else *padding-character* is used to pad for the remaining characters. The number of decimal places in the serialized representation depend on the desired precision.

Non scalar variables Our runtime libraries are organized around the definition of `BaseStruct`, the base class of all the *records* and *rows* of the tables in the program. In a language like ABAP, untyped records can be assigned to each other, inserted to a table, as well as dereferenced via explicit field names or indices. Such a requirement enforces a unified structure for all the records and table rows.

To enable reflection, `BaseStruct` stores all the field names and all the attributes of the fields (such as length, type, padding character and decimal precision). Each structure used in the program is represented using a class extending the `BaseStruct`, and adds new fields in the derived class, corresponding to the fields of the structure. The `BaseStruct` contains two `setValue` (and `getValue`) methods that are extended by the derived classes; to help update (and read) fields of the structure using the name of the field and the index of the field. The `compare` method does a field wise comparison and returns *true*, if all the fields of the current object match the fields of the argument. The `BaseStruct` class has a method to copy the fields by value, that is useful in the definition of the Table data structure. Figure 5 shows the (partial) code generated for a structure containing two fields.

To facilitate the creation of tables of scalar types (such as Table of integers), we create a wrapper class for each of the scalar types (such as `WrapperInt` for the scalar type `int`); these wrapper classes extend the parent class `BaseStruct`.

For efficient translation of ABAP code to Java, we have also implemented much of the underlying ABAP library functionality in Java. These include all the string processing, data processing, numerical process operations. These translations are mostly standard and are not discussed here.

We now discuss some features of our generic Table class that is used to represent internal tables. The ABAP language allows the programmer to access the work-area of a table, that contains the current record under consideration. Our `Table` class contains a field `WA` to represent the work area. We allow three different types of tables: sorted, indexed and standard (to represent tables other than sorted and indexed). Most of the implementation details of the `Table` class is standard. Some specific facets are discussed now. Each element of a table is a class that extends `BaseStruct` and thus we have a unified mechanism to read/update rows of tables, as well as records. The `Table` class has a method `add` to insert a new row/record; the elements of the record are copied by value (unlike the usual Java Collections where the references are directly stored); this ensures that changes made to the object (after the insertion) are not reflected in the rows of the table.

Generated program structure All variables declared in the ABAP report are declared as static variables in the generated Java class. All the `struct` type declarations are translated to Java classes. The entry point for the generated Java code is derived from translating the code present in different events such as `start-of-selection` (See [10]).

4.2 Translation of simple ABAP commands

We now present the translation rules for some of the ABAP commands and overview of the overall translation scheme. Figure 6 presents some rules to translate a few of the ABAP commands. We show a typical translation rule for a database statement (`SELECT`) over an internal table as a library call

(accessing of physical tables is discussed in Section 4.3). The `DELETE`, `INSERT`, and `SORT` commands are translated alike - we insert code to make appropriate transformation on the internal table (implemented in our library code for the class `Table`). Each ABAP statement results in one or more Java statement; each of these Java statements is annotated with the line number of the ABAP statement. Note: in our implementation, the annotations also include the file name, to take into account the multi-file ABAP program scenario.

An interesting aspect of ABAP language is that it allows numeric (integers, floating point) values to be stored in a string and accessed as desired. For instance, we can assign an integer to a string. A naive translation would lead to a type mismatch error in the generated Java code. Our ABAP to Java translator maintains and uses the type information to do a correct translation; for instance, see rules 2(a), 2(b), and 2(c). We omit the translation rules for `AT NEW` and `AT END` (handled as nested if statements), and `LOOP` (translated into Java loops).

Trace generation via annotated Java code Besides generating a semantically equivalent Java code, we also generate an instrumented translation, which on execution dumps the complete trace for the original ABAP program; this trace is used by the plugged-in dynamic trace analysis tool.

For each of the generate Java statement s, we emit code (after s) to output the values of all the variables that are used and defined in that statement. Such a translation helps output a forward path trace, by executing the generated Java program. The set of used and defined variables is obtained by analyzing the annotations of the AST (USE, DEF or USEDEF) for the input program.

4.3 Translation via Exception Handling

In this section, we discuss our efforts at handling incompleteness in the grammar and incompleteness in the translation, while ensuring that the resulting Java code generates a trace that matches the hypothetical trace generated by the input ABAP program. Our translator throws an exception when it encounters any of these incompletenesses. Further, in some rare situations our translator throws an exception (such as NullPointerException) because of some unhandled corner cases. There are also practical issues in our translator that leads to some bugs in the generated Java code that lead to a) compilation error or b) incorrect traces. Our translation tries to handle each of these cases. Such a scheme is also useful for developing the ABAP to Java translator in an incremental fashion wherein even the incomplete translator can be used in the framework in an effective way. We now discuss the details of these techniques.

Syntax not handled: These are the statements that are not yet handled by the translator. Instances of such commands include, physical database accesses, calls to unknown library functions (with no side effects) etc. The translator throws an exception for the code-repairer which performs *state-synchronization* to help ensure a correct trace generation.

1. Select :		
L1:SELECT <flds> FROM tab WHERE <conds> INTO itab } ⟹		/*L1*/ itab.select(tab, <flds>, <conds>);
2(a). Assign :	L1 : a = e //typeOf(a) = typeOf(e)} ⟹	/*L1*/ a = e;
2(b). Assign :	L1 : a = e//typeOf(a) = String, typeOf(e) = int} ⟹	/*L1*/ a = ""+e
2(c). Assign :	L1 : a = e//typeOf(a) = int, typeOf(e) = String} ⟹	/*L1*/ a = Integer.toInteger(e)

Figure 6. Rules to translate ABAP programs to Java. `tab` is an internal table in Rule 1.

The state-synchronization happens at two levels: 1) at the ABAP to Java translator side and 2) at the debugger side which creates a *partial trace*. The translator side steps are as follows: a) Roll back any code that might have been generated by the translator for the statement under consideration. b) Extract the *DEF* variables from the parse tree of the statement. c) Create a breakpoint in the source program, after the statement under consideration. d) In case the statement is a conditional/compound statement create a *predicate-marker* for the statement and a *target-marker* for each of the target statements. e) Generate code to read the values of the *DEF* variables from the partial trace. f) If the statement is a conditional/compound statement then generate code to read the target-marker from the partial trace and transfer the control to the statement corresponding to the target-marker.

At the debugger side, we create a partial trace file: For each breakpoint created by the translator the debugger stops to collect the values of the marked variables. Further, for conditional/compound statements it uses the introduced *target-marker* to note the statement that was executed after the statement marked with the *predicate-marker*.

We present a minor optimization for unhandled loop statements, whereby the number of lookups at the time of the execution of the Java code to the partial-trace are co-located. We create breakpoints for the `LOOP` and the `ENDLOOP` statements (which are executed for each iteration of the loop) to collect the partial trace in the debugger. The looping condition in the generate Java code is decided based on the total iteration count, which in turn is computed from number of contiguous patterns of the form `LOOP` <loop-body> `ENDLOOP` in the partial trace, for the particular instance of invocation. A limitation of state-synchronization approach is that it cannot handle statements with implicit side effects.
Parser Flagged Exception: These are handled exactly similar to the previous case of *syntax not handled*. Note that the parser exception handling also specifies the type of marker statement as - normal, conditional, or loop.
Exception while translating a statement: We encountered these when because of our limited knowledge about the language, certain variation of an ABAP statement were not handled in the translation. These exceptions are also handled similar to the case of *syntax not handled*.
Generated Java code does not compile: We maintain a mapping between the line numbers of the statements of the ABAP code and the generated Java code. On a compilation error, we identify the source statement in ABAP and invoke the state-synchronization method on that statement and repeat the process.

Incorrect Execution of the Translated Code: Considering the complexity of the source ABAP language and large coding effort involved in writing the complete framework, we do not give any formal guarantees about the correctness of translation. In lieu of the formal guarantee, our technique samples the generated trace statements against the actual execution. The sample size is determined as a threshold percentage over the whole code and the statements there are marked with a *verification marker*. For a statement carrying a verification marker, apart from the normal translation the translator does the following:
• flags this statement to be included in partial trace collection for both its use and def variables
• inserts an assert statement after the translated statement which compares the actual values of the def variables of the statement with the ones collected in the partial trace.

5. Pattern Checking

Identifying patterns in the code can be considered as the most effective and scalable technique for finding common bugs [8]. In this context we have built an automatic pattern detection engine for ABAP language. The important feature of our pattern detector is that it works on a given execution trace, instead of static code. This helps in a) allowing runtime patterns with actual values, and b) finding out the exact problem causing the buggy behavior, which is important from the ticket resolution perspective. However, it reduces the scope of pattern checking to only parts of the code that have been exercised by the trace. This pattern checker can be used as a plugin in our proposed framework.
Pattern Specification We use Extended Finite State Automata (EFSA) to describe patterns. Informally, EFSA extends finite state automata with state variables in states, and constraints and assignments in state transitions. The transition is only enabled if the constraints are satisfied, and then assignments are used to assign values to the state variables.

Formally, a Pattern-EFSA is an 9-tuple $\mathcal{E} = (Q, Q_0, F, X, E, G, A, T, D)$, where
• Q is a finite set of *states* ∪ the set of *variables* X,
• $Q_0 \subseteq Q$ is the set of *start states*
• $F = \{$Good, Bad$\} \subseteq Q$ is the set of *final states*.
• E is the set of *events*, each event is associated with a set of attributes. $Attr =$ set of all attributes over all the events.
• G is a set of *boolean conditions/guards* over the elements in X and all possible attributes of an event; the guards can use constant value, user inputs, and user-defined functions.
• A is a set of *assignment* statements which are of the form

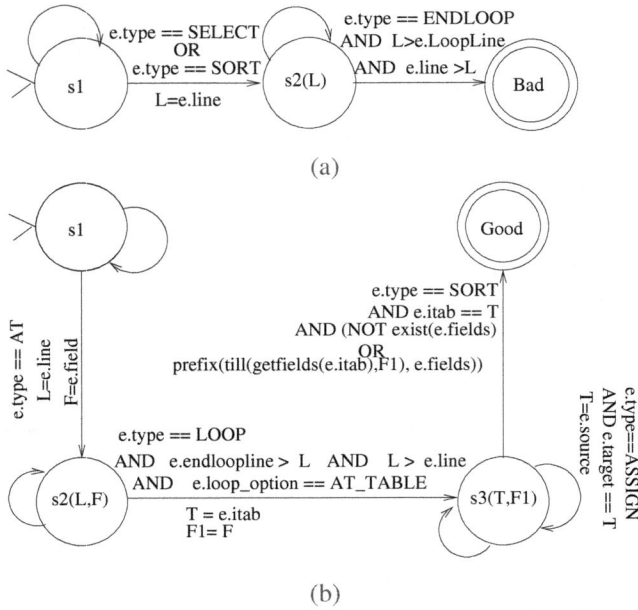

Figure 7. Sample EFSA: (a) InsideLOOP (b) SORT-AT

$x := y$, where $x \in X \cup Attr$, and $y \in X$.

• $T \subseteq Q \times (E \times G \times A) \times Q$ is a set of *transitions*. A transition $(q, (e, g, a), q')$ is *enabled* if in state q the event $e \in E$ is available and the boolean condition $g \in G$ is satisfied. When the transition is taken the assignment statements in a are executed. Additionally, a transition may be associated with a tag *non-vacuous* (discussed later).

• D is a direction property of the pattern which signifies whether the sequence of events should represent a trace from start to end ($D=\texttt{forward}$) or end to start ($D=\texttt{backward}$).

An execution trace is represented as a sequence of events (an event for each statement), each having a set of attribute-value pairs (for instance, `type` attribute of the sort statement is SORT) . Each attribute represents a static/dynamic property of a statement executed by the trace. We term a sequence of events as *good-accepted* (or *bad-accepted*) by an EFSA if it corresponds to a sequence of enabled transitions from the start state to the final Good (or Bad) state, leading to a a possible good (erroneous) execution.

We present two examples of pattern-EFSAs in Figure 7. The InsideLOOP Pattern-EFSA is an example of a forward pattern that represents a bad behavior of the trace. The InsideLOOP pattern represents a policy which states that having a *select and sort statement inside a loop is a bad behavior*, as it may lead to performance issues. The transition from state s1 to state s2, first checks whether the input event has a type attribute having value SELECT or SORT. The transition then records the line number (given by the attribute `e.line`) of the candidate statement in a state variable L in state s2. The presence of a loop statement around the candidate statement can be identified by comparing the line numbers of the END-LOOP and it's corresponding LOOP header. (the check for same filename is omitted for brevity). The self-loop transi-

tions do not alter the values of the state variables and are used to consume the events unrelated to the current pattern. Note that, the `type`, `line`, `LoopLine` attributes are all static attributes of the statements that are collected by traversal of the parse tree in *meta-data collection* phase (See Figure 1). Another pattern that accounts of erroneous behaviour is that of deleting rows from a table in a loop that iterates over the rows of that table.

If a trace is *bad-accepted* by a pattern, then the trace contains possible bad behaviors, and all the events in the input sequence which are enabled by the transitions are highlighted to the user as a possible fault. For instance, if a trace is *bad-accepted* by the InsideLOOP Pattern-EFSA, then the sort statement and loop statement are highlighted.

Consider the SORT-AT pattern-EFSA presented in Figure 7(b). The pattern represents a policy which states that, AT statement on a table should be preceded by a sort statement on that table, and the table should be sorted on all the (implicit and explicit) fields on which the AT check is done. As discussed in Section 2, the semantics of the AT statement states that along with the field f mentioned in AT, any change in values of the fields that occur before f in the declaration of the table also makes the condition to be true.

As the pattern check to be done from existence of AT statement first, and then existence of SORT statement, the D property of the pattern has value `backward`. We now describe some of the transitions.

• $s2 \rightarrow s3$: Finds an enclosing LOOP statement that loops over table rows (checked by loop_option = AT_TABLE). The name of the table and the fieldname are passed on to $s3$.

• $s3 \rightarrow$ Good: We find a sort statement on the same table on which AT check was done. The predicate ensures that the table is sorted on the fields on which AT check was done in the same order: if the sort statement mentions no field names, then the sort is done on all the fields in the order that exist in table definition and thus needs no further checks. In case the field names are mentioned in the sort statement, we use a helper function `getfields` to obtain the fields from the table declaration and compare with the implicit fields on which AT check was done (using function `till`).

• $s3 \rightarrow s3$: This transition enables us to capture the propagation of table names through assignments.

If a pattern is expressed with good final states, then the non-acceptance of a sequence of events may denote a possible bad behavior. However, it is possible that a non-acceptance of a sequence happened without enabling any "relevant" transitions (such as $s1 \rightarrow s2$ or other words without finding any AT statement). And that sequence should not be described as a bad behavior based on this pattern. To handle such cases, our pattern language allows certain transitions to be tagged non-vacuous in pattern-EFSAs that have a Good final state. This tagging is done by the EFSA writer. Non-acceptance of a trace along with enabling of non-vacuous transitions represents bad behavior.

The examples illustrated so far present cases where checks are performed on the static properties of statement. We now present some possible patterns on the dynamic properties (all with direction property D is forward).

• Unsuccessful db commands: In ABAP, execution of a database commands sets a status variable called sy-subrc. A non-zero value of sy-subrc denotes an unsuccessful database commands. The policy checks for non-zero value of sy-subrc after execution of a database command, before the updated records/tables are used.

• Large Internal Tables: One of the common problem noticed in ABAP is use of insufficient keys in select statement which returns more than expected number of rows. The policy checks for the length of the internal table exceeding an user input value.

• Overflow: After an assignment statement like a = b, whether the value of a is equal to b. This is not the case if length of b is greater than that of a and truncation of value occurs. This is important if the sizes of a and b are different.

• Missing check: Given a predefined set of key-value pairs whether any deletion was performed on a table which deleted the rows associated with the given set of key-value pairs; useful in finding missing entries in report output.

6. Rubber meets the Road

6.1 Uses of the trace

Trace for debugging input program Our framework, allows that arbitrary trace analysis tools can be plugged in. For instance, we have plugged-in the fault-detection tool of Saha et al [14] in our framework to derive expected results. The main requirement for plugin to work with our framework is that the plugin must conform to the interface requirements of our framework. We now discuss the details of the interface.

Our framework presents the details of the trace in two different files. The first file contains the variable and type information. For each variable used in the program, we store the name of the variable, scope (function name, class name or global), and the type details: an unique type id, structure of the type (scalar or *struct* or *table*), the declared type and the Java type. A struct type has additional attributes for the fields of the structure. A table type has additional attributes for the type of the table (standard, sorted, indexed) and the type of the rows of the table.

The second file is the complete trace file and is used to interface with the trace analysis tools. which contains the use-def data for each program statement. Each line in the trace has two identifiers: a) static line number, and b) the dynamic sequence number of this statement during the execution. Each trace line gives the details of all the variables and literals referred (used and/or defined) in the statement.

Trace for debugging the translation As discussed in Section 1, a naive way to generate the dynamic trace is to debug a program by stepping-into each statement, and use a screen-scrapping methodology to collect the use-def information

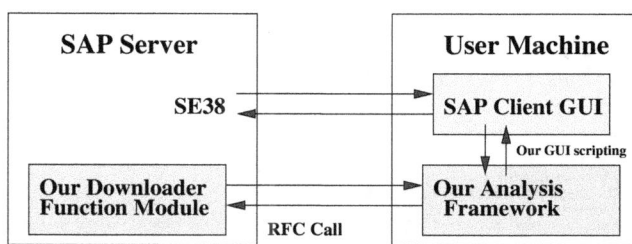

Figure 9. Interaction with SAP components

at each program point. We use this scheme (time consuming nevertheless) to establish the correctness of our translation. We generated the complete trace once using the screen-scrapping method, and then use it to compare the trace from our generated Java code. The translation is considered correct if both the traces match (both in terms of the order of the executed statements and values of the DEF variables at each program point). During the course of our initial development, this approach helped us to identify some corner cases in our implementation.

6.2 Application of standard tools

For a given ABAP program and its input, our framework generates its equivalent Java code, annotated with line numbers of the original ABAP code. One main advantage of such a translation is that since the generated code is written in Java, it allows a host of program analysis techniques written for Java; these can be plugged-in to our framework to derive desired results. Instances of the program analysis tools that can be applied are FindBugs [8], Khasiana [12] and so on.

6.3 Mapping the results

The results of all the plugged-in analyses is given in terms of the line numbers of the Java program or the line number of the trace. Since both the generated Java program as well as the dynamic trace are annotated with the line numbers of the original ABAP program, it is trivial to map the results back. We use this mapping technique to design a GUI based client (briefly discussed in the following section).

7. Implementation details

We have implemented the system illustrated in Figure 1. We now briefly discuss the implementation details.

• *Parser* - was generated for our ANTLR 3.2 based grammar for ABAP, with Java as the target. The complexity and the size of the ABAP grammar posed a unique challenge here. The compilation of the generated Java Parser ran into the "Code too large" problem. To deal with this we devised an automatic technique to partition the grammar into separate logical chunks. We have observed that even a naive partitioning of the grammar based on a threshold on the production-rule-count in each chunk has been found quite effective.

• *Fault Patterns Analyzer* It took pattern descriptions declared using XML as input and matched them on the trace.

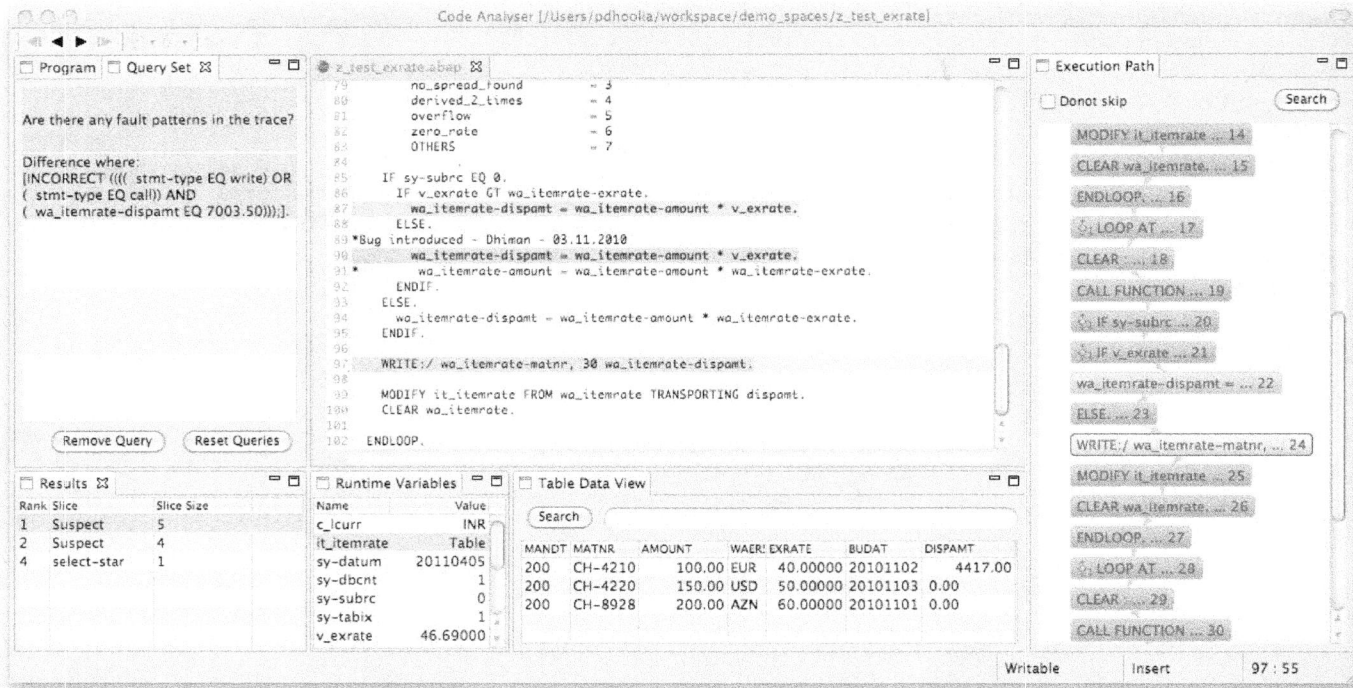

Figure 8. Snapshot of our ABAP Code Analysis Framework

- *GUI* - an Eclipse Rich Client Platform based GUI was implemented as the user-interface for tool. A snapshot of the tool in action is illustrated in Figure 8. This tool works as an interface to load the analysis, and displaying the results. The details of the GUI client (usability, speed, interactions etc) are beyond the scope of this submission.

- *Integration with SAP system* - Interfacing with the SAP system was done as illustrated in Figure 9. We implemented a function module in ABAP, which we upload to the SAP system, and then use via an SAP RFC call for the purpose of extracting the ABAP source, dependencies, and data-dictionary of built-in types. We use SAP Client GUI 7.10 installed on the user's machine for the purpose of collecting selective traces. Our system generates a VB script based on SAP GUI scripting language. This script automatically - (a) opens the ABAP program in SE38 (debugger) transaction; (b) puts required breakpoints on the lines indicated by the translator to be collected; (c) collects the partial trace at those breakpoints and dumps it to an XML file. An interesting issue we encountered here was that the SAP debugger transaction (SE38) puts a limitation of maximum 30 breakpoints; which was not sufficient for some of the large programs. We generated the partial trace collection for 30 breakpoints at a time and merged the final trace. In our experience this resulted only in minor additional cost.

8. Evaluation

In this section, we present our experience in using our ABAP Code Analysis Framework. We divide the presentation into three sections: experience with parser exception strategy,

Prog	LOC	# Err	Execution Time (in seconds)		
			Parsing	LineParsing	Writing
N1	198	1	1.8	0.3	0.01
N2	207	3	2.0	0.5	0.01
N3	630	5	1.9	0.5	0.07
N4	737	41	2.1	0.3	0.1
N5	925	2	2.1	0.6	0.1
N6	932	10	2.1	0.7	0.2
N7	966	2	2.1	0.4	0.2
N8	1078	3	2.0	0.6	0.2
N9	1401	2	2.0	1.1	0.3
N10	3281	1	2.7	1.8	1.0
N11	3330	3	2.7	1.7	1.0
N12	3838	6	2.2	3.1	1.2
N13	25766	238	4.1	46.7	23.9

Figure 10. Result: Parser Exception Strategy Handling experience with ABAP to Java translation, and the utility of our new pattern analysis technique.

Parser Exception Handling In our ongoing project, we started with an initial version of the ABAP grammar derived from the online language manual (http://help.sap.com). For reasons discussed before, that grammar was not able to parse the complete set of benchmarks we had at hand. But our analysis tool development and testing continued even in the presence of those unparsed statements. Eventually the grammar evolved to parse all our benchmarks. To test the effectiveness of the exception strategy handling we therefore chose a new set of ABAP programs that we had got recently. In Figure 10, we present the evaluation of our current grammar with respect to a subset of these programs that could not be parsed with our existing grammar and the grammar exception handling strategy was used used derive analyzable parse trees. For each benchmark we show, the number of lines of code (LOC), number of parse errors (# Err), and the breakup of the time taken by the our grammar exception handling strategy. The figure shows the time it took the parse the whole program ("Parsing"), time it took for parsing individual lines to identify and extract exact details for parsing failures ("LineParsing"), and the time taken to rewrite the updated file with relevant parse error statements. The total time taken went upto 75 seconds (for a large program with 25K lines of code), and rest all programs took just a few seconds. Overall, we conclude that a) there is a need for grammar exception handling strategy, and b) the overhead incurred by our proposed methodology is reasonable.

ABAP to Java translation To evaluate the coverage and correctness of our ABAP to Java translation scheme, we designed 165 unit testcases to cover all our known variations of ABAP. We compared the generated trace with the ideal trace to gain confidence on our translation.

For evaluating the efficacy of our ABAP to Java translation, we use a set of heavily used proprietary ABAP programs provided by our development teams; these are different from the newly obtained program benchmarks used earlier in this section. Some characteristics of these benchmarks can be found in the first two columns of Figure 11. We have used two sets of benchmarks - the first set is one from real applications, and the second set consists of all synthetic benchmarks. The third column lists the number of breakpoints that are used by the debugger mode partial trace collection. The performance benefits of using the our scheme compared to the complete trace obtained via the debugger are shown in the columns 4-6. It shows that our approach may result up to 11x speed ups.

Two observations: a) our approach may not yield benefit when the programs are trivially small which do not offset the overhead of our approach. b) For larger programs, the gains from our approach offsets the overheads we incur.

We have also used the FindBugs [8] tool on our generated Java code. It did correctly identify some simple warnings (such as unused variables, unused computation etc), but it did not find any programming bugs like null dereferences etc. This is quite expected as these programs are well tested and used in the industry for a while.

Pattern Analysis We encoded several static/dynamic patterns and run against traces of several programs. The results are shown in Figure 12. We give a short account of all the patterns in Figure 13. These patterns are suggested to us by ABAP practitioners. Only the pattern A8 has direction value D to be forward. To evaluate these patterns, the bugs were manually seeded in the benchmarks.

9. Conclusion

In this paper we shared our experience of building a framework for finding faults in ABAP programs in the context of

Prog	dbg mode time (s)	num lines	num breakpts	a2j mode time (s)	impr
B1	4854	393	2517	446	5.64 x
B2	860	235	355	183	1.94 x
B3	15746	900	1817	633	2.87 x
B4	1484	426	369	548	2.70 x
B5	4189	421	3298	576	5.73 x
B6	2542	530	587	194	3.03 x
B7	1694	427	5115	486	11.98 x
B8	1066	186	1424	136	10.41 x
S1	48	13	84	21	4.00 x
S2	48	13	26	19	1.37 x
S3	43	18	35	22	1.59 x
S4	49	24	43	22	1.95 x
S5	67	15	26	21	1.24 x
S6	86	16	32	60	0.53 x
S7	85	26	66	32	2.06 x
S8	35	11	14	67	0.21 x
S9	89	22	29	36	0.81 x
S10	133	36	470	97	4.85 x

Figure 11. ABAP to Java translation: evaluation

Pattern	Description
A1	SORT-AT pattern described in Section 5
A2	InsideLOOP pattern described in Section 5
A3	Similar to SORT-AT; field names existed in On-Change are compared with the fields in SORT
A4	Delete adjacent should be performed on same field names as sort for the same table
A5	Does not use select * or provide * syntax
A6	Is initial check needs to be done on a variable before it is used in forall clause in select statement
A7	read with binary search option should use the same keys on which the table is sorted
A8	database commands be followed by sy-subrc check

Figure 13. Sample Dynamic Patterns

ticket resolution. Due to the limited availability of debugging tools for localizing faults in such programs, we have taken the approach of generating equivalent translation to annotated Java programs, and executing it to generate the equivalent trace, such that we can use static and dynamic analysis tools for fault localization.

We present a new grammar annotation mechanism, along with different exception handling schemes to handle incompleteness in the grammar, and the translation. We observed that our proposed framework was able to cover all the benchmarks provided to us and the incurred performance overhead was kept to an acceptable limit. We have further developed and used a pattern matching tool which finds matching patterns in the generated traces. The use of both static and dynamic properties makes it particularly useful for fault localization in ABAP language.

Acknowledgements: The authors would like to thank Vibha Sinha, Satish Chandra, Sugata Ghosal, Sourin Ghosh, Dhiman Ghosh, Asidhara Lahiri, and Amitava Parui for many fruitful discussions and help at different stages of the project.

Prog	Static Patterns								Time	Dynamic Patterns				Time
	A1	A2	A3	A4	A5	A6	A7	A8	(sec)	unsucc-db	overflow	bigtbl	missing	(Sec.)
B1	58/1	0	3/2	0	4/3	1/1	0	30/2	5.7	1/1	0	0	1/1	3.0
B2	0	0	0	0	0	3/3	1/1	0	0.1	0	0	0	-	1.5
B3	0	0	0	0	0	2/2	0	0	0.7	22/4	0	0	-	3.0
B4	0	0	0	0	3/2	0	0	3/2	0.1	0	0	0	-	0.1
B5	0	62/2	0	0	1/1	0	0	5/5	3.5	0	0	0	1/1	9.0
B6	0	0	0	0	0	0	0	0	1.2	0	0	0	-	0.1
B7	166/2	0	0	0	1/1	0	0	86/4	60.0	0	0	0	-	6.0
B8	0	0	0	0	0	0	0	1/1	1.3	84/1	84/1	0	-	0.1

Figure 12. Static and Dynamic Pattern Analysis: statement instances/statements

References

[1] Java compiler compiler (JavaCC): The Java parser generator. http://javacc.java.net/.

[2] A. Aho, R. Sethi, and J. Ullman. *Compilers: Principles, Techniques, and Tools*. Addison-Wesley, 1986.

[3] H. Chen and D. Wagner. Mops: an infrastructure for examining security properties of software. In *CCS*, pages 235–244, New York, NY, USA, 2002. ACM.

[4] Julia Dain. Bibliography on syntax error handling in language translation systems.

[5] D. Evans and D. Larochelle. Improving security using extensible lightweight static analysis. *IEEE Softw.*, 19:42–51, Jan 2002.

[6] S.I. Feldman. A Fortran to C converter. In *ACM SIGPLAN Fortran Forum*, volume 9, pages 21–22. ACM, 1990.

[7] F. Fleurey, E. Breton, B. Baudry, A. Nicolas, and J.M. Jézéquel. Model-driven engineering for software migration in a large industrial context. *MDELS*, pages 482–497, 2007.

[8] D. Hovemeyer and W. Pugh. Finding bugs is easy. In *OOPSLA Companion*, pages 132–136. ACM, 2004.

[9] S. C. Johnson. YACC—yet another compiler-compiler. Technical Report CS-32, AT & T Bell Laboratories, 1975.

[10] Horst Keller. *The official ABAP reference*. SAP Press, 2004.

[11] R. Lämmel and C. Verhoef. Semi-automatic grammar recovery. *Softw. Pract. Exper.*, 31(15):1395–1448, 2001.

[12] M G Nanda and S Sinha. Accurate interprocedural null-dereference analysis for java. In *ICSE*, pages 133–143, Washington, DC, USA, 2009. IEEE Computer Society.

[13] Terence Parr. *The Definitive ANTLR Reference: Building Domain-Specific Languages*. Pragmatic Bookshelf, 2007.

[14] D. Saha, M.G. Nanda, P. Dhoolia, V.K. Nandivada, V. Sinha, and S. Chandra. Fault localization in ABAP Programs. In *FSE*, 2011.

[15] D. Saha and V. Narula. Gramin: a system for incremental learning of programming language grammars. In *ISEC*, pages 185–194. ACM, 2011.

[16] R. Sekar, V. N. Venkatakrishnan, S. Basu, S. Bhatkar, and D. C. DuVarney. Model-carrying code: a practical approach for safe execution of untrusted applications. In *SOSP*, pages 15–28, 2003.

[17] P.N. van den Bosch. A bibliography on syntax error handling in context free languages. *ACM SIGPLAN Notices*, 27(4):77–86, 1992.

[18] R.C. Waters. Program translation via abstraction and reimplementation. *IEEE Transactions on Software Engineering*, pages 1207–1228, 1988.

[19] David A Wheeler. Flawfinder. http://www.dwheeler.com/flawfinder/.

[20] K. Yasumatsu. SPiCE: a system for translating Smalltalk programs into a C environment. *Software Engineering, IEEE Transactions on*, 21(11):902–912, 1995.

Emscripten: An LLVM-to-JavaScript Compiler

Alon Zakai

Mozilla

azakai@mozilla.com

Abstract

We present Emscripten, a compiler from LLVM (Low Level Virtual Machine) assembly to JavaScript. This opens up two avenues for running code written in languages other than JavaScript on the web: (1) Compile code directly into LLVM assembly, and then compile that into JavaScript using Emscripten, or (2) Compile a language's entire runtime into LLVM and then JavaScript, as in the previous approach, and then use the compiled runtime to run code written in that language. For example, the former approach can work for C and C++, while the latter can work for Python; all three examples open up new opportunities for running code on the web.

Emscripten itself is written in JavaScript and is available under the MIT license (a permissive open source license), at http://www.emscripten.org. As a compiler from LLVM to JavaScript, the challenges in designing Emscripten are somewhat the reverse of the norm – one must go from a low-level assembly into a high-level language, and recreate parts of the original high-level structure of the code that were lost in the compilation to low-level LLVM. We detail the methods used in Emscripten to deal with those challenges, and in particular present and prove the validity of Emscripten's Relooper algorithm, which recreates high-level loop structures from low-level branching data.

Categories and Subject Descriptors D.3.4 [*Processors*]: Compilers

General Terms Languages, Algorithms

Keywords JavaScript, LLVM, Decompiler

1. Introduction

Since the mid 1990's, JavaScript [5] has been present in most web browsers (sometimes with minor variations and under slightly different names, e.g., JScript in Internet Explorer), and today it is well-supported on essentially all web browsers, from desktop browsers like Internet Explorer, Firefox, Chrome and Safari, to mobile browsers on smartphones and tablets. Together with HTML and CSS, JavaScript forms the standards-based foundation of the web.

Running other programming languages on the web has been suggested many times, and browser plugins have allowed doing so, e.g., via the Java and Flash plugins. However, plugins must be manually installed and do not integrate in a perfect way with the outside HTML. Perhaps more problematic is that they cannot run at all on some platforms, for example, Java and Flash cannot run on iOS devices such as the iPhone and iPad. For those reasons, JavaScript remains the primary programming language of the web.

There are, however, reasonable motivations for running code from other programming languages on the web, for example, if one has a large amount of existing code already written in another language, or if one simply has a strong preference for another language and perhaps is more productive in it. As a consequence, there has been work on tools to compile languages **into** JavaScript. Since JavaScript is present in essentially all web browsers, by compiling one's language of choice into JavaScript, one can still generate content that will run practically everywhere.

Examples of the approach of compiling into JavaScript include the Google Web Toolkit [8], which compiles Java into JavaScript; Pyjamas[1], which compiles Python into JavaScript; SCM2JS [6], which compiles Scheme to JavaScript, Links [3], which compiles an ML-like language into JavaScript; and AFAX [7], which compiles F# to JavaScript; see also [1] for additional examples. While useful, such tools usually only allow a subset of the original language to be compiled. For example, multithreaded code (with shared memory) is not possible on the web, so compiling code of that sort is not directly possible. There are also often limitations of the conversion process, for example, Pyjamas compiles Python to JavaScript in a nearly 1-to-1 manner, and as a consequence the underlying semantics are those of JavaScript, not Python, so for example division of integers can yield unexpected results (it should yield an integer in Python 2.x, but

---

[1] http://pyjs.org/

in JavaScript and in Pyjamas a floating-point number can be generated).

In this paper we present another project along those lines: **Emscripten**, which compiles LLVM (Low Level Virtual Machine[2]) assembly into JavaScript. LLVM is a compiler project primarily focused on C, C++ and Objective-C. It compiles those languages through a *frontend* (the main ones of which are Clang and LLVM-GCC) into the LLVM intermediary representation (which can be machine-readable bitcode, or human-readable assembly), and then passes it through a *backend* which generates actual machine code for a particular architecure. Emscripten plays the role of a backend which targets JavaScript.

By using Emscripten, potentially many languages can be run on the web, using one of the following methods:

- Compile **code** in a language recognized by one of the existing LLVM frontends into LLVM, and then compile that into JavaScript using Emscripten. Frontends for various languages exist, including many of the most popular programming languages such as C and C++, and also various new and emerging languages (e.g., Rust[3]).

- Compile the **runtime** used to parse and execute code in a particular language into LLVM, then compile that into JavaScript using Emscripten. It is then possible to run code in that runtime on the web. This is a useful approach if a language's runtime is written in a language for which an LLVM frontend exists, but the language itself has no such frontend. For example, there is currently no frontend for Python, however it is possible to compile CPython – the standard implementation of Python, written in C – into JavaScript, and run Python code on that (see Section 4).

From a technical standpoint, one challenge in designing and implementing Emscripten is that it compiles a low-level language – LLVM assembly – into a high-level one – JavaScript. This is somethat the reverse of the usual situation one is in when building a compiler, and leads to some unique difficulties. For example, to get good performance in JavaScript one must use natural JavaScript code flow structures, like loops and ifs, but those structures do not exist in LLVM assembly (instead, what is present there is a 'soup of code fragments': blocks of code with branching information but no high-level structure). Emscripten must therefore reconstruct a high-level representation from the low-level data it receives.

In theory that issue could have been avoided by compiling a higher-level language into JavaScript. For example, if compiling Java into JavaScript (as the Google Web Toolkit does), then one can benefit from the fact that Java's loops, ifs and so forth generally have a very direct parallel in JavaScript. But of course the downside in that approach is it yields a com-

piler only for Java. In Section 3.2 we present the 'Relooper' algorithm, which generates high-level loop structures from the low-level branching data present in LLVM assembly. It is similar to loop recovery algorithms used in decompilation (see, for example, [2], [9]). The main difference between the Relooper and standard loop recovery algorithms is that the Relooper generates loops in a different language than that which was compiled originally, whereas decompilers generally assume they are returning to the original language. The Relooper's goal is not to accurately recreate the original source code, but rather to generate native JavaScript control flow structures, which can then be implemented efficiently in modern JavaScript engines.

Another challenge in Emscripten is to maintain accuracy (that is, to keep the results of the compiled code the same as the original) while not sacrificing performance. LLVM assembly is an abstraction of how modern CPUs are programmed for, and its basic operations are not all directly possible in JavaScript. For example, if in LLVM we are to add two unsigned 8-bit numbers x and y, with overflowing (e.g., 255 plus 1 should give 0), then there is no single operation in JavaScript which can do this – we cannot just write $x + y$, as that would use the normal JavaScript semantics. It is possible to emulate a CPU in JavaScript, however doing so is very slow. Emscripten's approach is to allow such emulation, but to try to use it as little as possible, and to provide tools that help one find out which parts of the compiled code actually need such full emulation.

We conclude this introduction with a list of this paper's main contributions:

- We describe Emscripten itself, during which we detail its approach in compiling LLVM into JavaScript.

- We give details of Emscripten's Relooper algorithm, mentioned earlier, which generates high-level loop structures from low-level branching data, and prove its validity.

In addition, the following are the main contributions of Emscripten itself, that to our knowledge were not previously possible:

- It allows compiling a very large subset of C and C++ code into JavaScript, which can then be run on the web.

- By compiling their runtimes, it allows running languages such as Python on the web (with their normal semantics).

The remainder of this paper is structured as follows. In Section 2 we describe the approach Emscripten takes to compiling LLVM assembly into JavaScript, and show some benchmark data. In Section 3 we describe Emscripten's internal design and in particular elaborate on the Relooper algorithm. In Section 4 we give several example uses of Emscripten. In Section 5 we summarize and give directions for future work.

---

[2] http://llvm.org/

[3] https://github.com/graydon/rust/

2. Compilation Approach

Let us begin by considering what the challenge is, when we want to compile LLVM assembly into JavaScript. Assume we are given the following simple example of a C program:

```
#include <stdio.h>
int main()
{
  int sum = 0;
  for (int i = 1; i < 100; i++)
    sum += i;
  printf("1+...+100=%d\n", sum);
  return 0;
}
```

This program calculates the sum of the integers from 1 to 100. When compiled by Clang, the generated LLVM assembly code includes the following:

```
@.str = private constant [4 x i8] c"%d\0A\00"

define i32 @main() {
  %1 = alloca i32, align 4
  %sum = alloca i32, align 4
  %i = alloca i32, align 4
  store i32 0, i32* %1
  store i32 0, i32* %sum, align 4
  store i32 1, i32* %i, align 4
  br label %2

; <label>:2
  %3 = load i32* %i, align 4
  %4 = icmp slt i32 %3, 100
  br i1 %4, label %5, label %12

; <label>:5
  %6 = load i32* %i, align 4
  %7 = load i32* %sum, align 4
  %8 = add nsw i32 %7, %6
  store i32 %8, i32* %sum, align 4
  br label %9

; <label>:9
  %10 = load i32* %i, align 4
  %11 = add nsw i32 %10, 1
  store i32 %11, i32* %i, align 4
  br label %2

; <label>:12
  %13 = load i32* %sum, align 4
  %14 = call i32 (i8*, ...)*
        @printf(i8* getelementptr inbounds
          ([14 x i8]* @.str, i32 0, i32 0),
          i32 %13)
  ret i32 0
}
```

At first glance, this may look more difficult to translate into JavaScript than the original C++. However, compiling C++ in general would require writing code to handle preprocessing, classes, templates, and all the idiosyncrasies and complexities of C++. LLVM assembly, while more verbose in this example, is lower-level and simpler to work on. Compiling it also has the benefit we mentioned earlier, which is one of the main goals of Emscripten, that it allows many languages can be compiled into LLVM and not just C++.

A detailed overview of LLVM assembly is beyond our scope here (see http://llvm.org/docs/LangRef.html). Briefly, though, the example assembly above can be seen to define a function main(), then allocate some values on the stack (alloca), then load and store various values (load and store). We do not have the high-level code structure as we had in C++ (with a loop), instead we have labeled code fragments, called LLVM basic blocks, and code flow moves from one to another by branch (br) instructions. (Label 2 is the condition check in the loop; label 5 is the body, label 9 is the increment, and label 12 is the final part of the function, outside of the loop). Conditional branches can depend on calculations, for example the results of comparing two values (icmp). Other numerical operations include addition (add). Finally, printf is called (call). The challenge, then, is to convert this and things like it into JavaScript.

In general, Emscripten's main approach is to translate each line of LLVM assembly into JavaScript, 1 to 1, into 'normal' JavaScript as much as possible. So, for example, an *add* operation becomes a normal JavaScript addition, a function call becomes a JavaScript function call, etc. This 1 to 1 translation generates JavaScript that resembles the original assembly code, for example, the LLVM assembly code shown before for main() would be compiled into the following:

```
function _main() {
  var __stackBase__ = STACKTOP;
  STACKTOP += 12;
  var __label__ = -1;
  while(1) switch(__label__) {
    case -1:
      var $1 = __stackBase__;
      var $sum = __stackBase__+4;
      var $i = __stackBase__+8;
      HEAP[$1] = 0;
      HEAP[$sum] = 0;
      HEAP[$i] = 0;
      __label__ = 0; break;
    case 0:
      var $3 = HEAP[$i];
      var $4 = $3 < 100;
      if ($4) { __label__ = 1; break; }
      else    { __label__ = 2; break; }
    case 1:
      var $6 = HEAP[$i];
```

```
    var $7 = HEAP[$sum];
    var $8 = $7 + $6;
    HEAP[$sum] = $8;
    __label__ = 3; break;
  case 3:
    var $10 = HEAP[$i];
    var $11 = $10 + 1;
    HEAP[$i] = $11;
    __label__ = 0; break;
  case 2:
    var $13 = HEAP[$sum];
    var $14 = _printf(__str, $13);
    STACKTOP = __stackBase__;
    return 0;
  }
}
```

Some things to take notice of:

- A switch-in-a-loop construction is used in order to let the flow of execution move between basic blocks of code in an arbitrary manner: We set _label_ to the (numerical representation of the) label of the basic block we want to reach, and do a break, which leads to the proper basic block being reached. Inside each basic block, every line of code corresponds to a line of LLVM assembly, generally in a very straightforward manner.

- Memory is implemented by *HEAP*, a JavaScript array. Reading from memory is a read from that array, and writing to memory is a write. *STACKTOP* is the current position of the stack. (Note that we allocate 4 memory locations for 32-bit integers on the stack, but only write to 1 of them. See Section 2.1.1 for why.)

- LLVM assembly functions become JavaScript functions, and function calls are normal JavaScript function calls. In general, we attempt to generate as 'normal' JavaScript as possible.

- We implemented the LLVM *add* operation using simple addition in JavaScript. As mentioned earlier, the semantics of that code are not entirely identical to those of the original LLVM assembly code (in this case, overflows will have very different effects). We will explain Emscripten's approach to that problem in Section 2.1.2.

2.1 Performance

In this section we will deal with several topics regarding Emscripten's approach to generating high-performance JavaScript code.

2.1.1 Load-Store Consistency (LSC)

We saw before that Emscripten's memory usage allocates the usual number of bytes on the stack for variables (4 bytes for a 32-bit integer, etc.). However, we only wrote values into the first location, which appeared odd. We will now see the reason for that.

To get there, we must first step back, and note that Emscripten does not aim to achieve perfect compatibility with all possible LLVM assembly (and correspondingly, with all possible C or C++ code, etc.); instead, Emscripten targets a large subset of LLVM assembly code, which is portable and does not make crucial assumptions about the underlying CPU architecture on which the code is meant to run. That subset is meant to encompass the vast majority of real-world code that would be compiled into LLVM, while also being compilable into very performant JavaScript.

More specifically, Emscripten assumes that the LLVM assembly code it is compiling has **Load-Store Consistency** (LSC), which is the requirement that after a value with a specific type is written to a memory location, loads from that memory location will be of the same type (until a value with a different type is written there). Normal C and C++ code generally does so: If x is a variable containing a 32-bit floating point number, then both loads and stores of x will be of 32-bit floating point values, and not 16-bit unsigned integers or anything else.

To see why this is important for performance, consider the following C code fragment, which does *not* have LSC:

```
int x = 12345;
printf("first byte: %d\n", *((char*)&x));
```

Assuming an architecture with more than 8 bits, this code will read the first byte of x. (This might, for example, be used to detect the endianness of the CPU.) To compile this into JavaScript in a way that will run properly, we must do more than a single operation for either the read or the write, for example we could do this:

```
var x_value = 12345;
var x_addr = stackAlloc(4);
HEAP[x_addr]   = (x_value >> 0) & 255;
HEAP[x_addr+1] = (x_value >> 8) & 255;
HEAP[x_addr+2] = (x_value >> 16) & 255;
HEAP[x_addr+3] = (x_value >> 24) & 255;
[...]
printf("first byte: %d\n", HEAP[x_addr]);
```

Here we allocate space for the value of x on the stack, and store that address in *x_addr*. The stack itself is part of the 'memory space', which is the array *HEAP*. In order for the read on the final line to give the proper value, we must go to the effort of doing 4 store operations, each of the value of a particular byte. In other words, *HEAP* is an array of bytes, and for each store into memory, we must deconstruct the value into bytes.[4]

---

[4] Note that we can use JavaScript typed arrays with a shared memory buffer, which would work as expected, assuming (1) we are running in a JavaScript engine which supports typed arrays, and (2) we are running on a CPU with the same architecture as we expect. This is therefore dangerous as the generated code may run differently on different JavaScript engines and different CPUs. Emscripten currently has optional experimental support for typed arrays.

Alternatively, we can store the value in a single operation, and deconstruct into bytes as we load. This will be faster in some cases and slower in others, but is still more overhead than we would like, generally speaking – for if the code **does** have LSC, then we can translate that code fragment into the far more optimal

```
var x_value = 12345;
var x_addr = stackAlloc(4);
HEAP[x_addr] = x_value;
[...]
printf("first byte: %d\n", HEAP[x_addr]);
```

(Note that even this can be optimized even more – we can store *x* in a normal JavaScript variable. We will discuss such optimizations in Section 2.1.3; for now we are just clarifying why it is useful to assume we are compiling code that has LSC.)

In practice the vast majority of C and C++ code does have LSC. Exceptions do exist, however, for example:

- Code that detects CPU features like endianness, the behavior of floats, etc. In general such code can be disabled before running it through Emscripten, as it is not actually needed.

- *memset* and related functions typically work on values of one kind, regardless of the underlying values. For example, memset may write 64-bit values on a 64-bit CPU since that is usually faster than writing individual bytes. This tends to not be a problem, as with *memset* the most common case is setting to 0, and with *memcpy*, the values end up copied properly anyhow (with a proper implementation of *memcpy* in Emscripten's generated code).

- Even LSC-obeying C or C++ code may turn into LLVM assembly that does not, after being optimized. For example, when storing two 32-bit integers constants into adjoining locations in a structure, the optimizer may generate a single 64-bit store of an appropriate constant. In other words, optimization can generate nonportable code, which runs faster on the current CPU, but nowhere else. Emscripten currently assumes that optimizations of this form are not being used.

In practice it may be hard to know if code has LSC or not, and requiring a time-consuming code audit is obviously impractical. Emscripten therefore has a compilation option, SAFE_HEAP, which generates code that checks that LSC holds, and warns if it doesn't. It also warns about other memory-related issues like reading from memory before a value was written (somewhat similarly to tools like Valgrind[5]). When such problems are detected, possible solutions are to ignore the issue (if it has no actual consequences), or alter the source code.

[5] http://valgrind.org/

Note that it is somewhat wasteful to allocate 4 memory locations for a 32-bit integer, and use only one of them. It is possible to change that behavior with the QUANTUM_SIZE parameter to Emscripten, however, the difficulty is that LLVM assembly has hardcoded values that depend on the usual memory sizes being used. We are looking into modifications to LLVM itself to remedy that.

2.1.2 Emulating Code Semantics

As mentioned in the introduction, the semantics of LLVM assembly and JavaScript are not identical: The former is very close to that of a modern CPU, while the latter is a high-level dynamic language. Both are of course Turing-complete, so it is possible to precisely emulate each in the other, but doing so with good performance is more challenging. For example, if we want to convert

```
add i8 %1, %2
```

(add two 8-bit integers) to JavaScript, then to be completely accurate we must emulate the exact same behavior, in particular, we must handle overflows properly, which would not be the case if we just implement this as $\%1 + \%2$ in JavaScript. For example, with inputs of 255 and 1, the correct output is 0, but simple addition in JavaScript will give us 256. We can of course emulate the proper behavior by adding additional code. This however significantly degrades performance, because modern JavaScript engines can often translate something like $z = x + y$ into native code containing a single instruction (or very close to that), but if instead we had something like $z = (x + y)\&255$ (in order to correct overflows), the JavaScript engine would need to generate additional code to perform the AND operation.[6]

Emscripten's approach to this problem is to allow the generation of both accurate code, that is identical in behavior to LLVM assembly, and inaccurate code which is faster. In practice, most addition operations in LLVM do not overflow, and can simply be translated into $\%1 + \%2$. Emscripten provides tools that make it straightforward to find which code does require the slower, more accurate code, and to generate that code in those locations, as follows:

- Compile the code using Emscripten with special options that generate runtime checking. CHECK_OVERFLOWS adds runtime checks for integer overflows, CHECK_SIGNS checks for signing issues (the behavior of signed and un-

[6] In theory, the JavaScript engine could determine that we are implicitly working on 8-bit values here, and generate machine code that no longer needs the AND operation. However, most or all modern JavaScript engines have just two internal numeric types, doubles and 32-bit integers. This is so because they are tuned for 'normal' JavaScript code on the web, which in most cases is served well by just those two types.
In addition, even if JavaScript engines did analyze code containing &255, etc., in order to deduce that a variable can be implemented as an 8-bit integer, there is a cost to including all the necessary &255 text in the script, because code size is a significant factor on the web. Adding even a few characters for every single mathematic operation, in a large JavaScript file, could add up to a significant increase in download size.

signed integers can be different, and JavaScript does not natively support that difference), and CHECK_ROUNDINGS checks for rounding issues (in C and C++, the convention is to round towards 0, while in JavaScript there is no simple operation that does the same).

- Run the compiled code on a representative sample of inputs, and notice which lines are warned about by the runtime checks.

- Recompile the code, telling Emscripten to add corrections (using CORRECT_SIGNS, CORRECT_OVERFLOWS or CORRECT_ROUNDINGS) only on the specific lines that actually need it.

This method is not guaranteed to work, as if we do not run on a truly representative sample of possible inputs, we may not compile with all necessary corrections. It is of course possible to compile with all corrections applied to all the code, to make sure things will work properly (this is the default compilation setting), however, in practice the procedure above works quite well, and results in code is significantly faster.

2.1.3   Emscripten Code Optimizations

When comparing the example program from page 3, the generated code was fairly complicated and cumbersome, and unsurprisingly it performs quite poorly. There are two main reasons for that: First, that the code is simply unoptimized – there are many variables declared when fewer could suffice, for example, and second, that the code does not use 'normal' JavaScript, which JavaScript engines are optimized for – it stores all variables in an array (not normal JavaScript variables), and it controls the flow of execution using a switch-in-a-loop, not normal JavaScript loops and ifs.

Emscripten's approach to generating fast-performing code is as follows. Emscripten doesn't do any optimizations that can be done by other tools: LLVM can be used to perform optimizations before Emscripten, and the Closure Compiler[7] can perform optimizations on the generated JavaScript afterwards. Those tools will perform standard useful optimizations like removing unneeded variables, dead code elimination, function inlining, etc. That leaves two major optimizations that are left for Emscripten to perform:

- **Variable nativization**: Convert variables that are on the stack – which is implemented using addresses in the *HEAP* array as mentioned earlier – into native JavaScript variables (that is to say, *var x;* and so forth). In general, a variable will be nativized unless it is used outside that function, e.g., if its address is taken and stored somewhere or passed to another function. When optimizing, Emscripten tries to nativize as many variables as possible.

---
[7] http://code.google.com/closure/compiler/

- **Relooping**: Recreate high-level loop and if structures from the low-level code block data that appears in LLVM assembly. We describe Emscripten's Relooper algorithm in Section 3.2.

When run with Emscripten's optimizations, the code on page 3 looks like this:

```
function _main() {
  var __label__;
  var $1;
  var $sum;
  var $i;
  $1 = 0;
  $sum = 0;
  $i = 0;
  $2$2: while(1) {
    var $3 = $i;
    var $4 = $3 < 100;
    if (!($4)) { __label__ = 2; break $2$2; }
    var $6 = $i;
    var $7 = $sum;
    var $8 = $7 + $6;
    $sum = $8;
    var $10 = $i;
    var $11 = $10 + 1;
    $i = $11;
    __label__ = 0; continue $2$2;
  }
  var $13 = $sum;
  var $14 = _printf(__str, $13);
  return 0;
}
```

If in addition the Closure Compiler is run on that output, we get

```
function K() {
  var a, b;
  b = a = 0;
  a:for(;;) {
    if(!(b < 100)) {
      break a
    }
    a += b;
    b += 1;
  }
  _printf(J, a);
  return 0;
}
```

which is fairly close to the original C++ (the differences, of having the loop's condition inside the loop instead of inside the for() expression at the top of the original loop, are not important to performance). Thus, it is possible to recreate the original high-level structure of the code that was compiled into LLVM assembly.

306

2.2 Benchmarks

We will now take a look at some performance benchmarks:

benchmark	SM	V8	gcc	ratio
fannkuch (10)	1.158	**0.931**	0.231	4.04
fasta (2100000)	**1.115**	1.128	0.452	2.47
primes	**1.443**	3.194	0.438	3.29
raytrace (7,256)	**1.930**	2.944	0.228	8.46
dlmalloc (400,400)	5.050	**1.880**	0.315	5.97

The first column is the name of the benchmark, and in parentheses any parameters used in running it. The source code to all the benchmarks can be found at https://github.com/kripken/emscripten/tree/master/tests (each in a separate file with its name, except for 'primes', which is embedded inside runner.py in the function test_primes). A brief summary of the benchmarks is as follows:

- **fannkuch** and **fasta** are commonly-known benchmarks, appearing for example on the Computer Language Benchmarks Game[8]. They use a mix of mathematic operations (integer in the former, floating-point in the latter) and memory access.

- **primes** is the simplest benchmark in terms of code. It is basically just a tiny loop that calculates prime numbers.

- **raytrace** is real-world code, from the sphereflake raytracer[9]. This benchmark has a combination of memory access and floating-point math.

- **dlmalloc** (Doug Lea's malloc[10]) is a well-known real-world implementation of malloc and free. This benchmark does a large amount of calls to malloc and free in an intermixed way, which tests memory access and integer calculations.

Returning to the table of results, the second column is the elapsed time (in seconds) when running the compiled code (generated using all Emscripten and LLVM optimizations as well as the Closure Compiler) in the SpiderMonkey JavaScript engine (specifically the JaegerMonkey branch, checked out June 15th, 2011). The third column is the elapsed time when running the same JavaScript code in the V8 JavaScript engine (checked out Jun 15th, 2011). In both the second and third column lower values are better; the best of the two is in bold. The fourth column is the elapsed time when running the original code compiled with *gcc -O3*, using GCC 4.4.4. The last column is the ratio, that is, how much slower the JavaScript code (running in the faster of the two engines for that test) is when compared to gcc. All the tests were run on a MacBook Pro with an Intel i7 CPU clocked at 2.66GHz, running on Ubuntu 10.04.

---

[8] http://shootout.alioth.debian.org/

[9] http://ompf.org/ray/sphereflake/

[10] http://en.wikipedia.org/wiki/Malloc#dlmalloc_and_its_derivatives

Clearly the results greatly vary by the benchmark, with the generated JavaScript running from 2.47 to 8.46 times slower. There are also significant differences between the two JavaScript engines, with each better at some of the benchmarks. It appears that code that does simple numerical operations – like the primes test – can run fairly fast, while code that has a lot of memory accesses, for example due to using structures – like the raytrace test – will be slower. (The main issue with structures is that Emscripten does not 'nativize' them yet, as it does to simple local variables.)

Being 2.47 to 8.46 times slower than the most-optimized C++ code is a significant slowdown, but it is still more than fast enough for many purposes, and the main point of course is that the code can run anywhere the web can be accessed. Further work on Emscripten is expected to improve the speed as well, as are improvements to LLVM, the Closure Compiler, and JavaScript engines themselves; see further discussion in the Summary.

2.3 Limitations

Emscripten's compilation approach, as has been described in this Section so far, is to generate 'natural' JavaScript, as close as possible to normal JavaScript on the web, so that modern JavaScript engines perform well on it. In particular, we try to generate 'normal' JavaScript operations, like regular addition and multiplication and so forth. This is a very different approach than, say, emulating a CPU on a low level, or for the case of LLVM, writing an LLVM bitcode interpreter in JavaScript. The latter approach has the benefit of being able to run virtually any compiled code, at the cost of speed, whereas Emscripten makes a tradeoff in the other direction. We will now give a summary of some of the limitations of Emscripten's approach.

- **64-bit Integers**: JavaScript numbers are all 64-bit doubles, with engines typically implementing them as 32-bit integers where possible for speed. A consequence of this is that it is impossible to directly implement 64-bit integers in JavaScript, as integer values larger than 32 bits will become doubles, with only 53 bits for the significand. Thus, when Emscripten uses normal JavaScript addition and so forth for 64-bit integers, it runs the risk of rounding effects. This could be solved by emulating 64-bit integers, but it would be much slower than native code.

- **Multithreading**: JavaScript has Web Workers, which are additional threads (or processes) that communicate via message passing. There is no shared state in this model, which means that it is not directly possible to compile multithreaded code in C++ into JavaScript. A partial solution could be to emulate threads, without Workers, by manually controlling which blocks of code run (a variation on the switch in a loop construction mentioned earlier) and manually switching between threads every so often. However, in that case there would not be any utilization of additional CPU cores, and furthermore performance would be slow due to not using normal JavaScript loops.

After seeing these limitations, it is worth noting that some advanced LLVM instructions turn out to be surprisingly easy to implement. For example, C++ exceptions are represented in LLVM by *invoke* and *unwind*, where *invoke* is a call to a function that will potentially trigger an *unwind*, and *unwind* returns to the earliest invoke. If one were to implement those in a typical compiler, doing so would require careful work. In Emscripen, however, it is possible to do so using JavaScript exceptions in a straightforward manner: *invoke* becomes a function call wrapped in a *try* block, and *unwind* becomes *throw*. This is a case where compiling to a high-level language turns out to be quite convenient.

3. Emscripten's Architecture

In the previous section we saw a general overview of Emscripten's approach to compiling LLVM assembly code into JavaScript. We will now get into more detail into how Emscripten itself is implemented.

Emscripten is written in JavaScript. The primary reason for that decision was convenience: Two simple examples of the benefits of that approach are that (1) the compiler can create JavaScript objects that represent constant structures from the original assembly code, and convert them to a string using JSON.stringify() in a trivial manner, and (2) the compiler can simplify numerical operations by simply eval()ing the code (so "1+2" would become "3", etc.). In both examples, the development of Emscripten was made simpler by having the exact same environment during compilation as the executing code will have. This also helps in more complex ways, for example when the same code needs to be run at compile time and at runtime, and makes various dynamic compilation techniques possible in the future.

Emscripten's compilation has three main phases:

- The **intertyper**, which converts from LLVM assembly into Emscripten's internal representation.

- The **analyzer**, which inspects the internal representation and generates various useful information for the final phase, including type and variable information, stack usage analysis, optional data for optimizations (variable nativization and relooping), etc.

- The **jsifier**, which does the final conversion of the internal representation plus additional analyzed data into JavaScript.

3.1 The Runtime Environment

Code generated from Emscripten is meant to run in a JavaScript engine, typically in a web browser. This has implications for the kind of runtime environment we can generate for it, for example, there is no direct access to the local filesystem.

Emscripten comes with a partial implementation of a C library, mostly written from scratch in JavaScript, with parts compiled from an existing C library[11]. Some aspects of the runtime environment, as implemented in that C library, are:

- An emulated filesystem is available, with files stored in memory.

- Emscripten allows writing pixel data to an HTML5 canvas element, using a subset of the SDL API. That is, one can write an application in C or C++ using SDL, and that same application can be compiled normally and run locally, or compiled using Emscripten and run on the web. See, for example, Emscripten's raytracing demo at http://syntensity.com/static/raytrace.html.

- *sbrk()* is implemented using the *HEAP* array which was mentioned previously. This allows a normal *malloc()* implementation written in C to be compiled to JavaScript.

3.2 The Relooper: Recreating high-level loop structures

The Relooper the most complex module in Emscripten. It receives a 'soup of blocks', which is a set of labeled fragments of code, each ending with a branch operation, and the goal is to generate normal high-level JavaScript code flow structures such as loops and ifs. Generating such code structures is essential to producing good-performing code, since JavaScript engines are tuned to run such code very quickly (for example, a tracing JIT as in SpiderMonkey will only trace normal loops).

Returning to the LLVM assembly code on page 3, it has the following structure (where arrows denote potential paths of execution):

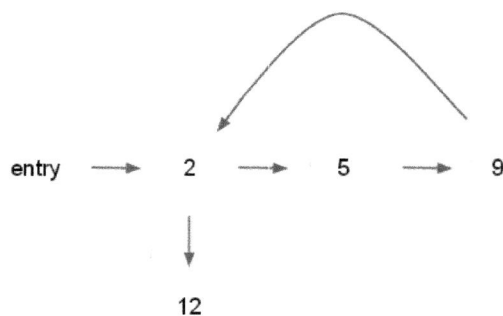

In this simple example, it is fairly straightforward to see that a natural way to implement it using normal loop structures is

---
[11] newlib, http://sourceware.org/newlib/

```
ENTRY
while (true) do
  2
  if (condition) break
  5
  9
12
```

In general though, this is not always easy or even practical – there may not be a straightforward high-level loop structure corresponding to the low-level one, if for example the original C code relied heavily on *goto* instructions. In practice, however, almost all real-world C and C++ code tends to be amenable to loop recreation.

We now begin to describe the Relooper algorithm. As mentioned before, it takes as input a 'soup of labeled LLVM blocks' as described above, and generates a structured set of Emscripten code blocks, which are each a set of LLVM blocks with some logical structure. For simplicity we call LLVM blocks 'labels' and Emscripten blocks 'blocks' in the following.

There are three types of Emscripten blocks:

- **Simple block**: A block with
  - One **Internal** label, and
  - a **Next** block, which the internal label branches to. The block is later translated simply into the code for that label, and the Next block appears right after it.

- **Loop**: A block that represents a basic loop, comprised of two internal sub-blocks:
  - **Inner**: A block that will appear inside the loop, i.e., when execution reaches the end of that block, flow will return to the beginning. Typically a loop will contain a conditional *break* defining where it is exited. When we exit, we reach the Next block, below.
  - **Next**: A block that will appear just outside the loop, in other words, that will be reached when the loop is exited.

- **Multiple**: A block that represents a divergence into several possible branches, that eventually rejoin. A Multiple block can implement an 'if', an 'if-else', a 'switch', etc. It is comprised of:
  - **Handled blocks**: A set of blocks to which execution can enter. When we reach the multiple block, we check which of them should execute, and go there. When execution of that block is complete, or if none of the handled blocks was selected for execution, we proceed to the Next block, below.
  - **Next**: A block that will appear just after the Handled blocks, in other words, that will be reached after code flow exits the Handled blocks.

To clarify these definitions, the example LLVM assembly code we have been working with could be represented in a natural way as

```
Simple
  entry
  Loop
    Simple
      2
      Simple
        5
        Simple
          9
          null
    Simple
      12
      null
```

where the first indented line in a Simple block is the Internal label in that Simple block, the second indented line is its Next block, and so forth.

Continuing to describe the Relooper algorithm, we will use the term 'entry' to mean a label that can be reached immediately in a block. In other words, a block consists of labels $l_1, .., l_n$, and the entries are a subset of those labels, specifically the ones that execution can directly reach when we reach that block. With that definition, the Relooper algorithm can then be written as follows:

- **Receive a set of labels and which of them are entry points.** We wish to create a block comprised of all those labels.

- **Calculate, for each label, which other labels it *can* reach**, i.e., which labels we are able to reach if we start at the current label and follow one of the possible paths of execution.

- **If we have a single entry, and cannot return to it (by some other label later on branching to it) then create a Simple block**, with the entry as its internal label, and the Next block comprised of all the other labels. The entries for the Next block are the entries to which the internal label can branch.

- **If we can return to all of the entries, create a Loop block**, whose Inner block is comprised of all labels that can reach one of the entries, and whose Next block is comprised of all the others. The entry labels for the current block become entry labels for the Inner block (note that they must be in the Inner block by definition, as each one can reach itself). The Next block's entry labels are all the labels in the Next block that can be reached by the Inner block.

- **If we have more than one entry, try to create a Multiple block**: For each entry, find all the labels it reaches that cannot be reached by any other entry. If at least one entry has such labels, return a Multiple block, whose Handled blocks are blocks for those labels (and whose entries are those labels), and whose Next block is all the rest. Entries for the next block are entries that did not become part of the Handled blocks, and also labels that can be reached from the Handled blocks.

- **If we could not create a Multiple block, then create a Loop block as described above** (see proof below of why creating a Loop block is possible, i.e., why the labels contain a loop).

Note that we first create a Loop only if we must, then try to create a Multiple, then create a Loop if we have no other choice. We could have slightly simplified this in various ways, but the algorithm as presented above has given overall better results in practice, in terms of the 'niceness' of the shape of the generated code, both subjectively and at least in some simple benchmarks.

Additional details of the algorithm include

- The technical mechanism by which execution flow is controlled in the generated code involves the _label_ variable, mentioned earlier. Whenever we enter a block with more than one entry, we set _label_ before we branch into it, and we check its value when we enter that block. So, for example, when we create a Loop block, its Next block can have multiple entries – any label to which we branch out from the loop. By creating a Multiple block after the loop, we can enter the proper label when the loop is exited. (Having a _label_ variable does add some overhead, but it greatly simplifies the problem that the Relooper needs to solve and allows us to only need three kinds of blocks as described above. Of course, it is possible to optimize away writes and reads to _label_ in many or even most cases.)

- As the Relooper processes labels, it replaces branch instructions accordingly. For example, when we create a Loop block, then all branch instructions to the outside of the loop are converted into *break* commands (since a break instruction in JavaScript will indeed get us to outside of the loop), and all branch instructions to the beginning of the loop are converted into *continue* commands, etc. Those commands are then ignored when called recursively to generate the Inner block (that is, the *break* and *continue* commands are guaranteed, by the semantics of JavaScript, to get us to where we need to go – they do not need any further work for them to work properly).

- Emscripten also does an additional pass after what has been described thus far, which was the first pass. The first pass is guaranteed to produce valid output (see below), while the second pass takes that valid output and optimizes it, by making minor changes such as removing *continue* commands that occur at the very end of loops (where they are not needed), etc.

We now turn to an analysis of the Relooper algorithm. It is straightforward to see that the output of the algorithm, assuming it completes successfully – that is, that if finishes in finite time, and does not run into an error in the last part (where it is claimed that if we reach it we can return to at least one of the entry labels) – is correct in the sense of code execution being carried out as in the original data. We will now prove that the algorithm must in fact complete successfully.

First, note that if we successfully create a block, then we simplify the remaining problem, where the 'complexity' of the problem for our purposes here is the sum of labels plus the sum of branching operations:

- This is trivial for Simple blocks (since we now have a Next block which is strictly smaller).

- It is true for Loop blocks simply by removing branching operations (there must be a branching back to an entry, which becomes a *continue*).

- For Multiple blocks, if the Next block is non-empty then we have split into strictly smaller blocks (in number of labels) than before. If the next block is empty, then since we built the Multiple block from a set of labels with more than one entry, then the Handled blocks are strictly smaller than the current one.

We have seen that whenever we successfully create a block, we simplify the remaining problem as defined above, which means that we must eventually halt successfully (since we strictly decrease a nonnegative integer). The remaining issue is whether we can reach a situation where we *cannot* successfully create a block, which is if we reach the final part of the relooper algorithm, but cannot create a Loop block there. For that to occur, we must not be able to return to any of the entries (or else we would create a Loop block). Assume that indeed we cannot return to any of the entries. But if that is so, we can create a Multiple block with Handled blocks that each include one of the entries (and possibly additional labels as well), since each entry label cannot be reached from any other label by our assumption earlier, thus contradicting that assumption and concluding the proof.

(We have not, of course, proven that the shape of the blocks is optimal in any sense. However, even if it is possible to optimize them further, the Relooper already gives a very substantial speedup due to the move from the switch-in-a-loop construction to more natural JavaScript code flow structures.)

4. Example Uses

Emscripten has been run successfully on several real-world codebases. We present some examples here to give an idea of the various opportunities made possible by Emscripten.

- **Python**: It is possible to run variants of Python on the web in various ways, including Pyjamas, IronPython on

SilverLight and Jython in Java. However, all of these are slightly nonstandard in the Python code they run, while the latter two also require plugins to be installed. With Emscripten, on the other hand, it is possible to compile CPython itself – the standard, reference implementation of Python – and run that on the web, which allows running standard Python code. An online demo is available at `http://syntensity.com/static/python.html`. (Another example of a language runtime that Emscripten can convert to run on the web is Lua; an online demo is available at `http://syntensity.com/static/lua.html`.)

- **Poppler and FreeType**: Poppler[12] is an open source PDF rendering library. In combination with FreeType[13], an open source font engine, it can be used to render PDF files. By compiling it with Emscripten, PDF files can be viewed on the web, without the use of plugins or external applications. An online demo is available at `http://syntensity.com/static/poppler.html`

- **Bullet**: The Bullet Physics library[14] is an open source physics engine, used in many open source and proprietary applications. An online demo is available at `http://syntensity.com/static/bullet.html`, showing a physics simulation of falling blocks that uses Bullet compiled to JavaScript. Bullet has in the past been ported to JavaScript[15], by porting JBullet (a port of Bullet to Java). The main difference in the approaches is that with Emscripten, there is no need for time-consuming manual conversion of C++ to Java and then to JavaScript, and consequently, the latest Bullet code can be run in JavaScript and not an earlier version (JBullet lags several versions behind the latest Bullet release).

5. Summary

We presented Emscripten, an LLVM-to-JavaScript compiler, which opens up numerous opportunities for running code written in languages other than JavaScript on the web, including some not previously possible. Emscripten can be used to, among other things, compile real-world C and C++ code and run that on the web. In addition, by compiling the runtimes of languages which are implemented in C and C++, we can run them on the web as well, for example Python and Lua.

Perhaps the largest future goal of Emscripten is to improve the performance of the generated code. As we have seen, speeds of around 1/10th that of GCC are possible, which is already good enough for many purposes, but can be improved much more. The code Emscripten generates will

become faster 'for free' as JavaScript engines get faster, and also by improvements in the optimizations done by LLVM and the Closure Compiler. However there is also a lot of room for additional optimizations in Emscripten itself, in particular in how it nativizes variables and structures, which can potentially lead to very significant speedups.

When we compile a language's entire runtime into JavaScript, as mentioned before, there is another way to improve performance. Assume that we are compiling a C or C++ runtime of a language into JavaScript, and that that runtime uses JIT compilation to generate machine code. Typically code generators for JITs are written for the main CPU architectures, today x86, x86_64 and ARM. However, it would be possible for a JIT to generate JavaScript instead. Thus, the runtime would be compiled using Emscripten, and at runtime it would pass the JIT-generated JavaScript to *eval*. In this scenario, JavaScript is used as a low-level intermediate representation in the runtime, and the final conversion to machine code is left to the underlying JavaScript engine. This approach can potentially allow languages that greatly benefit from a JIT (such as Java, Lua, etc.) to be run on the web efficiently.

Getting back to the issue of high-performing code in general, it is worth comparing Emscripten to Portable Native Client ([4], [10]), a project in development which aims to allow an LLVM-like format to be distributed and run securely on the web, with speed comparable to native code.

Both Emscripten and PNaCl aim to allow code written in languages like C and C++ to be run on the web, but in very different ways: Emscripten compiles code into JavaScript, and PNaCl compiles into an LLVM-like format which is then run in a special PNaCl runtime. As a consequence, Emscripten's generated code can run on all web browsers, since it is standard JavaScript, while PNaCl's generated code requires the PNaCl runtime to be installed; another major difference is that JavaScript engines do not yet run code at near-native speeds, while PNaCl does. In a broad summary, Emscripten's approach allows the code to be run in more places, while PNaCl's allows the code to run faster.

However, as mentioned earlier, improvements in JavaScript engines and compiler technology may narrow the speed gap. Also, when considering the speed of JavaScript engines, for purposes of Emscripten we do not need to care about *all* JavaScript, but only the kind generated by Emscripten. Such code is **implicitly statically typed**, that is, types are not mixed, despite JavaScript in general allowing assigning, e.g., an integer to a variable and later a floating point value or even an object to that same variable. Implicitly statically typed code can be statically analyzed and converted into machine code that has no runtime type checks at all. While such static analysis can be time-consuming, there are practical ways for achieving similar results quickly, such as tracing and type inference, which would help on such code very significantly, and are already in use or being worked on

---

[12] `http://poppler.freedesktop.org/`

[13] `http://www.freetype.org/`

[14] `http://bulletphysics.org/wordpress/`

[15] `http://pl4n3.blogspot.com/2010/07/bulletjs-javascript-physics-engine.html`

in mainstream JavaScript engines (e.g., SpiderMonkey). As a consequence, it may soon be possible to run code written in languages such as C and C++ on the web with near-native speed.

Acknowledgments

We thank the following people for their contributions to Emscripten: David LaPalomento, Daniel Heres, Brian Crowder, Brian McKenna, dglead and tuba.

References

[1] J. Ashkenas. List of languages that compile into JavaScript. Available at `https://github.com/jashkenas/coffee-script/wiki/List-of-languages-that-compile-to-JS`. Retrieved April 2011.

[2] C. Cifuentes, D. Simon and A. Fraboulet. Assembly to High-Level Language Translation. In Int. Conf. on Softw. Maint, pp. 228–237, IEEE-CS Press, 1998.

[3] E. Cooper, S. Lindley, P. Wadler and J. Yallop. Links: Web programming without tiers. In 5th International Symposium on Formal Methods for Components and Objects (FMCO), 2006.

[4] A. Donovan, R. Muth, B. Chen and D. Sehr. PNaCl: Portable Native Client Executables. Available at `http://nativeclient.googlecode.com/svn/data/site/pnacl.pdf`. Retrieved April 2011.

[5] D. Flanagan. JavaScript: The Definitive Guide. O'Reilly Media, 2006.

[6] F. Loitsch and M. Serrano. Hop Client-Side Compilation. In Trends in Functional Programming, vol. 8, pp. 141–158, Seton Hall University, Intellect Bristol, 2008.

[7] T. Petek and D. Syme. AFAX: Rich client/server web applications in F#. Draft. Available at `http://tomasp.net/academic/fswebtools.aspx`. Retrieved April 2011.

[8] C. Prabhakar. Google Web Toolkit: GWT Java Ajax Programming. Packt Publishing, 2007.

[9] T.A. Proebsting and S. A. Watterson. Krakatoa: Decompilation in Java (Does Bytecode Reveal Source?) In Third USENIX Conference on Object-Oriented Technologies and Systems (COOTS), 1997.

[10] B. Yee, D. Sehr, G. Dardyk, J. B. Chen, R. Muth, T. Ormandy, S. Okasaka, N. Narula, and N. Fullagar. Native Client: A Sandbox for Portable, Untrusted x86 Native Code. In IEEE Symposium on Security and Privacy, May 2009.

SPLASH and Onward! Workshop Chairs' Welcome

SPLASH and Onward! workshops are a great way to grow your knowledge and expand your professional network. They are highly interactive events that provide a creative and collaborative environment where attendees meet to discuss and solve challenging problems related to a variety of new emerging technologies and research areas.

Over the past two decades, the OOPSLA workshops provided an incubator for exploring many of the ideas that went on to shape general software practice (for example, design patterns, UML, aspect-oriented programming, and agile methods). That tradition continues this year both within the new charter for SPLASH established last year, and incorporating the visionary focus of Onward!

This year, SPLASH and Onward! offer twelve workshops that represent a diverse set of technology and research topics. Areas covered by the workshops include actors, agents, agile practices, cloud-based computing, decentralized control, embedded systems, evaluation and usability of programming languages and tools, foundations of object-oriented programming, free composition, legacy code, multicore programming, object-oriented and domain-specific modelling, programming languages and runtimes for internet clients, smartphone applications, and virtual machines. The summaries included in this companion provide an introduction to the goals and objectives of each workshop.

We welcome you to these workshops with the hope that the discussions are productive and fruitful, and assist in fostering new collaborations that extend beyond the borders of the conference!

The workshop proposals were reviewed and selected by the SPLASH Workshop Selection Committee, whose members we would like to thank for their collaboration:

- Dave Thomas *(Bedarra Research Labs, Canada)*
- Dirk Riehle *(University of Erlangen-Nuremberg, Germany)*
- Eric van Wyk *(University of Minnesota, USA)*
- Gary T. Leavens *(University of Central Florida, USA)*
- Jeff Gray *(University of Alabama, USA)*
- Jonathan Sprinkle *(University of Arizona, USA)*
- Joseph Yoder *(The Refactory, Inc., USA)*
- Paulo Borba *(Universidade Federal de Pernambuco, Brazil)*

Finally, we want to thank all workshop organizers and participants for their contributions. Thank you!

Ademar Aguiar
SPLASH Workshop co-Chair
Universidade do Porto, Portugal

Ulrik Pagh Schultz
SPLASH Workshop co-Chair
University of Southern Denmark

Pascal Costanza
Onward! Workshop Chair
ExaScience Lab, Intel Belgium

COOMP 2011: First International Workshop on Combined Object-Oriented Modeling and Programming

Ole Lehrmann Madsen

Alexandra Institute & Aarhus University,
Denmark
ole.l.madsen@cs.au.dk

Birger Møller-Pedersen

University of Oslo, Norway
birger@ifi.uio.no

Ragnhild Kobro Runde

University of Oslo, Norway
ragnhilk@ifi.uio.no

Abstract

Languages for modeling and programming are diverging, with the implication that developers that would like to model (in order to raise the abstraction level and become independent of implementation platforms) end up with the challenge of maintaining both model and program artifacts. In addition, modeling is hampered by poor tool support compared with programming tools. The trend in programming languages is that less attention is paid to the fact that programming should be a kind of modeling, while executable models will not cover what programs usually cover. The aim of this workshop is to investigate requirements for combined modeling and programming languages, by identifying candidate elements that should be supported by such languages, propose potential new combined language mechanisms, and by investigating implementation techniques for such languages.

Categories and Subject Descriptors   D.3.2 [*Object-oriented languages, Specialized application languages, Very high-level languages*]

General Terms   Languages

Keywords   Modeling, programming, Simula, UML

1. Introduction

Languages for modeling and programming are diverging, with the following implications:

- On one hand developers who would like to apply OO design to obtain a suitable model end up with the challenge of maintaining both model and program artifacts. And, since many modeling languages are at the same level of abstraction as programming languages, there is little benefit to using a separate modeling language.

- On the other hand we see that much OO code is written by developers with little appreciation of OO design and development disciplines [10], leading to complex code that is difficult to understand and maintain as the concepts and phenomena of the application domain are not properly reflected in the code.

It has not always been like this. The very first object-oriented programming language, SIMULA, was also considered (and used) as a modeling language. This was a great step forward compared to the dominating methodologies of that time where different languages were used for analysis, design and implementation.

Both modeling and programming have evolved since the days of SIMULA. *The aim of this workshop is to investigate requirements for combined modeling and programming languages as of today.*

This includes conceptual means as well as language constructs for modeling and programming, identification of modeling constructs that are currently not supported by programming languages, proposals for programming language support for such constructs, new abstraction mechanisms to raise the level of abstraction, graphical versus textual syntax, tools supporting modeling and programming, and implementation techniques.

There are many good reasons for combined modeling -and programming languages: Developers will not have to maintain both model and program artifacts; advanced language mechanisms (e.g. generics) that usually are developed for programming languages, become readily available for modeling; tools will require less effort (tools for executable models will have to compete with the best of tools for programming languages).

There a number of issues related to the design of such combined languages :

- *Graphical/textual syntax* While modeling languages are primarily graphical, and programming languages are primarily textual, an obvious requirement for such a new language is that it should have a mixture of graphical and textual syntax.

- *Constraints* While there are programming languages with support for e.g. both object-oriented and functional programming, constraints have so far not made it. An approach is described in [2].

- *Language mechanisms* Obviously some modeling mechanisms do not belong in such a language, or rather they are orthogonal to the (executable) elements of the language. Use Case models and Deployment models belong to this category. They apply to programming as well as to modeling, but with almost no implication on the semantics. Interaction Models (Sequence Diagrams), however, may not only be used to specify requirements, but also traces, and as such they can be used as the basis for the dynamic semantics of a combined language. State Machine models would belong to the language, one approach reported in [3]. However, they may to a large extent be provided through an implementation in a base language, but still should have special syntax. Some parts of Activity Models would also be part of such a language. Associations are obvious candidates, but despite some proposals ([4], [5]) they have not made it into programming languages.

SPLASH'11 Companion,   October 22–27, 2011, Portland, Oregon, USA.
ACM 978-1-4503-0940-0/11/10.

The goals of the workshop are to contribute to the resolution of these issues. We are therefore seeking contributions that e.g.

- Analyze current mainstream programming and modeling languages, identifying candidate elements that should be supported by such a unified approach and how they should be supported by language mechanisms. Similarly, the approach will have to identify and understand programming language mechanisms that do not apply for modeling – and the other way around. Low-level implementation mechanisms may not apply to modeling just as non-executable mechanisms cannot directly become part of a programming language.

- Propose the combination of modeling and programming language mechanisms, and even new language mechanisms that may come about as part of this combination.

- Device ways of implementing such languages, especially how to handle that some of the modeling mechanisms may be implemented as frameworks in an underlying language, but still should be provided by means of special syntax.

Note that we are looking for general purpose modeling –and programming languages, not Domain Specific Languages (DSLs). These have many of the desired properties, but they have these on the expense that they are domain specific. With the exception of embedded DSLs, they are modeling languages where models are executable, usually with a restricted repertoire of language mechanisms. We see DSLs as important in certain situations, so we would also like the general-purpose language to have mechanisms that support the embedding of DSLs, as e.g. demonstrated in [6].

2.   Tentative program

The program sketch so far is:

1. *Birger Møller-Pedersen, Ole Lehrmann Madsen*: Welcome and summery of keynote from Models 2010 [3]

2. *Dave Thomas* and *Thomas Weigert*: Positions from a programming and a modeling point of view (titles to be decided)

3. One or all of *James Noble, Andrew Black, Kim Bruce*: The role of modeling in Next Educational Language [11] (title to be decided)

4. *Klaus Ostermann*: Eliminating modeling from programming [9] (title to be decided)

In addition there will presentations and discussions on subjects such as:

1. Concurrency in relation to COOMP

2. Aspects in relation to COOMP

3. Constraints in relation to COOMP

3.   Organisation

Program Chairs

- *Ole Lehrmann Madsen*, Alexandra Institute & Aarhus University, Denmark

- *Birger Møller-Pedersen*, University of Oslo, Norway

- *Ragnhild Kobro Runde*, University of Oslo, Norway

Program Committee

- *Bjorn Freeman-Benson*, New Relic

- *Boris Magnusson*, Lund University

- *Mira Mezini*, Technical university Darmstadt

- *Oscar Nierstrasz*, University of Bern

- *Bran Selic*, Malina Software Corp

- *Dave Thomas*, Bedarra Research Labs

- *Antonio Vallecillo*, University of Málaga

- *Thomas Weigert*, University of Missouri-Rolla

- *Akinori Yonezawa*, University of Tokyo

Contact

For questions about the workshop, please contact one of the program chairs or send an email to `contact@coomp.org`.

References

1. OMG: Semantics of a Foundational Subset for Executable UML Models, 2009.

2. Freeman-Benson, B.N. and A. Borning: Integrating Constraints with an Object-Oriented Language, in ECOOP´92 - European Conference on Object-Oriented Programming, 1992.

3. Madsen, O.L.: Towards Integration of Object-Oriented Languages and State Machines, in Technology of Object-Oriented Languages and Systems (TOOLS Europe '99). 1999. Nancy.

4. Rumbaugh, J.: Relations as Semantic Constructs in an Object-Oriented Language, in OOPSLA'87 – Object-Oriented Programming, Systems Languages and Applications. 1987. Orlando, Florida, USA: ACM Press.

5. Østerbye: K. Associations as a Language Construct, in TOOLS'99. 1999. Nancy.

6. Hofer, C., et al.: Polymorphic Embedding of DSLs, in GPCE '08. 2008. Nashville, Tennessee.

7. Madsen, O.L., B. Møller-Pedersen, and K. Nygaard: Object-Oriented Programming in the BETA Programming Language, 1993: Addison Wesley.

8. Madsen, O.L. and B. Møller-Pedersen: A Unified Approach to Modeling and Programming, in MODELS 2010. 2010, Springer: Oslo.

9. Ostermann, Klaus, Paolo G. Giarrusso, Christian Kästner, Tillmann Rendel: Revisiting Information Hiding: Reflections on Classical and Nonclassical Modularity, in ECOOP´2011 - European Conference on Object-Oriented Programming, 2011.

10. Thomas, Dave: Programming with Models – Modeling with Code. The Role of Models in Software Development, Journal of Object Technology, 5(8):15-19, 2006.

11. Black, Andrew P., Kim B. Bruce James Noble: The Grace Programming Language, gracelang.org

The 11th Workshop on Domain-Specific Modeling

Juha-Pekka Tolvanen

MetaCase
Ylistonmaentie 31
FI-40500 Jyvaskyla, Finland

jpt@metacase.com

Jonathan Sprinkle

University of Arizona
ECE Department
1230 E. Speedway Blvd.
Tucson, AZ, USA

sprinkle@ECE.Arizona.Edu

Matti Rossi

Aalto University School of
Economics
Runeberginkatu 22-24
FI-00100 Helsinki, Finland

Matti.Rossi@aalto.fi

Jeff Gray

University of Alabama
Box 870290
Tuscaloosa, AL 35487
USA

gray@cs.ua.edu

Abstract

Domain-Specific Modeling (DSM) raises the level of abstraction beyond programming by specifying the solution directly using visual models to express domain concepts. In many cases, final products can be generated automatically from these high-level specifications. This automation is possible because both the language and generators fit the requirements of only one domain. This paper introduces DSM and describes the related 2-day workshop at SPLASH 2011 (23-24 October 2011, Portland, OR).

Categories and Subject Descriptors D 3.2 [**Languages**]: Specialized application languages, very high-level languages; D 2.2 [**Design Tools and Techniques**]: *Computer-aided software engineering* (CASE)

General Term Design, Languages

Keywords Modeling Languages; Metamodeling; Domain-Specific Languages; Code Generation

1. Introduction

The primary drawback of most software and systems modeling tools is that they are constrained to work with a fixed notation. That is, the tool vendor has defined a notation and environment that must be used in a prescribed way, regardless of the unique requirements of the user. Such inflexibility forces the user to adopt a language that may not be suitable in all cases for their distinct needs. Examples of such modeling tools include early flowchart tools, or more recent environments supporting object-oriented modeling. What is desired by most users is a customized modeling environment that has been tailored to contain the concepts needed in the user's problem domain.

Often, raising the level of abstraction can lead to a corresponding increase in productivity. In the past this has occurred when programming languages evolved towards a higher level of abstraction. Today, DSM languages provide a viable solution for continuing to raise the level of abstraction beyond coding, making development faster and easier.

Industrial experiences of DSM consistently show it to be several times faster than current practices, including current UML-based implementations of MDA. As Booch et al. [1] state, "the full value of MDA is only achieved when the modeling concepts map directly to domain concepts rather than computer technology concepts." Accordingly, in DSM the models are constructed using concepts that represent things in the problem domain, not concepts of a given programming language [8]. The

modeling language follows the domain abstractions and semantics, allowing developers to perceive themselves as working directly with domain concepts. The models represent simultaneously the design, implementation and documentation of the system. In a number of cases, the final products can be generated automatically from these high-level specifications with domain-specific code generators. This automation is possible because of domain-specificity: both the modeling language and code generators correspond to the requirements of a narrow domain, often in a single company.

This paper introduces DSM by describing a general framework for defining domain-specific modeling languages and code generators for a specific purpose. This is followed by describing the focus and topics of the 11th workshop on Domain-Specific Modeling [12].

2. Defining and using domain-specific languages

Three things are necessary to achieve full automatic code generation from domain modeling: firstly, a modeling tool supporting a domain-specific modeling language; secondly, a code generator; and lastly, a domain-specific framework. Figure 1 shows these three elements at two levels: the definition level and the use level.

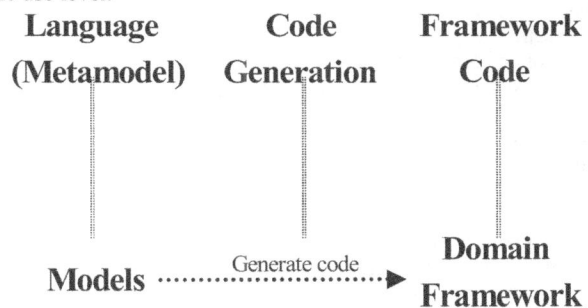

Figure 1. Framework for domain-specific modeling

The top-level (representing the definition) is made once by the organization for a given domain. This forms the start-up cost of the DSM approach [9]. Normally, one or two experts will define the modeling language (i.e., a metamodel) and related code generation, normally with a metamodeling tool [3, 6]. The metamodel is the implementation of the domain-specific modeling language, and includes the concepts and rules directly from the domain. The framework code will often have been made by developers in earlier projects in the domain, with some being added or modified specifically for the DSM creation project.

The bottom-level process represents the use of a domain-specific modeling language and code generator. This level is performed many times, once for each product, by normal developers. Development time can often be further reduced by reusing parts of the DSM model that are common to several products. The code generation and use of a domain framework or platform services require no effort by the developer. Together, these savings form the primary payback of the DSM approach.

This is unlike many visual modeling languages that are fixed to a specific notation that maps to semantically well-defined concepts of programming languages (like UML, SA/SD). With those languages, developers must leap straight from requirements into implementation concepts, and map back and forth between domain concepts, UML concepts, and program code. This requires significant time and resources, and can lead to errors.

In DSM, the specification models are built from instances of the domain concepts specified in accordance with the rules in the language metamodel. The code generator walks through the model and transforms the concept structures into code. In some cases the code will be fully self-contained; more often, significant parts of the code will be calls to reusable components and the domain framework. Because the code is generated, syntax and logic errors do not normally occur, and the resultant improvement in quality forms a significant secondary payback of the DSM approach [2].

3. Workshop focus and topics

DSM has been successfully applied in many different domains [9], including automotive manufacturing [7], digital signal processing [10], mobile devices [2], telecommunication [4, 11], finance [4], and electrical utilities [4]. However, more investigation is still needed in order to advance the acceptance and viability of domain-specific modeling.

There are general characteristics about these domains that suggest scenarios when DSM would be useful. Each of these examples represents a type of configuration problem with numerous choices (e.g., multiple "knobs" are available for tuning a system). Furthermore, each of these examples is based upon an underlying execution platform that may often change. The accidental complexities associated with evolving source code in the presence of platform adaptation are very hard to accomplish using ad hoc techniques based on low-level manual coding. This makes a system brittle because of the tight coupling to the execution platform. Moreover, these systems are constantly evolving by virtue of changes in the hardware and software platform, and due to changes in requirements. Therefore, there is a need to incorporate several degrees of concern separation through higher levels of system representation.

The goals of the workshop are to collect and exchange experiences related to building and using DSM; continue building and extending the DSM community; and address in focus groups the issues raised in the presented papers and at previous workshops. The workshop examines DSM in different ways, including:

- Full papers describing ideas at either a practical or theoretical level

- Experience reports on applying DSM

- Position papers describing work in progress or an author's position regarding current DSM practice

- DSM demonstrations describing a particular language, generator or tool for a particular domain

The presentations of papers and demonstrations form the basis for discussion in the group work sessions. The results of the group work sessions, along with presentation slides, will be made available on the workshop website [12] together with the papers.

The topics addressed in the workshop include:

- Industry/academic experience reports describing success/failure in implementing and using DSM languages/tools

- Approaches to identify constructs for DSM languages

- Novel features in language workbenches/DSM tools

- Approaches to implement metamodel-based modeling languages

- Metamodeling frameworks and languages

- Modularization technologies for DSM languages and models

- Novel approaches for code generation from domain-specific models

- Issues of support/maintenance for systems built with DSM

- Evolution of languages along with their domain

- Organizational and process issues in DSM adoption and use

- Demonstrations of working, or in-progress, DSM solutions (languages, generators, frameworks, tools)

- Identification of domains where DSM can be most productive in the future (e.g. embedded systems, product families, systems with multiple implementation platforms)

References

[1] Booch, G., Brown, A., Iyengar, S., Rumbaugh, J., and Selic, B., *MDA Journal*, May 2004.

[2] Gray, J., Tolvanen, J.-P., Kelly, S. Gokhale, A., Neema, S., and Sprinkle, J,, "Domain-Specific Modeling," *CRC Handbook on Dynamic System Modeling*, (Paul Fishwick, ed.), CRC Press, 2007.

[3] Kelly, S., Rossi, M., and Tolvanen, J.-P., What is Needed in a MetaCASE Environment?, *Journal of Enterprise Modelling and Information Systems Architectures*, Vol 1., 1, 2005

[4] Kelly, S., and Tolvanen, J-P, *Domain-Specific Modeling*, Wiley, 2008.

[5] Kieburtz, R., McKinney, L., Bell, J., Hook, J., Kotov, A., Lewis, J., Oliva, D., Sheard, T., Smith, I., and Walton, L., A Software Engineering Experiment in Software Component Generation, *Proceedings of 18th International Conference on Software Engineering*, Berlin, IEEE Computer Society Press, March, 1996.

[6] Lédeczi, A., Bakay, A., Maroti, M., Völgyesi, P., Nordstrom, G., Sprinkle, J., and Karsai, G., Composing Domain-Specific Design Environments, *IEEE Computer*, November 2001.

[7] Long, E., Misra, A., and Sztipanovits, J., Increasing Productivity at Saturn, *IEEE Computer*, August 1998, pp. 35-43.

[8] Pohjonen, R., and Kelly, S., Domain-Specific Modeling, *Dr. Dobbs Journal*, August 2002.

[9] Sprinkle, J., Mernik, M., Tolvanen, J-P., and Spinellis, D., What Kinds of Nails Need a Domain-Specific Hammer?, *IEEE Software*, July/Aug, 2009, pp. 15-18.

[10] Sztipanovits, J., Karsai, G., and Bapty, T., Self-Adaptive Software for Signal Processing, *Communications of the ACM*, May 1998, pp. 66-73.

[11] Weiss, D., and Lai, C. T. R., *Software Product-line Engineering*, Addison Wesley Longman, 1999.

[12] Workshop on Domain-Specific Modeling (DSM'11), http://www.dsmforum.org/events/DSM11

2011 International Workshop on Foundations of Object-Oriented Languages (FOOL'11)

SPLASH/OOPSLA'11 Workshop Summary

Jonathan Aldrich
Carnegie Mellon University
jonathan.aldrich@cs.cmu.edu

Jeremy Siek
University of Colorado at Boulder
jeremy.siek@colorado.edu

Elena Zucca
University of Genova
zucca@disi.unige.it

Abstract

The search for sound principles for object-oriented languages has given rise to considerable research during the last few decades, leading to a better understanding of the key concepts of object-oriented languages and to important developments in type theory, semantics, program verification, and program development. The purpose of this workshop is to provide a forum for discussing new ideas in the foundations of object-oriented languages and provide feedback to authors. Submissions to this workshop were invited in the general area of foundations of object-oriented languages, object-oriented languages, including integration with other paradigms and extensions, such as aspects, components, meta-programming.

Categories and Subject Descriptors D.3.1 [*Programming Languages*]: Formal Definitions and Theory

General Terms Languages, Security, Theory, Verification

Keywords foundations, object-orientation, programming languages, type theory, semantics, analysis, verification, concurrency, distributed systems, databases, security

1. Main Theme and Goals

The theme of the workshop is the general area of foundations of object-oriented languages, including integration with other paradigms and extensions, such as aspects, components, meta-programming. Topics of interest include language semantics, type systems, program analysis and verification, formal calculi, concurrent and distributed languages, databases, software adaptation, and language-based security issues. Papers are welcome to include formal descriptions and proofs, but these are not required; the key consideration is that papers should present novel and valuable ideas relating to foundations for object-oriented languages. The main focus in selecting workshop contributions will be the intrinsic interest and timeliness of the work, so authors are encouraged to submit polished descriptions of work in progress as well as papers describing completed projects. In addition to the sharing of research ideas, another goal of the workshop is to provide feedback to the authors, helping them prepare their papers for submission to top-tier conferences.

2. Papers and Activities

FOOL is a 1-day workshop that includes presentations of accepted papers as well as invited speakers and other technical sessions.

FOOL does not have formal proceedings, to enable authors to present preliminary work that they wish to later publish formally in a conference venue. Papers are peer-reviewed by the program committee above, however, and are posted online at the FOOL workshop site as an informal record of the workshop. Many past FOOL papers have had significant influence on object-oriented programming language research and revised versions appear in prominent conferences and journals. The home page of FOOL is at

    http://www.cs.cmu.edu/~aldrich/FOOL/,

and the web page for FOOL'11 is at

    http://www.disi.unige.it/person/ZuccaE/FOOL2011/

3. Location at SPLASH/OOPSLA

After many editions held in conjunction with POPL, last year the steering committee felt that the the object-oriented research community that is centered on OOPSLA and SPLASH would also provide a strong positive research community. Furthermore, FOOL fills a need for a foundational language workshop at SPLASH. Hence, this year for the second time SPLASH hosts FOOL, and we look forward to improved synergies between these communities.

4. Organization

FOOL is guided by a steering committee as follows:

- Jonathan Aldrich (Chair, Carnegie Mellon University)
- Viviana Bono (Universitá di Torino)
- Atsushi Igarashi (Kyoto University)
- James Noble (University of Wellington)
- John Reppy (University of Chicago)
- Jeremy Siek (University of Colorado)

The program committee this year is as follows:

- Elena Zucca (Chair, Universitá di Genova, Italy)
- Wei Ngan Chin (University of Singapore, Singapore)
- Ferruccio Damiani (University of Torino, Italy)
- Werner M. Dietl (University of Washington, USA)
- Dino Distefano (Queen Mary University of London and Monoidics Ltd, UK)
- Sophia Drossopoulou (Imperial College London, UK)
- Erik Ernst (Aarhus University, Denmark)
- Atsushi Igarashi (Kyoto University, Japan)
- Donna Malayeri (EPFL, Switzerland)
- Jan Smans (Katholieke Universiteit Leuven, Belgium)

Workshop: Beyond Green-Field Software Development: Reuse, Recycle, Refactor

Dennis Mancl

Alcatel-Lucent
Murray Hill, NJ, USA
dennis.mancl@alcatel-lucent.com

Steven D. Fraser

Cisco Systems
San Jose, CA, USA
sdfraser@acm.org

Bill Opdyke

JP Morgan Chase
Chicago, IL, USA
opdyke@acm.org

Abstract

There are many languages, tools, and design methodologies in the software community that are aimed at the creation of new software. But a lot of valuable software is the product of evolution, reuse, and reengineering. Some software is too expensive to "throw away and start over." A skilled software team will have an arsenal of techniques at their disposal for adapting, evolving, and refactoring existing code and designs. Adapting legacy software is a kind of recycling. If extending a legacy system is done well, it can help deliver business value sooner at a lower cost.

This workshop will explore some old and new techniques for building on existing code – wrapper classes, design patterns, test-driven approaches, refactoring tools, and others. The workshop will also address management issues: what factors to consider in the decision to reengineer or to build anew. This workshop revisits a topic discussed in an OOPSLA 2003 workshop.

Categories and Subject Descriptors D.2.7 [**Software Engineering**]: Distribution, Maintenance, and Enhancement.

General Terms   Management, Design.

Keywords   legacy code; refactoring; reengineering

1.   Reuse and legacy code

Legacy code can be an asset in the software business, but it can also create a considerable amount of extra work. Most software is not a product of "green field" development: many development efforts must reuse code and interfaces from pre-existing systems. Change and growth in require-ments and functionality occur in every system – and it is especially critical to manage the evolution process in modern agile software processes. The management of change and growth may in fact become a daily activity, so a well-defined set of techniques and tools for doing *reengineering* and *refactoring* are critical to success.

Leveraging existing software assets are even more important in today's web-centric and cloud-based environment. It is easier and faster to build new "apps" by building adapters and wrappers for legacy systems and components.

Successful projects that use legacy code must pay attention to people, processes, and tools. The goal of this workshop is to identify the issues facing individuals, teams, and companies that need to build on their legacy base. We are exploring these subjects:

- The techniques for wrapping and refactoring: software evolution techniques used to add new functionality to existing software systems – and which of the techniques are best for small systems, large systems, embedded systems, and open source software.
- The technical and organizational skills that are needed in a team that is constantly working with legacy systems and legacy modules.
- How to manage a software system that demands constant change and growth.
- Assessing the business value of refactoring and reengineering efforts.
- Impact of architecture on software reuse and evolution.
- How agile development practices affect the creation of long-lived software modules and components.
- How to measure the quality of reused, reengineered, and refactored code.
- When to abandon a legacy software reengineering effort.
- Exploration of some of the good "design for reuse" practices.

This workshop discusses some of the same topics as our OOPSLA 2003 workshop, and addresses some of the changes in the software industry in the past eight years:

- More tools-based support for code analysis, refactoring, and unit testing.
- More agile and iterative development in small teams, with less reliance on written design documents.
- More interest in "green technologies" and techniques for increasing reuse and improving efficiency.
- Increased use of refactoring and reengineering to help support moving software functionality to new environments: web apps, smart phones, cloud services.

2. Organizers

- Dennis Mancl, Alcatel-Lucent, Murray Hill, NJ 07974, USA
- Steven D. Fraser, Cisco Research, San Jose, CA, USA
- Bill Opdyke, JP Morgan Chase, Chicago, IL, USA

3. Post-workshop Poster

A post-workshop poster summarizing the most significant ideas shared and questions generated during the session is posted on the workshop website:

http://mysite.verizon.net/dennis.mancl/splash11/index.html

Workshop on Transitioning to MultiCore (TMC 2011)

Caitlin Sadowski   Jaeheon Yi

University of California at Santa Cruz

{supertri, jaeheon}@cs.ucsc.edu

Abstract

Multicore programming is both prevalent and difficult. Industry programmers deal with large amounts of legacy code and are increasingly relying on multithreading to provide scalability. For legacy systems, it may not be possible to change this programming model. The Transitioning to MultiCore (TMC) workshop is focused on tools and systems for parallel programming that are interoperable with legacy code, that minimize the annotation burden for developers, and match well with current industry practice. We solicit industry experience reports about working or unworkable examples of such tools or systems, as well as research reports.

Categories and Subject Descriptors   D.1.3 [*Programming Techniques*]: Concurrent Programming–*Parallel Programming*; D.2.2 [*Software Engineering*]: Design Tools and Techniques

General Terms   Design, Reliability, Human Factors

Keywords   Tools, Systems, Usability, Legacy Programs

1.   Background

In the early 2000s, we hit a power wall; the energy output of a chip with increased processor speed has become untenable [1]. Today, all major chip manufacturers have switched to producing computers that contain more than one CPU [12]; parallel programming has rapidly moved from a special-purpose technique to standard practice in writing scalable programs. Taking advantage of parallel processors often entails using concurrent software, where multiple threads work simultaneously. However, concurrent software suffers from concurrency-specific errors, such as data races, atomicity violations, determinism violations, and deadlocks [4, 8, 9]. Achieving parallel performance is also difficult. In fact, in previous studies which compared parallel programming models or techniques a large subset of the participants in different groups did not successfully complete a correct solution that exhibited *any* speedup (e.g. [5, 10]). Furthermore, a large survey on current development practices found that a large portion of developers have to regularly deal with multithreaded code [6].

2.   Main Theme and Goals

It is clear from the above discussion that multicore programming is both prevalent and difficult. To address that difficulty, numerous programming models and systems have been proposed, including transactional memory [7, 11], revisions [3], and type systems [2]. However, industry programmers face large amounts of legacy code, and so it may not always be feasible to change the programming model.

The TMC workshop is focused on tools and systems for parallel programming that are interoperable with legacy code, that minimize the annotation burden for developers, and match well with current industry practice. We solicit industry experience reports about working or unworkable examples of such tools or systems, as well as research reports. The topics for these reports may include:

- Surveys or empirical studies focused at measuring the current state of practice for multicore programming in industry

- Field studies identifying barriers and benefits to using existing tools

- Analysis tools focused on correctness, performance, or understandability analysis of existing programs

- New programming models which are interoperable with legacy multithreaded systems

We aim to bring together industry developers and researchers who are interested in improving the current transition to multicore.

3.   Participant Preparation

We accept shorter, two to four page *experience reports* focused on experiences with scalable systems used in industry, or problems with existing systems. We also accept longer, four to six page *research reports* focused on development of new systems, tools, or ideas in the multicore space. Additionally, we accept two page *position papers* focused on proposals for improving existing systems or tools. Although this is a small new workshop, we care about reviewers returning high-quality paper reviews and have picked our program committee accordingly.

4. Activities and Format

We plan to spend the morning on paper presentations. Each presentation slot will be approximately 10-15 minutes long, followed by a five minute question period.

We plan to start the afternoon with a panel presentation, moderated by the workshop organizers, comprising a mix of industry and academic panelists who can describe some of the challenges experienced with transitioning to multicore. The goal of this panel will be to highlight issues that may not be obvious within the research community.

Afterwards, we will facilitate a group discussion about what workshop participants feel are the largest issues raised in the workshop, and any issues they feel are not adequately addressed by current research literature. First we will break into focus groups (containing approximately 4-5 people per group) for about 30-45 minutes. These groups sessions will serve as a networking event so that participants will ideally make some new connections at the workshop. We aim to have at least one industry representative in each group. Each group will come together with 2-3 specific points for future or ongoing research which we will collate on the projected screen.

5. Organizers

Caitlin Sadowski (University of California at Santa Cruz)

Jaeheon Yi (University of California at Santa Cruz)

6. Program Committee

Michael Bond (Ohio State University)

Rachel Brill (IBM Haifa Research Lab)

Sebastian Burckhardt (Microsoft Research)

Joe Devietti (University of Washington)

Eitan Farchi (IBM Haifa Research Lab)

Benedict Gaster (AMD)

Ganesh Gopalakrishnan (University of Utah)

Shan Lu (University of Wisconsin - Madison)

Shankar Pasupathy (NetApp)

Neha Rungta (NASA Ames Research Center)

Koushik Sen (University of California, Berkeley)

Konstantin Serebryany (Google)

Stephen Toub (Microsoft, Parallel Computing Platform)

References

[1] K. Asanovic, R. Bodik, J. Demmel, T. Keaveny, K. Keutzer, J. Kubiatowicz, N. Morgan, D. Patterson, K. Sen, J. Wawrzynek, D. Wessel, and K. Yelick. A view of the parallel computing landscape. *Communications of the ACM*, 52(10):56–67, 2009.

[2] R. L. Bocchino, Jr., V. S. Adve, D. Dig, S. Adve, S. Heumann, R. Komuravelli, J. Overbey, P. Simmons, H. Sung, and M. Vakilian. A type and effect system for Deterministic Parallel Java. Technical Report UIUCDCS-R-2009-3032, Department of Computer Science, University of Illinois at Urbana-Champaign, 2009.

[3] S. Burckhardt, A. Baldassion, and D. Leijen. Concurrent programming with revisions and isolation types. In *Symposium on Object-Oriented Programming Systems, Languages, and Applications (OOPSLA)*, 2010.

[4] S. Choi and E. Lewis. A study of common pitfalls in simple multi-threaded programs. *ACM SIGCSE Bulletin*, 32(1):329, 2000.

[5] K. Ebcioglu, V. Sarkar, T. El-Ghazawi, J. Urbanic, and P. Center. An experiment in measuring the productivity of three parallel programming languages. In *Workshop on Productivity and Performance in High-End Computing (P-PHEC)*, 2006.

[6] P. Godefroid and N. Nagappan. Concurrency at Microsoft: An exploratory survey. In *Workshop on Exploiting Concurrency Efficiently and Correctly*, 2008.

[7] J. R. Larus and R. Rajwar. *Transactional Memory*. Synthesis Lectures on Computer Architecture. Morgan & Claypool Publishers, 2006.

[8] E. A. Lee. The problem with threads. *Computer*, 39(5):33–42, 2006.

[9] S. Lu, S. Park, E. Seo, and Y. Zhou. Learning from mistakes: a comprehensive study on real world concurrency bug characteristics. *SIGPLAN Notices*, 43(3):329–339, 2008.

[10] M. Luff. Empirically investigating parallel programming paradigms: A null result. In *Workshop on Evaluation and Usability of Programming Languages and Tools (PLATEAU)*, 2009.

[11] C. Rossbach, O. Hofmann, and E. Witchel. Is transactional programming actually easier? In *Symposium on Principles and Practice of Parallel Programming (PPoPP)*, 2010.

[12] H. Sutter. The free lunch is over: A fundamental turn toward concurrency in software. *Dr. Dobbs Journal*, 30(3):16–20, 2005.

AGERE! (Actors and aGEnts REloaded)

SPLASH 2011 Workshop on Programming Systems, Languages and Applications based on Actors, Agents, and Decentralized Control

Gul Agha

University of Illinois at
Urbana-Champaign, USA
agha@cs.uiuc.edu

Rafael H. Bordini

Institute of Informatics, Federal
University of Rio Grande do Sul, Brazil
R.Bordini@inf.ufrgs.br

Alessandro Ricci

University of Bologna, Italy
a.ricci@unibo.it

Abstract

The fundamental turn of software into concurrency and distribution is not only a matter of performance, but also of appropriate design and abstraction. This calls for programming paradigms that would allow developers to think, design, develop, execute, debug, and profile programs exhibiting different degrees of concurrency, reactiveness, autonomy, decentralization of control, and distribution in ways that are more natural than that supported the current paradigms. This workshop aims at exploring programming approaches explicitly providing a level of abstraction that promotes a *decentralized mindset* in solving problems and programming systems exhibiting such features. To this end, the abstractions of *actors* and *agents* (and systems of actors / systems of agents) are taken as a natural reference: the objective of the workshop is then to foster the research in all aspects of *actor-oriented programming* and *agent-oriented programming* and other *decentralized approaches* as evolution of mainstream paradigms (such as OOP), including the theory and the practice of design and programming, bringing together researchers working on the models, languages, and technologies, as well as practitioners developing real-world systems and applications.

Categories and Subject Descriptors D.1 [*Programming Techniques*]; D.2 [*Programming Languages*]; D.3 [*Software Engineering*]; I.2.5 [*Artificial Intelligence*]: Programming Languages and Software; I.2.11 [*Artificial Intelligence*]: Distributed Artificial Intelligence

Keywords agent-oriented programming, actor-oriented programming

1. Main Theme and Goals

The fundamental turn of software into concurrency, interactivity, distribution is not only a matter of performance, but also design and abstraction [19]. "The free lunch is over" calls for the devising of new programming paradigms — whether they are evolutions of existing ones or not — that would allow programmers to naturally think, design, develop, execute, debug and profile programs exhibiting different degrees of concurrency, reactiveness, autonomy, decentralization of control, distribution. Almost any application to-day includes the need of programming software components that actively — pro-actively and re-actively — do concurrently some jobs, react to various kind of events, communicate with each other by means of some interaction model. How to properly program such entities and systems of entities, what kinds of programming abstractions can help in systematically structuring complex reactive and proactive behavior, what kinds of programming abstractions can be effective in organizing applications as ensembles of relatively autonomous entities working together, and many other related issues are important open research questions.

The focus of this workshop is to investigate the definition of suitable levels of abstraction, programming languages, and platforms to support and promote a *decentralized mindset* [15] in solving problems, designing systems, programming applications, including the teaching of computer programming. That is, the question is how to think about problems and programs taking decentralization of control and interaction as the most essential features. To this end, we start from *agents* (and multi-agent systems) and *actors*, which can be recognized as two main broad families of concepts, abstractions and programming tools described in literature that explicitly promote such a decentralized thinking — even if assuming different facets depending on the context in which they are discussed, being it concurrent programming or distributed artificial intelligence. Accordingly, in this workshop we aim at promoting the discussion about agent-oriented and actor-oriented programming languages (models, theories, applications, systems), so as to explore agents and actors as a general-purpose computing paradigm explicitly supporting a decentralized mindset in solving problems and computer programming. Although we start from these two well known approaches, the workshop aims to promote discussion of any other approaches that also propose to contribute to the essential aspects of autonomous behavior and decentralized control. Any stage of software development is interesting for the workshop, including requirements, modeling, prototyping, design, implementation, testing, and any other means of producing running software based on actors and agents as first-class abstractions.

Overall, the workshop aims at fostering the development of the research in agent and actor oriented programming in the same vein that OOPSLA did for OOP at the beginning of the 80's. We hope to promote the investigation of all the features that would make agent-oriented or actor-oriented programming languages effective tools for developing software systems, as an evolution of the OO paradigm. Including aspects that concern both the *theory* and the *practice* of design and programming using such paradigms, so as to bring together researchers working on the models, languages, and technologies, and practitioners using such technologies to develop real-world systems and applications.

This overall perspective — which is oriented to impact on mainstream programming paradigms and software development — is

SPLASH'11 Companion, October 22–27, 2011, Portland, Oregon, USA.
ACM 978-1-4503-0940-0/11/10.

what distinguishes this event from related venues about agents and actors, organized in different contexts. Nevertheless, the event aims at being a good forum for collecting, discussing, and confronting related research that typically appears in different communities in the context of (distributed) artificial intelligence, distributed computing, computer programming and software engineering. Examples include: research on agent oriented programming and multi-agent programming [5, 6], either rooted in distributed artificial intelligence [7, 9, 12, 18] or computer programming contexts [14, 16, 17, 20]; research on actor-oriented programming [1, 11], including well-known programming languages/systems providing directly or indirectly support for actor oriented programming: examples are Erlang [4], Scala [10], Axum [21]; research on concurrent object-oriented programming [2, 3, 8], and on the extension of OO programming languages towards actor or agent-like levels of abstraction; research on new programming paradigms and reinvention of programming [13].

References

[1] G. Agha. *Actors: a model of concurrent computation in distributed systems.* MIT Press, Cambridge, MA, USA, 1986.

[2] G. Agha. Concurrent object-oriented programming. *Commun. ACM*, 33:125–141, September 1990.

[3] G. Agha, P. Wegner, and A. Yonezawa, editors. *Research directions in concurrent object-oriented programming.* MIT Press, Cambridge, MA, USA, 1993.

[4] J. Armstrong. Erlang. *Commun. ACM*, 53(9):68–75, 2010.

[5] R. Bordini, M. Dastani, J. Dix, and A. El Fallah Seghrouchni, editors. *Multi-Agent Programming Languages, Platforms and Applications - Vol. 1.* Springer, 2005.

[6] R. Bordini, M. Dastani, J. Dix, and A. El Fallah Seghrouchni, editors. *Multi-Agent Programming Languages, Platforms and Applications - Vol. 2.* Springer, 2009.

[7] R. Bordini, J. Hübner, and M. Wooldridge. *Programming Multi-Agent Systems in AgentSpeak Using Jason.* John Wiley & Sons, Ltd, 2007.

[8] J.-P. Briot, R. Guerraoui, and K.-P. Lohr. Concurrency and distribution in object-oriented programming. *ACM Comput. Surv.*, 30(3):291–329, 1998.

[9] M. Dastani. 2apl: a practical agent programming language. *Autonomous Agents and Multi-Agent Systems*, 16(3):214–248, 2008.

[10] P. Haller and M. Odersky. Scala actors: Unifying thread-based and event-based programming. *Theoretical Computer Science*, 2008.

[11] C. Hewitt. Viewing control structures as patterns of passing messages. *Artif. Intell.*, 8(3):323–364, 1977.

[12] K. V. Hindriks. Programming rational agents in GOAL. In Bordini et al. [6], pages 3–37.

[13] A. Kay. Programming and programming languages, 2010. VPRI Research Note RN-2010-001.

[14] J. J. Odell. Objects and agents compared. *Journal of Object Technology*, 1(1):41–53, 2002.

[15] M. Resnick. *Turtles, Termites and Traffic Jams. Explorations in Massively Parallel Microworlds.* MIT Press, 1994.

[16] A. Ricci and A. Santi. Agent-oriented computing: Agents as a paradigm for computer programming and software development. In *Proc. of the 3rd Int. Conf. on Future Computational Technologies and Applications – Future Computing 2011*, Rome, Italy, 2011. IARIA.

[17] A. Ricci, M. Viroli, and G. Piancastelli. simpA: An agent-oriented approach for programming concurrent applications on top of java. *Science of Computer Programming*, 76(1):37 – 62, 2011.

[18] Y. Shoham. Agent-oriented programming. *Artificial Intelligence*, 60(1):51–92, 1993.

[19] H. Sutter and J. Larus. Software and the concurrency revolution. *ACM Queue: Tomorrow's Computing Today*, 3(7):54–62, Sept. 2005.

[20] M. D. Travers. *Programming with Agents: New metaphors for thinking about computation.* Massachusetts Institute of Technology, 1996. PhD Thesis.

[21] Axum project, 2011. http://msdn.microsoft.com/en-us/devlabs/dd795202.

Agile and Object Oriented Practices in Embedded Systems

Charles E. Matthews
Fifth Generation Systems, Ltd.
Markham, Ontario, Canada
charles.matthews@acm.org

Bruce Powel Douglass
IBM Rational
Fairfax, VA, USA
Bruce.Douglass@us.ibm.com

Jim Kiekbusch
OMNI Engineering Systems, Inc.
Winona, MN, USA
jkiekbusch@omnimn.com

Abstract

Embedded systems are the most prevalent of all computer systems in the world. More than 99% of all computer/microcontroller products that are sold each year are single purpose embedded systems rather than workstations, desktops, laptops, or server systems. This workshop will gather embedded systems programmers and engineers to discuss how Agile and object oriented practices affect the design and implementation of embedded systems. We will explore how/whether a product design is affected when an embedded system implements functionality that is inherently object oriented in nature. We will explore how constraints that are unique to embedded systems affect the adoption of Agile and objected oriented processes and practices. The primary goal for this workshop is to provide feedback to the embedded systems community on which practices are judged as useful and which are not.

ACM Classification: D. Software; D.1 Programming Technique; D.1.5 Object-oriented Programming

General Terms: Design

Overview

The objective for this workshop is to review the principles of Agile and object oriented (OO) practices as they affect the design of embedded systems. We will explore the availability of modules, components, and tools that engineers use to build products. When an embedded system implements functionality that has characteristics of an inherently object oriented nature, e.g. ZigBee profiles/clusters or SNMP functionality, how is the product design affected? How well do tools like Rhapsody, which transforms UML diagrams to executable code for embedded systems, work in the real world? To what extent are engineers using OO principles when they use hardware description languages like VHDL or Verilog to design custom hardware?

This workshop will gather embedded systems programmers and engineers to discuss how Agile and object oriented practices affect the design and implementation of embedded systems. Because other forums exist for teaching the principles of Agile and object-oriented practices, we are more interested in sharing field experience from actual practitioners than in teaching these principles. Just as the purpose for a project post-mortem review is to provide feedback for an organization to improve its development processes, this workshop will provide feedback to the embedded systems community regarding which principles are useful and which are not.

Embedded systems are the most prevalent of all computer systems in the world. According to **EETimes**, more than 99% of all computer/microcontroller products that are sold each year are single purpose embedded systems rather than workstations, desktops, laptops, or server systems. Therefore, any productivity increase in the embedded systems community has the potential to result in a significantly higher cost savings to the computing industry as a whole than a similar increase in the traditional desktop computing field. Although the historical view of an embedded system is one of a real time operating system running on a minimal function hardware platform, current systems are quite complex and are often built with common off the shelf hardware and software components.

For this workshop, the definition of an embedded system is expanded beyond its historical hardware constraint to include any system that is intended to be used as a single purpose machine. Under this definition, systems that are built on Windows or Linux OS platforms are considered to be embedded systems as long as the deployed product is intended to be used for a single purpose.

We will explore the development of processes that engineers use to build products. What problems occur when designing with OO principles but implementing with non-OO languages? How do real-time constraints like interrupt handling affect an OO design? To what extent are common OO techniques used in the embedded system environment - data abstraction, encapsulation, messaging, modularity, polymorphism, and inheritance? We will identify those characteristics that are unique to embedded systems that affect the adoption of OO and Agile processes.

Historically, most SPLASH attendees come from "Big Iron" projects. Within this community, Agile and OO processes are well documented. However, the embedded systems community has not seen a large base of advocates for these practices. Based upon the interest in Agile and OO principles at conference that target the embedded systems market, the practice of these methodologies is increasing. This workshop provides a forum for engineers and programmers to discuss issues that are specific to the embedded systems community.

Each workshop participant will submit a 1-2 page position paper that describes their use of OO practices in their daily work. Please send this paper in PDF format to charles.matthews@acm.org. We are most interested in identifying reasons why specific practices work well or don't work well rather than simple reports of what techniques the participants are using. The primary goal for this workshop is to provide feedback to the embedded systems community on which practices are judged as useful and which are not. Sharing this feedback is an essential step for individual companies to determine how they can improve their development process.

Workshop Agenda
8:30 - 10:30 -- short presentations of the participants' position paper
10:30 - 11:30 -- focus session: identify characteristics that distinguish embedded systems development from enterprise level software systems; prioritize and select the primary factors that influence OO and Agile practices in embedded systems
11:30 - 4:00 -- perform at least three working sessions that explore in detail a system characteristic that was identified in the focus session
4:00 - 5:00 -- wrap up: creation of a poster for the SPLASH poster session

Workshop Website
http://www.fifthgensysltd.com/private/splash.htm

Workshop on NExt-generation Applications of smarTphones (NEAT)

Jules White

Virginia Tech
ECE Department
302 Whitemore Hall
Tucson, AZ 24060 USA

julesw@vt.edu

Jeff Gray

University of Alabama
Department of Computer Science
Box 870290
Tuscaloosa, AL 35487 USA

gray@cs.ua.edu

Abstract

The mobile sensing and networking capabilities of smartphones create a unique platform for building cyber-physical and other applications that sense and respond to the environment. Moreover, social networking capabilities of these platforms offer new paradigms for dissemination of knowledge, harvesting of user relationship information, and following current events. For example, recent research has yielded cyber-physical applications and cloud services to track patients lifestyle choices for health purposes, monitor CO_2 emissions around smartphone users, predict and respond to traffic accidents, measure traffic and derive road quality, and monitor cardiac patients. This workshop aims to investigate the key research challenges in this domain, such as software design impact on power consumption, synchronization of data with the cloud, and challenges of utilizing these services for mission-critical applications. The workshop will also investigate novel new methodologies for applying these computing paradigms to problems of societal importance.

Categories and Subject Descriptors D 2.10 [**Design**]: *Methodologies*; D 2.2 [**Design Tools and Techniques**]: *Software Libraries*

General Term Design, Human Factors, Languages

Keywords Mobile computing, smartphones, social computing

1. Workshop Introduction and Goals

Smartphone platforms, such as the iPhone and Google Android, are rapidly developing into rich platforms for building applications for cyber-physical systems [1], educational enrichment, enabling citizen scientists, disaster response, and environmental monitoring. For example, recent research has yielded cyber-physical applications and cloud services to track patients lifestyle choices for health purposes [2], monitor CO_2 emissions around smartphone users [3], predict and respond to traffic accidents [6], measure traffic and derive road quality [6,8], and monitor cardiac patients [7]. Many of these applications that combine sophisticated sensor capabilities of smartphones and cloud computing have become mainstream, such as Google Goggles, which provides an augmented reality overlay on a smartphone camera for situational awareness.

Smartphone sales are expected to outpace desktop/laptop computer sales in 2011. It is critical for software engineers to understand and research the key issues of building applications for this new platform. This workshop will foster new research and ideas that will be important for future software engineering research submissions to SPLASH.

The sophisticated capabilities of smartphones compared to previous mobile platforms provide a number of unique opportunities for research and development. For example, the latest smartphones can receive a variety of environmental stimuli, such as GPS location, acceleration, ambient light, sound, and imagery. Moreover, these smartphone platforms possess multiple network connections, such as WiFi and cellular data, which can be used with standard TCP/IP networking to connect them to external computing resources. Finally, smartphone platforms provide market-based software distribution mechanisms that can both push updates to phones and automatically track usage and report errors to researchers.

Building complex smartphone applications, however, is a new and challenging endeavor. Application developers must deal with limited resources, such as the battery capacity of the smartphone, which makes balancing the Quality of Service (QoS) concerns against resource consumption hard. Moreover, each platform has unique requirements that are placed on applications, such as Android's use of the specialized Binder inter-process communication mechanism with system services, which require careful consideration in the application's software architecture. Finally, application interaction with the physical world adds new challenges, such as resource conserving sensor data fusion.

This workshop aims to nurture new thinking on how to tackle the challenges of using smartphone computing at scale, as well as how these unique systems can be applied in novel ways to important societal problems. Our goal is to bring together a combination of academic research, industrial experience, and independent application development ideas. The workshop will compose a diverse set of perspectives on these topics and their applications. Some of the issues that are open to discussion at this workshop are:

- Summaries of experience and documented best-practices for introducing smartphones into the curricula (e.g., traditional software engineering, networking, software patterns, or network application design course, or a senior projects course)
- Industry/academic experience reports describing success/failure in implementing and using applications built on smartphones

- Approaches to building mobile cyber-physical systems using smartphones
- Tools for supporting early estimation of power, network bandwidth, and other types of resource consumption
- Cloud software architectures for scalably supporting data collection and synchronization across thousands of smartphones
- Novel software architectures for fusing streams of sensor data on smartphones
- Issues of support/maintenance for applications built on top of smartphone platforms
- Evolution and distribution issues of smartphone software stores
- New applications of smartphone computing
- Techniques for addressing portability and application retargeting across a very diverse and heterogeneous collection of devices and platforms
- Demonstrations of working smartphone-based systems that illustrate a novel development technique
- Specific research issues of building mission critical applications using smartphone platforms

2.   Activities of the NEAT Workshop

Prior to the workshop, the attendees are asked to read each of the submitted papers. During the first half-hour of the workshop, the organizers will present an introduction to the themes to be discussed, as well as a roadmap to the activities of the workshop that will occur throughout the day. Following the presentation by the organizers, a general introduction of all participants and their interests will occur. Several of the participants, all targeting similar kinds of issues, will be asked to give a 15-20-minute presentation of their submitted paper. During break periods, demonstrations of various smartphone applications that participants have built will be selected from the submitted papers.

In the afternoon, breakout groups will collaboratively explore unique ways of applying smartphone computing to important societal problems. The envisioned applications will be used as the context for discussion of critical research questions and challenges that must be addressed.

3.   Additional Workshop Information

The NEAT website (http://www.cs.ua.edu/neat/) documents all of the activities of the workshop and contains the final papers, presentations, and photos.

We appreciate the assistance from the following PC members who provided reviews of the submitted papers:

- Aniruddha Gokhale, *Vanderbilt University*
- Anthony Wasserman, *Carnegie Mellon Silicon Valley*
- Christelle Scharff, *Pace University*
- David Wolber, *University of San Francisco*
- Frank McCown, *Harding University*
- James Hill, *IUPUI*
- Jerry Gannod, *Miami University*
- Jing Zhang, *Motorola Mobility*
- Jonathan Sprinkle, *University of Arizona*
- Mark Goadrich, *Centenary College of Louisiana*
- Sean Eade, *Siemens Corporate Research*

References

1. J. White, S. Clarke, B. Dougherty, C. Thompson, D. Schmidt. R&D Challenges and Solutions for Mobile Cyber-Physical Applications and Supporting Internet Services, Springer Journal of Internet Services and Applications, vol. 1, no. 1, pp. 45-56, 2010.

2. T. Saponas, J. Lester, J. Froehlich, J. Fogarty, and J. Landay. iLearn on the iPhone: Real-Time Human Activity Classification on Commodity Mobile Phones. University of Washington CSE Tech Report UW-CSE-08-04-02, 2008.

3. J. Froehlich, T. Dillahunt, P. Klasnja, J. Mankoff, S. Consolvo, B. Harrison, and J. Landay. UbiGreen: Investigating a Mobile Tool for Tracking and Supporting Green Transportation Habits. In Proceedings of the 27th International Conference on Human Factors in Computing Systems, pages 1043–1052. ACM, 2009.

4. C. Thompson, J. White, B. Dougherty, A. Albright, and D. Schmidt. Using Smartphones and Wireless Mobile Networks to Detect Car Accidents and Provide Situational Awareness to Emergency Responders, Third International ICST Conference on MOBILe Wireless MiddleWARE, Operating Systems, and Applications (Mobileware 2010), June 30-July 2, 2010, Chicago, IL.

5. W. Jones. Forecasting Traffic Flow. IEEE Spectrum, 38(1):90–91, 2001.

6. G. Rose. Mobile Phones as Traffic Probes: Practices, Prospects, and Issues. Transport Reviews, 26(3):275–291, 2006.

7. P. Leijdekkers and V. Gay. Personal Heart Monitoring and Rehabilitation System Using Smart Phones. In Proceedings of the International Conference on Mobile Business, page 29. 2006.

ACM SIGPLAN International Workshop on Programming Language and Systems Technologies for Internet Clients (PLASTIC 2011)

Adam Welc
Adobe Systems
adam.welc@adobe.com

Michael Franz
University of California, Irvine
franz@uci.edu

Krzysztof Palacz
Adobe Systems
krzysztof.palacz@adobe.com

Abstract

Today's Internet users expect to access Internet resources using increasingly capable and ubiquitous client platforms. This trend has resulted in a wide-ranging diversification of hardware devices supporting various form factors and interaction modes, a choice of web browsers offering varying levels of performance, security and standards compliance, as well as the emergence of domain-specific uses of general-purpose Internet-related technologies, exemplified by Rich Internet Applications (RIAs) and site-specific browsers.

Despite the heterogeneity, all these platforms implement a common set of standards and technologies. While the resulting high level of interoperability can be seen as a major reason for the Internet's success, its constraints can also be viewed as limiting progress in client technologies. This workshop focuses on both innovative solutions in the area of Internet client software that improves on the current state-of-the-art while respecting the confines dictated by interoperability, as well as bold, new ideas that break with the status quo.

Categories and Subject Descriptors A.0 [*GENERAL*]: Conference Proceedings

General Terms Languages, Performance, Reliability, Security

Keywords Internet, Programming Languages, Systems, Compilation, Runtimes,

1. Overview

We firmly believe that, while the interest in the Internet-client related topics is on the rise, there is no single venue where people interested in these topics could meet, present their work, and exchange ideas. The main goal of this workshop is to fill out this niche. The workshop seeks contributions in the following (and also related) areas:

- compilation and runtime techniques for Internet client programming languages
- integration with server-side technologies, multi-tier programming languages and environments
- concurrency and parallelism support for Internet clients
- hardware acceleration of Internet client computational capabilities
- support for heterogeneity of Internet client environments (such as desktops, tablets and phones)
- Internet client security
- Internet client application deployment software engineering support (e.g. IDEs, refactoring, frameworks) for client-side Internet applications
- alternative Internet client programming languages and models
- novel approaches to Internet client software stack architecture

We solicit both regular papers (up to 10 pages) and position papers (up to 4 pages). The workshop will consist of a series of sessions where authors of the accepted papers will present ideas described in the papers. For the regular papers, we plan for 20-minute presentations and for the position papers we plan for 10-minute presentations. The intended time interval between the presentations would be at least 10 minutes. The the workshop will also include a panel session.

2. Organizers

The workshop is organized by two general co-chairs, Adam Welc (Adobe System) and Michael Franz (University of California, Irvine), and by the program committee chair, Krzysztof Palacz (Adobe Systems).

Adam Welc is a Senior Researcher at Adobe's Advanced Technology Lab. Adam's work is in the area of programming language design and implementation, with specific interests in web technologies, parallel programming and concurrency control, as well as compiler and runtime system optimizations. Some of his recent publications appeared in POPL'11, ECOOP'09 and EUROSYS'09.

Michael Franz is a Professor and the Director of the Secure Systems and Software Laboratory at the University of California, Irvine. He is well known for his research on dynamic compilation and continuous optimization. His work on trace-based compilation was subsequently adopted by Mozilla and became the TraceMonkey JavaScript engine in Firefox. He has been on the PCs of a large number of conferences and was one of the two founders of VEE, the ACM SIGPLAN/SIGOPS International Conference on Virtual Execution Environments.

Krzysztof Palacz is a Senior Computer Scientist in the Action-Script Engineering group at Adobe, where he is currently the tech lead of the Flash runtime concurrency effort. His previous research work has been focused on efficient implementation of programming languages and virtual machines, as well as reflection and communication frameworks. He is one of the authors of Lively Kernel, an Open Web malleable self-supporting application framework inspired by Smalltalk.

3. Program Committee

We have assembled a diversified program committee, consisting of leading experts in the field, coming from different institutions and backgrounds, and working on two different continents. The full list of program committee members is presented below:

- Ras Bodik (UC Berkeley)
- Andreas Gal (Mozilla)
- Brian Goetz (Oracle)

- Dan Ingalls (SAP)
- Chandra Krintz (UC Santa Barbara)
- Ben Livshits (MSR)
- Bernd Mathiske (Adobe)
- Mark Miller (Google)
- Florian Matthes (TU Munich)
- Tatiana Shpeisman (Intel)
- Laurence Tratt (Middlesex University)
- Jan Vitek (Purdue University)

VMIL 2011

The 5th Workshop on Virtual Machines and Intermediate Languages

Hridesh Rajan[λ], Michael Haupt[φ], Christoph Bockisch[β], Robert Dyer[λ]

[λ]Iowa State University, [φ]Oracle Labs, Potsdam, Germany, and [β]Universiteit Twente

[λ]{hridesh,rdyer}@cs.iastate.edu, [φ]michael.haupt@oracle.com, and [β]c.m.bockisch@cs.utwente.nl

Abstract

The VMIL workshop is a forum for research in virtual machines and intermediate languages. It is dedicated to identifying programming mechanisms and constructs that are currently realized as code transformations or implemented in libraries but should rather be supported at VM level. Candidates for such mechanisms and constructs include modularity mechanisms (aspects, context-dependent layers), concurrency (threads and locking, actors, software transactional memory), transactions, etc. Topics of interest include the investigation of which such mechanisms are worthwhile candidates for integration with the run-time environment, how said mechanisms can be elegantly (and reusably) expressed at the intermediate language level (e.g., in bytecode), how their implementations can be optimized, and how virtual machine architectures might be shaped to facilitate such implementation efforts.

Categories and Subject Descriptors D.3.4 [*Programming Languages*]: Processors—run-time environments

General Terms Design, Languages, Performance

Keywords Virtual machine, intermediate language

1. Motivations and Themes

An increasing number of high-level programming language implementations is realized using standard virtual machines. Recent examples of this trend include the Clojure (Lisp) and Potato (Squeak Smalltalk) projects, which are implemented on top of the Java Virtual Machine (JVM); and also F# (ML) and IronPython, which target the .NET CLR. Making diverse languages–possibly even adopting different paradigms–available on a robust and efficient common platform leverages language interoperability.

Vendors of standard virtual machine implementations have started to adopt extensions supporting this trend from the run-time environment side. For instance, the Sun standard JVM will include the *invokedynamic* instruction, which will facilitate a simpler implementation of dynamic programming languages on the JVM.

The observation that many language constructs are supported in library code, or through code transformations leading to over-generalized results, has led to efforts to make the core mechanisms of certain programming paradigms available at the level of the virtual machine implementation. Thus, dedicated support for language constructs enables sophisticated optimization by direct access to the running system. This approach has been adopted by several projects aiming at providing support for aspect-oriented programming or dynamic dispatch in general-purpose virtual machines (Steamloom, Nu, ALIA4J).

The main themes of this workshop are to investigate which programming language mechanisms are worthwhile candidates for integration with the run-time environment, how said mechanisms can be declaratively (and re-usably) expressed at the intermediate language level (e.g., in bytecode), how their implementations can be optimized, and how virtual machine architectures might be shaped to facilitate such implementation efforts. Possible candidates for investigation include modularity mechanisms (aspects, context-dependent layers), concurrency (threads and locking, actors, software transactional memory), transactions, paradigm-specific abstractions, and combinations of paradigms.

The areas of interest include, but are not limited to, compilation-based and interpreter-based virtual machines as well as intermediate-language designs with better support for investigated language mechanisms, compilation techniques from high-level languages to enhanced intermediate languages as well as native machine code, optimization strategies for reduction of run-time overhead due to either compilation or interpretation, advanced caching and memory management schemes in support of the mechanisms, and additional virtual machine components required to manage them.

SPLASH'11, October 22–27, 2011, Portland, Oregon, USA.
ACM 978-1-4503-0940-0/11/10.

2. Goals and Expected Results

We intend to solicit both technical and position papers. Our expectation is to receive contributions that, on the one hand, point out mechanisms and concepts worth to be supported at the level of the execution environment; and, on the other, provide more detailed descriptions of implementation approaches for such mechanisms and concepts. These papers should act as motivation for new researchers to include the topics of this workshop into their research. To accomplish this, we will make all papers available on the workshop web page; and we intend to publish the workshop proceedings—consisting of selected high-quality papers and extended abstracts of the remaining accepted papers—in the ACM digital library. The proceedings of the first four workshops in this series have already been published in the ACM digital library. We also intend to open the workshop to researchers without accepted papers.

It is our intention to receive submissions from researchers new to the field as well as experienced researchers and practitioners. For the former, we want to offer a platform for discussing their ideas and receiving feedback on them. This will be supported by question and answer sessions as well as by a session of group discussions. As in the past years, the program of VMIL 2011 will be complemented by high-quality invited talks.

3. Organizers

Hridesh Rajan is an Associate Professor of Computer Science at the Iowa State University. He received his Ph.D. from the University of Virginia in 2005. He is the recipient of a 2009 US NSF CAREER award and a 2010 Early Achievement in Research Award from Iowa State University.

Michael Haupt is a Principal Member of Technical Staff in the Maxine project at Oracle Labs. Previously, he has worked as a post-doctoral researcher in the Software Architecture Group at Hasso-Plattner-Institut in Potsdam. Michael holds a doctoral degree from Technische Universität Darmstadt.

Christoph Bockisch is an Assistant Professor on Software Composition with a research focus on the design and implementation of programming languages with advanced dispatching mechanisms. He received his doctoral degree from the Technische Universität Darmstadt in 2008. His PhD thesis was nominated for the German Dissertation Price 2009.

Robert Dyer is a fourth year Ph. D. student with a research focus on the design of intermediate language models and virtual machine support for advanced modularization techniques. He is the recepient of the 2009 Dr Robert Stewart Early Research Award and 2007 CRA Outstanding Undergraduate Award (Honorable Mention).

4. Program Committee

We are pleased to have assembled another excellent program committee for VMIL 2011. This year the program committee is chaired by Dr. Steve Blackburn from the Australian National University.

- Steve Blackburn (*Australian National U., Australia*)
- Cliff Click (*Azul Systems, USA*)
- David Grove (*IBM Research, USA*)
- Kim Hazelwood (*U. of Virginia, USA*)
- Antony Hosking (*Purdue U., USA*)
- Doug Lea (*State U. of New York, USA*)
- Guy Steele (*Oracle Labs, USA*)
- Ben Titzer (*Google, USA*)
- Olivier Zendra (*INRIA, France*)

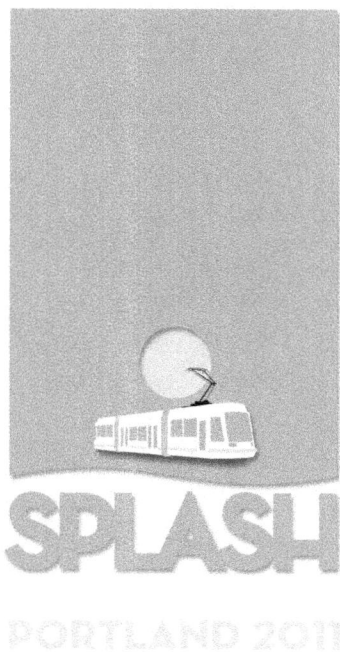

SPLASH 2011 Tech Talks

Welcome to the tech talks of SPLASH 2011! We have put together, in just three talks, a program, which will tell you about the past, the present and the future of developing software. First we hear from Jesper Richter-Reichhelm about the status of today, which is colored by the ridiculous number of users some systems of today have. Next, Dave Thomas will play the (not so far-fetched) role of a grumpy old man and tell us what is wrong with the industry of today. And last, but not least, Kresten Krab Thorup will give us his vision of where things are going. Enjoy!

How to Handle 1,000,000 Daily Users Without a Using a Cache

Jesper Richter-Reichhelm, *wooga GmbH*

Online games pose a few interesting challenges on their backend: A single user generates one http call every few seconds and the balance between data read and write is close to 50/50 which makes the use of a write through cache or other common scaling approaches less effective. Starting from a rather classic rails application as the traffic grew we gradually changed it in order to meet the required performance. And when small changes no longer were enough we turned inside out parts of our data persistency layer migrating from SQL to NoSQL without taking downtimes longer than a few minutes. Follow the problems we hit, how we diagnosed them, and how we got around limitations. See which tools we found useful and which other lessons we learned by running the system with a team of just two developers without a sysadmin or operation team as support.

Why Modern Application Development Sucks! Death by Objects, Agile, Middleware…

Dave Thomas, *Father of OTI, CEO of Bedarra Corporation*

In this talk we take a humorous but critical self-examination at modern application development - technology, practices and tools; to try to understand why building and evolving applications is so difficult and expensive. Why is technical debt of epidemic proportions given how great everything is? Where does all the effort and expense really go? We argue it is time to look at the application development value chain to obtain a sensible and balanced way forward so we can leverage new new tools while using the best of old old. Everyone is aware of the features and benefits of these technologies and practices but is the glass half full or half empty? Can we learn anything from the generations of developers before us? Are the problems due to skills or latent accidental technical complexity? Is the iPhone the only place where App development is cool? Can we help make application development in general much more enjoyable rather than blue collar programming with scrums?

Erlang, The Road Movie

Kresten Krab Thorup, *CTO Trifork*

In November 2009 I set out on a journey to learn Erlang. And not just learn it: I wanted to immerse myself in it, get under it's skin, feel it, get to think like Erlang. I took it for a test drive, and ended up spending 18 months in Erlang's company. This is the story of my trip. Not so much a talk about Erlang itself, but about what I realized on the way about where things are going. The systems that we build are getting increasingly integrated, distributed, and fragile. And becoming so at a disturbing rate when I think about it. Viewing the world from behind the steering wheel of this old beauty, I'll take you on a tour of some of the significant issues we're dealing with in today's software systems: cloud, multi-core, integration, high availability, and living with the fact that our software isn't perfect.

Aino Vonge Corry
SPLASH 2011 Tech Talks Chair
STLF, University of Aarhus, Denmark

Author Index

www.ingramcontent.com/pod-product-compliance
Lightning Source LLC
Chambersburg PA
CBHW080907220326
41598CB00034B/5506